Being and Intelligibility

Being and Intelligibility

ALBERT PETER PACELLI

WIPF & STOCK · Eugene, Oregon

BEING AND INTELLIGIBILITY

Copyright © 2017 Albert Peter Pacelli. All rights reserved. Except for brief quotations in critical publications or reviews, no part of this book may be reproduced in any manner without prior written permission from the publisher. Write: Permissions, Wipf and Stock Publishers, 199 W. 8th Ave., Suite 3, Eugene, OR 97401.

Wipf & Stock
An Imprint of Wipf and Stock Publishers
199 W. 8th Ave., Suite 3
Eugene, OR 97401

www.wipfandstock.com

PAPERBACK ISBN: 978-1-5326-3285-3
HARDCOVER ISBN: 978-1-5326-3287-7
EBOOK ISBN: 978-1-5326-3286-0

Manufactured in the U.S.A.   SEPTEMBER 5, 2017

Excerpts [pp. 6–437: 2210 words] from BEING AND TIME by Martin Heidegger. Translated by John Macquarrie and Edward Robinson. Copyright © 1962 by Harper & Row, Publishers, Incorporated and SCM Press Ltd. Reprinted by permission of HarperCollins Publishers and SCM Press Ltd. All rights reserved.

From: A HISTORY OF WESTERN PHILOSOPHY by Bertrand Russell. Copyright © 1945 Simon & Schuster. The use of six short extracts totaling 831 words from pp. 715–718 reprinted with the permission of Touchstone, a division of Simon & Schuster, Inc., and Taylor & Francis Books UK and The Bertrand Russell Peace Foundation. All rights reserved.

From: THE INFINITE by A.W. Moore, Routledge, 2nd ed., 2001. Copyright © 1990, 2001 A.W. Moore. Various extracts (including from pp. 41, 70–71, 123–28, 131–141, and 175–176) and summaries of discussion contained therein are used by permission of Taylor & Francis Books UK. All rights reserved.

From: INTRODUCTION TO METAPHYSICS, by Martin Heidegger. Translated by G. Fried and R. Polt. New Haven: Yale University Press, 2nd ed., 2014. 2nd edition copyright © 2014 by Yale University, new material; revised and expanded English translation, translators' introduction, prefatory material, and notes. First edition copyright © 2000 by Yale University. Used by permission. All rights reserved.

From: INTRODUCTION TO PHENOMENOLOGY, by Robert Sokolowski. Cambridge University Press, 2000. Copyright © Robert Sokolowski 2000. Summary of discussion including excerpts from pp. 22–41, 49–50, 65, 66–76, 78–84, 88–111, 130–145, and 152–155 totaling 528 words. Used and/or reprinted with permission of Cambridge University Press. All rights reserved.

From: PSYCHOLOGY FROM AN EMPIRICAL STANDPOINT, by Franz Brentano, translated by Rancurello, C., Terell, D.B., and McAllister, L. New York: Routledge, 1st ed., 1995. English translation © 1973, 1995 Routledge. Summary and various extracts totaling 1084 words, reproduced by permission of Taylor & Francis Books UK. All rights reserved.

To Marsha, my beloved wife,
whose patience and encouragement over the many years that this book was in
gestation are the true presuppositions of the philosophy presented in these pages.

Contents

Acknowledgments | xi

1 Introduction | 1

    The Why Question
    Transcendent Reality
    The Possibility of Metaphysics
    Agenda-Based Philosophy

2 The Death and Resurrection of Metaphysics | 22

    The Sundering of the Psychosome
    The Road to Nowhere
    Personhood

3 The Reach of Reason | 56

    Kant's Response to Skepticism
    Transcendental Epistemology
    Transcendental Illusion and the Ring-Fencing of Reason
    The Reductionist Assault on Kant: The Intuition of Space
    The Reductionist Assault on Kant: Causality
    A Critique of Kant's Metaphysics
    The Development of German Idealism from the Transcendental Platform
    The Platform of Transcendent Realism

4 The Possibility of Objective Knowledge | 109

    The Logos (Λόγος)
    Internal Cognition and Truth
    The Logical Grounding of Predication
    The Power of Abstraction
    The Necessity of Objective Reason

Contents

5 The Homogeneity of Reason | 124

    Rational Unity
    The Applicability of General Logic to Logical Objects
    The Logical Deduction of Natural Numbers
    Logical Objects and the Cardinality of Empirical Sets

6 Empirical Judgment | 150

    The Form of Empirical Cognition
    Intuition, Conception, and Science
    Causality and Implication
    Cognition Under Logical Concepts

7 Infinity, Countability, and Self-Reference | 174

    The Problem of Infinity
    Cantor and the Orders of Infinity
    The Ontology of the Infinite
    Self-Reference
    The Countability of Logical Objects

8 Propaedeutic to Ontology | 196

    The Birth of Phenomenology
    Brentano's Descriptive Psychology
    Husserl and the Philosophy of Phenomenology

9 Being and Intelligibility | 224

    Dasein
    The Being of Beings
    The Ground of Being
    Bergner's Credo
    The Meaning of Being

10 Duty and Desire | 281

    Morality and Agape
    The Fact of Morality
    The Possibility of Objective Practical Reason
    Subjective Reductionism
    Secular Deontological Ethics
    Kant and Nagel
    Internal Intuition of Agape

11   Moral Freedom | 308

   The Dependence of Freedom on Agape
   Freedom and Accountability
   The Failure of Compatabilism

12   The Supreme Principle of Being and Intelligibility | 320

   The Nature of the Subsistent World
   Unity and Preeminence
   The Ground of Being and Intelligibility
   Plato and the Idea of the Good
   Other Arguments for the Existence of God
   The Soul

13   Agape (Αγάπη) | 341

   Agape, Love, and Unqualified Good Will
   Agape and Ethical Behavior

Bibliography | 347
Names Index | 351

Acknowledgments

My formal studies in philosophy were undertaken at the University of Pennsylvania during the years 1970 to 1974, at the end of which I obtained a bachelor's and master's in political philosophy. Although I was very much interested in the broader questions of metaphysics and epistemology, the emphasis generally placed by Anglo-American universities (then and now), including Penn, upon positivism, analytical philosophy, and linguistics was for me a dissuasion to their pursuit. Instead, I elected to investigate the basic questions of how to live a philosophically good life and what sort of sociopolitical structures were best suited to that end.

By incredibly good fortune, my studies were guided by Dr. Jeffrey T. Bergner, who had obtained his PhD from Princeton University only a year or two before. Jeff, who at the time of this writing continues to teach at the University of Virginia, is a brilliant man and a superlative teacher who motivates and inspires in the most intellectually open and honest ways. For me, Jeff's greatest skill is his ability to guide one along one's own intellectual path without allowing his own views to interfere in the journey. Under Jeff's mentorship, I felt less that I was being taught than that I was being led to discover what I had already intuited. Indeed, Jeff rarely if ever volunteered what his thinking on a particular topic was; if you wanted to know that, you had to ask him!

As my graduation neared, I faced a choice between applying for admission to Princeton's graduate school of philosophy to pursue a doctoral degree or taking the more pecuniary road of becoming a lawyer and, after much handwringing, I elected the latter course. I remember quite clearly my reluctance to tell Jeff that, for primarily material reasons, I would not be following in his footsteps. I remember his supportive response with equal clarity. After telling me that Hegel would approve of my determination to become an officer of the court, Jeff told me that, no matter what I did, I would never be able to leave philosophy behind or to stop thinking critically about what the world presented to me.

As it turned out, in 1988, after seven or so years in the commodities business, I wrote a book called *The Speculator's Edge*, which presents a philosophy of markets and market speculation. In the intervening years, I had lost contact with Jeff and I sought mightily to find him to send him a copy of my book, just to show him that his assessment of me had been correct. But, alas, that was before the World Wide Web came into being and

I was unable to locate him. A number of years later, after the birth of my son, I turned my attention to what I came to regard as the more important matter of writing down the justification for my Roman Catholic faith so that, if I died or became incapacitated while my boy was still in his youth, he would have when he was ready the benefit of my thinking to guide him on his way. My specific concern was to provide my son with the wherewithal to withstand the atheistic pummeling that he was certain to confront during his university years in all aspects of his education. However, because, for me, faith and philosophy are intimately interwoven, I soon discovered that in order to competently justify my religious beliefs, I had to arrive first at a solid understanding of metaphysics. The task I was about to confront was a classic Patristic case of faith seeking understanding and one which I knew from the very start would be much bigger than I wished to undertake or fancied that I was capable of accomplishing. This book is the result of that metaphysical enterprise—the apologetics that are its motivation remain to be written.

It was not until 2013, after four years of solo investigation, that I completed a draft of this work that I assessed to be of sufficient quality to send to Jeff for his review. Fortunately, this time, with the aid of the Web, I was able to locate him and I asked whether he would grant me ten minutes of his time. Jeff had just published his own excellent book, called *Against Modern Humanism*, which will be the subject of some discussion in these pages. Although Jeff's book is not overtly phenomenological in its approach, I regard it as a fascinating review of the historical *Dasein* of Western philosophical culture, specifically with regard to the question of what it means to live a just life. Jeff, in a typical display of kindness, agreed to read my manuscript. After a couple of weeks, I received from Jeff a brief critique, several fundamental questions which he thought should be addressed, and an offer of encouragement to continue my investigations. During the ensuing three years, we exchanged numerous correspondences, Jeff reviewed a completely new draft of the book, and offered more guidance on points for clarification, gaps to be filled, and additional lines of related thinking that required to be investigated and addressed. With this book, I can finally say that I have done all of that.

With Jeff's facilitation, I was reintroduced to Professor Mark Blitz, another of my mentors at Penn, who is at the time of this writing Fletcher Jones Professor of Political Philosophy at Claremont McKenna College. Mark is the author of numerous books and articles, including of especial relevance to this work, on topics relating to Heidegger. Mark was kind enough to act as a peer reviewer of this book and to offer guidance with respect the publication process, for which I am deeply grateful.

As teachers who were both critical and encouraging at the same time and who fostered in me the nascent joy of philosophy that I brought to them as their student, Jeff and Mark had an enormous influence on my intellectual life and it is no overstatement to assert that this book could not have been completed without Jeff's guidance. To be clear, the philosophy presented here, especially its defects, is all mine, not Jeff's or Mark's, and, not surprisingly, although I imagine some of it (especially the critical aspects) is compatible with Jeff's own, I do not even know the extent to which that is the case. But that merely underscores Jeff's great ability as an educator, which is founded on the very openness to what is presented to one in life which is at the heart of Jeff's own philosophical thinking. I hope that the book is worthy of Jeff's and Mark's teaching.

1

Introduction

THE WHY QUESTION

Anthropologists tell us that human beings are distinguishable from all of the other beings on the earth in many interesting ways. Human beings are the only animals who walk upright in normal locomotion, who require clothing to survive in most of the locations in which they live, who possess opposable thumbs that can reach all the way across their fingers and fingers that can reach to the base of their thumbs, who cook their meals, who often belie their true feelings by blushing, who require parental care well into their teenage years, who live long after the end of fertility, whose mental capacities are by far the greatest of the animals, and who can communicate in oral and written speech. From an anthropological standpoint, these are profoundly important characteristics and together they make man what he is: *Homo sapiens*, the wise human. From a philosophical standpoint, however, with the exception of speech (which is important in and of itself as a mode of communication and socialization but equally because of the cognitive activity that renders it possible), none of these characteristics, not even human brain capacity, is particularly notable. In contrast, the list of human characteristics that achieve philosophical importance is substantially different and much shorter and, as far as the philosophy presented in these pages is concerned, is strictly limited to consciousness of self as a persistent entity, objective propositional thinking and speaking, unremitting angst about being in the world, and an abiding sense of moral obligation.

The respective nature of the two lists makes manifest the fundamental difference between science and philosophy. The anthropological list treats man as a species of animal and comprises his unique biological characteristics. It considers him objectively, as science does any other entity in the world that is of interest to it. It deliberately refuses to take into account that the scientist who studies man is himself the object of his study, and the fact that man studies and classifies himself and other animals is in itself unique. By contrast, the philosophical list treats man in the full sense of his *beingness* and identifies those characteristics which are most relevant to how he thinks about himself and engages with the world in which he finds himself and, as we will see in a moment, it takes as especially important (via self-consciousness and propositional thinking) that not only are the items in the list descriptive of man but the list itself is made by and for him.

Of all the beings in the world, only man both knows and knows that he knows and recognizes himself as a persistent entity in a manifold of empirical and conceptual experience. This capability and perspective ground all of the other characteristics which we have listed as philosophically important. Because man is self-conscious he can distinguish other entities in an *objective* manner and he can label them, consider them critically, and formulate, communicate, and test propositions about them. Man not only takes the world as it presents itself to him but his intellect demands that the world disclose the reasons for that which it presents. Man's reason does this on two levels. The first is imbedded in the very act of cognition; as Immanuel Kant teaches in his masterwork, *Critique of Pure Reason*, man organizes the material presented to his reason in space and time under the principle of *causality*. A world which presented itself to human reason *helter skelter* and not as a sequence of causes and effects would be incoherent and uncognizable. The second is a conscious act of thinking man. It occurs every time a child asks his parent why something is the way it is, or a scientist investigates empirical reality considered as a world of mind-independent objects, or a philosopher asks, as we will in these pages: *Why is there something instead of nothing?* This last question is one that we will call, following Martin Heidegger (in his *Introduction to Metaphysics*), the *Why* question. Indeed, thinking itself is the identification of the relations within and among its objects and their grounds.

It is also man's self-consciousness which enables him to consider *himself* and the world objectively; he can consider himself as part of the world in which he dwells or he can conceptually set himself over and against the world as if he does not belong in and to it. This is both a natural instinct and a cornerstone of philosophical inquiry. Man can appreciate and enjoy the world as the nurturing entity out of which he arises, but because he is self-conscious and finite, he can also see himself as alien to the very same world, as an unwitting warrior against it and his own physical nature, as the fighter of an inevitably losing battle with natural death. Indeed, of all the beings in the world, only man is *fundamentally* anxious about his place in the world and compelled by his own nature to live his life in the face of a pervading sense that it is fated to be short-lived and that after all is said and done it may very well amount to nothing objectively meaningful.

Yet man's brooding is also a great blessing to him because it impels him to be circumspect about how he makes use of his time on earth. Although all organisms have needs, only man is conscious of his in a way that allows him to formulate and prioritize his ends and to be aware that he is doing so; as a result, man can take the world and other men into account as both means and ends in themselves and he can measure his actions against other options available to him. Each decision that man makes at any moment to pursue a particular end is also a decision not to pursue a multitude of other ends open to him at the same moment. And the fact that such decisions by their very nature are made in the context of a world of other entities makes manifest what is perhaps the most interesting human characteristic of all: in acting and refraining from acting, in thought, word, and deed, man operates under an existential sense of *moral obligation*, that is, a perceived duty to comport himself in a certain way regardless of his own personal desires. Kant calls this the "fact of morality" and it is a characteristic about which we will have much to say in this work.

So *ecce homo* (behold the man): a self-concerned and anxious asker of the *Why* question, who is confronted until the day he dies with the question of how he ought to comport himself in and toward the world into which he is thrown. So far, so good. But what about the *Why* question itself, the one that is so profoundly important to man, and what is its relation to the beingness of man? On its face, the question seems simple enough—it appears to ask about the cause or ground of the beingness of beings (meaning all objects that can be perceived or conceived), which (again following Heidegger) we will call "Being." But immediately, a difficulty appears: What sort of thing can the answer to the *Why* question *be*? Is the ground of Being itself a being? If it is not a being, then either the *Why* question is unanswerable or it requires *knowledge of the existence* of at least one non-being that serves to explain all the beings that there are. But it seems that we cannot even inquire what sort of thing a non-being might be without hopelessly involving ourselves with incoherency and self-contradiction. How can a *non-being* be? And even if that were possible, how could we have any knowledge about it? Is Being therefore itself a being? If so, what is the ground of *that* being, which itself is a ground? If Being is an ungrounded being we must again ask how we might have any knowledge of it—doesn't knowledge of a thing mean knowledge of its ground? Must Being therefore ground itself? If so, that would make Being unique among all beings and, as such, one the knowledge of which would demark, if not exceed, the limits of our understanding.

The fact that we even ask the *Why* question seems to tell us something important because its asking presupposes that we already know something about the objects as to which we seek understanding. Certainly, it seems that we can only ask the *Why* question if we already have some knowledge of what beings are, which is to say that, at the very least, in the figurative sense, we seem to know beings when we see them. But, even taking that as true, we are only pushed deeper into the complexities of our inquiry, because we must then assess what it means to have that kind of knowledge. Saying, for example, that "(I know) there is a coffee cup on my desk," reduced to its essence, appears to be nothing more than an acknowledgment of a particular state of affairs, namely, of the Being of the coffee cup (a being) and the Being of the desk (a being), the relation of the two beings to one another, and their relation to me, as the one who has knowledge of their Being. The profound relationship between Being and intelligibility thus becomes conspicuous but in a way that seems hopelessly circular: Being seems to characterize that which *is* (i.e., said to be) in such a way that any attempt to explicate Being must be had in terms of Being itself and the explication of Being appears to represent an attempt at knowledge of *the* state of affairs that is the state of *all* affairs, including itself. So, once again, the *Why* question appears to float in the air in a way that belies that the ground of things must ultimately either be groundless or self-grounding. Ironically enough, if this is the case, the only two possible answers to the *Why* question seem to be, in the first case, "For no reason at all!" and in the second case, the one given universally by parents to children who ask "Why?" one time too many times, is, of course, simply, "Because!"

But is the question of Being so hopelessly intractable? Oddly enough, modern mainstream philosophy recognizes the circularity of the question of Being but in an utterly dismissive way, first, by acknowledging that knowledge of Being is both philosophically inaccessible and presupposed by all else and, then, by denying that this is a major difficulty or that its implications must be taken into account in its other investigations. This position may be fine for scientists who endeavor to account for beings, but, from a philosophical standpoint, it is patently unacceptable and its debunking occupies a substantial portion the excellent life work of Heidegger. Indeed, one of Heidegger's major themes is that philosophy unwittingly lost track of the question of *Being* as long ago as Plato and, instead, over the ensuing millennia, increasingly shifted its focus from the investigation of Being to the investigation of *beings* as such. In so doing, Heidegger argues, philosophy supplanted itself with empirical science and man increasingly came to define himself not in terms of his potentiality for Being but instead in terms of his own technology with the horrifying result that man's *tools* became his *ends* and man's historical Being was thereby obliterated. Heidegger asserts, quite rightly, that the failure of modern philosophy, in the first instance, and modern Western culture, consequentially, to take Being into account has led both philosophy and modern society to its current nihilistic mooring. Of course, Heidegger's indictment of mainstream philosophy would have limited value were it not accompanied by a viable alternative, which in the case of the apparently fundamental circularity of the *Why* question, requires a means of access to Being itself, which Heidegger provides by pointing out that *man himself is the one being whose Being is not presupposed by man but instead is disclosed to him in his asking of the* Why *question*. So, Heidegger tells us, the answer to the *Why* question must be had, if it can be had at all, by commencing with the interrogation of man as to his own Being.

Heidegger's superb methodological observation promises the possibility of yielding a presuppositionless philosophy, a goal which had been abandoned in the modern philosophical era until Edmund Husserl, Heidegger's mentor and the inventor of the philosophy of *phenomenology*, took it up at the beginning of the twentieth century. Husserl attempts to avoid all philosophical presuppositions by considering things simply in the way that they appear to consciousness, which is an approach that Husserl adopts from Franz Brentano, Husserl's mentor. Although Brentano describes his own work as the science of psychology, it is highly epistemological in its exposition and, from a historical perspective, Husserl's development of Brentano's methodology into a fully worked-out philosophical system represents an unsurprising step given Husserl's gifted mind and interest in philosophical investigations. But, as Heidegger quickly realized, taking things in their "giveness" (as the phenomenologists aptly characterize their methodology), although methodologically valuable, does not avoid the presupposition of the Being of the things so given, which remains uninvestigated by the phenomenologists. To achieve a presuppositionless philosophy, Heidegger demotes phenomenology from substantive philosophy to mere methodology and adopts it as such for his ontological investigations, including, especially, his interrogation of man as to his own Being. Heidegger calls man "*Dasein*" (literally, "Being-there" or "Being-open") because Heidegger understands him to be the ontological point at which the world discloses itself in its Being. It is difficult to imagine that anyone could ever characterize man more succinctly: for Heidegger, man is *the being for whom his own Being is an issue*. Given Heidegger's understanding of *Dasein*, it is easy to see why he would lament so vigorously the loss of man's historical Being that is implied in the confounding of *Dasein's* means with its ends.

The phenomenological method is distinguished, quite brightly, from the traditional methods of philosophy which consider the objects of philosophical investigation as independent of the mind and the Being of the one who studies them and which, as a result, are heavily imbued with presuppositions about Being, cognition, and underlying reality. Although I am not an acolyte of Heidegger and will offer in these pages a profoundly different understanding of the nature of things, Heidegger's claim, that cognition is a unified experience to which man brings his own Being in his grasping of what is disclosed to him and that science, which attempts to remove the cognizing "I" in order to understand entities objectively, *presupposes without understanding* the very Being of the entities it treats, seems unassailable. We can also agree with Heidegger that the result is that the scientific pseudo-philosophy that constitutes the contemporary mainstream, together with its analytical handmaiden, is not philosophy at all; that it fails to address, because it does not possess the scope or tools to do so, the most fundamental and important philosophical questions, and that in so doing *Dasein*, as the scientist-philosopher, completely loses sight of *itself*, the being to whom the world is disclosed.

Even so, the conclusion that a scientific approach to philosophical inquiry is by its very nature doomed to failure seems itself to presuppose that the Being of beings cannot be found by examining beings. This is a position with which we are in strong disagreement. Although our discussion has begun from a more or less phenomenological perspective with our depiction of man, the philosophy in these pages gives philosophical credence to both approaches, *with the caveat that the philosopher must take into account at all times the perspective from which he or she conducts his or her investigations in order to avoid tripping over his or her own presuppositions*, and we will utilize both approaches quite heavily in our analysis. This equanimity toward both phenomenological and traditional philosophical methods invites the question: How is it possible to regard as meritorious two seemingly exclusive approaches, the first of which considers man as a critical aspect of a unified act of cognition and the second of which considers the objects of cognition as if they simply exist on a mind-independent basis? The answer lies in the fact that we reach the same answer to the *Why* question under each methodology, *which is that Being and intelligibility are identical and arise under a necessary (as opposed to contingent) and supreme principle which is the ground of itself and of everything else, including human cognition and moral obligation*. This is possible only because the cognizing "I" who may be interrogated as to his own Being and the beings which may be considered scientifically *all have Being in common*. Just as we can arrive at an understanding of Being by phenomenologically interrogating man as to his Being, we can take an entity scientifically as a mind-independent object and, by a process of reduction, arrive at its fundamental objectivity. In both cases, we will find that Being consists of *a logical unity among manifolds*. In our interrogation of man as to his Being, we find that human rational experience fundamentally is that of a persistent and unified self among the manifold of its life experiences, which occur, in the case of sensible experience, under the ordered rubric of spatio-temporality, and, in the case of internal experience, under the logical rubric of the rules of thought. In the investigations of the objects of experience considered on a mind-independent basis, we find that their Being also consists of the unity among manifolds, this time as the unity of the ground of sensible predication with its predicates. The difference between the two approaches, however, is the one we have been emphasizing along with Heidegger, namely, that in the interrogation of man as to his Being we presuppose nothing whereas in the investigation of beings as such, we presume their mind-independent Being in the first instance. But, the identity between Being and intelligibility which arises as a result of the orderliness of Being inherent in the unity among manifold structure, in the end renders the starting point moot as a practical matter. In other words, when man brings his own Being to the world in the act of cognition of the Being of what is presented to him, he does not overwrite it.

The idea that Being and intelligibility are identical is, of course, not at all new, but it is not often recognized as such and certainly not in the radical way presented in this book. The identity between Being and intelligibility can be seen in God's self-characterization as the "I AM" in the book of Exodus, in Parmenides' statement that "thinking and Being are the same," in Heraclitus's *logos*, in Plato's Ιδέα του Αγαθού (Idea of the Good), in Descartes's *Ens Perfectissimum* (Most Perfect Being), and in Leibniz's Necessary Being, to name only a few. What *is* novel in the philosophy presented in these pages, however, is the *metaphysical* status we accord the identity relation. It will be argued here that *for a being to exist* it must be thinkable and that all thinkable entities share in common the just-described, irreducible unity among manifolds, which is inherently (indeed, definitionally) logical—in other words, that all beings are in their Being *logically grounded predication*, which we will assert consists of, at the most fundamental level, an identity (ground) of relations (predicates) of sequence, magnitude, proportionality, and other logical relations (e.g., negation, conjunction, disjunction, dependence), which we refer to herein as a "logical object." To emphasize the point, the central argument presented in these pages is not merely the epistemological one, namely, that we *understand* the world as unity among manifolds, but the *metaphysical* one, that world *exists as such and cannot exist otherwise*. We will show that logical objects ground: objective knowledge; the rules of thought, the deduction of natural numbers and the countability of the infinite; the structure of space, time, and causality; Being, including the Being of human beings; the connectedness of the phenomenological truth of disclosure and scientific propositional truth; and, finally, morality. Moreover, we will show that, as the structure of reality, logical objects imply the necessity of the Supreme Principle of Being and Intelligibility, which, following Heraclitus, we will sometimes also refer to herein as the *Logos*. To state the case most fundamentally, logic is not a set of rules that apply to objects but an articulation of the essential relation of grounded predication that constitutes objects and their relations, which is to say, *logic is an articulation of Being*.

Before proceeding, we should address ourselves to one last question: If it is possible to arrive at the Supreme Principle through either of the avenues of phenomenology or scientific philosophy, why have both approaches failed until now to do so? The answer is that the investigations which have been conducted to date under both methodologies fail to recognize the most important consequence of the identity between Being and intelligibility, namely, the *fundamental logicality* of all that there is. By disregarding Being and starting with empirical objects, scientific philosophy attempts to infer rationality from reality and in so doing demotes reason to an empirically reducible phenomenon. Thus, under modern materialism, intelligibility is a consequence of reality, not its essence. Even Kant, who seeks to reconcile rationalism and empiricism by arguing that sensible experience occurs under certain *a priori* categories of understanding, characterizes general logic as being derivative from such experience and therefore denies it any scope beyond such experience, which in turn is the basis for his rejection of the traditional arguments for the existence of God. Similarly, in the hands of Heidegger, the ontologist *par excellence*, Being is taken as the originary concept that is not itself a being and is accordingly placed above logic; in doing so, Heidegger makes allowance for the possibility of absolute nothingness and is forced to conclude that the very Being which grounds all beings is itself ungrounded. It is only when Being and intelligibility are seen to be the same thing that the fundamental logicality of all that there is and the self-grounding logical necessity of Being itself is revealed as the Supreme Principle. Therefore, while we agree with Heidegger's criticism of scientific philosophy, we must also level a similar charge at him as well: not only has modern mainstream philosophy lost sight of Being and of man in his Being, but modern philosophy, Heidegger included, has also lost sight of God, the *Logos*, the Being who is the Supreme Principle of Being and Intelligibility and the ground of all that there is.

TRANSCENDENT REALITY

There are certain aspects of human experience that do not appear to be part of or explicable in terms of sensible experience, considered from a reductionist perspective. These include: self-consciousness; objective, necessary, and universal knowledge; moral obligation; and moral freedom. Of them, only the first is manifestly particular to, and dependent upon, the individual with whom it is associated and only the last may be unequivocally said to derive from another, namely, moral obligation. Because they are independent of the empirical world, these aspects of human experience must be understood to have their grounds on a transcendent basis. The transcendent aspects of human experience may be identified by their direct accessibility to intuition or by prescinding from the totality of human experience all that is empirically known or explicable.

Transcendent knowledge is wholly *a priori* and yet has objective content, takes subject-predicate form, and is governed by certain rules of thought, which we understand as general logic. The rules of *a priori* thought are part of a single, unified intellectual experience, which includes cognition of empirical reality, and are directly associated with the way in which human beings understand the empirical (i.e., sensible) world in spatio-temporal terms through logical categories of understanding. It follows that the objects of empirical cognition, to be intelligible, must be orderly in a way that is susceptible of application by reason of its logically derived categories of understanding. If sensible objects were not susceptible to such application, then either cognition would be impossible altogether or it would require reason to create its own empirical objects, which is a special power not available to man.

The presuppositions of the possibility of objective knowledge, which govern its accessibility to rational minds include, on the side of reason, the form and rules of thought and its moral content, and the logical forms of empirical cognition (i.e., space, time, and causality) and, on the side of objective reality, objective empirical order. These are connected by reason in the process of empirical cognition under the categories of understanding, which represent the application of ontologically prior, general logic to spatio-temporal phenomena. The presuppositions of the possibility of knowledge provide an intuitively elegant order to the universe, which is utterly logical in nature.

The categories of understanding that will be postulated in these pages are structurally similar to those of Kant, which he derived from the work of Aristotle, insofar as all such categories are underpinned by logical judgments, but unlike the Kantian categories, the categories presented here include spatial, temporal, and mathematical classifications omitted by Kant on the ground that they provide the form of cognition and not the categories under which empirical objects are determined. The main reason for this difference is that, under the philosophy presented in these pages, which is called "transcendent realism," cognition has, depending upon its object, either internal or external reference, and although space and time are indeed the form of cognition of external and sensible objects, space and time are themselves determined by ontologically prior general logic, which in the case of space and time are mathematical, as the logically necessary means by which external objects (i.e., those of empirical cognition) may be recognized. Transcendent realism is also dramatically different from Kant's transcendental idealism because it is asserted here: that human reason has access to transcendent reality by *direct intuition*[1] of self, general logic, and moral obligation and freedom; that we have knowledge of the independent existence of objects of cognition (i.e., *things-in-themselves*) even if our knowledge of their attributes is limited to that which may be understood by application of the categories of understanding; and, most importantly, that general logic is ontologically prior to the categories and applies to all reality and not a mere abstraction from them, the applicability of which is limited to the empirical world.

The source of the moral obligation that is a component of transcendent reality is not the theoretical reason required as a precondition of its intelligibility. Theoretical reason can inform intelligent beings as to the logical course of action in a particular set of circumstances, but it can never *obligate* them to adopt such a course. Moral obligation is of a different source and character altogether. Moral obligation can only be understood as the intentionality of a transcendent will, called in these pages *Agape*, that exists independently of the morally conscious beings having access to it and which is ontologically prior to such beings. Such a transcendent will must be *good-in-itself* by definition and must intend itself as its own object or end. When morally conscious entities harmonize their will with *Agape* they instantiate it (to the extent of their ability) and, in doing so, act morally.

To the extent that God is knowable for man, he is most readily recognizable as the source of *Agape*, either in essential being or as its possessor (as a faculty). The term

---

1. "Direct intuition" is sometimes used to mean only that which is given to reason as immediately true, without further analysis or reference to sensible experience. In this book, by "direct intuition" we mean all that is objectively given to reason without reference to sensible experience, including that which is immediately known (e.g., the rules of thought), directly perceived as *objectively* existing (e.g., the soul as substance), and analytically known (e.g., logically derived from that which is immediately known or directly perceived).

Agape is thus used here to connote the divine good will that is the ground of Being and intelligibility. The Greek term "*Agape*" is chosen here over the equivalent notion of *unqualified good will*, which is the English translation that most closely corresponds to the manner in which it will be used in these pages, to underscore the important connection between the God of *Agape* as herein described and the God of Judeo-Christian conception as described in both the Old and New Testaments, which use the term *agape* in the Greek versions. That connection notwithstanding, this book is a work of metaphysics, not apologetics or theology. Although the God of *Agape* presented here is fully compatible with the God of orthodox Judaism and Christianity, to the extent God is presented to us by reason and not divine revelation, we know far less of him as philosophers than we do as believers and it is that narrower, philosophical understanding that is the subject matter of this book.

Agape, as used in these pages, connotes will, with all the mystical power given it by the German idealists, not emotive love, which is the common translation that appears in most English biblical translations. It is divinely intentional and creative, it provides the presuppositions by which human reason has access to it and to all reality, and it gives meaning to the human experience. However, it is not to be understood to be constitutive of reality in a pantheistic, immanent, or absolute way (as the German idealists would have it) but instead to operate separately from and above both the empirical and the supersensible worlds.

To be clear, *Agape* and the *Logos* are two ways of understanding a single Supreme Being; the self-intentionality of *Agape* and the self-grounding of the *Logos* are one and the same thing. Nevertheless, for emphasis, the tendency in the exposition presented in this book will be to speak of *Agape* when emphasizing the nature of God as divine good will, and to speak of the *Logos* when emphasizing God as the provenance of the identity of Being and intelligibility that provides and defines the orderliness of the universe. Moreover, because of the self-grounding nature of God as so conceived, it is sometimes necessary to emphasize God as the *source* of good will and moral obligation or the *Logos* as its own logical ground. So, it will be acceptable for us to speak of man instantiating the will of God through acts of good will or to say that logic *follows* the *Logos*. Similarly, when we speak of the Supreme Principle of Being and Intelligibility we have in mind both a transcendently real being and the ultimate ground of existence and reason. All of this is not to deny that God must be his own end, which is precisely the point to be understood. This is not an instance of circularity; rather, it reflects the conclusion that Being, intelligibility, and the divine good will constitute a necessary and ontologically supreme unity; conceptually, they come together in a Being that perfectly *is*.

One of the purposes of this book is to provide philosophical grounds for the proposition that there is a transcendent reality which comprises, at the very least, *Agape* and the *Logos* and the souls of morally conscious beings who have access to it. The term "soul" is used in these pages to refer to a persistent, *substantive* self that is not merely self-conscious but is, in addition, *morally* self-conscious. As used in these pages, a "self" is something less, namely, a unified (ground) manifold of conscious experiences the substance of which is the subject of much philosophical debate. David Hume, for example, asserts that the self is illusory, while Kant asserts that the self is a mere unity of apperception. Under transcendent realism, the self is asserted in fact to be a soul and the human being is said to be ensouled precisely *because it is a substantive entity that is the dative of Agape's disclosure and therefore obligated to comport itself in the world in a moral manner.* Moreover, under transcendent realism, transcendent reality is precisely that which is given to ensouled reason directly (i.e., by internal reference) and excludes all that is given to reason through the senses. That is not to say that there exist two different worlds; instead, it means only that the empirical world of extension does not constitute the entirety of reality.

The grounds of knowledge of God presented in this book include direct experience of moral obligation, an ontological proof from the logical impossibility of nothingness, and traditional cosmological and teleological proofs which are underpinned by the latter. Although none of these arguments are novel in form, to my knowledge, both the moral argument and the ontological argument presented here are new in substance and the latter provides what Kant and subsequent empiricists assert is missing from the cosmological and teleological proofs. All of them depend upon the identity of Being and intelligibility, the access to understanding of which depends upon the man's own, direct intuition of his own Being.

The premise of the ontological proof is not to be confused with the principle *ex nihilo nihil fit* (out of nothing, nothing comes) of Parmenides, which asserts that the existence of the world must be eternal and continuous, because the premise of the ontological proof makes a different claim which is that the existence of *something* is logically necessary and that that something must not only include the rules of its own conception, which means that it must be necessarily intelligible, but, in order to necessarily exist, it must also be self-instantiating. The ontological proof offered here differs from the one offered by St. Anselm and its subsequent variations in that it is not an argument from perfection. Although any conception of God must include his perfection by definition, I do not believe that there is warrant to infer the existence of God as the most perfect being from the conceivability of perfection as such. Since Kant, the usual formulation of the objection to the argument from perfection is that existence is not a predicate and, therefore, not a perfection, but I think there may be some merit to the counterargument that existence is analytical (i.e., the predicate is included in the concept of the subject) to a necessary transcendent being, so the question, if it were not circular, would become whether necessity (as opposed to existence) is a perfection. However, I believe that circularity is embedded in this whole form of ontological enterprise and that it arises because, if God is, as he must be, the sole reference by which perfection may be determined, then any predicate that reflects perfection must be by reference to God in the first place. So, even if existence is a predicate, it can only be shown to be a perfection if it is possessed by God and the premise that existence is a perfection assumes *sub silentio* the existence of the God it purports to prove.

The question of the existence of God is not one to be considered casually. If the universe is merely a causally determined, infinite contingency (which I believe is logically impossible), as many atheists contend, then man is different from other animals only in the scope and power of his intellect and there can be no moral obligation or responsibility. This is a conclusion that most material reductionists find unpalatable but their efforts to escape it are demonstrably futile. If God is an indifferent creator, the conclusions are the same. But if God is *Agape* (or anything like the God of Moses, Abraham, Elijah, and Jesus), then man engages with God through moral will and is both morally responsible and free to be so and how man exercises that freedom may determine his fate for all eternity.

THE POSSIBILITY OF METAPHYSICS

The question of the existence of God is a metaphysical one; indeed, it is the ultimate metaphysical one. Unlike epistemology, which asks what we know and how we know it, metaphysics seeks to go behind epistemological knowledge to describe the ultimate nature of things. That there is an ultimate nature of things seems undeniable; whether it exists in reality in form and substance identical to human cognition of it is a different question; whether the human intellect can have access to reality beyond that which is presented to it by the senses is yet another. Current mainstream philosophy, in the form of material reductionism, answers only the first two such questions affirmatively. But the position of the mainstream today is remarkably unexplanatory and it comes at the cost of abandoning philosophy as a meaningful discipline altogether. If reason demands, as it does, answers to metaphysical questions, then any philosophy which asserts that such answers are beyond the reach of reason must also provide rational grounds for that unhappy circumstance.

Unlike the physical sciences, where the current thinking on a particular topic generally represents the complete body of usable knowledge, Western philosophy comprises a dialectic that has been ongoing for at least several millennia. Modified versions of arguments that were originally advanced by the Ancient Greeks and other classic thinkers and which were thought to have been definitively disposed of have risen again and again to command the stage, oftentimes after many centuries in hiatus. It is therefore not sufficient for a philosopher to study the current mainstream; he or she must also know fully how it came to be such or risk having no understanding of it at all. A physical scientist can be completely competent without knowing the history of science, but a philosopher, to be comparably competent, must be a student of the history of philosophy and, indeed, the distinction between philosophy and its history is largely illusory. In the instant case, it is important to understand, specifically, how mainstream philosophy came to deny both the possibility of metaphysics and the significance of its own epistemological investigations beyond supporting the empirical knowledge of the physical sciences, in order to determine whether those conclusions are well-supported and, if not, whether metaphysics remains to be reclaimed as the ultimate philosophical prize.

As Kant observed, it is possible to understand the history of modern philosophy specifically as a dialectic between rationalism and empiricism. In simple terms, rationalists hold that knowledge depends upon innate reason for its warrant and empiricists hold that all knowledge, including reason itself, comes through the senses. The classic modern philosophical debate began with the philosophy of René Descartes, the first of the three great continental rationalists, who, in 1647, posited *a priori* self-consciousness as the basis of all knowledge, and ended nearly a century later with Hume, who as the last of the three great British empiricists posited a radical skepticism about not just the self but any causal connection between empirical events. In between Descartes and Hume were: Baruch Spinoza, whose rationalism led him to posit a pantheistic God with man being a mere mode of divine substance; John Locke, who as the father of modern empiricism (a title sometimes given to Francis Bacon instead) posited the mind as a *tabula rasa* (blank slate) and defined knowledge as the mind conforming to reality; Gottfried Wilhelm von Leibniz, whose rationalism led him to posit a universe comprising completely closed monads (including as such each human soul) existing in a divinely coordinated harmony; and George Berkeley, whose empiricism led him to posit an ideal reality dependent upon its being perceived for its existence.

That each of these philosophers offers the world much brilliance cannot be denied, but neither can be the utter confusion that their divergent philosophies represent. Kant despaired of the state of the philosophy of his time, especially because metaphysics seemed to be developing in a progressively more chaotic manner while the physical sciences were making great advances. Kant's empiricism is such that he admits no possibility of metaphysics, but he resolves to rescue epistemology from the confusing array of systems of rationalists and empiricists by critiquing reason itself. Kant locates the source of the confusion in what he asserts is the misapplication of principles of empirical knowledge to non-empirical matters as to which they have no validity. Although a detailed argument will be presented in these pages to the effect that Kant errs in limiting reason to a transcendental empirical abstraction, he is commendably thorough in presenting a justification for his empirical premise, an explanation of the phenomenon of self-consciousness (as the unity of apperception), a theory of moral obligation, and the origin of what he regards as the transcendental "Ideas" of soul and God. One can reject (as will be done in these pages) Kant's transcendental idealism, but one cannot deny the great merit of his endeavors and of his willingness to confront all of the complicated issues that are associated with a philosophical system.

Kant was a traditional empiricist insofar as he believed that all knowledge originates in sensory experience; however, Kant also believed that in the process of the cognition of empirical objects reason contributes certain *a priori* concepts under which such cognition must take place. *Importantly, for Kant, these concepts are structural in nature and do not rise to the level of directly intuited, innate ideas.* For Kant, all empirical knowledge is therefore of reality as understood under the structure of human rational cognition, which Kant arranges under a table of categories, and not necessarily as it might independently be; indeed, that reality, called *"noumenal"* by Kant, cannot even be conceived of except as the limit of human empirical cognition because any attempt at a metaphysical understanding of *noumenal* reality can only be made by means of application of the categories of empirical understanding to a reality as to which they do not apply. According to Kant, general logic is nothing more than abstraction of all empirical content from categories of empirical cognition and therefore general logic has no applicability except in relation to such categories and to the objects of thought considered as abstract concepts. The problem of metaphysics arises, concludes Kant, because the intellect insists on answers to metaphysical questions even though it does not have the intellectual tools to provide them.

Introduction

Although the various versions of empirical philosophies that developed in the late nineteenth and early twentieth centuries in England and the United States, including, especially, logical positivism and material reductionism, draw upon Kant where convenient to refute rationalist arguments and other competing claims, current-era empiricists regard Kant with great suspicion. The reasons are of more than historical interest. First, the totality of Kant's philosophy retains much that is traditionally regarded as metaphysics because, although he denies that we can have knowledge of its basic problems, including God, eternality of the soul, and freedom, Kant argues that reason requires their acceptance as a matter of *compelled faith*. Apparently, in drawing a line between knowledge and compelled faith, Kant used too fine a pen for subsequent empiricists, so those philosophers have tended to cherry pick from Kant with limited or no justification of the grounds of their selectivity. In this regard, Bertrand Russell, who happily accepts Kant's refutation of the scholastic arguments for the existence of God but is otherwise generally dismissive of Kant's transcendental philosophy upon which Kant's refutation is based, is a glaring example.

Second, certain difficulties with Kant's philosophy that relate to his unwillingness to acknowledge *noumenal* reality except as representing the limits of empirical cognition and to acknowledge the self as anything more than a formal condition of thought, left the door open for the German idealists to seize upon Kant's transcendental philosophy to formulate their own unabashedly radical idealistic system, which is, of course, anathema to empiricists. Although Kant offers a theory of how objective and universal logic derives from the process of abstracting all empirical content from empirical cognition, he is precluded by the limitations of his own philosophy from offering an explanation of how it is possible for there to be a reality that is organized in a manner such that the categories of human understanding of it can logically be applied to that reality. If reality does not exist *noumenally* or is not compatibly organized, then human reason must be regarded as creative in the sense that we normally attribute to the divine and a solipsistic conclusion is inevitable. Neither does Kant connect an organized objective reality with human consciousness considered as an aspect of empirical man such that we can understand how the faculty of reason *evolves* from an organized material world; instead, Kant accepts conscious cognition as an empirical fact. Worse still, Kant's theory of self-consciousness is impermissibly circular because the self, considered as the *unity of apperception*, is determined by reference to the objects it knows, which knowledge requires its presence in the first place. Kant acknowledges this circularity but somehow finds it both necessary and permissible because in his conception the self is only knowable as the form of representation of thought and not the representation of a thought about the self as an object. The German idealists responded vigorously to these difficulties by transferring human consciousness to the universe in a constitutional way and in its ultimate expression by Georg Wilhelm Friedrich Hegel, characterized the universe as "thought thinking itself."

Finally, if one accepts Kant's system as representing the pinnacle of empiricism, then its failure is suggestive of the inherent deficiency of that philosophical line and it is quite natural and predictable for those subsequent empiricists who are unwilling to abandon empiricism to distance themselves as much as possible from Kant's version.

Instead of attempting to address the difficulties of Kant's empiricism (perhaps because doing so would necessarily expose the fruitlessness of the empiricist line), the modern British and American empiricists have gone in a different direction altogether, sometimes lumping Kant together with the German idealists, and pursuing a wholly reductionist approach with much more limited epistemological ambitions. In its current reductionist form, empiricism adheres to a strict doctrine that states that all knowledge comes from the senses, that reality is precisely as it appears to the human intellect to be, and that there is no knowledge that cannot be scientifically demonstrated or that is not analytically determined by examination of the relationship between the objects of such scientific knowledge. The main difficulty with reductionism is that it fails to describe great portions of human experience, including the evolution of the world, human consciousness, universal and objective knowledge, moral experience, and freedom (which it must reject). Reductionism does not deny its limitations; instead, it asserts that its limitations are *human* limitations and that, to the extent, a phenomenon is not reducible, reductionism is not required to provide an explanation. The following paradigmatic excerpt from the famous debate on the existence of God between Frederick Copleston, SJ, and Bertrand Russell on the Third Program of the British Broadcasting Corp., 1948, demonstrates, via the words of Russell, the predominant view of analytical philosophers on metaphysics:

> RUSSELL: But when is an explanation adequate? Suppose I am about to make a flame with a match. You may say that the adequate explanation of that is that I rub it on the box.
>
> COPLESTON: Well, for practical purposes—but theoretically, that is only a partial explanation. An adequate explanation must ultimately be a total explanation to which nothing further can be added.
>
> RUSSELL: Then I can only say that you're looking for something which can't be got, and which one ought not to expect to get.[2]

In taking this line, modern reductionism has no recourse for the explanation of the things it considers explicable but to appeal to science for answers and in the process of doing so, it has, together with the scientists, declared metaphysics to be impossible and philosophy to be dead.

It is important to remember that although skepticism and subjectivism have from time to time held sway, for most of the history of philosophy man's access to objective and universal truth has not been subject to serious doubt. The skeptical views are unstable because the demonstration of skepticism cannot be made on skeptical grounds and, similarly, the subjectivist views ultimately can be supported only by resorting to objective reason and objective reason can only rest in its inquiry upon direct intuition, which must be regarded as fundamental to sentient beings existing in an intelligible universe. Kant's attempt to abstract the rules of thought from the categories of empirical cognition cannot explain how those categories arise or how man acquires the ability to abstract general logic from them or why the objects of such cognition are intelligible in

---

2. Copleston and Russell, "Debate on the Existence of God."

the first instance. In asserting that the categories themselves are transcendental, Kant walks up to the cognitive divide between sensible and supersensible reality, but because he is unwilling to cross it, he is left with a circularity that corresponds to his circular thinking on the self-concept. The materialist response is to argue that reason is subjective and dependent upon man considered as animal, individual, or group.

There is another, far better alternative, one which answers reason's call to metaphysics by postulation of the *Logos* and by considering intelligibility (not universal consciousness) to be a fundamental ordering characteristic of the universe including the transcendent and the empirical world. Such a view requires direct intuition of the soul and the placement of general logic above the categories of empirical cognition so that the latter might be conceived of as the implementation of the former in the determination of contingent sensible objects. By so doing, an explanation of the possibility of universal, necessary, and objective knowledge of the sensible and supersensible worlds can be provided and the attributes of the objects of theoretical, empirical, and moral knowledge, which are necessary for such objects to be intelligible, can be worked out. Postulation of the *Logos* also renders possible the ultimate ontological task of identifying the relationship between the directly intuited objects of transcendent reality, namely, the soul and God, who is known to reason by the direct perception of moral obligation and analytically, by virtue of the ontological proof of his existence. Indeed, if metaphysics has for a time been dead the time for its resurrection is at hand.

Of course, it is one thing to say that the rules of logic are known with certainty and quite another to say that such knowledge comes from direct intuition and, indeed as has just been mentioned, Kant argues otherwise. But by its nature, logic is abstract, without content or reference to the empirical world, and self-justifying; therefore, the burden of the argument must lie with those who would assert, nevertheless, that the source of the rules of logic is somehow given in empirical reality. Moreover, not only must the empirical case be made in the face of all appearances to the contrary, but it must be built from the ground up and include not just the logic of cognition, but the power to abstract from such logic, including the power to critique itself. Kant's transcendental idealism represents a mighty attempt to do just this; however, that philosophy cannot overcome its own circularities and neither Kant nor any empiricist since has succeeded in overcoming the presumption of the direct intuition of the rules of thought and, indeed, the project, like most other philosophically important ones, has been ceded by the material reductionists to the scientific community.

It is similarly the case with the soul and moral obligation. The soul is disclosed to itself from within itself as a persistent, morally obligated, and substantive unity among a manifold of life experiences. The substance of the soul is given to itself both as the internal perception of a unique "me-ness" and as the perspective from which objectivity is obtained. Because the self is the locus of personal experience there can be no experience of the self that is not by the self and, indeed, in my view, that is what self-consciousness is. Self-consciousness must be more than the unity of apperception or any other formality because it includes not just a bundle of perceptions but also the perception of perceiving. That the self, in turning its attention inward in search of itself, finds nothing but the search does not mean there is no self; to the contrary, because an object cannot be both the subject and predicate of a non-trivial thought, if an internal search for self were to yield anything but internally intuited predicates (such as moral responsibility or freedom), our concept of self would logically have to be held to be in error. Being is given to itself as grounded experience and never as the experience of mere ground. Moral experience implies a soul as its own ground. Although moral obligation governs empirical (as well as spiritual) relations, it is itself given to reason internally both in the direct intuition of being an object of *Agape* and in the analytical intuition of the Supreme Principle of Being and Intelligibility and is externally reflected in the empirical fact of morality.

AGENDA-BASED PHILOSOPHY

Since the Renaissance, metaphysics has been a central part of the politically charged battle between church and state. During the medieval era, metaphysics, along with mathematics and the physical sciences, was conducted under the heavy-handed scrutiny of Rome and was compelled, sometimes under penalty of torture and death, to support church doctrine. Perhaps the most significant development of the period was the introduction of Aristotle into Western philosophy and the formulation by St. Anselm and St. Thomas Aquinas of important Aristotelean arguments for the existence of God. But from the Enlightenment onward the pendulum has swung increasingly away from the church, and philosophy in general has become ever more secular in its orientation and ever more closely aligned with the physical sciences in its doctrines. The Reformation challenged the authority of the church and the French Revolution sought to subordinate it to the state. The tendency toward secularism gained impetus from the movement of philosophy away from the private studios of philosophers who labored on their own into the halls of the great universities, which in the century just concluded have become increasingly dependent upon relations with the nation-states in which they are located for grants and other financial support. Since Kant offered his refutation of the scholastic arguments for the existence of God, modern mainstream philosophy has done its best to treat such arguments as anachronisms. Modern mainstream philosophy, which is the grandchild of classic British empiricism, does not like the idea of God any more than does the modern nation-state. God is seen as the source of natural human rights, which stand in opposition to the power of government and government-controlled science and, indeed, it is the formal recognition of God's endowment to humanity that is the source of the genius of the founding fathers of the American Revolution. Christianity, in particular, puts the individual above the state and the laws of God above the desires of man. Theism stands in opposition to humanism, which is the populist religion of the day, and to which the modern nation-state can pander in its assertion of authority over the individual.

That mainstream philosophy has come to embrace materialism during a political era of secularism in and of itself is not an indictment of the philosophy because, even so, that philosophy is entitled to consideration on its own merits. But the fact that material reductionism has done so by paying the ultimate price of declaring itself to be irrelevant is nothing less than self-damnation and belies an underlying agenda that is not only inapposite to the advancement of its own discipline but, considered together with the vitriol of its proponents against those who would argue in opposition to it, tellingly indicates that it is not merely atheistic but rather fully anti-theistic. John Stuart Mill declared that "God is a word to express, not our ideas, but the want of them." Karl Marx called religion "the opiate of the masses." Frederick Nietzsche declared God to be dead and himself to be the Antichrist. Russell published a collection of atheistic essays under the title *Why I Am Not a Christian*. And consider this passage from Thomas Nagel, one of the best of living philosophers, which, tellingly, appears in a chapter entitled "Evolutionary Naturalism and the Fear of Religion," from his very interesting book, *The Last Word*:

> In speaking of the fear of religion, I don't mean to refer to the entirely reasonable hostility toward certain established religions and religious institutions, in virtue of their objectionable moral doctrines, social policies, and political influence. Nor am I referring to the association of many religious beliefs with superstition and the acceptance of evident empirical falsehoods. I am talking about something much deeper—namely, the fear of religion itself. I speak from experience, being strongly subject to this fear myself: *I want atheism to be true and am made uneasy by the fact that some of the most intelligent and well-informed people I know are religious believers. It isn't just that I don't believe in God and, naturally, hope that I'm right in my belief. It's that I hope there is no God! I don't want there to be a God; I don't want the universe to be like that.*[3] (Emphasis added.)

The charge against reductionism of unphilosophical anti-theistic bias is further supported by the *ad hominem* nature of the outcry that is heard when one of the noteworthy among their members separates himself on this issue. Examples include the mainstream criticism of Antony Flew, who in his last years abandoned atheism in favor of a belief in a disinterested, Aristotelian God, and Nagel, the atheist philosopher just quoted above, after he published his anti-reductionist book, *Mind and Cosmos*, in which he asserts that reductionism is insufficiently robust to explain the evolution of the universe, including human rational experience of it.[4] This sort of blatant bias far exceeds the bounds of legitimate intellectual discourse and cries out for reprimand, and, even more so, justifies the strictest sort of scrutiny about the ideas in favor of which it is demonstrated.

Since Kant, the empiricist project has been conducted on a piecemeal basis, without the support of an encompassing system or even a broad-based epistemology. Indeed, in retaining and working out select Kantian themes, for example the need for precision of definition and consistency of syllogistic terms, and rejecting certain others, for example the supplantation of the traditional Aristotelean logic upon which Kant relied with the predicate logic which the logical positivists invented, not only do the post-Kantian empiricists utterly ignore the importance of presenting a complete epistemology in support of their claims but they flaunt their unwillingness to do so, asserting instead that it is a badge of philosophical prowess. Russell, in characterizing the analytic philosophy that he was instrumental in popularizing and which is embraced at present

---

3. Nagel, *Last Word*, 130. It should be noted that Nagel is not himself a material reductionist but the quoted passage is offered here as an example of the agenda-driven philosophy that typifies the anti-theism that the material reductionists share in common with Nagel.

4. See, e.g., Chorost, "Where Thomas Nagel Went Wrong."

by the overwhelming majority of Anglo-American university philosophy departments, brags about its independence from any such system:

> Modern analytical empiricism . . . differs from that of Locke, Berkeley, and Hume by its incorporation of mathematics and its development of a powerful logical technique. It is thus able, in regard to certain problems, to achieve definite answers, which have the quality of science rather than of philosophy. *It has the advantage, in comparison with the philosophies of the system-builders, of being able to tackle its problems one at a time, instead of having to invent at one stroke a block theory of the whole universe.* Its methods, in this respect, resemble those of science. I have no doubt that, in so far as philosophical knowledge is possible, it is by such methods that it must be sought; I have also no doubt that, by these methods, many ancient problems are completely soluble.[5] (Emphasis added.)

Not too many decades later, A. J. Ayer, one of the founders of positivism, argued that metaphysical statements are meaningless because they are not verifiable and a few decades after that Flew argued that for a claim to be meaningful it must be refutable and that since religious claims may not be refuted they are essentially meaningless, in each case without grounding their claims in an epistemological system. The positions of Ayer and Flew seem to represent a view that not only is truth propositional in nature but so is human experience of the world, neither of which can be maintained on a merely analytic basis and without addressing its presuppositions, including its presuppositions of Being. Moreover, it has been pointed out by many that Ayer's claim itself is not verifiably true and therefore does not pass its own test. As for Flew's assertion about religious claims, it is of course true that one cannot perceive God with one's senses; however, one *can* endeavor to logically infer God's existence from human rational experience and one can also endeavor to refute such inferences and it seems that good philosophy depends, in the case of all arguments for and against the God-proposition, that they be openly grounded upon a sound epistemological foundation.

The anti-theistic agenda of contemporary empiricism notwithstanding, the demand for precision of analytical philosophy will, to the extent possible, be taken to heart in the presentation of transcendent realism in this book, and it is only fair that I confess in advance my own biases in the development of the philosophy presented in these pages. The qualification on precision is required because, in my view, as reason approaches its limits and attempts to peak beyond them in considering God *as an object*, it is inevitable that such precision yield somewhat to metaphor. We have already suggested that God, as *Agape* and as *Logos*, must be self-willing and self-grounding, and in these respects both unique and beyond sensibility in an empirical world that is organized under the principle of causality. God is important to most lay people in their daily lives and many assert a personal relationship with him. Those who have even a rudimentary Western religious education will describe God as having the attributes of omniscience, omnipotence, and omnipresence. The God of the scholastic proofs is naturally characterized in accordance with the nature of the proofs and many such formulations end with the words "and this Being we call *God*," such that God is seen to be the most perfect possible Being, the creator of the world, the designer of the world, the sufficient reason for all that

---

5. Russell, *History of Western Philosophy*, 834.

exists, etc. Such formulations can be viewed in several ways. One is merely definitional, which is to say, for example, that God is by definition the entity who created the world, if there is such an entity. Another is a shorthand for the additional metaphysics that would be necessary to connect God, perhaps defined as an ontologically necessary being, with the God of the particular proof. This is one way of understanding Kant's assertion that all proofs other than the ontological proof presuppose that proof for their validity. It is clear that claims about God are attended by a unique difficulty. One need be especially careful not just about the nature of God, considered as the object of the argument, but also about the applicability of the argument to an object of the type God is asserted to be and whether God is even intelligible as an object of thought in the first place.

As noted, the grounds asserted here for the proposition that God, as *Agape* and as *Logos*, exists include both direct intuition of moral obligation and an ontological argument that has the consequence of supporting traditional scholastic arguments for the existence of God. Once the notion of direct intuition is adequately described, the assertion that moral obligation is directly intuited seems straightforward enough. In transcendent realism, the source of moral obligation is *Agape*. In this case, *Agape* can be understood in most important respects like any other will, that is, the determination of a mind that its object be instantiated. Whether there is such a faculty as direct intuition or that moral obligation is recognized by such a faculty are fair grounds for discussion. There does not seem to be an insurmountable conceptual or linguistic problem with the analysis. Moreover, since access to *Agape* is asserted to arise by virtue of the *Logos*, which is the ground for the intelligibility of the world, there is no basis for denying the applicability of the other structural components of reason to the idea.

The ontological proof to be offered in these pages requires some additional anticipation here. As noted, the gist of the argument is that because absolute nothingness is impossible there must be a necessary object that is the ground of Being and intelligibility. But in this case, it must be clear from the outset that the word *object* is used in a uniquely metaphoric sense. In the *Logos* of transcendent realism, we have direct experience of *Agape* but not necessarily of God as the divine Being whose will it is understood to be. In the ontological proof, we are setting God up against absolute nothingness and therefore as the ground of Being and intelligibility. But, because God is asserted uniquely to be its own ground, we have no direct intuition of God as an *ordinary* object and, therefore, we cannot be certain that our categories of theoretical knowledge are directly applicable. This is even clearer in the case of the scholastic arguments. We might, for example, conclude that there must be an uncaused cause, an unmoved mover, a designer of himself and the universe, etc., but because we cannot fully relate them to any experience, external or internal, it is doubtful that they have any significance other than metaphorically. The closest we can come to an understanding of the necessary is in our understanding of the self-grounding of the rules of thought and in their identical Being. That does not mean that the traditional ontological and cosmological characterizations of God have no significance or even less than the intended significance. In my interpretation, they assert the need for something that is their functional equivalent and can only be understood as such. In other words, there appears, beyond the point of our ability to comprehend fully but before our ability to comprehend ends altogether, an ambiguity that nevertheless may fruitfully be filled metaphorically by accepting, in lieu of the concrete understanding demanded everywhere else, a vaguer notion of a function to be served without requiring knowledge of how it might be accomplished.

Although the God of *Agape* is wholly compatible with the Judeo-Christian deity, the philosophy presented in these pages is not intended as apologetics. Judaism and Christianity are profoundly broader and deeper. They include portrayals of the human fall from grace, direct communication with God, prophesies, miracles, God's presence on earth in the form of Jesus, and his crucifixion, death, and resurrection, the eternality of the soul, and descriptions of heaven and hell. Except for the elucidation of the concept of *Agape*, the possibility of the eternality of the soul, and some brief remarks about Kant's portrayal of life after death, none of these matters will be discussed in these pages. Nevertheless, it is only fair to confess here another possible bias, which despite my best efforts may be presumed to influence my philosophy, namely, my religion, which is Roman Catholicism, which, as G. K. Chesterton once summarized so succinctly, may be taken as simply stated in the Apostle's Creed.[6] My faith includes, on an intellectual basis, the philosophy included here and all of the doctrines that go along with Roman Catholicism, which I accept as a matter of divine revelation. I should probably go the further step of acknowledging that if I were to determine that my faith conflicted with my philosophy, I would almost certainly go to my grave investigating where my reason failed me. Fortunately enough, that is a fate of which I have been spared.

Additionally, as a matter that is in part intellectual and at least equally as much sentimental, I should state that I cannot accept any philosophy that cannot *positively* justify any limits it would impose on the ability of human reason to understand the world of human rational experience. That is why I have such great respect for Kant who aspires mightily to do so, even though I believe the fatal flaw in his transcendental idealism lies in where he places that limit, and very little regard for positivists or reductionists, whose assertions as to such limitations often go without even an attempt at justification, beyond my admiration of the physical sciences with which they have aligned themselves. How can an understanding of human experience, which is rational in character, be beyond the ability of a reason that has the power to ask metaphysical questions? In a related vein, I should confess bias against any understanding of the world that includes as its highest form of intellect a creature such as man, pitifully conceived as a being whose rationality has reached a pinnacle at which he is only sufficiently intelligent to recognize that his life is fleeting and brutish, lived as an automaton with a perverse illusion of ego and freedom, devoid of any meaning yet subject to a moral obligation that he cannot possibly uphold, and without any ability to understand why it should be so. I cannot imagine a creature that is more pathetic and it is not in my nature to be so pessimistic or self-effacing. It is undeniable that there remain many important, unsolved metaphysical puzzles. The solution to them will not come from science because they are not the subject matter of science. Neither will the solution come from philosophers who abandon their posts. What I take from the desolate state of mainstream metaphysics is only that

---

6. Chesterton, *Othodoxy*, 10–11.

there is much work left for philosophers to do. In this I am not alone and I think that the following words of C. E. M. Joad are especially poignant:

> Unless I thought that philosophy had some contribution to make to the answering of such questions as "What sort of universe is this in which we are living?" and "How ought we to live in it?," I, for one, should have no interest in philosophy. I believe that most philosophers are in similar case. In spite of the scantiness of the light which philosophy has managed to throw upon the constitution of the universe and the status of human existence, in spite of the meagerness of the rules which it has succeeded in drawing up for the right conduct of life, we are, most of us feel convinced, not knocking at a door irrevocably closed, when we look to it to provide understanding and guidance.[7]

---

7. Joad, *Guide*, 258.

2

The Death and Resurrection of Metaphysics

THE SUNDERING OF THE PSYCHOSOME

When René Descartes, the father of modern philosophy, posited as the foundation of his system the three most famous words ever written by a modern philosopher, "*Cogito ergo sum*" (originally stated in French as "*je pense, donc je suis*" and translating into "I think, therefore I am") and divided the human being into body and soul, he sent metaphysics down a series of blind alleys from which it has yet to return. Descartes was anxious to show that man's substance is spiritual and that his soul is immortal but, despite great effort, Descartes was unable to connect soul with body in a way that offered satisfactory explanation of many of the basic problems of metaphysics, including man's experience of moral obligation, free will, and consciousness. Descartes's failure to do so made manifest that his assertion that man's essence is a thinking being temporarily *occupying* a physically extended body is a mistake and it set Descartes and his apologetics up as an easy target for what has grown over the centuries into the mainstream secular philosophy that prevails today.

The questions of the essence of the human being and the nature of self-knowledge must of necessity be fundamental to any comprehensive philosophical system because the philosophical investigation into the nature of knowledge and the world can never be undertaken independently of human knowledge and experience. For there to be knowledge, cognition must start with an understanding of itself as the "cognizing-I." As a result, the answers to the questions of whether the self of self-consciousness is real and, if so, whether it can be known by direct intuition, which were raised and answered affirmatively by Descartes, will largely determine the lines that are available to the philosopher in undertaking other metaphysical and epistemological investigations.

At its core, human experience is quite different from the dualism offered by Descartes. Man's self-consciousness is of a psychosomatic unity, that is, of a fully integrated person comprising a persistent, incorporeal self and a spatio-temporally extended body. Predictably, therefore, the result of Descartes's philosophy was to set an agenda for some sort of monistic response. In most of the systems that come after Descartes, the self, if it is considered real at all, is conceived of as either body or mind existing as (1) a wholly material organism whose consciousness and intellect are fully material phenomena, which to the extent they are remarkable at all, are nothing more than a curious, species-specific attribute (e.g., Locke, scientific reductionism, and much of modern philosophy of the mind); (2) an entity of doubtful substance (a) to which a stream of thoughts either appear in an illusorily connected fashion (Hume), or (b) which is a mere form of the representation of thought (Kant) or other formality (John Searle), or (c) which is a mere limit on experience (Ludwig Wittgenstein); or (3) a mere mode or aspect of a universal, pantheistic consciousness (e.g., Spinoza and Hegel). However, the solutions offered by these systems sacrifice one or the other genuine aspects of human experience that Descartes errantly sought to explain by his dualism precisely because these systems lead to the utter obliteration of the real, persistent self upon which human consciousness is anchored. As a result, instead of offering an understanding of man's rational experience of reality, modern philosophy has pulled the rug out from under him. It is not an exaggeration, then, to say that one of the unintended consequences of Cartesian dualism was to effectively divert the attention of mainstream philosophy from the explanation of human rational experience in all its fullness to explaining away however much of that experience is deemed necessary to deny man his soul.

This state of affairs has profound implications which run throughout contemporary society because the philosophical understanding of self is at the core, not merely of metaphysical understanding, but also at the very heart of what action is conceivable and even morally required. Consider these words from Jeff Bergner in his book *Against Modern Humanism*:

> What difference does it make how we think about who or what we are? What difference does it make how we understand ourselves and our purpose(s)? One who thinks of oneself as a servant of a god named Allah, commanded to die in a glorious and holy act of destruction, can fly an aircraft into the World Trade Center at 400 miles an hour. Such an action is not possible, and barely even comprehensible, to a person who thinks of himself or herself as a businessman in a commercial republic or as a suburban soccer mom. One who thinks of himself as a member of a tribe (or a family, or gang, or nation) whose perpetuation is prized above all else can act with honor and lay down one's life for that end. One who believes one is everlasting soul briefly trapped in a physical body, can act with little concern about preserving that body. And one who believes one's entire psychosomatic being is at risk of permanent bliss or torment will take seriously indeed the path to salvation.[1]

Left out in the modern dialectic on the soul is the fact that the diremption between the persistence of the self of consciousness and the temporary nature of its body does not necessarily imply that man is a duality of mind and body, or that one possesses or imprisons the other, or that one or the other is an illusion. To be sure, the dichotomy raises particularly challenging metaphysical questions which cannot be avoided, but any philosophy that proposes to consider man on any terms other than those of common human rational experience must provide compelling grounds for doing so. The position of the reductionists has the advantage of relying exclusively on material which is, to most

---

1. Bergner, *Against Modern Humanism*, 19.

reasonable minds, indisputably presented to the senses. It suffers from the great disadvantage, however, of being remarkably incapable of explaining human experience, including, especially, self-consciousness, the access of reason to universal and objective truth, and moral obligation and freedom. The view of man as a psychosomatic unity has the great advantage of explaining virtually all of human experience, but it requires resorting to an objective reality that is supersensible and raises the extremely difficult questions concerning the substance of objects, including the human soul, and the existence of God. The view of man as a psychosomatic unity is the traditional Judeo-Christian view, but it is not one which has found much favor in the modern philosophical community.

If human reason is not materially reducible it cannot be the subject matter of science. Science can tell us about the make-up of the material world and the relationship among its objects insofar (and only insofar) as they are presented to the senses. Science must operate within the context of the sensible world but it cannot tell us whether that world as perceived by the mind of man fully exhausts reality or only mirrors all or a portion of it. The metaphysical aspects of human rational experience are not only inexplicable scientifically but fly in the face of what is discoverable on that basis.

Certainly one of the best measurements of the robustness of a philosophy is the extent to which it fully explains human rational experience and, to the extent that it is unable to do so, the reasons for its incompleteness. Any view that does not take into account both man's direct intuition of himself as a real, persistent, incorporeal being and his existence in the empirical world as a mortal entity in a fully integrated way is therefore *prima facie* deficient and its caliber may fairly be assessed by whether it offers a compelling explanation of the grounds for its omission to do so. By this standard, modern mainstream philosophy is an abysmal failure. In limiting the scope of philosophy to the support of the validity of the judgments of physical science, modern mainstream philosophy has not only abdicated its throne as queen of all sciences but it has also pronounced philosophy, its own discipline, to be dead. In making such a pronouncement, however, modern mainstream philosophy exceeds the very authority it grants itself, because the reach of reason and the stuff of its objects are philosophical questions which may not be answered by science. Philosophy can no more declare itself to be dead than can a person declare himself to be dead because, in the case of philosophy, the grounds for any such declaration are the subject of philosophical investigation and, in both cases, the fact of the declaration contradicts its substance. To make the point by standing Descartes on his head, it as if modern mainstream philosophy declares "*Non cogito, ergo non sum!*" ("I do not think, therefore I am not") but such a declaration is, of course, itself an unthinkable thought. It is material reductionism, therefore, which must be declared dead, not metaphysics, and the demise of modern mainstream philosophy cries out for an examination of how it could have possibly arrived at this point not merely anecdotally but, far more importantly, as a prelude to the restoration of metaphysics on sound grounds. To fix philosophy, it is essential to begin with Descartes and to follow in greater detail the road taken by him and the succession of philosophers, including the quantum scientists who covet, but may never possess, the crown of the queen of all sciences.

THE ROAD TO NOWHERE

As has been emphasized, under the traditional Roman Catholic view that prevailed at the time of Descartes and continues to this day, man is understood as a psychosomatic unity which survives death and is resurrected on a day of final judgment to enjoy eternal life in the presence of God or to suffer eternal despair in separation from God. Although this view, which was developed by the church over the first several centuries after Jesus, has its roots in both Judaic and Greek religious and philosophical traditions, it gained unprecedented acceptance primarily on the grounds of what Christians consider to be the revealed truth of the New Testament. As Roman Catholic doctrine was worked out and formalized, the perceived opposition between spirit and flesh came to be viewed not as a dualistic battle that is internal to man but as a reflection of the orientation of the whole person toward or away from God.

As the early centuries of the first millennium passed and ancient Greek philosophy became available in Latin, Christian scholars developed a number of Aristotelian logical arguments for the existence of God. These arguments were initially discouraged by the church because of its concerns not only that philosophical arguments might distract from the primacy of faith-based revelation but also about the consequences of the counter-arguments that they would inevitably attract. By the early centuries of the second millennium, as the church's control over scholarship waned and the Enlightenment dawned, medical scientists were learning much about the human organism and, although they could not explain the phenomenon of life, their increasing knowledge of biological processes offered no evidence of even the possibility of resurrection. By the time of Descartes, church doctrine was under increasing attack from a growing number of skeptics, including scientists, men of commerce, and secular philosophers, all of whom were enjoying the liberation from church-controlled thought and the libertine mores that the Renaissance and early Enlightenment brought them. The church therefore had no choice but to defend its faith in the arena of philosophical ideas. Descartes, in a stunning gambit that was to have a greater impact on the direction of philosophical thought and discourse than any other, determined to embrace the skeptical methodology but not its conclusion. After surveying his own conscious experience, Descartes found that there was only one thing that he could not doubt, namely, that he must exist because, in doubting everything, he was engaged in *thinking*. Starting with that simple conclusion, Descartes reasoned that if he exists, then so must a more, and in fact most, perfect being and, because such a perfect being would not deceive him, Descartes could confidently rely not only on his direct intuition of self but also on the evidence of the empirical world presented to him by his senses.

As already remarked, in dividing man into the dual components of mind and body, Descartes's motivation was to show that man's essence or substance is mental and not physical and therefore could survive corporeal death. Descartes's dualism also offered something of a truce with the increasingly secular scientific community of which Descartes was himself an important part because, in effect, Descartes proposed to retain for the church man's mental component while ceding the study of man's body to science. But Descartes's suit for peace was summarily spurned and Descartes found that, in proposing mind-body dualism, he had set himself up for a withering attack which followed almost immediately from both the philosophical and scientific communities.

The first challenge to Cartesian dualism was originated by Pierre Gassendi, a French priest and contemporary of Descartes, and was later championed by Hume, the ultimate classical British empiricist. Under the Gassendi-Hume line of argument, it was asserted that there is no unified thinking self but only a constant stream of thoughts which seem to assemble themselves in a connected order. The Gassendi-Hume argument is that associating a *self* with the act of thinking and then concluding that the presence of thought proves the existence of that self assumes what it seeks to prove. The argument proceeds that all that can be asserted is the presence of cognitive activity along the lines of "*there is thought.*"

The Gassendi-Hume argument is important because it has been adopted in some shape or form expressly or implicitly by many, if not most, subsequent philosophers including Spinoza, Kant (who, as will be seen, is nevertheless subject to this same criticism), Hegel, and the modern reductionists. If correct, it leads to two possible alternative conceptions of the human being. The first is that instead of a persistent, conscious being, man is both temporary and in constant flux. This is the view that is most compatible with the empiricism of Locke, Hume, Kant (although not his rationally-compelled faith), and modern reductionism. The second is that consciousness is not individual but universal in nature and that, instead of representing the substance of human beings, universal consciousness is something that is experienced by human reason as a consequence of its participation in nature (Spinoza, Hegel, and, under at least one interpretation to be described below, Wittgenstein).

The Gassendi-Hume argument is deeply flawed for many reasons. One of the objections to the Gassendi-Hume argument, namely, that it ignores the nature and structure of cognition, merits immediate consideration because it is relevant to virtually the entirety of subsequent philosophy that will be discussed in turn in the following pages; the other objections are best raised as such to the systems to which they most specifically relate. The Gassendi-Hume argument is certainly supported by the grammatical form of the *Cogito* because (as translated to English) it begins with the word "I" and therefore apparently assumes its conclusion. However, Descartes's point is that the "I think" *is* the "I am" and that, for there to be any thinking at all, it must be the thought of a persistent thinker. Whether Descartes considered the importance of separating the thought itself from its thinker, the fact that the *Cogito* is formulated in an apparently tautological way merely underscores the necessity of the self in the process of thinking. As Kant importantly points out, in the subject-predicate logic by which human reason operates, every thought is accompanied by an implicit "I think" so that a thought such as "it is raining outside" is really the thought "*I think* thinks that it is raining outside," whether the thinker is aware of himself in the act of thinking about rain or not. In modern predicate logic, the *Cogito* might be restated as "there is one and only one S such that S is the subject and the object of a thought T about the existence of S." It is no accident that this formulation begins with the existential quantifier, *there is one and only one*. In contemporary parlance, Descartes's self-reflection consists of Descartes having a thought about the fact that he is thinking.

This predicate-logical formulation obviously represents a special sort of privileged assertion because it is known to be true only by the direct intuition of the one who asserts it. That such is the case can be seen by considering a second major problem with the Gassendi-Hume argument, namely, that in its attempt to eliminate the "I think" from the *Cogito*, the Gassendi-Hume argument has to treat thought as though it were an empirically verifiable phenomenon. If I am asked to justify my statement that "I think it is raining," I might convincingly respond by saying that I see what appear to be droplets of water falling from the clouds above and that when I go outside I feel what appear to be droplets of water on my skin and I sense that they are wet, and that, because all of these are phenomena that I associate with rain, I conclude that it is raining. But if I am asked to justify the Gassendi-Hume argument that "there is thought," how shall I respond except to say that I conclude that there is thought because I am the one who is thinking it? A proponent of the Gassendi-Hume argument might assert that I should ignore the natural structure of thought, which transforms "there is thought" to "I think there is thought" and respond only that "there is experience of a thought." But how can such an experience occur *except by the direct intuition of its thinker*? It is not just thought of which I am aware, but thought the access to which I have unique privilege. Moreover, even if disassociate awareness of the existence of thought might somehow arise, then the only other possibility is that the thought must be both thinking about itself, not as thinker but as thought, and experiencing itself in the process. But how can a thought, which is an idea, think about or experience anything? A thought can be about any conceivable entity other than itself (as a thought) because in the latter case the thought would be its own subject and object. *Logically, a thought,* T, *cannot be about* T *without entailing an infinite loop of thinking.* To avoid circularity there must be a persistent self, S, that has a thought, T, about S, such that S is not T but the thinker of T. Such a self may, of course, also have thoughts about thinking in general as well as thoughts about thoughts about thinking in general, but how can there be an experience of a thought about me as an existing entity if I do not exist? Surely, such an experience is not the same as one of a thought about a unicorn and the difference is that such an experience both is about *and belongs to* me.

It will be illuminating to consider by way of contrast to human conscious experience the unconscious data processing of a weather monitoring computer that detects and reports upon the occurrence of rain. The computer can state that "it is raining" but it cannot know or even think that such is the case. Conscious thought occurs when a conscious entity formulates a thought. Consciousness is objective *self-reference*. The statement "there is consciousness" is awkwardly incomplete and in concept is no more meaningful than the thought of one hand clapping; it requires reformulation as "I am conscious" because it means that there is an entity *thinking about itself as a thinking entity*. Although a computer may be designed to detect and report the occurrence of brain waves of human subjects, it cannot consciously detect and report that consciousness is occurring because the computer is not a self-conscious entity and it is only the self-consciousness of the person asserting its own consciousness that may be known and reported to others. The computer may process by manipulating its embedded symbols a series of related "observations" and store them sequentially in its "memory," and it may even report by further symbol manipulation that observations are being so made and stored, but it cannot have any knowledge of itself as a computing entity and, indeed, no knowledge resides in the computer itself but instead knowledge arises as the result of *human interpretation* of the symbols manipulated, recorded, and displayed by the machine. If one were metaphorically to characterize the data processing of the computer as "thinking," then the Gassendi-Hume argument would apply to its illusorily connected "thoughts" but that argument utterly mischaracterizes Descartes's self-consciousness. For Descartes to have been conscious that "there is consciousness" he must have been conscious of himself and speaking only about his own consciousness.

Spinoza followed Descartes as the second great modern rationalist and, although Spinoza's philosophy reflects his deep knowledge of Cartesian principles, Spinoza does not accept Cartesian doubt or its subjective starting point.[2] Instead, Spinoza argues that the starting point of all metaphysics must be its highest ontological object. Spinoza starts with a definition of "substance" as that which is in itself and conceived through itself, a definition of "attribute" as that which the intellect perceives as constituting the essence of substance, and a definition of "mode" as the modifications of substance, or that which exists in, and is conceived through, something other than itself, and Spinoza proceeds in linear fashion, expressing his philosophy in a series of additional definitions, axioms, and corollaries. Of particular relevance to the instant discussion, Spinoza's metaphysics include a pantheistic God, who, as the one and only infinite substance, equates fully with nature and who may be understood by human reason solely under the attributes of thought and extension. Under Spinoza's scheme, man's substance must also be God but his identity is that of a mode that may be understood under the attribute of extension as his physical body and under the attribute of thought as his mind. The dual attributes under which man is understood apply to all other objects but they do not result in a dualistic reality; rather, they are proposed by Spinoza as two different ways of understanding their monistic objects. For Spinoza, man's mind is the idea of, and as complex as, his body and when his body dies so must his mind.

Although there are differences of opinion about Spinoza's stance on immortality, it follows that man as an individual mode perishes along with his body, although his substance, as part of the infinite divinity, continues in eternity. Spinoza's philosophy specifically solves the problem that plagued Descartes, namely that the mind and body act as a unit, although for Spinoza because man is a mere mode of a necessary Supreme Being man is fully determined. Although Spinoza's philosophy includes several interesting metaphysical points, for example, its proof that there can be only one God and its equating (not described above) of the logic of implication with causality, it is fatally flawed in two respects that are important here. The first and more obvious difficulty faced by Spinoza's philosophy is that it depends from the very beginning upon a traditional ontological proof and therefore is subject to the criticisms of that proof.[3] The second is that his pantheism depends upon an impermissible application (and misunderstanding) of the concept of infinity to his idea of substance. It is at best doubtful that the concept of infinity can be meaningfully applied to the concept of God and, even if it applies, in some way, whether specifically or as a metaphor, it is doubtful that God's infinite

---

2. The work of Spinoza summarized here is set forth in Spinoza, *Ethics*, 408–617.
3. See the discussion at 10 and also at 328–331.

nature would be such as to preclude the existence of anything that is not-God. Spinoza's mistakes in this regard are examples of the type of scope error that neither Kant nor the modern materialists will allow. For Spinoza's conception of human substance to be justified, he must prove both the existence and immanence of God; because he accomplishes neither, that conception fails.

Locke is the first of the three great classic British empiricists and his thinking appears after Spinoza but before the rationalist Leibniz and the other classic empiricists, Berkeley and Hume. Locke argues: that man's mind is a blank slate at birth containing only the capacity to reason; that all knowledge comes through the senses; that objects are supported by a featureless substance that causes in the mind ideas which represent both the object's primary qualities of extension and its secondary qualities, such as its sensible temperature, color, taste, and odor, which are dependent upon the disposition of the perceiver; and that truth consists of the conformity of such ideas to reality. As for man's substance, Locke argues that it should be understood not as an immaterial thinking being, but as a participant in a single continuous life. For Locke, the essence of man as a species *is his species* and his essence as an individual human is his *existence as an organism*. In this regard, Locke asserts that man is no different than any other animal species. For Locke, thinking is an activity but not the essence of man and is of indeterminate origin, the possibilities of which include both a psychosomatic unity and a materially reducible being:

> We have the ideas of matter and thinking, but possibly shall never be able to know whether any mere material being thinks or no; it being impossible for us, by the contemplation of our own ideas, without revelation, to discover whether Omnipotency has not given to some systems of matter, fitly disposed, a power to perceive and think, or else joined and fixed to matter, so disposed, a thinking immaterial substance: it being, in respect of our notions, not much more remote from our comprehension to conceive that GOD can, if he pleases, superadd to matter a faculty of thinking, than that he should superadd to it another substance with a faculty of thinking; since we know not wherein thinking consists, nor to what sort of substances the Almighty has been pleased to give that power, which cannot be in any created being, but merely by the good pleasure and bounty of the Creator.[4]

Locke explains personal identity, that is, the sense of persistent self, by a process of conscious memory such that the same person can be conscious of himself at a particular time and also conscious of a memory of the past conscious events of his life. As for consciousness itself, Locke simply identifies it with the act of thinking, without explaining how such consciousness is associated with the thoughts of which it is conscious. Locke directly challenges Descartes and the notion of an immaterial thinking substance:

> But the question is, whether if the same substance which thinks be changed, it can be the same person; or, remaining the same, it can be different persons?
>
> And to this I answer: First, this can be no question at all to those who place thought in a purely material animal constitution, void of an immaterial substance. For, whether their supposition be true or no, it is plain they conceive personal identity preserved in something else than identity of substance; as animal

---

4. Locke, *Essay Concerning Human Understanding*, Book IV, Chapter III, §6, 540–41.

> identity is preserved in identity of life, and not of substance. And therefore those who place thinking in an immaterial substance only, before they can come to deal with these men, must show why personal identity cannot be preserved in the change of immaterial substances, as well as animal identity is preserved in the change of material substances, or variety of particular material substances, or variety of particular bodies: unless they will say, it is one immaterial spirit that makes the same life in brutes, as it is one immaterial spirit that makes the same person in men; which the Cartesians at least will not admit, for fear of making brutes thinking things too.[5] (Section number omitted.)

Interestingly, Locke departs from the Gassendi-Hume line by accepting the *Cogito* and expanding it to cover human empirical experience in general (e.g., I see, therefore I am), acknowledging that man could know of his own existence by reference to his empirical experiences just as much from his own thought. But in Locke's formulation of individual substance there are several slights of hand. By equating self with continuous organic existence he effectively denies the inner sense of a persistent, *unchanging*, self, which is inexplicable in Locke's conception, completely glossing over the diremption between that inner sense and the real, constant flux of the organism. Additionally, in attaching consciousness to organic thought processes he adds the "I think" to thought in a circular way because in Locke's understanding the "I" of "I think" is known by tying immediate consciousness to conscious memory, which is a process that can only occur if there is consciousness in the first place.

Berkeley is the second of the classic British empiricists and is known as the inventor of subjective idealism. Because in Berkeley's philosophy the world is ideal in nature there is no room for dualism and his conception of soul, which follows from his epistemology, is one of simple spirit. Berkeley accepts the empiricist premise that all knowledge comes through the senses but denies any knowledge of a material reality or any reason to postulate one. Berkeley argues, following Locke, that knowledge of external reality consists exclusively of ideas about it and, *contra* Locke, that as a result we cannot have any knowledge of the materiality of the objects of cognition. Berkeley challenges Locke directly on a number of points which are critical to the latter's version of empiricism, including, most importantly, his doctrine of material substance:

> If we inquire into what the most accurate philosophers declare themselves to mean by material substance, we shall find them acknowledge they have no other meaning annexed to these sounds but the idea of Being in general, together with the relative notion of its supporting accidents. The general idea of Being appeareth to me the most abstract and incomprehensible of all other; and as for its supporting accidents, this, as we have just now observed, cannot be understood in the common sense of those words; it must therefore be taken in some other sense, but what that is they do not explain. So that when I consider the two parts or branches which make the signification of the words material substance, I am convinced there is no distinct meaning annexed to them. But why should we trouble ourselves any farther, in discussing this material substratum or support of figure and motion, and other sensible qualities? Does it not suppose they

---

5. Ibid., Book I, Chapter XXVII, §12, 336.

have an existence without the mind? And is not this a direct repugnancy, and altogether inconceivable?[6] (Section number omitted.)

Berkeley does not dispute the existence of physical reality but argues that, because our experience of reality is limited to cognition of ideas, we have no reason to conceive of reality as being anything other than those ideas, which Berkeley considers to be passive in nature. For Berkeley, the minds which perceive the ideal objects of physical reality are not themselves passive ideas but actively perceiving entities, which he calls, interchangeably, mind, spirit, soul, and self. It follows, according to Berkeley, that the existence of any object depends upon its being perceived by a mind:

> That neither our thoughts, nor passions, nor ideas formed by the imagination, exist without the mind, is what everybody will allow. And it seems no less evident that the various sensations or ideas imprinted on the sense, however blended or combined together (that is, whatever objects they compose) cannot exist otherwise than in a mind perceiving them—I think an intuitive knowledge may be obtained of this by any one that shall attend to what is meant by the term exists, when applied to sensible things. The table I write on I say exists, that is, I see and feel it; and if I were out of my study I should say it existed-meaning thereby that if I was in my study I might perceive it, or that some other spirit actually does perceive it. . . . For as to what is said of the absolute existence of unthinking things without any relation to their being perceived, that seems perfectly unintelligible. Their *esse* is *percipi*, nor is it possible they should have any existence out of the minds or thinking things which perceive them.[7]

When Berkeley addresses the spirit, his philosophy takes an interesting twist in which he identifies the spirit as being incorporeal substance:

> We perceive a continual succession of ideas, some are anew excited, others are changed or totally disappear. There is therefore some cause of these ideas, whereon they depend, and which produces and changes them. That this cause cannot be any quality or idea or combination of ideas, is clear [from prior discussion]. It must therefore be a substance; but it has been shewn that there is no corporeal or material substance: it remains therefore that the cause of ideas is an incorporeal active substance or spirit.
>
> A spirit is one, simple, undivided, active being as it perceives ideas it is called the understanding, and as it produces or otherwise operates about them it is called the will. Hence there can be no idea formed of a soul or spirit; for all ideas whatever, being passive and inert [citation omitted], they cannot represent unto us, by way of image or likeness, that which acts. A little attention will make it plain to any one, that to have an idea which shall be like that active principle of motion and change of ideas is absolutely impossible. Such is the nature of spirit, or that which acts, that it cannot itself be perceived, but only by the effects which it produceth.[8] (Section numbers omitted.)

---

6. Berkeley, *Treatise Concerning the Principles of Human Knowledge*, §17, 186.

7. Ibid., §26, 190.

8. Ibid., §27, 190–91.

It is noteworthy that Berkeley avoids the Cartesian problem of the apparent impossibility of mind moving matter by eliminating matter altogether and replacing it with ideas which are manipulatable by minds. In doing so, Berkeley acquires a subtler difficulty, the discussion of which will be postponed, namely whether it is permissible to conflate the idea of an object with the object itself; we have already seen that in the case of self-consciousness, it is not.

Although Berkeley contends that objects do not exist independently of their being perceived, as noted, he accepts the existence of physical reality independently of any particular mind. To avoid solipsism and a reality that switches on and off when we turn our attention to and away from it, Berkeley must identify an independent ground for its existence. Since human minds are not themselves divinely creative and reality is consistent, connected, and organized under natural laws which are beyond the power of human minds to alter, Berkeley concludes that the world must depend for its existence on God, conceived of as infinite spirit who holds all reality in his divine mind and gives it order and intelligibility.

Leibniz is the third and, in my opinion, the greatest of the three rationalists. Leibniz's philosophy occupies a unique place among the modern rationalists because it represents a rejection of both materialism and substance dualism in favor of an objective, monistic idealism, which it reaches by treating space and time as an illusion that represents relationships among beings rather than the real structure of the universe. Specifically, Leibniz rejects materialism on two grounds. The first is that inner, unified conscious experience cannot be explained materially. The second is expressed in a more complex argument. Leibniz's position is essentially that for an object to exist it must ultimately either be individual, unified, indivisible substance or an aggregate of such substances and that because matter is infinitely divisible it cannot be substance. Leibniz calls the basic substantive elements "monads," which, although unextended, have certain fundamental characteristics, including "perception," which I understand to be the internal representation of the relationship of each monad to the rest of the universe as to which, under Leibniz's conception, it has no external representation, and "appetition," which is the internal principle of change within the monad. Significantly, monads are, in Leibniz's terminology, "windowless" and cannot be affected by each other or anything but God:

> [T]here is no way of explaining how a Monad can be altered in quality or internally changed by any other created thing; since it is impossible to change the place of anything in it or to conceive in it any internal motion which could be produced, directed, increased or diminished therein, although all this is possible in the case of compounds, in which there are changes among the parts. The Monads have no windows, through which anything could come in or go out. Accidents cannot separate themselves from substances nor go about outside of them, as the 'sensible species' of the Scholastics used to do. Thus neither substance nor accident can come into a Monad from outside.[9]

To connect the monads with real experience, Leibniz's metaphysics proceed along the following lines. Each monad must have unique qualities, otherwise the world would be featureless and each monad would be indiscernible from each other monad. Since

---

9. Leibniz, *Monadology*, §7, 219.

each monad is windowless, all change must occur within and be expressed as a continuous sequence of changes in its perception in accordance with its appetition. But change can only occur within a simple substance if it contains within itself "multiplicity," which Leibniz justifies by reference to the human experience of self:

> We have in ourselves experience of a multiplicity in simple substance, when we find that the least thought of which we are conscious involves variety in its object. Thus all those who admit that the soul is a simple substance should admit this multiplicity in the Monad.[10] (Section number omitted.)

Leibniz offers a famous and important argument for the inexplicability of consciousness in material terms:

> And supposing there were a machine, so constructed as to think, feel, and have perception, it might be conceived as increased in size, while keeping the same proportions, so that one might go into it as into a mill. That being so, we should, on examining its interior, find only parts which work one upon another, and never anything by which to explain a perception. Thus it is in a simple substance, and not in a compound or in a machine, that perception must be sought for. Further, nothing but this (namely, perceptions and their changes) can be found in a simple substance. It is also in this alone that all the internal activities of simple substances can consist.[11]

In Leibniz's thought, there are four different types of monads: matter, plants, animals, and humans. Matter's internal properties are limited to expressions of external relationships, plants internal properties include those of matter plus an expression of their form, animals include those of plants plus memory, and humans have the properties of animals plus reason. In this understanding, all simple substances are similar in state to unconscious human beings. For Leibniz, it is reason that sets man apart and it is by reason that man conceives of self, substance, and God:

> But it is the knowledge of necessary and eternal truths that distinguishes us from the mere animals and gives us Reason and the sciences, raising us to the knowledge of ourselves and of God. And it is this in us that is called the rational soul or mind [spirit].
>
> It is also through the knowledge of necessary truths, and through their abstract expression, that we rise to acts of reflection, which make us think of what is called, I, and observe that this or that is within us; and thus, thinking of ourselves, we think of being, of substance, of the simple and the compound, of the immaterial, and of God Himself, conceiving that what is limited in us is in Him without limits. And these acts of reflection furnish the chief objects of our reasonings.[12] (Section numbers omitted.)

Leibniz next articulates what he regards as the two great principles of reason, the first of which dates back to the ancient Greeks and the second of which is new, forms the basis of a novel argument for the existence of God, and will be much discussed by

---

10. Ibid., §16, 226.
11. Ibid., §17, 228–29.
12. Ibid., §§29–30, 233–34.

subsequent philosophers, including, especially, Heidegger, upon whom we will focus in chapter 9, "Being and Intelligibility":

> Our reasonings are grounded upon two great principles, that of contradiction, in virtue of which we judge false that which involves a contradiction, and true that which is opposed or contradictory to the false;
>
> And that of sufficient reason, in virtue of which we hold that there can be no fact, real or existing, no statement true, unless there be a sufficient reason, why it should be so and not otherwise, although these reasons usually cannot be known by us.[13] (Section numbers omitted.)

For Leibniz, space and time are a well-founded illusion by virtue of which the soul is able to *perceive* the relationship among those monads and that if one thinks space and time away, one can see that each monad must contain within itself all that it was, is, and ever will be, including, perhaps most importantly, its relationship with each other monad. There is no cause and effect or any other natural law; instead, the organization of the natural world is simply the expression of the preestablished harmony of the monads, which is established by God. Leibniz believes that God is the demonstrable sufficient reason for all that exists.

As is the case with Spinoza, Leibniz has bequeathed to us many brilliant and useful concepts, including the idea that space and time do not exist independently in reality, the principle of sufficient reason (about which we will have much to say later), and the overarching importance of the individual soul in understanding reality. However, Leibniz's metaphysics as a whole have never gained wide support and will not do so here. In order to maintain his notion that space and time are a well-founded illusion, Leibniz has to invent an incredibly complex system and, speaking metaphorically, it is as if Ptolemy's astronomy is supplanting that of Copernicus. With respect to the soul as monad, Leibniz's conception is such that each human being contains *within himself* his own identity and his relations to the rest of the universe as to which he has no external representation; he is, in essence, both himself and an encapsulation of the entire universe from his own perspective and, in this regard, would seem to be, at the individual level, not unlike Hegel's universal consciousness (described below). But it is at best difficult to understand how the individual can be anything other than at once a solipsistic entity (since he is windowless) and fully determined.

As the last of the three classic British empiricists, Hume follows Locke and Berkeley and all three of the rationalists. Hume's adoption of the Gassendi line of argument was part of his broader radical skepticism. Like Locke, Hume believed that the human mind is a blank slate at birth, but, unlike Locke, Hume would not allow even an innate propensity to reason. For Hume, all knowledge, including the ability to reflect upon what is known, comes through the senses. But Hume argues that such knowledge is of doubtful nature because it is based upon an inductive association of ideas that cannot include any grounds for its validity. Accordingly, Hume voices skepticism about all natural laws, including, most importantly, causality. For Hume, careful examination of events commonly thought to be causally connected yields no universal or necessary connection

---

13. Ibid., §§31–32, 235.

but only a sequence that appears to repeat itself. We have already objected to Hume's skeptical conception of the self in our discussion of the Gassendi-Hume line. We need only add here the observation that Hume's entire skeptical project is logically unstable because it must either include skepticism about its own skeptical philosophy or be based upon objective reason, both of which contradict it.

Before turning to Kant, whose transcendental idealism, which although flawed, represents a brief moment in the history of modern philosophy of clear correspondence with human experience of empirical reality, it is worthwhile to reflect upon the utter chaos represented by the extraordinary dialectic among the three great modern rationalists and empiricists who preceded him. Starting with the rationalists, Descartes's methodical doubt leads him to only knowledge of self, from which he is able, by ontological argument, to prove the existence of God, and, by virtue of God's goodness, the reliability of his senses. For Descartes, there are the three substances readily accessible to the common understanding of the world, namely, God, soul, and matter. Spinoza, starts with an ontological proof of the existence of God and based upon divine perfection concludes that he must be limitless and therefore immanent in all reality. For Spinoza, there is only one substance, namely, God, and man is a mode of that substance. This of course represents a departure from common thinking. For Leibniz, because of the infinite divisibility of matter, substance must be located in immaterial monads, but in order to preserve the diversity of empirical experience, Leibniz must allow for infinitely many monads each of which includes within itself the history of the universe from its unique perspective as to which it has no external representation and which therefore requires the orchestration of God.

The empiricists do not fare any better. Locke's philosophy represents a brilliant start to modern empiricism in which he postulates a common sense understanding of the possibility of knowledge, namely, that there must be a knowing mind, the idea that is known, and the object that causes the idea. Berkeley shows that there is no knowledge of any such object but only of ideas of such objects, so, to avoid solipsism, postulates that God is the source of all such ideas. Hume shows that Berkeley's idealism is inconsistent with his empirical premise that knowledge comes through sensory experience and further argues that there is no warrant for the existence of God. What is left for Hume, then, is a stream of illusorily connected ideas that cannot even be associated with a particular mind. This is the Gassendi-Hume line of criticism of Descartes, which, as we have already seen, is itself unmaintainable.

As previously remarked, Kant greatly despaired of the confusion and utter lack of progress that metaphysics had made from the time of the ancient Greeks. The impact of Hume's arguments was to tear at the very fabric of human cognition, which was a result that Kant, who was Hume's contemporary, could not accept. Although Kant embraces the fundamental premise of the classic British empiricists that all knowledge originates in the senses, Kant does not accept the uncertainty that Hume asserts must attend that knowledge. In what may be the most brilliant philosophical idea since the *Dialogues of Plato*, Kant justifies his assertion of the certainty of empirical cognition, including causation, by proposing that such certainty arises because the human mind contributes certain rational concepts in the process of comprehending the raw material of the senses. In Kant's system, causation does not exist necessarily in nature but rather in the way that human reason organizes what nature presents to human senses and, because causation is fundamental to empirical cognition, its presence in nature as understood by the human mind is as reliable as reason itself. In Kant's system, because the mind-dependent, empirical world represents all that can be known about reality, we can have no knowledge as to whether there is a *mind-independent, noumenal* reality behind such phenomena or anything else about such a reality.

It is important to understand that, for Kant, what is contributed by the mind in the process of cognition of empirical objects has applicability only to objects that are given to the senses and that, perhaps even more importantly, reason has access to what is contributed by the mind not, as would naturally be assumed, by direct examination of reason in the first instance but instead by a process of abstraction from empirical cognition. So, according to Kant, there is a strict correlation between logic and the categories under which objects are understood by reason precisely because the former abstract from the latter, and logic, which is devoid of all of the empirical content that the senses provide, has no applicability to anything that is not sensibly experienced. Logic, for Kant, is transcendental in nature in the sense that it is devoid of empirical content and therefore is *a priori* but, even so, it has no existence or applicability except with respect to the empirical world. According to Kant, when reason succumbs to its natural impulse to apply its own rules of thought to anything that is outside of that which is experienced empirically, fallacies, in the form of antimonies (valid proofs of opposite conclusions) and paralogisms (proofs that are sound as to form but contain the *transcendental* error of such misapplication) are bound to occur.

Kant distinguishes two kinds of objects within the concept of the representation "I," one being the soul, which he describes as the inner sense of self as a thinking being (sometimes referred to as the "transcendental Ego"), and the other being the empirical, sensible locus of personality, which can be an object of knowledge (and can be thought of as the object of the study of psychology). But unlike Cartesianism, Kant's empiricism will only allow knowledge of the latter because only it is given to reason by sensory perception. For Kant, the "I think" that purports to represent the soul does not even rise to the epistemological status of a concept but instead merely provides the vehicle by which all empirical cognition and analytical thought can occur and is therefore nowise empirical in nature. As a result, the categories of understanding of empirical objects and the logic that abstracts from them is utterly inapplicable to philosophical psychology. According to Kant, when reason, operating under the irresistible impulse to apply transcendental logic to all objects of understanding, considers the soul it incorrectly treats it as though it were an empirical object, and in so doing, mistakenly concludes under the categories of understanding that the soul is substance, simple, persistent, and existing in relation to all possible objects of experience. In his introductory discussion of the *paralogisms* of pure reason,[14] Kant explains this as follows:

> All concepts of pure psychology arise from these elements, simply by way of combination, and without admission of any other principle. This substance, taken merely as object of inner sense, gives us the concept of *immateriality*; and

14. Kant's exposition of his famous four paralogisms (i.e., fallacious arguments) of the soul is discussed in greater detail at 69 and 95–97.

as simple substance, that of *incorruptibility*; its identity as intellectual substance gives us *personality*; and all these three together, *spirituality*; the relation of the substance to objects in space gives us *commerce* with bodies; and so it represents the thinking substance as the principle of life in matter, that is, as soul (*anima*), and as the ground of *animality*; and animality again, as restricted by spirituality, gives us the concept of *immortality*.

To these concepts refer four paralogisms of a transcendental psychology, which is falsely supposed to be a science of pure reason concerning the nature of our thinking being. We can, however, use as the foundation of such a science nothing but the simple and by itself perfectly empty representation, "I," of which we cannot even say that it is a concept, but only that it is a mere consciousness that accompanies all concepts. Through this I, or he, or it (the thing), which thinks, nothing is represented beyond a transcendental subject of thoughts = x.[15]

Ironically, as will be discussed below, although Kant believes that as a matter of reason-compelled faith there are grounds for belief in the immortality of the soul, he could not be more clear (in his characteristically obscure way) that as an object of philosophical knowledge, the soul is literally a non-entity. It remains therefore for Kant to explain how and why we come in the first place to have any idea of the soul as to which we might mistakenly apply the categories of understanding of empirical objects. Kant's explanation is as follows:

> [The soul] is known only through the thoughts that are its predicates and apart from them we can never have the slightest concept of it; therefore we revolve around it in a perpetual circle, since before we can form any judgment about it we must already use its representation. And this inconvenience is really inevitable, because consciousness in itself is not so much a representation distinguishing a particular object, but really a form of representation in general, insofar as this representation is to be called knowledge; of such representation alone can I say that I think something through it.[16]

In positing the transcendental Ego as the form of representation of thought, or as Kant sometimes calls it, "the unity of apperception," Kant is attempting structurally to connect the thoughts of a thinker in a way that refutes Hume's skeptical "stream of consciousness" characterization of the self. But in doing so in a way that does not add any objective existence to the self-concept, Kant has merely added gloss to Hume, and worse, Kant has painted himself into a corner from which, by his own admission, he can only attempt escape by circular reasoning. Under Kant's system, the self, as a non-substantive unity of apperception, is a precondition of empirical cognition that can only arise by virtue of empirical cognition that depends upon the self in the first place. Moreover, Kant's reduction of the transcendental Ego to a mere form of representation of thought leaves the thoughts of the transcendental Ego disconnected from any substantive being and reduces the transcendental Ego to a mere perspective upon an underlying reality as to which it affords no assurances. By contrast, had Kant been willing to posit the self as a real entity, he would have been able to assert that the self is a supersensible precondition to empirical

---

15. Kant, *Critique of Pure Reason*, B403–4. Cited by reference to the standard B pagination of the second (1787) edition.

16. Ibid., B405.

cognition that may be known by direct intuition or by inference from such cognition; however, Kant's strict empiricism will allow him no such intuition or inference.

As it turned out, Kant's transcendental idealism utterly failed to bring an end to the dialectic between rationalism and empiricism or to achieve its goal of resolving, once and for all, the question of the certainty of empirical experience. Before Kant had even finished the development of his system, the German idealists began to pick it apart. The German idealists were not satisfied with Kant's sheepish admission that his transcendental subject of thoughts involved the circularity of a subject thinking about itself as an object because that formulation, if correct, undercuts not just the thinker but all thought. The solution of the German idealists was to liberate consciousness from the individual and place it in empirical reality in a constitutive way, giving substantive life to the Gassendi-Hume line that all that Descartes was entitled to assert is that "there is thinking." The efforts of the German idealists culminated in the absolute idealism of Hegel, in which man is understood to be part of a larger universal, conscious unity (sometimes referred to as the "Absolute" or the "absolute Ego") and the universe is understood to be mind, *that is, thought thinking itself*. The path that German idealism took is difficult and obscure. For Hegel, the absolute Ego is the ultimate creative-destructive force which defines not only empirical reality but also the supersensible reality that exists behind it. Flipping Kantian empiricism on its head, Hegel argues that what is perceived as presented to the senses is not positive reality but an absolute Ego-imposed limitation on positive reality which exists supersensibly and is known, not by direct intuition, but by a process of conceptual reasoning which, not surprisingly, reaches its endpoint in Hegel's own thought. In other words, for Hegel, that which is not absolute Ego is only such because the absolute Ego has created it as such and it is that as to which we attain knowledge.

However valid the criticism of Kant by the German idealists may be, the solution offered by German idealism of separating thought from an individual thinker is unworkable for a number of reasons including, most importantly, the structural one already discussed in connection with the Gassendi-Hume criticism, namely, that thought cannot think nor can it experience itself, especially not in a way that includes human experience of such a process. Therefore, for all the sublimity and complexity of Hegel's absolute idealism, it may be dispensed with by the asymmetrically simple observation that nowise does absolute idealism bear resemblance to, or connection with, human experience. Human beings are rational *individuals who think for themselves* and it is therefore too far removed from human experience to assert that individual thinkers are either part of an absolute mind to which they have such infinitesimal access and of which they have no common intuition or are mere limitations on such a mind that it imposes upon itself.

It is crucial to observe that Hegel's system is as lawless as his absolute Ego must be. If Kant teaches us anything (and indeed he teaches us much), it is that metaphysics must follow epistemology and epistemology requires an understanding of the rules of its own understanding. For Kant, these are identified and set forth in sophisticated schema and are said to derive from and apply only to empirical objects. It is one thing to disagree over the origin of logic and the scope of its applicability, but, in positing absolute consciousness not as the cause or explanation but rather as constitutive of the universe, Hegel has not merely removed the source of consciousness from the individual person but he has liberated it from all rules of thought and he has liberated the individual from himself altogether. As a result, Hegel renders the absolute Ego comprehensible only to itself on its own terms which presumably it is free to invent and reinvent at its own whim. The rules of thought and of cognition of objects as they are known to human reason are nothing like this; they cannot possibly apply to an entity such as the absolute Ego and, therefore, Hegel, who is subject to such rules, is not entitled to posit the existence of the absolute Ego or make any other intelligible statement about it. If Hegel's point was that the universe is utterly incomprehensible, then he would be required by logic to stop with that assertion; although that is not his intent, it is all he can be understood to assert and he is wrong in doing so. Nevertheless, Hegel's idealism is an admonition to theistic philosophers: *if you wish to make statements about the divine, they must not extend beyond any intuition of the divine and they must not be of a nature to render the rules of thought under which you assert them unstable.* That admonition will be taken to heart in these pages.

However great the deficiencies of the positive philosophy of the German idealists may be, such deficiencies should not be allowed to obfuscate the importance of their argument against Kant that it is contradictory to maintain that the self is somehow inferable from experience that is in the first instance dependent upon it. Although that criticism was directed at Kant, it applies equally to all empirical philosophies. If one denies direct knowledge of self because it is not an object of sensory knowledge, one is left with a small number of unpalatable choices, namely, to follow Hume in the denial of the self and the acceptance of the skepticism that necessarily follows or to recognize the necessity of the self in some non-substantive form (e.g., as a mere logical necessity or formal necessity), which entails the same circularity of reasoning that is by Kant's own admission circular and which, as was noted, is mere gloss upon and not dispositive of such skepticism.

Inasmuch as Hegel's absolute idealism represents a system in which an individual's consciousness is merely a fragmentary component of a larger, unexperienced conscious unity, it is, as already remarked, utterly disconnected from the nature of human experience and, as a result, it could not and did not hold sway for long. Nietzsche, the last great German rationalist philosopher of the nineteenth century, took his countrymen to task, declaring that nature displayed no God, no absolute Ego, and no objective morality. Nevertheless, Nietzsche sought to resurrect the human soul as pure will and to install the value-defining *ubermensche,* its greatest possible *human being,* as nature's greatest possible achievement. It is easy to see how Nietzsche's philosophy might be easily abused to justify unintended political ends; and it was only a few decades before Hitler and his national socialist movement selectively utilized it to support their doctrine of German global supremacy. Not surprisingly, when the Nazis were defeated, Nietzsche, his reputation profoundly sullied by their misappropriation of his philosophy, and the entire line of German idealism that preceded him lost whatever claim they may have had to the mainstream of continental philosophy.

German idealism had never enjoyed much popularity in England or the United States and, simultaneously with its rise, a modern version of classic British empiricism was under development. When German idealism ceased to be a widely held philosophy, the field was clear for this form of empiricism to assume preeminence, at least for a time in the twentieth century, which it accomplished in the form of logical positivism. Logical positivism and similar empiricist schools reject the possibility of metaphysics altogether and, although they generally accept in whole or in part Hume's skepticism about the self as a substantive entity, they reject Hume's skepticism about the empirical world. Logical positivism is characterized by: an aversion to philosophical systems; emphasis upon precision in language, logical statement, and analysis of philosophical problems considered independently of any particular philosophical system; and verifiability of all propositions.

The school developed out of the work of Gottlob Frege, George E. Moore, and Bertrand Russell. Wittgenstein, the Austrian philosopher who may be regarded along with Russell as one of the most influential philosophers of the twentieth century, argues in his *Tractatus Logico-Philosophicus* that the self is a mere limit of empirical knowledge:

5.621   The world and life are one.

5.63   I am my world.

5.631   There is no such thing as the subject that thinks or entertains ideas. If I wrote a book called *The World As I Found It*, I should have to include a report on my body, and should have to say which parts were subordinate to my will, and which were not, etc., this being a method of isolating the subject, or rather of showing that in an important sense there is no subject; for it alone could not be mentioned in that book.

5.632   The subject does not belong to the world: rather, it is a limit of the world.[17]

This formulation by Wittgenstein is particularly interesting because it hearkens back to Gassendi, Hume, Kant, and the German idealists so reviled by the twentieth-century empiricists. In it, Wittgenstein utterly obliterates the self, reducing it to a mere limit. But what sort of limit can a nonentity be? In Kantian terms, Wittgenstein seems to suggest that the self is *noumenal* in the negative sense; however, since the self is associated with conscious perception of reality, it must represent, if not substance, then reality itself considered from a particular non-substantive perspective and, that being the case, it is difficult to see how the self and the reality of Wittgenstein are meaningfully different from the self and reality of Hegel.

The fundamental epistemological tenet of the logical positivists is that for an assertion to be warranted it must be *verifiable* and, therefore, only scientific knowledge is possible. The implications for metaphysics are immediate and obvious: scientific, and only scientific, explanations of human experience are valid and pursuit of metaphysical understanding is a fool's errand. This is the position of Ayer, one of the founders of positivism, who argues that metaphysical statements are meaningless because they are not verifiable,[18] and of Flew, who argues that for a claim to be meaningful it must be falsifiable.[19] Under these tests, only empirical and analytical propositions have significance. Both Ayer and Flew reject religious claims as meaningless on these grounds (although near the end of Flew's life, he adopted the view that there exists a disinterested

---

17. Wittgenstein, *Tractatus*, 74.
18. Ayer, *Language, Truth and Logic*, 35–45.
19. Flew, "Theology," 48–49.

God). However, neither succeeds in providing grounds for their assertions other than in a definitional way because neither assertion survives the test of its own content.

With the advent of logical positivism, philosophy has become a mere handmaiden of science and as the philosophical community at large first retreated and then altogether capitulated, the scientists, rather than rejecting metaphysics, sought full charge of it. No clearer example can be found than the following very recent passage from *The Grand Design* by Stephen Hawking, one of the leading astrophysicists of our day:

> How can we understand ourselves in the world in which we find ourselves? How does the universe behave? What is the nature of reality? Where did this all come from? Did the universe need a creator? . . .
>
> Traditionally, these are questions for philosophy. But philosophy is dead. Philosophy has not kept up with modern developments in science, particularly physics. Scientists have become the bearers of the torch of discovery in our quest for knowledge.[20]

However, Hawking's hubristic declaration neither tells the whole story nor ends it as he would have it. Over the course of the twentieth century and continuing to the present day in the twenty-first century, the scientific approach to the metaphysical questions has proceeded along two lines, one of which may be described as the philosophy (or science) of the mind and the other of which is essentially quantum astrophysics. These lines have in common the rejection of Cartesian mind-body dualism and its supplantation with one or another form of *materialist monism*, which holds that there is no separation between mind and body and that the mind can be explained in, or reduced to, wholly material terms. Both may be thought historically to refer back to Locke.

The first of the materialist approaches is psychological in its consideration and grew naturally from the emphasis that German idealism had placed on consciousness. This line includes behaviorism (which holds that the mind is simply the behavior of the body), physicalism (which holds that the mind is reducible to the brain), functionalism (which holds that mental states are phenomena which are causally related to perceptions and desires), and computer functionalism (which holds that the mind is a computer and consciousness is its software). Each of these approaches has its specific deficiencies, which are ably chronicled by Searle in his *Mind: A Brief Introduction,* and all of them suffer from the larger common fatality (also chronicled by Searle) that they leave too much of the human conscious experience unexplained.[21] To see that computer functionalism, for example, does not explain human mental states, take the simple example of a chess program that enables a computer to "defeat" the world's greatest chess masters. Following literal instructions contained in the program and receiving input about the state of a virtual chess board, the computer runs electricity through its circuitry, effectively

---

20. Hawking and Mlodinow. *Grand Design*, 5.

21. Searle says: "In general, these attacks have the same logical structure: the materialist account leaves out some essential feature of the mind such as consciousness or intentionality. In the jargon of philosophers, the materialist analysis fails to give sufficient conditions for mental phenomena, because it is possible to satisfy the materialist analysis and not have the appropriate mental phenomena." Searle, *Mind*, 83.

For a list and explanation of compelling objections to the various forms of materialism, see ibid., 84–95.

manipulating symbols to yield output which humans *interpret* as chess moves. The point is this: the computer together with its software may be "unbeatable" at chess but *the computer will never know it is playing chess*; indeed, all the computer does is manipulate symbols that it cannot itself interpret and to which it cannot attach any meaning and, to the computer, there is no such thing as playing anything at all.

More generally, Searle rightly points out that materialist explanations of consciousness do not explain the *qualia* of human experience, the individual nature of such experience, or man's perception of human freedom and moral obligation. Searle, having criticized with devastating effect earlier materialistic approaches, offers his own, which he calls "biological naturalism"; however, because it is a materialist philosophy in organic clothing, it is no more convincing than the ones that Searle rebukes. Searle asserts that consciousness must be a natural, neurobiological function, which is fully implemented in the brain, that it inherently possesses freedom, and that it requires a "self" in order to fully describe our experience. But he seems to arrive at that conclusion by the process of eliminating the other materialist philosophies rather than force of reason. Searle insists that the problem of consciousness is not difficult if we think about the distinction between the mind and the body and the other basic issues of philosophy of the mind "differently." Searle purports to solve the mind-body problem with the following observations and argument: (1) conscious states, with their subjective, first-person ontology, are real phenomena in the real world; (2) conscious states are entirely caused by lower-level neurobiological processes in the brain; (3) conscious states are realized in the brain as features of the brain system and thus exist at a level higher than that of neurons and synapses; and (4) because conscious states are real features of the real world, they function causally.[22] Although Searle's argument is unavoidably instinct with materialist assumptions, it is distinctly scientific, not philosophical, in nature, with the implication that its justification must come from science. Searle's argument is merely a list of propositions for testing in the laboratory and all Searle can do in support of his position is to implore the neurobiologists somehow to "figure it out." In doing so, Searle expressly acknowledges that inert matter and the laws governing it are to no avail (except to the extent that they offer a first-order explanation of the existence and operation of living organisms) and, because of Searle's self-avowed naïve realism, he is left to turn to the only other possible materialist explanation, namely, that consciousness must be an organically explicable phenomenon. But Searle gives us no reason to believe that organic matter is any different from inert matter in a way that is relevant to metaphysics and the burden of proof on this essential point is his.

Most importantly, after acknowledging that virtually all modern philosophers have accepted Hume's view that we have no, and cannot have any, experience of a self, even Searle concludes reluctantly that because of rationality, free choice, decision making, and reasons for action, it is necessary to postulate a formal (as opposed to substantive) notion of self:

> It has to be an entity such that one and the same entity has consciousness, perception, rationality, the capacity to engage in action, and the capacity to organize

---

22. Ibid., 113–14.

perceptions and reasons, so as to be able to perform voluntary actions on the presupposition of freedom. If you have got all of that, you have got a self.[23]

Oddly, although Searle makes his proposal expressly as a supplement to Hume, his position seems remarkably closer to those of Locke, who argued for the possibility of materially reducible consciousness, and Kant, in the latter case, with an important fillip. As has already been mentioned, Kant argues that the transcendental Ego is a precondition of experience about which we can therefore have no knowledge but, as a result of doing so, Kant is charged by the German idealists with circular reasoning. Searle seems to be inferring the existence of self for the same reasons as Kant but, in order to avoid the charge of circularity leveled against Kant by the German idealists, Searle argues that the self is a formality that is fully implemented as part of the neurobiological phenomenon of consciousness (which, somehow, also possesses freedom). But Searle's formal conception of self does not succeed in avoiding circularity. Searle's explanation of the persistence of the sense of self is based on conscious memories, which, in Searle's view, require a self in the first place:

> My sense that I am exactly the same person over time, from my first-person point of view, is in large part a matter of my ability to produce *conscious* memories of earlier conscious events in my life.[24] (Emphasis added.)

This was precisely the criticism that we leveled at Locke. It should also be noted that by causally tying the self with consciousness Searle subjects the self to the same criticism already leveled at his theory of consciousness, namely, that Searle has no explanation for the phenomenon and must resort to exhorting the neurobiologists to figure the self out too. Finally, by Searle's own admission, Searle's theory leaves out any explanation of the actual sense of self that accompanies consciousness as a unique entity:

> A second worry that I have is that I do not know how to account for the fact that an important feature of our experiences is what one might call a "sense of self." One way to put this is to say that *there is definitely something that it feels like to be me*.[25] (Emphasis added.)

Because Searle has disposed of all of the *inert* materialist approaches and appears to have unsuccessfully made the only organic monist argument (by adding little that was not already present in Locke and Kant), he may be considered to be the endpoint of the philosophy of mind, which is the first of the two lines of scientific metaphysics mentioned above, at least so far as it has developed to date. But before concluding that

---

23. Ibid., 297.

24. Ibid., 288–89. I do not think that this explanation is consistent with our common experience of consciousness. A simple example to make the point: people awaken from surgery under general anesthesia find their bodies altered by the surgical process, which can be long and radical, and, without any conscious memory of the surgical process, have no identity crises whatsoever. Moreover, under some forms of general anesthesia, patients can be conversant, access their own memory in response to questions from the doctors and yet have no memory of the surgery itself; such patients still awaken with their unified self-identity intact.

25. Ibid., 298–99.

science has played out its metaphysical string there remains to be addressed the metaphysics of quantum physics, which is the other line of scientific metaphysics.

Quantum physics has yielded a host of natural laws which depart markedly from the laws that govern the objects larger than atoms. From the laws of quantum physics, the quantum metaphysicians argue that scientific determinism, founded on quantum mechanics and not Newtonian physics, yields answers to the fundamental problems of metaphysics. For reasons that are far beyond the scope of this paper, quantum theory, and in particular the approach to quantum theory called "alternative histories," has yielded the view that the universe does not have just a single existence or history, but rather every possible version of the universe exists simultaneously in what is called a quantum superposition. This is the quantum metaphysician's answer to the questions of why there is something rather than nothing and why this particular universe exists. Under this theory, at each point in time a new parallel universe is spun off from each extant one. To take an example of personal importance, there is a parallel universe, about to occur, in which I die before completing this sentence. There are (too) many problems with the *philosophy* of quantum astrophysics, including that the actual quantum phenomena *do not apply* to objects larger than atoms, but one is especially important to us in the present inquiry.[26] If I have a persistent unified self that I experience and which cannot be explained in material terms, then I cannot be constantly spun off into infinitely many other selves. In other words, if I am and can only be a single, real, transcendent ego, then there can be only a single sensible universe for me to experience at any given time.

As already noted, the twentieth-century philosophy of mind and quantum metaphysics are part of a broader, modern approach to the metaphysical questions previously regarded as being the exclusive province of philosophy, which may be loosely encompassed under the heading "material reductionism," which relies heavily on neo-Darwinism. The fundamental idea behind material reductionism is that the history of the universe and human experience of it may be fully explained in material terms. According to materialist reductionism, the history of the universe includes the following important steps: (1) the universe began with the Big Bang;[27] (2) after the Big Bang, matter

26. One such problem, which occurs to me as an occasional lay reader of scientific literature, is where the energy to support each parallel universe comes from. If the amount of energy in this universe is limited, as it is generally supposed to be, and in the next instance this universe splits off into two parallel universes, it seems that either the energy contained in each such universe must be one-half of the energy in the single universe that preceded them, or the total energy of the two universes has somehow doubled that of the single preceding universe, or both of the new universes share the same energy. None of these alternatives seem feasible to me. A second problem attends an important related premise of the would-be quantum metaphysicians. To offer a complete "theory of everything," the question of why this particular universe exists must be answered. The answer of the quantum metaphysicians is that the quantum superposition includes all possible universes, which include universes in which a completely different set of physical laws is applicable. The problem with that theory is that because each of these infinite universes has a single common ancestral universe, presumably with its own set of physical laws, then it must be assumed that the physical laws which govern any universe may cease to do so at any instant. This also seems untenable to me.

27. Although the Big Bang theory is not without its detractors in the astrophysics community, it is the most widely accepted theory of the beginning of the universe. Under the theory, all of the matter and energy currently in the universe was concentrated into a "singularity," which exploded to create the expanding universe. Based upon the rate at which the constellations are moving apart from one another, scientists estimate that the Big Bang occurred approximately 13.7 billion years ago.

separated into the various atomic elements; (3) matter then began to undergo a series of self-sustaining chemical reactions; (4) a small number of these chemical reactions became animated (i.e., acquired life); (5) those early life forms, through an infinite series of lucky mutations, became increasingly complex, with the best of the mutations displacing all near competitors; and (6) after a long period, those complex creatures started to acquire characteristics of mind, including objective cognition, reason, intentionality, and morality. As far as a history of the universe, the preceding represents the best scientific thinking of our day and can be accepted as such. The problem is that it is a *mere* history which is devoid of any meaningful explanation of how or why that sequence of events occurred. Material reductionist explanations fail on at least five grounds: (1) as already noted, they leave too much of human conscious experience unexplained; (2) they offer no explanation for the quantum leap from dead matter to live matter; (3) they offer no explanation for the leap from mere organism to conscious organism; (4) they offer no explanation for the leap from consciousness to objective reason (and in fact would lead us to subjective reasoning via induction and quantum mechanics); and (5) they offer no explanation for the leap from objective reason to objective moral reason. In addition, an apparently strong case can be made that the development of the universe, as described by the best science of our day, could not have occurred within the amount of time since the Big Bang as a result of the purely physical forces assumed to be at operation and that some form of nonphysical teleology must be assumed to be part of the process.[28]

The conclusion that science has not supplanted and cannot supplant philosophy is inevitable. In fact, in the century and one quarter that science has held sway, its remarkable achievements within its own discipline have yielded little of direct importance to philosophy other than demonstrating the futility of materialism. The march of psychologists and physicists that has yielded relativity, behaviorism, computer science, quantum mechanics, string theory, and other materialist ideas has left us no closer to the answers to the fundamental metaphysical questions acknowledged above by Hawking. Under the current circumstances, the only reasonable conclusion to be reached is that modern science, robust beyond imagination as its own discipline, never was, is not, and never will be able to constitute or supplant metaphysics.

Four centuries after Descartes sought to lay compatible metaphysical grounds for Christianity and secular science by abandoning Christianity's fundamental view of man as a psychosomatic unit, modern mainstream philosophy has concluded its investigation with the verdict that there is no God, no soul, and no meaningful metaphysics. But the supplantation of the Cartesian version of Christianity with religion of materialist reductionism does not represent an advancement; indeed, at the current juncture, we are in a position remarkably similar to, if not (for want of any meaningful opposition to reductionism) worse than, the one lamented by Kant. Cartesian dualism cannot explain the interaction between its two substances; subjective idealism with its roots in Locke's representationalism and its expression in Berkeley's philosophy leads unacceptably to solipsism; the rationalism of Spinoza and Leibniz yield, respectively, pantheism and an

---

28. *See*, Nagel, *Mind and Cosmos*, 6–9. Not surprisingly, Nagel has come under substantial fire from the reductionist community for this position and his related conclusion that the universe reflects teleological design (but not a divine designer). See 4n, 17.

infinity of blind and disconnected souls each of which contains the universe within it; Hume requires suspension of our experience of reality; Kant's transcendental idealism is closed, circular, and yields nothing but a unified perspective upon an unknowable ultimate reality; the German idealists leave us with an impossible universe of thought thinking itself that is shackled by its own freedom; and material reductionism has declared itself to be dead as philosophy. The philosophers who took the bait of Cartesian dualism have all failed in their metaphysics. Those who accept such dualism cannot explain unified human experience of mind operating upon matter. Those who assert that the world is mind and challenge matter cannot avoid solipsism either at the individual or universal level and those who assert the world is matter cannot explain human mental experience.

The state of modern philosophy in general and metaphysics in particular is, indeed, no less a mess than it has ever been. But if metaphysics is dead, it can be resurrected by returning to the conception of man as a psychosomatic unity of mind and body that Descartes discarded, which unity is the only characterization that enables a full description of human experience.

PERSONHOOD

It has always struck me as odd that modern mainstream philosophy in general and, upon its ascendance to that position, empiricism in particular have held the position that man has no direct knowledge of self, even while coming to acknowledge the direct intuition of logic and mathematics. The primary reason for my puzzlement is that it is difficult to understand why, if we had no such experience, there would be anything to deny. It is important to observe that the question of self-consciousness is fundamentally different from the question of the nature and certainty of cognition of objects other than the self. In this regard, we may agree with the empiricists that knowledge of empirical objects comes to us from the senses and, for the most part, is limited to their empirical predication; however, with respect to the self, it is undeniable that the experience of each sentient entity includes the apparently non-sensory, fundamental intuition of a persistent, central unity of all other experience and that, in each such case, that self-experience is a *uniquely privileged* one. The task for the self-skeptics, therefore, must be to take the internal experience of self as given and show that it is nevertheless illusory. However, even if an explanation were offered, it is difficult to see how it might be other than an unstable one because it would of necessity entail answering the questions of what sort of entity or non-entity it is that purports to characterize its own intuition of self as mere illusion and how it is that any such non-self can have all of the other experiences common to rational creatures, including a coherent experience of empirical reality that is external to the self, access to objective and universal truth, moral obligation, and freedom. It is difficult to see how it is possible to deny the self without falling into the abyss of utter skepticism or for a non-self to recognize that is has come under such a misconception and to act on that recognition by discourse with other non-selves the objective of which is to convince them that their similar experiences of self are also illusory. Indeed, if the experience of self is both non-sensory and also illusory, how is it possible to even have an intelligible conversation about it (which we obviously do)? It must be remembered that, illusion or not, each self is the unity of all of its human experience; how, then, can we communicate about the illusory nature of the self without also demolishing the perspective from which that experience is had and from which any such discussion must take place? And if we are able to communicate effectively about what is commonly understood as a *universally* persistent internal experience, how is it possible to demonstrate that it is illusory solely by reference to sensible experience? The case is not analogous to hallucinations which accompany the taking of a pill. In that case, we can connect the empirical fact of drug taking with the consequent internally experienced hallucinations and the absence of drug taking with the absence of hallucinations, but, because of the universal nature of experience of the self, a similar proof is impossible.

We have already dismissed Kant's explanation of the unity of apperception because of its circularity. But any attempt to unwind the circularity by retaining the idea that rational entities determine the self by distinguishing it from all non-self reality, while discarding the idea that the self is a precondition to cognition of such non-self reality, is not possible. If cognition of the real world does not depend upon the self as a precondition, then it becomes impossible to maintain the division between self and non-self or, if you will, internality and externality; elimination of the self as a precondition to experience can only lead to solipsism, Humean skepticism, or the absolute Ego of German idealism. Since Hume, one of the common lines offered by skeptics is to begin with the observation that, when one turns one's mind inward in search of the self, one finds that nothing is there. However superficially appealing this line may be, it leads directly to the opposite conclusion because, if the self is persistent and indivisible substance to which all predication attaches and is therefore the subject of all experience, one ought not to expect to have any experience of the self as anything other than the unity of such experience, which is to say, as the perspective from which any such inquiry must be had. Additionally, the self-skeptical position raises too many questions that it cannot possibly answer. For example, how is it possible and what does it mean for a non-self to turn its attention internally and find that there is no self there? Or, how is it possible for a mere, illusorily connected stream of consciousness to come to recognize that it is in fact a disconnected stream of consciousness? Doesn't the fact of the inquiry presuppose that there is a self to conduct it?

The second reason that I find the entire mainstream challenge to the reality of the self so puzzling is that I am quite convinced, based upon my own experience and upon my being on this point in the company of virtually everyone other than the modern philosophical community, that what we perceive to be direct experience of self is, and can be nothing other than, precisely that. It is, of course, the role of philosophy to expose and explain any and all illusions of reason and perception, but unless the self-concept can be disposed of with the same degree of certainty that it is intuited, it would seem a far better course to accept the persistent self as a presupposition of any epistemology and proceed, if not from there, then at the very least in a manner that is consistent with that presupposition. That all experience ultimately is internal experience was recognized by Descartes, Locke, and others and it has rarely been seriously challenged since. Sensible experience is internal experience of the external world. Knowledge of logic and—as will be demonstrated in chapter 5, "The Homogeneity of Reason"—mathematics is purely internal in nature and so, it would seem, is experience of thought itself and of self as thinker. Why should we trust our sensible experience, which is notoriously unreliable, and doubt our internal experience, which is direct and not subject to error in observation and transmission from the senses? My experience of self (which I will endeavor to describe in a moment) is more clear and distinct, to employ Cartesian criteria, than any other experience I can possibly have and no amount of philosophical argument can change that simple fact. The question is particularly acute when it is observed that any such doubt arises by virtue of the application of one and the same faculty of internal reason upon which my intuition of self is based in the first place.

The conclusion seems inescapable that the mainstream position reflects a secular agenda that prioritizes anti-theism over good philosophy. Modern philosophy of mind began with Cartesian mind-body dualism, which was proposed by Descartes with an unabashedly theistic motivation and, if the post-Cartesian history of philosophy is anything at all, it is a rebellion that parallels the rebellion of science against the church that had repressed it for so many centuries during the Middle Ages. As has been discussed in some detail, mind-body dualism is an easy target because of the many difficulties that lie within the confines of its doctrine, including, most importantly, that there is no satisfactory explanation of how the mind is connected to the body or how the immaterial mind can have any causal effect on it. Idealism also lends itself to theistic interpretations and is therefore anathema to scientifically oriented philosophers and it carries the additional burden of its unfortunate history of leading from the defective empiricism of Kant to the idealism of Hegel, the rationalism of Nietzsche, and the national socialism of Hitler. So it is not hard to see how materialism, coupled with a selective dose of Humean skepticism, easily became the religion of the twentieth century.[29] Although Descartes begins, reasonably enough, with internal self-knowledge and ends with external knowledge, because he mischaracterizes man's substance as mental, to rebut his own presumptive doubt and get to assurances with respect to the external world, Descartes has to invoke God and his goodness. That, of course, was wholly unacceptable to the majority of Descartes's contemporaries of the Enlightenment who were racing away from church repression. In rebuking Descartes, modern empiricism starts with external knowledge given by the senses and, for the reasons that have been covered already, is unable ever to get to non-empirical, internal knowledge, which the empiricists readily reject in order, it would seem, to preclude any possibility of theism. But the empiricists are faced with a paradox, namely, how to allow for internal knowledge of external experience while disallowing pure internal experience. Unless the empiricists can identify an objectively valid reason for rejecting the appearance of pure internal experience, the empiricist position is really

---

29. This characterization belongs to Searle who is himself a materialist:

> There is a sense in which materialism is the religion of our time, at least among most of the professional experts in the fields of philosophy, psychology, cognitive science, and other disciplines that study the mind. Like more traditional religions, it is accepted without question and it provides the framework within which other questions can be posed, addressed and answered. The history of materialism is fascinating, because though the materialists are convinced, with a quasi-religious faith, that their view must be right, they never seem able to formulate a version of it that they are completely satisfied with and that can be generally accepted by other philosophers, even by other materialists. (Searle, *Mind*, 48–49)

nothing more than a restatement of their premise that, if it is the case that all knowledge comes from the senses it must be the case that there can be no direct internal knowledge because such knowledge, by definition, is removed from the senses.

The reason for rejecting the internal experience of self most commonly given over the first centuries of the modern philosophical era comes from Hume, which is that internal reflection renders the presumed internal knowledge of self to be mere illusion and requires supplanting the self with a stream of consciousness. However, Hume's characterization is no longer representative of the mainstream. Critics of Hume, including Kant and most mainstream philosophers of the mind, argue that the stream of consciousness is the illusion and that, instead of a sequence of vaguely connected thoughts, internal experience comprises a unified conscious field. Although the contemporary position comes perilously close to the admission of the existence of a real self, these philosophers are unwilling or unable to accept or explain the human sense of the self as a real entity and instead focus on explaining it as a mere phenomenon. But it is readily apparent that, in rejecting internal knowledge, the mainstream leaves our basic conscious self-experience wholly unaccounted for. Not only have they failed to explain the self but they cannot explain consciousness, they cannot explain free will, they cannot explain morality, and, despite the mightiest of efforts starting with Hume and continuing through the materialist monists, *they have not been able to explain these phenomena away*. As between Hume and such subsequent philosophers, it seems the latter are clearly correct that consciousness occurs in the context of a unified field and not solely sequentially. But Hume's mistake also highlights the mistake of Descartes, whose view Hume is seeking to rebuke. In making his observation, Hume picks up and seeks to destroy the Cartesian concept of self *as a mind*. Taken all together, the Cartesian proposal, the rebuttal by Hume, and the ineptitude of modern materialism suggest that man is something other than a mind and that framing the debate as pro and con that proposition has fundamentally restricted the development of modern philosophy.

We are now many centuries removed from the beginning of the Enlightenment and, under the circumstances in which philosophy finds itself and in the prevalent climate of anti-theism, it is still relevant to ask whether there exists valid reason to doubt our internal knowledge other than in service of the secular agenda that has been superimposed upon the modern philosophical discourse. In response, it would be tempting to take the view, which is diametrically opposed to the empirical one, that internal knowledge is the only knowledge that we have. Certainly, there are many reasons to suspect the information presented to us by our senses. But yielding to the temptation to simply assert the exclusivity of internal knowledge leads one unacceptably to solipsism. Instead, it will be better to accept a very weak form of empiricism that all *empirical* knowledge originates in the senses and to proceed from there by acknowledging (and investigating) direct intuition of the self and other aspects of human rational experiences that are not empirically sourced. It is true on these premises that we have no direct *sensible* experience of self but this merely shows that the self is not, in essence, a material object. Neither does it mandate a dualistic solution to the mind-body problem. Descartes was correct that he could not doubt that he was considering the question of whether there was anything that he could not doubt but he was not correct in concluding that he was therefore, in substance, a mere mind in temporary occupation of a material body. As Descartes's critics, following the Gassendi-Hume line, gleefully point out, before Descartes can reach the conclusion that he exists, he must not only identify that thought is occurring but also satisfactorily answer the question: Who and what is doing the thinking? Descartes's dualistic answer to that question simply does not work.

If man's essential Being is not mere mind, then what else might it be? And if the self is not a sensible object, where will we find it and how can we know it when we do? In answering these questions, we will do well to start with a description of the experience of self. Admittedly, although few would argue with a concept of self as representing the perspective from which an individual rational entity experiences reality, any commonality among the major philosophers and philosophical schools seems to end there. For Descartes, the self is mind, which he, along with many other subsequent thinkers, equates with soul, which is the substance of the human being and under his dualism is distinguishable from the body. For Spinoza, the self is a mode of the divine substance that is immanent in all reality. For Leibniz, the self is a monad, which in the case of humans is a substantive soul that includes all of the predicates that may be attached to a person, including its infinite relationships with all other objects in the universe and all the events of its existence. For Hume, the self is an illusion that arises from the apparent connection of ideas that present themselves in a stream of consciousness. For Kant, the self as known and the self as believed to be are quite different; the first is a mere unity of thought and the second is eternal substance (not unlike that asserted in these pages to be known). For Wittgenstein, the self is a limit on human experience of the physical world. In many reductionist philosophies, the self is a formal condition of consciousness that has no real existence apart from the conscious experience it supports (not unlike Kant's transcendental Ego). And, as we will see shortly, for Heidegger, the human being is *Dasein* and the self is a being who is the point at which the world opens up to it and who, in its essential concern for its own Being, temporalizes it.

That there are many different philosophical conceptions of the nature of self does not imply that there is not a common intuition of self, any more than the existence of many different philosophical conceptions of the nature of the experience of empirical objects implies that there is no empirical reality or that it is subjective in nature. We have already noted the close association of the understanding of self under a particular philosophy with the understanding of other metaphysical questions, including especially the question of the existence of God, and observed that modern mainstream philosophy seems to have placed primary emphasis on serving a secular agenda and, indeed, the philosophical diversity on the question of self only buttresses that argument, as one after another unsupportable explanation of the self as illusion has been offered in a seemingly desperate attempt to ground the anti-theistic platform. It is important, therefore, to understand the position of a particular philosophy on the nature of the self-concept in the broader context of the rest of the philosophy of which it is a part. If the self is illusory, then one is a rudderless nothing, free to invent and reinvent its experience as it sees fit and some form of solipsism, skepticism, or absolute idealism seems to inescapably follow. If the self is amoral substance, then the world is merely the context in which the determination of the individual will plays itself out. For reductionists, the self must be explained as a mere material phenomenon and direct intuition must be denied altogether; otherwise the view of the world as materially limited and causally closed will be undercut. For rationalists, the self must be directly intuited as an elemental object and therefore must be regarded as substance and, if the self is moral substance, then one is a morally conscious entity whose freedom comes at the price of a moral obligation to act without regard for his or her subjective needs.

Regardless of the motivation of mainstream philosophers, the fact of the diversity of philosophical views of the self-concept suggests that there is great difficulty associated with our understanding of the way in which we come to know it as a phenomenon and, indeed, the differing views described above are less about the nature of the self as the elemental perspective of human experience than they are about how the self can be categorized within an epistemology. Even the most extreme views of Hume and Wittgenstein do not deny the experience of a self but, instead, deny that the self of such experience is real, in the case of Hume, or accessible to reason, in the case of Wittgenstein. Characterization of the nature of self-cognition as being by direct intuition has the *prima facie* advantage of reflecting the common sense of that experience and, therefore, other ways of thinking about self-cognition have the burden of showing why the appearance of direct intuition of self is illusory. To do that, such systems must start someplace other than direct intuition of the self and then infer the proper location of the self within the system based upon epistemological or metaphysical premises that do not take the self-concept into account in the first instance. But that is a procedure that almost assures error because it treats the self-concept, which undeniably lies at the very root of cognition, as being of secondary epistemological importance. Under such circumstances, the characterization of self-cognition within a system may be more revealing about the system than it is about the nature of the epistemology of the self.

Most of the philosophical literature on the self-concept treats it in the same impersonal terms as any other concept of philosophical importance. For example, as we have seen, the self might be described as substance to which all predicates of a life are attached or as an illusionary stream of consciousness. There is nothing wrong with this way of thinking about the self-concept as long as it is held in mind that the self is a unique ontological *object* because it is the object that engages in philosophical inquiry about itself. Insofar as the intuition of self is personal to anyone who would trouble themselves to think about it, if it is a real, directly intuited entity, each philosopher should be expected to have a uniquely privileged experience of it that, although personal, may be described to others in a way that they may understand it as representative of their own experience of self. Accordingly, it should also be expected that personal description of the self as it is experienced will be both valid and enlightening and, given the diverse and confused state of modern philosophy of the self, such a description commends itself as a fresh starting point in developing a philosophical understanding of the self which may follow from it.

That we think of ourselves as real entities all the time is a fact that only a philosopher would question. The fact that we are internally quite comfortable with self-statements suggests that the philosophers who would deny the self as a real entity have gone completely astray on this question. It is human nature to engage in conversation (indeed, too much conversation) in which the speaker makes empirical statements about his or her current state of empirical affairs. "I am so busy at work, I hardly have any time for myself," "I am too fat for my own good," "Yesterday, I got caught outside in the rain without an umbrella," and "I didn't mean to offend you when I said that" are examples. These are contingent statements and are either verifiable by reference to the external world or to the internal state of mind of the speaker (which is of course only known to him or her). But we are also able to make *meaningful* non-empirical statements about ourselves as subject and object, namely, "I am," "I am conscious," "I am free," "I am morally responsible," and "I am a person who engages in philosophical inquiry including asking questions about my own essential Being."[30] These statements roughly correspond or relate to what Kant characterized as transcendental Ideas but they are not mere Ideas; rather they reflect the direct, objective intuition of the speaker about himself as a being, *understood not as a mere mind but as a real, existing, ontological object to which both empirical and non-empirical predication attaches.* Therefore, such statements describe some aspects of transcendent reality, which may be reflected in human empirical experience but is not *of* the sensible world. Understood as such, the self of self-consciousness is not an entity that is known by reference to the sensible world but is instead a human being as known to himself from the inside out and who is the subject of his own empirical experience. Additionally, it is in these statements that we find the character of the self and see the horrendous errors of both the Cartesian *Cogito* and the Gassendi-Hume line of criticism of it. Consciousness neither creates nor explains personal identity; rather, it is a fundamental characteristic of a human person. The self cannot be reduced to consciousness; rather, consciousness is an *attribute* of the self. Consciousness does not exist independently of a conscious entity any more than ideas exist independently of a thinker of them. Instead, consciousness is *self*-consciousness. Revisiting in slightly different terminology the formulation proposed near the beginning of this chapter, each person is a unique conscious being such that it can and does think about itself as the subject and object of a thought, each of which is different from the thought itself. Accordingly, consciousness is an intuition by which human Being reveals itself to itself.

It is crucial to distinguish between the awareness apparently characteristic of many higher order vertebrates and the self-consciousness that is presumably a faculty possessed on this earth solely by man. Animal awareness does not require a concept of self at all; it merely requires sufficient cognition to enable purposeful interaction with the physical environment, even if that interaction is wholly mechanistically determined. Even if such animal awareness is accompanied by a self-concept, the self of such awareness is, unlike human self-consciousness and more like the mistaken Humean conception of it, presumably wholly contingent, empirical, constantly changing, and motivated by mechanistically determined physical, chemical, and biological forces.[31] The self of human

---

30. Although it would be wholly ungrammatical, it would be more accurate (and illustrative) to substitute the self-assertion "I am" for the pronoun "I" in first person sentences, so that "I think" becomes "I am is thinking." We can see that, contrary to Kant, the self is both a subject and an object. Recognizing this disposes of the entire Gassendi-Hume line of argument that ran from Gassendi all the way to Søren Aabye Kierkegaard, the nineteenth century Danish existentialist.

31. Although we can never know what it is like to be a dog, for example, and inferring the state of mind of a dog from its behavior is inevitably polluted with anthropomorphism, to all appearances dogs are always "in the moment" and seem free of concerns about what the future will hold for them.

self-consciousness is something altogether different because, in addition to the features of animal self-awareness as a contingent and changing being, human self-consciousness includes both an abstract concept of self and the direct intuition of a persistent self as a *morally responsible being*. Indeed, it is the direct intuition of moral responsibility which illuminates the direct intuition of self as a persistent entity and, as will be explained in chapter 10, "Duty and Desire," provides morally rational creatures with freedom. If, as Heidegger teaches, man is the being for whom his own Being is an issue, then man must be a persistent, substantive self and if he is morally obligated, as is asserted here, man is indeed more than that: he is a soul.

Perhaps the point will become clearer if I make it in an experiential way. When I reflect inward, I find, like Hume, a stream of conscious focus. But behind that consciousness I find a person that I uniquely and directly identify as myself. That person, it turns out, has a few surprising characteristics, namely, persistence as a unity over time, confidence in his freedom of thought and action, and a profound and inescapable sense of moral obligation and responsibility. My thoughts may be discreet and sequential but my intuition of self is continuous, unified, and identical during and in between them. So, for example, the person typing these words at age sixty-five can recall, with deep regret, impulsively coaxing little Megan to run by and then sticking his leg out and tripping her when we were nine or ten years old. At the time, I thought it was funny even though I knew it was wrong to do; looking back today, I do not regard it in the least as having been humorous. But the critical fact for discussion here is this: my experience is such that I identify the person who acted badly many decades ago *as the same person* who is expressing these ideas about myself today, even though there is not a single physical cell in my body today that was present then, and *I consider, with nagging regret, myself, the current scrivener of these words, to be morally responsible for that idiotic and childish act of long ago*. It is important to note that I might, as people often do, make the statement that "I am a different person today than I was then—I would never trip a little girl today because I now know it is morally repugnant." But that is just a mode of speech and it, in fact, contains an internal contradiction, namely, that I cannot be different today from the "I" of yesterday unless the word "I" is merely a placeholder for something that is not a unity. The "I" then is the same being as the "I" now, notwithstanding the change in perspective. The "I" is a real, ontological entity. In order for me to be morally responsible for my actions, I must be the same person who committed them and not merely a contingent being who is constantly changing at the most fundamental biological level.

It is important to delineate what we mean when we say, as Searle did in the passage quoted earlier, that there is something that "it feels like to be me." In normal parlance, in my case, those words might be understood to be shorthand for "there is something that it feels like to be a sixty-five-year-old man living in New Jersey in the year 2017 and undertaking philosophical investigations for the sheer joy of doing so." Those words do express, to a limited degree, some idea of what it is like to be the *empirical* "me" of the moment, the "me" who woke up with a slight pain in his left knee this morning and is hoping to have sausage and eggs for breakfast. The empirical "me" is the contingent, ever-changing, empirical self of my animal awareness. It is known to me (and to others who observe me) by reference to contingent, ever-changing, empirical facts. At age sixty-five, I do not possess a single cell that I possessed forty-seven years earlier when I was capable of running a mile in 4:28. In what sense, then, may I intelligibly say that I am the same person who accomplished that feat? Certainly, I may be understood, as Locke would have it, as being the uninterrupted continuation of the same living organism, but it is difficult to see how the mere continuity of life provides anything like a self, including all of the aspects of internal human experience that we have repeatedly chronicled here. Metaphysically speaking, my body seems more comparable to the ship of Theseus whose planks were changed one at a time or to Heraclitus's ever-changing river. Am I the same empirical person today that I was at age eighteen? Certainly not, for biologically, I am completely different than I was then and I cannot even run a mile in twice that time. Indeed, the connection that I have today with the physical person of my youth is more memory than reality.

But the empirical self-description says nothing about what it is like to be the essential, persistent me, the *me* that is *substance* in Cartesian terms. That person is unique and describable only in supersensible terms because it is a *transcendent* entity. Although I know myself better than anything else, I can tell you little about myself as a transcendent entity other than *I am, I am free, I am concerned about my Being in general and, in particular, I hold myself to be morally responsible for my actions past, present, and future*, precisely because my transcendent Being is the indivisible substance that is me. Each person will comprehend quite clearly what those sentences mean because each person experiences the same things; but, because each of us is a mere morally responsible entity to which transcendent and empirical predicates relate, our language, indeed our thought, fails us as we attempt to describe that object apart from its predication. My consciousness of myself as an empirical entity, which extends far beyond any possible self-awareness of lower order primates, can only be explained as a feature of my self-consciousness as a transcendent being. My self-consciousness is not merely quantitatively different from animal self-awareness but is qualitatively different because it has a different subject. The difference between the two types of consciousness cannot be explained by my having a greater grey matter; it can only be explained by the fact that, as a human being, I am fundamentally different from the other organisms which inhabit the planet Earth, with the difference being that I am self-conscious of my essence as a morally responsible being. The essential me is confronted with the contingencies and necessities of my physical existence and environment, but my consciousness of them and my relationship to them is determined not mechanistically but through the free exercise of my will in light of my direct intuition of moral obligation, as I continually ask myself how ought I respond to what is before me. My freedom is known to me because even though I know I am obligated to conduct myself in a certain manner I (far too) often *elect* not to do so.

I presume that this personal description of my intuition of self is not substantially substantively different from the experience of other human beings. From this intuition, therefore, a philosophical exposition of the self of universal applicability can be identified, which exposition will only be briefly presented here because further groundwork must be undertaken for its complete elucidation and because the present purposes are limited to identifying a conception that both avoids the difficulties of the self-concept of modern philosophy already described and expresses the foundation upon which the philosophy of transcendent realism will be built. The self of self-consciousness may be understood as relating to its conscious experience in the same way that an object, considered as the subject of its predication relates to that predication, which, in the case of morally conscious beings, includes transcendent and empirical properties and relations, including individual conscious experiences. For consciousness to occur the predication of the self-object must therefore include as substance both the capability to think of the self as an object and the power of abstraction that flows from that capability and, because any attempt to infer these capabilities from empirical reality presupposes them, it follows that they can only arise by direct intuition. Importantly, from the association of the self-object as the subject of both transcendent and empirical predication it follows that the self is neither wholly transcendent nor wholly empirical but rather a psychosomatic unity. In the philosophy of transcendent realism, the self-object represents the persistent and unified subject of conscious experiences and characteristics. The self-object is the subject of each experience and, as part and parcel of its intuition of moral obligation, it understands itself to possess a moral status that depends upon the characteristics of such experiences which are determined both by empirical contingencies and the free exercise of will in response to them. That the self-object has moral status means that it is more than a mere collection or bundle of its predicates and that it must exist as a real ontological object. It is important to emphasize that the self-object, as the subject of predication, provides both the unity of its persistent identity as such and the multiplicity of each of its predicates, which are the elements that Leibniz correctly recognized as essential, although it is worth noting in passing that, because of its transcendent character, it is ontologically different from a subject to which only the predicates of contingent experience are attached (which is how Leibniz described the substance of human personality).

Because postulation of the transcendent self is necessary to supply the persistent being necessary for consciousness and the fullness of human experience, philosophers who acknowledge only the empirical self are doomed to the frustration of the impossibility of manufacturing perdurance where there is none and are forced to live with wholly unsatisfactory concepts of self as formality, logical construction, or mere transcendental Idea. The understanding of self as a psychosomatic unity is not only important because it provides the basis from which self-consciousness can occur that is missing from all reductionist explanations, but also because it demonstrates that there is a transcendent reality that includes an entity that is present to reason by direct intuition. In knowing ourselves as objects, we also know that knowledge is not limited to that which is presented to the senses and, philosophically, it becomes not only possible but necessary to begin to lay out an epistemology that includes such knowledge. To the poet, the eyes may be the windows of the soul; for the metaphysician, the soul is the window to metaphysics and the transcendent reality which it depicts.

3

The Reach of Reason

KANT'S RESPONSE TO SKEPTICISM

It is no understatement to say that if Descartes set the agenda for modern philosophy, Hume nearly succeeded in tabling it. Although Descartes's mind-body dualism was quickly rejected by subsequent philosophers, his rationalist philosophy was taken up by other men such as Spinoza and Leibniz, but, after Hume's devastating attack on rationalism and also on his predecessor empiricists, it seemed as though there might be little left of philosophy for discussion. As has already been mentioned, Hume denied knowledge of self, real empirical objects (retaining only the ideas that represent them), and the principle of causality which appears to connect such objects. Hume's ground for denial of causality is based upon an important discernment, namely, that a critical review of empirical events shows no evidence of the *necessity* or *universality* implied by our understanding of that concept. The following is a famous passage from *An Enquiry Concerning Human Understanding* in which Hume expresses his skepticism regarding causality by reference to a collision of billiard balls:

> But to convince us that all the laws of nature, and all the operations of bodies without exception, are known only by experience, the following reflections may, perhaps, suffice. Were any object presented to us, and were we required to pronounce concerning the effect, which will result from it, without consulting past observation; after what manner, I beseech you, must the mind proceed in this operation? It must invent or imagine some event, which it ascribes to the object as its effect; and it is plain that this invention must be entirely arbitrary. The mind can never possibly find the effect in the supposed causes, but the most accurate scrutiny and examination. For the effect is totally different from the cause, and consequently can never be discovered in it. Motion in the second billiard ball is a quite distinct event from motion in the first; nor is there anything in the one to suggest the smallest hint of the other. A stone or piece of metal raised into the air, and left without any support, immediately falls: but to consider the matter *a priori*, is there anything we discover in this situation which can beget the idea of a downward, rather than upward, or any other motion, in the stone or metal?[1]

---

1. Hume, *Enquiry Concerning Human Understanding*, Section IV, Part I, 325. The view that natural

Like Hume, Kant was troubled by the deficiencies in both rationalism and empiricism, which Kant regarded as the two primary strains of epistemology and metaphysics, but he was not prepared to accept the alternative of Hume's skepticism. Kant saw correctly that insofar as rationalism is not dependent upon the senses for its knowledge, it offers an apparent certainty that empiricism does not, but the trade-off is that rationalism is able to tell us very little about the sensible world. Empiricism, on the other hand, starts with a tenuous acceptance of the information provided by the senses but, although it appears to tell us much, it cannot escape the criticisms of Hume. Kant thought, with a great deal of justification, that he found an alternative approach which provides the certainty of the applicability of universal laws of nature to sensible experience while at the same time strictly limiting their applicability to such knowledge. In the working out of his transcendental idealism, Kant's concern for restoring the credibility of empirical experience in a way that can withstand a Humean skeptical critique is apparent throughout and, arguably, that concern led Kant to err on the side of skepticism to such a degree that his philosophy failed to achieve its potential, leaving open the door for the disparate and far less laudable philosophical approaches that developed in the void of Kant's reticence.

Kant, in direct contrast to Hume, asserts that we *do* have scientific knowledge. Kant's justification for his position lies in a genuinely unique brew of rationalism and empiricism. Kant holds that although all knowledge originates in the sensation of the empirical world, the mind contributes *a priori* certain rational metaphysical concepts to synthesize sense data in the process of understanding it.[2] For Kant, empirical knowledge occurs in the context of space and time[3] and is understood under the rubric of the universal law of causation, all of which are contributed by the mind as a condition, not just of knowledge, but of the *sensible experience from which such knowledge arises*. In other words, Kant is saying that if an object is not susceptible of comprehension as a caused entity that exists in space and time, then we cannot even become aware of it and, further, that what we experience is a sort of mentally *preprocessed* reality that stops completely short of any cognition of the underlying *thing-in-itself* of each object. Indeed, Kant argues that we cannot even know that there is a *thing-in-itself* and that it must be considered only as a limit of empirical cognition. Kant is therefore in direct opposition to Locke, who asserts that knowledge consists of the mind conforming to reality, insofar as Kant asserts that *reality must conform to transcendental reason* and also in direct opposition to Hume, insofar as Kant asserts that man does have true knowledge of the necessary and universal connections between empirical phenomena because *such connections are a condition of such phenomena being experienced in the first place*.

---

laws are contingent (and may be different in different universes) continues to be prominent today. See, Searle, *Mind*, 147, and Hawking and Mlodinow, *Grand Design*, 118, on M-Theory.

2. Kant employs the term "transcendental" to denote those *a priori* concepts of reason which constitute the mode of cognition of empirical objects and not the objects themselves. Kant, *Pure Reason*, B25.

3. Since Einstein, it has been commonplace to speak of space and time to be unified in a four-dimensional continuum called "space-time." However, that space and time are intuitively separate in the act of cognition of objects is evidenced by the fact that it took many millennia for science to unify them. As a result, it will enhance the clarity of discussion to refer to space and time as separate intuitions except where the concept of space-time as a unified dimensionality is relevant to the discussion.

Although Kant is widely regarded as the greatest of all modern philosophers, his transcendental idealism is not generally accepted today and his importance is understood by the mainstream for the most part to consist of his recognition that reason includes certain *a priori* knowledge which is not merely analytical, such as logic, and that any consideration of metaphysical questions must proceed first from consideration of epistemological questions. The latter point may be understood simply as stating that before we can explore the real nature of things we must first answer the questions of what we know and how we know it. There is a third aspect of Kant's philosophy which is widely underestimated but which, in my opinion, is the most important of all, namely, *Kant's depiction of reason as constituting a single, unified faculty through which abstract reasoning, including both theoretical and practical reasoning, and empirical understanding, which occurs through the transcendental categories of understanding, occur*. In this regard, Kant's transcendental idealism represents the completion of the idea, which to my knowledge originates with Spinoza, that the principles of implication abstractly underpin the law of causation in space and time.

Of course, because reductionist philosophy is the mainstream of the day, Kant's current stature reflects the criticism of that school. But as already explained in the prequel to this chapter, before reductionism reached preeminence, Kant received from the German idealists the perverse flattery of having his philosophy rebuked in order that they might adopt a version of it as a platform for developing their own, comprehensive idealist systems, and in pursuing their program, which the German idealists understood to be the conversion of Kant's critical philosophy into pure idealism, the German idealists made the two important and enduring points against Kant already detailed, namely, that Kant's insistence on the primary role of causation in cognition is inconsistent with his argument that we cannot understand the existence of the *thing-in-itself* as the cause of our sensation of objects and that Kant's explanation of the idea of the transcendental Ego as the mere form of the representation of thoughts is circular insofar as its inference from empirical reality presupposes its prior existence. As already explained, the German idealists took these two criticisms to a logical extreme and postulated not just the existence of a supersensible reality but the existence of a fully unified universe that can only be understood as thought thinking itself.

Although reductionism is Kant's *empiricist* successor, in its current positivist/analytical iteration, reductionism immediately followed German idealism and therefore had to contend with that philosophy before reductionism could ascend to prominence. Although reductionist philosophy is far more successful in its refutation of German idealism than it is in its critique of Kant, reductionism, in its own selfish interest of maintaining the closed causality of the empirical world, disregards the fundamental contributions made by German idealism and is able to do so not because such contributions are at all insignificant but because, when the grand system of German idealism came crashing down, it engendered wholesale ridicule from its critics who were not at all disposed to recognize the importance of its critique of Kant.

Transcendent realism is similar to Kant's transcendental idealism, to the extent, but only to the extent, that transcendent realism recognizes reason as a unified faculty and that all cognition, including the determination of empirical objects, entails the making of judgments under logical concepts. The differences between the two philosophies are otherwise numerous and great and they are largely centered on the question of the relationship between general and transcendental logic and the scope of their applicability. Although transcendent realism has little in common with German idealism, it shares in the criticism of Kant's conception of the *thing-in-itself* (albeit on significantly different grounds) and in the criticism of the circularity of Kant's transcendental Ego (and I must confess in passing a certain fascination for the audacious way in which German idealism annihilates the distinction between the sensible and supersensible worlds, even though I consider it to be fundamentally flawed).

After Kant's critical philosophy, it is no longer satisfactory for any philosophical system to ignore the necessity of articulating as a starting point its assessment of the nature and scope of reason itself, which may explain why few such systems have arisen subsequent to him. Perhaps the most interesting aspect of Kant's two *Critiques* is that although they represent a denial of the possibility of metaphysics as a science they possess all the scope of a complete system. Transcendental idealism provides in rigorous detail an empirical epistemology that borrows from rationalism only so much as is necessary to ensure the integrity of human experience. With respect to metaphysics, it addresses both the *self* and the *thing-in-itself* in each case by recognizing their important role in human experience while denying any metaphysical knowledge of either. And it offers on a philosophically scientific basis a reason-based ethics from which, through its reliance on the human experience of a freedom that cannot be empirically grounded, supports a robust, faith-based, quasi-metaphysical system that extends all the way to heaven. Additionally, Kant's philosophy, especially as presented in the first *Critique*, is not merely important for its substance but also its architecture. Kant, in presenting the categories of understanding and judgment and in his treatment of the paralogisms and antimonies, sets out a structure that no modern philosopher who aspires to system building can blithely hope to ignore and still achieve success. Although history has placed the German idealists and the material reductionists in the strategic position to pound away at Kant, these post-Kantians uniformly pale by comparison to Kant on the important questions of the nature, scope, and even the possibility of objective human knowledge and it is Kant alone who remains the point of embarkation for understanding the important questions of philosophy, starting with the question of the reach of reason itself.

TRANSCENDENTAL EPISTEMOLOGY

In delimiting the field on which Kant is prepared to confront Hume, Kant springs upon us a great philosophical surprise by asserting that there is *a priori* knowledge but that it is only applicable to sense experience and that such *a priori* concepts cannot be extended in their application beyond the sensible world to achieve metaphysical knowledge. Kant contends that attempts to apply such concepts to anything other than those which we do have sensible experience can be demonstrated to lead to logical fallacies and antimonies and, accordingly, Kant argues that man cannot have knowledge of the existence of God, freedom, immortality, or the substance of which matter is comprised, all of which are inaccessible to the senses, because they are beyond the scope of the categories of understanding, which together with the logic that Kant asserts is abstracted from them, completely circumscribe human reason. But Kant, unlike his purely empirical predecessors, is not prepared to dismiss these transcendental Ideas as superstition and neither does he consider them unimportant. To the contrary, Kant asserts that such metaphysical ideas arise *as man seeks the unconditioned unifying principles of empirical cognition* and that such ideas are useful in conceptualizing objective experience. Moreover, Kant asserts that practical moral faith is justifiable based upon human *experience* (as distinguished from knowledge) of freedom and develops an imposing ethical artifice based upon it. In doing so, Kant hopes to have removed belief in God from challenges on scientific grounds all the while affirming its reasonableness on the basis of faith.[4] In Kant's own words:

> Hence I had to suspend expansion of knowledge in order to make room for belief. For the dogmatism of metaphysics, that is, the presumption that it is possible to achieve anything in metaphysics without a preceding critique of pure reason, is the source of all that disbelief which opposes morality and which is always very dogmatic.[5]

It is of paramount importance to note that although Kant is certainly correct in his assertion that empirically sourced laws may not be applicable to supersensible experience, Kant's relegation of metaphysics to the realm of faith cannot follow from that assertion unless he can show that such laws constitute the whole body of rules that govern human reason. It will be argued in these pages that, for reasons which are thematic to transcendent realism, Kant fails to support that claim and, therefore, it appears that Kant's treatment of metaphysics may be understood as an unnecessary concession to Hume and, therefore, may very well constitute the greatest modern philosophical error after the Cartesian division of body and soul.

Kant divided knowledge into three types: (1) analytic *a priori*; (2) synthetic *a priori*; and (3) synthetic *a posteriori*. Analytic *a priori* propositions are propositions whose predicate concept is included in their subject concept and are known without reference to experience. A common example of an analytic *a priori* statement is that "all bachelors are unmarried." It is important to note that such propositions can be shown to be *a priori* because they are *universally* and *necessarily* true, which, as Hume points out with such force, can never be true of empirical (i.e., *a posteriori*) statements. Synthetic *a priori* propositions are known in the first instance by reference to experience but upon examination can be seen to be universally and necessarily true. One example of such propositions (used by Kant) is that the shortest distance between two points is a straight line. Synthetic *a posteriori* propositions are propositions whose predicate concept is not included in its subject concept and are known solely by reference to particular experiential instances. These propositions are neither universal nor necessary but instead are wholly contingent, meaning that both their occurrence and non-occurrence are possible. An example of such a proposition is that it is raining outside my home. Logically, there is a fourth possible type of knowledge, namely, knowledge that is analytic *a posteriori*. Such

---

4. Kant, *Critique of Pure Reason*, Bxxv–xxx.
5. Ibid., Bxxx.

propositions would be propositions whose predicate subject is included in its subject concept but known solely by reference to experience. Kant did not recognize the existence of such knowledge and its existence or nonexistence is neither relevant to the discussion of transcendental idealism nor transcendent realism and therefore will not be further mentioned here.

Kant argues that all scientific knowledge is synthetic *a priori* and gives examples from three disciplines, namely, mathematics, geometry, and physics. In mathematics, Kant provides the famous example of the equation that $7 + 5 = 12$. Kant asserts that this equation is seen to be universally and necessarily true even though the concept of "12" does not contain the concept of "7" or "5." In geometry, Kant provides the example mentioned earlier that the shortest distance between two points is a straight line. Kant asserts that this proposition is seen to be universally and necessarily true even though straightness is a quality not a quantity and, because shortest is quantitative, the concept of straightness can be seen to be adding to the proposition and therefore not analytically known. With respect to physics, Kant provides the example of the law of conservation of mass.[6] Kant asserts that this law is seen as necessary and universal but originates from observation of the permanence of matter/energy because the concept of matter entails extension in space but not permanence in time.

Kant then sets out to show, as his fundamental epistemological task, how synthetic *a priori* knowledge is possible. Before following along with Kant, it is important to note that philosophers of certain empirical schools, most notably the logical positivists, have devoted great effort to challenging these categories, arguing instead that all knowledge is either analytic *a priori* or synthetic *a posteriori*. On this view, there is no synthetic *a priori* knowledge and therefore Kant's inquiry, indeed, his entire project, is misguided.[7] For reasons that will be discussed in detail in the next section, Kant has the better of this argument, at least in general, if not with respect to each of his examples. Kant's question can be rephrased in a narrower and more focused way as follows: *How is it possible to have knowledge of necessary and universal propositions concerning the empirical world?* To avoid getting bogged down in argument over other examples given by Kant and disputed

---

6. The *Encyclopædia Britannica* (Editors of the Encyclopaedia Britannica, "Conservation of Mass") states:

> [Conservation of Mass is the] principle that the mass of an object or collection of objects never changes, no matter how the constituent parts rearrange themselves. Mass has been viewed in physics in two compatible ways. On the one hand, it is seen as a measure of inertia, the opposition that free bodies offer to forces: trucks are harder to move and to stop than less massive cars. On the other hand, mass is seen as giving rise to gravitational force, which accounts for the weight of an object: trucks are heavier than cars. . . .
>
> With the advent of relativity theory (1905), the notion of mass underwent a radical revision. Mass lost its absoluteness. The mass of an object was seen to be equivalent to energy, to be interconvertible with energy, and to increase significantly at exceedingly high speeds near that of light. The total energy of an object was understood to comprise its rest mass as well as its increase of mass caused by high speed. . . . The new conservation principle is the conservation of mass-energy.

7. It is worth noting that the statement that all knowledge is either analytic or *a posteriori* would, if true, seem to be a synthetic *a priori* statement because it entails argument for the necessity and universality of the observation that some knowledge is empirical.

by empiricists, unless otherwise expressly stated, the term *synthetic a priori* will be used in this work to refer to such propositions.

Kant holds that although all knowledge originates from *a posteriori* sensible experience (which is an empirical concept), the precondition of such experience is that it conforms to certain formal conditions and categories of understanding (which is a rationalist concept) *which are the* a priori *fundamental ordering principles of reason.* According to Kant, all empirical experience occurs in space and time, which provides the form or framework of the object.[8]

Copleston summarizes Kant's position on space as follows:

> The very lowest level conceivable of anything which could be called a knowledge of or acquaintance with objects involves at least an adverting to the representations produced by the action of things upon our senses. But we cannot advert to sensations without relating them in space and time. For instance, to advert to two sensations, that is to be conscious of them, involves relating the one to the other within time, within an order of temporal succession. One sensation comes before or after or at the same time as another. Space and time constitute the framework, as it were, in which the manifold of sensation is ordered or arranged. They thus at the same time diversify and unify (in spatio-temporal relations) the indeterminate matter of substance. . . .
>
> This does not mean, of course, that we are at first aware of unordered sensations, and that we then subject them to the *a priori* forms of space and time. For we are never faced, as it were, with unordered sensations. Nor could we be. Indeed, Kant's main point is that space and time are *a priori* necessary conditions of sense-experience.[9]

This is an enormously important point not only because it is the foundation of Kant's epistemology but because, together with the transcendental deduction of the categories of understanding, which will be discussed next, it reflects the rationalist element in Kant that is in direct opposition to traditional empiricism, which insists that space and time exist in reality external to reason and are not contributed by the human mind. To be clear, Kant is not asserting that space and time are not empirically real; to the contrary, Kant holds that there can be no cognition of objective reality that is not in space and time. But, for Kant, space and time are the form of the cognition, are contributed by the mind, and *are not presented to the mind by the senses.* There are two far-reaching implications of Kant's position in this regard. First, insofar as cognizable objects exist in themselves (without the contribution of the cognizing mind) they are not in space and

---

8. Kant says time and space are *a priori* concepts which cannot be determined empirically and cannot be thought away. But consider that virtual reality can be created by the purely logical parameters of machine programming, which suggests that time and space is the sensible representation of the logic of four-dimensional arrays. One implication is that sensible reality (as well as internal reality) must be logical, which in turn suggests that although the forms of time, space, and the categories may not be applied beyond empirical reality, the logic of the related judgments may. This is a fundamental principle of transcendent realism and is discussed at great length in chapter 4, "The Possibility of Objective Knowledge," chapter 5, "The Homogeneity of Reason," and chapter 6, "Empirical Judgment."

9. Copleston, *French Enlightenment to Kant*, 238.

time. Second, it is possible to conceive, without ever having the possibility of actually knowing, of entities that cannot affect our senses or be understood in space and time.[10]

For Kant, the *thing-in-itself* that affects the senses is forever unknown to the subject. Instead, by affecting the senses the *thing-in-itself* produces an *appearance* (i.e., the content of a sensation) to which reason then applies its categories (which correspond to formal logical judgments)[11] in coming to an understanding of the objects of the sensible world and their relation to one another. The following table shows the categories of understanding that are applied to appearances to produce the object as cognized and the related logical judgments inferred from the categories (which will be discussed shortly):

Table 1—Categories and Judgments of Reason	
A Priori Categories of Understanding	Judgments (Logical)
1. Quantity	1. Quantity
a. Unity	a. Universal
b. Plurality	b. Particular
c. Totality	c. Singular
2. Quality	2. Quality
a. Reality	a. Affirmative
b. Negation	b. Negative
c. Limitation	c. Infinite
3. Relation	3. Relation
a. Inherence and Substance	a. Categorical
b. Causality and Dependence	b. Hypothetical
c. Community (Reciprocity)	c. Disjunctive
4. Modality	4. Modality
a. Possibility—Impossibility	a. Problematic
b. Existence—Non-Existence	b. Assertoric
c. Necessity—Contingency	c. Apodictic

10. Kant also argues that time, and not space, is the "form of our internal sense, that is, of the intuition of ourselves and of our internal state." Kant, *Critique of Pure Reason*, B50.

11. Kant's contribution on this point is not in the identification of the categories, which for the most part dates back at least to Aristotle, but in showing that such categories are correlated on a one-for-one basis with the judgments of general logic upon which they are based. Kant would say that the latter are abstracted from the former and therefore are inapplicable beyond empirical experience. In transcendent realism, the ontological priority of general logic and the categories of understanding is reversed.

Kant offers little by way of explanation of the judgments, apparently on the assumption that his readers are competent classical logicians. Nevertheless, it is important to devote a little time to their elucidation and that of the related transcendental categories of understanding because they will figure largely in the exposition of how, under transcendent realism, general logic, as the ontologically prior rational power, governs both the form of cognition of objects in space and time and their determination under categories that arise from the application of general logic to extended objects. It should be noted that although Kant's list is deduced from the Aristotelian logic that prevailed in Kant's day, it will aid the analysis to employ the robust set of tools available to us today under modern predicate logic. We should begin, as does Kant, by noting that in each of Kant's triadic list of judgments under the four headings, the third judgment is not required as a matter of general logic but is added by Kant as a logical correspondent, which Kant asserts results from the combination of the first two and is required to complete the transcendental categories applicable to empirical cognition. The triadic judgments under the heading of Quantity correspond to the quantification in modern predicate logic, so that universality, plurality, and singularity, in the table correspond to the predicate quantification of "all x," "some x," and "the x," respectively. Kant's explanation of the necessity of adding the last (which is not necessary in predicate logic to achieve singular predication), seems to be that although in the case of universal and singular statements with respect to logical objects the predicate applies to the subject without exception, in the world of empirical cognition, the difference between a universal judgment and one that is only applicable in an individual instance is significant.

Similarly, the triadic judgments under the heading of Quality correspond to the way in which properties are predicated of variables in predicate logic, so that affirmation, negation, and infinity, correspond to having a property, not having a property, and having an opposing property, respectively. Kant's explanation of the necessity of adding the third judgment in the triad seems to be that, while general logic asks only whether a predicate may be ascribed to a subject and therefore in the case of general logic the first two judgments are sufficient, where the object is sensible the distinction between the inapplicability of a predicate and the applicability of its opposite is important and must therefore be acknowledged. In this regard, Kant offers the seemingly poor example of the distinction between the statement that the soul is not mortal and the soul is non-mortal, with the former negating the ascription of mortality to the soul and the latter placing the soul in the infinite category of non-mortal things. A better example might be the difference between asserting that an object is not black and that an object may be seen to reflect color.

With respect to the triadic judgments under the heading of Relation, Kant's exposition becomes more descriptive in character. Kant asserts that in logic, there are only three types of relations, namely that of predicate to subject, that of ground to consequence, and that of "the subdivided knowledge and the collected members of the subdivision to one another."[12] These are characterized as categorical, hypothetical, and disjunctive judgments, respectively, which correspond to the categorical concepts of understanding of inherence and substance, causality and dependence, and community and reciprocity. Kant has nothing to say about the first case, but presumably it treats of the ascription of

12. Kant, *Critique of Pure Reason*, B98.

a relation to a subject as being either essential or contingent, which is common to categorical logic and which, when applied to empirical cognition, comes under the concept of substance or inherence. With respect to hypothetical judgments common to propositional logic, Kant offers the premise of *modus ponens* (i.e., if A, then B), and with respect to disjunctive judgments Kant offers the logical opposition within a field that includes all possibility (e.g., if the field comprises A and B, then x must either be an A or a B), which combines both categorical and propositional logic in a manner that is common to modern predicate logic. Kant explains, obscurely, that in the case of empirical cognition, the category of "community is causality of a substance as reciprocally determining another substance."[13]

Finally, Kant explains that modality is a special function of judgment that adds nothing to the content of a judgment, which is fully determinable under the other categories, but only concerns the value of the copula in relation to the thought in general. Under the heading of Modality, Kant lists problematic, assertoric, and apodictic, which reflect possibility, actuality, and necessity, respectively. In the case of the last, Kant asserts that necessity arises as a combination of possibility and actuality because necessity is nothing but existence, which is given through possibility itself.

The function of the categories of understanding in the process of cognition is to provide the logical structure under which the imagination can organize the manifold of appearances presented to the senses. The categories are *ontological* predicates which may be applied to any or all possible objects and which must be applicable to the appearances given to the senses *as a condition to the thinkability of the objects to which such appearances relate*. The judgments are related thoughts or words about objects which constitute general logic acquired by abstraction of all empirical content from empirical objects; in other words, the judgments reflect both the general logic of pure reason and of empirical cognition. In order for reason to think about an object, (i.e., make a judgment about it), there must be a corresponding category of cognition that supports the judgment and in fact Kant, in order to ensure that his table is complete, builds his taxonomy of categories after completing his survey of the forms of logical thought, which because they are abstracted from empirical cognition, are ontologically subordinate to the concepts of understanding.

In Kant's system, the appearances, after organization under the categories of understanding, result in cognition of a known *phenomenon*. Kant's explanation of this process of objective understanding may be summarized as follows. An object (presumably, a *thing-in-itself*) affects the senses thereby giving rise to an appearance. The senses provide the raw data of objective experience. Such data in its raw state is unordered and indeterminate and there can be no awareness of it until reason renders it comprehensible, which happens under a process called synthesis, in which the imagination acts as a mediator between the logical categories and the manifold of representations by employing certain schemata to subsume the latter under the former. The schemata are internal rules for the production of the images that represent the determination of sensible objects in the act of empirical cognition.[14]

---

13. Ibid., B112.
14. The schemata are discussed in greater detail at 172–173.

Significantly for Kant, because our knowledge of the objective world is limited to the categories of our own internal reason, we have no right to assert that our knowledge exhausts objective reality and, indeed, Kant assumes that objects represent the appearance in space-time of *things-in-themselves* that are not fully known. Kant argues that if one abstracts from an object all that is susceptible of being understood of it, what is left behind is an unknown and unknowable "something." This something is the transcendental object, which Kant refers to as the "*noumenon*," and is wholly indeterminate. The *noumenon* of a sensible object is the correlative transcendental object (i.e., the object to the extent it is not known), which is referred to by Kant as a *noumenon* in the *negative* sense. Because Kant's epistemology is dependent upon the contribution by the mind of the categories of understanding in the act of cognition, he must presume the existence of *noumena* in order to avoid the conclusion that the human mind *creates* its own objects in the same way that theists presume that divine intuition does. Indeed, *noumena* are so important to Kant's philosophy that he says that "[t]he doctrine of sensibility is at the same time the doctrine of *noumena* in the negative sense of the term."[15] Nevertheless, Kant holds true to his basic premise that we cannot apply the categories beyond sensible experience and therefore states that not only can we not know the characteristics of *noumena* but we cannot assert dogmatically that they exist. As a result, Kant concludes that *noumena* are *problematical* and can only be understood as a limiting concept.[16]

Given Kant's epistemology, *noumena* in the negative sense are not the only conceivable *noumena* that may exist. According to Kant, if it were possible for there to be a *transcendent* object that is not correlative to a sensible object (in the way *noumena* in the negative sense are presumed to be), we could have no knowledge of the transcendent object because all such *noumena* (which Kant calls *noumena* in the *positive* sense) would be outside space and time and, therefore, outside the categories of human understanding. So, for Kant, while it is possible that there are real objects that are not in any way sensible, because we do not have any non-sensible (i.e., purely intellectual) intuition of them, they are wholly and completely unknowable to us. And, although Kant does not say so, there is no reason within his framework that an object cannot be *noumenal* in both the negative and positive sense, (i.e., to be partially but not wholly correlative to a sensible object) and, in fact, it is asserted in these pages that this is precisely the condition of man considered as a psychosomatic unity.

In response to the criticism of the German idealists that, to be consistent, Kant must accept that the *thing-in-itself* must be said to *cause* the representation of its object, Copleston responds that the idea of the *noumenon* arises "not through inference to a

---

15. Kant, *Critique of Pure Reason*, B308. The postulation of *noumena* by Kant render him a realist and not an idealist as he is commonly mischaracterized. When Kant postulates transcendental Ideas he is speaking of concepts that cannot constitute knowledge and, in so speaking, does not embrace idealism.

16. It is interesting to contemplate the consequences of Kant's refraining from asserting the existence of *noumena* in the negative sense. If such *noumena* do not exist, then the only conclusion (which Kant strives to avoid) is that sensible objects are created by human reason, which seems to lead inexorably to solipsism. Conversely, it seems that if we are to reject solipsism, then it follows that we should be able to assert non-dogmatically that *noumena* in the negative sense do in fact exist.

cause of sensation, but as an inseparable correlate of the idea of the phenomenon."[17] Copleston's position may be stated in another way, namely, that although the existence of the *thing-in-itself* (either as wholly represented or not) cannot be asserted non-dogmatically to be cause of sensation, the existence of the cognizable sensation of an object justifies the presumption of the existence of the correlative *noumenon*. The significance of Copleston's position as so restated is difficult to exaggerate, not because of the support it offers Kant, but because it hints that, although the categories of understanding may not permissibly be applied beyond sensible experience, the general *a priori* logic that is correlative to them must apply to the supersensible world.[18] It should also be noted, however, that this is a point as to which Kant would vehemently disagree, precisely because of his ontological prioritization of the categories over such logic, and the criticism of German idealism must therefore stand as at least pointing to the secondary inconsistency, not of the asserted inapplicability of causation to the sensation of the *thing-in-itself* but of the presumed existence of the *thing-in-itself* notwithstanding the admittedly dogmatic nature of that presumption.

According to Kant, the application of the categories to the synthetized object can only occur within the *unity of consciousness*. Kant expresses this by saying that the "I think" must be capable of accompanying all of one's representations; in other words, knowledge of an object cannot occur unless accompanied by the possibility of awareness of such knowledge. When Kant refers to the unity of consciousness or the "I think" he is not referring to the fragmentary, empirical ego (which is the province of psychologists) but, instead, to what we have already referred in Kant's terminology as the transcendental Ego. Kant's transcendental Ego is also to be distinguished from Searle's formal notion of self and the self that the phenomenalists assert is a logical construction comprising the series of psychical events. But Kant is faced with a serious problem, namely, how to justify the unity of consciousness within an epistemology that requires strict limitation of the categories of understanding to sensible objects which do not include the self. Kant criticizes Descartes's *Cogito* as entailing an assumption that we have knowledge of self independently of, and prior to, experience of external things; Kant instead argues that internal experience is possible only through external experience and that *consciousness is consciousness of external things*. In other words, because all knowledge originates in the senses, the "I think" can only know sensible objects and the transcendental *Idea* of self arises only because of their existence.

Kant says that the empirical ego is determined in time (i.e., successive states of consciousness) but that such cannot occur except by presupposition of something persistent; in other words, the transcendental Ego is a necessary condition of thought (but not itself susceptible of being by itself thought as an object). For Kant, this presupposition is

---

17. Copleston, *French Enlightenment to Kant*, 271.

18. The rightmost column of Table 1 shows the judgments that Kant says arise as the result of application of categories and *not* that the logic of such judgments *underlies* the categories. One of the fundamental points of disagreement with Kant upon which transcendent realism is based is that, in order for there to be cognition under the categories and related logical judgments, the universe, including the subject and objects of cognition, must reflect an underlying logical order. This topic is more fully addressed in chapter 4, "The Possibility of Objective Knowledge," chapter 5, "The Homogeneity of Reason," and chapter 6, "Empirical Judgment."

neither itself a knowable object nor a logical construction; it is *the unifying element of the process of thinking an object*. It seems that the transcendental Ego is similar to *noumena* in the negative sense (and, as we shall see, to freedom) insofar as they are both presumptions that are justified by objective experience but cannot be asserted non-dogmatically to exist. Not surprisingly, as already noted, the German idealists see in Kant's formulation of the transcendental Ego a contradiction similar to the one that is the object of their criticism of the doctrine of *noumena* in the negative sense, namely that the transcendental Ego that is supposed to constitute empirical experience is dependent upon such experience in the first place. But, in the case of the transcendental Ego, the criticism of the German idealists has substantially more bite because the transcendental Ego is not a limitation on knowledge (as it is for Wittgenstein) but is asserted to be a *precondition* that plays an active part in the process of knowing, and the contradiction therefore undercuts the entire foundation of Kant's epistemology. However, instead of attempting to solve this problem as the German idealists do by separating consciousness completely from the individuals who experience it, which for reasons already explained take us further away from the reality of human rational experience, a far better solution is to reverse Kant's prioritization of general and transcendental logic, by placing the former ontologically at the pinnacle of reason.

TRANSCENDENTAL ILLUSION AND THE RING-FENCING OF REASON

Although the just-summarized epistemology of Kant is as substantial as any ever produced and therefore merits serious consideration in its own right, it must be remembered that Kant's epistemology is only one part of a philosophy that also includes Kant's rationally compelled, faith-based metaphysics and Kant's critique of modern philosophy, which is offered as the ground for Kant's foundational premise that *a priori* categories of understanding may not be applied to anything that we do not experience sensibly.[19] As noted earlier, Kant's argument is that because rationalism and empiricism are capable of producing valid proofs of opposite propositions, by virtue of the principle of non-contradiction, neither can be correct and, therefore, an alternate approach to metaphysical questions must be found by identifying and correcting the contradictory presuppositions of each. In the case of rationalism, Kant argues that the primary difficulty lies in its presupposition of knowledge that is non-sensibly sourced (including, importantly, knowledge of *noumena* in both the negative and positive senses); in other words, the difficulty is that rationalism treats *noumena* as though they are phenomenal objects of cognition. In the case of empiricism, Kant asserts that the primary difficulty lies in its presupposition that reality as empirically understood strictly conforms to reality as it is, so that knowledge consists in the conformity of the understanding to the sensible world; in other words, the difficulty is that empiricism treats phenomena as though they are identical with their correlative *noumena*. Kant characterizes the application of logic beyond sensible experience

---

19. In *Critique of Pure Reason,* Kant's epistemology is set forth in the "Transcendental Analytic," the first of two divisions of the "Transcendental Logic," and Kant's critique of modern philosophy is set forth in the "Transcendental Dialectic," the second of two divisions of the "Transcendental Logic."

as "transcendental illusion" and the correction of this error forms the basis for Kant's transcendental epistemology in which he asserts that, as a precondition of empirical experience, the appearances affecting the senses must conform to the *a priori* categories of the understanding but that, even though such categories are not empirically sourced, they have no applicability beyond the world of sensation. In support of Kant's premise, Kant offers four paralogisms of the soul and four antinomies of pure reason. Although there is undeniable elegance in the way that Kant grounds his positive epistemology in a logical critique of rationalism and empiricism, unfortunately, Kant's analysis suffers yet again from a circularity of reasoning insofar as his critiques of modern philosophy presuppose the rectitude of the epistemology that he purports to build upon them.

Kant begins his elucidation of the paralogisms of the soul with the assertion that the common understanding of the soul as persistent, indivisible, immaterial, and immortal does not constitute knowledge but, instead, results from the attempted application of the categories of understanding beyond the sensible world. The gist of the paralogisms is that the common understanding mistakes the unity of apperception (i.e., the "I think" or transcendental Ego) for the soul as it is commonly understood as a substantive, albeit supersensible, being. In Kant's view, the "I think" that accompanies every thought is merely the logical background of conscious thought and as such it can never be the object of knowledge and therefore cannot be understood by application of the categories of understanding. In the first paralogism, Kant makes this point directly by basing his refutation of the argument that the soul is substance upon his assertion that the "I think" is nothing more than the unity of apperception. In the second paralogism of the soul, Kant argues that we cannot know that the soul is simple and therefore distinguishable from matter because we cannot have knowledge of the substratum of either, in each case because we do not have direct, sensible experience of it. In the third paralogism of the soul, Kant contends that the conclusion that the soul is a *person* results directly from confusing the unity of apperception with individual identity. Finally, in the fourth paralogism of the soul, Kant argues that the idea that the soul is separate from the external world cannot be proven because all experience ultimately is internal experience.[20]

Kant next turns to what he calls the antinomies of pure reason. According to Kant, in the process of trying to conceive of the true nature of external experience, human reason continues to seek the cause of each cause of natural phenomena in a vain search for the unconditioned cause, which is presumably a metaphysical conception. But we have already seen that, in Kant's view, any such cause must lie beyond the realm of knowledge because, if it exists at all, it lies beyond the scope of the categories of understanding upon

---

20. In order for the paralogisms to be such, one must agree that Kant is correct in his equating the self with the empirical thinker (i.e., the "I think"). However, this is precisely the error committed by Descartes. Correcting this error, it seems that the paralogisms show the opposite of that which Kant intended, namely, that the self is not the same entity as the empirical thinker. With respect to the second paralogism, it should be noted that the soul is distinguishable from the "substratum" of objective reality on the grounds that when empirical knowledge is prescinded from the totality of human knowledge, we have direct knowledge of the human substratum which is in fact separate and apart from the empirical world. To argue, as Kant does, that we cannot distinguish between soul and matter because all experience is internal experience represents an inexcusable relapse into solipsism. For additional criticism of Kant's paralogisms, see the discussion at 95–97.

which such knowledge is preconditioned. Kant claims to be able to prove that such is the case because there assertedly are equally valid proofs for and against the transcendental Ideas that result from the regressive process of metaphysical inquiry. Kant says:

> If we apply our reason, not merely to objects of experience, in order to make use of the principles of the understanding, but venture to extend it beyond the limits of experience, then there arise sophistical doctrines which may neither hope to be confirmed nor fear to be refuted in experience. Every one of them is not only in itself free from contradiction, but can even point to conditions of its necessity in the nature of reason itself—although, unfortunately, the assertion opposing it can produce equally valid and necessary grounds in its support.[21]

If Kant is correct, the solution is not to discard reason altogether but to avoid logical contradiction by limiting the scope of reason to empirical experience. It is important to note that for Kant's methodology to be valid four conditions must be met. The first is that it is not sufficient for the conclusions of each argument in an antimony to be contradictory because, unless the premises are the same, there will be no true antimony and the contradiction may be resolved by rejecting one of the premises or the other or both. The second is that each of the two arguments in an antimony must be based upon application of reason to an element that is beyond empirical experience because, if it is not, then it cannot be said to demonstrate the invalidity of applying reason outside of the empirical experience to which Kant asserts it is limited. The third is that analysis of each such argument must not assume what Kant purports to prove, namely, that all knowledge originates from empirical experience and that the categories of understanding and the intuitions of space and time, and the logic which Kant argues is abstracted from them, are all inapposite to anything that is not given to reason in empirical experience. The fourth condition is that each argument must be valid and contradict the other.

Kant's four antimonies may be summarized as follows.[22]

First Antimony

Thesis: The world has a beginning in time and is limited also with regard to space.

Antithesis: The world has no beginning and no limits in space, but is infinite as regards both time and space.

A. *Proof of Thesis*: Assume the antithesis is correct. If there were no beginning in time, then an infinite series of successive states of things must have passed away in the world. However, the infinity of a series consists in the fact that its completion in the empirical world is impossible. Hence, an infinite prior sequence of empirical events is impossible and therefore the world must have had a beginning. With respect to the second part of the thesis, that the world is limited with regard to space, again assume that the antithesis is correct. In that case, the world would have to be given as an infinite whole of

---

21. Kant, *Critique of Pure Reason*, B449–50.
22. Kant's full discussion of the antimonies is at ibid., B433–90. The antimonies as set forth herein are as Kant stated them. The proofs are the author's paraphrase of Kant's arguments.

simultaneously existing empirical objects, which could never be given to reason by the senses or even thought except, in each case, as an infinite totality synthesized over an infinite time, which is impossible.

B. *Proof of Antithesis*: Assume the thesis is correct. The existence of a beginning to the world presupposes that there was "empty time" prior to its commencement. But in empty time there can be no distinction of one part or another with respect to any condition of existence and hence nothing can come into being either of its own accord or as a contingency which depends upon an antecedent. With respect to the second part of the antithesis, that space is infinite, again assume the thesis is correct. In that case, space would be limited and there would need to be "empty space" outside of it that is not limited and therefore objects would not only be in relation within space but also to space. However, since the world is a totality outside of which no object can exist, the latter would entail relation to nothing (i.e., no object) and such a relation, as well as the relation of the totality of space as limited by empty space, is nothing and therefore space cannot be limited.

C. *Analysis and Commentary*: In Kant's view, both the thesis and the antithesis treat the world, conceived as a totality of extended objects, as though it were a possible object of experience. Kant's position is that human rationality is incapable of experiencing the world in this way and, instead, merely conceives of the world as an Idea based upon the extrapolation of individually limited experiences.[23] Accordingly, Kant's argument is that both the thesis and the antithesis entail the attempted application of reason to something it never experiences, namely, the world as a whole. However, implicit in Kant's characterization is that the world as conceived in both arguments contains not only the totality of empirical objects but that the empirical world exhausts reality, including space and time. This is plainly only true of the antithesis. If such an understanding of the world is correct, then the conclusion of the antithesis that the world has no spatio-temporal limits is sound. On the other hand, the thesis, which is a classic rationalist proof, treats the *empirical* world as a totality of extended objects that does not exhaust human *rational* experience. Upon this understanding, the application in the thesis of the law of causality to the world as a whole may be justified. Kant's argument is that, because we have no experience other than that which originates from the senses, we cannot abstract to non-empirical conditions, to a world that includes space and time (which are not in the world but rather conditions of the possibility of the experience of external objects), or to the world as a totality and, therefore, that neither thesis is correct. Of course, Kant's epistemology may or may not be correct, but his methodological conclusion that the antimony arises because both the thesis and antithesis attempt to apply reason to objects which are not given in empirical experience remains subject to doubt.

We should consider Kant's analysis in the light of the four conditions we have imposed upon his methodology. The common premise in each argument is that the world

---

23. Whether certain infinities can be given to reason as completed totalities is a controversial issue that has persisted since Aristotle. It remains important in contemporary philosophy of mathematics and, because the philosophy presented in these pages equates Being and intelligibility, its resolution is of great importance. Accordingly, chapter 7, "Infinity, Countability, and Self-Reference," is largely devoted to analysis of this issue and its implications.

exists as a totality so the first condition is met upon the assumption that by "world" both arguments mean the same thing. For the second condition to be met, Kant must show that we have no experience of the world as a totality. Certainly no human being has experienced the entire history of the world or voyaged throughout all of space. On the other hand, there seems to be no impediment to describing the world as the totality of its objects and events. If the world, considered as such, comprises an independently existing space and time, and human reason is fully contained in it along with the rest of its objects (as asserted by mainstream empiricism), then the world can only be experienced from the inside out and can only have reference to itself. On the other hand, if space, time, and causality are *a priori* intuitions under which empirical phenomena are understood and if we have direct intuition of the supersensible (such as the soul and its freedom), then it is not at all clear that the empirical world exhausts human experience or that it cannot be objectively understood. Under this view, the empirical world is not a container of all that there is but a description of that group of objects given to ensouled reason as possessing spatio-temporal predication. That even if the world is taken to be a totality there remain different conceptions of it complicates Kant's task, because he must now show that we have no experience of the world as a totality no matter how the world is understood. Instead of taking this issue on directly, Kant asserts that our limited experience of empirical phenomena cannot provide a sufficient basis for extrapolation of the world as a possible object of metaphysical analysis and endeavors to dispose of the rationalist view by application of his own epistemology to the possibility of transcendent reality, which takes us headlong into examination of the third condition we have imposed on Kant's methodology.

Unfortunately for Kant, the third condition requires that the arguments in the antimony not be made upon the assumption of Kant's epistemology, which is to say that although Kant may use his epistemology to resolve the antimony, he cannot use it to create the antimony in the first place by making the case for either argument within the antimony on Kantian terms. This condition is clearly not satisfied. Kant's disproof of the thesis is based upon the assertion of the impossibility of "empty time" and "empty space" as limitations upon the world. That this analysis is in itself heavily imbued with Kantian epistemology is readily apparent from Kant's argument in support of it:

> For as to the plea by which people try to escape from the conclusion that if the world has limits in time or space, then the infinite void must determine the existence of real things, as far as their magnitude is concerned, it is really no more than a disguised attempt at putting some unknown intelligible world in the place of our world of sense, and an existence in general that presupposes no other condition in the world in the place of a first beginning (an existence preceded by a time of nonexistence), and boundaries of the cosmic whole in the place of the limits of extension; and thus one gets rid of time and space. But we have to deal here only with the *mundus phaenomenon* and its magnitude, and we cannot abstract from the conditions of sensibility, without annulling the very essence of that phenomenal world. The world of sense, if it is limited, lies necessarily in the infinite void. If we ignore this void, and with it space in general as an *a priori* condition of the possibility of appearances, then the whole world of sense vanishes. This world alone is given to us in our enquiry. The *mundus intelligibilis* is nothing but the universal concept of a world in general, in which abstraction

is made from all conditions of its intuition, and in reference to which, therefore, no synthetic proposition, whether affirmative or negative, is possible.[24]

In introducing the concepts of "empty time" and "empty space," Kant treats each as though it were alternative time and space before concluding, upon his own epistemology, that because alternative time and space are not given to the senses they cannot exist. This is certainly a position that mainstream empiricism would embrace and it shows the fundamental empiricism of Kant's transcendental idealism. However, in supporting the antithesis with his own philosophy, Kant creates the first antimony in at least two ways. The first is that Kant's argument may simply be false, which is evidenced by the facts that it is not the position of those modern cosmologists who embrace the multiverse and that it assumes the impossibility of the transcendent reality which we assert in these pages is in fact given to reason in internal experience. The second difficulty is that Kant's argument, in support of the antithesis, relies upon the impermissibility of taking the world as a whole, which is contrary to the premise of the antithesis, in order to set the world as conceived in the thesis in opposition to a void out of which Kant asserts that the thesis suggests that the world came. Once again, although it is possible that Kant is correct (and the cosmologists and we both are wrong), Kant may not use his empiricism *to create* an antimony for the purpose of supporting his argument that the problem which the antimonies manifest is that traditional rationalist and empiricist arguments are flawed because they employ the categories and intuitions to objects that are not knowable.

This leads to a final point which, together with our observations on the importance in analyzing the first antimony of the different understandings of how we experience the world, casts further doubt on Kant's methodology. If one regards the world as given at least in part in intuition, its beginning and extent may be understood in logical terms (for example, by substituting for causality the concept of sufficient reason), whereas if one regards the world as wholly given to the senses, then the very question of its beginning or extension (which may only be understood from within the world about which it inquires) may be largely unintelligible. Viewed in this light, the thesis and the antithesis treat such different conceptions of the world that, although both arguments may be valid, their contradiction of each other follows directly from their contradictory understanding of the subject matter. Kant does not appear to deny this. It follows that, although both arguments may be valid, it is not possible for both arguments to be sound, and for the antimony to serve Kant's purpose, he must show that neither is sound for the specific reason that their subject matter includes objects as to which we cannot have knowledge, which he does not appear to accomplish.[25]

---

24. Kant, *Critique of Pure Reason*, B462.

25. In furtherance of the point, it can be observed that the purported antimony can be restated as a lengthy syllogism which begins with the major premise that "the empirical world is a totality which either comprises everything that there is, including space and time, or only all extended objects," and which then proceeds with arguments for or against the world being limited or unlimited, each of which can be challenged upon its own terms.

Second Antimony

Thesis: Every composite substance in the world consists of simple parts, and nothing exists anywhere but the simple or what is composed of it.

Antithesis: No composite thing in the world consists of simple parts, and nowhere in the world does there exist anything simple.

A. *Proof of Thesis*: Assume that the antithesis is true. In that case, if all composition were reduced in thought, then there would remain no composition and, upon the assumption that no simple parts exist, there would remain no simple part either and, therefore, the result of such reduction would be to eliminate the object altogether. Therefore, it must either be impossible to reduce composite objects in thought or simple parts must exist. However, it cannot be impossible to think away all composition because composition is a contingency which cannot, therefore, ground its own existence. Therefore, simple parts must exist.

B. *Proof of Antithesis*: Assume that the thesis is correct. Because all composition of substances is only possible in space, space must consist of as many parts as there are parts in the composite, and the simple substance that is the absolutely first part of the composite must occupy space. But since everything that occupies space must consist of a manifold of parts, a composite cannot be reduced to something that is both simple and occupies space. (By this, I understand Kant to be saying that since space is a totality and not a composition of individual spaces, simple substance cannot occupy space.) Therefore, no simple substance exists.

C. *Analysis and Commentary*: Kant's conclusion is that because neither proposition is an assertion about objects of experience it cannot be known to be true. For Kant, a simple substance cannot give rise to an appearance, and, therefore, if it exists it must be *noumenal* in the negative sense. In the thesis, the distinction between phenomena, about which we have knowledge, and *noumena* as to which we may have none, is disregarded. In the antithesis, the proposition that because we can have no sensible experience of substance it must not exist reduces to an impermissible assertion that for *noumena* to exist they must be phenomena.

This is perhaps a good place to emphasize one of the recurrent themes expressed in these pages, which is the fundamental problem with analytical philosophy, namely, that the premises must be given as part of an entire metaphysics and not freely chosen from a hodgepodge of possibilities. There is an important distinction between philosophic intuition and scientific analysis.[26] Underlying the antithesis is that space must be divisible without limit, which, although philosophically possible, may not reflect actual phenomena; indeed, neither the quantum physicists (since Max Planck, the German theoretical physicist responsible for the development of quantum physics) nor I believe in the infinite divisibility of empirical space. In addition, in challenging the thesis, Kant is arguing in favor of the possibility that the universe may be an infinite contingency.

---

26. This distinction will be discussed in detail at 92–93 and in in chapter 6, "Empirical Judgment."

For reasons that will be explained in chapter 12, "The Supreme Principle of Being and Intelligibility," I do not believe this to be correct either.

We can see that the first two conditions that we have placed upon Kant's methodology are met in the second antimony. With respect to the first, the premise of both arguments is that composite objects exist and are either composed of other composite objects or simple substance. With respect to the second, we have no empirical experience of simple substances in the external world, so application of the categories and intuitions to them is outside that experience. Thus, it is fair for Kant to argue here with respect to empirical reality that it is impermissible to treat phenomena as *noumena* and *vice versa*. With respect to the third condition, it appears that Kant successfully refrains from incorporating his epistemology into the antimony in order to create it. However, with respect to the fourth condition, it does not appear that the two arguments are equally valid and therefore create an antimony that requires the circumscription of the categories and intuitions to resolve. With respect to the thesis, although we do not have experience of empirical substance, we do have experience of transcendent reality (including our own souls) which supports that argument in favor of the existence of substance. Of course, this calls into question not just this antimony but Kant's entire epistemology. Additionally, the antithesis is particularly doubtful given our experience of transcendent reality and the scientific evidence in favor of the limited divisibility of space, so not only do we not have experience of space as being empirically infinitely divisible, contemporary science, which represents our empirical experience, suggests that it is not.

Third Antimony

Thesis: Causality according to the laws of nature is not the only causality from which all the appearances of the world can be derived. In order to account for these appearances, it is also necessary to admit another causality, that of freedom.

Antithesis: There is no freedom, but everything in the world takes place solely according to laws of nature.

A. *Proof of Thesis*: Assume that there is no causality other than natural causality. In that case each event must be preceded by an event that causes it in accordance with the law of natural causality and each such prior event must also be preceded by an event that causes it in accordance with the same law, which yields an infinite regression. But such an infinitely contingent sequence contradicts the law of natural causality according to which it occurs. Therefore, there must be another causality through which something takes place without its cause being determined any further, according to necessary laws, which is to say that "we must admit an absolute spontaneity of causes, whereby they start by themselves in a series of appearances that proceeds according to natural laws; and we must consequently admit transcendental freedom, without which, even in the course of nature, the series of appearances on the side of causes can never be complete."[27]

---

27. Kant, *Critique of Pure Reason*, B475.

B. *Proof of Antithesis*: Assume the thesis is correct. In such event, freedom, conceived as a faculty of *absolutely beginning* a sequence of subsequently caused events, exists. But on this assumption, the subsequent events cannot be presumed to be caused, since their ultimate event was uncaused freedom. Therefore, nothing is caused in accordance with natural law. Therefore, freedom contradicts natural law.

C. *Analysis and Commentary*: Kant is willing to allow for the possibility that freedom may exist as the absolutely spontaneous cause of the world and, having opened that door, also with respect to other aspects of a non-sensible reality as to which Kant maintains we can have no knowledge. On the other hand, with respect to empirical cognition, where causality is a category of understanding and therefore a condition of determining phenomena, Kant is constrained to assert that the antithesis is correct. Kant attempts to reconcile the two by advancing the concept of causality in time, which is given under the categories and therefore present in all cognition, and comparative causation of a series of events that begins as the result of an action freely taken but that is nevertheless understood empirically in accordance with the law of temporal causation. Kant provides the example of one freely arising from one's chair, which may then absolutely begin a sequence of causally connected events. In the example, although the determination to arise from the chair is freely made in the context of a prior and subsequent sequence of determined events, Kant argues that the entire sequence is *fully caused* in time. Nevertheless, given Kant's unwillingness to acknowledge any direct intuition of freedom or any other supersensible reality, his defense of the possibility of freedom seems forced and one would need to be forgiven if they concluded that Kant's motivation in doing so is to provide the presupposition upon which his ethics and reason-compelled faith is based. We can agree with Kant that physical objects are understood under the rubric of natural causality and therefore are fully determined to the extent of our knowledge. However, because transcendent realism is predicated upon direct intuition of the soul and its freedom in moral action, freedom of will is accordingly embraced as an undeniable aspect of the *Logos*.

Turning to an examination of the conditions we imposed upon Kant's methodology, we find Kant in a somewhat different position than he was with respect to the first two antinomies. As was the case with the first two antinomies, the premise of temporal causality supports both arguments. With respect to the second condition, however, there appear to be two difficulties. The first is that, insofar as the antithesis speaks only to the determinism of empirical phenomena, it is difficult to see how it can be characterized as entailing the application of reason beyond the scope intended by Kant and, thus, our second condition is unmet. The second is that Kant's assertion that we have no empirical experience with respect to freedom except to the extent that it is implied from the empirical fact of morality, flies in the face of our actual experience, and depends upon acceptance of the antithesis for its support. To be clear, the argument here is not that Kant's reconciliation of freedom and causality is itself incorrect but rather that Kant's analysis fails to meet the conditions that we have established in order for an antinomy to support his broader contention that application of the categories of understanding outside of the world of phenomena yields metaphysically important contradictions.

Fourth Antimony

Thesis: There belongs to the world an absolutely necessary being, either as its part or as its cause.

Antithesis: An absolutely necessary being exists nowhere, neither in the world nor outside the world as its cause.

A. *Proof of Thesis*: The sensory world is a series of alterations, each of which is subject to its condition. Because each conditioned event presupposes a complete series of conditioned events leading up to the unconditioned, which is necessary, something necessary must exist. Moreover, this necessary thing must exist in time because the beginning of a series of time can only be determined by that which precedes it in time. It follows that the sensible world must include something that is necessary, whether it be the whole series of the world itself or only part of it.

B. *Proof of Antithesis*: Assume that the world contains within it a necessary being either as the whole series of the world or as part of it. If the latter, then the necessary being would be itself uncaused yet existing in time, which contradicts the law of causation in time. If the former, then the entirety of the world would be necessary even though it comprises only contingent parts, which is self-contradictory. Assume, then, that there exists an absolutely necessary cause of the world that lies outside of the world itself. For the sensible world to come into being, the necessary cause would have to begin to act, and for an agent to begin to act it must be within time. Therefore, a necessary cause of the world cannot exist outside of time.

C. *Analysis and Commentary*: Kant argues that because the thesis by its terms is confined to the existence within the world of a necessary being it must stand or fall solely upon the law of natural causation in accordance with which all empirical change must occur and that the existence within the world of a necessary being that is itself uncaused is contradictory and therefore impossible. Kant observes that logical (i.e., pure) contingency, which means that either a thing or its opposite may be true, and temporal contingency, which means that an actual state of being may be *succeeded in time* by its opposite, are different concepts and may not be used interchangeably. Following along this line, Kant explains that logically an event A is contingent if it's opposite not-A is also possible at the same time, but that the existence in time of A and the subsequent existence of not-A does not support any inference that A was, at the time of its existence, contingent, and concludes that change in time does not imply any logical contingency or require inference of a logically necessary regression to an uncaused cause. On the other hand, because the disputation of the thesis depends upon application of causality as a category of understanding which is applicable only to the empirical world, it has no bearing on the possibility of the existence of a necessary being outside of that world.

The flaws in both these arguments are obvious and undercut their impact as Kantian antimonies. The thesis asserts not only that there must be a first cause but that it must exist in time, which makes it much easier to refute than other similar arguments. The antithesis refutes the existence of a first cause within the empirical world and asserts that, to the extent that the first cause must be outside the world, it cannot be said to be a (temporal) cause at all. For the arguments to be equally valid, they must, of course, be valid. But the premise of the thesis, namely, that the first cause must be in time in order to set the sequence of contingent events in motion, is by no means clear and is disputed here. As was discussed in connection with the first antimony, all that is required for the existence of the world is a sufficient *reason* and, if time itself is merely an intuition of human reason, there is no logical reason why the explanation of the existence of the world must be itself a temporal one. Kant's distinction between logical and temporal contingency and his reliance upon the latter in support of the antimony is a reflection of his privileging of the categories over the related logical judgments, which we have repeatedly asserted to be incorrect. Because, as stated, the validity of the thesis is dubious at best, the antimony itself must fall by the wayside.

Notwithstanding our disagreement with the antimonies and their significance, Kant's treatment of them offers much information about his thinking in general. First, it will be recalled that the antimonies are not presented as a random set of metaphysical paradoxes but as four specific ideas that come to light as man seeks to understand at its very root his empirical experience. Kant identifies these as the questions of the beginning of the world, the nature of matter, freedom and determinism, and the existence of God. These ideas, in the view of Kant, constitute the primary questions of metaphysics.

Second, the presentation of thesis and antithesis follows Kant's articulation of a traditional rationalist formulation and a traditional empirical response. As has been emphasized, Kant's fundamental criticism of traditional metaphysics is that it is predicated on a false epistemology in which the categories of understanding are attempted to be applied beyond sensible experience with catastrophic effect. Since each of the rationalist theses is an example of such flawed metaphysics, Kant must reject it and so he does. However, Kant's position forces him to reject the first two empiricist antitheses as well, because in each case the subject matter (the totality of the universe and the substratum of matter) is assertedly beyond the realm of experience. When we come to the final two antimonies, Kant's philosophy is made fully manifest. Kant is clearly on the side of the empiricists in their treatment of determinism and the impossibility of an uncaused cause to the extent that the empirical position is considered with respect to sensible experience. But, unlike the empiricists, Kant is unwilling to leave the matter at that and in fact, however awkward the conclusion, Kant is forced to concede that the rationalists may very well be correct when it comes to the existence of freedom and God, even if we can never know it. A more formal way of stating Kant's position is that Kant regards the rationalists as being dogmatic in their misapplication of the categories of understanding to non-sensible experience (but he is unwilling, nevertheless, to dismiss the human experience of freedom or human faith in God) and the empiricists as being comparably dogmatic insofar as they treat sensible objects as *noumenal* objects (i.e., *things-in-themselves*) to rule out the undeniable human experience of freedom.

Kant's presentation of the antimonies is designed to ground his epistemology and is not his final word on the fruitlessness of attempting to prove that God exists, although there is a close relationship between Kant's discussion of the antimonies and Kant's refutation of the traditional proofs of the existence of God. Kant categorizes all such proofs as falling into one of three categories, to wit, *cosmological, ontological,* and *teleological*.[28] Under the heading of cosmological proofs, Kant lumps all arguments that purport to show there must be a sufficient reason for the existence of the world, whether as a necessary unconditioned comprising all or part of it or existing wholly external to it. Ontological arguments are rationalist arguments to the effect that an *Ens perfectissimum* is conceivable only if it, in fact, exists. Teleological arguments are those commonly known as arguments from the order and design of the universe to an intelligent designer. As seen in the fourth antimony, Kant refutes cosmological arguments on the by now predictable ground that they rely on misapplication of the categories of pure reason outside the sensible world. Kant refutes ontological arguments on the grounds that, under the categories of understanding, existence is a modality and not a predicate that adds anything to the concept of perfection and therefore perfection does not entail existence. Kant refutes teleological arguments on the same grounds as cosmological arguments and notes that at most they may show the existence of a designer, not a creator.

It serves to reemphasize that Kant's purpose in refuting the traditional arguments for the existence of God is not to promote a secular worldview but rather to remove the question from the realm of science, thereby protecting it from criticism on scientific grounds, and to place it in the realm of faith, where Kant believes he can show it to be rationally compelled and useful in living life. Kant's unwillingness to dismiss the human intuition of freedom and commonly held belief in God even though they cannot be supported by knowledge of empirical reality takes him headlong into metaphysics not as a scientific subject but as reason-compelled faith. As noted briefly above, even though Kant was adamant that there can be no knowledge of the theses of the antimonies, he finds them to be inherently valuable, especially the final two. In seeking the unconditioned, Kant argues that human reason ultimately leads to the transcendental Ideal, as the unconditioned cause of all perfection, which reason then objectifies as the most perfect Being (*Ens perfectissimum*) and the most real Being (*Ens realissimum*). Kant is very much impressed with the valuable nature of the transcendental Idea of freedom and the transcendental Ideal (of God) because it places human experience in a moral context and liberates man from the mechanistic determination of the empirical world. The apparent circularity of Kant's admiration for these characteristics of human nature (which presupposes their value in the first instance) is, to my knowledge, not discussed by Kant. From the presupposition of the transcendental Idea of freedom, Kant attempts to construct a nontheistic moral philosophy, which culminates in his famous categorical imperative but which, like all other such philosophies of an empirical character, ultimately falls of its own weight.[29] Unfortunately for Kant, because his attempted removal of the metaphysical questions from the realm of science was only partial insofar as it still provides that faith is rationally compelled upon the presupposition of freedom, the secularly oriented,

---

28. Kant refers to this category as the physico-theological argument.
29. The specific deficiencies with Kant's moral philosophy are summarized at 296–301.

empirical philosophers who followed him have been unwilling to accept Kant's religiosity and, although Kant's transcendental philosophy yields a causally-closed, empirical world of sensation that, deficiencies notwithstanding, represents an empirical view that is far more robust than that of contemporary philosophy, Kant's entire program has been rebuked by the mainstream, albeit on grounds that are less than convincing.

THE REDUCTIONIST ASSAULT ON KANT: THE INTUITION OF SPACE

To the extent that Kant's philosophy can be fairly described as a response to the question of how scientific knowledge is possible, it must be regarded as a huge success and as being head and shoulders above the traditional approaches of rationalism, empiricism, and skepticism (to the extent not subsumed in the first two). No rationalist philosopher has been able to tell us much that is meaningful about the sensible world. No empirical philosopher has been able to explain the certainty that we find in our sensible experience. Tellingly, few if any philosophers of any of these stripes, especially the empiricists and skeptics, seem willing to live their lives on the basis of their philosophical positions. In the case of the empiricists, few are willing to deny the necessity of moral action even though they can find no compelling basis for it. With respect to the skeptical philosophers, worth noting is the proposal of Saadya Gaon, a prominent Jewish philosopher, who suggests that it might be worthwhile to throw a skeptic into a fire to see if he has doubts whether he feels heat or pain or whether such an act is immoral.[30]

Accordingly, Kant's philosophy has much to commend itself and it is not an accident that in an age where Kant's views are for the most part rejected, he is still regarded as among the greatest philosophers and perhaps the only modern philosopher worthy of ranking alongside Plato and Aristotle. Kant shows that for metaphysics to be compelling one must first set forth a credible epistemology and, in doing so, make manifest that subsequent analytic attempts at addressing discrete philosophical problems in the absence of an expressed and comprehensive epistemology are mere sophistry. Kant's philosophy also addresses many of the shortcomings of idealism and empiricism. It provides a laudable (if not fully correct) explanation of the structure and process of cognition. It correctly sets the limits of *empirical* knowledge at the bounds of the *noumenal* world, even if it is willing only to posit such as a limiting concept.

Most contemporary philosophers side with Hume against Kant, rejecting the reality of self and causality (but substituting probability) and denying that human reason constitutes reality in any meaningful way. As noted in chapter 2, "The Death and Resurrection of Metaphysics," this position is a complete epistemological capitulation and because it aspires to so little, it is difficult (though by no means impossible) to challenge, except on these most fundamental of points. It is clear that Kant's philosophy is critically flawed but the reason is not, as the modern empiricists would have it, the injection of human reason into the cognition of the sensible world. To the contrary, the fundamental problems with Kant's presentation are his steadfast refusal to allow for the *direct intuition* of the self as a substantive entity, to allow for the ontological primacy of general logic

---

30. Popkin, *Columbia History*, 145.

over the categories of understanding which result from their application in space and time, and to allow for the real existence of *things-in-themselves* as orderly objects that are correlative with, if not identical to, phenomena.

In an attempt to confine all human experience to the empirical world, empiricists generally challenge Kant on two major points. The first line of attack is to dispute Kant's argument that space and time are contributed by the understanding and not part of empirical reality itself. The second line of attack is to deny the existence of any synthetic *a priori* knowledge. Both of these lines have in common the empiricists's motivation to hold all reality as external to observing reason, where it is subject only to sensation and conscious awareness, and to avoid any prospect of encountering the divine in a supersensible world of internal experience.

Kant offers five *expositions* with supporting arguments in favor of his conception of space (he also offers five corresponding arguments in favor of time, the consideration of which will be postponed until chapter 6, "Empirical Judgment"), four of which he characterizes as metaphysical and one of which he characterizes as transcendental. The former four expositions are metaphysical insofar as they present the concept of space without reference to empirical content and the last exposition is transcendental insofar as it presents space as a presupposition of other synthetic *a priori* knowledge, which Kant argues can only be the case if space itself is an *a priori* intuition (with that term being used by Kant in this context to mean *a way of looking at things*).

The four metaphysical expositions and the arguments in support of them are as follows:

(1) Space is not an empirical concept which has been derived from outer experiences. For in order that certain sensations be referred to something outside me (that is, to something in a different part of space from that in which I am), again, in order that I may be able to represent them as outside and alongside one another, that is, not only as different but as in different places, the representation of space must already be at the basis. Therefore, the representation of space cannot be borrowed from the relations of outer appearance through experience, but, on the contrary, this outer experience is possible only through that representation of space.

(2) Space is a necessary *a priori* representation which underlies all outer intuitions. It is impossible to have a representation of there being no space, though one can very well think of space without objects to fill it. Space is therefore to be regarded as the condition of the possibility of appearances, not as determination dependent upon them. It is an *a priori* representation which necessarily underlies all outer appearances.

(3) Space is not a discursive or, as we say, general concept of the reality of things in general, but a pure intuition. For first of all, we can represent one space only; and when we speak of many spaces, we mean only parts of one and the same unique space. Nor, secondly, can these parts precede the one and all-embracing space, as its constituents, out of which it can be assembled; rather they are thought only as in it. Space is essentially one; the manifold in it, and therefore the general concept of spaces in general, arises entirely from limitations. Hence it follows that, with respect to space, an *a priori* intuition of it (one that is not empirical) must underlie all concepts of it. In the

same manner, all geometrical principles, e.g., that in a triangle two sides are greater than the third, are never derived from the general concepts of line and triangle, but from intuition, and derived moreover *a priori* with apodictic certainty.

(4) Space is represented as an infinite *given* magnitude. Now it is quite true that every concept must be thought as a representation which is contained in an infinite number of different possible representations (as their common characteristic), and therefore the concept contains these *under itself*; but no concept as such, can be thought as containing an infinite number of representations *within itself*. Nevertheless, space is so thought (for all parts of space, up to infinity, are simultaneous). Consequently, the original representation of space is an *a priori intuition*, not a *concept*.[31]

Kant's fifth (transcendental) exposition follows the four metaphysical ones in a separate section and is not enumerated as such:

> Geometry is a science which determines the properties of space synthetically and yet *a priori*. What, then, must the representation of space be if such a knowledge of it is to be possible? Space must originally be intuition; for from a mere concept it is impossible to obtain propositions which go beyond the concept, such as we do, however, obtain in geometry. This intuition must, however, be encountered in us *a priori*, that is, prior to any perception of an object, and must therefore be pure, not empirical, intuition.[32]

In his *History of Western Philosophy*, Russell attempts a comprehensive refutation of Kant's exposition, which is important because it is emblematic of the response of logical positivists to Kant's transcendental philosophy and also because, although it fails to accomplish its purpose of rebutting the understanding of space as an intuition, it does make clear the glaring deficiency in Kant's failure to acknowledge the underlying order of empirical reality. Russell's arguments are point-by-point as follows.

With respect to Kant's first exposition:

> The phrase *outside me* (i.e., *in a different space from that in which I find myself*) is a difficult one. As a *thing-in-itself*, I am not anywhere, and nothing is spatially outside me; it is only my body as a phenomenon that can be meant. Thus all that is really involved is what comes in the second part of the sentence, namely that I perceive different objects as in different places. The image which arises in one's mind is that of a cloak-room attendant who hangs different coats on different pegs; the pegs must already exist, but the attendant's subjectivity arranges the coats.
>
> There is here, as throughout Kant's theory of the subjectivity of space and time, a difficulty which he seems to have never felt. What induces me to arrange objects of perception as I do rather than otherwise? Why, for instance, do I always see people's eyes above their mouths and not below them? According to Kant, the eyes and the mouth exist as things-in-themselves, and cause my separate percepts, but nothing in them corresponds to the special arrangement that exists in my perception.[33]

---

31. Kant, *Critique of Pure Reason*, B39–40.
32. Ibid., B40–41.
33. Russell, *History of Western Philosophy*, 714–15.

With respect to Kant's second exposition:

> The second metaphysical argument maintains that it is possible to imagine nothing in space, but impossible to imagine no space. It seems to me that no serious argument can be based upon what we can or cannot imagine; but I should emphatically deny that we can imagine space with nothing in it. You can imagine looking at the sky on a dark cloudy night, but then you yourself are in space, and you imagine the clouds that you cannot see. Kant's space is absolute, like Newton's, and not merely a system of relations. But I do not see how absolute empty space can be imagined.[34]

With respect to Kant's third exposition:

> The gist of this argument is the denial of plurality in space itself. What we call "spaces" are neither instances of a general concept "a space," nor parts of an aggregate. I do not know quite what, according to Kant, their logical status is, but in any case they are logically subsequent to space. To those who take, as practically all moderns do, a relational view of space, this argument becomes incapable of being stated, since neither "space" nor "spaces" can survive as a substantive.[35]

With respect to Kant's fourth exposition:

> It is difficult to see how anything infinite can be "given."[36] I should have thought it obvious that the part of space that is given is that which is peopled by objects of perception, and that for other parts we have only a feeling of the possibility of motion. And if so vulgar an argument may be intruded, modern astronomers maintain that space is in fact not infinite, but goes round and round, like the surface of a globe.[37]

With respect to Kant's fifth exposition:

> "Geometry," as we now know, is a name covering two different studies. On the one hand, there is pure geometry, which deduces consequences from axioms, without inquiring whether the axioms are "true"; this contains nothing that does not follow from logic, and is not *synthetic*, and has no need of figures such as are used in geometrical text-books. On the other hand, there is geometry as a branch of physics, as it appears, for example, in the general theory of relativity; this is an empirical science, in which the axioms are inferred from measurements, and are found to differ from Euclid's. Thus of the two kinds of geometry one is *a priori* but not synthetic, while the other is synthetic but not *a priori*. This disposes of the transcendental argument.[38]

---

34. Ibid., 715.

35. Ibid., 716.

36. In yet another example of the sophistry to which analytic philosophy lends itself, this argument directly contradicts both the axiom of infinity, upon which Russell's set-theoretic deduction of the natural numbers is based, and the foundational premise of Georg Cantor's theory of the infinite, which was wholeheartedly embraced by Russell. Because the philosophy presented in these pages equates Being and intelligibility, these matters are profoundly important and are discussed in great detail in chapter 5, "The Homogeneity of Reason," and chapter 7, "Infinity, Countability, and Self-Reference."

37. Russell, *History of Western Philosophy*, 716.

38. Ibid., 714–17.

Russell then provides his own exposition of space-time in which he argues that space, considered separately from space-time, is no different from our perception of other empirical qualities insofar as it is a subjective appearance of correspondent real relationships among empirical objects. Russell argues that time, considered separately from space-time, cannot be in any sense subjective, because an objective sequence of events is necessary to maintain order in the universe. Russell concludes with the following:

> The above arguments assume, as Kant does, that percepts are caused by *things-in-themselves,* or, as we should say, by events in the world of physics. This assumption, however, is by no means logically necessary. If it is abandoned, percepts cease to be in any important sense *subjective,* since there is nothing with which to contrast them.[39]

It is difficult to read Russell's criticism of Kant without receiving the impression that Russell is sometimes doing his best not to understand Kant's meaning and at other times to argue that non-critical mistakes are fatal to his exposition. As an example of the former, Kant's entire exposition is expressly predicated upon a distinction that he makes throughout his critical philosophy between internal experience (inner sense) and external experience (outer sense), with latter being empirical in character. When Kant says in the first exposition that an appearance (which, it will be remembered, is the action of a *thing-in-itself* upon the senses prior to its being understood as a phenomenon in completion of the act of cognition) is referred as being outside him, he simply means that the experience is sensory (empirical), not intellectual (without empirical content). There is nothing difficult about Kant's statement and one would presume that Russell, a great man who demonstrated the extraordinary ability to reduce mathematics to pure logic,[40] should have no difficulty in understanding it. As an example of the latter, Russell makes in several places the valid and important point that Kant seems to assume that the universe is orderly (in the sense, as Russell illustrates, of eyes appearing above noses) without ever explaining how this should be so and argues, quite disingenuously, that Kant's exposition of space and time fails as a result. Of course, it does not; the positing of an orderly universe is not at all inconsistent with the positing of space and time as intuitions by virtue of which the human mind experiences that order.

For purposes of evaluating Kant's exposition then, it will be helpful to assume that the empirical world is in fact orderly and consider whether Russell's other criticisms successfully rebut Kant's philosophy. In doing so, it should be remembered that for Kant to win the day, his exposition needs to stand up only once, because each of his five expositions is independent of the others.

In Kant's first exposition, Kant is arguing that space is a precondition of empirical experience without which there could be no cognition of empirical objects. This is evident from Kant's depiction of the process of cognition itself, which proceeds first with appearances which are referred to as external (i.e., in space and time), then synthesis, then cognition of phenomena. Kant concludes as a result that reason must locate the

---

39. Ibid., 717–18.

40. Admittedly, Russell's deduction falls somewhat short in this regard but it is nevertheless brilliant. See the discussion in chapter 5, "The Homogeneity of Reason."

appearance as being in space and time prior to having any empirical cognition of it. Russell says nothing to suggest that Kant's fundamental description of the cognitive process is incorrect and upon the assumption (for the sake of argument) that Kant's description is, in fact, correct then his first exposition seems sound. Russell's rebuttal is therefore of the wrong point; to support his contention that space is empirically understood, Russell needs to show that cognition of externality is simply an aspect of a unified act of cognition of an object itself as it exists in spatial relation to other objects (or the perceiving subject), which Russell does not do.

In Kant's second exposition, Kant argues that one can think away all of the objects in the universe but one cannot think away space and that, therefore, space must be a condition of the possibility of empirical experience and not part of empirical reality itself. Contrary to Russell's snide rebuttal to the effect that no serious argument can be based upon what we cannot imagine, where the question is the nature of *a priori* intuition, consideration of that which is imaginable is important, relevant, and valid, in the instant case because under any epistemology one cannot logically think away the condition of the possibility of empirical experience and retain the contents of cognition at the same time. If space and time are part of the external experience of the object, then they may be thought away with the object; if only the object can be thought away, then what remains must be an intuition of the possibility of its cognition.[41] Russell cannot, therefore, effectively challenge Kant's exposition by dismissing the form of Kant's argument in this manner and instead Russell must show that it is substantively incorrect, and in this regard it is Russell's argument, not Kant's, which one ought not to take seriously. In particular, Russell's assertion that one cannot think of empty space because such a conception requires elimination of the thinker from space is a strikingly silly one because it represents the denial of the existence of objective reason which is essential to Russell's naïve empiricism. On this point, then, it seems to me that Kant is correct with the following clarification. I can conceive of empty space and a world that continues after I cease to exist but what I cannot conceive of is absolute nothingness because that would entail negation of the very basis of its conception (i.e., the rules of thought). This clarification is a point with respect to which much attention will be given in chapter 12, "The Supreme Principle of Being and Intelligibility," in which an ontological argument for the existence of God will be offered upon that premise.

In Kant's third exposition, Kant argues that there is one and only one space of our conception and that although space may be conceptually divided into parts for purposes of location within it, space cannot be assembled from partial spaces into a whole as if they are constituent parts, because any such partial spaces can exist only as arbitrary divisions with the whole. In rebuttal, Russell seems to be making three points, the first of which is linguistic, with the second two being substantive. The first is that in asserting that space is an infinite and indivisible *a priori* condition of the possibility of extension, Kant is not linguistically allowed to employ the term "spaces" to signify anything less than a totality. This, of course, is not correct. When Kant speaks of space generally he

---

41. Oddly, Russell seems to contradict himself when he asserts, with uncharacteristic ambiguity, that the portion of space not populated by objects nevertheless supports the "feeling of the possibility of motion."

is referring to the form of the cognition of extended phenomena; when he speaks of "spaces" he is referring to referential subdivisions within an indivisible totality and he is making the point that while you may delineate subspaces within space you may not remove them physically or in thought from the unified totality of space because such subspaces are not substantive parts that combine to make up a whole. Russell's second point seems to be that there must be something in the real world that corresponds to the relationship of objects within space in order for the universe to be orderly; in other words, that cognition entails not just objects but their objective relations and, to the extent that such relations are spatial, space must be an empirical substantive that is given to the senses together with the objects themselves. Russell's third point is that on a *relational* view of space one may not consider it as existing separately from empirical objects and therefore to speak of space as being a unified whole that cannot be composed of its parts is incoherent. It is uncertain as to whether Russell, in making these two arguments, is speaking past Kant in the sense that Russell is attributing empirical substance to Kant's intuition of space in a way that Kant would not abide. In Kant's philosophy, although the intuition of space is not divisible it still provides the means by which relations between extended phenomena may be understood. That being the case, Russell's position that space is relational, which I understand to mean that space is the empirical representation of the extended relation between phenomena, is clearly a different view of the nature of space, which itself requires justification and which therefore does not, without such justification, succeed as a rebuttal of Kant. Consider in support of Kant's third exposition, the example of three billiard balls arranged in a row, with a red billiard ball to the left, a blue billiard ball to the right, and a yellow billiard ball in between. Removal of the yellow billiard ball from the row causes there to be empty space where it was located, but such removal does not alter the spatial relation between the red and blue billiard balls. Under Kant's view the space in which the three billiard balls is located constitutes the *a priori* condition of the possibility of the cognition of the three billiard balls in space and not the empirical relation among them; removal of the three balls neither causes the space to disappear, nor does it eliminate the possibility that the three billiard balls may be replaced in their original positions.

In Kant's fourth exposition, Kant bases his argument for space as being intuition upon his assertion that space is *given* to reason as being infinite or unlimited even though we can have no conception of an infinite number of empirical objects within it. In this regard, Kant points out that, unlike the categorical concepts, which characterize objects (as being under them), space *contains* its objects. In any case, Kant is saying that no matter how many objects exist, there will always be room for more as they, and not the space in which their modality is intuited, are instantiated and space is understood as without limit or dependence upon the number of empirical objects contained within it for its size. Kant concludes, therefore, that space is not a concept given to the understanding via sensory experience (in which case it would be only so large as is necessary to express the relationships among the objects existing within it) but rather an intuition by which all of the objects of the universe may be cognized without any *a priori* limitation. Taking Kant's fourth exposition together with Russell's rebuttal, the difference between Kant's intuition of space and Russell's relational conception becomes clear. The distinction is not, as Russell asserts, that, whereas Kant's space exists absolutely, Russell's exists as the relational predication of the objects within it, but rather that, whereas, in Kant's conception of space as a condition of the possibility of empirical experience, space cannot be anything but infinite (i.e., there is no limitation upon the scope of reason or upon the logical *possibility* of phenomena), in the case of Russell's conception, space is only as large as it has to be to accommodate actually extant matter. As a result, Russell's rebuttal falls short. An infinite space can indeed be *given* (in precisely the same way as an intuition of the infinity of the series of natural numbers can be given) if it is an intuition by which any magnitude of empirical objects can be cognized. Russell is correct that it cannot be *given* if it exists empirically in relation to an objective reality that is quantitatively limited and as not as an intuition, but as is the case with Russell's rebuttal of the third exposition, Russell is merely asserting that Kant's theory of the spontaneous process of cognition is incorrect and that Russell's naïve empiricism is the better view, which, of course, requires justification that Russell does not provide.

In Kant's final exposition, Kant argues that if space were an empirically understood concept in which geometric figures were synthesized, then the *a priori* science of geometry could never be abstracted from such figures. In this instance, it appears that Russell has the better view. Kant never succeeds in convincing that geometry is synthetic *a priori*. Indeed, although in the philosophy of transcendent realism there is synthetic *a priori* knowledge which arises by application of general logic to the empirical world in the discovery of its physical laws, because geometry is wholly deducible as a part of general logic it is regarded as analytical notwithstanding that we may very well have discovered the science of it by drawing triangles in the sand.

Additional support for Kant's position that space and time provide the framework of cognition in accordance with the principle of causality comes from modern quantum mechanics, which ironically is usually incorrectly cited as contradicting Kant's claim that causality is a synthetic *a priori* category of understanding. In an attempt to solve fundamental problems of quantum physics, modern science has postulated the necessity of ten or eleven additional space-time dimensions under the rubric of what is called String Theory and M-Theory. Although I do not presume to understand the rationale behind these theories to any significant degree, if they are accurate, it seems that such additional dimensions are only intelligible as concepts which arise by inference and analogy to the spatio-temporal intuitions given to reason and not by direct observation. It seems, therefore, that these theories should support Kant and not the empiricists on the question of on which side of the observer lay the four dimensions of space-time. If the dimensions of String Theory and M-Theory exist *out there* in the real world, why are they not wholly empirically sensible? Moreover, asserting, as do the empiricists, that space and time are themselves phenomena that exist independently of human observation is to add a level of complexity to empirical reality that is unnecessary and therefore unwarranted.

THE REDUCTIONIST ASSAULT ON KANT: CAUSALITY

It will be recalled that, at root, the debate between Hume and Kant is the question of the validity of the human experience of necessary and universal rules that enable reason to identify the causal connection between events. The view of the empiricists is one in which the universe is no more than a chain of events following one after another that is at best understood on an inductive basis and that upon close observation of empirical events the so-called causal relationship is nowhere to be found in either the causal event or its effect.[42] Under Kant's philosophy, causality is a synthetic *a priori* category of the understanding that provides the order to the sequence of events (Kant refers to this as "alteration") in time and supports the inference to the general logic of implication.

When we say that A is the cause of B, one of the things we are saying is that A precedes B *in time*. Another thing we are saying is that there is a *logical* order to the sequence of events, which, it is important to note, does not need to be measured in time in order to hold as being logical,[43] provided that our intuition of time is replaced with the consequential logic of implication underlying cause and effect. In fact, this seems to be precisely what we do when our current experience trails away into memory of past experience. For example, I can recall one summer of my early forties during which I spent most of my weekend days at the behest of my wife building an enormous tree house for our then young boy. That building the tree house was a labor of love did not make it any less difficult, painful, or time consuming (since it required skills that I had to acquire as the project progressed) and, indeed, there were times when I thought the job would never end. Today, when I recall it, the element of time, as such, is completely removed and replaced by a merely qualitative memory that it took a long time; instead, I remember the process, with each step being taken in tandem with the other contemporaneous events of my life and the world around me. I know it took a long time to build the tree house in the same way that, having read Hemingway's *For Whom the Bell Tolls*, I know the story is long and I have an idea of the passage of time in that tale. In the case of the tree house, what I have today is a fading cognition of the *idea* of having built the tree house over an extended period of time that is now only accessible to my memory as a lengthy sequence of events that I understand both as a whole and as the composition of its parts and about which I may mentally dart at my volition while the integrity of the whole remains intact.

Hume's position is that there is no synthetic *a priori* knowledge at all, including, in particular, knowledge of causality. However, Hume's position is difficult to maintain unless one is as courageous as Hume is in pursuing his line of reasoning all the way to

---

42. Many empiricists would say according to the laws of probability.
43. The *Encyclopædia Britannica* (Editors of the *Encylopædia Britannica*, "Causation") states:

    [Causation is the] relation that holds between two temporally simultaneous or successive events when the first event (the cause) brings about the other (the effect). According to David Hume, when we say of two types of object or event that "X causes Y" (e.g., fire causes smoke), we mean that (i) Xs are "constantly conjoined" with Ys, (ii) Ys follow Xs and not vice versa, and (iii) there is a "necessary connection" between Xs and Ys such that whenever an X occurs, a Y must follow. Unlike the ideas of contiguity and succession, however, the idea of necessary connection is subjective, in the sense that it derives from the act of contemplating objects or events that we have experienced as being constantly conjoined and succeeding one another in a certain order, rather than from any observable properties in the objects or events themselves. This idea is the basis of the classic problem of induction, which Hume formulated. Hume's definition of causation is an example of a "regularity" analysis. Other types of analysis include counterfactual analysis, manipulation analysis, and probabilistic analysis.

skepticism about everything other than ideas themselves. Most modern empiricists are not so courageous and, instead, allow only knowledge of a scientific nature (based upon mathematical probability, not causality) to be possible (in doing so, they are more in line with Locke). Such empiricists seek to keep the world of experience *out there* in the realm of the senses and independent of the presence of man (although, as it turns out, the presence of the observer is especially important in quantum physics). For these empiricists, a proposition that is true on its own terms is analytic and everything else is *a posteriori*.

Not surprisingly, Russell is one such empiricist who argues against Kant that instead of causality there is only probability and that scientific reasoning is based upon induction:

> It is obvious that if we are asked why we believe that the sun will rise to-morrow, we shall naturally answer, "Because it always has risen every day." We have a firm belief that it will rise in the future, because it has risen in the past. If we are challenged as to why we believe that it will continue to rise as heretofore, we may appeal to the laws of motion: the earth, we shall say, is a freely rotating body, and such bodies do not cease to rotate unless something interferes from outside, and there is nothing outside to interfere with the earth between now and to-morrow. Of course it might be doubted whether we are quite certain that there is nothing outside to interfere, but this is not the interesting doubt. The interesting doubt is as to whether the laws of motion will remain in operation until tomorrow. If this doubt is raised, we find ourselves in the same position as when the doubt about the sunrise was first raised.
>
> The *only* reason for believing that the laws of motion will remain in operation is that they have operated hitherto, so far as our knowledge of the past enables us to judge. It is true that we have a greater body of evidence from the past in favour of the laws of motion than we have in favour of the sunrise, because the sunrise is merely a particular case of fulfillment of the laws of motion, and there are countless other particular cases. . . . It is to be observed that all such expectations are only *probable*; thus we have not to seek for a proof that they *must* be fulfilled, but only for some reason in favour of the view that they are *likely* to be fulfilled.[44]

It is interesting to note that if Russell is correct, then either Kant is incorrect in his assertion that the logic of implication is abstracted from causation, in which case the rationale for limiting its applicability to empirical experience must also go by the wayside, or the logic of implication itself is not sound and has no applicability to empirical experience at all. In any event, it follows from Russell's argument that one cannot deny causality without also denying there is any corresponding judgment to be made based upon the logic of necessary implication in the order of events of nature. Therefore, the position that all sensible experience is inductive, and therefore based on probability, entails that at any moment the so-called natural laws may, and given sufficient time at some point will, be suspended or overturned altogether. Taken to its *logical* conclusion, Russell's argument is that empirical reality, which in Russell's understanding is all that there is, is not only not governed by causality but is also essentially only provisionally coherent, which requires that Russell follow Hume all the way to skepticism. And, in this

---

44. Russell, *Problems of Philosophy*, 42.

regard, it is fair to ask how one comes to understand the nature of inductive reasoning and the laws of probability or their applicability to, and the provisional coherence of, the physical world.

There is a thematic difficulty with Russell's argument that runs through this entire line of reductionism. Russell's premise that the sole basis for believing that physical laws govern the world is that we have observed them in operation for a limited period of time. This is patently false. It is true that we derive our understanding of the laws of nature from empirical observation. However, such laws are the result of logical analysis, require integration into a cohesive scientific understanding, must be isomorphic with our intuition, and must be able to predict outcomes with respect to heterogeneous events within their scope. Only if these conditions are met can we consider a scientific principle to represent a law of nature. Indeed, not only do we know that the sun rises as the result of physical laws, and not induction, but we also know that one day it will fail to rise not because of the laws of probability but because universal physical laws require the ultimate annihilation of the sun and the earth. Moreover, consider the consequences of the failure of a real physical law (as opposed to a provisional human understanding of one). If such a failure were uniform throughout physical reality, the fabric of our intuition of it would almost certainly be torn and, even if we survived such circumstances, we would either be unable to understand the events or would consider ourselves to be mad or dreaming.

Kant would argue in response to Russell that you cannot *think away* the law of cause and effect as it applies to human experience and I think he is right. That is not to say that we cannot dream up fictional *Alice In Wonderland* worlds in which the natural order of things is suspended or reversed; rather, it is to say that we cannot conceive of reality behaving that way and remaining at all coherent. Moreover, if it is the case that there is no logical order to the world other than the mathematics of probability, it is difficult to understand how a human intellect that is predicated on logic could ever come into existence.[45] In fact, on a strictly empiricist interpretation of the world, it would seem that all of the logic inherent in human reason, including both the logic of implication underpinning causality and the mathematical logic of probability theory, would of necessity govern the material world because the human being, and along with him, human reason, are wholly part of, and fully explainable by, material factors. In other words, given the undeniable existence of logic, if according to one's philosophy, there is nothing about which knowledge can be had that is not empirical, then the empirical world must be ordered in a manner that is fully consistent with *a priori* logic. Of course, as has just been observed, Russell's entire argument in favor of probability is based upon a purportedly logical interpretation of inductive events and not upon some probability-based reason.

Additionally, it is difficult to understand how and why we should consider the limitations of induction and probability theory applicable to world that shows no sign of their relevance. It is easy to understand that if there are a billion black marbles in a hat and one white one, many black marbles are likely to be drawn before the white one

---

45. This argument anticipates the discussion in chapter 4, "The Possibility of Objective Knowledge." The rules of logic (including the rules upon which probability theory is based) are not highly probable but absolutely certain.

is removed, because the rules of probability theory are demonstrably applicable to such a case and the certainty of the characterization that there is uncertainty, however miniscule, in whether a black marble will be drawn at any time is predicated upon the fact that we can peek into the hat and *see all of the marbles, including the white one.* But where is the white marble in our experience of nature?[46] Indeed, it is worth noting that one of the mainstream arguments against cosmological proof of the existence of God is that the world is an infinite contingency and, if that is the case, we would expect to have observed some evidence of failures of the laws of nature in the infinity of already lapsed time. To my knowledge, no evidence of the occurrence of any such anomaly exists. Causality is the application of logical implication in the cognition of events in space-time. Probability applies where there is more than one possible outcome; for appeal to probability theory to be warranted, there must be warranted belief that the outcome is not certain. What is the basis for thinking that the laws of Newtonian physics might ever cease to apply to the sensible world? The principle of causality and the Newtonian laws of physics explain why if I release a ball it falls to the ground each and every time. What if one time it rose? If that were to occur and I survived the experience with my intellect intact should I shrug my shoulders and appeal to probability or should I seek understanding of where Newton erred in positing his laws?

It should be observed that the principle of causation, together with the laws of physics, offers the additional benefit of enabling extrapolation to heterogeneous events. Consider as an example the phenomenon of gravity. We observe that a ball held at eye level, when released, falls to the ground each and every time. After years of experiment and analysis, we conclude that the reason that such occurs is that the relatively massive earth bends space to a greater degree than the ball and as a result *causes* the ball to move toward it. If the theory that massive objects bend space is correct, we should be able to observe that when a beam of light passes in proximity to such an object the beam will bend. We conduct an experiment and, lo and behold, we observe the bending of light from a distant star as it moves near the sun.[47] It seems that explaining the phenomenon in terms of probability is a difficult proposition. Do we postulate that the earth *probably* bends space-time or that the path of entities as heterogeneous as physical objects and light waves will *probably* be altered when passing through bent space-time? Do we not then need to predict and verify that there may occur an event in which the path of an object will not be affected when it passes through bent space-time before we can conclude that the laws governing gravity are merely probabilistic?

---

46. Some, including Russell, are wont to make much of the probabilistic nature of physical behavior at the quantum level. See, Russell, *Why I Am Not A Christian*, 8. But, as M-Theory makes clear, although there may be random behavior at the quantum level (which we do not directly observe) such behavior is not a feature of nature when objects larger than atoms are considered; in other words, the theorized randomness of quantum particles does not translate into randomness at the Newtonian levels of reality.

47. In 1919, Arthur Eddington, a noted British astronomer and professor at Cambridge, with the help of globally situated colleagues, conducted this experiment and concluded that Einstein's theory was correct. Decades later the results were disputed and Eddington was accused of allowing his pro-Einstein bias to unduly influence his findings. In an interesting article, Daniel Kennefick reviews Eddington's original results and concludes that Eddington had ample grounds for his conclusion. See, Kennefick, "Testing Relativity," 37–42.

Russell seeks to buttress his argument in favor of induction by explaining that reason errantly infers causation as the result of reason being misled by the frequent repetition of associated events to infer cause where there is none.

> A horse which has been often driven along a certain road resists the attempt to drive him in a different direction. Domestic animals expect food when they see the person who usually feeds them. We know that all these rather crude expectations of uniformity are liable to be misleading. The man who has fed the chicken every day throughout its life at last wrings its neck instead, showing that more refined views as to the uniformity of nature would have been useful to the chicken.[48]

Of course, Russell's point is that mere repetition of associated events should not be confused with causality. But it is not clear how Russell's observation is relevant to Kant's transcendental philosophy, or, more generally, to the law of causality. Kant asserts that for an appearance to become a cognized phenomenon the appearance must be susceptible to being ordered by the reason according to the law of cause and effect; it does not follow and Kant does not assert that human reflection upon sensible experience is free from error in the conclusions that are drawn from it. It should be noted that the chicken in Russell's example erred in relying upon inductive reasoning when he should have understood that the daily presence of the farmer was a necessary condition of his being fed from which no inference about the chicken's continued well-being could be drawn because the unknown intention of the farmer when so present was also important. In other words, the difficulty with the chicken's understanding is not that his continued feeding is probabilistic under the laws of induction but rather that the principle governing his feeding is to fatten him for slaughter and that his demise at the hands of the farmer is certain to occur.

Finally, it should be noted that the laws of Newtonian physics are concerned with the behavior of physical objects in space and time, which is the fundamental framework of human empirical cognition. It is not necessary that the laws of physics strictly conform to human intuition of empirical reality; what is required is that any scientific understanding be isomorphic with that intuition. The cessation of applicability of such laws in a manner that could not be understood within the human intuition of space and time would entail fundamental alteration of cognition itself and would almost certainly result in a breakdown of the cognitive process. So it would not be just a case of the ball rising upon release instead of falling to the ground; rather, the ordered fabric of the universe, as understood by human reason, would have to come apart. Moreover, if, as is asserted in the philosophy of transcendent realism, that the physical world must be inherently orderly, it is difficult to imagine how it might cease to be so.

The distinction between philosophic and scientific understanding and the necessity only of isomorphism is shown in Russell's attempts to refute the other examples of synthetic *a priori* knowledge provided by Kant. In *Principles of Mathematics*, Russell's *magnum opus*, Russell claims to prove that, contrary to Kant, mathematics is not empirical at all but can be reduced to the analytic *apriority* of set theory which Russell argues

---

48. Russell, *Problems of Philosophy*, 43.

is wholly logical in nature.⁴⁹ Russell then argues that since post-Kantian modern science has come to regard space in non-Euclidian terms, Kant's argument that Euclidean geometry is synthetic *a priori* could not be true.⁵⁰ We may agree with Russell that mathematics is wholly logical in nature (for reasons that will be presented in chapter 5, "The Homogeneity of Reason") even if we disagree that he succeeded in so demonstrating and therefore that the science of geometry is not a valid example of synthetic *a priori* knowledge. However, for the reasons already given, Russell's conclusion that the intuition of space and the scientific explanation of the behavior of entities within space demonstrates that space is not an *a priori* intuition is not only ostensibly flawed but leads to a conclusion that would horrify him (i.e., that we have directly intuited knowledge). We start with the observation that the scientific explanation of space, which was Euclidian from the time of Euclid until early in the twentieth century and was, at least for a time, supplanted with a non-Euclidean explanation, has nowise affected how we sensibly perceive objects in space-time. If space is spherical, I do not *see* the arrangement of phenomena within it as such. If it is the case that in a spherical universe a powerful laser shot directly out in front of me would, given sufficient time and upon the condition of its being unimpeded, hit me in the back, I can only understand it by thinking space a sphere, which is a Euclidean concept, even though in the cognition of phenomena I continue to organize them in a Euclidean manner. Indeed, it is worth noting that in one important non-Euclidean system, a "straight" line is not straight at all but is defined as a great circle!

A profound difficulty would arise, however, if science determined that phenomena behave in space in a manner that is not only non-Euclidean but that cannot be mapped onto a Euclidean intuition of space, which would indeed contradict Kant's argument, with which I agree, that we could never have any such understanding. The conclusion to be reached, therefore, is that although Russell is correct that geometry is not a synthetic *a priori* science, space, together with time, must be the *a priori* framework of cognition of phenomena. And, for what it is worth, it should be noted that the question of the scientific character of space as Euclidian or non-Euclidian has reemerged and is today an open question.⁵¹

With respect to Kant's characterization of the laws of physics as examples of synthetic *a priori* knowledge, Russell predictably makes his challenge on the same inductive basis as his challenge of causality, namely, that such "laws" are merely observations about highly probable relationships and, accordingly, in so doing, Russell is subject to the same rebuttal. Finally, Russell holds in utter contempt Kant's views concerning moral laws, which Kant attempts to ground in pure reason based upon the empirically observed moral conduct, and argues instead that moral obligation is nothing more than a set of rules learned at mother's knee.⁵² It will readily be observed that what is learned at mother's knee would not necessarily govern the conduct of a mature adult, yet the understanding of moral obligation persists throughout the lives of healthy people. Because it is a fundamental thesis of transcendent realism that the source of moral obligation lies in the *Logos*

---

49. Russell, *Principles of Mathematics*, v.
50. Russell, *History of Western Philosophy*, 716.
51. Castelvecchi, "What Do You Mean?"
52. Russell, *Why I Am Not A Christian*, 11.

itself as a fundamental aspect of the structure of the universe and that such obligation derives from direct intuition of *Agape*, full discussion of moral obligation will be had in these pages but must be postponed until additional groundwork has been completed.

A CRITIQUE OF KANT'S METAPHYSICS

Although Kant's epistemology ranks among the very greatest achievements in the history of philosophy, his metaphysics does not. This is because of his empiricist bias and correspondent unwillingness to acknowledge (except as mere possibility) knowledge of anything beyond sensible experience. So, oddly enough, Kant's metaphysics is asserted not to be metaphysics at all, but instead, an exposition of rationally compelled faith. Nevertheless, what makes Kant's metaphysics so interesting is that, unlike other empiricists, because Kant's epistemology leans heavily on internal sense in the process of cognition, he cannot bring himself to ignore internal sense completely in considering questions traditionally left to metaphysics. Kant attempts to resolve the conflict inherent in his system by creating a world of Ideas, which, although they result from the misapplication of the categories of understanding to objects that are not given to the senses, have the support of the human empirical experience of freedom that cannot be explained in a causally closed empirical reality. However, in so doing, it is clear that Kant paints himself into a corner. Although Kant's metaphysics is comparably brilliant to his epistemology in its conception, because Kant's metaphysics starts with the incorrect premise that we cannot have any direct intuition of supersensible reality, the result is an odd inconsistency between Kant's reality-based epistemology and his faith-based metaphysics, the latter of which must ultimately be regarded a castle in the air.

One need not delve too deeply to see how Kant's epistemological errors lead to his fundamental misconceptions about the possibility of metaphysics and the substance of his metaphysical claims (in the case of Kant on an Ideal, as opposed to real basis). In this regard, to prepare the way for the philosophy presented in these pages, we need consider only the following four points:

1. Kant's denial of direct intuition leads him to swallow the Cartesian premise that man is a thinking being and to concoct a transcendental Ego that is nothing more than the unified background of all conscious thought. However, insofar as Kant's characterization of the self as the unity of apperception is based upon circular reasoning, Kant does not meet the burden of proving the incorrectness of the metaphysical human experience of itself as soul.

2. Kant's invention of the concept of *noumena* in the negative sense as a limit to knowledge leads him to reject as dogmatic any metaphysical assertions about the nature of anything other than sensible phenomena. However, if Kant's foundational epistemological claim that man brings to cognition certain *a priori* concepts and intuitions is correct, then knowledge of the existence of *noumena* as corresponding to phenomena is necessary to avoid solipsism.

3. Kant's reversal of the ontological priority of general logic and transcendental logic, which he bases upon his foundational epistemological assertion that all knowledge originates in sensible phenomena, leads him to incorrectly limit the applicability of general logic to sensible phenomena (and objects of thought abstracted from them), and to reject as dogmatic any metaphysical claims based upon logic. However, as will be explained in the ensuing chapters, it is unfettered general logic that underpins the access of human reason to universal and objective truths, that constitutes the concepts of cognition, and that, in its essence, is the articulation of Being.

4. Kant's denial of direct intuition underpins his heroic invention of the concept of transcendental Ideas as the basis of his metaphysics of compelled faith. However, his arguments in support of transcendental Ideas of God and freedom are flawed and the conclusion to be drawn from the fact of morality upon which they are based is that we have direct intuition of transcendent reality.

Little more than has already been said is necessary to address the first point. In chapter 2, "The Death and Resurrection of Metaphysics," the observation was made that the human being intuits itself a persistent, substantive, and morally obligated soul and that, as a result, the burden of proof lies with anyone who would propose a philosophy that does not take that intuition into account. Obviously, Kant cannot meet that burden by proposing that the human soul is nothing more than the *unified perceiver of* the objects it knows, which knowledge requires the presence of the self in the first place, which Kant himself admits is circular.

Before moving on, however, it is worthwhile to reconsider Kant's paralogisms in the light of the failure of the doctrine of the unity of apperception, because, in so doing, we will find that they support the intuition of self as soul which is universally given to human beings. It can readily be seen that on the premise of direct intuition of self the four paralogisms all fall away. In the first paralogism, which is a refutation of the doctrine that the soul is substance, Kant argues that the "I think" that accompanies every thought is merely the logical background of conscious thought and does not rise even to the level of a concept. Kant's argument proceeds that, as such, the "I think" can never be the object of knowledge and therefore cannot be understood by application of the categories of understanding. The rebuttal should be readily apparent. If the self were the same as the "I think," then Kant's point would be well taken. But if the self is a morally responsible entity that possesses the faculty of reason but that is separate from its thoughts, then the self is not the "I think" but an "I am" and, as such, it is quite capable of being the subject and object of its own thought. In other words, self-consciousness consists of *a self thinking about itself*, not thought thinking itself. It should be noted that, unlike the "I think," the "I am" has the capacity to apply the categories to its *sensible* experience and the *Logos* (including direct intuition of moral obligation which cannot be, as Kant would have it, solely based upon reason) to both its internal experience and its external experience.

In the second paralogism, Kant argues that the soul cannot be known to be simple, different from matter, or immortal. Kant's argument is that we can have no knowledge of the substratum of either and therefore we can make no comparison between them or conclude that the substratum of the soul is such that, unlike the substratum of matter, the substratum of the soul supports the conclusion that the soul is outside of space and time. Kant is correct that we have no sensible experience of the substratum of *matter* as permanent substance; however, valid direct intuition of self as a *moral being* entails knowledge of characteristics that are wholly outside space and time which are therefore *noumenal* in the positive sense. In contrast, there is no evidence of moral obligation or freedom of action (neither do we understand how they might arise) in strictly material phenomena or any other reason to believe that such phenomena have *noumenal* characteristics in the positive sense (as does the soul) and it is impossible to see how a mere unity of apperception could ever come to know either. The soul, as the *ground* and the object of self-consciousness, is precisely what Kant asserts that it is not, namely, simple, immaterial, persistent, and unified, and it is through ensouled reason that man has the ability objectively understand his own internal and external experience.

The third paralogism is that the soul is a person. Here, Kant's position is that in order for a stream of thought to be coherent, it must occur in the context of a single unchanging subject but that because that subject cannot be an object of its own thought it cannot be considered to be a person, which is defined by Kant as the consciousness of the identity as its own substance as a thinking being in all change and variation of all circumstances. But we have just seen that the contrary is true. Insofar as the third paralogism is predicated on the notion that the "I think" can never be both the subject and the object of its own thought, Kant's position appears to be little more than further development of his analysis of the first paralogism and the refutation is the same in both cases. Contrary to Kant's assertion of the Cartesian conclusion that a person is conscious of identity as its own substance as a *purely thinking being*, as has been indicated, self-consciousness consists of a *morally responsible being* with the faculty of reason entertaining thoughts about itself. Accordingly, the *personhood* of morally responsible beings is an analytical proposition.

The fourth and final paralogism is that the soul is separate from the material world. Kant states:

> That I distinguish my own existence, as that of a thinking being, from that of other things external to me—among which my body also is reckoned. This is also an analytical proposition, for other things are exactly those which I think as different or distinguished from myself. But whether this consciousness of myself is possible without things external to me; and whether therefore I can exist merely as a thinking being (without being man)—cannot be known or inferred from this proposition.[53] (Paragraph enumeration omitted.)

There are several points to note in this paralogism. First, the quote makes clear (as does the original text of the preceding three paralogisms) that Kant is incorrectly speaking of the soul in Cartesian terms, that is, as a thinking being. Second, Kant states that the proposition that the self is separate from the external world is analytic because, viewed from the first-person perspective, there is the self and then there is everything that is not the self. Third, having defined the self in a way that is dependent upon the external world, Kant argues that it cannot be known that the self can exist in the absence

---

53. Kant, *Critique of Pure Reason*, B409.

of the external world. If, by this, Kant means that if there were no external world, then the only things that might exist would be supersensible, non-extended, *noumena* in the positive sense, then, given the limits of Kant's epistemology (i.e., that there can be no knowledge of the supersensible world), his conclusion must be correct. The approach to be taken in rebuttal should be obvious. Justification of the premise that the self is not a mere thinking being but a morally responsible being with the faculty of reason has been provided on both direct intuition and on the fact that human experience cannot be explained in wholly empirical terms. That which cannot be explained in empirical terms cannot be wholly empirical in nature and that human experience cannot be fully explained empirically is a matter of direct knowledge to us. That is not to say that the person is not a psychosomatic unity or that the soul is eternal to the extent that it is *noumenal* in the positive sense, both of which are separate propositions.

It is worth noting that Kant's assertion that the self cannot be understood as existing separately from the empirical world and is therefore a non-object provided much fuel for the German idealists, including of course, Hegel, and seems also to be compatible with Wittgenstein's less well defined statement that the self is a limitation on empirical experience. For reasons already explained that are directly relevant to Kant's assertion, neither of these philosophies is meritorious. To be a mere limitation on empirical reality, I must be a non-object, but what in the world (or outside of it) is that? If I am a *non-object*, then I am indistinguishable from all other non-objects and there must be only the empirical world, *period*. That is why German idealism and reductionism must yield to solipsism or worse; if I am, in essence, a limitation on reality, then how can I have access to any consciousness, let alone a consciousness that I identify with myself? To see the utter vacuity of this line, consider this: what is the difference between a universe in which there is a non-entity that correctly understands itself as a limitation on reality and one in which there is no such non-entity? I submit that there is no difference.

Kant, by virtue of the failure of his paralogisms, leads us to precisely the opposite conclusion that he wishes us to reach, namely, that it is his concept of self as the form of the representation of thought that is incorrect and not our direct intuition of real human substance as a non-empirical entity that has the faculty of reason. The premise of the paralogisms that man is a thinking organism is a false premise that began with Descartes and that has been embraced by empiricism. Since human experience cannot be fully explained in material terms, it follows that man must be something other than a mere thinking organism and the place to find him must lie in the realm of that part of human experience which is not materially reducible.

Turning to our second point, which concerns knowledge of *noumena* in the negative sense, it will be remembered that Kant is compelled to postulate them because it is central to his epistemology that man never has direct knowledge of sensible objects as they are presented to the senses as a manifold of appearances but only as phenomena which represent such appearances after complete organization under the categories of understanding through the process of cognition. Kant, staying rigidly true to his premise that knowledge starts at the level of phenomena, is unwilling to assert any knowledge of *noumena* in the negative sense, including whether they exist at all. A comparison to Berkeley is helpful in understanding Kant's difficulty. It will be recalled that Berkeley argued that, because we have only mental representations of objects, we have no basis for concluding objects exist independently of such representations. Kant, on the other hand, is asserting that although we have only mental representations of objects, it does not follow that they do not independently exist, but the assertion that they do in fact exist is fully dogmatic and can never be known. Kant goes one step further by describing a complete cognitive process that starts at the moment of sensation, even though he must remain agnostic as to whether the sensation corresponds to anything real.

Kant's problem becomes obvious when one considers the implication of the possible nonexistence of such *noumena*. Under the Kantian epistemology, if there are no *noumena* in the negative sense, cognition is a fully creative act. In other words, without *noumena* in the negative sense, cognition entails creation by the cognizing subject of the object of its cognition and that is a capability that can only be assigned to God or a solipsistically rational being. The real issues, therefore, can only be not whether such *noumena* exist but whether our objective knowledge is exhaustive so that *noumena* are identical with phenomena or, if not, whether we can have any substantive knowledge of the nature of such *noumena*. The position that our knowledge of objects is exhaustive is the one held by naïve realists. However, under that portion of Kantian epistemology already accepted and defended in these pages, where the mind contributes the categories of understanding and the intuitions of time and space in the process of cognition, it can be known is that *noumena* must exist in some correspondent form.

But that is not all we can say about *noumena* in the negative sense. Not only must *noumena* in the negative sense logically exist but they must also be such that they are susceptible to being *thought about logically*, which is to say that they must be subject to logical organization that it is not dependent upon the forms of cognition, namely, space and time and causation. The following can therefore be said about *noumena* in the negative sense: (1) such *noumena* cannot be self-contradictory or substantively chaotic; (2) such *noumena* must be such that reason may cognize them as individual objects with relations that are correspondent to those which are understood in their empirical determination; and (3) they must be subject to the forms of thought and be logically orderable either sequentially or ontologically or both.

We turn now to our third point, which is the ontological priority of logic over the categories and the difficulties that Kant faces because he has this priority reversed. We have just examined one such difficulty which is the problem of the existence of *noumena* in the negative sense. Under the Kantian structure of cognition, Kant is reduced to presuming that such *noumena* exist even though asserting their existence is dogmatic. However, as we have just seen, the existence of *noumena* in the negative sense constitutes knowledge. Because we know that *noumena* must exist and affect the senses, we have an instance of the applicability of the rules of implication (as well as the category of modality), which Kant asserts is abstracted from causality, applying beyond empirical reality. It follows that general logic must be ontologically prior to the transcendental logic of the categories of understanding.

The priority of general logic over the categories can also be seen by careful examination of the relationship of the categories to their associated logical judgments in Kant's table of the categories (shown in Table 1). Under Kant's scheme, each logical judgment about an object requires first that the object be cognized under a corresponding category of understanding. The judgments may be thought of as the application of the *a priori* form of the logical judgment to objects that are extended in space and time. For example, that A is the cause of B (the category being causality) is a reflection of the logical judgment that A implies B sequentially, and if A is a necessary and sufficient cause of B, then the occurrence of A in space and time can be said to imply the subsequent occurrence of B in space and time, and the absence of the occurrence of A in space and time can be said logically to ensure that B has also not occurred. Kant rightly repeatedly asserts that it is impermissible (although often irresistible) for reason to apply the categories of understanding outside of the sensible world because, by their very nature, the categories are essentially *logical concepts as applicable in space and time.*

But further analysis yields that the intuitions of space and time are themselves inherently logical in their structure. Kant as much as acknowledges this in his association of arithmetic with time and geometry with space. In subsequent chapters, we will devote much attention to the homogeneity of logic and mathematics and to a theory of cognition in which all thought, including empirical, theoretical, and practical cognition, occurs under a fundamentally logical rubric and, indeed, we will go all the way to the ultimate ontological conclusion of identifying Being with intelligibility. But the point to be made here is a simple one. If, as Kant asserts, the categories occur under, and not prior to, the intuitions of space and time (which are not themselves categories or abstractions from them), and space and time are themselves inherently logical, then general logic must be ontologically prior to the categories of understanding.

Copleston, in concluding his chapter on Kant's epistemology makes the following important observation:

> It does not follow . . . that if we accept the existence of synthetic *a priori* knowledge, we are bound to accept also the hypothesis of Kant's Copernican revolution. It is possible to allow that there are synthetic *a priori* propositions and at the same time to hold that there is an intellectual intuition which grounds such propositions. . . . I am thinking, not of the propositions of pure mathematics, but of metaphysical principles, such as the principle that everything which comes into being has a cause. And by intuition I do not mean a direct apprehension of spiritual realities, such as God, but an intuitive apprehension of being, implied by the existential judgment concerning the concrete object of sense-perception. In other words, if the mind can discern, in dependence on sense-perception, the objective, intelligible structure of being, it can enunciate synthetic *a priori* propositions which have objective validity for *things-in-themselves*.[54]

And, indeed, with this observation, Kant's Copernican revolution comes apart at the seams. His brilliant observation that reason brings *a priori* concepts in the act of cognition cannot be reconciled with the ring-fencing of reason to the field of sensible phenomena. Kant's core empiricism simply does not hold up. It is belied by our knowledge of soul that is based upon direct intuition. It is belied by the failure of the paralogisms, which are based upon the ill-conceived, circular notion of self as the form of representation of thought, to demonstrate the fallacy of that direct intuition. It is belied

---

54. Copleston, *French Enlightenment to Kant*, 275–76.

by the failure of the antimonies to justify the limitation of general logic to empirical phenomenon, which has been discussed in detail earlier in this chapter. And it is belied by our implicit knowledge of the *noumena* underlying empirical objects as their correspondents and all that follows from it.

We cannot find the answer to *why* there is logic in the universe by examining its contents. We can only note that there is and we should not be amazed because the universe cannot exist under any other condition and it cannot not exist.[55] The empirical world as it is cannot simply be; it does not contain enough to explain its own existence, our experience of it, or the logical principles that govern it. The world is intelligible and it reflects an underlying order that corresponds to the categories and the forms of logical thought in which reason occurs. Man *recognizes* the logic of the world in the process of *cognition*; in doing so, he is not bringing order to chaos but perceiving the logic that inheres in the objects and relations of a *noumenal* universe which are the necessary conditions of the possibility of cognition in the first place.

We turn at last to our fourth and final point, concerning the flawed concept of transcendental Ideas and its implications for direct intuition of transcendent reality. It will be recalled that in Kant's view, as man seeks the unconditioned explanation of reality beyond the realm of sensible experience he formulates Ideas, which do not constitute knowledge, and those Ideas culminate in the objectification of the most perfect being (*Ens perfectissimum*) and the most real being (*Ens realissimum*) in the form of one God. The most real being is the *uncaused cause* of reality, the knowledge of which Kant attempts to dispose of upon his errant empirical epistemology. The most perfect being is the prototypical sum of all possible perfections. The problem here lies not in Kant's formulation of it but in the manner in which Kant constructs it. To build God from the ground up (i.e., starting with the sensible world and reasoning backward to the supersensible), as Kant wants to do, he must first presume that there is an idea of *goodness* in objective reality that is independent of, and procedurally (i.e., sequentially) prior to, the objectification of such goodness in a single perfect being. But how is that possible? If I have no direct intuition of *goodness*, how do I find it in sensible reality? The answer is that I cannot, because, unless I bring goodness into the sensible world, the world will forever exist as a morally neutral, materially reducible state of nature. That is why the empiricists fail whenever they try to address ethics. They seek morality in the material world but only find brute facts and brutish self-expedience.

Practical proof of this deficiency in Kant's formulation lies in the fact that his process of construction of the transcendental Ideal, however brilliant, cannot possibly reflect the manner in which the ordinary man comes to know God, freedom, and moral obligation and consequence. Any such explanation must deal with the reality that the majority of human beings believe in God under one depiction or another and only a very few of them are metaphysicians willing to, or capable of, developing such a system. It is one thing to assert that many, if not most, people seek the ultimate cause of the world and objectify God as the *Ens realissimum* (even five-year-old metaphysicians are in the habit of incessantly asking *why?*) but it is quite another to assert that man derives his

---

55. The grounds for this assertion will be provided in chapter 9, "Being and Intelligibility," and chapter 12, "The Supreme Principle of Being and Intelligibility."

sense of free will from his belief in God. To the contrary, there are most certainly many atheists who believe that they are free agents. Moral obligation can only come from a moral source that has authority to bind man and recognition of it, and the freedom to obey it, can only be had on the basis of direct intuition.

THE DEVELOPMENT OF GERMAN IDEALISM FROM THE TRANSCENDENTAL PLATFORM

Sandwiched in the middle of the historical dialectic between transcendental idealism and logical positivism lies an utterly different critical voice, namely, that of German idealism, which, instead of seeking to tear Kant's work down wholesale, aspires to build upon its platform. Kant was still an active philosopher when the German idealism that was to surpass temporarily his critical philosophy began to arise. Among the various criticisms of Kant's philosophy by the German idealists are two which we have been emphasizing all along. One is the apparent inconsistency inherent in Kant's insistence upon the problematic conception of the *thing-in-self* (considered as the object to the extent it is not known) as a limitation on objective cognition and his refusal to allow inference of its existence as the cause of objective cognition. The other is the circularity of Kant's conception of the self as a mere form of the representation of thoughts about objects because, under Kant's system, such objects must first be understood before the self can be known as the form of their representation.

Nevertheless, the German idealists held Kant's critical philosophy in high regard and they had in common the notion that correction of its flaws would allow for the development of a complete metaphysical system that reason requires to be fully idealistic in nature. Indeed, Johann Fichte, the first of the trio that also includes Friedrich Schelling and Hegel, met personally with Kant and, after an early period of compatible work, turned to the unsanctioned task of converting Kant's critical philosophy into such a system. Although Fichte, Schelling, and Hegel reached three very different conclusions about the logical completion of the conversion of Kant's philosophy to idealism, their systems include the following important commonalities which are, therefore, characteristic of German idealism as a whole.

First, each of the German idealists attempts (not unlike Spinoza) to analyze human experience of reality from a first principle, and, indeed, this is what makes German idealism systematic. The core metaphysical concept of German idealism is that *reality is the self-expression of infinite reason*. Hegel expresses this succinctly as "the real is the rational and the rational is the real." The German idealists reach this conclusion by removing the *thing-in-itself* as a limitation on cognition and recharacterizing empirical objects as fully ideal objects of *mind-independent* thought. To avoid the equally unacceptable conclusions that man is individually creative (in the sense of the divine) of the objects of his cognition and that man's knowledge is solipsistic, the German idealists posit a superhuman intelligence as constitutive of reality, which is either seen as the ground of consciousness, in the case of the early thinking of Fichte, or as universal consciousness itself, in the case of Schelling and Hegel. For Hegel, such consciousness is Absolute subject or ego and, because it creates the objects of its own cognition, is understandable as *thought thinking itself*. It bears mentioning in passing that, although Hegel is the philosopher whose thinking is identified with the culmination of German idealism, Fichte is of particular interest to transcendent realism because in Fichte's philosophy, the Absolute ego is distinctly moral in character and is seen as infinite practical reason or *moral will*, which posits Nature as a field and instrument for moral activity and which, as a result, is in some ways compatible with the conception of the God of *Agape,* which is central to transcendent realism.

Second, under German idealism, because reason is reality and *vice versa*, there can be no limit on the scope of reason. The German idealists certainly did not accept Kant's division of the world into an empirical one, which is accessible to reason in the process of cognition, and a supersensible one, which is only available to faith however compelled by reason it might be. For the German idealists, if reality is the unified process by which Absolute thought or reason manifests itself, it must be accessible to human reason provided that human reason can ascend to the comprehension of the totality of the Absolute, whereupon the human mind becomes the vehicle by which the Absolute ego reflects upon itself. This, of course, is an extraordinarily humanistic proposition which places human reason at the pinnacle of existence in participation with the divine. Under German idealism, philosophy is seen as a reflective reconstruction of the dynamic rational process of the infinite mind. One important example of the consequences of the breaking of the barrier between the supersensible and sensible worlds is Fichte's positing the Absolute as moral will on rational grounds and not as a matter of faith.

Third, the equation of reason with reality results in the obliteration of the distinction between general and transcendental logic, which in turn allows causality to be seen to be correspondent to the rules of implication and time to be seen as the medium by which man's finite mind is able to grasp the totality of an Absolute reality which is simply too much for his immediate comprehension.

Finally, inasmuch as reality is considered to be a rational process, there is an emphasis on intentionality and on history, the latter of which must be understood from a teleological standpoint. And that teleology is a highly spiritual, if not overtly religious one. Fichte sees Nature as the instrument by which the human spirit moves towards the ideal moral world order. Schelling sees history as the story of the return to God of fallen humanity. Hegel, who emphasizes the idea of the dialectic of national spirit, the importance of world-historical figures, and the movement of history towards the realization of spiritual freedom, says that the subject matter of philosophy is *God and nothing but God* and Hegel regards himself as having proved Christianity.

Hegel's metaphysics was considered for much of the nineteenth century to be preeminent and, even though it is no longer so regarded, it receives approbation from some philosophers as representing an admirable working out of the entire line of idealism. Of particular fame is Hegel's triadic method of logical inquiry, which, by nature of the equation of reason and reality that is fundamental to German idealism, is both a method of reasoning and the process by which the Absolute expresses itself in reality. Hegel's triad is usually referred to as a sequential reasoning method (in the case of critical thinking) or process (in the case of history) which includes a thesis, an antithesis, and a synthesis, although apparently Hegel never used that nomenclature. Because Hegel's universe is that of a unified Absolute mind, everything in the universe stands in relation to everything else as part of the whole and cannot be understood except in a complete context that includes all of its relations, and any particular item of knowledge that is less than an understanding of the whole is, of necessity, incomplete. Hegel makes two assertions as a result of this position. The first is that any partial consideration of objects is bound to yield contradictions. The second is that by application of the Hegelian analytical triad, human reason can push beyond such partial knowledge and its attendant contradictions to a complete understanding of the whole. Russell aptly analogizes Hegel's position to that of a comparative anatomist who, by examination of a single bone, can reach conclusions as to the description of the entire animal to which it belonged.[56] According to Hegel, any initial analysis of an abstract concept will, as a result of its incompleteness, lead to its opposite concept, which will also contain its own deficiencies, but which, together with the initial concept, will point the way to a synthesis of the two that will be less incomplete than either; however, because even the synthesized concept will be incomplete, it will require consideration of its opposite and synthesis of a new concept, and so on until the totality of its participation in the Absolute is understood. The elegance of Hegel's methodology, if only it were true, is that a philosopher can gain access to the Absolute by starting with any abstract concept because the method leads inexorably to the Absolute from all points of entry.

The classic example of Hegelian analysis, given to us by Hegel himself, is the consideration of the Self as a unique, particular substance that is ontologically separate from the rest of the universe. Hegel argues that such a concept is incomplete because, following Kant and the earlier German idealists, the Self knows itself only by distinguishing itself from everything else, that is, the Not Self. Without each other, Hegel argues, both concepts are empty and, in fact, self-contradictory because their initial definition excludes that which they depend upon for their existence. Hegel's solution lies in recognizing that the Self can only be known in relation to the Not Self and vice versa and that the synthesis of the two concepts yields that what really exists is neither Self or Not Self, considered independently, but an act of knowledge of both of them.

An expressed premise of this principle of German idealism is that all of the relations of an object to the rest of the universe are *fundamental* to its comprehension and not merely anecdotal contingencies. Under this view, no completely true statement can be made about a thing that does not describe its relationship to everything else in the universe and, in order to do that, it must also describe the relationship of each other object to everything else; a coffee cup in the cupboard is a different object from the cup when it is placed on the kitchen table. Hegel is not the first to espouse such a view; a very similar one is contained in Leibniz's human monad. Hegel's philosophy, which aspires to completeness, covers other areas of philosophical interest, including a political philosophy which emphasizes the relationship of the individual as a participant in the all-important state and which served as the basis for certain statist philosophies that were to have a profound impact on subsequent world history. As a result, Hegel's many commentators have offered criticism of him with a high degree of emotion.

The essential difficulty with German idealism is particularly apparent when one considers its implications for establishing the identity of a particular person. An example

---

56. Russell, *Problems of Philosophy*, 103–4.

in this regard will be illuminating. It might be said, for example, that Kant is the man who wrote the *Critique of Pure Reason*.[57] For Hegel, that statement is only partially true because the world includes much more than just Kant and his book. Under Hegel's philosophy, to understand those, it is necessary to know everything about Kant's parents, siblings, and spouses, and their parents, siblings, and spouses, including where and when they were born, raised, and educated, and where they lived and died. One would also need to know about the earth which they inhabited, its relationship to the sun and the other planets, their relationship to the galaxy, and the relationship of the galaxy and each of its objects to the rest of the universe. A similar inventory of facts would need to be assembled to understand Kant's *Critique*. Only after attaining such knowledge, which obviously extends well beyond a normal understanding of that which is contained in the statement that "Kant is the author of the *Critique of Pure Reason*," can we arrive at an understanding of who Kant was.

The example just given makes no distinction between facts that are particular to Kant and those which apply to the rest of the universe. But it seems there is something gravely wrong with such an approach. Here is Russell's wry criticism:

> To put the matter abstractly: we must distinguish properties of different kinds. A thing may have a property not involving any other thing; this sort is called a quality. Or it may have a property involving one other thing; such a property is being married. Or it may have one involving two other things, such as being a brother-in-law. If a certain thing has a certain collection of qualities, and no other thing has just this collection of qualities, then it can be defined as *the thing having such-and-such qualities*. From its having these qualities, nothing can be deduced by pure logic as to its relational properties. Hegel thought that, if enough was known about a thing to distinguish it from all other things, then all its properties could be inferred by logic. This was a mistake, and from this mistake arose the whole imposing edifice of his system. This illustrates an important truth, namely, that the worse your logic, the more interesting the consequences to which it gives rise.[58]

In order to evaluate the contribution of the German idealists, it is helpful to recognize some of the specifics effected by the conversion of Kant's critical philosophy into an idealistic system. These include: (1) the elevation of the transcendental Ego (as the form of representation of a thought) to the Absolute ego (as fully constitutive of all reality); (2) the elimination of the *thing-in-itself* and its supplanting with the objective ideas of a self-manifesting infinite reason; (3) the obliteration of the distinction between the sensible world of empirical cognition and the supersensible world of faith and the corresponding obliteration of the distinction between *a posteriori* and *a priori* knowledge; (4) the elevation of the categories of understanding from subjective conceptual classifications to categories of reality; (5) the elevation of teleology from a normative or regulatory principle to a real, description of the progression of Nature, conceived as the manifestation infinite reason as it works out its self-conception; and (6) the elevation of

---

57. This example is freely based upon a similar one given by Russell in *History of Western Philosophy* at 744–45.

58. Ibid., 745–46.

Kant's epistemology (i.e., the critical philosophy) to the full-blown metaphysics of the infinite mind becoming aware of itself through human philosophical expression.

In my opinion, which in this regard is in accord with the current mainstream, German idealism is far more successful in its criticism of Kant than it is in accomplishing its objective of converting his critical philosophy into a satisfactory system. The reasons are highly illuminating in pointing the way to a successful metaphysics. First, there is the problem, already described in detail, of Hegel's understanding that an object's essence includes all of its infinite relationships with the rest of the objects of the world and with the Absolute totality that comprises, creates, and knows them. Second, in removing the *thing-in-itself* but positing ideal objects in its place the German idealists are unable to connect *Being* with *thought*, leaving only the latter intact. To retain Kant's concept of the critical philosophy (i.e., philosophy is thought's reflective awareness of its own spontaneous activity) it was necessary to elevate philosophical reflection to the self-awareness of Absolute reason in and through the human mind. Fichte insists upon a divine Absolute which transcends the reach of human reason, Schelling allows a personal God who reveals himself to man, and Hegel's is the standard conception of infinite reason becoming aware of itself through man. But their premise is that the universe is *thought* thinking itself, not *Being* thinking about itself. This is the Gassendi-Hume problem writ large. A thought cannot be its own subject and object; a mind requires a being for self-consciousness. Although the structure of German idealism follows logically from its premises, in its adoption, German idealism altogether annihilates reality, including, importantly, the very structure of thought. The consequences cannot be overstated—truth becomes subjective, the past can be rewritten, and there is no morality, and in all of this, freedom is lost because the Absolute cannot liberate itself from itself. Here is how Bergner expresses the last in *Against Modern Humanism*, the thesis of which is that mainstream reductionism, in placing the individual above any semblance of objective moral obligation, has made a surreptitious peace with the German idealism that it outwardly decries:

> What could possibly shape or guide—or for that matter inhibit—the choices of an ego which lies behind the empirical world? What does the radical freedom of ego really mean? If ego or *I* is essentially a thought which willfully appropriates other thoughts, from what is the ego free? It must be free from all that is not ego. It must act only in and of itself, determined in no way by what is *outside* the ego. Such an ego must be free not only of the external material world, and of other humans and their desires, but also of its own body, its own location, and its own history, including even the immediately prior thought or choice of ego itself. If ego were shaped by its prior choices, the *me* would shape the *I*; but as we have seen, it is the *I* that creates the *me*.[59]

Third, as so aptly described by Bergner in the preceding quote, the closely related result of the dissociation of thought from Being is the deconstruction of the self, itself. Fourth, there is the peculiar incongruity of an infinite intelligence so great as to produce the universe through its own thought and yet so apparently feeble as to require the mind of such a brooding, plodding, and immoral creature as man to understand and realize itself.

---

59. Bergner, *Against Modern Humanism*, 210.

THE PLATFORM OF TRANSCENDENT REALISM

Mainstream metaphysics, as a systematic attempt to understand reality, ended in a highly unsatisfactory state with the death of Hegel and left the ground clear for the materialists to reduce philosophy to the role of supporting knowledge gained from physical sciences. But that Kant did not allow reason sufficient scope for metaphysics to survive and that the German idealists made too much of reason in response to Kant's circumspection does not mean that there can be no metaphysics and, to the contrary, the efforts of Kant and the German idealists yield a great number of important ideas upon which a new metaphysics might be based. That is precisely what the philosophy of transcendent realism represents and, indeed, if I favored German idealism more than I do, I might even be disposed to argue that transcendent realism represents the synthesis of the thesis of transcendental idealism and the antithesis of German idealism. Although this comment is made largely tongue-in-cheek it is not fully so, because, as will be seen, although transcendent realism draws substantially more from Kant than Hegel, there are elements of both imbedded in its foundation. As a final preliminary to the presentation in the ensuing chapters of the philosophy of transcendent realism, a summary of those elements follows next.

The starting point is Kant's transcendental idealism. Kant's philosophy represents the most comprehensive critique of reason ever conducted and although it comprises most famously his two works bearing that title, namely, *The Critique of Pure Reason* and *The Critique of Practical Reason*, Kant is eminently clear in his assertion that *there is only a single faculty of reason to which man has access and from which his knowledge of what is and what ought to be is derived*. This is a point of which sight is easily lost but one which will be kept in the forefront of transcendent realism's working out of its unified conception of the faculty of reason. Kant also made clear both theoretically and in his presentation that, although metaphysics may be philosophically senior to epistemology, one cannot get at a clear metaphysics without first systematically identifying what is known and how it is known. Hence, the beginning point cannot be, as some rationalists have it, at the ontologically highest point. Instead, knowledge itself must be studied critically and only after its nature has been firmly grasped can the scope of reason be assessed and a metaphysics be developed that is fully within that scope. Kant is undoubtedly correct that if one exceeds the scope of reason, he leaves philosophy behind and enters the realm of faith or superstition and, therefore, identifying reason's reach is of paramount importance.

These two points, when taken together, show Kant's genius most clearly in his complete integration of general logic with the transcendental categories of understanding. In Kant's epistemological system there is one reason, operating logically, whether it considers empirical objects, theoretical objects, or moral obligations. The integration of general and transcendental logic has as its presupposition Kant's Copernican revolution that man brings to the process of empirical cognition the *a priori* concepts of the categories and, in doing so, achieves the same certainty in his empirical experience that logic provides to his theoretical experience. Although most reductionists argue otherwise to ensure that their exclusively material reality remains hermetically sealed off from any idealist vapors, they are unable to explain any of the elements that support the possibility of knowledge and have no grounds for the understanding of reality.

This much of Kant's transcendental philosophy is stunningly brilliant and when it is compared to the history of philosophy that preceded it one must go all the way back to the Ancient Greeks to find any philosophy that is comparably so. Although Kant appears after a number of great modern philosophers, his philosophy undeniably represents the dramatic start of a new era, even it if has not been designated as such. The unsuccessful attempt of the German idealists to convert Kant's critical philosophy to full-blown idealism may represent the culmination of a certain kind of idealistic thought, but it neither has the final say on the merit of Kant's work as he presented it nor on other possible rationalist lines. Nevertheless, it is beyond doubt that Kant's epistemology, to the extent summarized here, is itself sandwiched between the two great mistakes made by Kant, both of which were quickly identified and seized upon by the German idealists. At one end is the *thing-in-itself*, conceived by Kant as an unknowable limit on empirical cognition and at the other end is the transcendental Ego, which Kant describes as the unity of apperception and which Kant asserts does not even rise to the level of a concept but is instead the mere form of representation of thought.

At this point, attention needs be turned to the German idealists, because in rebuking Kant for these errors they opened a great door to cognition of supersensible reality. This was an important achievement, but because they did so in a highly flawed manner, it did not last. Therefore, if transcendent realism is to regain access to the supersensible, it can only do so with full awareness of the errors of German idealism. As described in detail, the first point that the German idealists make is that Kant is inconsistent in his insistence on the *thing-in-itself* as an unknowable limit on empirical knowledge and his denial of an inference from it to causation of that knowledge. In this, the German idealists are correct. However, the resolution of the inconsistency does not require the elimination of the *thing-in-itself*; instead, what is required is the recognition that although the *thing-in-itself* may lie beyond the boundaries of the categories it is the ontological correspondent of the object which is cognized and, logically, it must exist as an ordered but indirectly known correlative. The categories of understanding of empirical objects are precisely that; they are not categories of sensation of such objects. But the logical inference of the real existence of the *thing-in-itself* indicates that Kant is incorrect in characterizing theoretical reason as an ontologically subordinate abstraction from the categories of understanding, because the *thing-in-itself* must be intelligible in order for the categories to determine the representation of it. The real may not be identical with the rational, but the real, in order to be knowable, must be ordered in a manner that is amenable to cognition under rational principles, which is to say that it must be intelligible.

With respect to Kant's transcendental Ego, the German idealists are also correct in their rebuke of Kant for the positing of a self that is required for cognition and yet depends upon that cognition in order to be known. But the German idealists err again in refusing to accept the common sense intuition of self as persistent substance, and instead replacing it with a synthesis of subject and object that results in its annihilation. Instead of the individual subject existing under God, the German idealists merge all reality into a unified Absolute mind, which is incoherently characterized as thought thinking itself through the medium of human reason and instead of a great teleological progression of reason and history, they reap an utterly rudderless, changing, subjective, and unknowable will that is nothing more than omnipotent solipsism writ universally large.

That is not to suggest the contribution of the German idealists is by any means limited to recognition of the flaws of Kant's epistemology. In my opinion, the most significant features of German idealism are in opposition to materialism, namely, the recognition of the reality of non-empirical self-consciousness and non-empirical, universal reason, both logical and practical, and the unification of the two into a single act of knowledge and will. In sum, Kant's critical philosophy brings reason to the world but he refuses to include with it a requirement that reality itself be orderly; the German idealists do that, but only at the cost of the destruction of the self.

The profile of the foundation of transcendent realism can be seen to emerge from the philosophy of Kant and the German idealists. The new philosophy will identify Being with intelligibility under logically structured unity among multiplicity. It will posit via direct intuition the existence of entities which are conscious of their own existence as substantive beings independent of any external object. It will posit the existence of an empirical reality that is mind-independent but understandable in terms of an intelligibility that is both on the side of the subject and the object and it will exclude the possibility of the *existence* of anything that is not intelligible. It will posit direct intuition by ensouled reason of a supersensible reality that includes the *Logos*, *Agape*, and the freedom that accompanies such intuition. It will not allow any limitations on the reach of reason. If Kant had to suspend expansion of knowledge of God in order to make room for belief, transcendent realism accomplishes the opposite. Under transcendent realism man is a psychosomatic unity whose soul can be understood as the human *thing-in-itself* in the positive sense, outside of space and time, and which appears phenomenally and acts in space and time as a morally responsible being, and not, as Descartes would have it, a thinking being.

4

The Possibility of Objective Knowledge

THE LOGOS (ΛΟΓΟς)

Although most important philosophers have treated the question of human knowledge in one way or another, the attention given by philosophers to the first order question of how such knowledge is even possible has been sporadic, at best. In the modern era, most of the focus has been on the traditional questions of epistemology (namely, the nature, methods, and scope of knowledge) and not on the more fundamental question of how it is that human beings have access to objective truths. Rationalists, who by nature of their philosophy have an easier time with this question than do the empiricists, generally argue that knowledge is acquired by some sort of direct intuition but in many cases that still leaves open the question of how such intuition arises. The German idealists stand out on this question as having provided a complete answer, namely, that as a participant in Absolute reason man is part of the process of thought thinking itself, but, because only a thinker can think about thought and *thought* cannot think about itself, this position is one that cannot stand up under its own weight. Among the empiricists who argue that all knowledge comes through the senses, only Kant, by arguing that theoretical reason is an abstraction from empirical cognition, which is itself objective in form, seems to have advanced a colorable explanation of the possibility of objective knowledge, but, like the others, Kant's explanation is fatally flawed. On the side of the thinker, Kant posits *a priori* transcendental reason as the precondition of empirical cognition but, instead of explaining how the process of abstraction of objective truth from such cognition is possible, Kant simply incorporates the power of abstraction, which is utterly heterogeneous with the other rational faculties, into the cognitive process. With respect to the objects of empirical cognition, because Kant is unwilling to allow for any knowledge of reality as it may actually exist beyond the mere possibility of the existence of mind-independent *noumenal* objects, Kant does not provide any objective matter to support a claim of the objectivity of human cognition of it. To the contrary, for Kant, sensation is the matter of cognition, not any objects that might affect the senses, and it would seem that sensation itself is always subjective, regardless of what reason may do with it in the process of cognition, with the implication being that even under Kant's system, solipsism is not ruled out. Skeptics argue that we have little or no knowledge at all, although they must resort to objective reason to justify their position that what we perceive cannot be known. In any event, the point is that whatever these philosophies assert to be known or knowable they often do not take on directly the question of how it is even possible that human beings can know anything objectively. Instead, rationalists, empiricists, and skeptics are all too often content to accept tacitly or expressly that some form of objective or subjective knowledge exists and then move on to the questions of its scope and truth criteria.

Because the answer to the question of the possibility of knowledge is inexorably connected with the question of the certainty of knowledge and the question of its certainty is an essential aspect of its nature and scope, assertions about the nature and scope of knowledge are ungrounded if they do not accompany a consistent and satisfactory explanation of how such knowledge is accessible to human reason. Indeed, the evasion of the question of the possibility of knowledge has left open a gaping hole that has succored the mistaken positions of those contemporary philosophies, which hold that reason is subjective or that its reach is limited to supporting scientific inquiry.

In Nagel's introduction to *The Last Word*, his book in favor of the objectivity of reason over what he calls modern irrationalism, Nagel acknowledges the importance of the problem with customary eloquence but, nevertheless, asserts that it appears, ultimately, to be indeterminable:

> I am prompted to this inquiry partly by the ambient climate of irrationalism but also by not really knowing what more to say after irrationalism has been rejected as incoherent—for there is a real problem about how such a thing as reason is possible. *How is it possible that creatures like ourselves, supplied with the contingent capacities of a biological species whose very existence appears to be radically accidental, should have access to universally valid methods of objective thought?* It is because this question seems unanswerable that sophisticated forms of subjectivism keep appearing in the philosophical literature.[1] (Emphasis added.)

I do not believe that the question of the possibility of universally valid methods of objective thought is indeterminable but rather that the answer to that question begins with the observation that in order for there to be knowledge there must be something *knowable*, which is to say that there must be an underlying order to the universe that is applicable both on the side of the objects to be known and on the knowing subject, *which, as it turns out, is an object itself*. This underlying order is what we have been hitherto referring to as the *Logos*. The *Logos* comprises the orderliness that must characterize empirical reality in order for reason to make sense of it, the form of thought about empirical reality, and the form and, to some degree the content, of thought about internal human experience, including reason, itself. The *Logos* renders reality intelligible and is necessary, universal, self-justifying, and the condition of its own possibility. The *Logos* is both human- and mind-independent (except, perhaps for the mind of the divine) and indeed, as to the latter, it is the presupposition of the existence of the minds which can do nothing other than reason in accordance with its preconditions and rules. All

---

1. Nagel, *Last Word*, 4.

rational creatures, by virtue of their reason, have access to the *Logos*, but only souls, as fully self-conscious creatures who have the ability to consider themselves as objects, can have the power of abstraction and, therefore, are capable of asking and answering Nagel's question. Stated more concretely, the possibility of knowledge depends upon three conditions: (1) mind-independent, self-justifying *a priori* rules of thought; (2) an empirical reality that is orderly in a manner that may be understood under the auspices of general logic; and (3) consciousness of self as a persistent, rational entity. In short, (non-divine) objective knowledge is always and everywhere exclusively a faculty of *ensouled* reason.

Immediately, three important questions arise. The first such question has two components: what are the rules of thought and how do they relate to reality in the process of cognition? Addressing this question is required as grounds for the assertion that the *Logos* comprises the form of thought about both empirical reality and internal human experience. The second question that arises is this: what can be said of the structure of reality that explains its susceptibility to cognition? Addressing this question is required to provide content to the assertion that reality itself must be orderly to be intelligible. The third question is: how is it possible that human knowledge of reality and the rules of thought about it are known objectively? This is the question that Nagel is asking and that philosophy is derelict in ignoring. Because the answers to these three questions are dependent upon one another, they may only be understood collectively as aspects of a homogenous philosophy of knowledge.

INTERNAL COGNITION AND TRUTH

Our initial point of inquiry must be to determine the criteria by which we can satisfy ourselves that we have any knowledge at all. In its essence, the question reduces to what we mean when we say that something is true. This, of course, is one of the ancient questions of philosophy and it is one which received an extended flurry of attention during the twentieth century. Some of the more prominent theories include correspondence with fact, coherence with a system of facts, social constructivism, and pragmatism. Of these the first has been perhaps the most widely held and it will provide a sufficient platform for our own investigations.

Not surprisingly, the place to begin is with Kant. One of the more interesting passages in the *Critique of Pure Reason* appears in Kant's discussion of transcendental logic, where he disposes of the standard empirical formulation of knowledge of the correspondence theory:

> If truth consists in the agreement of knowledge with its object, then that object must thereby be distinguished from other objects; for knowledge is false if it does not agree with the object to which it is referred, even if it contains something which may be valid of other objects. Now, a general criterion of truth would be one that is valid for all knowledge, wherever its objects may be. *But it is clear that such a criterion abstracts from all contents of knowledge (reference to this object), while truth concerns these very contents.* It is impossible and absurd, therefore, to

ask for a sign of the truth of such contents, and therefore a sufficient and at the same time general indicator of truth cannot be given.[2] (Emphasis added.)

Kant goes on to say, quite rightly, that logic, as supplier of the general and necessary rules of understanding, is a *sine qua non* of empirical knowledge, but one which cannot provide any criteria by which factual error might be discovered. Kant's point is twofold: first, that the statement that *truth is the agreement of knowledge with its object* is, by reason of its generality, not itself susceptible of being characterized as true under its own criteria; and, second, that, however necessary general criteria may be for truth validation, such criteria can never provide substantive knowledge of a particular object, whether it be sensible or supersensible, even though, in the case of the latter, human nature cannot resist the temptation to apply general logic to non-empirical objects. In introducing the concept of transcendental illusion, which was discussed in the prequel chapter, Kant says:

> [T]here is something so tempting in the possession of this specious art of giving to all our knowledge the form of understanding however utterly poor and ignorant we may be in regard to its content, that general logic, which is merely a canon of judging has been used as if it were an organon for the actual production of at least the semblance of objective assertions, and has thus been misused. . . .
>
> Therefore, any attempt at using general logic as a tool (organon) in order to extend and expand our knowledge, at least supposedly, can end in nothing but idle talk, where one can assert or, if one prefers, deny, anything one likes, with a certain semblance of plausibility.[3]

Of the two points Kant makes in the preceding passages on the criteria of knowledge and its misapplication, only the first is undoubtedly true. But, if truth is not, as is generally held, the agreement of knowledge with its object, then what is it? For Kant, the objectivity of human knowledge emanates from the corresponding objectivity of the logic which underpins human cognition; in other words, human reason is objectively valid because human cognition of empirical reality is an objective process of making logical judgments about what is given to the senses. Kant sets as his task the exposition of this logic, which he calls transcendental because, although it is *a priori*, it governs all empirical experience and therefore transcends human empirical cognition. Transcendental logic contains both the elements of the pure knowledge of the understanding of objects and the principles without which no objects can be thought. Transcendental logic presupposes the intuition of objects in space and time, which provides the transcendental aesthetic. In Kant's view, the application of transcendental logic to such intuition represents the complete exposition of the process by which reason understands the representations given to its senses and there can be no true knowledge of empirical reality beyond that. *In short, according to Kant, understanding how human reason operates in the process of empirical cognition yields the entirety of that which can be known with absolute certainty.* Such a process yields the certainty of scientific knowledge while making allowance for the error-prone nature of each individual act of empirical cognition.

---

2. Kant, *Critique of Pure Reason*, B82–83.
3. Ibid., B86.

The Possibility of Objective Knowledge

As was discussed in detail in the prequel chapter, there are many difficulties with Kant's theory of judgment insofar as it relegates general logic to an inference from the categories of understanding. We have seen that, as an integral part of Kant's broader epistemology, the transcendental analytic is subject to the criticism that it tells us nothing about the self or things-in-themselves, including, in this context, making any representation as to the orderliness of the universe that is a precondition to knowledge. In the prequel chapter, we emphasized the importance of knowledge of the soul and the things-in-themselves in allowing reason its full scope to consider metaphysical concepts and, in the case of the *things-in-themselves,* to provide the order inherent in an orderly universe. Here, we will see that the soul, as the object of self-consciousness, is necessary to provide the power of abstraction which is required for objective knowledge. Moreover, although Kant asserts that transcendental logic has the scope to critique itself, he offers no explanation of how the inferential process by which reason derives general logic from the categories fits together with the categories themselves. To the contrary, it would seem that the sort of abstractive process required for inference of general logic from the categories is so fundamentally different from cognition under the categories themselves that abstractive reasoning should be considered separately from, *and ontologically prior to*, empirical categorization, which again undercuts Kant's core limitation on the scope of reason. In sum, it is fair to ask of Kant: If the self is the mere form of representation of sensible objects and the categories are prior to general logic and the categories do not apply to anything other than sensible objects, then by what power is reason able to abstract from empirical cognition to general logic?

It should seem obvious and trivial, indeed, that any criteria of truth must include within its scope its own truthfulness in order to be well grounded. If it were otherwise, then there would either necessarily exist an independent criterion of the truthfulness of truth itself, and still another independent criterion of the truthfulness of the criterion of truthfulness of truth, and so on, or truth would be utterly ungrounded, in which case, it is difficult to see how we could regard it as truth. Yet, obvious and trivial as the proposition that truth must be self-grounding is, it is utterly disregarded by the contemporary mainstream because its implications take them far outside the scope of their empirical zone of comfort and cast doubt upon the very foundations of their philosophy. When Kant criticized the notion that truth consists in the agreement of knowledge with its object he was doubtlessly referring to Locke (if not to earlier philosophers); yet nearly three hundred years after that great philosopher, we find Ayer, the twentieth-century logical positivist, asserting a similarly ungrounded criterion of verifiability.

Can it be possible, it must be asked, that a criterion of truth include itself without entanglement in endless (and beginningless) circularity? The answer to this question is in the affirmative and it lies, where it can only be, in the realm of direct intuition. Let us begin with the laws of thought, which are given precisely and immediately to reason. We take these fundamental laws, (i.e., the principle of identity (each thing is the same with itself and different from another), the principle of non-contradiction (contradictory statements cannot both be true in the same sense at the same time), and the principle of the excluded middle (for any proposition, either that proposition is true, or its negation is true)) literally for granted, for without them *we could not even think an object.* And it is of the utmost importance that these are indeed *laws of thought*. They are not mere assumptions, for if they were, it would remain to be asked, what are the rules of the thought by virtue of which the election to make such assumptions is justifiable? Neither are they axioms, which appear to be true but do not admit of proof, because we would then be compelled to ask by what criteria do we assert their apparent (though unprovable) truth? To the contrary, they are *the essence of thought itself*; they require neither benefit of the doubt, nor proof of their truthfulness, nor external criteria for their truthfulness, for they are the preconditions of all assumption, proof, and truthfulness, and contain, within themselves, their own credentials. The rules of thought are therefore known by *direct intuition* in its narrowest sense, which is to say immediately and directly without deduction, and it can be seen that the reason that reason so comfortably rests at this direct intuition is that it is reason's fountainhead without which no rational thought may be had at all.

Direct intuition also includes what we are calling in these pages "analytical intuition." Analytical intuition is intuition that is given by logical inference from the directly intuited rules of thought. Two examples that lie far apart on the logical spectrum are *modus tolens* and Fermat's last theorem. The former states:

1. If A, then B.
2. Not B.
3. Therefore, not A.

Modus tolens is a rule of inference which says that if a consequent of a conditional statement is false, then the antecedent must also be false. For many (if not most) people, *modus tolens* is not immediately seen to be correct and requires some additional thought before it is accepted. In logic courses, *modus tolens* is usually explained to students by an empirical example, such as the following syllogism:

1. If it is raining, then the ground will be wet.
2. The ground is not wet.
3. Therefore, it is not raining.

Once such an example is given, the truth of *modus tolens* is apparent. Most importantly, although the demonstration of *modus tolens* given above is an empirical one, the truth of *modus tolens* is entirely grounded in the logic of direct intuition and is not in any way synthetic. Fermat's last theorem states that no three positive integers a, b, and c satisfy the equation $a^n + b^n = c^n$ for any integer value of n strictly greater than two. Fermat's last theorem was proposed by Pierre de Fermat in 1637 but went unproven for more than three and a half centuries until Andrew Wiles proved it in 1995 in a work that took 150 pages to present and seven years to accomplish. Even so, because Fermat's last theorem has been mathematically[4] proved, it is known to be true by analytical intuition with the same certainty as *modus tolens* and as the rules of thought given by direct intuition.

---

4. In the next chapter, we will provide an unaxiomatic deduction of the natural numbers to support our claim here that mathematical proofs are entirely logical.

The Possibility of Objective Knowledge

To buttress the claim just made that the rules of thought are known to be true by direct intuition we might ask another question: is it possible for us to think coherently under the rubric of rules other than those which we identify as logical? The question answers itself: it is impossible to do so. The rules of thought therefore are objective, necessary, and universal. The *apriority* of the rules of thought requires that they be either self-justifying or logically deducible from something that is self-justifying. An essential characteristic of self-justifying entities is that they be at once the condition and the object of their own existence. So, we see that *the existence of objective reason is given by reason as its own condition*, and objectivity must therefore inhere in the structure of reason itself. And we will see shortly that this is precisely the case when we discover that there underpins each thought a substantively predicateless (i.e., contentless), *logical object* that is both a precondition of thought and an object of it, each of which is given to reason as logical predication and its ground.

Because internal cognition comprises more than direct intuition of the rules of thought and analytical intuition of logical propositions, it is necessary to take a moment to remark upon its other content. One of the reasons that internal cognition is feared so by the empiricists is that it may be asserted to justify the real existence of all manner of immaterial entities (gods and numbers being two examples) and historically has been utilized to provide metaphysical justification for various sorts of religious claims. The demand that those who would rely on internal cognition as a foundation of knowledge be specific about its nature and scope is therefore fairly made. Under transcendent realism it is held that direct intuition includes not only the immediate intuition of the rules of thought and the analytical intuition of all other logically valid propositions (including mathematic propositions), but also the *direct perception* (meaning knowledge that is grasped directly without reference to reason or any particular empirical object) of soul, including its components of a persistent and substantive self and its being subject to moral obligation. It is undeniable but quite acceptable that the immediate intuition of the rules of thought and the direct perception of the individual soul are different in nature although, insofar as both are given to reason independently of empirical experience, both must be held to come under the category of internal cognition. The distinction lies in the intentionality of the intuition; in the former case, the intuition targets objects that are independent of the thinker, whereas in the latter case the object of the intuition is the intuiter itself. For reasons just mentioned, that the rules of thought and the analytical logical propositions are self-justifying is beyond serious doubt (notwithstanding the contemporary prevalence of what Nagel calls irrationalism). But, as we have already seen, the internal cognition of the soul has historically been a matter of great dispute. To be clear, the *internal perception* of self as a persistent entity and the subject of consciousness is not controversial but what is hotly contested is *the philosophical status of that perception*.

The position of transcendent realism on this matter has already been made clear on multiple occasions and will require much of the remainder of this work for full justification. The persistence of the soul is disclosed to itself from within itself (and not circularly by reference to the empirical change which depends upon it), as is its substance, which is given in the "I-am-ness" of its Being and the uniquely known "me-ness" of each individual's experience, and in its abiding direct intuition that it is both an object of *Agape* and subject to moral obligation. Moreover, the cognition of moral obligation that binds the soul may be had by direct perception and also analytically, by logical deduction (from the Supreme Principle of Being and Intelligibility), and it is empirically evidenced by the brute fact of morality which flies in the face of an empirical world which not only cannot explain it but is often antagonistic to it.

We have thus identified three types of direct intuition, namely, immediate intuition, analytical intuition, and direct perception. In doing so, we have provided the grounds of objective knowledge in a manner in which such grounds are also included within their own scope, but we have not explained what *truth* is and there remains to be seen whether we can be said to have knowledge of matters other than logic and soul. We begin by provisionally adopting a definition of truth as *the cognition of internally grounded objects*, or, alternatively, *cognition of that which is given to reason internally*. This definition comprehends the propositional truth of logic, analytical truth, the truth of the disclosure of soul, the truth of internal states of mind, the truth of the disclosure of external reality taken as a whole (i.e., space, time, and the existence of the world and the logicality of its structure), and the truth of the possibility of science (i.e., the possibility of knowledge of necessary and universal truths about the empirical world but never of any individual, empirical object, or any particular scientific proposition). This definition recognizes the representational character of cognition and asserts that what is critical to knowledge is whether *the ground* of its object is referred to reason as being internal or external to it.

Starting with cognition of external objects, we can make the following observations. Each external object is given to reason as an external unity among a manifold of *extended* predication. Because the predicates of an object cannot exist independently of the object, we understand the cognitive unity of the object to be given by the ground of such predication. That is not to say that a predicate, such as "redness" cannot itself be an object of thought; instead, what we are saying is that the collection of predicates of an object, in order to be such, must have a common ground. Even though all representations are internal in the sense that they are given to reason, which is itself internal, the nature of the representation of empirical objects given to reason is that they exist externally to reason. The object, then, is understood as a mind-independent, instance of *externally grounded* predication. The predicates of an empirical object must include the spatial and temporal predicates that determine the object's relation to the cognizing "I" and to other extended objects together with the qualities of the object that correspond to the senses by virtue of which they may be perceived. All such objects are contingent and are given to reason under the organizing principle of causality. The knowledge of any particular empirical object is never absolute and can only be had on a pragmatic basis that is heavy with presuppositions both about external reality and the state of mind of its percipient. Therefore, we cannot be said to possess knowledge of the existence of any particular empirical object. The statement that "there is a bottle of ink on my desk" entails a degree of certainty upon which I would stake much but I can never be certain that my perception is not illusory or otherwise in error.

Cognition of external reality as a whole is on an entirely different footing than the individual objects that it comprises. We have already defended Kant's exposition of space as being an intuition that is a precondition to the cognition of sensible objects. Here, without undercutting our essential agreement with Kant, we will recharacterize space as an internally grounded *and predicated* structural intuition of externality, which, along with time, in their essence, are the conditions of the possibility of the existence of extended objects. The representation of external reality itself (as opposed to the intuition of externality) is given to reason as an *internally perceived unity* among its constituent external objects and their relations in space and time. The intuition of space is wholly *a priori*; knowledge of individual empirical objects is *a posteriori*. It is precisely because of the *apriority* of our intuition of externality that we know that the empirical reality exists. In the act of cognition of *extended* objects, we bring them under our *internal* intuition of space, which is the cause of the confused conclusions of the subjective idealists that *esse est percipi* (to be is to be perceived) and of the solipsists that only the cognizing "I" exists.

Science, considered as the possibility of knowledge of necessary and universal truths about external objects, events, and relations, is also given to reason internally. Following Kant, we can say that the possibility depends upon the logical nature of cognition (albeit under a structure that differs markedly from Kant's). Scientific propositions (considered as general propositions about the nature of empirical reality) are about the systematic relationship between our intuition of externality and the objects of that intuition. Scientific propositions are those which may be tested and verified. The propositions themselves are *provisionally* universal and necessary statements about the grounds of manifold states of external affairs (objects and events). Because such propositions, which seek to identify the systematic *causes* of empirical events, are either directly logical or entail the applicability of the derivative logicality of causality, their ground is always internal to reason. As synthetic *a priori* propositions they are known to reason to be *discoverably* true but cannot be determined to be so in the absence of empirical experience of their objects. Thus, it cannot be said that any particular consensus scientific proposition is *absolutely* true. Instead, we can say, indeed insist, that every empirical event (other than action taken under the intuition of freedom) must be explicable on a scientific basis, whether we know what the explanation is.

With respect to the existence of *subjective* internal objects and internal states of affairs (as distinguished from objective intuitions of logic, soul, and externality), we have knowledge of the fact and contents of mental observations but never of the objective existence of such contents. If I state that I am thinking about a multi-colored unicorn, I have privileged knowledge of the truth of the statement (i.e., that I am thinking about the object) but my thinking about an object cannot bring the object into empirical reality or render it internally real on an objective basis. If I state that "I believe there is a bottle of ink on my desk," I have privileged knowledge of the truthfulness of the statement (i.e., my belief) but not the existence of the bottle of ink itself. In the first case, the object of the thought is presented to me as a wholly internal unity (i.e., the idea of the unicorn) among the manifold of its predication (e.g., striped with different colors, horse-like, single horn), the qualities of which are all only imaginarily existing and are not given to me under my intuition of externality.[5] In the second case, it is tempting, especially for empiricists, to

---

5. Interestingly, the experience of an external illusion, such as a mirage, can be understood as internal representation of an internal object that is incorrectly given to reason under the intuition of externality.

seek truth in the conformity of the mental representation with the mind independent object of its intentionality, but we can never make the connection between the two on an absolute basis. Instead, our certainty about particular sensible objects is primarily contextual; it comes from a supporting survey of our internal mental state (which is for the most part consciously unobserved), our life experience, and the coherence of the cognition, and it arises from the absence of a compelling, present reason for doubt.

We have already discussed the truth of the rules of thought as self-grounded in thought itself. In the ensuing chapters, we will see that mathematical truth is deducible logically on an unaxiomatic basis and of the same priority as logic itself.

Finally, we come to truths about substantive transcendent objects, where the internal cognition is such that the object itself comes into view. The most obvious and important one is perception of soul. In self-consciousness, I directly perceive myself to be a real substantive entity. Moreover, the soul of self-consciousness is a necessary and universal condition of the act of *objective* thinking. It is therefore also an analytically intuited object and must be understood to exist transcendently. The soul is given to itself as a unity among its manifold experiences which include cognition of internal and external objects, which are always and everywhere given as unities among their respective manifolds of predication. It should be noted that the soul is more than the internal experience of the ground of the external predication of the body which might be the case if the soul were materially reducible. We have provided many reasons against reductionist arguments in earlier chapters and we may add here that a materially reducible soul could never be given to reason via sensory perception and neither could such a soul be the basis for the bootstrapping of objectivity by an utterly subjectively existing entity. Moral obligation and freedom are of equal accord with knowledge of the soul. Freedom is identical with *will* because without freedom there can be no will in a causally closed material world. Freedom is given to the self internally on a privileged basis, but because, as we will show in chapter 10, "Duty and Desire," freedom is analytically deducible from moral obligation, which in turn is analytically deducible from the *Logos* and from *Agape*, we know that freedom is necessary and universal to ensouled reason and therefore exists transcendentally. And, as is to be expected, cognition of moral obligation and freedom, although abstract in concept, is always as a unity among the manifold of moral and circumstantial predication.

THE LOGICAL GROUNDING OF PREDICATION

There underpins each thought a substantively predicateless (i.e., contentless), logical object that is both a precondition of thought and an object of it. In the ensuing chapters, we will have much to say about the nature of logical objects and their relations to thinkers, themselves as grounded predication, and other logical objects, and their nature as progenitors of substantive objects in the process of cognition. Here will we say only so much about the nature of the relation of logical objects to empirical ones as will illuminate the general theme of the ontological priority of logic in all aspects of rational experience, including empirical cognition, all in furtherance of the current investigation of the question of the objective intelligibility of the universe.

We begin by making a few observations about rational experience itself. All thought is about objects and their relation to themselves (i.e., the ground of their intelligibility as objects), their thinker, and other objects. Although a thought may be *about* a mind-independent entity, the thought about it cannot be *itself* mind-independent and must belong to the rational being who thinks it. The object of a thought can be empirical (i.e., existing in space and time independently of its thinker), theoretical (i.e., existing as the creation of the mind that thinks it), or transcendent (i.e., existing as an unextended, mind-independent object). Here, the first will be referred from time to time as "empirical objects," which are understood to include events as well as things and to exclude thoughts about such objects that are not cognitive of appearances given to the senses and the second will be referred to from time to time as "theoretical objects," which will include abstract objects and theoretical thoughts about empirical objects which are not cognitive of appearances. Discussion of the third category, which largely relates to moral reasoning, will be postponed until chapter 9, "Being and Intelligibility," and the subsequent chapters.

To support the claim just made, it is necessary to identify the minimal characteristics of an object that renders it thinkable. This may be accomplished by considering any object, even an empirical one, and stripping away its substantive predicates, one by one, until any further such reduction will eliminate the object as a thinkable entity altogether. To be clear, in doing so, we are not seeking the substance of the object as a species of object but rather the essence of all objects, which is to say, their *Being*. When one prescinds an object's substantive predicates, one is left with a thought kernel (to which we are referring as a logical object), which is a uniquely identifiable entity that stands in relation to itself as such as grounded predication (and so acquires its character as an object) and to its thinker either as theoretical or empirical, and which has the possibility of being posited in an ordered relation to other objects. Although a more technical meaning will be provided shortly, for present purposes, "ordered" will be used to mean susceptible of consideration in relation to other objects in accordance with a principle of sequence, magnitude, proportionality, and/or other logical relation (which will be referred to as "logical predicates"). It is easily demonstrated that elimination of any of the characteristics of logical objects renders a logical object unthinkable. One cannot conceive of an object of a thought existing independently of a thinker (although one can, of course, think that mind-independent objects exist); one cannot think of an object that is ungrounded, free-floating predication (and therefore not an object); and one cannot think of an abstract object that, *by its nature*, does not have the possibility of logical relation to other objects. Logical objects are therefore irreducible and have no substantive content (i.e., characteristics other than relation to their thinker and their grounded logical predication, which includes the possibility of relation to any other objects to which reason assigns an ordered relation). Yet another way of making the point is that all characteristics other than those which define a logical object as such are contingent to thought.

When any object (logical or otherwise) is instantiated, whether in theoretical reasoning or empirical cognition, it must have a unique reference to reason so that reason can *keep track* of it as an object and of its relations to other objects. In the discussion that follows, this referential quality is referred to as an object's "handle" and all objects of thought or cognition are referred to as being "enhandled."

Without a unique handle, an object may not be thought as a unique object of thought separately from other objects or even at all.

The general and specific objects commonly employed in predicate logic are to be understood as logical objects which have been substantively predicated (even variables have the properties of placeholders and are therefore something more than logical objects); such objects will most often hereinafter be referred to as "substantive objects." Of primary importance, the susceptibility of substantive objects to logical analysis (including the variables often employed to represent other substantive objects) exclusively depends upon their inclusion (called "inheritance") of the essential qualities of logical objects and not in any way on their substantive predication. So, as will be shown in the sequel chapter, the rules of thought are applicable ontologically in the first instance to logical objects and then more generally to substantive objects by virtue of the fact that substantive objects may be reduced to logical objects through the prescinding of their substantive predicates without undermining the rules of thought. Indeed, to refer to logic itself as "rules" of thought is a misnomer; instead, the rules of thought are merely descriptions of the fundamental logical relations of the grounded predication of logical objects.

It is easily anticipated from the foregoing argument that in logical objects lay the clue to the objective intelligibility of the world. The unique enhandlement of logical objects renders them to be intelligible as such and their orderability provides the overarching structure of reason, including, as just mentioned, general logic and also mathematics, the intuition of space and time, and the arrangement and countability of empirical objects within it. All of these will be discussed in subsequent chapters. The mathematical character of logical objects allows for the purely logical deduction of the natural numbers on an unaxiomatic basis and, from them, the basic mathematical operations of addition, subtraction, multiplication, and division, and also geometry. From arithmetical and Euclidian geometry come the fundamental intuitions of space and time, which together with causality (which entails the application of the logic of implication in space and time), are the preconditions of all empirical cognition. Mind-independent empirical reality may only be understood by the application of reason to the appearances it gives to the senses under the intuitions of space and time, which must also be sufficiently ordered to be susceptible to such application. And all of the foregoing occurs under the principle of sufficient reason, which states that everything must have its ground.

The world, therefore, must be inherently logically ordered and it is this order to which we refer when we speak of the *Logos*. *In short, Being and intelligibility are one and the same thing.* For a being to exist, it must be intelligible. If something is intelligible, it may be said to *be*. Obviously, these are major assertions and their grounds will be provided in chapter 5, "Homogeneity of Reason," chapter 6, "Empirical Judgment," and chapter 9, "Being and Intelligibility," but, for purposes of the present discussion, it serves to have presented them briefly here as part of the explanation of the possibility of objective knowledge.

THE POWER OF ABSTRACTION

The final element in the explanation of reason's access to universally valid methods of objective thought requires yet another reversion to the phenomenon of consciousness, in this case, as the precondition to the capacity of abstraction. In order for reason to make the improbable journey from subjective experience to mind-independent, objective knowledge it must not only have the capacity to receive and process data but it must also be capable of finding what is general in a given set of particular experiences (i.e., the unity among a particular manifold), including, importantly, those elements of such experience which are particular to the individual thinker.

The process of deriving the general from the particular and measuring the results against actual and possible empirical experience is a theoretical one and entails exercise of reason's highest power, namely, the power of *abstraction*. The process of categorization of an object of experience under increasingly narrower categories (from general to specific) is an ancient one. In the biological domain, the taxonomy of organisms dates back at least to Aristotle. The contemporary system of such categorization is credited to Carl Linnaeus, the Swedish botanist, and entails classification according to life, domain, kingdom, phylum, class, order, family, genus, and species. For the purposes of the instant discussion the particulars of systemic understanding are not important. What is important is not the result of the abstractive process but how it is possible at all.

The question posed by Nagel, which has been used to frame the exposition in this chapter, is a decidedly humanistic one and, accordingly, one that requires a correspondingly humanistic response. In order for there to be objective knowledge, the field of such knowledge must include not just the particular facts which it comprises but also knowledge of the field itself. In other words, in order for reason to rise above subjectivity, it must first *know that it knows*. At various stages in the previous pages, the assertion, accompanied by much supporting discussion, has been made that in order for there to be any conscious thought at all there must be a soul who possesses the thinking mind. Here we can add two items of importance. The first is that when we say that a soul possesses a thinking mind we mean that there is a rational *being* that is a persistent entity *in relation to which all thought of the mind of that being must occur*. Earlier we referred to the thinking subject as the "I am" that is thinking; now we are in a position to state that in order for a thought to occur, there must be two objects, one of which is the thinking object (i.e., a being) and the other of which is the object of the thought of that being. *A being is thus a precondition of thought and self-consciousness but thought is not Being itself.* Inasmuch as self-consciousness entails the consideration of a rational entity of itself as an object, that object must be referred to reason uniquely by a persistent handle just as is the case with all other objects that come under reason's consideration. This is direct intuition of *Being* at its very fundament. All conscious experience of uniquely enhandled objects other than the soul must contain a reference to the self-object in relation to which such experience occurs. This is what is meant when it is said that each logical object must exist in relation to its thinker. The second point regards the consideration of the profoundly important process of abstraction as it relates to self-consciousness. Ironically enough, what makes the power of abstraction so important is that it is an aspect of self-consciousness (the improbability of the existence of which among purportedly materially reducible organisms has engendered so much controversy) which requires the additional rational capacity to ignore the soul in the process of intellectual experience. The accessibility to reason of the soul as a uniquely and *persistently* enhandled object also enables reason intellectually to abstract the self from experience and to consider whether a given intuition is objective or subjective in nature. In so doing, the soul, as thinking object, must evaluate its own relation to the thoughts under consideration. So, for example, if I have some objective knowledge of the physical laws of color subtraction, I know that a magenta light filter will absorb (and not allow through) green light and therefore that if I am wearing magenta glasses and looking at black ink, the ink is either in fact black or it is green, even the though color presented to me is black and not green. My conclusion is arrived at by treating my subjective perception objectively, which I can only accomplish by abstraction. If I then remove my magenta glasses and in fact find either green or black ink before me, I will have completed a scientific experiment which provides evidence for the objective truth about color filtration. The conclusion and confirming experiment are only possible because I am consciously able to consider myself as an object. The implications of the answer to the question of the possibility of knowledge of universal and objective truth are as profound as reason itself because the explanation of objective reason entails not only the necessity of an orderly (not to be confused with *ordered*) universe but also the existence of persistent being as a precondition of thought.

THE NECESSITY OF OBJECTIVE REASON

Before moving on to discussion of the relations among logical and empirical objects in the sequel chapters, there is a profoundly significant aspect of the question of the possibility of objective knowledge that requires consideration and arises from the nature of the question itself. It will be recalled that Nagel poses the question in the context of the faculties of *a biological species whose very existence appears to be radically accidental*. The premise of the question as so posed is that contingent species whose organic nature renders them in constant flux ought not to be expected to have objective knowledge, especially if one makes the further, empirical assumption that all such knowledge comes through the senses and therefore is of a correspondingly radically accidental subject matter. Nevertheless, for the reasons briefly mentioned here and so brilliantly presented by Nagel, which, in essence, reduce to the idea that any alternative conception of knowledge can only be supported on objective grounds which contradict it in the process, the *fact* of objective knowledge is undeniable. And if the faculty of objective reason is, as seems inevitably to be the case, utterly incongruous with the organic nature of its possessors and the material nature of its subject matter, then it follows that either the knowing subject or the objects of its knowledge must be of a very different nature than their empirical appearance. One possibility is that matter contains within it something more than that which is sensible, which explains both its own intelligibility and the evolution of objectively rational, yet nevertheless organic, beings. Of course, this in itself is a denial of empiricism and is little more than a lonely speculation in search of a philosophy and, if one wishes to pursue a line of reasoning based upon such a premise, it is incumbent upon him to provide the full line.

The other possibility is that the knowing subject is exactly what he intuits himself to be, namely, a persistent knowing soul whose physical body exists in the context of an orderly empirical world, however contingent it may be. And it is not difficult to explain how this might be so. For reason to have access to objective truth the world must be objectively rational in the first place. It must have an order to it that defines reason and its objects and thought and that about which thought may be had, and it must be defined by its own *Logos*. Because the *Logos* can only be known by its own lights, access to it can only be had by direct intuition and logical deduction. Under the auspices of the *Logos*, reason has access to its objects and their relations to reason, themselves as objects, and to other objects, and the mind of man is able to see man himself as both the thinking subject and an object of thought. These are the preconditions to abstraction and it is by the power of abstraction that universally valid methods of thought are given to man. A mere unity of apperception (Kant), thinking thought (Hegel), limit on experience (Wittgenstein), logical construction (phenomenalism), or formal notion (Searle) can have no such power of abstraction or objective understanding of reality or self. Other non-ensouled organic creatures, which are presumably without the capacity of abstraction may still process and respond to the orderly information given to them by their senses, even in a tactical way, but there is no reason to expect that they have any objective understanding of it or that they are even doing so.

And here we come to the final point. Not only does the existence of objective knowledge fly in the face of empiricism, but such knowledge carries with it the grounds of its own *necessity*. That is to say, given that such knowledge is objective one cannot even think of the possibility of its negation because to do so would negate the grounds of such a thought. And, if the subjectivity or contingency of objective reason is unthinkable, then not only is the existence of objectivity undeniable but so also must be its necessity, and it follows that the principle of order represented by the *Logos* is not merely characteristic of the universe but necessarily so.

5

The Homogeneity of Reason

RATIONAL UNITY

It is probably fair to say that one of Kant's achievements most revered by those who admire him (the present author included) is his connection of theoretical reason, which is to say logic, to empirical cognition (and to practical reason, as well) in a comprehensive way. In doing so, Kant presents a unified, rational model of human experience. With respect to empirical cognition, Kant specifies categories of understanding under which appearances that are given to the senses externally via the *a priori* intuitions of space and time are spontaneously understood as empirical objects. In Kant's theory, although theoretical reason is *a priori* it represents an abstraction from these categories of understanding and therefore has no application beyond empirical experience, and, indeed, much of the *Critique of Pure Reason* is devoted to demonstrating how the failure to recognize this limitation on reason lies at the root of the broader failure of metaphysics. This is the main reason that Kant is regarded in these pages as an empiricist (however unique his version of empiricism may be) although in many if not most other places Kant is considered to be an idealist or a mixed rationalist-empiricist. In support of the characterization of Kant as an empiricist, one need only consider that for Kant rational experience is wholly sense-based because it consists of empirical cognition and that which may be abstracted from it, and, indeed, Kant calls sensation "the matter of sensible knowledge" and notes that sensation presupposes the actual presence of its object. The main reason that the empiricists find so much fault with Kant is that, notwithstanding his presupposition of the existence of real objects, Kant refuses to allow for any knowledge of the *noumenal* world beyond recognition of *noumena* in the negative sense, and, in so doing, leaves open the door for an idealistic development of his ideas, which indeed occurred in grand style with the advent of the German idealists.

Theoretical reason, constituting as it does for Kant mere abstraction from the concepts of empirical cognition, is ontologically subordinate to objective cognition under the categories of understanding. In introducing the transcendental analytic, which entails the deduction of the categories of understanding from the logical judgments implicit in them (which, given Kant's subordination of general logic to such categories, can only be regarded as an egregious case of the tail wagging the dog), Kant employs a remarkably dubious sleight of hand which undercuts the entirety of his transcendental philosophy and which is strikingly (and oddly) similar to the defective rationale of the standard empirical criteria of truth he so strongly criticizes. It will be recalled from the prequel to this chapter that Kant disposes of the notion that truth consists in the agreement of knowledge with its object by pointing out that, as so stated, the criteria of truth is not itself within the scope allotted by it to truth and therefore may not be regarded as true under its own criterion. In the case currently under consideration, Kant asserts that transcendental logic is abstracted from empirical experience and therefore is applicable only to empirical experience *and to its own critique*. Predictably, the grounds for Kant's foundational claim that the general logic that may be inferred from the spontaneous judgments made by reason in determining objects is limited to empirical experience are nowhere to be found in Kant's treatment of transcendental logic, for it is difficult, if not impossible to see how the power of abstraction would even fit into a system of reason comprising *a priori* logic, the form of empirical cognition, and the unity of apperception as the background of thought. Instead, Kant is content to assert that there emerges from empirical judgment a self-critical rational capacity which, when applied to reason, yields that the application of general logic is limited to empirical experience, and he offers as evidence a dubious set of antinomies and paralogisms.

It is, of course, *logically* impossible to handcuff *logic*; Kant would have done better to deny the existence of general logic at all. But this is, of course, impossible because as we have seen the grounds for irrationalism must ultimately be made by recourse to objective reason. The claim that logic is inapplicable in a certain realm of thinking may not be made if the result is to disavow the very logic upon which it is founded. The same logic that applies to empirical experience must apply to pure judgments and to inferences about all that is known or accessible to reason because that logic governs all thought. This is one of the foundational claims of transcendent realism, which in positing the *Logos*, asserts that the entirety of human empirical, theoretical, and practical experience is, as it must be, part and parcel of an orderly universe which includes all knowable objects and supports the reason of the knowing subject. Logic, therefore, is ontologically prior to empirical cognition and the act of understanding under categories must itself be understood as the spontaneous application of universally applicable, transcendent logic to orderly appearances that affect the senses in space and time. And, it is worth noting that this claim is supported by the very logic to which it attaches ontological priority.

In the prequel to this chapter, the concept of "logical object" was introduced as the irreducible object of all thought and undeniably bold assertions were made about the homogeneity of mathematics and logic and about the deductibility of mathematics, geometry, space and time, and the judgments and categories of understanding from them. It is now time to offer grounds for the claims in this chapter, for the asserted relation between logic and mathematics, and, in the next, for the assertion that logic and mathematics provide the form of empirical cognition and the certainty that physical objects must behave logically in accordance with the rules of their cognition.

It will be recalled that logical objects are the cognitive progenitors of all substantive objects and, as such, are contentless and substantively predicateless thought kernels, which are uniquely referred to reason and which stand in relation themselves as grounded logical predication and to their thinker and any other logical objects to which reason may assign (or recognize) logical relations. The foregoing can easily be seen from the following: (1) we neither experience nor can conceive of (the German idealists notwithstanding) thinking without thinker, hence the necessary and universal relation between logical object and its thinker; (2) contemporary predicate logic, which reflects the current state of theoretical reason, concerns objects and relations among objects, which although often expressed in terms of variables, in the purely logical realm reduces to relations among logical objects; and (3) because of (1) and (2) no thought can be conceived of that is not about an object that does not have relation to its thinker and the possibility (which may be negated in actual conception) of relation to other objects of thought.

Before proceeding with the exposition of the homogeneity of logic and mathematics, a point of clarification is necessary. The discussion which follows lays heavy emphasis upon the distinction between logical and substantive predicates, with the former being limited to the necessary relation of a logical object to its thinker and the possible logical relations among logical objects, and the latter including all other non-logical relations, whether or not they are empirical. This distinction is by no means artificial and neither is it a matter of convenience; to the contrary, it recognizes both the fundamental rational boundary between the purely logical and all other types of rational experience and the ontological priority of logic over empirical understanding. Logical objects may be conceived of without relation to the empirical world, but, as we shall see, empirical objects can only be understood in logical terms.

As a further prelude to the exposition of the homogeneity of logic and mathematics, it is essential to provide a specific set of definitions of the terms that are used with other than ordinary meaning:

"descendant" means the substantive object that is reducible to an identically enhandled logical object (i.e., its *progenitor*) by prescinding the predicates of the substantive object.

"enhandled" means having a handle. *"Enhandlement"* has a correlative meaning.

"handle" means the unique, identifying reference of an object to reason. Because an object cannot be thought except by reference to its handle, a handle is not a predicate of an object (i.e., saying that an object of thought has a handle is tautological).

"inherit" means the taking by a descendant substantive object of its identifiability and orderability from its progenitor logical object. *"Inheritance"* has a correlative meaning.

"logic" means the rules of formal inference about objects and their relations to themselves and other objects. Alternatively, *"logic"* is a description of the orderable predication of logical objects.

"logical object" means a thinkable (i.e., enhandled) entity which has only logical predicates and no substantive predicates.

"logical predicate" means, of an object, relation to itself and to its thinker and the possibility of any ordered relation to other objects that reason my assign to it.

"*object*" means a logical object or a substantive object.

"*orderability*" means the susceptibility of the object to being considered in relation to other objects in accordance with a principle of sequence, magnitude, proportionality, and/or other logical relation. "*Ordered*" and "*orderable*" have correlative meanings.

"*progenitor*" means the logical object from which a descendant substantive object inherits its identifiability and orderability.

"*sequence*" means a following of one object after another in accordance with a rule or rules.

"*series*" means a sequence which is characterized by asymmetry, transitivity, and connectivity (each of which is used in its technical meaning which is provided below for convenience).

"*substantive object*" means a thinkable entity that has logical and substantive predicates.

"*substantive predicate*" means any predicate other than a logical predicate.

"*substantively predicateless*" or "*substantively unpredicated*" means, with respect to any logical object, not being thinkable except in relation to itself, to its thinker, and to other logical objects in a logically orderable way.

Logical objects are the most basic elements of thought. Logical objects are enhandled and are distinguishable by their handle, which is to say, by definition, that even though they represent the most primitive form of object, each logical object is uniquely referred to the understanding upon its conception. By this, nothing more is meant than reason is able to *grasp and hold* its objects separately. Logical objects are predicable but substantively unpredicated and therefore contentless. Upon additional predication, logical objects become substantive objects but do not lose their orderable qualities. Although the cognition of a substantive object under categories of empirical understanding depends upon its empirical predicates, the thinkability of a substantive object *qua* object depends solely upon its being a descendant of a logical progenitor and not upon any substantive predicate of the object. To be clear, in empirical (or transcendent) cognition, reason does not bring the logicality of its objects to unordered predication; instead, as we have been stressing all along, such objects are orderable (in their very Being), else they could not be thought or understood as such.

Purely logical objects may not be thought of as in Being without relation to their thinker or without the possibility of logical relation to other objects; however, care must be taken about what is meant here because this notion brings us to the threshold of an ontological discourse that has been ongoing since at least Plato. Under Platonism, it is held that numbers and other abstract entities exist transcendently, which is to say that they have objective existence that is not spatio-temporal. This is a view with which we are in disagreement and, in fact, in a moment we will proceed to the logical *deduction* of the natural numbers as a special case of logical objectivity. Under transcendent realism, Being and intelligibility are the same thing, by which we mean that all that may be said "to be" or characterized as "in Being" must be *intelligible,* which we assert means to be reducible to *grounded logical predication*. When we think of a purely logical object as such, we do not pluck an existing logical object out of the air (so to speak) to examine it, but instead we bring to mind for analysis that by which the very orderliness of the universe is manifest, which is to say we bring under consideration Being itself. This is what we have been referring to as the *Logos* and its conception is foundational to transcendent realism. Because of its complexity and its centrality to the themes investigated in these pages, its additional exposition must be postponed until chapter 8, "Propaedeutic to Ontology," and chapter 9, "Being and Intelligibility," so that we may first understand how reason homogeneously understands its objects.

The thinker is the *ground* of the *thought* of a logical object and therefore the ground of the Being of the thought; the ground of the logical object itself is the ground of its predication, and neither the ground of logical predication nor the logical predication can exist without the other. Logical objects may be assigned by reason such ordered relations to other logical objects as reason may determine without any limit or restriction other than the rules of logic. The distinguishability of objects in thought depends upon their enhandlement and not upon their predication, and the distinguishability of objects in their Being depends upon their separate grounding. Each predicate of an object may, at the whim of reason, be thought of separately as its own enhandled, substantive object. The enhandlement and orderability of logical objects are the ontologically prior characteristics of all objects, which render all such objects cognizable, orderable, countable, measurable, and commensurable.

Consider in support of the foregoing the example of two billiard balls that are only distinguishable by virtue of their color, one being red and the other blue, and by virtue of their different location in space and time. The spherical shape of such objects, their color, and their position in space and time are all sensible (empirical) predicates. If each sensible predicate is removed, including location in space and time, one at a time, the billiard balls will cease to be sensible objects, but at no point in the process will they lose their separate thinkability as objects whose predicates have been prescinded, which is to say that at completion of the process they will still be thinkable as two different logical objects. This will be the case as long as we do not give up their separate enhandlement; if we do that, they will cease to have any relation to one another as objects of thought and will have been reduced by reason into a single logical object (having a single ground and set of logical predicates) of thought. Of course, we can do either as we may elect. We can say that two billiard balls, one formerly red and one formerly blue, one formerly to the left and the other formerly to the right, having been stripped of all unique predicates, including their separate enhandlement, are now a single logical object with a single reference to reason (indeed, this is one formulation of the principle of the identity of indiscernibles) which, if reason so chooses, may be duplicated by separate enhandlement and substantively predicated with all of the characteristics of billiard balls, or we can say that we have two logical objects, each of which is the progenitor object of a unique billiard ball and, if we so desire, we can begin to reattach predicates separately to them. Indeed, the foregoing is a rare example of *saying making it so*, for the very intelligibility of these assertions depends upon their being true in the first place. We should note the one-to-one correspondence between the ground of the predication of an object and its reference to reason. We should also note that the reduction of a billiard ball into a single logical object does not entail the instantiation of a new object of thought, which shows that logical objects themselves do not have the sort of transcendent existence that Platonism would suggest.

Logical objects, in their own right and as progenitors of substantive objects, are the provenance of the applicability of general logic to all objects of thought and cognition.[1] But that is not all that logical objects account for. One can easily see how logical objects and the descendant substantive objects, which inherit the properties of their progenitors, whether of thought or the empirical world, are themselves *essentially mathematical*, insofar as they cannot be thought of as objects without being inherently orderable and therefore no object, logical or substantive, may be thought which cannot be counted or placed in an ordered relation to other objects. And, indeed, the identifiability and orderability of logical objects underpin both the science of mathematics (by supporting the *unaxiomatic* deduction of the natural numbers and, therefore, all traditional pure mathematics, including analytical geometry, which follow by the application of logical principles to them) and its applicability to empirical objects.

Thus, general logic and mathematical logic are part and parcel of a *homogeneous* set of rules of thought, the former of which concern the defining qualities of logical objects and the latter of which concern rules of their arrangement. Logicism, the theory that mathematics is reducible to general logic, which arose in earnest in the nineteenth century but has never been proven, turns out to be correct, not because mathematics is derivable on logical principles but rather because general and mathematical logic are simply artificial divisions within a homogenous field of reason and, indeed, if anything, because of the nature of logical objects and *the quantified nature of predicate logic,* it may be more illuminating to treat logic as being mathematical in character. In support of this last proposition, I would suggest that distinguishing a purely logical relation, such as the relation of antecedent to consequent in *modus ponens*, from a mathematical relation, such as the relation of antecedent to subsequent (defined below and more commonly referred to as the relation of predecessor to successor), is an artificial act. To further the point, in response to the argument that *modus ponens,* without which the deduction of mathematics would be impossible, applies to all logical objects, not merely such objects when considered mathematically, I would point out that all logical objects are countable and orderable in a mathematical way.

---

1. In anticipation of the objection that logical rules such as the principle of noncontradiction may apply to empirical objects by virtue of their predicates, I would point out that such predicates are themselves objects of thought subject to its laws. So, for example, to say that a billiard ball cannot both be green and blue at the same time is, of course, true, but its truthfulness reduces to the broader empirical claim that a color cannot be one and another at the same time, which further reduces to the purely logical statement that a logical object cannot both have and not have a single unique handle and any logical relations that may be assigned to it. Perhaps another way of making the point is to say that the statement that a billiard ball cannot both be red and blue at the same time has nothing to do with the fact that the predicate under consideration is color and everything to do with the fact that color, like all other sensible objects of thought, inherits from logical objects. This and related ideas are discussed in more detail below at 130–133.

THE APPLICABILITY OF GENERAL LOGIC TO LOGICAL OBJECTS

We would not do harm to our understanding of Being simply to define logical objects as entities the predication of which is reducible to that which we understand as being logical and to assert that entities may not be further reduced. Nevertheless, it is worthwhile to investigate how general logic may be understood to apply objects which are so minimal. Demonstration of the applicability of general logic to logical objects may begin with the observation that logical objects fit within the definition of the objects to which predicate logic claims domain; in other words, logical objects are entities that may fall within the range of first-order or second-order bound variables and for which *identity* conditions can be provided. This is a technical way of saying that variables may represent logical objects. A simple example would be the statement:

$$\sim\exists(x)(x \neq x)$$

where x is a logical object, which translates into the true statement that there is no logical object that is not equal to itself or, more precisely, that each logical object is uniquely grounded and enhandled. We can think of an object in its most abstract form and, if we so choose, we can think of two such objects separately and simultaneously, but, even though such objects are contentless, we cannot think of two such objects as being a single object without merging them conceptually under a single ground and handle.

It is important to note that logical objects are *not* variables. Variables are symbols that stand for other things, which may or may not be substantively predicated; a logical object is a substantively unpredicated object which does not stand for anything other than itself. First order bound variables are themselves substantive objects, because they possess the quality of being able to take on any objective quality; such variables inherit from logical objects and are effective for their purposes because of that inheritance. It follows that rules of thought apply to objects by virtue of their inheritance from substantively predicateless logical objects and not by virtue of their predication.

The effort to consider specifically how the rules and postulates[2] of thought apply to logical objects as such will be amply rewarded even if it is unnecessary in light of the foregoing. To be discussed are the three classic rules mentioned in the preceding chapter, namely, the principle of identity, the principle of non-contradiction, and the principle of the excluded middle, and two additional rules, both the work of Leibniz, which are sometimes included as such in the taxonomy of rules of thought, namely, the principle of the identity of indiscernibles (which states that there cannot be separate things that have all their properties in common), and the principle of sufficient reason (which states

---

2. The terms "postulate" and "axiom" are often used interchangeably to denote a self-evident or universally recognized truth. In contemporary times, a distinction is sometimes made between the latter, which is so defined, and the former, which is used in cases in which an element of doubt must be recognized. Following this usage, the rules of thought described above would be axioms, because they are understood on the grounds of direct intuition to be beyond dispute, but Russell's axiom of infinity, which states that there are "infinite collections" in the world, cannot be regarded as an axiom because it is by no means certain to be true. Until now, we have used these terms interchangeably to accord with the relevant common practice. Going forward, we will adhere to the distinction between postulates and axioms described in this footnote.

that everything has a cause or sufficient explanation). It should be mentioned in passing here, with detailed discussion reserved for chapter 9, "Being and Intelligibility," that although the validity of principle of sufficient reason is sometimes contested on empirical grounds, in the philosophy presented in these pages not only is the opposite position taken but, following Leibniz and Heidegger, the principle of sufficient reason is regarded as the *principium principia* (i.e., the principle of principles) because it applies not merely to itself and its objects but to all of the other rules of thought as well.

Having so noted, the task before us is to show that such rules apply to contentless objects whose characteristics include only enhandlement and orderability. The principles of identity, non-contradiction, and the excluded middle can be seen to be applicable to logical objects because the enhandlement of each logical object, by definition, provides reason with a *unique* reference to it and because orderability according to a principle of sequence, magnitude, or proportion (or other logical relation) means that propositions about the sequence, magnitude, or proportion (or other logical relation) of logical objects must either be true or not true but not both. Even though a logical object is contentless and in that regard is identical with all other logical objects, its unique enhandlement and ground means that it cannot be identical with any logical object other than itself and, accordingly, the principle of identity applies to it. Similarly, the propositions about the enhandlement and definitional relations (to thinker, to itself as grounded predication, and to other logical objects) of logical objects, which are instantiated in their conception as part of such propositions, cannot both be true and not true at the same time. Speaking generally, each logical object must be orderable even if it is not assigned an order by reason, and it cannot both have and not have the possibility of assignment of a sequential, magnitudinal, or proportional relation to another logical object. Speaking more particularly, a logical object, which by definition has a unique ground of its predication, cannot both have and not have a unique handle and, indeed, if there is a single, unique handle there can only be a single object which cannot both have and not have any other relations or predicates. Because unique enhandlement is the precondition of the thinkability of a logical object and the assignability of an ordered relation to it, for there to be a plurality of logical objects there must be a corresponding plurality of object handles, where there is only a single handle there can only be a single object, and, accordingly, the principle of the identity of indiscernibles applies to logical objects. With respect to logical objects, the relevance of the principle of sufficient reason may appear to be obscure, but it reduces to this: inasmuch as a logical object is an essentially contentless object of thought the only *reason* that may be given for it is that *it is before a mind.* In other words, the ground of all logical objects is the soul that thinks them and nothing more should be expected of contentless objects. The demonstration that the eighteen rules of logical inference apply to logical objects follows from the fact that they may be stated in predicate logical form and is also trivially similar to the preceding discussion of the rules of thought and, as a result, will not be specifically undertaken here.

With this understanding in mind, we are in a position to make two important observations about thinking, itself, and about the nature of the rules of thought, themselves. In *Introduction to Metaphysics,* Heidegger identifies three elements of thinking as such: (1) voluntarily bringing an object before the mind (Heidegger calls this re-presenting);

(2) in a mode of analysis; (3) in which the universal is sought.[3] Under our understanding, the voluntary re-presenting occurs by establishing a reference to reason, which is what we are referring to as "enhandling." By mode of analysis, Heidegger means the breaking up of the object into elements for further consideration. In the case of logical objects, these elements are its handle, its ground, and its logical predicates. Finally, Heidegger tells us that the objective of the analysis is to identify the universal in the object. With respect to logical objects, in our understanding, this means to seek out the logical predication of the object. The foregoing leads to a perspective on the very nature of thinking that is striking in its fundamentality: thinking *essentially* amounts to perception of logical predication and the rules of thought are thus seen not so much as rules that stand on their own and apply to logical objects but rather as articulations of that which is universal in all thinkable objects, that is, their predication. Thus, as the irreducible and universal progenitor of all conceivable objects we see that the logical object is literally the Being of all conceivable objects and we also see, once again, the identity of Being and intelligibility.

The next step in the presentation of the homogeneity of general and mathematical logic is to show that the applicability of general logic to substantive objects depends not on their possession of substantive predicates but only on their inheritance from logical objects. The demonstration is not difficult. Consider as an example of an empirical object Bertrand Russell's beech tree. How is it that we are able to conclude that his beech tree is identical with itself, cannot both be and not be a beech tree, and that either it stands outside his study window or it does not stand there? The first proposition refers to an object that appears to be a beech tree. Whether it is one or not is irrelevant to its self-identity; it either has the required beech tree predicates or it does not. What is relevant is that it be distinguishable as a unique object of empirical cognition and that is a fact that in the first instance depends upon its essence as mind-independent, grounded substantive predication, and secondarily upon the ground of such predication having a unique reference to reason. If these conditions are satisfied, the beech tree will be thought to exist distinguishably from other possible objects. If there is one and only one beech tree under consideration, there is one and only one enhandled beech-tree-object under consideration, and, as has been shown, that object must be identical with itself and no other enhandled object. The second proposition may be similarly analyzed. Whether the tree is or is not a beech tree is again irrelevant. The point is that it cannot both be a beech tree and not be a beech tree and that is not a proposition that in any way depends upon what sort of tree it is but only upon whether it is a uniquely enhandled object (which, considered as a mind-independent object means that is also a unique instance of grounded predication), which cannot both be and not be something because it cannot have and not have a unique ground and handle. If there are two handles, then there are two objects and they must be different unless reason has been fooled into thinking that what is actually a single object is two different ones (in which case we would have one physical object but two separate conceptions of it). The analysis of the third proposition is again quite similar. Whatever the criteria of determining the *truth content* of a proposition about an object, such as whether Bertrand Russell's beech tree stands outside his study may be, that truth content depends upon the object, in this case the beech tree,

---

3. Heidegger, *Introduction to Metaphysics*, 131.

having a unique reference to reason (which again means that is also a unique instance of grounded predication). If it did not, then there would be more than one object to consider and it is possible that one might stand outside Bertrand Russell's study and the other might not. The proposition that Bertrand Russell's beech tree either stands outside Bertrand Russell's study is translatable to:

$$(\exists x)(Bx \ \& \ (Sx \ \vee \ \sim Sx))$$

which in turn translates into there is an x such that x is Bertrand Russell's beech tree and x either stands outside his study or it does not and which, stripped of all predication, reduces to:

$$(\forall P)(TP \ \vee \ \sim TP)$$

which also in turn translates into *for all propositions P, either P is true or P is not true* and which (even in the case of propositions) only requires inheritance from a logical object to be true.

THE LOGICAL DEDUCTION OF NATURAL NUMBERS

The exposition of the homogeneity of general and mathematical reason will be greatly benefitted by a few preliminary words on the history and importance of the epistemological and metaphysical nature of mathematics, in particular by putting the exposition in the context of the deduction of the natural numbers by Giuseppe Peano in the late nineteenth century and its more or less contemporaneous mainstream supplantation by the set-theoretic explanations of Georg Cantor, Frege, Russell, and Ernst Zermelo. Acknowledgement of the intimate connection between mathematics and knowledge dates back at least to the Ancient Greeks. Pythagoras posited that empirical objects are or resemble numbers, meaning that things are measurable and commensurable or proportional in terms of number, which is an idea not too remote from the thesis presented here. Plato thought that numbers, along with *forms* of all empirical objects, exist as real but immaterial ideas, and, although his broader metaphysics is not widely popular among contemporary philosophers, it does inform certain popular modern schools of mathematical philosophy including mathematical Platonism and Neoplatonism, which incorrectly hold that the subject matter of mathematics includes supersensibly existing numbers. As we will show momentarily, however, the *deduction* of the natural numbers from logical objects and relations renders the positing of transcendent numbers unnecessary. In any event, in the modern era, the importance of the philosophy of mathematics emerges in full force in the philosophy of Kant. Kant's central thesis in the *Critique of Pure Reason* is that certain sciences, including mathematics, geometry, and physics, owe the certainty of their postulates to the fact that they are known on a synthetic *a priori* basis. In this regard, Kant's philosophy represents a very minimal compromise with rationalism, which he accepts in order to defend his otherwise empirical philosophy from skepticism. But the mainstream empiricists, including especially in this context, Russell, could not abide any obeisance to rationalism and, Russell, working independently and initially without knowledge of the very similar work of Frege, sought to demonstrate that mathematics is deducible from general logic and does not require any reference to empirical reality for its validity. If correct, logicism would appear to support the argument that there is no such thing as synthetic *a priori* knowledge and as a result would completely undercut transcendental idealism. It should be noted that the idea that mathematics is reducible to logic had been expressed by Leibniz, who, in parallel with Newton invented the calculus, but Leibniz was unable to demonstrate the logicistic proposition.

Russell was concerned not only with discrediting transcendental idealism but, more generally, with severing any cord that might bind mathematics to time, which Kant ties in his exposition of the transcendental aesthetic. Ironically, although the Frege-Russell project failed, even had it succeeded in demonstrating the independence of mathematics from empirical preconditions, the success of the Frege-Russell project would have been limited to the denigration of Kant's transcendental idealism and would not have at all militated in favor of Russell's broader positivist philosophy. The reason is that logicism is fully compatible with, if not, supportive of rationalism and it is therefore quite possible, as is asserted to be the case in transcendent realism, that empirical reality acquires its certainty not on a transcendental basis but on a transcendent one. Indeed, under transcendent realism, the orderliness of the universe is a precondition of its intelligibility and the logic of logical objects applies not just to theoretical reason but also to empirical cognition because all empirical objects inherit from their progenitor logical objects and cognition of empirical objects depends upon the same general logic, including the *a priori* arithmetical and geometrical reasoning that applies ontologically in the first instance to logical objects. This is precisely the theme the development of which begins in this chapter and which will be completed in the sequel chapter, "Empirical Judgment."

It is generally accepted that if the deduction of the natural numbers may be accomplished on logical grounds, then the subsequent deduction of arithmetical, analytical geometry, and the rest of pure mathematics may also be had on such a basis. This, of course, is a proposition that ought not to be accepted on faith and the examination of which could fill many pages. It is also a proposition that extends far beyond the scope of the metaphysical investigation being herein conducted. For our purposes, limiting the discussion to the natural numbers, and to a lesser degree to arithmetical operations and least of all to analytical geometry, will suffice to demonstrate the homogeneity of reason and the logical structure of empirical cognition, at least insofar as such may be accomplished in a book of this type.

The first credible attempt at logicism belongs to Peano.[4] In Peano's system, three primitive (i.e., undefined) terms are employed together with five postulates. The

---

4. The discussion of Peano's philosophy of mathematics in these pages leans heavily upon two examinations of it. One is the discussion in Bertrand Russell's *Introduction to Mathematical Philosophy* and the other is an article entitled "On the Nature of Mathematical Proof," by Carl Hempel. The material in Russell's treatment is largely prefatory to the exposition of his set-theoretical philosophy of mathematics (which in turn leans heavily upon the work of Cantor and Frege) and the material in Hempel's article is part of a broader discussion of the difference between mathematical and scientific proof. See, Russell, *Introduction to Mathematical Philosophy*, 5–10; and, Hempel, "On the Nature of Mathematical Proof."

primitives of Peano's system are the terms "0,"[5] "number," and "successor." The symbol "0" is intended to designate 0 (zero) in its usual numeric sense, while the term "number" is meant to refer to the natural numbers, 0, 1, 2, 3.... By the "successor" of a natural number n, which successor will sometimes be referred to as $n^{\#}$, is meant the natural number immediately following n in the natural order. Before proceeding any further it is worth making two points. One is that Peano's primitives leave much undefined on the grounds of intuitive common understanding. The other is that this is not entirely indefensible; although all understandings ultimately rely upon undefined primitives of some sort and it seems undeniable that there is a solid common understanding of the primitives chosen by Peano, in presenting a logical deduction, it is not satisfactory to assume understanding without definition or proof that cannot be shown to be the case on the basis of direct or analytical intuition and, as will be shortly explained, others, including Russell, have attempted to do better than Peano does, and we will do the same.

In addition to Peano's primitives, Peano's work includes the following five postulates:

1. 0 is a number.

2. The successor of any number is a number.

3. No two numbers have the same successor.

4. 0 is not the successor of any number.

5. If P is a property such that (a) 0 has the property P, and (b) whenever a number n has the property P, then the successor of n also has the property P, then every number has the property P.

Postulate 5 represents a common formulation of the principle of mathematical induction, which, because it facilitates the assessment of the truth value of general statements, including statements about presumably infinite series such as the natural numbers, is among the most important postulates in mathematics.[6] In more simple terms, postulate 5 states that (a) if 0 has a particular property *which is not unique to it* and (b) it is the nature of that property that when any number has it so does its successor simply by virtue of its being such a successor, then (c) because 0 is a number, its successor number (i.e., 1) and each and every subsequent successor number (2, 3, 4 ...) will also have that property.

In Peano's system, the natural numbers are defined as sequential successors of 0. "1" is defined as the successor of 0 (also as $0^{\#}$), "2" is defined as the successor of 1 (also as $1^{\#}$ or $0^{\#\#}$), "3" is defined as the successor of two (also as $2^{\#}$ or $1^{\#\#}$ or $0^{\#\#\#}$), and so on. By virtue of postulate 2, each such successor of 0 and its successors is a number and, by virtue of postulate 5, this process of deducing numbers as successors of prior numbers

---

5. One of the interesting and important open issues with respect to the natural numbers is whether it is appropriate to include 0 among them. Apparently, Peano did not include 0 in the natural numbers. In the philosophy of transcendent realism, 0 is treated for ease of comparison with contemporary mathematics, although it seems more natural to think of the natural numbers as "counting" numbers, as they had been for most of human history.

6. Although the principle of mathematical induction is referred to here as a postulate, it is almost assuredly more accurately referred to under our nomenclature as an axiom. See 2n, 130.

can be continued indefinitely. Because of postulate 3 the deduction never leads back to one of the numbers previously defined and, because of postulate 4, neither does it lead back to 0.

In the Peano system, addition is defined in a way such that the addition of any natural number to some given number reflects the repeated addition of 1, with the addition of 1 being expressed by means of the successor relation. The stipulated definitions of addition are as follows:

1. The sum of any number n and 0 equals the number n (i.e., $n + 0 = n$).

2. The sum of any number n and any number other than 0, which can be expressed as the successor of a number k (i.e., $k^\#$, the successor to k), is equal to the successor of the sum of n and k (i.e., $n + k^\# = (n + k)^\#$).

From these two definitions, the sum of any two integers may be calculated. Consider, for example, the sum $3 + 2$:

1. According to the definition of the number 2, we can substitute $1^\#$ for 2, which gives us:

$$3 + 2 = 3 + 1^\#$$

2. According to the definition of the number 1, we can substitute $0^\#$ for 1, which gives us:

$$3 + 1^\# = 3 + (0^\#)^\#$$

3. By definition 2:

$$3 + (0^\#)^\# = (3 + 0^\#)^\# = ((3 + 0)^\#)^\#$$

4. By definition 1:

$$((3 + 0)^\#)^\# = (3^\#)^\#$$

5. Substituting back for $(3^\#)^\#$ and $4^\#$ the numbers $4^\#$ and 5, respectively, we get:

$$(3^\#)^\# = 4^\# = 5$$

It can be seen from the above example that in the Peano system, addition reduces to counting, which seems to be in accordance with our everyday experience. In the Peano system, the definition of multiplication is: $n \times k^\# = n \times k + n$, which also reduces to counting. If, as is often done, one includes 0 among the natural numbers, then, as was the case in addition, a special definition of multiplication by 0 is also needed and is as follows: $n \times 0 = 0$.

Subtraction and division are the inverse operations of addition and multiplication, but it is important to note that the results of such operations are not necessarily natural numbers and so, to enable their employment, other categories of numbers, namely, integers, rational numbers, irrational numbers, and complex numbers, are necessary. It should also be pointed out that, although we are in agreement with Peano's characterization of the basic arithmetical operations as forms of counting, this view is inconsistent with mainstream set-theoretic systems and, most importantly, creates difficulties concerning whole segments of modern mathematics based upon Cantor's theories of multiple orders of infinity. To the extent one accepts the notion that Cantor and his progeny have sufficiently well worked out the rules governing infinite numbers and their relations, a circumstance that we will critically investigate shortly, the topic may very well be considered the province of mathematics. Under the philosophy of transcendent realism, however, human rational experience intersects with mathematical logic in three important regions. The first is the topic under consideration in this chapter, namely, in the intuition of pure mathematical logic itself. The second is the topic in the sequel chapter, which is the relation of such logic to empirical cognition. The third is purely metaphysical and concerns, to a very large degree, the relationship of the concept of infinity to questions such as whether the world has a beginning and whether God exists and how he might be understood. Thus, we will merely note here that one's view of a topic so apparently simple as counting may have the broadest possible consequences, including providing the basis of an entire philosophy of the infinite and related metaphysics, and leave for discussion in chapter 7, "Infinity, Countability, and Self-Reference," and subsequent chapters on metaphysics the working out of some of these ideas.

Although the Peano system marks a significant advance in the philosophy of mathematics, it has suffered much criticism, a good portion of which has been aimed at its dependence upon its primitives, and in the early twentieth century, the Peano system was supplanted by set-theoretic philosophies which are of a substantially different character. Oddly, the deficiency of leaving the terms "0," "number," and "successor" undefined is not merely a curse but also a blessing, because instead of providing a unique deduction of the natural numbers, the Peano system yields a highly useful, general logical structure which applies to any domain that may be described by definitions which satisfy its five postulates. Because of the breadth of the applicability of the Peano system, it is regarded as demonstrating a *progression* of which the natural numbers must be understood as representing a special case. Carl Hempel demonstrates the generality of the Peano system by offering the simple example of a linear representation of the natural numbers:

> [L]et us understand by "0" the origin of a half-line, by the successor of a point on that half-line the point 1 cm behind it, counting from the origin, and by a number any point which is either the origin or can be reached from it by a finite succession of steps each of which leads from one point to its successor. It can then readily be seen that all the Peano postulates as well as the ensuing theorems turn into true propositions, although the interpretation given to the primitives is certainly not the customary one.[7]

For reasons which will become apparent shortly, it is important to note that the objects in Hempel's example of are substantive and not logical in nature.

---

7. Hempel, "On the Nature of Mathematical Proof," 9.

Russell, the most prominent figure in the set-theoretical deduction of the natural numbers, characterizes the problem with the Peano system in this way:

> [T]hat "0" and "number" and "successor" cannot be defined by means of Peano's five axioms, but must be independently understood, is important. We want our numbers not merely to verify mathematical formulae, but to apply in the right way to common objects. We want to have ten fingers and two eyes and one nose. A system in which "1" meant "100," and "2" meant "101," and so on, might be all right for pure mathematics, but would not suit daily life. We want "0" and "number" and "successor" to have meanings which will give us the right allowance of fingers and eyes and noses. We have already some knowledge (though not sufficiently articulate or analytic) of what we mean by "1" and "2" and so on, and our use of numbers in arithmetic must conform to this knowledge. We cannot secure that this shall be the case by Peano's method; all that we can do, if we adopt his method, is to say "we know what we mean by '0' and 'number' and 'successor,' though we cannot explain what we mean in terms of other simpler concepts." It is quite legitimate to say this when we must, and at some point we all must; but it is the object of mathematical philosophy to put off saying it as long as possible. By the logical theory of arithmetic we are able to put it off for a very long time.[8]

Although Hempel, who devoted much academic attention to the relationship between mathematical and scientific reasoning, is kinder in tone than Russell, his criticism is substantially the same. Hempel asserts:

> The Peano system permits of many different interpretations, whereas in everyday as well as in scientific language, we attach one specific meaning to the concepts of arithmetic. Thus, for example, in scientific and in everyday discourse, the concept "2" is understood in such a way that from the statement "Mr. Brown as well as Mr. Cope, but no one else is in the office, and Mr. Brown is not the same person as Mr. Cope," the conclusion "exactly two persons are in the office" may be validly inferred. But the stipulations laid down in Peano's system for the natural numbers, and for the number 2 in particular, do not enable us to draw this conclusion; they do not *implicitly determine* the customary meaning of the concept "2" or of the other arithmetical concepts. And the mathematician cannot acquiesce in this deficiency by arguing that he is not concerned with the customary meaning of the mathematical concepts; for in proving, say, that every positive real number has exactly two real square roots, he is himself using the concept "2" in its customary meaning, and his very theorem cannot be proved unless we presuppose more about the number 2 than is stipulated in the Peano system.[9]

It is undeniable that the Peano system, however elegant and intuitive it may be, has no fully satisfactory response to the criticisms offered by Russell and Hempel, a fact upon which Russell seized in one of the great masterworks of mathematical philosophy, *The Principles of Mathematics*, to introduce his version of the set-theoretic methodology for the deduction of the natural numbers. Russell's work was based upon then-recently developed set theory initiated in the 1870s by Cantor, who is also known for his groundbreaking work in the theory of infinite sets, and Richard Dedekind, who is also known

---

8. Russell, *Introduction to Mathematical Philosophy*, 9.
9. Hempel, "On the Nature of Mathematical Proof," 9–10.

for his work in abstract algebra and the foundations of real numbers. Russell proposed to demonstrate the deduction of the natural numbers from what is today known as naïve set theory, which is one of several set theoretic approaches and which is distinguished from the subsequently developed and more axiomatic set theories by the sparsity of its axiomatization. Although, as an accomplished mathematician, Russell's motivation in doing so may be presumed to grow out of his interest in his subject matter, as has been mentioned already, the successful demonstration of the logicism of mathematics would undercut Kant's transcendental idealism, which regards mathematics as synthetic *a priori*, and, indeed, was a fact often explicit in Russell's mathematical as well as in his philosophical writings.

In Russell's system, a number is that which is characteristic of all numbers (in the same way that "man" is characteristic of all men) and each natural number is regarded as *the defining characteristic a set of all similar sets*.[10] So, for examples, the number "2" is defined as the number of the set of all sets of duos and the number "3" is defined as the number of the set of all sets of triads. For reasons that will become apparent almost immediately, it is important to understand that, as would be expected, the definition means what it says quite literally; in the case of the number "2" (or "3" or any other number), the number is the defining characteristic of all possible collections of duos (or triads or other similar sets) of empirical objects existing in the world and each such collection is an *instance* of the number "2" (or "3" or other such number). Russell's definition of "number" offers three advantages over the primitive in the Peano system. The first is the obvious advantage of precisely replacing Peano's primitive with a meaningful definition. The second is that Russell's definition practically addresses the Russell/Hempel criticism that numbers must be effective for counting things and not so general as to constitute all manner of progressions. The third is that this definition of number is the foundation of the set-theoretic approach to natural numbers, which offers much information about the practical use of numbers in the real world.

Russell's set-theoretic approach also possesses its own difficulties, however, which do not attend the Peano system. The main problem that Russell faces lies in the process of deducing the entirety of the natural numbers from his definition of number. In the Peano system, that deduction follows from the five postulates and leans heavily on the fifth such postulate, namely, the principle of mathematical induction. Russell, on the other hand, required two attempts to accomplish the deduction, neither of which was wholly successful. In Russell's first attempt to achieve the deduction of all of the natural numbers, Russell sought to automate Peano's successor function to actually generate the natural numbers on a set-theoretic basis, but, in the process of doing so, Russell unearthed a profound paradox that required him to substantially modify the foundations of his entire set theory. In Russell's second attempt, he abandoned the troublesome set-theoretic definition of the inductive process and in its place adopted Peano's fifth postulate as a definition; however, in giving up the former, Russell found himself in need of the axiom of infinity, a new axiom which states that there are in the world infinite sets of objects. Both of Russell's approaches, and the reasons for their failure, are important

---

10. In naïve set theory, a set is a collection of objects and two sets are said to be "similar" when their members may be mapped to one another on a one-one basis.

to understand in order to clear the ground for presentation of a mathematical system that is complete, consistent, and exclusively based upon logical principles.

Russell's initial approach is simple in its design. Having defined number as the set of all similar sets, Russell attempts to deduce the entirety of the natural numbers, which, it follows from the definition of natural number, must be the set of all numbers or, more precisely, the set of all sets of similar sets. In Russell's first attempt, he defines "0" as the number of the members in the null set (i.e., an empty collection), which he posits as the first member set of the set of all similar sets, and then he proceeds to generate the entire series of such sets (i.e., the natural numbers) by repeatedly adding a new member consisting of the last member plus a new element not already included such last member. In more formal terms, the definition of "number" is given as follows:

1. define each natural number n as the set, A, of all sets, X, that have n elements;

the definition of 0 is given as follows:

2. define 0 as $\emptyset$ (i.e., the empty set);

and the deduction of the set of natural numbers N is given by adding a new set A to N comprising the union of each X in the last such A with a *new* element y that is not in X:

3. define $N(a)$ as:

$$\{X \cup \{y\} \mid X \in A \land y \notin X\}$$

In (1) above, each natural number (n) is defined as A, the set of all sets having that number of members; in (2) above, 0 is defined as the set that has no members (i.e., $\emptyset$); and in (3) above, the set of all natural numbers, N, is obtained by successively adding to every member set X of the last A in N, a new element y (i.e., one that is not already included in X). So, starting with the natural number 0, the first step in defining N is to add a new set to its member sets, A, which new set is formed by the union of $\emptyset$, which is the first (and last) member set of both A and N, with a set that contains an element, y, which is not contained in $\emptyset$. The second member set in N is therefore $A\{y\}$, which, it can be seen, is the set of all sets having 1 member. Under Russell's definition, N is now $\{\emptyset, A\{y\}\}$ and has two members. But Russell's definition will not allow us to stop there because it postulates that to each member set X of $A\{y\}$ another a new y (since y is already a member, we would be well advised to call this new y, $y^\#$) must be added with the result that N now becomes $\{\emptyset, A\{y\}, A\{y, y^\#\}\}$. It can be seen that the set N *automatically* implements the successor function in a way that allows definition of the natural numbers as successors of 0, so that one can define $1 = N(0)$, $2 = N(1)$, $3 = N(2)$, and so on. Each number so obtained is the set whose members include sets having the corresponding number of elements.

Russell's approach addresses the deficiencies he identifies in the Peano system by clearly defining Peano's primitives and by obviating the need for Peano's postulates by implementing the set-theoretic successor function. But that is where the good news ends. As Russell (and Frege) quickly discovered, naïve set theory entails a fatal contradiction, which appropriately enough has come to be known as Russell's Paradox and which precludes the use of self-referential sets to automatically implement the successor

The Homogeneity of Reason

function upon which Russell's deduction of the natural numbers depends. Since Russell's deduction of the natural numbers is founded upon the notion of collecting all similar sets in the universe, at some point in what is intended to be an infinite process, one must add to the set of all sets, all sets that are not included therein as members. The paradox arises when one attempts to determine what the new sets are because, if a set does not include the set being determined as a member, then it is a member of that set, but if it is a member of the set being determined, then the set includes itself as a member! This paradox absolutely precludes the deduction of the natural numbers under naïve set theory. In other words, one cannot create the natural numbers by adding to the set of all of the natural numbers a new number that is not a natural number.

Ultimately, Russell and Zermelo eliminated Russell's Paradox by employing additional definitions and axioms which prohibit the use of self-referential sets in the set-theoretic deduction of the natural numbers. As noted, in Russell's case, he retained the definitions of "number" and "zero" but instead of automating the successor process in a way that leads to the paradox that bears his name, Russell adopted Peano's fifth postulate as a definition. Russell's new line, briefly summarized, is as follows:

1. define each natural number n as the set, A_n, of all sets, X, that have n elements;
2. define 0 as $\emptyset$ (i.e., the empty set);
3. define "successor" of a given number n as the number of the class obtained by adding a new member y to any set having n members; and
4. define the "natural numbers" as the posterity of 0 with respect to the relation "immediate predecessor," with the following definitions:
    a. a property is "hereditary" in the natural number series if, whenever it belongs to a number n, it also belongs to $n + 1$, the successor of n;
    b. a property is "inductive" when it is a hereditary property which belongs to 0 and a class is "inductive" when it is a hereditary class of which 0 is member;
    c. the "posterity" of a given natural number with respect to the relation "immediate predecessor" is all those terms that belong to every hereditary class to which the given number belongs; and
    d. the term "immediate predecessor" means the converse of successor.

By swapping out the set-theoretical successor operation upon which Russell's first attempt depends and replacing it with a definition (not a postulate) of induction, Russell has avoided his famous paradox. Russell has offered precise definitions of Peano's primitives in the paragraphs enumerated above as (1), (2), and (3). Additionally, Russell's definitions obviate the need for the first four of Peano's five postulates. From Russell's definitions, we may: (a) remove postulate 1:0 is a number, by the definition of "0"; (b) remove the successor of any number is a number, by the definition of "successor"; (c) prove postulate 4:0 is not the successor of any number, because the definition of "successor" requires the addition of a term to a given set and therefore a successor set must have at least one member; and (d) remove postulate 5: if P is a property such that (y) 0 has the property P, and (z) whenever a number n has the property P, then the successor of n also has the property P, then every number has the property P, which we have adopted definitionally as a term within the definition of "natural number." But postulate 3: No two numbers having the same successor creates a subtle problem, because, even under Russell's scheme, it is only true if one assumes that there are an infinite number of individuals in the world. So Russell's advances have come at a heavy cost, which is a new dependence upon at least one axiom, namely, the axiom of infinity. Russell recognizes the difficulty and explains it as follows:

> The difficulty does not arise unless the total number of individuals in the universe is finite; for given two numbers m and n, neither of which is the total number of individuals in the universe, it is easy to prove that we cannot have $m + 1 = n + 1$ unless we have $m = n$. But let us suppose that the total number of individuals in the universe were (say) 10; then there would be no class of 11 individuals, and the number 11 would be the null-class. So would the number 12. Thus we should have $11 = 12$; therefore the successor of 10 would be the same as the successor of 11, although 10 would not be the same as 11. Thus we should have two different numbers with the same successor. This failure of the third axiom cannot arise, however, if the number of individuals in the world is not finite.[11]

Thus, Russell must accept axiomatically that which he cannot demonstrate, namely the existence in the world of infinite terms. On this point, Russell says:

> It cannot be said to be *certain* that there are in fact any infinite collections in the world. The assumption that there are is what we call the "axiom of infinity." Although various ways suggest themselves by which we might hope to prove this axiom, there is reason to fear that they are all fallacious, and that there is no conclusive logical reason for believing it to be true. At the same time, there is certainly no logical reason *against* infinite collections, and we are therefore justified, in logic, in investigating the hypothesis that there are such collections. The practical form of this hypothesis, for our present purposes, is the assumption that, if n is any inductive number, n is not equal to $n + 1$. Various subtleties arise in identifying this form of our assumption with the form that asserts the existence of infinite collections; but . . . [f]or the present we shall merely assume that, if n is an inductive number, n is not equal to $n + 1$. This is involved in Peano's assumption that no two inductive numbers have the same successor; for, if $n = n + 1$, then $n - 1$ and n have the same successor, namely n. Thus we are assuming nothing that was not involved in Peano's primitive propositions.[12]

Having expressed the need for such an axiom, Russell remains content that he has demonstrated logicism:

> Assuming that the number of individuals in the universe is not finite, we have now succeeded not only in defining Peano's three primitive ideas, but in seeing how to prove his five primitive propositions, by means of primitive ideas and propositions belonging to logic. It follows that all pure mathematics, in so far as it is deducible from the theory of the natural numbers, is only a prolongation of logic. The extension of this result to those modern branches of mathematics

---

11. Russell, *Introduction to Mathematical Philosophy*, 24.
12. Ibid., 77–78.

which are not deducible from the theory of the natural numbers offers no difficulty of principle, as we have shown elsewhere.[13]

It is an odd bit of philosophy, indeed, to declare that one has demonstrated the logicism of mathematics all the while acknowledging that the demonstration depends upon an empirical assumption and Russell cannot be allowed to get away with it. Russell's dependence upon the axiom of infinity is the direct result of Russell's empirical proposition that numbers are the defining characteristic of *real* things and, as a result, it casts doubt on the empirical premise that all knowledge comes directly from the senses. Not only is it a stretch to characterize the proposition that there exists an infinite set as an axiom, but it contradicts Russell's fourth point of rebuttal against Kant's exposition of space which relies upon the contemporary scientific evidence that the amount of matter in the universe is limited.[14] Moreover, because the axiom of infinity is not itself logical in nature, its employment in this context wholly undercuts the logicism of the Russell (and Zermelo) set-theoretical deductions of the natural numbers. As to this last point, it must be emphasized that contemporary philosophy of mathematics has not rejected set-theoretic approaches to number theory but has either rejected the claim of logicism or accepted Russell's impermissible fallacy.

Ironically, taking the set-theoretic exposition on its face, including recognition of the empirical assumption regarding infinite items, would seem to support the claim of Kant that mathematics is in fact synthetic *a priori*. Since Russell and Zermelo, alternative axiomatic set theories have been developed and although the prevailing view remains that the natural numbers represent the defining characteristic of similar sets the presence of alternative sets of axioms casts further doubt on the logicism of set theory in general. Additionally, many philosophers now hold (apparently upon empirical grounds) that set membership is not a logical concept, although this is a point as to which we will offer disagreement in a later chapter. Finally, mention must be made of the widely accepted theories of Kurt Gödel, who asserts that any recursive axiomatic mathematical system that is sufficiently robust to provide for the deduction of the natural numbers must be either incomplete or contradictory.[15]

Given that set theoretics cannot support the logicist conclusion, the question which must be asked is whether the logicist project must be abandoned altogether. The answer to this question is crucial to transcendent realism because transcendent realism holds that all rational experience, including empirical cognition, must be founded in logic itself and that empirical reality must be so ordered as to be accessible under logically grounded cognitive concepts. If transcendent realism is correct in this fundamental respect, then arithmetic and geometry, which govern the organization of objects in space and time, must be fully *a priori* (which is to say that they must be deducible from direct intuition of the rules of thought without reference to empirical experience). The demonstration of the logicism of the natural numbers and, by extension, arithmetic and

---

13. Ibid., 24–25.

14. See 83. This is yet another example of doing analytical philosophy on shifting premises.

15. Some observations upon Gödel's work in this regard will be offered in chapter 7, "Infinity, Countability, and Self-Reference."

geometry, within the context of transcendent realism will proceed by application of logical principles to logical objects. The strategy will be to revisit Peano's system from this perspective. In so doing, it will be shown that such objects represent numbers as they are commonly understood and that the deduction of arithmetic follows from the properties of logical objects without any need for primitive concepts or axioms.

Within transcendent realism, the natural numbers N are a *prioritized series* of logical objects and the priority of logical objects in the N-series is determined solely by reference to the logical relations of *antecedence* and *subsequence*. It will be helpful to set forth the definitions of the nature of this priority.

1. A logical object a in a series is an antecedent of another logical object b in the series if b cannot be posited in the series without a having been posited in the series but a can be posited in the series without b having been posited in the series.

2. A logical object a in a series is the immediate antecedent of another logical object b in the series if the only antecedent of b in the series that is not also an antecedent of a in the series is a itself.

3. A logical object b in a series is a subsequent of another logical object a in the series if a is an antecedent of b in the series.

4. A logical object b in a series is the immediate subsequent of another logical object a in the series if a is the immediate antecedent of b in the series.

The definitions of priority will allow for the placement of logical objects in a *serial* relation to one another. A "series" is a sequence that meets certain generally accepted logical criteria which are utilized here with a few changes to accommodate our terminology. These criteria are *asymmetry*, *transitivity*, and *connectedness* and are employed as follows:

1. The priority relation between two objects, a and b, in a series is "asymmetrical" if it is the case that if an object a is an antecedent of b, then b cannot also be an antecedent of a.

2. The priority relation between three objects, a, b, and c, in a series is "transitive" if it is the case that if a is an antecedent of b and b is an antecedent of c, then a must be an antecedent of c.

3. The priority relation between objects in a series is "connected" if it is the case that for all pairs of objects, a and b, in the series it must be the case that either a is an antecedent of b and b is a subsequent of a or *vice versa*.

The serial criteria determine its linear nature so that the logical objects in the series will follow a progression that corresponds to the one in the Peano system. If we are, however, to progress, as Russell does, beyond the generality of the Peano system, but without the need of any axioms that might subterfuge our deduction as the axiom of infinity does to the set-theoretic approaches, still more definitions are required. Specifically, definitions of the concepts of "induction," "natural number," and "zero" must be provided unaxiomatically.

1. A "logically inductive" series is a series comprising logical objects posited by reference to a logical object which does not have any antecedents (the "referent object") and in which each of the referent object and each other logical object is the immediate antecedent of another logical object (i.e., for every logical object n in the series, including the referent object, there is another logical object $n^\#$, that is its immediate subsequent).

2. The natural number series is the logically inductive series whose referent logical object is 0. Alternatively, the N-series is the logically inductive series comprising 0 and its subsequent logical objects in the series.

3. "zero (0)" is the logical object that is posited as being antecedent to all other logical objects in the N-series (i.e., 0 is not subsequent to any other logical objects in the N-series and therefore has no antecedents).

4. Each *natural number* is a logical object in the N-series the defining characteristic of which is the number of logical objects that are antecedent to it in the N-series. Alternatively, each natural number is a logical object the defining characteristic of which is its position in the N-series, determined by reference to its antecedent logical objects in the N-series.

We are now in a position to formalize the process of the deduction of the natural numbers (i.e., N-series) by stating that the deduction of the natural numbers proceeds by positing (without end) 0, as the immediate antecedent of the number 1, and each immediate subsequent natural number in accordance with the definitions thereof. Mention should be made that 0 is the referent in the series and, consistent with modern mainstream mathematical theory, is included as a natural number despite the fact that, unlike all of the other logical objects in the series, 0 has no antecedent. It should also be noted that, throughout the vast majority of the history of mathematics, zero has not been considered to be a natural number or, for that matter any other kind of number. In the Roman numeral system, for example, there is no number "0," and the use of zero as a substantive (as opposed to mere placeholder) does not appear to have occurred until its employment in ninth-century India. The basis for the historic exclusion of 0 from the system of natural numbers seems to be the intuitive observation that the *counting numbers* (the concept of counting is the etymological basis for the use of the term *natural*) start with 1 and if 0 is considered as meaning the absence of any object under consideration, then including it in the counting numbers is equivalent to treating *nothing* as if it were *something*. However, 0 serves many important purposes in the development of higher mathematics, including of particular importance, the calculus and set theory, so, the only productive alternative to including 0 among the natural numbers is to distinguish between the *counting numbers* (as being definitionally identical to the natural numbers) and the *non-negative integers* and to regard higher mathematics as representing the working out of the relations among the latter. This is a matter of convenience insofar as one might just as easily define the initial logical object posited in the series as the number 1 and characterize the entire N-series by reference to the subsequence relation. We could, for example, define the number 1 without reference to 0 using the sentential calculus as follows:

$$(\exists x) (Lx \vee \sim Sx \& \forall y (Ly \& \sim Sy \rightarrow y = x))$$

which translates into that there is a logical object x that is in a prioritized series and that is not a subsequent of any other logical object in the prioritized series and for all logical objects y in the prioritized series, if y is not a subsequent of any other logical object, then y is equal to x. In this formulation, the number "1" would be the referent object and also the first natural number.

The unaxiomatic deduction of the natural numbers exclusively from logical objects and logical relations, demonstrates the pure logicism of the natural numbers and, considered in the light of the prior exposition of the nature of logical objects in general, the homogeneity of mathematics and general logic. The uniquely important feature of this deduction is that it is implemented by positing logical objects in accordance with definitions which are wholly logical in nature and which are without any reference to empirical reality. This deduction removes all primitives from the Peano system: "0" is defined. "Natural number" is defined. "Successor" is supplanted with priority, antecedent, immediate antecedent, subsequent, and immediate subsequent, all of which are defined. Peano's postulate 5 is adopted as a definition and the other four postulates are true by virtue of the definitions. Unlike Peano's system, this deduction is not of a generic progression but of the special case of progression that constitutes the natural numbers N as a logically inductive series of logical objects whose referent logical object is 0 and, therefore, this deduction is not subject to any of the objections raised by Russell and Hempel against Peano.

It will be worthwhile to briefly revisit the discussion of the applicability of the rules of thought to logical objects with a few remarks about the application of such rules to natural numbers. Consider, first, the principle of identity. The principle of identity states that each thing is the same with itself and different from each other thing. As was noted, this principle plainly applies to logical objects by virtue of their being enhandled and it should therefore be expected to apply, as it in fact does, to natural numbers. Certainly, the statement that $5 = 5$ is true. It might be objected that the number 12 is not only equal to itself but is equal also to the number 5 added to the number 7 and that this violates the principle of identity. It will be recalled that Kant took the opposite position, namely that there is nothing in the concept of "12" that includes the concept of "5" or of "7." In any case, in the logical object system the number "5" cannot be added to the number "7" as such to come up with a new logical object. Instead, the addition of 5 and 7 merely requires identifying 12 as the logical object posited at the end of the process of repeated succession required by the statement "7 + 5." To be sure, the set of all numbers the sum of which is equal to 12 is infinitely large, but, in the logical object system, each member of that set merely points to the same logical object, which is the twelfth number after 0 in the sequence of logical objects constituting the natural numbers. Addition is not logical alchemy; it is merely a process of counting (i.e., identifying the appropriate subsequent) among ordered logical objects.

The principle of non-contradiction states that contradictory statements cannot both be true and false in the same sense at the same time. As applied to logical objects, the principle of non-contradiction simply means that two logical objects cannot be reduced to one while maintaining their separateness. 12 cannot both equal 7 + 5 and not equal 7 + 5 because the twelfth logical object in the *N*-series cannot both be and not be the twelfth logical object in the *N*-series. Stated in predicate formulation:

$$\sim\exists(x)(x \neq x).$$

The principle of the excluded middle states, with respect to any proposition, either that proposition is true or its negation is true. The principle of the excluded middle can be understood to be a statement about relations between numeric logical objects which are either true (i.e., consistent with the ordered relations) or untrue (i.e., inconsistent with the ordered relations). So, for example, the statement 7 + 5 = 12 is either true or it is not true; it cannot be both or something else.

The principle of the identity of indiscernibles states that there cannot be separate things that have all their properties in common. Two different arithmetical statements, for examples, 7 + 5 and 3 + 9, considered as statements have different properties and are each uniquely enhandled; the evaluation of both statements to 12 yields a single logical object with one and only one unique handle.

LOGICAL OBJECTS AND THE CARDINALITY OF EMPIRICAL SETS

As was just noted, because the logical deduction of the natural numbers is unaxiomatic, it is not subject to any of the criticisms leveled against set-theoretic deductions. The axiom of infinity required under both naïve and ZFC set theory is not necessary because there can be no logical limitation on the existence of the subsequence relation that is characteristic of each logical object in the *N*-series. Set-theoretic deductions of the natural numbers require adoption of the axiom of infinity because the existence of an infinite set cannot be proved from the other axioms of set theory. However, the axiom of infinity is not required in the case of the deduction of the natural numbers in the logical object system because the theorem that there is no limit on logical objects is analytically true from the definition of them as being orderable. To see that this is so, assume the contrary, namely that there is a greatest logical object. If that is the case, there cannot be posited a logical object that is its immediate subsequent. But we have defined "immediate subsequent" as the ordered relation (as assigned by reason) of a logical object to the logical object, if any, that is posited as being immediately before it and we have seen that this definition merely expresses the possibility of sequential relation that is part of the essence of a logical object as being inherently orderable. In other words, placing a limitation on the sequential orderability of a logical object is to predicate it in a way that changes its nature into a substantive object, which is not part of the logical object system. Therefore, reason may always posit a logical object after any given logical object in a sequence of logical objects and holding otherwise would contradict the idea of a logical object as such and violate the definition of "immediate subsequent," which follows naturally from it.

This deduction does not depend upon a concept of set membership, which, as employed in modern set theory, is regarded by most as an empirical concept. The analysis underpinning the logical deduction reduces set-theoretic systems to a zero-based positive integral progression because the essential features of *set of set-membership* which governs the similarity relation which is the defining characteristic of "number" in such systems are reducible to a single series of sets logical objects. For example, the duality of each set of duos in the set of all sets of duos is determined solely by reference to their enhandlement, which is a logical predicate not an empirical one, so that considering a set of all sets of duos is no more informative than considering a single set of duos and determining the cardinality of such a single set reduces to counting antecedents in an inductive series.[16]

It will be worthwhile to investigate further the relationship between mathematical logic as understood in these pages and set theory in general. That we have disposed of the set-theoretic deduction of mathematics does not mean that we have discounted set theory altogether and, in fact, to the contrary, the introduction of logical objects and their relations provides a purely logical field upon which set theory may be employed. Of particular importance in this regard is the elevation of the idea of a set to logical status because, reduced to its purely logical conception, a set of logical objects, which we might appropriately call a *logical set,* may be defined as those objects having a given logical predicate, and a logical set is, itself, therefore a logical object. The obviously relevant example of this is the *N*-series, which has the serial and subsequence predicates described above. Proceeding further, consideration of such sets as comprising exclusively logical objects obviates the need for the axiom of infinity because there can be no limit on the number of logical objects. So, even though the set-theoretic deductions of the natural numbers represent an excessive artifice over the more straightforward logical deduction in these pages, set theory can be said to be unaxiomatically logical when applied to logical objects as its members.

Which brings us to a final point in furtherance of the theme of the ontological priority of logic over empirical cognition. The reason that set theory understood within the domain of empirical objects is so powerful and compelling is because it represents one way of applying ontologically prior pure reason in the empirical context, which serves to illustrate the importance of careful consideration of the relation between the two. Russell may be quite correct that the defining characteristic of all sets of (empirical) duos is the number "2," but that merely tells us something about how the number "2" operates in empirical cognition and it certainly does not tell us what the number "2" is. To achieve that understanding, much deeper investigation is required (the results of which have been presented here). The reason that the number "2" is the defining characteristic of all empirical duos has absolutely nothing to do with their empirical character at all but everything to do with the fact that in order for them to be understood as pairs objects, they must be referred to reason as pairs of their progenitor *enhandled* logical objects.

16. On this view, the cardinal members are an inductive series which undercuts, on a metaphysical basis, one of the major presuppositions of Cantor's theory of uncountable sets of numbers. This topic is discussed at length in chapter 7, "Infinity, Countability, and Self-Reference."

The multitude (which Russell presumes to be infinite) of sets of empirical duos depends upon their empirical predicates; their "twoness" does not. When such objects are reduced by reason to their logical progenitors, they may be placed by reason in a series (as defined above) and counted, the first (i.e., 0) as having no antecedents and the second (i.e., 1) as having one antecedent (i.e., 0) and the third (i.e., 2) as having a pair of antecedents (i.e., 0 and 1). That such pairs are similar to all other sets of empirical pairs and may be comprehended under the definition of "2" depends not at all upon their similarity with each other or on their similarity with two logical objects. We can match similar sets without counting them but we cannot know how many members they have until we do.

In the introduction to this chapter, the view that a fundamental error which Kant makes, and which separates transcendental idealism from the philosophy presented in these pages, regards general logic as being inferential from, and therefore ontologically subordinate and limited in applicability to empirical cognition under the categories of understanding. It is readily apparent that the set-theoretic definitions and deduction of the natural numbers is based upon an error that is remarkably similar to the one made by Kant. It is, of course, the case that you can perform mathematical operations on empirical objects and it is the case that infants are taught to count using empirical objects. But that does not mean that mathematics is empirical in nature or that its independence from the empirical world is based upon mere abstraction. Infants learn to count by reference to empirical objects because communication is sensory and that is the only way we can communicate the logical relations that govern such objects to them.

6

Empirical Judgment

THE FORM OF EMPIRICAL COGNITION

In an earlier chapter, we devoted not a small amount of attention to Kant's exposition of space (largely skipping over his parallel exposition of time) and to Russell's mainstream empirical rebuttal of that exposition. It will be recalled that, in Kant's philosophy, space and time are each an *a priori* condition to the possibility of empirical appearances and as such space and time are contributions of the mind to the experience of mind-independent empirical reality, whereas, in Russell's view, empirical cognition consists of the perception of the objective relations among empirical objects as such relations actually exist in mind-independent space-time. Kant is asserting that space and time are entirely mental and that for cognition of an empirical object to be possible it must be such that it can be ordered and placed within the mind in relations that we understand to be spatial and temporal and, therefore, that we do not perceive space or time at all but, instead, we merely organize our *external* sensations within our *internal* representations of space and time. In introducing his exposition of space Kant says:

> That in an appearance which corresponds to sensation I call its matter; but that which brings about the fact that the manifold of the appearance can be ordered in certain relations, I call the form of the appearance. *Now, that in which alone sensations can be ordered and placed in a certain form cannot be sensation again.* Consequently, despite the fact that the matter of all appearance is given to us only *a posteriori*, its form must lie ready for the sensations *a priori* in the mind, and must therefore allow of being considered apart from all sensation. (Emphasis added.)[1]

Kant's refusal to allow for perception of space-time as a mind-independent reality is perfectly consistent with his unwillingness to make any assertions with respect to *noumenal* reality. If Kant is justified in his unwillingness to assert anything with respect to *things-in-themselves*, surely he is equally justified in declining any assertions as to any ultimate reality that might be understood by reason to constitute the space between empirical objects or any change in their relations (i.e., the *space-in-itself* or the *time-in-itself,*

---

1. Kant, *Critique of Pure Reason*, B34.

EMPIRICAL JUDGMENT

as it were). In other words, given the premise that we know nothing about that which affects the senses at the start of empirical cognition, it is impossible that we can know anything about the actual conditions which correspond to the possibility of sensation and the presence and absence of sensation in particular instances. However, in arguing that reason must therefore have an *a priori* representation of space, Kant apparently glosses over the distinction between a representation and a condition of a representation. It is one thing to say that for a sensation to be empirical it must be referred to reason as having mind-independent existence (i.e., not being of the cognizing self but existing of independent account and therefore being *metaphysically* (as opposed to empirically) external to the observer) but it does not follow, without more, that the means by which such independence must be understood in the process of cognition is by the *ab initio* perception of such an object as being in space. To make this point clearer, we can distinguish between the recognition of externality, defined not in terms of space, but in terms of the mind-independence of the object of a thought from the thinker and the form in which such recognition takes place, which, in the case of extended objects, is universally understood as space. In so doing, it is possible to replace Kant's pure intuition of space with a *pure intuition of externality*. Under this view, although empirical cognition starts in the same way as it does with Kant, by reason referring the sensation of an object that is independent of the self, the process is quite different because such referral does not require any internal representation of space but instead only such intuition as may be understood in terms of the basic relation of a substantive object, inherited from its progenitor logical object, to its thinker. A more practical way of making the point is that empirical objects are only knowable by referral of sensory information and that, in commencing the act of empirical cognition, it is arguable that all that reason must know is that under determination is data received from the senses.

That reason does not need to begin with an intuition of space and time as such to distinguish between internal and external cognition does not imply that Kant is wrong on the broader question of whether space and time are directly intuited as the form of empirical cognition or empirically perceived. Space and time are, as Kant asserts, conditions to the possibility of empirical objects. What we perceive when we perceive an object in space and time is not only the object but also its *relation* to ourselves and other objects, including the space around them which, upon consideration, can only be understood *as the absence of all possible objects*. Of course, what does not exist cannot be given to the senses as an empirical object or anything else, and the absence of what might exist can only be understood as the *a priori* intuition of the uninstantiated possibility of empirical objects. Consider the following example: As I look across the field outside my window I see some distance away a Norwegian spruce tree. I assess (with my mind's eye) that perhaps a dozen similarly sized Norwegian spruce trees or one large house *could possibly but do not* stand in between me and the tree at the border of the field. My faculty of sight, by virtue of which I am able to sense the existence of the Norwegian spruce tree, cannot give me any positive sensation of the absence of the two dozen possible trees any more than it can give me the positive sensation of the absence of a house that might also fill the space between me and the tree that actually exists. Indeed, the reason that I know that *nothing* stands between me and the spruce tree is that, if something did exist in between us, I would see it and it would eliminate or affect my ability to see the tree and I cannot *perceive* nothing (i.e., the absence of a thing) as an empirical object itself, although I very well can *conceive* of it as a possible but non-existing object. Neither does my faculty of sight tell me the size of the tree relative to the distance between us. My senses can only tell me what is there to be perceived; my intuition of space, that is, of the possibility of objects some of which exist and others of which do not, must supply the missing details of its relations.

That the form of my intuition of the possibility of extended objects, some of which are instantiated and others of which are not, is spatial does not mean that space, even as an internal representation, possesses the status of ontological priority and, indeed, it is one of the fundamental premises of transcendent realism that space itself is further reducible to logical objects and their relations, possible and actual. Under this understanding, that we sense space and spatial relations as we do must be regarded as a mere contingency. But there is nothing about the form of our sensation that is not utterly reducible to logic and logical relations. To see that this is so, one need only consider as an example of such a reduction of space and time the completely logical encapsulation of virtual reality within the correspondingly logically structured binary symbol manipulation of the computer.

It is hardly deniable that Kant is correct that our intuitions of space and time are essentially those of three-dimensional Euclidian geometric space in a sequential context of the fourth dimension of time. However, that the intuition of the *geometry* of space is, contrary to Kant and consistent with Russell, wholly *a priori* (and not synthetically so) can be shown using the work presented in the prequel chapter on the pure deduction of the natural numbers from the logic of logical objects. A series of numbers, such as the N-series, may be understood to represent not just a numeric sequence but also a magnitude or extent, which is commonly understood as a dimension. So, for example, the series of natural numbers may be considered as a *number line*, with each number representing a location in the linear dimension and the distance or difference between two such numbers representing a magnitude within that dimension. It will be recalled that the N-series was deduced unaxiomatically from its constituent logical objects and their attendant logical relations. In our number line, such logical objects take on a new characteristic, namely, that which is understood in geometry as a point, which is a location within the dimensions of the system in which it appears. But reason is not merely one-dimensional and, in fact, in mathematics and the disciplines which depend upon it, it is common to speak of two-dimensional space, which comprises a plane, the three-dimensional space that comprises the space of our intuition, and many more possible dimensions which underpin theoretical mathematics and physics. It is not hard to see that to locate a point in a line, a single number is needed, to locate a point in a plane, two numbers are needed, to locate a point in three-dimensional space, three numbers are needed, and to locate a point in n-dimensional space, n numbers are needed. Again, it is important to note that in each such case, the numbers representing the location of objects are wholly logical relations among wholly logical objects. If we restrict for simplicity's sake the numeric values of the points to natural numbers, then each point in a one-dimensional linear structure would be represented by such a number (e.g., 0, 1, 2 . . .), each point on a plane

EMPIRICAL JUDGMENT

would be represented by an ordered pair of such numbers (e.g., (0, 0,), (0, 1), (1, 0), (1, 1), etc.), and each point in three-dimensional space would be represented by ordered triples (e.g., (0, 0, 0), (0, 0, 1), (0, 1, 1), (1, 0, 0), etc.). In order to comprise a Euclidian structure, it is also necessary to modify the antecedent-subsequent relations of the N-series so that, in a planar space, each logical object has not one but two immediate antecedent and immediate subsequent objects, which enforces the perpendicularity and parallelism of the planar matrix, and in a three-dimensional Euclidian space, each logical object has three immediate antecedents and immediate subsequent objects, which enforces the perpendicularity and parallelism of its component planar spaces.

It is interesting to note what happens when we add additional dimensions to the three dimensions that are comprised in our spatial intuition. From a strictly mathematical standpoint, it is obvious and intuitive that to locate an object in a theoretically four-dimensional space, one need only to provide for ordered quadruples instead of ordered triples and modify the antecedent-subsequent definition to all four such immediate increments and decrements. But what does such space look like? The simple answer would be to say that it does not *look like* anything because human sensibility is such that we cannot see anything that is not extended in at least three dimensions and can only see it to the extent of such dimensions. Nevertheless, to say four-dimensional space is not accessible to our senses does not mean that it is beyond our powers of conception. Indeed, four-dimensional space may be thought of as a series of three-dimensional spaces and visualized substituting a cubic structure (such as a common die) for three-dimensional space and then locating the entirety of the cubic structure in the linear structure provided by the fourth dimension (as in a string of cubic beads).

That Einsteinian physics nevertheless suggests the desirability of treatment of space and time as a homogenous, four-dimensional unity notwithstanding the heterogeneous appearance of space and time would seem to be additional evidence that Kant is correct in his assertion that space and time are *a priori* intuitions and that Russell is incorrect in his assertion that what we experience accurately reflects reality. In support of the interpretation of space as Euclidean and time as a separate intuition, one need only review the literature prior to Einstein's exposition of the concept of space-time, in which space and time are almost universally referred to as separate intuitions and in which the Euclidean nature of space is not questioned. That is not to say that the debate about the real nature of space and time is not an ancient one. Indeed, one of the earliest recorded philosophical issues consists of whether the world is in constant flux, as Heraclitus argued, or whether motion is an illusion, as was held by Parmenides, and, historically, the main point of controversy has been, and continues to this day to be, whether time is real and exists absolutely without dependence upon the existence of any extended objects within it (this is the view of Plato) or whether time is relationally dependent upon the existence of such objects (this is the view of Aristotle). The Platonic view, that time is outside of space, is palpably incoherent, for what would it mean for time to pass while nothing in the world changed? On the other hand, the Aristotelian assertion that time is dependent upon the existence of alteration of physical objects seems equally incoherent because it renders time as the by-product of alteration the possibility of which is left unexplained. In any case, prior to the Middle Ages, both space and time were generally considered to be absolute and not relative, with the universe revolving around earth which was understood to stand motionless at its center and with time ticking away in a manner that was universally and necessarily the same for all beings at all times, and there was little disagreement between our perception of empirical reality and our understanding of the science of it. However, great men such as Copernicus, Galileo, and Einstein changed all of that and, with his development of the theory of relativity, the last irrevocably tore a rift between the form of perception and our understanding of reality.

Although our intuition of time is sequential and therefore arithmetical in nature, it is radically different than our intuition of space. We sense that objects exist in space and move about within it over time, the latter of which is not given to reason as an *external* sensation in and of itself. We do not see, hear, feel, smell, or taste time; instead, we sense the existence of extended objects and the irrepressible presence of change in them. Considered in the abstract, the most striking difference seems to be that we sense ourselves to be able to move about freely in space but that time passes inexorably and involuntarily forward. Unlike space, we intuit time as being a unidirectional phenomenon that impinges upon us without regard for our own volition. Time seems to move forward whether we like it or not; we do not intuit any innate ability to go backward in time or to control the pace at which we move forward in time. So, for example, I may go from the kitchen to the study and back again and I intuit the reality of that movement as being strictly in accord with my perception of space as unrestrictedly geometric and my perception of time as serial so that upon my return to the study I seem to be in the same place as I was when I began the short journey but at a different time.

That our intuition of time is of different character from our intuition of space is almost certainly the reason that we speak of space and time as though they are separate intuitions. But it is important to distinguish between the intuition and the actuality. I can imagine a billiard ball with all of its predicates of extension that does not change or exist in time but I cannot conceive of the existence of a real billiard ball except in time. Similarly, as I sit in my study writing these words, I know that my kitchen exists but I cannot both be here and there at the same time and if I wish to go to the kitchen I know that it will take some time to do so.

That our intuition of time as being of a completely different nature than our intuition of space, renders inapposite a simple four-dimensional geometric explanation of our intuition of time. In Kant's metaphysical exposition of time, which parallels his metaphysical exposition of space, Kant argues as follows: (1) time is not an empirical concept that in some way is derived from experience; (2) time is a necessary representation that underlies all intuitions; (3) time has only a single dimension and is successive (as distinguished from the three simultaneous dimensions of space); (4) as is the case with space, time is a pure form of sensible intuition; and (5) time is unlimited. Kant's transcendental exposition of time is especially interesting:

> Here I may add that the concept of alteration, and with it the concept of motion (as alteration of place), is possible only through and in the representation of time; and that if this representation were not an (inner) *a priori* intuition, then no concept, whatever it may be, could make comprehensible the possibility of alteration, that is of a combination of contradictorily opposed predicates in one

and the same object (for instance, the existence and nonexistence of one and the same thing, that is, one after the other).[2]

There is nothing that surprises in points (1), (2), and (4) of Kant's metaphysical exposition of time. That Kant regards time equally with space as the necessary and universal form and condition of the possibility of empirical cognition is itself necessary to make his transcendental aesthetic work. But in point (3) and his transcendental exposition of it, Kant is making a truly remarkable point, for it is here that Kant asserts that time must be understood as a condition of empirical cognition because for the presence of alteration in the world to be understood by reason there must be an *a priori* intuition *that renders possible the existence of a single object containing opposing predicates*. It must be recognized that Kant is making two different but closely related and important points. The first is that the intuition of time is not merely a condition of empirical cognition but, more precisely, it is *the condition of the possibility of alteration,* and the second is the implicitly *logical* one that for reason to understand one and the same object as having different and sometimes contrary predicates *reason must contain within itself* the ability to serialize the predication of an object while retaining its identity. It follows that if change in time was merely an empirical phenomenon, then reason would not be able to determine any logically comprehensible continuity in the objects of its cognition. That is to say if at each instant both the objects of cognition and observer, considered as the perspective from which such cognition occurs, are constantly changing, then there would be no unity from which change could be determined.

Here the compatibility of the transcendent exposition of the intuition of time with Kant's exposition is obvious: Kant's conception of time as the condition of the possibility of alternation is grounded in the principle of non-contradiction, which, it will be recalled, states that contradictory statements cannot both be true in the same sense *at the same time*. Since, under the transcendent philosophy presented in these pages logic is ontologically prior to empirical cognition, the principle of non-contradiction, which applies both to logical objects and their relations and the substantive objects (including empirical ones) which inherit from them, the only way that change over time can be understood is if the field in which it occurs is one which reason may interpret logically and serially, with the latter term being used here in its fully rigorous mathematical sense as entailing asymmetry, transitivity, and connectedness. Time, then, is not merely a fourth dimension of cognition, but it is one that imposes logical order upon the three dimensions of the intuition of spatial extension by bringing to bear upon its objects the pure logic of both the principle of non-contradiction and the laws of implication (i.e., *modus ponens* and *modus tolens*). And it follows from the foregoing that, as was the case with our intuition of space, insofar as our intuition of time is reducible to an arithmetical series of the predication of substantive objects which inherit from logical objects, it is the latter and not the former that must wear the crown of ontological priority.

---

2. Ibid., B49.

INTUITION, CONCEPTION, AND SCIENCE

So far, we have been speaking only of our *intuitions* of space and time and contrasting those intuitions with the notion that space and time are purely *a posteriori*, empirical phenomena given to the senses. For Kant, who was unwilling to allow for any knowledge of *things-in-themselves*, there could be no discussion of space and time beyond their consideration as such intuitions. But this is not the case with the transcendent understanding of reality because one of its foundational principles is that empirical reality must be sufficiently organized to be accessible to objective, logically-based cognition and therefore under transcendent realism there must be an isomorphism between the objects as determined by reason and the *things-in-themselves*, which in turn raises the question of the nature of that isomorphism.

In addressing that question, the starting point must be the human experience of space and time. As a psychosomatic unity, man's consciousness includes consciousness of his existence as an extended being. That means that man experiences space and time from within space and time. Although I may conceive of time before and after me, I cannot remove myself from the experience of time. Man's consciousness includes not only the unified perspective from which he experiences empirical reality in space and time but also his memory of that experience which is augmented over time. As a result, man not only experiences change in the objects of his empirical cognition of objects other than himself but also change in himself as a result of each such experience. So, the serial alteration of the predication of objects of cognition entails a corresponding serial alteration of the predication of the cognizing self that includes the experience of events in time, even though the cognizing entity remains a psychosomatic unity.

Because man experiences the empirical world from within it, his experience of reality is relative to himself both as an observer and as a participant and because man, in the act of cognition, organizes his empirical experience within his own internal logical framework, there can be no absolute location in space and there can be no absolute moment in time to orient cognition. That this is the case can be seen by considering cognition within the context of a representation of space and time as a set of four integer coordinates which represent locations in time and along traditionally conceived x, y, and z axes, respectively, such that the sagittal plane (front and back) is described by the y and z axes, the frontal plane (side to side) is described by the x and y axes, and the transverse plane (surrounding) is described by the x and z axes. The set will be in the form of (T, X, Y, Z) which maps (time, left or right, up and down, front or back) in accordance with the foregoing conventions. To begin with, it is important to note that there is no absolute reference point in our cognition of space and time to which we might conceptually anchor our set of coordinates. All extended objects are perceived from the standpoint of the individual observer, who for purposes of cognition is always located at the four spatio-temporal coordinates of (0, 0, 0, 0). This is especially interesting in the case of the sensation of time, because although the observer persists over time, each intuition, being relative to the observer at a moment in time, is located in the present and therefore *the observer's time coordinate is always* 0 and the time coordinates of each event that has been observed is always decrementing (or incrementing, depending upon arbitrary designation) as it recedes into the past. The respective locations in space-time of a universe of extended objects can be placed relative to the observer, which is consistent with the subjective intuition of each such observer, or to an artificially chosen reference point, such as the North Star, which is necessary for intellectual and physical commerce.

Not only is there no absolute reference point in our cognition of space and time, but there cannot be any because any such reference point would have to be outside of space and time. Because space and time are conceptually limitless, they cannot be located within "empty space" and "empty time," which would of course have to be space and time again to have any meaning. To demonstrate such to be the case, I ask you to assume the opposite and show where in absolute space-time point (0, 0, 0, 0) exists. Because there is no absolute reference point in our cognition of extended objects in space-time, it follows that space-time is merely the form in which the relationships of extension are understood. If I exist at a given time at relative space-time location (0, 0, 0, 0) and from my standpoint you are three meters in front of me, then I can locate you at coordinates (0, 0, 0, 3). But from your perspective you will be at coordinate (0, 0, 0, 0) and, if you are facing me, I will be at coordinate (0, 0, 0, 3). If there is a third person who is standing three meters behind me, then from my perspective he will be at (0, 0, 0, -3) and, from your perspective he will be at (0, 0, 0, 6). Note that not only is my cognition of space and time relative to me, but it requires that I arbitrarily assign its dimensions directionally, as in designating that which is in front of me to be placed at positive horizontal coordinates and that which is behind me to be placed at negative horizontal coordinates. So, we can see that the positions of objects in space are all relative to one another and, taking a geographical example, although we may all agree that New York is north of Philadelphia, if I am standing at any point in a line between those two cities and facing eastward, New York will be to my left and Philadelphia to my right, and if I am facing westward, the former will be to my right and the latter to my left. Similarly, the computer on which I am typing these words may be located in Mendham, New Jersey, but my experience is that the keyboard is under my hands and that the screen upon which the letters I am typing appears is approximately two feet directly in front of me. But even that measurement is utterly relative, for where in the universe does one go to determine what the magnitude of two feet is? With respect to time, the situation is even clearer. We may all agree that, as I write these words, it is 7:46 p.m., GMT, on June 27, 2015, but from the standpoint of my empirical cognition of the lines on the screen that represent them, the time is *now* and, indeed, *all of my cognition always occurs in the here and now*.

At the time of Newton and Kant, the world was understood to operate in accordance with the laws of physics which were then understood to be part of what we now call "classical relativity theory." Under those laws, motion was understood as being relative to the observer. So, for example, two people sitting at a table on a moving train would appear to one another to be stationary while, from the standpoint of an observer who is standing alongside the train track, the people on the train would appear to be moving at the same speed as the train. If a man capable of throwing a ball at ninety miles per hour stood atop the train and threw one in the direction of the train while it was moving at sixty miles per hour, to the man throwing the ball it would appear to move at ninety miles per hour while to an observer standing alongside the track the ball would appear to move at one hundred fifty miles an hour, which is the sum of the velocity of the ball and the train. Under Kant's transcendental idealism, although nothing can be known about the *things-in-themselves* presumed to act upon the senses of the actors and observers in our examples, the form of their intuition under Euclidean geometric space and internally arithmetical time is fully isomorphic with their explanation under the principles of Newtonian physics. From the standpoint of transcendental idealism, it matters not whether you are on the train or alongside the tracks on which it runs; in either case, space and time are the form of the cognition of the train and its passengers and the ball.

Under modern relativity theory, which began to be developed in the mid-nineteenth century (after Kant's death) and which is the mainstream physics of the day, classical relativity is considered to be an approximation of reality as it actually exists which is only fully adequate within the frame of reference of human beings with limited ability to move about the universe. In 1865, James Maxwell made the remarkably counterintuitive discovery that light travels at the same speed, namely 186,000 miles per second, in all directions and under all circumstances. To understand the enormous implications of Maxwell's observation, consider the example, which corresponds to the example of the man throwing a ball off of the top of a train, of an astronaut in a spaceship that is traveling at 93,000 miles per second (i.e., one-half the speed of light). If the astronaut points a flashlight in the direction in which the spaceship is traveling, the beam of light will appear to him to travel forward at 186,000 miles per second. In both the case of the man throwing the ball and the astronaut pointing the flashlight, from their perspective the laws of classical physics will hold and their perceptions will be exactly the same as if they were stationary. However, unlike in the train example, a stationary observer of the astronaut with the flashlight would not see the beam of light traveling at 279,000 miles per second (i.e., the sum of the speed of the light and the speed of the spaceship) but instead would see the light traveling at the same 186,000 miles per second that the astronaut does! Since velocity is by definition the relationship between distance and time (i.e., $v = d/t$), if the observed velocity is the same, then either the distance that the light travels or the time as measured by the observers or both must differ. And, indeed, recognizing that this is the case was the great achievement of Albert Einstein in his development of modern relativity theory. Under Einstein's theory, which has been scientifically verified many times over the ensuing decades, since the laws of physics, including the speed of light, must hold for all observers under all conditions each observer must have his own, relative experience of space and time. As a matter of scientific explanation, Einstein described space and time not as separate dimensions but as a unified, four-dimensional framework of empirical reality, which he called "space-time." Einstein's exposition includes the notion that objects "travel" through a space-time continuum and that, as one travels faster and faster through space, time increasingly slows until at the speed of light time stops altogether and distance increasingly shortens in the direction of travel until it disappears.

Oddly, Russell seized with relish on Einstein's theory as evidence that space and time are empirically real phenomena the existence of which render Kant's transcendental aesthetic invalid, while, it would seem, precisely the opposite conclusion should be drawn. In asking the question how, if space and time are the preconditions of empirical experience, it is possible that a scientific understanding of empirical reality can differ from that intuition, Russell is attempting to stand transcendental idealism on its head. The whole point of Kant's transcendental philosophy was to explain the certainty of science in an empirical world by imposing upon the empirical world the condition that it be understandable under certain *a priori* categories and forms of intuition; Russell's argument is that any valid science that is inconsistent with transcendental intuition must therefore disprove it because the science would entail cognition of facts that contradict and therefore cannot be conditioned on such intuition.

In rebuttal to Russell, as has already been observed, there is a difference between philosophical intuition and the scientific analysis that occurs under that intuition. One must take care to distinguish between a science that yields results that are not identical with the intuition of space and time and one that requires its abandonment. One also must be careful to distinguish between facts as they are given to reason via empirical cognition under the intuition of space and time and what reason tells us about those facts. Finally, one must be careful to identify the field upon which intuition operates in the cognition of empirical objects under the intuition of space and time and the field upon which science is operating when it purports to yield results that are incompatible with that intuition.

In furtherance of these points, it is worth considering the relationship between philosophical intuition and scientific knowledge, first with respect to space and second with respect to relativity. We begin by noting that there exists a modern (but heavily contested) notion that empirical space is, contrary to human intuition, non-Euclidean. At the time of Kant, geometry and Euclidian geometry, which was developed circa 300 BC, constituted one and the same body of understanding and non-Euclidean geometry did not exist. Euclidian geometry is based upon five axioms:

1. A straight line segment can be drawn joining any two points.

2. Any straight line segment can be extended indefinitely to form a straight line.

3. Given any straight line segment, a circle can be drawn having the segment as radius and one endpoint as center.

4. All right angles are congruent.

5. If two lines are drawn which intersect a third in such a way that the sum of the inner angles on one side is less than two right angles, then the two lines inevitably must intersect each other on that side if extended far enough.

In Euclidean geometry, by virtue Euclid's fifth axiom, given a straight line and a point outside of it, there will always be one and only one line that can be drawn through that point which will be parallel to, and never intersect, the reference line. For more than two millennia, it appeared to mathematicians that Euclid's fifth axiom should be demonstrable from the first four axioms. However, after all that time and much effort by many leading mathematicians no such proof had been found and in the nineteenth century mathematicians began to explore other axiomatic geometric systems which included alternatives to Euclid's fifth axiom. Two such systems, which are relevant to the current inquiry, are hyperbolic geometry, in which many lines may be drawn through the point outside the line, each of which curves hyperbolically farther away from the others as the distance from the point increases; the other is elliptical geometry, in which each line drawn through the point curves elliptically toward the others, finally intersecting with them so that it is impossible to draw a line through the point that does not intersect with it (this requires a special interpretation of what is meant by straight line). In parabolic geometry the space described by its postulates is saddle-shaped and in elliptical geometry the space described by its postulates is circular. It was found that both parabolic and elliptical geometry could be applied to empirical experience within the limits of scientific investigation to yield results that were consistent with that experience. As a result, certain empirical philosophers, Russell among them, gleefully argued that, given the presence of multiple, contradictory geometric systems that appeared to conform to reality, it was no longer possible for Kantian philosophers to maintain their foundational argument that geometry was a synthetic *a priori* science and, instead, geometry could only be regarded as pure mathematics. Interestingly, and importantly, after the development of Einstein's relativity theory in the early 1900s, gravity came to be conceived as resulting from the curvature of space around massive objects and the question of whether space-time is flat (i.e., Euclidian), parabolic, or elliptical became an important focus of cosmology in the twentieth century.

The crux of the philosophical challenge posed by Russell to Kant's synthetic *a priori* theory of Euclidian geometry seems to be that if it turns out that the universe is not flat, then even if Euclidian geometry is derived from nearby empirical experience, because it does not accurately describe reality on a cosmological scale, it cannot be universally and necessarily applied in the empirical domain to explain scientific certainty and, further, that the necessity and universality of Euclidian geometry, which follows logically from its five axioms can only be regarded as a purely mathematical system on the basis of such axioms. This can be expressed in another way, which is that Russell is asserting that Kant's system requires that intuitive space and time and scientific space and time be one and the same. However, as long as intuitive and scientific space and time are able to coincide without contradiction, it would seem that the presence of other geometric systems does not subvert Kant because it can hardly be argued that such other systems provide the form of human empirical cognition. In other words, if one can understand a scientifically non-Euclidian space in intuitively Euclidian terms, then the former does not require abandonment of the latter or undercut its *philosophical* importance. And, indeed, such is the case under consideration. One need only consider that to understand elliptical geometry one typically draws a globe or parabolas *on a flat surface* (which one intuits in the usual Euclidian way), and then proceeds to draw lines and measure angles of intersection on it to demonstrate how they behave in non-Euclidian space. To be more clear, we do not directly intuit space in any form other than Euclidian; for example, in elliptical geometry a straight line is defined and understood as a *great circle* and is given to the senses as a circle intuited in Euclidean space.

There is an important distinction between cognition of facts under philosophical principles and scientific analysis of facts of such cognition. For example, that astronomically heavy objects bend Euclidian-intuited space and in doing so cause the visual siting of stars whose light passes nearby to such objects to be physically offline is nevertheless understood in the Euclidian terms of its intuition, even though that understanding depends upon conceptually bending what is provided by reason in the act of cognition as normal Euclidian space. Contrast the example of a curveball thrown by a major league pitcher which, like the bent starlight, moves in a curved line without apparent external affect. In both cases, reason demands a logical explanation for their departure from the expected linear motion and it turns out that the explanations are quite different but completely compatible with science and philosophy. The curveball curves because of the spin on it as it moves through the air. The starlight bends because the space in which it travels is best understood to bend under the influence of gravity. The two explanations are not at all inconsistent and work under a Euclidean intuition of space. The point to be made is that we expect that objects in space will behave in accordance with philosophical intuition of our understanding of it; when their behavior is observed by science to depart from such expected behavior it is noted to be anomalous and investigation and analysis is made to bring the actual behavior under a satisfactory scientific theory but such observation does not require wholesale reconsideration of our epistemology unless the scientific theory is shown to be valid and incompatible with our philosophical understanding of the intuition of space in which science makes it observations. Kant is not saying that there can be no departures from Euclidian behavior; what he is saying is that there can be no departures from such behavior by objects of empirical cognition that cannot be explained in Euclidean terms.

The final reason for the failure of Russell's argument is that, even if at universal scope space is curved, over the field of natural sensory cognition there is no difference between a Euclidian and non-Euclidian interpretation of reality and, indeed, the circumference of a circle as large as that which might be represented by the outer reaches of space is, for purposes of empirical cognition, a straight line.

Examination of the compatibility of our intuition of space and time with modern relativity theory yields a similar conclusion. Whether it is heuristically desirable to unify space and time in understanding the laws of physics applied to events occurring at high speeds has no bearing on whether our cognitive intuition of extended objects is of a strictly Euclidean geometry and an internal time that is intuitively absolute even though science tells us it is relative. To the astronaut on our spaceship the laws of physics remain intact and his experience is not that time is slowing down as he moves ever faster; instead, the world external to the spaceship appears to be moving faster! Moreover, one need only consult the literature by which difficult, counterintuitive theories such as Einstein's relativity are explained to novice readers to see that they inevitably consist of the mapping of those theories to the basic terms of our ordinary intuition of space and time, precisely as given to us by Kant. For example, consider the idea of a space-time continuum in which everything that ever existed, now exists, and will exist, is contained at once. This idea, which is part of mainstream relativity, is far from our everyday intuition. Yet, that it is fully isomorphic with that intuition can be seen from the common heuristic description of the continuum as a series of connected space-time slices (akin to a loaf of bread). From that description, it is explained that two motionless people, far apart in the universe, may be said to exist on the same space-time slice, but, as one moves relative to the other, the space-time slice of the person in motion either cuts in diagonally in front (if the person in motion approaches) or diagonally behind (if the person in motion moves away from) the one who is stationary. That the concept of the continuum is inconsistent with our intuition of space and time and our perception of objects within it is beyond a doubt; nevertheless, such an arcane theoretical understanding can only be presented to reason in a manner that is isomorphic to our Euclidean/arithmetical intuition of space and time. In support of this fundamental idea one need only be reminded that the just-described explanation of the space-time continuum of modern relativity theory is analogous to the description of an ordinary loaf of bread and the direction in which it is sliced! Or consider the example of the heuristic description of the effect of the velocity of movement within the space-time continuum, which is typically given on a simple two-axis graph. In the description, the y-axis represents space (reducing its three dimensions to one) and the x-axis represents time. If one is stationary, he is described to be moving exclusively through time, which is depicted as a line that follows along the x-axis. At the other extreme, if one moves at the speed of light, then he is described to be moving exclusively through space, which is depicted as a line that follows along the y-axis, with the result that for him, time stops (i.e., all external objects appear to freeze in space). Again, that the concept of our perception of time speeding up or slowing as we move about the universe is counter-intuitive cannot be doubted; yet its presentation to reason is given in a manner that is isomorphic to our Euclidean/arithmetical intuition of space and time, which in this case utilizes a simple graph that an elementary school child can understand.

In attempting to rebut Kant's transcendental aesthetic by demonstrating the inconsistency between the science of space-time and Kant's description of space and time as being the *a priori* forms of cognition of empirical objects, Russell appears to be misconstruing Kant's assertion that space and time are conditions of empirical cognition without which no empirical phenomenon could ever arise. Russell's argument is that if scientific space-time differs from the *a priori* form of the intuition of space and time and yet we still have empirical cognition, then space-time must be extant in the real world on a mind-independent basis. But the rebuttal to Russell has already been made. The *a priori* form of space and time governs the cognition of empirical objects as the condition of their possibility; their behavior must accord to physical laws that are isomorphic with the form of their cognition. In other words, Kant's edict is only that in order for objects to be cognizable they must be *determinable* under the forms of human intuition (in the case of space, Euclidean geometry), even if, strictly speaking, the rules governing their physical behavior as phenomena are different (in the case of physical space at cosmological scope, perhaps, non-Euclidean geometry) and the problem of which Russell attempts to make so much only arises if the science of space-time contradicts the *a priori* intuition of space and time, which Kant would assert, and with which we agree, is impossible.

Before moving on, it should be noted that Russell's argument, even if persuasive, is of only parochial significance to transcendental idealism because it is, in any event, inapposite to transcendent realism. In the philosophy presented in these pages, logic, and not empirical cognition, is paramount and the logicism of mathematics, including Euclidian geometry which is the form of the intuition of the spatial dimensions of space and time, requires that for reality to be at all intelligible, it must be, and be understood to be, strictly logical. In transcendent realism, it matters not whether scientific space-time is best understood against a spherical template that is given to reason as Euclidean because, under all conceivable circumstances, the rules of logic must govern both.

It was briefly mentioned only a few moments ago that modern relativity theory regards space and time as a unified continuum in which all things that have ever existed, now exist, or will in the future exist, are permanent. This understanding requires the further conclusion that our intuition of space and time is an illusion and the acceptance of the notion that reality constitutes a completed infinity. It will be recalled that this was precisely the position of Leibniz, whose philosophy predates modern relativity theory by more than one hundred years. Although Leibniz's complete metaphysics yields an infinity of windowless monads, each of which experiences reality in a divinely conducted symphony that is difficult to accept, his fundamental concept and that of modern relativity theory of the permanence of objects is certainly theoretically possible precisely because of its isomorphism with our *a priori* intuition of space and time. However, as will be discussed in the sequel chapter, I do not believe that the idea of a completed infinity is conceptually coherent or, even if it were, that it would be empirically possible, and, in my admittedly lay understanding of modern physics, I do not believe that Einstein's relativity theory necessitates the conclusion that the entire history (past, present, and future) of the universe exists all at once as a fully determined unity. Under modern relativity theory, an astronaut traveling toward us at the speed of light from a distance four light-years away will, from our perspective, arrive in four years although from his perspective his trip will take no time at all. It is argued from this by some modern physicists that because what is four years in the future for us as stationary entities is the present from the perspective of the astronaut the future must already exist. But this is far from clear for at least three reasons. One is that if time stops for the light-speed traveling astronaut, then it would seem that he can no longer be said to be *in time* (or, therefore, *in space* either) during his trip (i.e., he must cease to exist as a spatio-temporal entity). From the perspective of the astronaut, it is we who cease to exist for the duration of his trip, which of course cannot be the case because we are stationary entities. A second, closely related reason which seems to buttress the view shared by Kant and transcendent realism that time is the condition of the possibility of change is that for the astronaut traveling at the speed of light *no change is possible*. The third reason is foundational to transcendent realism and identical to the one leveled against the idea of the multi-verse, namely that as a psychosomatic unity who continuously experiences reality from a single (albeit serially progressing) point in space and time it is not possible for me to exist in more than one place and time separately from my consciousness of them.

Certain implications of Kant's treatment of space and time buttress the argument of transcendent realism against his placement of the categories of understanding as ontologically prior to general logic. For Kant, space is undeniably of geometric nature and time is undeniably arithmetical in nature and both are provided by reason *a priori* as a precondition of empirical cognition. Kant is concerned with showing how we experience mathematics empirically but understand from that experience the necessity and universality of mathematics as a science precisely because of the *apriority* of space and time. That is the basis of Kant's claims that arithmetical and geometry are synthetic *a priori*. If Kant is correct, it seems that he cannot hold that the logical judgments associated with the categories are of understanding are mere abstractions from them because space and time (and therefore the logic of mathematics) are preconditions to empirical cognition under the categories and must therefore be prior to the categories. Because of the special nature of space and time as a precondition to such experience, Kant appropriately omits space and time and the related mathematical judgments from the categories of understanding and the table of judgments. It follows that the mathematical logic that underpins space and time must be ontologically prior to any empirical understanding and, indeed, this is one of the foundational principles of transcendent realism.

In transcendent realism, the description of the structure of the intuition of empirical objects is similar to the one that was described in the context of computerized productions of virtual reality. Logical objects, being uniquely enhandled and orderable, may be arranged by reason across any number of dimensions. As is the case with Kant's incorrect pure intuition of space and time, our logical matrix is a pure intuition which is ready to be populated with both the empirical objects and the absence of such objects given to us by the senses. We are left with a separate intuition of space and time, each of which is logically mathematical in structure, and both of which are necessarily unified as the form of intuition of empirical objects. Unlike transcendental idealism, which depends upon synthetic *a priori* reason, transcendent realism requires that reality must be ordered so that pure reason, which is part of a logical reality that is not materially limited, finds what it needs for cognition when it considers what is given to the senses. Under transcendent realism, the universe is governed by the *Logos,* including the ontologically prior logical relations that govern theoretical reason and cognition in space-time and, accordingly, the world cannot behave illogically because such would be incomprehensible and any apparent inconsistencies between reason and reality must be interpreted as reflecting a deficiency in scientific knowledge which requires further investigation to be understood.

CAUSALITY AND IMPLICATION

As has been emphasized from time to time in these pages, Kant's development of transcendental idealism was substantially motivated by his desire to respond to Hume's extreme skepticism generally and in particular to Hume's dismantling of causality. The gist of Hume's position is that close examination of two events in a sequence that are presumed to be causally connected yields that the purported cause and effect are such completely different events that the former cannot be found to exist in the latter. Kant's response is typically brilliant; instead of seeking the cause in the effect, Kant finds causality in reason itself as an organizing concept of the understanding, which he closely associates with the aesthetic of time. As was noted a moment ago, for Kant, time is a *form* of empirical cognition that allows an object to have serially contradictory predication without losing its identity. It follows that all change (succession) of appearances consists in alteration, as distinguished from coming into being and ceasing to be, because if it were otherwise the appearance and disappearance of different predicates would entail the appearance and disappearance of the objects to which they attach (including their ground and their enhandlement). In such event, reason would not be able to determine the existence of any unified objects over time and reality would be correspondingly chaotic and incoherent.

Since, for Kant, all cognition of empirical objects is the apprehension of appearances that are given to the senses and not of *things-in-themselves*, the perception of successive appearances entails the connection by the imagination of two perceptions in time, which is an internal representation and not an empirically observable phenomenon. If reality is to be objective (and solipsism is to be avoided) the connection of appearances must occur according to an objective rule. Such a concept, under which synthetic unity of appearances may be accomplished by the imagination, must be *a priori* because it cannot be contained in the perception which is dependent upon it and is known as the law of cause and effect. Kant says:

> Experience itself, therefore, that is, an empirical knowledge of appearances, is possible only by our subjecting the succession of appearances, and with it all alteration, to the law of causality; and appearances themselves, as objects of experience, are consequently possible only in accordance with this law.[3]

Kant notes that the apprehension of the manifold of appearance is always successive and distinguishes between the apprehension of the appearance of an object, such as a house, and an event, which is the coming into existence of an object or a state which did not exist at an earlier time. In the former case, the order in which the object is understood is at the discretion of the observer in the sense that the observer may, for example, survey the object in any chosen order (e.g., up, down, left, right). In the latter case, no discretion is involved and the cognition of an event constitutes the apprehension of a perception following upon another perception in conformity with an objective rule of cognition. Even where apprehension is subjective in order, as is the case with the house, it must consist of apprehension of an underlying objective succession of appearances. Thus understood, the law of causality gives order and objectivity to understanding of the succession of appearances and, without causality, all apprehension would be utterly subjective. Kant also distinguishes between the empirical causation of science, which is discovered by repeated empirical observation and only tentatively universal in character, and the *a priori* causation which governs the apprehension of the appearance of objects and events which constitute the reality upon which scientific analysis may be performed. In other words, for empirical cognition to occur events must be causally related even if science has not yet determined in a particular case what the scientific cause actually is.

Kant's response to Hume is devastating in its scope. Instead of attempting to show that causally related events have particular commonalities from which they may be inferred, Kant asserts that causation is a necessary and universal law of the sensibility of objects in the first place, with the determinate place of objects in the temporal series of events being based upon *the presupposition of antecedent causes and subsequently caused events*:

> If, then, it is a necessary law of our sensibility, and therefore a formal condition of all perceptions, that a preceding time necessarily determines the succeeding time (because I cannot arrive at the succeeding time except through the preceding one), then it is also an indispensable law of the empirical representation of the series of time that the appearances of past time determine every existence in

3. Ibid., B234.

succeeding time; and that these existences, as events, cannot take place except insofar as the appearances of past time determine their existence in time, that is, fix it by a rule. For it is only in appearance that we can know empirically this continuity in the coherence of times.[4]

We take Kant's account of causation as essentially correct insofar as it is summarized here (there are additional aspects of Kant's characterization not addressed here which go beyond the philosophy of transcendent realism) with the usual caveats that should now be expected of transcendent realism, namely, that the appearance of causation in time reflects the ontologically prior logical rules that govern all objects and their relations, the mathematics of space and time, and in particular the principle of sufficient reason, the principle of non-contradiction and *modus ponens* and *modus tolens*. With this understanding, we are in a position to complete the discussion of the form of empirical cognition under wholly logical terms. We take as given to us as really existing in the world objects that may be understood by reason in wholly logical terms. The objects of empirical cognition are substantive objects that inherit from logical progenitors. Their predication must be such that they may be ordered by reason in space and time under an utterly logical structure. That structure includes the geometry of Euclidian space and the arithmetically serial alteration of predication in time both of which operate under the principle of non-contradiction and the rules of implication. The existence and predication of objects and events must occur serially, objects cannot have and not have contradictory predicates at the same time and cannot be in two places at once. That which is experienced in the empirical world and understood in scientific terms must be reducible in form and substance to the terms of logic. To be sure, logic does not create empirical reality but it absolutely and completely governs reason's access to it and, indeed, Being and intelligibility are one and the same.

COGNITION UNDER LOGICAL CONCEPTS

As has been repeatedly emphasized, it is central to the thesis of transcendent realism that because theoretical reason is the logical antecedent to the form and categories of empirical cognition, knowledge does not stop at the borderline of sensation. Therefore, if we are to assert the applicability of logic to all thought and the existence of an empirical reality that must correspond to empirical cognition, we must answer the question of how logical concepts apply to cognition of objects in space-time.

It was noted earlier that Kant's categories of understanding are taken largely from Aristotle's foundational work and it is worth taking a moment to identify that great philosopher's taxonomy. Aristotle identifies ten classifications which he intends to encompass everything that may be said about simple objects and which, therefore, may be the subject or predicate of a proposition. The ten Aristotelian categories (it must be mentioned that, as to some, I have been so presumptuous to employ my own nomenclature) are: (1) substance, (2) quantity, (3) quality, (4) relation, (5) spatial *locus*, (6) temporal

---

4. Ibid., B244

locus, (7) attitude (i.e., position, posture, attitude for action), (8) condition (i.e., state of having been affected), (9) affecting, and (10) under effect.

The table of Kant's categories of understanding and associated logical judgments has been set forth previously in these pages.[5] As has already been presented, Kant's categories appear under the four main headings of quantity, quality, relation, and modality. Several observations on Kant's tables will be useful to set the table for discussion from the perspective of transcendent realism. First, the obvious must be stated, namely, that the tables not only represent an integral part of the elucidation of transcendental idealism but they are also predicated on the validity of the transcendental approach. That is to say, if it is not the case that in the process of empirical cognition the mind brings to sense data certain *a priori* concepts which dictate the process, then the tables are of no validity. Second, given that the Kantian categories are the concepts under which the logical judgments are made with respect to representations that are already given to reason under the intuition of space and time, to avoid redundancy Kant appropriately omits from Aristotle's list those which are spatio-temporal in nature. In other words, because space and time are the forms of empirical cognition and not themselves sensible, empirical cognition represents categorization via logical judgments that are spatio-temporalized in character before they even appear to the senses. Third, Kant's table reflects logic as it was understood at Kant's time, which was without significant advancement from the time of Aristotle. Since Kant, logic has undergone robust development, including evolution from the categorical and nascent propositional logic available to Kant to first and second order predicate logic, which has been used by Kant's critics to call into question the efficacy of Kant's tables. Fourth, Kant completely omits mathematical relations from his table, which again is appropriate under the assumptions of transcendental idealism because of Kant's characterization of mathematics as synthetic *a priori* and not purely logical. Finally, it should be noted that there are alternative theories to Kant's logic-based theory of empirical cognition, including those as ancient as Plato's theory of Ideas, and modern psychological ones.

Kant's tables represent one of the ways in which a core compatibility of transcendent realism and transcendental idealism may be clearly seen because under both philosophies empirical cognition occurs by spontaneously logical judgments in space and time. In this regard, it should come as no surprise that under transcendent realism, the logic-based approach is ratified on the grounds that cognition is a rational function that can only be conducted under the rules of thought as understood in their operation upon substantive objects as inheritors of logical objects. Under transcendent realism, empirical objects, being as they are descendants of logical objects, are given to reason as enhandled and can only be understood in a manner that is consistent with the rules of thought just as is the case with respect to their logical progenitors. However, unlike their logical progenitors, empirical objects are given to reason within the framework of space and time which, although themselves mathematically logical, provide the framework for determination of substantive objects to which sensory predicates must attach. So the question for transcendent realism is: How does reason start with purely logical objects and relations and apply its rules to the appearances given to the senses?

---

5. See Table 1, 63, and subsequent discussion.

The transcendent view is similar to the transcendental one insofar as empirical cognition is regarded as entailing logical judgments under spatio-temporal categories but, placing logic first as the transcendent philosophy does, such categories are wholly derivative of logic and not vice versa. Although, as has been said, Kant's omission of the spatio-temporal categories and judgments from his table is consistent with his division of cognition between the transcendental aesthetic of space and time and the transcendental analytic, that rationale is inapplicable to the transcendent cognition because the logic which underpins transcendent cognition operates across the entire field of rational experience, including the logical construction of space and time. So, the transcendent table of judgments must start with logic and show its application in space and time and, to do so, must include the transcendent logic upon which the spatio-temporal framework is based.

In order to appropriately present the concepts of cognition under transcendent realism, two tables will be required. The first table, shown below as Table 2, will contain the core constitutional concepts of logical and empirical objects considered solely as such. The second table, shown below as Table 3, will present the concepts of general logic and their application in space and time in the cognition of empirical objects.

Table 2—Constitutional Concepts of Logical and Empirical Objects and Relations			
		Logical Objects and Relations	Empirical Objects and Relations
	(A)	(B)	(C)
(1)	Identity	Uniquely enhandled logical object (under principles of identity and identity of indiscernibles)	Uniquely enhandled, synthetically unified object extended in space-time
(2)	Predication	Logical predication	Substantive predication
(3)	Relation to thinker	Internal object of reason	External object given to reason as sensible
(4)	Relation to self	Uniquely enhandled object	Synthetically unified object
(5)	Relation to other objects	Logically related	Spatio-temporally related under rule of causation in time
(6)	Non-contradiction	Logical consistency under the principle of non-contradiction	Consistency of predication at each instant

The concepts presented in Table 2 were introduced in the discussion of general logic in the prequel chapter. It will be recalled that logical objects are uniquely enhandled objects of thought the predication of which is limited exclusively to *a priori* logical relations and relations to self (as grounded predication), as a thinkable entity capable of bearing such predicates and being in relation to thinker and such other logical objects as reason may, in its discretion, determine. Logical objects are unified, individual, and indivisible *logical substance*. Empirical objects, as descendants of logical objects, inherit unique enhandlement, relation to thinker as a mind-independent external object of empirical cognition, and the possibility of relation to other empirical objects. Empirical objects are synthetically unified in the process of cognition and are entities capable of bearing all of the rich predication of sensibility.

Logical concepts may be arranged mathematically to produce the N-series (i.e., the natural numbers) and geometrically, to produce an internal *a priori* Euclidean matrix as the field upon which reason may arrange logical and empirical objects as well as the form in which their empirical cognition occurs. Following Kant, empirical cognition occurs when reason refers an appearance as being external but with one crucial difference. Under transcendental idealism, such externality is determined by immediate location in space and time, whereas under transcendent realism, such externality is determined by mere reference of an appearance as originating in the senses on a mind-independent basis and the placement of an empirical object in space and time occurs as part of the spontaneous act of cognition under logical concepts.

Finally, a few words about the application of the laws of thought to logical objects and to empirical objects as extended in space and time. With respect to logical objects, the principles of identity and non-contradiction are of especial importance to the identity of a logical object and its unique enhandlement and to its logical predicates to the extent that they are considered as logical objects in their own right. The applicability of *modus ponens* and *modus tolens* and other rules of thought to logical objects are known by direct intuition. With respect to empirical objects, the principle of identity applies across time as a result of its synthetic unity without which such objects could not be understood at all, and the principle of non-contradiction applies to their predication at any given instant but not across time; taken together, these two logical rules give empirical objects their unity in cognition but their characteristic of constant change and provide reason with a *sense of the passage of time* even though time itself is an *a priori* condition of empirical cognition and is not itself sensible. Lastly, of the other rules governing logical relations, *modus ponens* and *modus tolens*, considered together as the rules of implication, apply in space and time as the philosophical causality which Kant so aptly recognizes and describes as the principle according to which reason arranges the series of temporal appearances given to it in sensation.

We are now in a position to present in tabular form a logic-based categorization of the concepts of theoretical understanding. It should be anticipated by now that the table will start with logical judgments and describe their relation to corresponding judgments in space and time.

	(A)	(B)	(C)
	Logical Concept	Logical Formulation	Empirical Judgments
Quantity			
(1)	Universality	$(\forall x)$	Unity
(2)	Particularity	$(\exists x)$	Singularity or Plurality
(3)	Negation	$\neg(\exists x)$	Negation
Quality			
(4)	Predicated	$(\forall x) Fx$ or $(\exists x) Fx$	Existence
(5)	Unpredicated	$\neg(\exists x) Fx$	Non-Existence
Relation			
(6)	Categorical	Fx	Substance or Inherence
(7)	Conditionality	$x \rightarrow y$	Causality and Dependence
(8)	Disjunctive (excluded middle)	$Px \vee Qx$	Community (reciprocity)
(9)	Conjunctive	$Px \wedge Py$	Community (complementation)
(10)	Arithmetical	$x > y; x < y; x = y$	Temporal (before, after, contemporaneously)
(11)	Geometric	$x > y; x < y; x = y$	Spatial (location, magnitude, proportion)
Modality			
(12)	Necessity	$\Box x$ (directly or analytically intuited)	Permanent in Being
(13)	Contingency	$\Diamond x \wedge Ax \vee \neg Ax$	Temporary in Being

Table 3—Logical and Empirical Judgments

Table 3 is similar in purpose to the Table 1, which contains Kant's categories of understanding and his table of judgments insofar as Table 3 contains a taxonomy of logical judgments in narrative (Column A) and logical (Column B) form and the related empirical judgments (Column C). In Table 3, such judgments are broken down into the same four groupings as appear in Table 1, namely, Quantity, Quality, Relation, and Modality. However, the placement of logical judgements in Column B ahead of the corresponding empirical concepts in Column C, Table 3, reflects the prioritization under transcendent realism of general logic over the concepts under which empirical cognition occurs. Ironically, it will be recalled that although the ontological prioritization is reversed in transcendental idealism Kant starts with general logic first as the principle by which assurance can be had that no empirical categories are being omitted. By comparison, the

EMPIRICAL JUDGMENT

Table of Logical and Empirical Judgments of transcendent realism has the advantage of being consistent in concept and the manner in which it is formulated.

With respect to the judgments of Quantity, the quantification alternatives of predicate calculus, namely, all, some, and none, are sufficient to yield the full scope of the corresponding empirical judgments. The first two such judgments listed in Table 3, namely, Unity and Plurality, correspond with Kant's Categories. The third logical judgment in Table 3, that of negation, translates to an assertion that no object having relevant predication exists. In Kant's categorization, negation is listed under the grouping of Quality, which presumably reflects Kant's focus on predication and his assertion that empirical qualities have magnitude that ranges from reality down to negation by degrees. The reason that negation is included under the Quantity grouping in Table 3 is that under transcendent realism, thought relates to *enhandled objects* not mere predicates or predicate groups and therefore, existence and nonexistence is determined by reference to a logical object, which may include a predicate if considered as such and not unattached predicates. The treatment in Table 3 is also consistent with the quantification rules of predicate calculus. Omitted from Table 3 is Kant's third concept of Quantity, namely Totality, which Kant asserts is a necessary combination of Unity and Plurality but which, to the extent I understand it, seems to be an unnecessary complexity.

In predicate calculus, all predication under consideration in any particular case either attaches to all, some, or no objects. Therefore, with respect to a particular quality an object may be said either to be predicated or unpredicated of it. Thus, under the grouping of Quality, Table 3 includes only the ideas of *predicated* and *unpredicated*, which are asserted to be correlated to the existence or nonexistence of the predicate of its object. Under Kant's categorization, quality-judgments are reality, negation, and their supposed combinatory limitation.

With respect to Relation, Table 3 includes, under slightly variant nomenclature, the three relational categories of transcendental idealism plus three additional categories, namely, conjunctive, arithmetical, and geometric. The conjunctive category of general logic is correlated with the empirical judgment that two objects belong together, not as alternatives, but as complements, and also provides the underlying logic of set membership. The arithmetical and geometric relations have already been treated at length and they comprise all of the empirical judgments of extension in space time.

Finally, with respect to Modality, Kant's three categories of possibility-impossibility, existence-nonexistence, and necessity-contingency, have been reduced in Table 3 to the two categories of necessity and contingency to reflect that all objects of thought are either necessary, in which case, they must obtain and be self-justifying, or contingent, in which case, they might or might not obtain and are conditional. Necessity is correlated with self-instantiating permanence and contingency is correlated with conditionally instantiated impermanence in the empirical world. It is an open question whether any necessary empirical object exists. Kant's concept of existence or nonexistence, which he famously asserts in opposition to ontological proofs of the existence of God as not being a predicate but a modality, has been eliminated from the Modality group because it is included in the Quantity group as being fundamental to quantification under predicate logic.

There are other important differences been the judgments of transcendent realism and transcendental idealism, which require renewed reference to Kant's presentation first. In *Critique of Pure Reason*, the Table of Judgments and the Table of the Categories of the Understanding are only the beginning of Kant's exposition of the process of empirical cognition. Subsequent to the presentation of the judgments and categories, Kant proceeds through an obscure and difficult elucidation of the *schema* of the concepts (of categorical understanding), which represent the process of the imagination by which disparate and unorganized sensory appearances are subsumed under the concepts in the process of cognition. For Kant, all cognition of objects, the appearances of which are *ab initio* referred by reason to be externally located in space and time, occurs sequentially as part of the internal representation of time. Kant concludes that the schemata of each category yield the internal representations of time:

> [I]n the case of the schema of magnitude, the production (synthesis) of time itself, in the successive apprehension of an object; in the case of the schema of quality, the synthesis of sensation (perception) with the representation of time, or the filling of time; in the case of the schema of relation, the relation of perceptions to one another at all times (that is, according to a rule of the determination of time); lastly, in the case of the schema of modality and its categories, time itself, as the correlate of the determination of an object as to whether and how it belongs to time.[6]

Kant concludes:

> The schemata, therefore, are nothing but *a priori* determinations of time according to rules; and these rules, as applied to all possible objects, refer in the order of the categories to the series of time, the content of time, the order of time and, lastly, the sum total of time.[7]

So far, Kant has set forth the concepts and process of empirical cognition but it remains for Kant to provide the principles under which the process occurs. Kant tells us that the general principle of application of the category of quantity to appearances is that *all intuitions are extensive magnitudes*. With respect to application of the category of quality, Kant tells us that the principle is that *in all appearances the real, which is an object of sensation, has intensive magnitude, that is a degree*. With respect to the category of relations, Kant offers a general principle and three so-called *analogies of experience*.[8] The general principle is: *experience is possible only through the representation of a necessary connection of perceptions*. The three analogies are: *in all change of appearances substance is permanent and its quantum in nature is neither increased nor diminished; all alterations take place according to the law of the connection of cause and effect;* and *all substances, insofar as they can be perceived as simultaneous in space, are in thoroughgoing interaction*.[9] Finally, with respect to the category of modality, Kant offers three postulates of empirical thought in general, namely: *that which agrees with the formal conditions of experience (in*

---

6. Kant, *Critique of Pure Reason*, B184.
7. Ibid., B184–85.
8. Ibid., B202–8.
9. Ibid., B218–65.

intuition and in concepts) is possible; that which is connected with the material conditions of experience (with sensation) is actual; and that the connection of which with the actual is determined in accordance with universal conditions of experience is (exists as) necessary.[10]

Transcendent realism is compatible with transcendental idealism insofar as they both understand judgment under logical rules of thought as reason's main cognitive faculty and empirical judgment as entailing the ordering of sensible representation under logical concepts. However, transcendent realism, by placing general logic ontologically prior to the form of empirical cognition and the empirical concepts under which cognition takes place, averts any need to explain, on a philosophical basis, the process by which the mind associates the rules of thought with the objects of cognition. Starting as it does from the standpoint that all knowledge is of directly intuited logical objects or their descendants and their respective relations, transcendent realism provides reason with the power to think empirically in terms of space and time, which can be fully understood in such terms and, given transcendent realism's assertion of the essential orderliness of empirical reality, under transcendent realism reason may naturally associate substantive objects (as descendants of logical objects) with the representations that are real, empirical correlates of such objects. Contrary to transcendental idealism, the *a priori* geometric idea of a circle under which Kant's plate is understood as such is in fact in the circularity of the plate itself in an unknowably direct or correlate form. A plate on the table before me is understood as a uniquely enhandled object that is: (1) singular (Quantity); (2) predicated of those necessary and contingent properties of a plate, including, for example, circularity and flatness, and unpredicated of those properties which would preclude it from being understood as a plate (Quality); (3) comprising the essential and incidental plate-properties given in their representations (Relation); and (4) contingently persistent for a limited time (Modality). The organic and imaginative processes by which I come to judge that the plate is before me, the accuracy of the representations upon which my judgement is based, and the importance which I attach to the presence of the plate are all physical and/or psychological but the epistemological process by which I judge that such representations are of a plate is wholly and objectively logical.

10. Ibid., B265–74.

7

Infinity, Countability, And Self-Reference

THE PROBLEM OF INFINITY

Of all of the problems of philosophy, none has caused more persistent difficulty than that of the existence, the nature, and the metaphysical and epistemological implications of the infinite. Of course, that the problem of the infinite has continued through the ages without resolution hardly renders it unique among philosophical concerns. What distinguishes the problem of the infinite is not its intractability but that it impinges upon so many diverse areas of philosophical inquiry. For example, without having decided upon a particular conception of the infinite, one cannot adequately address the nature of space (e.g.: Is it finite or infinite? Is it infinitely divisible?) or time (e.g.: Did it have a beginning? Will it ever end? Is it infinitely divisible?), the cause of the existence of the universe or the reason for the existence of the particular universe in which we find ourselves (e.g.: Did the universe have a beginning? If so, what came before it? Does the multiverse exist?), the idea of God (e.g.: How are the omniscience, omnipotence, and omnipresence of God reconcilable with an empirical reality that appears to be finite and includes pain and evil? If God is omnipresent, then is he immanent, and why do we not have continual empirical experience of him?), the idea of substance (e.g.: Is there anything in or behind empirical objects that is not divisible or are all things infinitely divisible?), and the idea of immortality (e.g.: Does man have an eternal existence, that is, a soul, that exists outside of space and time?)

Although contemporary discussion of the infinite tends to have at its core a mathematical focus, such has not always been the case.[1] In Ancient Greece, the idea of the infinite, known as *apeiron*, appears in the seventh century BC, in the philosophy of Anaximander as the limitless, boundless, indeterminate metaphysical stuff that underpins all reality, in the sixth century BC, in the philosophy of Pythagoras, which emphasized both the metaphysical and aesthetic importance of numbers, as the chaotic and abhorrent counterpoint to the arithmetical and geometrical beauty of the empirical

---

1. In the historical overview presented and related mathematical explanations summarized in this chapter, in addition to consulting original sources where available, I have often selectively followed the discussion in Moore's *The Infinite*.

world, and in the fifth century BC, in the philosophy of Zeno of Elea, who presented his famous paradoxes of infinite divisibility which, although posing mathematical problems the complexity of which is evidenced by the fact that they went without solution for two millennia, were primarily intended by Zeno to support the philosophy of Parmenides, Zeno's mentor and the founder of the Eleatic school, who held that motion and change are illusions and that the universe exists as a complete and infinite universe. It should be mentioned in passing that, although Zeno's paradoxes were solved with the invention of the calculus, the Eleatic idea of a completed infinity is one that persists, quite problematically, to this very day and supports the modern conceptions of infinity first offered by Cantor, which will be criticized as part of the central theme in this chapter, and the space-time continuum, which was challenged in an earlier chapter. Zeno's use of the mathematics of infinity thusly must be understood as part and parcel of his metaphysics and it was not until two centuries afterwards that Aristotle shifted the focus of the discussion of the infinite to its mathematical nature as such. In his *Metaphysics*, Aristotle takes a view of infinity that is in direct opposition to Zeno by making an important distinction between actual and potential infinities. Aristotle says:

> But also the infinite and the void and all similar things are said to exist potentially and actually in a different sense from that which applies to many other things, e.g., to that which sees or walks or is seen. For of the latter class these predicates can at some time be also truly asserted without qualification; for the seen is so called sometimes because it is being seen, sometimes because it is capable of being seen. But the infinite does not exist potentially in the sense that it will ever actually have separate existence; it exists potentially only for knowledge. For the fact that the process of dividing never comes to an end ensures that this activity exists potentially, but not that the infinite exists separately.[2]

Aristotle's application of this distinction to various paradoxes of his day is subtle and quite interesting but it is his thinking on the natural numbers that is important to us here. A. W. Moore summarizes it thusly:

> It seemed necessary to accept the existence of the infinite given the infinitude of the natural numbers (which, for Aristotle, were abstractions from things and processes in the natural world). But Aristotle felt able to accommodate this. Such infinitude did not mean that there were actually infinitely many numbers. Nor, certainly, did it mean that any individual number was infinite. *(There was, for Aristotle, no such thing as the number of numbers.)* It was to be understood rather in terms of there being no end to the process of counting.[3] (Emphasis added.)

It should be mentioned in passing that although Aristotle's distinction between actual and potential infinities is no longer mainstream, it is undeniably one of the greatest and most persistently influential philosophical innovations and it will be shortly supported here.

During the Middle Ages, when the church dominated western philosophical thought, the religious significance of the idea of the infinite became the focus of discourse, with the main theme of God's metaphysical infinitude being asserted by St. Thomas Aquinas in the

---

2. Aristotle, *Metaphysics*, IX, 6, 1048^b.
3. Moore, *Infinite*, 41.

thirteenth century and the idea of the infinite permeating his Five Ways of proving the existence of God. Although, with Aquinas, the common metaphoric understanding of God as omniscient, omnipotent, and omnipresent was fully developed, the concept of infinity continued to profoundly impact the development of metaphysics, including, especially, the philosophy of Descartes (who held that matter is an infinitely divisible substance and that, because a cause must be at least as real as its effect, God, as an infinite being, could be proven from the human idea of an infinite being), Spinoza (who concluded that an unlimited God must also be an immanent one), Hegel (who regarded the universe as the Absolute thinking about and limiting itself) and the ersatz metaphysics of contemporary cosmologists (who, for example, offer the completed space-time continuum, the multiverse, and probabilistic explanations for the existence of this particular universe).

The mathematical aspects of the problem of infinity took much longer to develop than the metaphysical ones and, it was not until the late seventeenth century, when Leibniz and Newton independently developed the calculus, that the modern mathematics of infinity could be said to be substantially under way. That development, with its concepts of continuity, convergence, and divergence, made possible final solutions to many puzzles and paradoxes, including the most famous paradoxes of Zeno.[4] Other major developments relevant to the instant inquiry came with the invention of predicate logic and set theory by Frege, Cantor, and Russell, which have been discussed in previous chapters, and Cantor's related theories of the cardinality and countability of infinite sets and infinite orders of infinity, upon which a substantial portion of this chapter will be focused.

Although these modern achievements resolved many ancient controversies, they also created new ones. In general, the ancient and modern paradoxes fall under a discrete number of categories, including paradoxes of the infinitely small, paradoxes of the infinitely large, and paradoxes of self-reference. Although the development of the calculus all but eliminated the first category, it left the latter two such categories virtually unscathed. From a metamathematical standpoint, the contemporary urgency of the extant paradoxes is primarily associated with the development of set theory and, in particular, the development of metamathematical theories of the existence of uncountable domains (i.e., domains of numbers that are larger than the infinitely large domain of the natural numbers) and multiple orders of infinity and their related paradoxes, which depend heavily upon self-reference for their justification.

Modern set theory, metamathematics, and transfinite mathematics are each broad, deep, and difficult disciplines, which, to be fully understood and presented, are far beyond the scope of this work and require mathematical competence which I do not possess. Nevertheless, as philosophers we are in a position not only to demand of contemporary mathematics that it be metaphysically well-founded but also to assess whether and the extent to which it passes that test. An example of the critical intersection between metaphysics and mathematics is the previously discussed problem of the existence of infinite sets. If one asserts that mathematics is reducible to set theory, then analysis of the mathematics of the actual infinite requires demonstration of the existence of infinite sets. This is in the first

---

4. Moore argues that the calculus is not necessary to solve the paradoxes of the infinitely small but instead that they may be seen to dissolve upon careful analysis of their coherence and/or determinancy. Ibid., 70–71.

instance a metaphysical question not a mathematical one and the lengths to which the set theorists have been willing to go to try to address it are revealing. Bernard Bolzano argued that the set of propositions and propositions about propositions (and so on) was infinite in size. Dedekind made a similar argument about thoughts and thoughts about thoughts. Frege and Russell rejected these approaches, arguing instead as we have seen that sets and sets of sets could be infinitely assembled, only to discover that the set of all sets that does not include itself as a member presented set-theoretic mathematics with an impassable obstacle, which, as we have seen, motivated Russell to assert in a grand capitulation that the existence of the actual infinity of empirical objects may and must be maintained axiomatically. Russell's final conclusion is precisely of the sort for which the philosophy in these pages requires that metamathematicians be held to account.

In making such metaphysical demands upon the mathematicians of infinity, we have at our disposal our understanding of logical objects and their ontological importance. Under transcendent realism, all thought is about logical objects and their substantive descendents, one of the distinguishing characteristics of which is their unique enhandlement and it is such enhandlement which supports the logical deduction of the natural numbers. Under the homogenous logicism of transcendent realism the connection between thinkability and countability is airtight; any object that may be thought may also be counted and, conversely, objects that are somehow uncountable cannot be accessed by human reason and, therefore, cannot be thought or said to exist. Accordingly, our assessment of modern metamathematics will depend in large part upon whether it meets or transgresses these basic metaphysical criteria and, conversely, we will look to see whether we learn from it anything that casts doubt upon our own metaphysics.

CANTOR AND THE ORDERS OF INFINITY

Although the central focus of this chapter is the seminal work of Cantor on the infinite in the late nineteenth century, our starting point will be the customarily clear exposition of Russell on the distinction between "numbers," in general, and "natural numbers" (also called "inductive numbers" by Russell). As will be recalled from our discussion in chapter 5, "The Homogeneity of Reason," in set theory, the cardinality of a set is a measure of the number of its members. For example, the cardinality of the set comprising a dog, a cat, and a chicken is 3 and a "number" is the defining characteristic of each set of similar sets. In set theory, "number" means "cardinal" number not "natural" number. The importance of the idea that there is a "number" that comprises other types of what are commonly understood as numbers, including most importantly natural numbers, but which is not necessarily attended by what we understand as arithmetical properties cannot be overstated in this context. Because any set of natural numbers from 0 to n contains $n + 1$ members, we can say that the cardinality of the set of natural numbers is 1 greater than any set of natural numbers from 0 to that natural number. The cardinality of the natural numbers is not an inductive number itself and as a result those cardinal numbers which represent the number of infinite sets such as the set of natural numbers will not have all of the arithmetic properties associated with inductive numbers. Russell describes this as follows:

> Now it is easy to see that this [cardinal] number is not one of the inductive numbers. If n is any inductive number, the number of numbers from 0 to n (both included) is $n + 1$; therefore the total number of inductive numbers is greater than n, no matter which of the inductive numbers n may be. If we arrange the inductive numbers in a series in order of magnitude, this series has no last term; but if n is an inductive number, every series whose field has n terms has a last term, as it is easy to prove. Such differences might be multiplied *ad lib*. Thus the number of inductive numbers is a new number, different from all of them, not possessing all inductive properties. It may happen that 0 has a certain property, and that if n has it so has $n + 1$, and yet that this new number does not have it.[5]

Russell then characterizes the foundational importance of the non-inductive nature of the cardinal numbers.

> The difficulties that so long delayed the theory of infinite numbers were largely due to the fact that some, at least, of the inductive properties were wrongly judged to be such as must belong to all numbers; indeed it was thought that they could not be denied without contradiction. The first step in understanding infinite numbers consists in realising the mistakenness of this view.[6]

In sum, under the set-theoretic definition of "number," we have a cardinal number which is not itself a natural number and does not contain all of their inductive properties, and which designates the *size* of the set of natural numbers. Given this understanding, the cardinality of any finite set can be determined by placing its members in a one-to-one correspondence with the natural numbers (not including 0) and identifying the natural number that corresponds to the last member so mapped. However, because infinite sets have no last term, the question arises as to whether such sets may be said to have any cardinality and, if so, how it is to be defined.

To see how Cantor answered this question, a brief reversion to the great Galileo Galilei will be helpful. In *Dialogues Concerning Two New Sciences*, Galileo's final work, Galileo discussed a paradox which, although not of his invention, has come to bear his name. Galileo noted an apparent contradiction between the numerosity of the natural numbers and their squares, which may be paraphrased as follows:

1. Because every natural number has a square but only some natural numbers are squares of natural numbers, the set of natural numbers, which include both squares of natural numbers and non-squares of natural numbers, must be more numerous than the set of squares of natural numbers.

2. Because, for every square of a natural number, there is exactly one natural number that is its square root and for every natural number there is exactly one natural number that is its square, the number of natural numbers and the number of squares of natural numbers must be the same.

---

5. Russell, *Introduction to Mathematical Philosophy*, 78–79.
6. Ibid., 79.

INFINITY, COUNTABILITY, AND SELF-REFERENCE

Galileo's paradox may be graphically illustrated as follows:

Table 4—Bijection of Natural Numbers and Their Squares										
N	1	2	3	4	5	6	7	8	9	...
	↕	↕	↕	↕	↕	↕	↕	↕	↕	↕
N^2	1	4	9	16	25	36	49	64	81	...

The arrows in Table 4 indicate that each natural number (which is a member of N) can be mapped directly onto its square (which is a member of N^2) and *vice versa*. This, in set-theoretical terms is called a "bijection" and, as Table 4 shows, N^2 is a bijection with N. Since both of Galileo's observations cannot be true, Galileo concluded that the basic arithmetical relations of <, >, and =, all of which apply to finite sets, do not apply to membership of infinite sets.

Cantor accepts Galileo's observation (2) but not his observation (1), the latter of which is undeniably an intuition that is applicable to finite sets but not one that applies to infinite ones. Cantor begins by adopting from Dedekind the definition of an infinite set (i.e., a set of infinite cardinality) as one that has the same cardinality as one of its proper subsets. In Dedekind's terms, the set of natural numbers is infinite precisely because of observation (2) above, that is to say, because the set of squares of natural numbers is a proper subset of the set of natural numbers and yet has the same cardinality as (i.e., is a bijection with) the set of natural numbers, the set of natural numbers is definitionally infinite. Cantor then defines the notion of a "countably infinite set" as any set that is a bijection with the natural numbers (i.e., any set that can be placed in a one-to-one relation with the natural numbers). By this definition, it is readily apparent that N^2 is a countably infinite set. But Cantor does not stop there. Cantor offers a proof, known as Cantor's Diagonal Proof, which has received mainstream but not universal acceptance, that the cardinality of all real numbers R (i.e., numbers that can be represented on a number line) is greater than the cardinality of N and further, as Cantor purports to show by additional proof, that there are infinitely many *orders* of infinity.

Cantor's Diagonal Proof proceeds as follows. Cantor begins by assuming the opposite of that which he intends to prove, namely, that R is countably infinite and that a complete list of R can therefore be made as a function of N. Table 5 below represents a list of randomly selected real numbers and is analogous to the list that Cantor utilized in his proof:

[Table 5 appears on the next page.]

	Table 5—Diagonalization Method							
	d_1	d_2	d_3	d_4	d_5	d_6	d_7	...
$r_1=$	2	3	4	5	6	1	7	...
$r_2=$	6	3	5	7	9	2	8	...
$r_3=$	3	4	1	9	2	7	3	...
$r_4=$	6	8	5	6	5	4	8	...
$r_5=$	5	2	9	4	3	9	6	...
$r_6=$	2	1	0	3	0	8	3	...
$r_7=$	9	5	1	5	1	0	2	...
...								

Note: The boxes are placed to draw attention to the nth digit (d_n) of r_n.

If it could be shown that there is a method for constructing a real number r_{new} that cannot possibly be included in any complete list of R such as the one purported to be set forth in Table 5, then it would appear to follow that R is not countably infinite.

In the Diagonal Proof a new real number, r_{new}, the digits of which can be represented as 0. $d_1 d_2 d_3 d_4 d_5 d_6 d_7$ ..., is created by applying a rule, which we will refer to as the "Diagonal Rule." Under the Diagonal Rule, r_{new} will be populated as follows: taking each real number r_n in the order it appears in Table 5, if the nth digit of r_n is a 1, then d_n of r_{new} will be a 2; otherwise, d^n of r_{new} will be a 1. It should be noted that the choice of 1 and 2 as the digits of r_{new} into which the digits of each real number will be added is arbitrary and has no effect on the proof; the important feature of the Diagonal Rule is that its application must yield for every n a d_n that is different than the nth digit of r_n. Applying the Diagonal Rule to Table 5, we see that the string of digits in Table 5 upon which the Diagonal Rule will operate (delineated by surrounding boxes) is 0.2316382 and that, upon such application, the r_{new} that is generated thereby will be equal to 0.1121111. . . .

Of course, because both the number of real numbers on the list and the number of digits contained in each such number, in each case when fully expanded as symbolized by the inclusion of the ellipses, is infinite, the application of the Diagonalization Method can never be actually completed *in time*. However, it is clearly the case that application of the Diagonalization Method to the digits of the finitely many numbers that are specified in Table 5 will always yield a r_{new} that cannot possibly appear on the list in Table 5. This result obtains because by changing the nth digit of the nth number on the list, r_{new} cannot be any place on the list between 1 and n. To see why this is so, simply observe that r_{new} cannot be first on the list, because its first digit has been changed from the first digit of the first number on the list, r_{new} cannot be second on the list because its second number has been changed from the second digit of the second number on the list, r_{new} cannot be third on the list because its third number has been changed from the third digit of the third number on the list, and so on. It can be seen that the Diagonalization Method is self-referential insofar as it refers to a list to create a new number that is not on the list. This is a point to which we will return a bit later on. The Diagonal Proof concludes by asserting that, because the construction of r_{new} can proceed through the list of real numbers indefinitely, an r_{new} can always be created that will never be on the list and, therefore, *there must be more real numbers than any purported countably infinite list might contain.*

Although it is not worthwhile for our purposes to explain how, the Diagonalization Method is an extraordinary logical tool which can, on certain assumptions, be used to show that there are more *sets* of natural numbers than the natural numbers themselves, that N is smaller than its own power set,[7] and that there exist an infinity of sets of power sets, and it was the existence of these sets which motivated Cantor's endeavor to determine the cardinality of infinite sets other than N. Even if one were to agree that there may be more real numbers than natural numbers, it is far from intuitive that we can coherently speak of the *size* of infinite sets, let alone of their *relative sizes*. Nevertheless, with characteristic genius, Cantor proposed the following means of doing so.[8] Cantor defined a new set of numbers called "ordinal numbers" to designate the size of well-ordered sets. "Well-ordered" sets are those as to which each non-empty subset contains a least element. Moore explains well-ordered sets thusly:

> *Definition of a well-ordering:* A well-ordering of a set X (finite or infinite) is an imposition of order on the members of X satisfying the following conditions: it singles out one of the members of X as the first, unless, of course, X has no members (that is, unless X is the empty set); it singles out another member of X as the second, unless X has only one member; it singles out another as the third, unless X has only two members; and quite generally, it singles out, for each member of X that has already been singled out, another as its immediate successor, unless there are none left; more generally still, it singles out, for each *set* of members of X that have already been singled out (finite or infinite), a first to succeed them all, again unless there are none left.[9]

For example, N is a well-ordered set because the least element of the set N {0, 1, 2 ... } is 0 and the first number to succeed 0 is 1, the least element of the subset of N {1, 2, 3 ... } is 1 and the first number to succeed 1 is 2, and the least element of the subset of that subset of N {2, 3, 4 ... } is 2 and the first number to succeed 2 is 3, and so on *ad infinitum*. The first number to succeed them all is $\aleph_0$, which Cantor used to designate the cardinality of N. By the definition of a well-ordering, we can see that each of the following sets is a well-ordered set:

1. As just shown, the set N of all natural numbers.

2. The set N of all natural numbers (other than 0), followed by the number 0:

$$\{1, 2, 3 \ldots 0\}$$

3. The set of all of odd natural numbers followed by all of the even natural numbers:

---

7. A power set is the set of all subsets of a given set. For example, the power set of {a, b, c} is {{}, {a}, {b}, {c}, {a, b}, {a, c}, {b, c}, {a, b, c}}. A set having n members will have a power set the cardinality of which is equal to 2^n.

8. The discussion here (through the Burlati-Forti paradox) is largely based upon Moore, *Infinite*, 123–28.

9. Ibid., 123.

$$\{1, 3, 5 \ldots, 2, 4, 6 \ldots\}$$

We can describe the "shape" of the foregoing sets as follows. Set 1 is an infinite set, set 2 is an infinite progression (1, 2, 3 ...) followed by a single element (0), and set 3 consists of two infinite progressions (1, 3, 5 ...) and (2, 4, 6 ...). Ordinal numbers are designations of the size and shapes of sets. The first ordinals are identical to the natural numbers. The first ordinal to succeed the natural numbers is designated as "ω" and is equal to $\aleph_0$. Like the cardinal numbers, ω is not a natural number. The first ordinal to succeed ω is $\omega + 1$ which is not an arithmetic statement but one that describes and infinite progression (ω) followed by a single element, such as set 2 above or such as $\{1, 2, 3 \ldots \omega)$. The ordinal describing set 3 above is $\omega + \omega$ and also $\omega \times 2$. It is readily apparent that a progression of ordinals can be constructed to describe sets whose subsets include finite and infinite subsets as follows:

> 0, 1, 2, ...
>
> $\omega, \omega + 1, \omega + 2 \ldots$
>
> $\omega \times 2, (\omega \times 2) + 1, (\omega \times 2) + 2 \ldots$
>
> $\omega \times 3$
>
> $\omega \times 4$
>
> $\omega \times 5$
>
> ω^2
>
> ω^3
>
> ω^4
>
> ω^5
>
> ω^ω

It is postulated that there is a first ordinal to succeed all of the sets of ordinals, which is called ε_0.

Not wholly unlike Russell's set-theoretic deduction of the natural numbers, Cantor's method of measuring the shape of infinite sets yielded a paradox named for its discoverer, Cesare Burlati-Forti. Moore describes the Burlati-Forti Paradox as follows:

> The ordinals are well-defined mathematical objects, just as the natural numbers and real numbers are. They seem to constitute a perfectly determinate mathematical totality. Can we not therefore collect them together and consider the set of ordinals, say Ω (just as we have been considering the set of natural numbers N, and the set of real number R)? Given that there *are* infinite sets, there can surely be no objection to this. But consider: if Ω does exist, then it is a set of ordinals like any other, and so ... there must be another ordinal which is the first to succeed all its members, thus contradicting its pretension to contain *all* the ordinals. It is as if the very endlessness of the ordinals precludes their being collected together into a set. No set can be "big enough." We can think of it like this. If Ω exists, then it has a well-ordering, so there must be an ordinal which acts as a

INFINITY, COUNTABILITY, AND SELF-REFERENCE

measure of how long this well-ordering is. But obviously none of the ordinals in Ω is itself big enough to do this. So Ω cannot after all contain all the ordinals.[10]

Burlati-Forti concluded that the ordinals could not be well-ordered themselves and therefore could not measure infinite sets as Cantor proposed. Cantor, however, took quite a different view. Cantor argued that some totalities, which he called inconsistent totalities, are simply immeasurably big—too big in fact to be regarded as a set. Cantor took the view that Ω does not exist and, on the same grounds, that neither does the set of all sets which led to Russell's paradox. Cantor referred to these inconsistent totalities as the truly infinite and in a way that is obviously anathema to transcendent realism:

> The Absolute can only be acknowledged and admitted, never known, not even approximately.[11]

Cantor's conclusion left set-theoretical mathematics in a strangely indefensible place which, if it was to be saved at all, required much additional work. For purposes of our exposition we can summarize two additional important developments. The first was the attempt to address the difficulties of naïve set theory by developing axioms. In this regard, Ernest Zermelo and Abraham Fraenkel are proponents of the most famous system, although there are others. Zermelo and Fraenkel developed what is called ZFC, which stands for Zermelo-Fraenkel set theory with the axiom of choice. We will note, without comment, the axioms of ZFC: (1) axiom of extensionality; (2) axiom of regularity; (3) axiom schema of specification; (4) axiom of pairing; (5) axiom of union; (6) axiom schema of replacement; (7) axiom of infinity; (8) axiom of power set; (9) well-ordering theorem; and (10) axiom of choice. The second, which occurred almost immediately, was the development by Gödel of his incompleteness theorem, which states that any robust axiomatic system such as modern set-theoretic mathematics must be either incomplete or inconsistent. Although we will have a few words to say about Gödel's work shortly, it is sufficient to note here that all of this left set-theoretic mathematics far from achieving its goal of proving logicism or that there exist orders of infinity beyond that of the natural numbers.

Burlati-Forti was not the only mathematician who expressed doubts about Cantor's accomplishments. Indeed, Cantor was vehemently and publicly opposed from the start by Leopold Kroenecker, Cantor's teacher, who stated notoriously that that "God made the integers; all the rest is the work of man." Henri Poincaré, the French polymath, argued that the Diagonal Proof could just as well be interpreted as showing that it is impossible to devise a way of listing the real numbers or even that R is not a genuine set. Poincaré stated:

> There is no actual infinity, the Cantorians have forgotten that, and they have fallen into contradiction. It is true that Cantorism rendered services, but that was when it was applied to a real problem whose terms were clearly defined, and we could walk safely. Logisticians as Cantorians have forgotten.[12]

---

10. Ibid., 126.
11. Ibid., 128.
12. Heinzmann and Stump, "Poincaré," §3.1.

C. S. Peirce, the American polymath known as the founder of pragmatism, concluded in a more Aristotelean vein that R did not exist as a completed whole but only as a potential infinity and proposed his own complex, non-Cantorian theory of the continuum.

Kroenecker, Poincaré, and Peirce were joined by still other mathematicians in criticizing Cantor's work and, indeed, there are at least three comprehensive schools of thought that arose subsequently to Cantor's exposition which were motivated, at least in substantial part, by a desire to respond to it.[13] The first was the development by L. E. J. Brouwer, a Dutch mathematician, of a philosophy of mathematics known as intuitionalism, in which it is held (similarly to Kant) that mathematics is a mentally created activity that arises out of the human experience of time. For Brouwer, time exists as a seamless whole that in our thought we separate into past and future. From this cognitive structure, Brouwer argued that we develop the idea of a progression from which the notion of infinitude by division and infinitude by addition arise. With respect to Cantor, Brouwer argued that transfinite mathematics is a formal structure that is disconnected from human experience of temporally-based infinitude. Like many of the others mentioned, Brouwer's view was that R did not exist as a completed whole (because we had no experience of one) but that, instead, only individual real numbers could be created by specification of laws for their creation through, for example, decimal expansion. Importantly for Brouwer, in this matter R differs from N; the natural numbers can be thought as a completed whole because all that is required for their construction is the simple principle of mathematical induction. Nevertheless, with respect to the Diagonalization Method, Brouwer argued that all that it shows is that given any progression of real numbers, there is a means by which a real number that is not in the progression can be specified.[14]

The second school of thought, called finitism, was developed by David Hilbert in the hopes of laying a foundation upon which the core features of Cantor's work could be placed in a way that avoided some of these criticisms. In recognition of scientific developments that suggest that the empirical world is not infinitely big and that space-time is not infinitely divisible, Hilbert's approach was to seek wholly within mathematics itself the conditions upon which Cantor's transfinite mathematics could be justified. Specifically, Hilbert's concept was to start with unassailable principles of finite mathematics and then to examine how generalizations from them to ideas about infinity (such as N) as a completed whole are useful in the development of mathematical proofs. In finitism, finite mathematical operations and statements are called "finitary" propositions and infinite mathematical operations and statements are called "ideal" propositions. Ideal propositions have no meaning but instead are formalities which facilitate the demonstration of finitary proofs. Hilbert argued that, not unlike Kantian Ideas, although ideal propositions are never experienced in reality, they transcend experience in a way that enables us to understand reality as a concrete totality. Unfortunately, Hilbert sought to formalize his finitist project through axiomatization, an approach that was overwhelmed by Gödel's emasculation of axiomatic systems on the grounds that they must either be incomplete or inconsistent. Nevertheless, Hilbert's approach to ideal propositions (not

---

13. See Moore, *Infinite*, 131–41.
14. Ibid., 131–32.

unlike Kant's concept of Ideas) continues to have appeal and it remains influential to this day.

We come at last to the work of Wittgenstein, who was responsible for the third and final philosophical development that must be discussed before we are able to present our own views on the metaphysical aspects of the mathematics of infinity. Wittgenstein, whom we have already met critically on the concept of self, approached Cantor's mathematics from Wittgenstein's own, unique linguistic perspective and in this matter we are highly sympathetic with him. Wittgenstein believed that the meaning of words were a matter of their use. Since we do not have experience of a completed infinity, the term "infinity" could not mean that—instead we use the term "infinity" to generalize about the endless possibilities of certain types of infinities. For example, when we say there are infinitely many numbers, we mean that however many we count there remain more to be counted and therefore, when we speak of a last term, we indulge in incoherency because there is no last term to which we refer, and when we refer to space and time as being infinite, we simply mean that there is no limit on how far or how long things may move or exist in the empirical world. Interestingly, Wittgenstein felt that it was not his business, as a philosopher, to interfere with mathematics as a science but rather to observe how mathematics is practiced and to bring his philosophical (in Wittgenstein's case, linguistic) concerns to bear upon what he observed, which is a sentiment we share.

THE ONTOLOGY OF THE INFINITE

Cantor's opponents notwithstanding, it is important to recognize that the view of contemporary mainstream mathematics is that Cantor's work is sound, especially because, at the most general level, there exists an incompatibility between Cantor's transfinite mathematics (considered metaphysically) and the philosophy presented in these pages. The tension between the two views of the infinite results from our identification of Being with intelligibility—if all that exists or can be thought, including numbers, is reducible to logical objects, then it is not possible to speak of the actual existence of things, including, especially the real numbers, in unthinkable quantities. Let us see how this plays out.

We begin by noting that Cantor's philosophy is set-theoretical in nature and that, as we have seen in our examination of Russell's work, set theoretical constructions of even the simplest of mathematical concepts such as the natural numbers depend upon axioms, including, especially, the axiom of infinity. An axiom is supposed to be something more than an assumption. Russell's characterization of the existence of an actual empirical infinity seems to have been based upon the "large" quantity of matter in the observable universe and the fact that the contrary proposition that the world is finite cannot be proved. Cantor's position on this foundational matter is even less supportable. Cantor asserts that "[e]ach potential infinite . . . presupposes an actual infinite."[15] On its face, this statement, upon which Cantor's entire mathematics is based, reverses the logical order of things insofar as it would ordinarily be thought to be the case that for something to actually exist it must first

---

15. Ibid., 117. It is at least odd that Russell, who wholehearted embraces Cantor's work, seems to have taken the opposite view on this fundamental metaphysical point in his disputation of Kant's exposition of space. See text accompanying 36n, 83.

have existed in its potentiality. Human experience tells us that not all potentialities come to fruition but that for something to occur it must have been logically possible. And it should be noted that this particular criticism is buttressed by the presence of the alternative of the unaxiomatic deduction of the natural numbers from logical objects, which is not premised upon the existence of an actual infinity of anything.

There is a second ground upon which set-theoretic philosophies may be criticized, which is perhaps more important because, as we shall see in the following chapters, it is one which is not limited to mathematical philosophy. This is the critique that Heidegger leveled against scientific philosophy generally and even against the phenomenology proffered by his mentor, Edmund Husserl. Simply stated, scientific philosophies presuppose the Being of their subject matter. What this means for metaphysics generally will be explained in great detail a little later on. In the case of set theory, it means that the Being of sets and their elements are taken for granted, without examining what their Being means and how that Being impacts its set-theoretical conclusions.

It is sometimes argued against set-theoretical based logicism, such as that proposed by Russell, that a set is not, as Russell assumes, a logical object. Such arguments are presumably based upon the notion that although sets are different from their members they are determined by them and that, under the empirical view, since their members are empirical so must sets of empirical members be. We are in disagreement with this view and in favor of Russell on this matter but for our own reasons. In considering this issue, it is appropriate to begin with the definition of a set. Cantor defined a set as "any gathering into a whole . . . of distinct perceptual or mental objects" and also as "a many which allows itself to be thought of as a one."[16] As such, a set is clearly a thinkable object and is therefore at the very least a substantive object the predicates of which in any given instance would include its members. To be clear, as earlier noted, a set is different from its members insofar as it is a collection of them (Russell tells us that a set of dogs is not a dog), unless the set is a set of sets. The question here, though, is not whether a set is a substantive object but a *logical* one. Certainly, the members of any and all sets either are logical objects or are reducible to their progenitors. It is clearly the case that we can coherently speak of a set whose members include only logical objects, such as {1, 2, 3}, and that such a set does not require reference to empirical reality. So, we are able to conclude that, as an abstract idea, a set is indeed a logical object which is distinct from its elements (so long as they are not sets) be they logical or substantive.

What of the Being of the members of sets themselves? It will be recalled that set theoretical number theory defines numbers as the defining characteristic of similar sets. So, as we have seen, it takes sets of duos such as sets of duos of cats, and sets of duos of dogs, and sets of duos of chickens, and assigns the number 2 to them as their defining characteristic. But set theory does not address the question of the Being of its elements. It does not tell us what it is about dogs and cats and chickens that qualifies them to be elements of a set in the first place and to be put in such a relation to one another that they may be paired off one-to-one. The answer to this question is much more profound than the obvious one that dogs have "doggy" predicates and cats are "catty" and it lies in the fact that each of the elements of a set is either a logical object or a descendant of

16. Ibid., 10.

one. While an understanding of sets of all the animals of the earth may be of paramount importance to a veterinarian, there is little if anything of importance to a metaphysician that can be said about them that cannot be said about sets of logical objects alone. We see, therefore, that the concept of duos of objects itself is reducible to a single concept of a duo of logical objects and that the natural number 2 is not an empirical one but a wholly logical one. And, equally important, we have deconstructed the concept of sets of things to a logical object whose predicates are its logical relation to its member objects and their logical relation to each other.

We turn next to the idea of an infinite set. As we have just noted, under mainstream set theory, which is empirical in nature, the existence of infinite sets poses a problem which ultimately requires solution by axiom. Transcendent realism is free of this difficulty because its deduction of the natural numbers is unaxiomatic and non-set-theoretic and it allows for, at the very least, their *logical* infinity. But the question of the infinity of the natural numbers is not, strictly speaking, what is at issue here. Instead, the question is whether the presupposition of an actually infinite set, upon which Cantor's theory of the uncountability of the real numbers is based, is a coherent one. To be a bit more precise, when we say that modern mathematics is premised upon the existence of actually infinite sets, we mean that the subject presupposes the existence of sets which are determinate and complete and that, without such sets, its propositions could not be advanced and its operations could not be conducted. All sets, to be intelligible, must by definition be determinate. The determinateness of a set is given either by listing its members or by describing them in such a way that its membership may clearly be understood. But completeness is another matter. Clearly, the set of all planets orbiting the sun can be considered to be determinate and also complete. The set of all natural numbers is also determinate. It can be specified as such or by partial listing (e.g., {0, 1, 2 . . . }). But is it complete? Aristotle, Kant, Hilbert, and Wittgenstein would answer in the negative and that is a position with which we are in agreement. For metaphysical purposes, for a set to be complete, it must have a last term, which no infinite set can claim to possess. As we just saw, Hilbert would argue that even though there are no infinite sets we can act as if there are in performing mathematical operations. Wittgenstein would argue that infinitude means endless or without limit, which, on any understanding of the term, means that it is incomplete.

As we have seen, some mathematicians (Brouwer is an example) who were contemporaries or who followed Cantor distinguished between the natural numbers and the real numbers in this regard. However, it seems that the argument in favor of the completeness of the natural numbers, which is inevitably based upon mathematical induction, misconstrues determinateness for completeness. Mathematical induction is a species of *modus ponens*. In any proof, no matter how long or complicated, there is an endpoint, which is its conclusion. A valid proof is a complete proof. However, just because we employ *modus ponens* in deducing the natural numbers, does not mean that the set of natural numbers is complete. We do not *prove* the natural numbers we *deduce* them. It will be recalled that the cardinality of the natural numbers is founded upon a claim about all finite sets, namely, that their members may be counted. In set theory countability depends upon the matching of similar sets and the countability of infinite sets depends upon the axiom of infinity. But we have already seen that such an analysis assumes the Being of the membership of sets. When one reduces the membership to a single set of logical objects the result is its utter deconstruction; countability no longer depends upon similarity but instead depends upon the prioritization of the series of logical objects by reference to the logical relations of antecedence and subsequence. We do not look at a set of logical objects to see how many members it has, we *count* them. To do that, we do not require a set-theoretic concept of similarity; instead we need only to understand that the nature of the natural numbers is a prioritized series of logical objects. As a result, the entire concept of cardinality generally as a non-inductive number disappears and cardinality of the natural numbers (notice here that it adds nothing to say the *set* of natural numbers) becomes meaningless. All of which is not to say that mathematicians, Cantor included, are not free to proceed theoretically on any assumption they choose and to work out its implications in a logical and consistent manner.[17] But the philosophy presented in these pages precludes acceptance of the metaphysical foundations of transfinite mathematics and we are left in apparently similar condition to Wittgenstein with a profound degree of unease about its meaning.[18]

A couple of additional points need be made on the topic of the intersection of transcendent realism and metamathematics. One is against Brouwer's notion that our concept of the infinite is based upon our experience of temporality. It will be recalled that in the

---

17. In this footnote, I will indulge in a bit of mathematical fancy as to which I have already admitted my own limited capabilities in order to suggest that there appears to be an inherent contradiction in Cantor's Diagonal Proof that suggests not that the real numbers are countable but that the natural numbers cannot be taken as a completed totality. The argument runs as follows. We will list all of the real numbers between 0 and 1 inclusive ($R_{[0,1]}$) in groups according to the degree of their decimal extension. The first group will be all tenths (starting with .0), the second will be all hundredths, the third will be all thousandths, and so on *ad infinitum*. In order to avoid repeating any, we will do this by mirroring the number of the line in which each real number is listed. For example, in line 0, the number .0 will be listed, in line 1, the number .1 will be listed, in line 2, the number .2 will be listed, in line 10, the number .01 will be listed, in line 11, the number .11 will be listed, in line 57, the number .75 will be listed, and so on, in each case (followed by an infinite number of 0's). We can define a function that generates our list as follows:

$$D_m\left(\sum_{i=0}^{n} a_i 10^i\right) = \sum_{i=0}^{n} a_i 10^{-(i+1)},$$

for a_i integers between 0 and 9.

This list is clearly determinate. We are entitled to assume, upon an understanding that is the same as Cantor's, that the list is also complete (and includes 1.000 . . . by virtue of its including .999 . . .). If we take the list as a completed totality, application of the Diagonalization Method to the list must yield a number that is not on the list. However, we just saw that the list is determinate and complete and contains all numbers in ($R_{[0,1]}$). This is a contradiction which would seem to indicate that the list cannot be taken as a completed totality. I note that if we take the list as determinate but not complete, applying the Diagonal Method to the list one number at a time will always yield a new number *that is on the list and has the same degree of decimal extension as the number changed* and never one that is not on the list.

18. One possible way of resolving our differences with Cantor is to reinterpret him as having established that even if it were possible to count all of the natural numbers it would not be possible to count all of the real numbers. Because transcendent realism does not regard numbers having objective existence, we do not have to deal with the difficulty of there actually existing more real numbers than natural numbers, so we can think of both in such quantities as our mental endurance allows. But even upon this analysis, it appears that we run afoul of the fundamental prohibition of transcendent realism against any assertion that the *unthinkable* can coherently be *thought* to exist.

prequel chapter we proposed a structure of temporality that privileged logic over it and formed its basis. Upon such an understanding, Brouwer's analysis is readily seen to be superficial. The perceived progression of time is a logical one and the idea of an infinite progression cannot, therefore, ultimately be founded on our experience of time but instead must be founded upon our experience of logical relations. Another such point relates to a common sentiment that the infinite and all of its paradoxes do not reflect reality so much as the finitude of human reason. This argument is attended by its obvious corollary that, if only human reason were more powerful, human beings could experience the world all at once as a complete totality. Again, we must reject this notion. We have identified Being with intelligibility. For the reasons already given and to come, to suggest that Being is somehow different from the way in which we understand it is incoherent.

SELF-REFERENCE

The Diagonalization Method is an important example of the use of self-reference in metamathematics. As noted, the self-referential nature of the Diagonalization Method consists in its application to a purportedly complete domain of all real numbers to generate a new real number that demonstrates its incompleteness. Since Cantor, the Diagonalization Method and variations upon it have been used as part of other metamathematical proofs, including, of special importance, Gödel's incompleteness theorem which, as already noted, is a demonstration of the theorem that any minimally robust and consistent axiomatic theory of mathematics will contain true propositions that are not provable within the theory itself.[19]

The misuse of self-reference underlies many paradoxes and sometimes even plays a foundational role in philosophical positions that have been important in the history of philosophy. One such example which was discussed early on in chapter 2, "The Death and Resurrection of Metaphysics," is the distinction between a thinker having a thought about himself and the impossibility of a thought being about the thought itself. Accordingly, it is worth taking a few moments to identify some of the difficulties that attend self-reference and to see how they relate (beyond the earlier discussion of the soul) to the philosophy presented in these pages.

The discussion can appropriately begin with the *Cogito*. It can readily be seen that a self-referential syllogism such as "I think, therefore I am" would hold as much truth and content if it stopped at the word "I," for an entity must first exist in order to assert its existence. Consider the contrary statement "I do not exist." That such a statement is false on its face should be apparent even to those who have never taken an elementary logic course. Nevertheless, it is important to understand why it is false because it appears insidiously in various forms and places in philosophy, including the Liar's Paradox, the Barber's Paradox, and Russell's Paradox, and it figures prominently in the Gödel

---

19. See, Moore, *Infinite*, 175–76, for a proof of Gödel's incompleteness theorem based upon the application of the Diagonalization Method to a theoretically infinite table of sets containing numbers according to whether they satisfy arbitrary arithmetical statements. Of course, this proof is subject to the same doubts that we expressed with respect to the Diagonalization Method itself. See 17n, 188.

sentence (upon which the proof of his incompleteness theorem is based) which was carefully crafted to avoid the pitfalls of self-contradiction.

The self-referential statement "I do not exist" is different in nature from other false statements such as "unicorns exist in the real world," because the falsity of the former can be determined solely by reference to the words it comprises, while the falsity of the latter requires reference to the empirical world. In the case of the statement "I do not exist," the subject *I* by assertion of the statement purports to negate itself, which violates the principle of non-contradiction. Under that principle, an entity cannot be and not be at the same time.

The Liar's Paradox, which consists of a similar statement, namely "I always lie," suffers from the same fatal flaw but more subtly so. If the assertion in the Liar's Paradox is true, then it must be a lie, but, if it is a lie, then it cannot be true. Again, the statement which contains the implicit representation of truthfulness purports to negate that representation in its assertion that it is false.

The Barber's Paradox is even more abstract. It consists of the following puzzle. There is a village in which the barber shaves each man who does not shave himself. The question, then, is: Who shaves the barber? The paradox arises because if the barber shaves himself, then according to the premise he does not do so but, if he does not shave himself, then according to the premise he must in fact shave himself. The Barber's Paradox is yet another example of a proposition that contains within itself an inherent contradiction; in other words, the premise that the barber shaves all men who do not shave themselves, if interpreted to include the barber in its domain, is logically impossible. Interestingly, as a matter of logic, the statement that "there is a village in which the barber shaves each man who does not shave himself" is analytically false because logically there can be no such village (assuming the barber lives there).

We come next to Russell's Paradox, which was discussed in chapter 5, "The Homogeneity of Reason." It will be recalled that Russell's Paradox consists in the analysis of *the set of all sets that do not include themselves as a member*. The paradox arises because if the set of all such sets includes itself, then it cannot be a set that does not include itself and if it does not include itself it must, by definition, do so. As is the case with respect to the Barber's Paradox, logically, there can be no such set but, unlike the Barber's Paradox and the other paradoxes previously described, which have the appearance more of parlor games than important philosophy, Russell's Paradox had the profound impact of rendering his initial attempt at logicism a failure and, because it impelled Russell to commit further to axiomatization, it set the stage for Gödel's proof that there is a logically necessary deficiency in all axiomatic systems such as that presented by Russell in his *Principia Mathematica* (in which Russell's second attempt at logicism appears).

Gödel's proof is difficult and abstract and it is at least as interesting for the methodology that Gödel employed as it is for the conclusion he reached. In the most grotesquely summary terms, Gödel developed a system by which the entirety of Russell's predicate calculus and each and every theorem that can be expressed in its terms is translatable into a single, unique number (called a *Gödel number*) the generation of which is accomplished by the multiplication of powers of prime numbers in accordance with the rules of Gödel's system. Importantly, the system is designed such that not every number is a

INFINITY, COUNTABILITY, AND SELF-REFERENCE

Gödel number and that, given any Gödel number, because of its uniqueness, the symbol, sentence, or theorem which it encodes can be reverse-engineered by an inverse process of factoring. Next, Gödel shows that not only can Gödel numbers represent symbols, statements, and theorems within Russell's predicate calculus, but because of the way in which Gödel numbers map onto Russell's predicate calculus they may also represent metamathematical statements about the predicate calculus itself such as the statement that "the initial symbol of ~(0 = 0) is the tilde." Gödel then demonstrates that there is a Gödel number that represents the statement, "The sequence of formulas with the Gödel number x is a proof of the formula with the Gödel number z" and finally that "there is no number x that is the Gödel number of any formula with the Gödel number x." The former may be translated into the statement that the formula with the Gödel number z is demonstrably true. The latter, which because it includes within itself a reference to its own Gödel number, is the self-referential statement that "this theorem is not provable (using the axioms of the predicate calculus)."

By formulating a statement within *Principia Mathematica* that asserts *of itself* that it is not provable, Gödel has shown that *Principia Mathematica* is *incomplete*. Nevertheless, it is argued that the statement can be shown outside *Principia Mathematica* to be true. The proof proceeds by *reductio absurdum*. As is the case with the Liar's Paradox, the statement "this statement cannot be proved," if false, yields its opposite, namely the statement that it can be proved. However, unlike the Liar's Paradox, the Gödel sentence is not bi-conditional but, rather, it is tri-conditional: (a) it might be false; (b) it might be true and provable; or (c) it might be true, but not provable (within *Prinicipia Mathematica*). The first two possibilities are ruled out because they are logically contradictory, which leaves only the last. The argument concludes that the Gödel sentence, therefore, can only be shown to be true *outside* of *Prinicipia Mathematica* and therefore that *Principia Mathematica* is incomplete.[20]

20. Acknowledging as was the case with Cantor's Diagonal Proof that I am stepping far beyond the bounds of my expertise, I would like to express two reservations about Gödel's incompleteness theorem. One is with respect to the Gödel sentence itself (which I assume is a translation of the actual formula proposed by Gödel that is valid for the purposes of our analysis). If one considers the statement as a logical proposition *outside* of *Principia Mathematica* it seems to be *meaningless*. The sentence "this sentence is not provable" has no content beyond an assertion about the indemonstrability of the truthfulness of its content, which raises the question: How can the demonstrability of a contentless statement have any meaning at all? What does it mean to say "*this sentence* is true" and "*this sentence* cannot be proved"? This leads me to a second, related concern. It will be recalled that part of the genius of Gödel's system is that it maps the symbols, sentences, and theorems of *Principia Mathematica* into a single, unique Gödel number and that the system depends upon there being a Gödel number for every formula within *Principia Mathematica*, which Gödel purports to demonstrate. I cannot help but ask the question whether the absence of a Gödel number for the Gödel sentence proves that *Principia Mathematica* is incomplete or whether it merely shows that some meaningless statements within *Principia Mathematica* have no Gödel number. Because of the way in which the Gödel sentence is structured it reduces to the plainly true statement that

$$\forall(x \neq 0) \sim \exists(y): y = y + x$$

which translates into for all x not equal to 0, there is no y such that y is equal to y plus x. Of course, there is a Gödel number for the proof of this statement which would seem to show that the Gödel sentence is in fact provable within *Principia Mathematica* as a special case of the proof that there can never be a Gödel number for any formula that includes the Gödel number itself. Having said all of this, if Gödel's

As noted, Gödel's incompleteness theorem is widely accepted in the current mainstream and applies not only to *Principia Mathematica* but to any axiomatic system sufficiently robust to provide for basic arithmetic. Moreover, Gödel's incompleteness theorem has been asserted to have implications far beyond metamathematics. For example, in *Gödel, Escher, and Bach: An Eternal Golden Braid*,[21] Douglas Hofstadter relies upon its self-referential nature to build a theory of self-consciousness. Ironically, in a completely contrary vein, some theists assert that it demonstrates that any complete explanation of human rational experience requires reference to something outside of that experience, which they assert to be God.[22]

We come now to the main point of our discussion of Gödel's incompleteness theorem in this book. One way of interpreting Gödel's incompleteness theorem is that it shows that any axiomatic system designed by human reason must be done so outside that system. That would suggest that either reason is itself incomplete or that it is unaxiomatic. In our ontology, which identifies Being with intelligibility, because there is no separation between the rules of thought and the objects of thought to which they relate, if reason were incomplete, then so would cognition be and, more fundamentally, our understanding of Being. Under the philosophy presented in these pages, neither reason nor cognition nor Being is axiomatic. As will be explained in the following chapters, under transcendent realism it is fundamental to human Being that the Being (of things) is *disclosed* to it in rational experience and that the truth of propositions is not determined axiomatically or by identification of their meaning within a system but rather by that disclosure which, as it turns out, is fundamentally logical in nature. As has already been said, logic does not *apply* to beings but is, instead, the articulation of Being, itself.

THE COUNTABILITY OF LOGICAL OBJECTS

Insofar as transcendent realism places logical objects and their relations to thinker, themselves, and each other at the pinnacle of human rational experience, its approach to the problems presented by the infinite and self-referential logic should be obvious. In the case of the infinite, it will be observed that most of the difficulties chronicled here arise as the result of several insidious errors of analysis, including treating infinity as though it is a number and not the absence of limitation, inappropriately applying to the problems of the infinite concepts that are applicable to finite collections and finite numbers, and treating numbers as though they are things and not logical objects.

A series of paradoxes developed by Hilbert and grouped under the provocative title of Hilbert's Grand Hotel, is particularly enlightening in this regard. The first two paradoxes may be paraphrased as follows:

> *Premise*: Hilbert postulates a fully occupied hotel containing countably infinite number of rooms.

---

point is that formal axiomatic systems can never adequately prove all arithmetical truths, we offer no objection because we hold that arithmetic is unaxiomatically logical.

21. See Hofstadter, *Gödel*.
22. See Raatikainen, "Gödel's Incompleteness Theorems," §6.1.

Paradox No. 1: The question proposed by Hilbert's first paradox is whether and how to accommodate a new guest.

Solution: Each existing guest may be asked to move to the next higher room in the hotel, leaving the first room empty for the new guest.

Paradox No. 2: Hilbert asks whether and how all of the guests on a bus containing an infinite number of them can be accommodated in his already full hotel.

Solution: Each existing guest may be asked to move to a room number that is equal to his existing room number multiplied by 2, leaving infinitely many odd-numbered rooms open for the new guests.

The remaining paradoxes contain greater and greater numbers of new guests, including, in one case, the arrival of uncountably infinite guests, which, of course, cannot be accommodated in Hilbert's Grand Hotel.

Considered together, Galileo's and Hilbert's paradoxes present typical themes of paradoxes of the infinitely large. The common analysis of these paradoxes may be summarized as follows. These paradoxes play upon the different mathematics of finite and infinite sets. For any finite set of natural numbers, there will be fewer squares (in the case of Galileo's paradox) or even or odd natural number subsets less than the cardinality of the finite set. However, because the cardinality of infinite sets by definition is equal to the cardinality of certain of its proper subsets, in these cases, squares, odd numbers, and even numbers, new members can be added without altering their cardinality, in each case which is equal to $\aleph_0$. This understanding derives from Russell's point, made earlier, that the cardinal numbers are not inductive.[23]

Because the deduction of the natural numbers under the homogenous logicism of transcendent realism does not depend upon set-theory, a different analysis of these problems will be undertaken. Under the philosophy presented in this pages, the natural numbers are a series of logical objects the priority of which is determined solely by reference to the logical relations of antecedence and subsequence. As such, the *N*-series is endless and not susceptible of quantification under any limit and, accordingly, *the concept of cardinality is inapplicable to it*. It will be helpful if we substitute for Hilbert's quaint hotel, a simple series of logical objects that can be mapped on a one-for-one basis with the *N*-series. We can call the series that so corresponds to the *N*-series, the *N*-correspondent series. The question that corresponds to the question asked in Hilbert's first paradox is whether it is possible to add to the *N*-correspondent series a new logical object and if so what is the effect of such addition. The answer is that of course we can, but doing so is of no consequence, because, after the operation, we are in precisely the same state of affairs as before, which is that we have an infinite series of logical objects that, just like the *N*-correspondent series, is mapped on a one-for-one basis with the *N*-series. The number of logical objects is unchanged and although it may be the case that the handle-to-handle mapping of the logical objects comprising each series has been modified that is a meaningless alternation because the *logical* structure of the mapping is the same in both cases.

---

23. See text accompanying 5n and 6n, 179.

Consider Hilbert's second paradox, which is resolved by moving all guests to even numbered rooms so that the new quests can be accommodated in the vacated odd numbered rooms. Note that if instead of moving each guest to an even numbered room we asked each guest staying in an odd numbered room to leave the hotel, we would have precisely the same availability and yet we would have displaced an infinite number of guests to achieve it! The counterintuitive nature of the paradox is generated in the first instance by the introduction of the empirical concept of a hotel and its guests and its rooms, all of which are naturally understood to be finite and, in the second instance, by the concept of cardinality. But the point is this: after you fill Hilbert's hotel any way you like and reduce the rooms and their occupants to their fundamental Being as logical objects, the *logical* structure of the mapping is always the same.

Galileo's and Hilbert's paradoxes only seem paradoxical because intuitively we ascribe limitation to that which is unlimited and because we consider natural numbers as though they are things, so that, in the case of Galileo's paradox, when we match a natural number with its square it seems that we must run out of squares long before we run out of the natural numbers from which they are derived and, in the case of Hilbert's paradoxes, it seems impossible that we should be able to find rooms for guests who arrive at a fully occupied hotel. Because numbers are logical objects, they and their relations are potentially unlimited. The paradoxes that arise from attributing cardinality to infinite sets, such as $\aleph_0 + 1 = \aleph_0$, evaporate when we realize that infinity is not a number, infinite sets have no numeric cardinality, and that these set-theoretic concepts needlessly introduce complexity to what is a straightforward logical analysis.

That logical objects are potentially unlimited does not imply that they are uncountable and, indeed, the contrary proposition is true. Logical objects are *limitlessly* countable and therefore may not be quantified. It will be remembered that under transcendent realism, the countability of all objects of thought is preconditioned by their enhandlement. In other words, anything that is thinkable is countable as an object of thought because it either is or inherits from an enhandled logical object. Natural numbers are infinitely countable by definition, not by bijection with any other set. The notion that there should be twice as many natural numbers as there are even natural numbers presupposes that there is some number that may be associated with each and then compared but, of course, that is not the case.

Moreover, it is impossible to imagine how any thinkable object or collection of objects (such as the real numbers) could be uncountable. It is, of course, true that a logical object that represents a collection of objects will, by virtue of its unique enhandlement and ground, be countable as a single object. The question, then, becomes whether the elements of the collection can ever be uncountable. Again, taken individually, each such element will be uniquely enhandled and grounded and, therefore, countable. It will be recalled that Cantor does not purport to provide a comprehensive list of real numbers that is longer than the infinitely long list of natural numbers and, indeed, although he purports to provide a means for identifying a real number that is not included in a purportedly complete list of real numbers, he does not profess to provide a number that is itself uncountable or the digits of which are uncountable. Instead, Cantor's argument is that given an infinite list of real numbers, Cantor can always identify a real number that is not on the list. A corollary argument is that while we may be able to think about many individual real numbers and count each one we will never be able to think about all of them. Of course, that is also the case with the natural numbers, so it would not suffice to say that we cannot list all of the real numbers (although we have shown that we can do so logically). It seems, therefore, that given the unique enhandlement of all objects of thought understanding transcendent realism for there to be an uncountable collection it would have to include members that could be shown *individually* to be unthinkable. However, if an object were unthinkable, it could not logically be thought to exist. We may often speak of that which is unthinkable but such statements are substantively the same as statements about objects that are not objects, which, of course, are patently incoherent.

8

Propaedeutic to Ontology

THE BIRTH OF PHENOMENOLOGY

It will be recalled that the three presuppositions of objective knowledge are mind-independent, self-justifying *a priori* rules of thought, an empirical reality that is orderly in a manner that may be understood under the auspices of general logic, and consciousness of self as a persistent, rational entity. In our exposition of that topic, we treated each such precondition as a separate element. Although this approach is heuristically desirable, it does not reflect reality as it is actually constituted, and, in fact, in the real world, transcendent and physical, the elements of objective knowledge are constitutionally unified. The rules of thought are the fundamental principles describing the orderability of logical objects and their relations and, as such are *properties* of logical objects, logical objects are the progenitors (cognitive grounds) of their descendent empirical objects and of the spatio-temporal horizon in which they are present to reason, and self-consciousness is possessed by beings that are themselves objects and that, as such, must be understood under the same rational aegis as the rest of world. In other words, in the real world, for man considered as a rational being for whom objective knowledge is possible, *Being, intelligibility (of Being), and self-consciousness (of self-Being), coincide in and constitute a harmonious whole.* For the same heuristic reasons, our prior exposition of self-consciousness was couched in terms of internal cognition and presented in a logically formalistic manner. But, in the real world, self-consciousness is anything but formal. Indeed, self-consciousness represents the most immediate and intimate cognition of reality from within the very reality that is its object because self-consciousness is present knowledge of the soul, as revealed by itself to itself, and of the relation of the soul to all other objects, physical and theoretical, that are present to it. Self-consciousness is therefore originary knowledge and, because it is part and parcel of the Being and intelligibility of the world, it is *the point of access* to all objective knowledge that is attainable by man. So, although our exposition of the possibility of objective knowledge in terms of its three presuppositions is correct, it provides only the formal structure of rational experience and, in order to understand the *actualization* of objective knowledge, not only must the *Being* of self-conscious beings be understood but it must be understood as the starting point of all such knowledge and as the horizon of all experience.

In our earlier presentation of the modern death march of metaphysics, with the exception of our passing mention of Nietzsche, we largely ignored the philosophical lines that were developed in continental Europe during the nineteenth and twentieth centuries. These philosophies include Marxism, neo-Kantianism, phenomenology (which in some of its iterations may appropriately be considered as neo-Kantian), nihilism, existentialism, and others (some of which, together with nihilism and existentialism, may appropriately be considered as versions of phenomenology). The scholarship during this period, which was dominated by the German and Austrian schools, reflects the chaos of the historical, cultural, and economic changes that were transpiring contemporaneously at a breath-taking pace. These philosophies developed to some degree in cooperation with pioneering advances in mathematics, physics and cosmology, psychology, biology, and other sciences. Although these philosophical schools are fundamentally diverse in their presuppositions, claims, and purposes, they share a profound dissatisfaction with both the speculative character of German idealism, which oddly (given the strong and overtly nationalist current of German intellectualism) had lost most of its currency in Germany several decades before it did in England, and with the dubious materialist philosophies that arose in conjunction with the massive expansion of industrialism and science during that era. As a result, nineteenth and twentieth century continental philosophy can fairly be understood as a rush to fill the chasm between German idealism and Anglo-American pragmatism/materialism and perhaps it is no surprise that so many different schools came and went during the period, which provided it with the character of being more of an effervescing of themes than an enduring, progressive development of any particular system. This understanding is confirmed to a large degree by the fact that most philosophy of the period consists of monographs rather than the treatises that had historically characterized important philosophical thinking and also by the fact that, to the extent that there is in them any sustained progression of ideas, in most cases, only a short period of time was required to reach their patently dissatisfactory endpoints. The exclusion of these lines from our earlier discussion on the decline of philosophy was appropriate on the ground that none of them achieved the mainstream gravitas necessary to interrupt the supplantation of metaphysics with the pseudo-philosophy of modern science and, with the exception of a particularly important strain of phenomenology, we will continue to disregard continental philosophy of the period, in the case of (non-phenomenological) neo-Kantianism on the same grounds as our criticism of Kant's philosophy and, in the case of the others, on the grounds of their lack of substantive merit or relevance. "Phenomenology" is a loose locution that is often understood to comprehend much of the nineteenth and twentieth century continental philosophy other than Marxism (and is sometimes uninformatively characterized as representing the mainstream there), but under that broad umbrella, there is a distinctly narrow but dominant line that commences with Franz Brentano and runs next to Edmund Husserl and finally to Martin Heidegger, who were teacher, pupil, and pupil's pupil, respectively. The philosophy of these three men represents an undeniably robust exposition of human experience and its psychological, metaphysical, and ontological underpinnings, and, indeed, when it comes to understanding Being as such, *no* line of thinking, before or after, is more important. So it is with this strain of phenomenology that we will initiate our investigation of the *actualization* of objective human knowledge of the world.

Brentano's philosophy, which is called "descriptive psychology," is primarily set forth in his masterwork, *Psychology from an Empirical Standpoint* and, as the name implies, it reflects his determination to develop a philosophy of the mind by describing and categorizing mental operations and objects. Although there is disagreement as to the meaning of the term "phenomenology" and as to whether, under any given definition of phenomenology, Brentano should be considered to be its grandfather, its father, or merely its precursor, we will include him as the first important phenomenologist under a definition of phenomenology as the philosophical study of perceptual and sensory phenomena without any claim as to the existence, nonexistence, or nature of physical objects independently of their mental representation. Husserl started out as an adherent of his teacher but in a series of important works, including *Philosophy of Arithmetic*, *Logical Investigations* (two volumes), and *Ideas for a Pure Phenomenology and Phenomenological Philosophy*, he gradually progressed from the student of Brentano's empirical psychology to the creator of a full-blown philosophical system, which Husserl named "phenomenology." Husserl's central claim is that the *essences* of mental objects (including physical objects to the extent presented to the mind) can be determined by subjecting the presentation of such objects to processes of philosophical purification, which he calls "phenomenological" and "eidectic" reduction. Brentano's descriptive psychology and Husserl's phenomenology accordingly share a focus upon mental phenomena as the empirical matter of investigation and the premise that, in so doing, their respective philosophies, directly, in the case of Brentano, and indirectly (after application of a process of reductive analysis) in the case of Husserl, constitute expositions of reality that are *purportedly* free of any metaphysical presuppositions. However, Husserl's investigations are of a distinctly different character than Brentano's because Husserl insists that such investigations must include, in addition to mental phenomena, consciousness itself as the field in which such phenomena occur. Heidegger, like Husserl, began his philosophical career as a proponent of his teacher, and, also like Husserl, after only a short while, found it necessary to forge his own path. Heidegger asserts that the goal of avoiding the presuppositions of all philosophy can only be achieved by placing ontology ahead of epistemology and metaphysics and, instead of starting investigation with consciousness, one must first refer to Being itself as the most fundamental concept of all. In both *Being and Time* and *Introduction to Metaphysics*, two of the three great works of Heidegger upon which we will focus (the other being *The Principle of Reason*), Heidegger begins by acknowledging both the necessity and the difficulty of beginning an ontology with an interpretation of the very Being it seeks to explain, because Being is the most originary[1] (and therefore presumably indescribable) concept, but Heidegger, taking a cue from Brentano, starts from the standpoint of human familiarity with its own Being and carefully and methodically builds a metaphysical system the goal of which is nothing less than a complete and concrete exposition of the meaning of Being.

---

1. Heidegger employs the term "primordial" in *Being and Time* and "originary" in *Introduction to Metaphysics* and *The Principle of Reason*.

As is to be expected with the philosophers of the same line of thought, the journey from Brentano to Husserl to Heidegger is highly thematic. Although each philosophy is fundamentally psychological, all three are staunchly opposed to psychologism, which is the view that all knowledge, including logic and mathematics, is reducible to mental phenomena, and also to subjective idealism, and, of course, solipsism. Each philosopher believes that his philosophy represents the highest form of science, that is, the science to which the physical sciences and all others must ultimately refer for validation. Each philosopher harkens back to much earlier philosophers for his inspiration—Aristotle and the Scholastics in the case of Brentano, Descartes and Kant in the case of Husserl, and the pre-Socratics and Aristotle, in the case of Heidegger. There is the interesting and overarchingly important development that starts with Brentano's revitalization of Aristotle's concept of intentionality, which is adopted and broadened by Husserl into the study, not just of the objects of consciousness but also consciousness itself, and finally into Heidegger's study of Being as Being-in the world and whose intentionality is nothing less than the means by which human reason gains access to the world in which it is itself included. There is also a parallel development that begins with Brentano's attribution of affirmation and emotion (love and hate) in the act of judging objects, to Husserl's emphasis on the subject's empathetic cognition of other humans, to Heidegger's notion of care, which is the structure of humanity as the being for whom its own Being is an issue and which includes the Being-with other people. There is also in all three the ever-present concern with the formal importance of unity among manifolds, although none of the three philosophies place logic at the pinnacle of human thinking—for Brentano and Husserl, logic is not subordinate to other knowledge while, for Heidegger logic is subordinate to Being. All three philosophers stress the temporal nature of human experience and prioritize temporality over extension in the cognition of objects, although in at least one of Husserl's articulations it constitutes the originary residuum of consciousness and in Heidegger it is raised to the fundamental horizon of *Dasein*. All three consider reason to be engaged with its objects in the act of their cognition and not merely their detached, dispassionate determiner, as the physical scientists would have it.[2] As a result of these last two ideas, the current circumstances, personal history, and history of man are all factors that each of these philosophers consider to be important in understanding the basic philosophical propositions at any time. Finally, there is an especially interesting development in methodology that begins with Brentano's "inner perception" of mental presentations, is followed by Husserl's early adoption of "reflection" and subsequent adoption of the two reductions, and culminates with Heidegger's "interrogation" of *Dasein*.

Heidegger's criticism of Brentano and Husserl that the presupposition of Being remains unexpurgated from (and unexplained in) their philosophies is undoubtedly correct and we will attach much importance to it in the discussion that follows in the next chapter; however, it should be acknowledged here that there seems to be under development a body of scholarship along the lines that Heidgegger himself makes more of it than is merited. Although the details of Heidegger's criticism that ontology must precede

2. In Brentano's case, this engagement occurs as the "lived experience" of inner perception, in Husserl's case, as that of the "life-world" of consciousness and its correlates (i.e., intentional objectivities), and, in Heidegger's case, as *Dasein's* Being-in the world of which it has a primordial understanding.

any science of consciousness (which Heidegger calls the "immanent critique" because it is established within the confines of phenomenology itself) must await a more complete discussion of Heidegger's philosophy in the sequel chapter, it is worthwhile to point out here that because it is one thing to identify a problem and quite another to solve it, and because it is by no means clear that identifying a presuppositionless starting point from which metaphysical investigations may be undertaken is even possible, the fact that, and the manner in which, Heidegger faces these challenges projects a high degree of philosophical bravado. And that Heidegger starts with man's vague idea of his own Being and fights his way all the way through to a metaphysics that is ontologically founded is nothing less than an exercise of raw philosophical power and will. Nevertheless, in unfolding of the meaning of Being, Heidegger makes several fundamental errors, the implications of which undermine his entire philosophy. Of these, the most important is that Heidegger incorrectly treats Being and logic as though they are wholly independent of one another and incorrectly assumes that his claim that one must start with Being entails the privileging of Being over logic. It should come as no surprise that we hold this idea to be incorrect. As will be explained, the result of Heidegger's privileging of Being over logic is to allow nothingness (he calls it "Nothing"), which is demonstrably self-contradictory, suddenly to leap forth as a real possibility and an important perspective from which Being must be understood. This error is as profoundly problematic as Heidegger's recognition of the importance of Being is ingenious because it precludes ontology from reaching its necessary and sublime objective, namely, the Supreme Principle of Being and Intelligibility and leaves ontology languishing instead in what Heidegger calls the *abgrund* (which translates into "abyss" and is used to connote ungroundedness). Even so, Heidegger's philosophy is as fresh, rich, and informative as any in history and it is in Heidegger's exposition of Being as experienced by human beings that we will find our orientation for ascent from the foothills of the formal logical epistemology of the preceding chapters to that metaphysical pinnacle, by virtue of which we will find the answer to the meaning of Being generally and the Being of man in particular.

In this chapter, we will cover the work of Brentano and Husserl, which, although interesting and important in its own right, is considered in these pages as propaedeutic to Heidegger's ontology, the discussion of which will be postponed until the next chapter, where it will serve as the springboard for our own investigation of the meaning of Being.

BRENTANO'S DESCRIPTIVE PSYCHOLOGY

We commence our investigations with Brentano's *Psychology*, which was published in 1874. Brentano begins his work with an assessment of the state of psychology that is reminiscent of Kant's assessment of metaphysics in his introduction to the *Critique of Pure Reason*. Brentano tells us that psychology was zealously investigated by the great men of antiquity, that, if anything, their findings have been obscured instead of advanced by subsequent thinkers, and that only metaphysics is a subject held by the masses in greater contempt. And just as metaphysics was esteemed by Kant as the Queen of All Sciences, Brentano expresses his assessment that psychology should be regarded as the crowning discipline above all sciences. Brentano's initial step in advancing his argument is to refer us to Aristotle, in whom he finds great inspiration, as the first to classify science as such, emphasizing that Aristotle referred to science as "psychology," which derives from the Greek word ψυχή (*psychí*) for soul and therefore means "science of the soul." In Aristotle's essay *On the Soul* (*Perì Psūchês*), the great philosopher is concerned with the classification of living things, which he characterizes as those beings which are able to nourish themselves, to grow and to reproduce, or which possess either or both of the faculties of sensation and thought. For Aristotle, *ensouled* beings include animals and plants, even though only some of the former and none of the latter may be said to be conscious. Brentano then recounts the continual historical division of what was encompassed by Aristotle's psychology into other fields of a biological nature, such as botany, biology, and physiology, and the corresponding narrowing of the concept of soul from that which enlivens to that which is the substantial bearer of mental "presentations" and related activities all of which are known through inner perception. Brentano tells us that the circumscription of the soul was attended by a corresponding circumscription of the field of psychology, finally yielding the contemporary epistemological division between psychology, which studies the properties and laws of mental phenomena, and the natural sciences, which study the properties and laws of physical objects. Brentano makes the important observation that the phenomena of consciousness and the phenomena of the physical world are given to us *under the same mode of perception* and are in this and other ways related to such a degree as to merit their study as a unified scientific domain. In support of this claim, Brentano tells us that phenomena of inner perception are subject to laws, including, for example, the laws of coexistence and succession of mental phenomena. As a result, Brentano regards the distinction between psychology and the physical sciences as it is commonly understood to be a fundamental error that leads to mistaken epistemological conclusions. For Brentano, a more accurate and fruitful approach is to define the field of psychological (philosophical) study as comprising all mental phenomena and to distinguish between such phenomena according to whether they constitute presentations of mental or physical objects. Placing all phenomena under a single psychological umbrella does not imply the denigration of the physical sciences or their methods, but it does require viewing them from a different epistemological perspective and, following Locke, Brentano asserts the unreliability of the absolute correspondence of mental presentations of physical objects to the objects as they are presumed to be in reality (the example Brentano provides is John Locke's famous experiment of the immersion of a hot and cold hand into water simultaneously yielding completely different sensations) and emphasizes that the only clear and distinct knowledge accessible to human reason is of the objects of our inner perception which is given to us by immediate insight. This distinction is especially profound because, in Kantian terms, science can never get at the *noumena* of its objects of study, but objects of inner perception are their own *noumena* and are therefore fully knowable objects. Brentano brings home the distinction between knowledge of presentations of mental objects and physical objects as follows:

> We have seen what kind of knowledge the natural scientist is able to attain. The phenomena of light, sound, heat, spatial location and locomotion which he studies are not things which really and truly exist. They are signs of something real,

> which, through its causal activity, produces presentations of them. They are not, however, an adequate representation of this reality, and they give us knowledge of it only in a very incomplete sense. We can say that there exists something which, under certain conditions, causes this or that sensation. We can probably also prove that there must be relations among these realities similar to those which are manifested by spatial phenomena shapes and sizes. But this is as far as we can go. We have no experience of that which truly exists, in and of itself, and that which we do experience is not true. The truth of physical phenomena is, as they say, only a relative truth.[3]

Brentano concludes, because the phenomena of inner perception are true as regards themselves, and because they are the provenance of sensation, imagination, judgment, will, and, in turn, art, knowledge, and virtue, and because they are our own more than any physical objects can ever be, psychology is the highest science. And Brentano takes pains to make clear that psychology studies only mental phenomena without making any metaphysical claim as to whether such phenomena are borne by a substantial soul and that the question of the immortality of the soul, which since at least the time of Plato was regarded as the most important psychological investigation, is, on Brentano's definition, beyond the reach of its subject matter. Interestingly, Brentano, following a pattern not unlike Kant's when he sought to "suspend expansion of knowledge in order to make room for faith," holds out hope on a non-scientific ground for those who cherish the prospect of immortality:

> For even though it is self-evident that those who deny the existence of a substantial soul cannot speak of the immortality of the soul in the proper sense of the word, it still does not follow that the question of the immortality of the soul loses all meaning because we deny the existence of a substantial bearer of mental phenomena. This becomes evident as soon as you recognize that with or without a substantial soul you cannot deny that there is a certain continuity of our mental life here on earth. If someone rejects the existence of a substance, he must assume that such a continuity does not require a substantial bearer. And the question whether our mental life somehow continues even after the destruction of the body will be no more meaningless for him than for anyone else. It is wholly inconsistent for thinkers of this persuasion to reject, for the reasons mentioned, the question of immortality even in this, its essential sense, though it certainly would be more appropriate to call it immortality of life than immortality of the soul.[4]

In supporting his argument in favor of the scientific primacy of psychology, Brentano makes a one-off remark that suggests his support of psychologism, thereby igniting a controversy that continues to the present day: "[S]uffice it to say that the important art of logic, a single improvement in which brings about a thousand advances in science, also has psychology as its source."[5] As will be seen, Husserl will rely upon Brentano in Husserl's earliest works and will embrace a psychologistic philosophy of mathematics, which will draw caustic rebukes from both Frege and Brentano and which may have prompted

3. Brentano, *Psychology*, 14.
4. Ibid., 12–13.
5. Ibid., 15–16.

Husserl to abandon psychologism as the first step in his development of the philosophy of phenomenology. Brentano's subsequent protestations to the contrary notwithstanding, there is additional support for psychologism (which it is safe to assume did not go unnoticed by Husserl) in Brentano's inclusion of mathematics in a comprehensive spectrum of sciences even though it is located at the end of the spectrum opposite to psychology.

Brentano's next step is one of the truly revolutionary ones in all of philosophy. Although he seeks to establish psychology on an empirical basis, Brentano astutely refrains from the blind adoption of the methods of the physical sciences to his subject matter. Brentano's thesis is that the scientific method that is appropriate for inquiry into physical objects draws its propriety from the relation of its concepts to its subject matter and he therefore identifies his objective as the determination of a scientific method *that is specifically appropriate to psychic life*. Brentano tells us that the adoption of such a method requires the development of a natural classification of mental phenomena not based upon observation and hypothesis testing, which is the methodology of the physical sciences, but upon consideration of the experience of mental phenomena *as they are presented* to the mind without any presupposition. This, along with Brentano's minimization of the importance of extension in the determination of physical objects and his adoption of the Aristotelian concept of intentionality, is perhaps the most important aspect of Brentano's entire philosophy because the goal of rooting out all presupposition will drive the entire development of Husserl's phenomenology and Heidegger's ontology. Brentano tells us that inner perception, not introspection (observation), must be the source of psychological experience and makes the distinction between the lived experience of the psychological phenomena as a true fact in and of itself (regardless of the conformity of its content to any objective conditions), and the separate act of observing the occurrence of the psychological phenomena, the content of which differs from the content of the perception itself. The truth of the lived experience as such is another important concept that is developed along with phenomenology, which will manifest in a similar concept of truth in Heidegger's ontology, which he will stand against the mainstream empirical notion of truth.

For Brentano, the highest laws governing the succession of mental phenomena are, strictly speaking, empirical laws. Because Brentano asserts that we can never have an experience and observe the experience at the same time, he is compelled to provide us with an understanding of how we are to access true perceptions and, in this regard, he offers five means: (1) consideration of earlier mental phenomena through memory; (2) indirect knowledge of other people's mental phenomena from their outward expressions; (3) study of conscious lives simpler than our own; (4) observation of diseased mental states; and (5) study of prominent features in both the lives of individuals and of peoples. According to Brentano, these means provide us with the raw material of experience from which we may identify the universal characteristics common to all psychological phenomena and their basic classification from which the fundamental laws of psychology may be deduced. Brentano tells us that even though exact laws governing the succession of mental phenomena cannot be discovered in the absence of a way of measuring their intensity (which in Brentano's day was not available), special laws governing the succession of mental phenomena may be deduced from observations (made by the means of access to perception of presentations just identified) and tested by reference to further observation.

It should come as no surprise that Brentano's broadest classification of mental phenomena is between those which are mental and those which are physical. However, Brentano asserts that it is sometimes difficult to differentiate the two because we have no presentation of physical data as such and, in order to give a sense of the difference, Brentano gives examples of each type, which demonstrate his intention that mental phenomena be understood as *mental activity* (e.g., hearing, seeing, feeling, imagining, conceptualizing) and that physical phenomena be understood as *objects* which are given in perception (e.g., sounds, colors, heat and cold, and objects of imagination or conceptualization). Brentano clarifies that mental phenomena are presentations or are based on presentations, so that taking a mental activity as the object of a thought does not render it physical in nature. In a point of profound importance, Brentano notes that Descartes, Spinoza, and Kant all distinguish that which is mental from that which is physical in a completely different manner, which is according to whether the object is extended. Brentano also notes that some (citing Berkeley, A. Plainer, David Hartley, Thomas Brown, James Mill, John Stuart Mill, and Herbert Spencer) object to this distinction on the basis that some or, indeed all, physical phenomena (such as sounds and olfactory phenomena) appear to be without extension, and that some mental phenomena, such as pleasure or pain in the extremities, even after amputation of a limb, appear to have extension. Brentano expresses skepticism about both objections but in effect renders the debate moot by adopting *intentionality* as the sole criteria by which one can distinguish mental from physical phenomena. Brentano tells us that what is characteristic of mental phenomena in general is their reference to a content, direction to an object, or immanent objectivity, and their inclusion, in each case, of an object within themselves. The inclusion of objects within mental phenomena differentiates them from physical phenomena and is called "in-existence," which allows for a definition of mental phenomena as "those phenomena which contain an object intentionally within themselves."[6]

Brentano offers several other distinguishing characteristics of mental and physical phenomena which will facilitate their classification and the deduction of scientific principles that apply to them. Specifically, Brentano notes that: (1) mental phenomena can only be perceived through inner consciousness, whereas it is only possible to perceive physical phenomena through outer perception; (2) physical phenomena can exist only phenomenally, whereas mental phenomena exist in reality as well; and (3) mental phenomena which we perceive, in spite of all their multiplicity, always appear to us as a unity, while physical phenomena, which we perceive at the same time, do not all appear in the same way as parts of one single phenomenon. It is impossible to overemphasize that in Brentano's assertion of the importance of intentionality and his minimization of the importance of extension in the determination of physical objects within the span of a few paragraphs, Brentano, notwithstanding that he did not consider himself to be a phenomenologist, cleared the field for the elaboration of the importance of subject-object relationship and time-consciousness that were to become central to the phenomenological investigations of Husserl and Heidegger and to which we will attach great significance in the development of the (albeit much different) philosophy that follows in these pages.

---

6. Ibid., 68.

Brentano next turns to a description of conscious experience from which he will elicit several important principles, including: (1) that all mental acts are conscious (although many may be promptly forgotten); (2) that each lived experience directs itself towards it objects in a way that depends upon the character of the experience itself and that the ways in which intentionality occurs may be characterized as a presentation (i.e., the appearance of a phenomenon), judgment (i.e., the determination of the truth or falsity of the presentation), and interest (i.e., anything that is not included in the first two, such as love, hate, desire, fear, etc.); (3) that the relationship of the intensity of a presentation and its object differs according to the character of the experience; and (4) that consciousness is a unity. We will consider the first three principles according to the type of experience before considering the all-important question of the unity of consciousness.

(1) *Presentations.* For Brentano, consciousness *means* mental phenomena or mental act. This definition renders possible the apparent oxymoron of "unconscious consciousness" (i.e., engaging in mental activities of which we are unaware) the impossibility of which Brentano shows by refuting the four possible arguments in its favor. The first such argument is to infer unconscious consciousness from some known mental phenomenon such as clairvoyance, presentiment, premonition, and acts of great genius. The refutation is that the first three examples cannot be factually verified and with respect to acts of genius there exist other explanations that are equal, if not better. The second argument is by means of implication of a known mental phenomenon to a necessary cause as to which we have no consciousness. The refutation is threefold: first, the cause could have occurred but been forgotten; second, with respect to mental phenomena, it is not always clearly correct to connect an apparent effect with another mental phenomenon as its necessary cause; and third, the argument depends upon demonstration that the causes which prevented the missing, and therefore presumably unconscious, phenomenon from manifesting itself in a conscious presentation, and which were obviously not present in other similar cases in which such a presentation manifested, did not also prevent the mental phenomenon, the actual existence of which is to be inferred, and, in general, that no special obstacle lay in the way of this phenomenon. The third argument for unconscious consciousness is based upon the assertion that, unlike the directly proportional relationship between the strength of a presentation and its content, *the consciousness of a conscious phenomenon is a function of its own strength and is not related to the intensity of the conscious phenomenon.* The refutation of the third argument proceeds by showing that the assertion is false and that, instead, there is a directly proportional relationship between the intensity of the consciousness of a conscious phenomenon and the strength of the phenomenon itself. The fourth and final argument in favor of unconscious consciousness is based upon the assertion that the contrary argument (i.e., that every mental phenomenon is the object of a mental phenomenon) leads to an infinite regress which would render consciousness impossible. An example of the argument is that if there are no unconscious mental acts, then an act of hearing would be accompanied by consciousness of the act of hearing which in turn would be accompanied by consciousness of the consciousness of the act of hearing, *ad infinitum.* Brentano's refutation is ingenious and profoundly important. Instead of breaking the infinite loop imbedded in the argument by assuming the existence of unconscious consciousness, Brentano asserts that

each presentation entails a corresponding presentation of that presentation in one and the same act. Brentano then asserts that it is impossible both to have a perception of a mental phenomenon and observe the perception at the same time:

> Do we perceive the mental phenomena which exist within us? This question must be answered with an emphatic, "yes," for where would we have got the concepts of presentation and thought without such perception? On the other hand, it is obvious that we are not able to observe our present mental phenomena. But how can we explain this, if not by the fact that we are incapable of perceiving them? Previously, in fact, no other explanation seemed possible, but now we see the true reason clearly. The presentation which accompanies a mental act and refers to it is part of the object on which it is directed. If an inner presentation were ever to become inner observation, this observation would be directed upon itself. Even the defenders of inner observation, however, seem to consider this impossible.[7]

Next, Brentano asserts that the intensity of the presentation of the act varies with the intensity of the act itself because the content of the act is also included in the content of the presentation and concludes from this that there can be no unconscious mental activity. Accordingly, whenever a mental act is the object of an accompanying inner cognition, it contains in itself its entirety as presented and known, in addition to its reference to a primary object. This alone makes inner perception infallible and limits knowledge of the real object to knowledge of the object as presented in the mental act:

> The truth of inner perception cannot be proved in any way. But it has something more than proof; it is immediately evident. If anyone were to mount a skeptical attack against this ultimate foundation of cognition, he would find no other foundation upon which to erect an edifice of knowledge....
>
> We can say that the force of this argument extends beyond the evidence of inner perception and it even serves to confirm the way in which the inner presentation is connected with its real object, a connection which we have already come to recognize in other ways. The cognition of a real object cannot be more intimately united with it than its presentation is, since presentation forms the basis of cognition.[8]

(2) *Judgements.* Brentano next turns to judgements about mental acts which often accompany them. The accompanying inner judgement does not exhibit a combination of subject and predicate but only an affirmation of the mental phenomenon that is present. Interestingly, Brentano mentions in passing the nature of the affirmation as the *existence* of the mental phenomenon in virtually the same way that Heidegger will later speak of our intuition of "something like" Being as the starting point for his phenomenological ontology of *Dasein*. Brentano says:

> In the case of cognition through inner perception, the judgement is undoubtedly affirmative, but the predicate which is attributed to the subject would have to be existence, for what we perceive is that a mental act exists. Philosophers are not in agreement as to what the term "existence" really means, even though not only they, but any ordinary person, knows how to apply the term with confidence. But

7. Ibid., 99.
8. Ibid., 109.

it does not seem difficult to see that it is a very general and hence a very abstract concept, even if it really was derived from experience and did not exist in us as an *a priori* concept prior to all experience (always an awkward assumption).[9]

Brentano tells us that the affirmation is absolute and does not vary with the intensity of the mental phenomenon or its presentation.

(3) *Interest.* Brentano tells us that often there is within us a third kind of consciousness of the mental act in addition to presentation and knowledge, namely, a feeling directed toward it and likewise included in it. For examples, we think and desire things and know we think and desire them. This kind of inner consciousness, too, accompanies all mental activity without exception. Unlike the other two types of consciousness, the intensity of feeling is neither directly proportional nor constant. Although these emotive elements are of central importance to practicing psychologists, because we are not undertaking an analysis of aesthetics in these pages and do not consider moral obligation to be predicated upon empathy, no further consideration of them is necessary.

(4) *The Unity of Consciousness.* Brentano next turns to the all-important question of the unity of consciousness. As initially posed by Brentano, the question is whether there is a real unity of consciousness which encompasses all of the mental phenomena (as to which we are reminded that each is a unity which encompasses the mental act, its presentation, its affirmation, and related sentiments). Brentano tells us that although one thing cannot be a multiplicity of things, unity (of multiplicity) and simplicity are not interchangeable. Brentano reformulates: "in the case of more complex mental states, do we have to assume a collective of things, or, does the totality of mental phenomena, in the most complex states just as in the simplest, form one thing in which we can distinguish divisives as parts?"[10] Brentano observes that there are two types of complexities, neither of which rule out the unity of consciousness. One occurs when we are conscious of a single object in multiple ways (e.g., perceiving, judging, desiring) and the other occurs when we are conscious of a multiplicity of objects at the same time. Brentano argues that although (1) our simultaneous mental acts may be independent of one another (e.g., seeing a thing while listening to another), and (2) the intimacy between such acts is nowhere near as close as the unity among the three aspects of inner consciousness (mental act, perception of mental act, affirmation of mental act), the complexities themselves could not arise in the absence of a real unity because neither the multiplicity of the simultaneous mental acts nor the unity of the aspects of each such act could ever become known to us. To make the point, Brentano offers various examples, including the comparing of seeing and hearing simultaneously, devising strategies for accomplishing ends out of a multiplicity of means and steps, seeing and desiring an object, and recognizing the temporal order of the individual notes in a song. Brentano concludes that our simultaneous mental activities all belong to one real unity:

> The unity of consciousness, as we know with evidence through inner perception, consists in the fact that all mental phenomena which occur within us simultaneously such as seeing and hearing, thinking, judging and reasoning, loving

---

9. Ibid.
10. Ibid., 121.

and hating, desiring and shunning, etc., no matter how different they may be, all belong to one unitary reality only if they are inwardly perceived as existing together. They constitute phenomenal parts of a mental phenomenon, the elements of which are neither distinct things nor parts of distinct things but belong to a real unity. This is the necessary condition for the unity of consciousness, and no further conditions are required.[11]

The last point of interest to us in the current investigations is the telling blow that Brentano deals to Kant's transcendental ego. Brentano says:

> Of course the unity of consciousness would fare ill if the phenomena of inner perception too had only phenomenal truth. Not even the existence of consciousness would be assured. But we have already pointed out repeatedly that Kant and Lange, who follows him here, are on the wrong track. It is an out and out contradiction to attribute a mere phenomenal truth both to inner and outer perception, as Kant does, for the phenomenal truth of physical phenomena requires the real truth of mental phenomena. If mental phenomena did not exist in reality, neither physical nor mental phenomena would even exist as phenomena. The contradiction, then, cannot be removed in this way.[12]

Before moving on to a discussion of the development by Husserl and others of the philosophy of phenomenology, a word of summary of Brentano's philosophical importance is appropriate. At the highest level, Brentano's science of mental phenomena provides the basis for the psychologically oriented philosophies of Husserl's phenomenology (science of consciousness) and Heidegger's ontology (science of Being considered as the situs at which the world discloses itself). More specifically, Brentano introduces with some success concepts that will be adopted or developed by the subsequent thinkers. These include: (1) the critique of modern philosophy/psychology as having obscured the important findings of the ancient philosophers/psychologists and as having narrowed what is essentially the highest and all-encompassing science; (2) the restoration of the Aristotelian and Scholastic concept of intentionality as the core principle; (3) the rejection of the mainstream propositional definition of truth in favor of one that is based upon the lived experience of mental phenomena; (4) the description of the structure of mental acts as comprising presentation, judgment, and interest; and (5) the defense of the real unity of consciousness.

HUSSERL AND THE PHILOSOPHY OF PHENOMENOLOGY

Although Edmund Husserl received his doctorate in mathematics from the University of Vienna, shortly afterward he attended certain of Brentano's lectures and Husserl's interest began to shift, first to the philosophy of mathematics, then to epistemology, and lastly to metaphysics and ontology. As a result of this somewhat unusual career path, Husserl received relatively little formal training in philosophy other than from his close relationship with Brentano, which is a fact that has emboldened some of his critics to assert

---

11. Ibid., 126.
12. Ibid., 133.

that Husserl frequently repeats errors that had been identified and resolved long before him in the history of philosophy. Like his mentor, Husserl's objective was to develop a scientific philosophy that is free of metaphysical presuppositions. It is not a disservice to Husserl to characterize his work not as a radical departure from Brentano's descriptive philosophy but instead as a generalization of it into a full-blown metaphysics of all realms of conscious experience. Husserl's philosophy culminates in his own version of transcendental idealism under which knowledge reaches its limits at pure consciousness, which Husserl asserts is the precondition of all experience.

Although Husserl's doctoral dissertation was on the calculus, he wrote his habilitation thesis, "On the Concept of Number: Psychological Analyses," after spending two years of study under Brentano. Husserl's thesis formed the basis of his *Philosophy of Arithmetic*, which set forth Husserl's psychologistic number theory. As noted, Husserl's early psychologism engendered public rebuke from both Frege, a Platonist, on straight philosophical grounds, and from Brentano, on the grounds that, to the extent that it purports to represent an application of descriptive psychology to number theory, it contains metaphysical claims that were not held by Brentano. Whether these criticisms were a factor in Husserl's abandonment of psychologism is unclear; however, a little less than a decade later Husserl's two volume *Logical Investigations* was published, with the first volume, which is called the *Prolegomena to Pure Logic*, being devoted to the rebuttal of psychologism as being indefensibly subjective, relativistic, and incoherent. In the *Prolegomena*, Husserl makes clear his new understanding of logical entities (e.g., numbers, geometric forms, propositions) as objective in nature and, in the second volume of *Logical Investigations*, called *Investigations in Phenomenology and Knowledge*, Husserl presents his epistemological description of the phenomenology of logical experiences as so understood. In 1913, Husserl published *Ideas for a Phenomenology and Phenomenological Philosophy*, which is the first of a trilogy of books devoted to his developing philosophy, the latter two of which were published posthumously many decades later. In *Ideas I*, Husserl announces phenomenology not merely as a theory of knowledge but as *the* methodology of philosophical investigation (which to a large extent was already implicit in the *Logical Investigations*) the goal of which is to uncover epistemological, metaphysical, and ontological truths concerning the entire realm of conscious experience.

Although Husserl's philosophy is deeply rooted in Brentano's descriptive psychology, Husserl's work is highly innovative and profoundly more ambitious, and includes, among other advancements: a new interpretation of intentionality and the expansion of intentionality to include consciousness itself as an object; the formal division of consciousness into regions within which that which is given to consciousness can be taken as true in accordance with the rules governing the region; the concept of ordinary experience as constituting a life-world (*Lebenswelt*); and what Husserl calls the methods of eidetic and phenomenological reduction as the necessary procedures for ascertaining the essence of the phenomena as given to consciousness. Interestingly, as Husserl's philosophy evolved from a theory of logical knowledge, to metaphysics, to ontology, it became more and more closely aligned in various important respects with those of Descartes, Hegel, and, especially, Kant and, by the middle of Husserl's career, Husserl himself came to regard phenomenology as a form of transcendental idealism, albeit one that is fundamentally different from that of Kant. Of particular interest to our own investigations is Husserl's development of the phenomenological understanding of the self, which although always presented as a unity of conscious experience, sometimes seems to be a reinterpretation of Kant's unity of apperception relative to objects as given to consciousness and other times seems indistinguishable from Hegel's absolute Ego.

It is safe to say that most continental philosophers would regard Husserl's phenomenology as either the first or second most important philosophical achievement of the twentieth century, depending upon where they would place it in relation to that of Heidegger, his student. Although it is the latter who, because of his focus on ontology, is more germane to the exposition of transcendent realism, it cannot be overemphasized that Heidegger could not have developed his philosophy without standing upon Husserl's shoulders and we should also note that Husserl near the end of his career (if not earlier) acknowledged the metaphysical connection between thinking and Being that is so important to us in our own investigations. In this regard, Dermott Moran, in his *Introduction to Phenomenology*, tells us:

> Underneath the diversity of themes and approaches adopted by Husserl there lies a deep unity of project, the project of "first philosophy": the relation between being (*das Seindes*) and reason (*Vernunft*). Thus, in the *Crisis* [*of the European Sciences*], he asks, "Can reason and that-which-is be separated, where reason, as knowing, determines what is?"[13]

Nevertheless, as we shall see, that Husserl saw this relation as being between *consciousness*, as such, and its *objects*, and not with *intelligibility* and *Being*, leaves Husserl open to criticism upon grounds that do not apply to the stricter identification that is professed in these pages, including, especially, the immanent critique leveled at Husserl by Heidegger that in starting with consciousness Husserl presupposes the Being of its objects and, therefore, that ontology must take precedence.

For our purposes, then, without in any way denigrating Husserl's philosophical stature or appeal, Husserl's importance lies in his relation to Heidegger, which means that our summary of Husserl's work must serve certain limited purposes relevant to our subsequent critique of Heidegger. One is to understand the ways in which phenomenology represents both a systematic philosophy and a methodology for understanding consciousness and its phenomena. The former is important to us because Husserl's phenomenology is central in the line from Brentano to Husserl to Heidegger, the last of whom will serve as a springboard to our own understanding of the Being of human beings. The latter will serve as a useful prelude to the understanding of Heidegger's own unique methodology, which, in *Being and Time*, consists of the interrogation of man as to his own Being through an iterative interpretation of his "everydayness" and justifies its characterization as phenomenological ontology (although Husserl will critically characterize it as being "anthropology").

In accessing Husserl's philosophy we are immediately presented with the difficulty that his work, which comprises an enormous volume of treatises, articles, lecture transcripts, and personal notes, represents a process of continual development, clarification,

---

13. Moran, *Introduction*, 61, quoting Husserl, *Crisis*, §5, 11.

self-criticism, and renewed expression of earlier concepts. Accordingly, there is no single work, or even discreet subset of his work, which one can say represents a definitive statement of Husserl's phenomenology, which leaves us with at least three possible avenues for the explication of Husserl's work. One approach, which is frequently if not most often taken by scholars, is to selectively progress through Husserl's writings on a chronological basis. This approach offers the advantage of providing the context of the actual development of Husserl's philosophy; however, it also entails working through material that will later be superseded, sometimes clearly and sometimes ambiguously so. Another approach is to try to restate Husserl's philosophy as a consistent, complete, and determinate system, which has the advantage of fixing the target of inquiry, but this approach requires acceptance of some amount of misstatement and omission as an unavoidable cost. A third option, of course, is a combination of the first two, which will be the approach taken here in order to highlight such of Husserl's themes and overarching principles (as in a completed system) which will advance our stated objectives, while at the same time allowing us the flexibility of using the chronology of Husserl's development to clarify how he came to arrive at particular understandings.

As noted, in the *Investigations*, Husserl's initial philosophical concern was essentially an epistemological one, namely, the structure of cognitive acts involved in *logical* experiences. Husserl distinguished the field of his inquiry from that of pure logic, traditionally understood as the necessary, formal relationships among ideal objects, from that of psychology, considered as the study of natural mental processes and events of individuals, and from that of traditional epistemology, which considers whether we have any knowledge at all. Instead, Husserl sought a *pure* understanding of the structure of all acts of thinking and knowing that are necessary to address the basic questions of traditional epistemology. Husserl tells us:

> The above mentioned motives for phenomenological analysis have an obvious and essential connection with those which spring from basic questions of epistemology. For if these questions are taken in the widest generality, i.e. in the "formal" generality which abstracts from all matter of knowledge—they form part of a range of questions involved in the full clarification of the Idea of pure logic. We have, on the one hand, the fact that all thought and knowledge have as their aim objects or states of affairs, which they putatively "hit" in the sense that the "being-in-itself" of these objects and states is supposedly shown forth, and made an identifiable item, in a multitude of actual or possible meanings, or acts of thought. We have, further, the fact that all thought is ensouled by a thought-form which is subject to ideal laws, laws circumscribing the objectivity or ideality of knowledge in general. These facts, I maintain, eternally provide questions like: How are we to understand the fact that the intrinsic being of objectively becomes "presented," "apprehended" in knowledge, and so ends up by becoming subjective? What does it mean to say that the object has "being-in-itself," and is "given" in knowledge? How can the ideality of the universal *qua* concept or law enter the flux of real mental states and become an epistemic possession of the thinking person?[14]

---

14. Husserl, *Logical Investigations II*, Introduction §2, 169. Volume references in footnotes are to the German editions.

In accord with the scope of Husserl's targeted investigations, Husserl provides six meditations, each of which focuses on concepts that Husserl considers to be required by any science. These include expression and meaning, universality and abstraction, mereology, pure meaning and grammar, consciousness and intentionality, and the theory of knowledge. A limited summary of these expositions will be included in the general summary of phenomenology that will be provided a little later on.

For Husserl, to achieve a *pure* understanding means to get at the essence of the conscious acts themselves, objectively and without any ontological commitment as to the existence of their intentional objectivities. However, Husserl tells us that doing so is attended by certain challenges which inhere in the *unnatural* intuition required for this sort of phenomenological analysis, and, parting company with Brentano,[15] Husserl asserts that it is not *introspection* that is required but instead a process of *reflection*, which is especially important because reflection represents an early articulation of what, in the ensuing decade, will become Husserl's foundational method of phenomenological reduction:

> Psychologists usually discuss such difficulties when they consider introspection as a source of our detailed psychological knowledge, not properly however, but in order to draw a false antithesis between introspection and "outer" perception. The source of all such difficulties lies in the unnatural direction of intuition and thought which phenomenological analysis requires. Instead of becoming lost in the performance of acts built intricately on one another, and instead of (as it were) naïvely positing the existence of the objects intended in their sense and then going on to characterize them, or of assuming such objects hypothetically, of drawing conclusions from all this etc., we must rather practice "reflection," i.e. make these acts themselves, and their immanent meaning-content, our objects. When objects are intuited, thought of, theoretically pondered on, and thereby given to us as actuality in certain ontic modalities, we must direct our theoretical interest away from such objects, not posit them as realities as they appear or hold in the intentions of our acts. These acts, contrariwise, though hitherto not objective, must now be made objects of apprehension and of theoretical assertion.[16]

In 1913, the second edition of the *Investigations* and Husserl's new work, *Ideas for a Pure Phenomenology and Phenomenological Philosophy*, were published. During the period from 1901, when the first edition of the *Investigations* was published, to 1913, much had changed in Husserl's thinking.[17] For one thing, it became apparent to Husserl that phenomenological methods had applicability not just to logic and epistemology but to the entire range of conscious experience, including sensible experience, social and ethical experience, and even consciousness itself. As might be expected, Husserl's

---

15. It should be stated that my interpretation entails reading Husserl's use of the word "introspection" to mean the same thing as Brentano's "inner perception," which, as noted, Brentano *expressly distinguished* from "introspection." I am making this judgment based upon the context in which Husserl uses introspection as being a sort of psychological habit of distinguishing between inner and outer intentional objectivities, which to me seems compatible with Brentano's using "inner perception" to make clear that there is no process of introspection by which one may have a lived experience of a mental object and observe that experience at the same time.

16. Husserl, *Logical Investigations II*, Introduction, §3, 170.

17. See, Moran, *Introduction*, 92–93.

understanding of consciousness underwent a similar expansion such that, in place of Brentano's view of consciousness as a continuous stream of mental processes, Husserl now saw consciousness as a fundamentally temporal, *world-constituting* experience of each individually conscious entity. Moreover, the transcendental ego, which Husserl had previously considered to be inaccessible to consciousness, now became its ultimate object, the accessibility to which was obtained by a corresponding expansion of the process of reflection (as so described in the *Investigations*) to a fully worked out two-pronged phenomenological methodology that includes phenomenological and eidetic reduction.

Husserl announced his transition to transcendental thinking in the very first pages of *Ideas I* by contrasting his new understanding with that of psychology, which Husserl characterizes as a science of facts and realities (i.e., phenomena which really occur):

> In contrast to [psychology], *pure or transcendental phenomenology* will *be established, not as a science of facts, but instead as a science of essences* (as an "*eidetic*" science), a science that aims exclusively at securing "knowledge of essences" and *no "facts" at all*. The corresponding reduction that leads (in the sort of thinking involved in making a judgment) from the factual ("empirical") universality to the universality of an "essence" is the *eidetic reduction*.
>
> *[T]he phenomena of transcendental phenomenology will be characterized as irreal*. Other reductions, i.e., the specifically transcendental reductions, "purify" the psychological phenomena of what lends them reality and thereby any fit or classification in the real "world." Our phenomenology is to be a doctrine of the essences, not of real but of transcendentally reduced phenomena.[18]

Husserl will conduct the transcendental phenomenology under a "principle of all principles," which Husserl identifies as follows:

> *that each intuition affording* [something] *in an originary way is a legitimate source of knowledge*, that *whatever presents itself to us in "Intuition" in an originary way* (so to speak, in its actuality in person) *is to be taken simply as what it affords itself as*, but *only within the limitations in which it affords itself there*.[19]

However, even with the field of inquiry so clearly delineated, it will readily be seen that taking things given to consciousness in the manner in which they are given is easier said than done and, therefore, requires a powerful methodology, which Husserl provides in the form of the two different types of ideal reductions. To understand them, we must first identify their field of operation. In §§27–29 of *Ideas I*, Husserl describes, in what is striking prose, what he calls the world of the "natural attitude," which includes "I and my environment," "The cogito, my natural environment, and the ideal environments," and "The 'other' ego-subjects and the intersubjective natural environment," from which Husserl elicits in §30 of *Ideas I*, what he calls the "giveness of the natural attitude." All of this represents a factual but stylized depiction of how each subject, as a conscious being, finds itself in a world of sensible, logical, and social experiences that are always "on hand." Additionally, we "move" within and among these worlds by constantly directing and redirecting our conscious focus, and we have attitudes (such as liking and disliking) and make judgments

---

18. Husserl, *Ideas I*, Introduction, 5–6.
19. Ibid., §24, 43.

(such as "useful or not," "good or bad," and "beautiful or ugly") about what is there, on hand, before us. Husserl summarizes the natural attitude as being one of *belief* or, as we have been calling it, an ontological commitment (to its existence as understood):

> In the following propositions, we stress once again a most important point. I find constantly on hand opposite me the one spatiotemporal actuality to which I myself belong, as do all other human beings who find themselves in it and related to it in a similar way. I find the "actuality" (the word already says as much) to be there in advance and I also take [it] *as it affords itself to me, as being there*. No doubt or rejection of anything in the natural world changes anything in *the natural attitude's general thesis*. As an actuality, "the" world is always there; at most it is here or there "other" than I supposed; this or that is to be stricken *from it*, so to speak under the title of "illusion," "hallucination," and the like, stricken from it as the world that—in the sense of the general thesis—is always there [*immer daseinde Welt*]. To know it more comprehensively, more reliably, and more perfectly in every respect than the naïve experiential information can, to solve all the tasks of scientific knowledge that present themselves on its basis, that is the goal of the *sciences in the natural attitude*. (Brackets in original.)[20]

There is, of course, nothing wrong with the natural attitude or the world which is lived in and disclosed to us by it. Neither is there anything wrong with natural science. The difficulty is that the natural attitude does not and cannot reveal anything other than the natural world, which is of no interest as such to phenomenological philosophers. Instead, to phenomenological philosophers, who take consciousness as the precondition of all experience and are seeking a theory of knowledge about how consciousness *constitutes* its objects, the need is to get behind the natural world to consciousness itself. The natural world is given to consciousness as conscious phenomena and not the other way around. To understand consciousness and its phenomena we must suspend the natural attitude and all judgments about the natural world that it entails and look only at the conscious phenomena themselves. Husserl explains, by reference to Cartesian doubt, how it is possible to do so. As is the case with Descartes's famous epistemological method in which everything that can be doubted is doubted, suspension of our ontological commitments is possible because it is part of our faculty of reason which we are free to exercise. But unlike Cartesian doubt, phenomenal reduction does not entail negation of, or skepticism about, the natural world. Instead, in the phenomenological reduction, the natural world is "bracketed" and only the conscious phenomena themselves in precisely the manner in which they are given are analyzed. In his *Introduction to Phenomenology*, Robert Sokolowski explains bracketing thusly:

> When we so bracket the world or some particular object, we do not turn it into a mere appearance, an illusion, a mere idea, or any other sort of merely subjective impression. Rather, we now consider it precisely as it is intended by an intentionality in the natural attitude. We consider it as correlated with whatever intentionality targets it. If it is a perceived object, we examine it as perceived; if it is a remembered object, we now examine it as remembered; if it is a mathematical entity, we consider it as correlated with a mathematical intention, if it is a merely possible object, or a verified one, we consider it as the object for an

---

20. Ibid., §30, 52.

intentionality that intends something only possible, or an intentionality that intends something verified. Bracketing retains exactly the modality and the mode of manifestation that the object has for the subject in the natural attitude.

... In the natural attitude we head directly toward the object; we go right through the object's appearances to the object itself. From the philosophically reflective stance, we make the appearances thematic. We look *at* what we normally look *through*.[21]

As has been noted, one of Husserl's motivations in writing the *Ideas* was to provide the grounds for and details of the expansion of the logical phenomenology of the *Investigations* into a complete philosophical system. With respect to bracketing, which Husserl also calls the *epoché* (ἐποχήας) (which is an ancient Greek philosophical term connoting the suspension of judgment), the question naturally arises whether it can be turned upon consciousness itself. Husserl recognized this issue and tells us early on in *Ideas I* that pure consciousness is revealed by the *epoché* but cannot itself be subject to it:

> In these studies, we go as far as is necessary to achieve the targeted insight; namely, the insight that consciousness in itself has a being of its own that is not affected in its own absolute essence by the phenomenological suspension. It accordingly remains as a "phenomenological residuum," an intrinsically sui generis region of being that can indeed become the field of a new science-phenomenology.[22]

We will shortly endeavor to ascertain the *ontological* significance of Husserl's understanding of consciousness as the ultimate phenomenological residuum and the precondition of all experience, but first we need to identify the philosophical fruits of the suspension of the natural attitude, the bracketing of the natural world, and the eidetic reduction of the phenomena as revealed thereby. In order to do so, as promised, we will now temporarily switch our methodology from an exegesis of Husserl's large body of work, to a concrete summary of phenomenology.[23]

Most phenomenological questions entail analysis according to three structures that are present in conscious acts, namely parts and wholes, identity[24] in a manifold, and presence and absence.[25] The three are interrelated but not identical with one another. The concept of parts and wholes was important in Aristotle's thinking, and identity in a manifold was important in Plato's thinking (often referred to in reference to Plato as "one over many") and is central to the philosophy in these pages. The equally important phenomenological notion of cognition through presence and absence[26] is, by contrast,

---

21. Sokolowski, *Introduction*, 49–50.

22. Husserl, *Ideas I*, §33, 58.

23. This summary of phenomenology generally follows the outline of the related portions of *Introduction to Phenomenology* by Robert Sokolowski, which is a wonderfully lucid, comprehensive, and pithy assembly of phenomenology as understood today. It should be emphasized that Sokolowski deliberately presents phenomenology as a current philosophy without reference to the author of its particular concepts. As a result, although the majority of the summary presented here may be attributed to Husserl, it almost certainly includes some of Heidegger's and Sokolowki's own ideas.

24. Instead of "identity," Husserl speaks of the "unity" of the object. *Ideas I*, §131, 314.

25. See generally, Sokolowski, *Introduction*, chapter 3, 22–41.

26. Instead of "presence" and "absence," Husserl speaks in terms of "fulfilled" and "unfulfilled" intentions. See, *Investigations II*, Investigation VI, §14b, 218.

new to phenomenology. In the doctrine of parts and wholes, "pieces" are parts that can subsist on their own and, when separated from a whole, become wholes themselves, and "moments" are parts that cannot subsist on their own and, when separated from the whole to which they relate, cannot become wholes themselves.[27] An acorn is a piece of a tree. The color red is a moment of a cherry. Phenomenologists argue that many historically intractable philosophical problems arise as the result of confusion between pieces and moments. For example, under phenomenology, which rejects Platonism, the *idea* of a geometric form (such as a circle, triangle, or square) is not a piece and therefore cannot exist independently of the instantiated geometric forms as to which it pertains as a moment, and the soul, which is considered to be a *moment* of a human being must therefore perish along with the body.[28]

The doctrine of identity in a manifold begins with the simple observations that an object is *presented* as an identity in a manifold of appearances and that the identity *transcends* its presentations and is not merely a sequence of apparently connected appearances or the sum of them. Husserl tells us:

> Thus each noema contains such a pure something-qua-object as a point of unity, and we see at once how, in a noematic respect, two concepts of the object must be distinguished: this pure point of unity, this *noematic "object simply,"* and the *"object in terms of how it is determined"*—including the respective indeterminacies that "remain open" and are co-meant in this mode.[29]

Under phenomenology, the object is a really existing presentation and is of a different dimension from its parts. A cube is not one of its aspects or profiles (these terms are phenomenological terms of art, which we need not define here) presented to us in its perception. A proposition is not one of its uttered sentences. A play is not one of its performances.[30]

The doctrine of presence and absence describes the manner in which all extended objects and many other objects are given to consciousness and can be identified in what is perceived and hidden from perception in an extended object, what has been, is being, and will be temporally disclosed in an extended object or a temporal sequence, and what is given in an unextended sequence. So, for example, from a phenomenological perspective, when I see an object such as a coffee cup on a table, I see as present only those portions of it which reflect light towards my eyes and the rest of the cup, which is blocked from my view, is not merely inferred but is *given as absent*. Presence and absence is also used in phenomenology to describe intentions themselves; fulfilled intentions are intuitions of an object (such as the coffee cup on my desk as I write) that is present, and empty (unfulfilled) intentions are of an object (such as one of the coffee cups in the cupboard in my kitchen) that are absent (from me) while I work in my study.

---

27. Husserl also speaks of "independent" and "non-independent" objects. See, Husserl, *Investigations II*, Investigation III, §§1–25, 4–46.
28. Sokolowski, *Introduction*, 26.
29. Husserl, *Ideas I*, §131, 260.
30. Sokolowski, *Introduction*, 27–30.

In phenomenology, simple cognition occurs under three noetic categories of intentionality, namely, perception, memory, and imagination or anticipation.[31] Obviously, these categories correspond to our natural temporal notions of present, past, and future, which have their own unique characterization under phenomenology. Because consciousness always occurs in the present, so also must perception, memory, and imagination. Perceptive intending is sensory in nature, and, as just noted, is of objects that are given directly to consciousness in a mixture of presences and absences. We need only add here that we can overcome some absences only at the cost of abandoning other presences (for example, by moving about an extended object of perception), that the continuous presencing and absencing of objects is a constantly changing manifold of the presentation of one and the same object, and the object as given is a different dimension from its sides, aspects, and profiles. The characterization of memory under phenomenology represents a more radical departure from our understanding in the natural attitude because memory is treated not as the picturing of a past experience but rather as the present summoning of a perception under the noetic structure of the past. In other words, in remembering, we *reactivate* a past experience (given as such) so that the experience, now a memory, is given in the present. The memory is a present experience of a *noematic* object that is given not as present but *as past*. Under phenomenology, imagination and anticipation are similar to memory; imagination is the present experience of a future event under a conditional modality (as if) of belief, and anticipation is a species of imagination that includes a present belief in its futurity.[32] Husserl emphasizes that, notwithstanding these noetic structures, consciousness occurs for each conscious entity in a single continuous stream.[33]

Under phenomenology, there is another important type of intentionality, called "signitive intending,"[34] by virtue of which meaning is attributed to an intention. Signitive intending usually occurs in the cognition of words, pictures, and symbols. In signitive intending, we understand sounds as words, pictorial shapes and colors as representations of extended objects, and symbols as letters, numbers, words, and signs. The ability to perceive the meanings signified by sounds, words, symbols, and markings is a specifically human rational power. The object of signitive intentions is empty but given through meaning. Associating a picture with a word is an imaginary act that occurs in conjunction with the empty intention of understanding the word itself. Unlike objects of perception, the objects of signitive intention are given directly, immediately, and all at once. The introduction of signitive intentions in turn introduces three elements: a word, a meaning, and a reference. Because we can name and articulate something in its absence, we can also determine whether a present thing is the thing named (i.e., we can verify propositions about them).

---

31. See ibid., chapter 5, 66–76.
32. Ibid., 73–74.
33. Husserl, *Ideas I*, §82, 158–59.
34. One of the places in which Husserl focuses on signitive intentionality is in chapter 1, "Meaning-Intention and Meaning Fulfilment," of Investigation VI of *Investigations II*, §§1–12, 191–216. The summary here follows Sokolowski, *Introduction*, 78–84.

One of the most important concepts in phenomenology is called "categorial intending," in which the subject takes an articulated state of affairs as its intentional object.[35] Unlike mere cognition, categorial intending entails the making of judgments about objects and articulating states of affairs and propositions about them through predicating, relating, collecting, and applying logic. For example, an apple is an object but the statement that "there is an apple that is green" is a categorial judgment that tells us something about the apple. The process of making categorial judgments entails three steps: (1) passive perception of an object as a unity among manifolds; (2) identification of one or more parts of the whole, which comes to the foreground against the background of the object's unity; and (3) recognition that the whole contains the part. Sokolowski gives the example of a damaged car: we perceive a car, we perceive a dent in the car as being a moment of the perception, and we recognize that the car contains the dent.[36] Categorial judgments are the basis of language. In Sokolowski's example, as a result of the first three steps, we are able to declare "The car is damaged!" Having associated the car with its damage, we have intellectualized a new unity that is not merely a car but a damaged car. Significantly, the new object, that of the damaged car, which was perceived in a temporal sequence of sensibility, is given all at once as a *categorial object*.

The establishment of a categorial object is called *constituting* the object. In constituting the object, the subject does not create the object but accepts it as it is given. Sokolowski says:

> In phenomenology, to "constitute" a categorial object means to bring it to light, to articulate it, to bring it forth, to actualize its truth. We cannot manifest a thing any way we please; we cannot make an object mean anything we wish. We can bring a thing to light only if the thing offers itself in a certain light. The thing has to show up with certain aspects that we can spotlight if we are to be able to declare that it has certain features. If we did not experience something like the abrasions in the car, we would not be able to constitute the car as damaged. Of course, we might be misled by false appearances, in which the car merely seems to be scraped, and we might erroneously declare that it is damaged when it is not; but then we remedy this situation simply by further and closer experience of the car, or by listening to what other people have to say about it, or by figuring out what must really be the case; we will then come to see that we were wrong. We have to submit to the way things disclose themselves. To submit in this way is not to place limitations on our freedom, but to achieve the perfection of our intelligence, which is geared by its nature to disclosing the way things are. To submit in this way is to bring about the triumph of objectivity, which is what our minds are supposed to do. To "constitute" a state of affairs is to exercise our understanding and to let a thing manifest itself to us.[37]

---

35. Categorical intentionality is discussed at length by Husserl in chapter 6, "Sensuous and Categorical Intuitions," and chapter 7, "A Study in Categorical Representation" of Investigation VI of *Investigations II*, §§40–58, 271–94, and in Sokolowski, *Introduction*, chapter 7, 88–111.

36. Sokolowski, *Introduction*, chapter 7, 90.

37. Ibid., 92–93

Because the constitution of individual objects applies to constitution of the world of conscious objects as a totality, it is important to keep in mind that for Husserl in the act of constitution of the world its facticity is not disregarded.[38]

One of the most important developments in all of phenomenology is its conception of truth, not of the correspondence of our ideas with their objects, but in the satisfaction of the conditions of fulfilment of intentional acts, which may vary according to the region of the intentionality. In the phenomenological understanding, in making categorial judgments, we take the world as it is given to us and we establish states of affairs based upon the *giveness* of things. If we have no reason to doubt what is given, we simply take it as being true. So, for example, in the region of sensible intentionality, as I write these words, I see that there is a pen lying on my desk. To support the many judgments underpinning the proposition that there is a pen on my desk, I have the full context of having purchased the desk and placed it in my study, of having worked at it daily for over twenty years, of perceiving the object that I identify as a pen to have all of the properties that I would expect, of having a memory of having brought the pen into the room and placing it on my desk, and so on. The conclusion that I may confidently reach is expressible as a true state of affairs: There is a pen on my desk. Or, as an example in the region of rational intentionality, consider the simple example of the grasping of a mathematical truism given by Moran:

> Thus, in mathematics, when I grasp that the three angles of a triangle are equal to two right angles, I have an object which is given with [direct self-evidence]. I experience this simple truth not just as something that can be validated or which has been validated, but as validated right now. Furthermore, intuitions can be grasped as not possible otherwise, that is not just as adequate but as apodictic.[39]

Now suppose I have reason to question whether the object on my desk is a pen. Suppose I do not remember putting it there and I have a novelty gift flashlight that looks like my pen and I use it to see in the darkness behind my desktop computer where various peripheral devices are attached. I see the object and it looks like a pen, but it also looks like my flashlight. The perception in either case is identical and the context is consistent with either state of affairs. As in the first case, the categorial object is what it is but the moments that I am able to attach to the whole are different. I do not know whether when I press on the button the cartridge will extend for writing or whether a bulb will light up. What changes in the scenario is not the object as presented to me but *my attitude to the presentation*, which has gone from treating it as a state of affairs to a proposition that must be investigated. The new attitude is called "propositional," or "judgmental," or "apophantic." The truth of the statement: "there is a pen on my desk" depends upon my acquiring additional information through acts of perception. If I press the button and it causes the cartridge to extend I will confirm that the statement was indeed a true state of affairs and return to straightforward intending of the pen. In such a case a unity is established between my unfulfilled intention and my intention as now fulfilled. For example, we sometimes speak of things which are absent and verify them by making them present. On the other hand, if the bulb lights up, I will reject the proposition that "there

---

38. See, Moran, *Introduction*, 165–66.
39. Ibid., 128.

is a pen on my desk" and consider it merely to be a proposition that does not correspond with the state of affairs, which is that "there is a novelty flashlight pen on my desk." I will replace my unfulfilled intention of the pen on my desk with a fulfilled intention that there is a flashlight on my desk.

The phenomenological view differs from the mainstream correspondence theory of truth. The mainstream view is that ideas, meanings, and judgments are mental things that are always directly present to our minds and that truth consists in the correspondence between them and empirical reality. But the positing of meanings and judgments raises more questions than it answers in supporting the notion of truth, including: How do we know them if they are not given to the senses? Where do they reside if not in the world? Do they have continuous existence, nowhere and nowhen, or are they created as needed by categorial reason? On what ground can we postulate them in order to define truth? If they merely copy the world why do we need them and how do we know that the copy is genuine? This phenomenological understanding of truth eliminates the necessity to postulate propositions and meanings as subsistent, conceptual entities and the existence of the empirical objects to which they are asserted to correspond.

Perhaps most importantly the making of categorial judgments and their expression in language manifest the intentionality of the speaker who takes responsibility for them. As a result, they reveal a transcendental ego who is an agent of intentionality and evidence and the emergence of an elevated self as an *agent of truth*.[40] But we can go much further in our characterization of the transcendental ego. Under phenomenology, as is the case with such objects, *the conscious self or ego establishes and presents itself to itself as an identity in a manifold of appearances*. However, the self-manifold differs from its objects because it is never presented as a mere object but instead stands out as being central to conscious experience, as the agent of intentional life, as the one who *has* the world and the things in it given to him. So, in the phenomenological understanding, the ego is both empirical, that is, *in the world* as a physical phenomenon, and *over and against the world* as a center of disclosure to whom the world and everything in it manifests themselves. As the agent of truth, the transcendental ego is the perceptual and cognitive "owner" of the world. The empirical and transcendental egos are a single entity considered in two different ways, the possibility of which corresponds to the manner of its being.

The essential structure of consciousness is temporality.[41] All *noetic* and *noematic* things are pervaded by time. In the case of natural objects, we perceive their temporal character as part of natural cognition, and in the case of objects of inner perception, we perceive their "timelessness" over the time of their perception. Stating the case more strongly, all conscious experience is preconditioned upon time consciousness. It is important to note that spatiality does not hold the same priority as temporality, because spatiality does not apply, for example, to non-spatial sequences (such as the natural numbers) or to melodies or categorial statements. We have already considered the temporal character of perception under the noetic structures of past, present, and future. Here we are concerned with the temporal character of consciousness itself. In the natural attitude,

---

40. Sokolowski, *Introduction*, 110–11.

41. See generally, ibid., chapter 9, 130–45. See also, Kelly, "Phenomenology and Time-Consciousness," §1.

we understand time in three different ways. The first is part of the spatio-temporal container given to us (or so the positivists would say) in sensory perception. The second is the scientific construct by which we observe, measure, and coordinate events. The third is the subjective time of our internal experience of the passing of time. The application of the phenomenal reduction to temporality also yields a tripartite understanding, but one that is of a strikingly different structure. As is to be expected, phenomenology brackets the metaphysical time first described above and recognizes only the second and third experiences as "world" or "transcendent" time and "internal" or "immanent" time, respectively. Phenomenology introduces its own, third element of time consciousness, which is *consciousness of immanent time*. This level is necessary to account for self-awareness of what occurs in immanent time. It is the ultimate horizon or context in which consciousness of all phenomena—*it founds all experience but is itself unfounded*. It is interesting to note the parallel between this account of time consciousness and Brentano's assertion that each presentation entails a corresponding presentation of that presentation in one and the same act.[42] There is much more to be said about time consciousness, but we will postpone that for the corresponding discussion of Heidegger's version of it.

Finally, we should say a few, and only a few, words about the concept of intersubjectivity which, once again, is of interest in these pages primarily because of its relation to what Heidegger will call "Being-with Others." An obvious problem arises because phenomenology is what some commentators call "methodological solipsism," meaning that it entails analysis of conscious phenomena as given to a particular subject, and because, fundamental to its methodology, is that the natural world, in which all other egos are given, is bracketed. The question becomes whether it is philosophically permissible to treat others as mere conscious phenomena, without any ontological commitment as to their existence. The answer is a perplexing one. Other egos are not given to us fully in the same way as any other objects. It is true that we can perceive them under the same conscious structures, but what we perceive as their physical being is precisely what we would expect if they were just like us. Moreover, in our interaction they give us signs of possessing a conscious world that is just like the one we possess, albeit from a different perspective of their own "here and now." We can both perceive the same sensible objects and make the same categorial judgments and statements about them. But there is a limit on our intersubjective connection, which arises because we can never experience directly what others experience—instead we can only live what they appear to be experiencing in our own intuitive empathy. For example, if we perceive another crying in pain, we cannot know what they are feeling or even if they are feeling anything at all, and, if we believe they are in pain, we can only intuit that it is something like what we feel when we are in pain. There is a third aspect to intersubjectivity that is both interesting and controversial, which seems to be a limit on it. It seems that underlying our consciousness of others is what Husserl called a sphere of ownness, where consciousness of others is eliminated.[43]

With this summary understanding of phenomenology, we are able to return our focus to its founder as teacher and predecessor to Heidegger. Specifically, it remains only to

---

42. See text accompanying 7n at 206.
43. See, Moran, *Introduction*, 175–79; see also, Sokolowski, *Introduction*, 152–55.

examine the philosophical endpoint of phenomenology which is pure consciousness itself. As noted, as early as *Ideas I*, Husserl understood there to lie, at the end of all phenomenological analysis, a "phenomenological residuum" of consciousness which is impervious to phenomenological reduction. This, it would seem, is a logically predicable resting point because, if the case were the contrary, then Husserl would have to privilege phenomenology over the consciousness which discovers and applies it. In *Ideas I*, Husserl tells us:

> Difficulties present themselves at one limit-point. The human being as a natural being and as a person in a personal union, in that of "society," is suspended; so, too, is every animal being. But how do matters stand with the *pure ego*? Has the phenomenological ego (the one that is doing the investigating from the outset) also become a transcendental nothing by means of the phenomenological reduction? Let us practice the reduction to the stream of pure consciousness. In reflection, every implemented cogitatio takes on the explicit form of the cogitatio. Does it lose this form if we perform the transcendental reduction?
>
> From the outset, this much is clear. After performing this reduction in the flow of a manifold of experiences, a flow that remains as a transcendental residuum, we will nowhere hit upon the pure ego as an experience among other experiences, not even as a genuine piece of the experience, emerging [with it] and vanishing in turn.[44]

So, after all possible phenomenological reduction has been undertaken and completed, we are left with a transcendental world that consists of consciousness (pure subjectivity) and all of the objects that it comprises (pure objectivity). Although Husserl preceded Nagel by decades, we can see that Husserl's answer to the question asked by Nagel at the outset of chapter 5, "The Possibility of Objective Knowledge" (i.e., how is it possible for contingent beings to attain objective knowledge), is a wholly transcendental one—Husserl would say that the source of all objective meaning lies in the pure subjectivity of the transcendental ego and that the transcendental ego is itself responsible for the Being of the world.[45] Obviously, since Nagel is asking the question long after Husserl purported to answer it, we may safely assume that Nagel is not satisfied with this answer and, for the reasons set forth in chapter 5, as next to be clarified, neither are we.

Describing the transcendental ego as such, or as an agent of disclosure of the world, or as an agent of truth, or as a pure residuum of consciousness, or in other similar fashion, still leaves us short of an understanding of its Being, and, sadly, Husserl left us without one, although not for lack of trying. Instead, over the course of Husserl's long and productive career, his understanding of the Being of the transcendental ego changed repeatedly and this fact is highly illuminating of the deficiencies of the phenomenological ontology. Moran has identified at least six different conceptions of the transcendental ego which were held by Husserl chronologically: (1) in the first edition of the *Investigations*, Husserl followed Brentano and Hume in treating the ego merely as a bundle of conscious acts; (2) in the *Idea of Phenomenology*, Husserl expressed the view that bracketing the natural ego leaves the transcendental ego as a depersonalized stream of consciousness; (3) in the second edition of the *Investigations*, Husserl treats

---

44. Husserl, *Ideas I*, §57, 105.
45. Moran, *Introduction*, 168–69, citing Husserl, *Cartesian Meditations*, §28, 62.

the "phenomenologically reduced ego" as the unity of the set of structures which cause the various acts of consciousness to glue together into a single self-related stream; (4) in *Ideas I*, Husserl presents the transcendental ego as the residuum which resists reduction; (5) in *Ideas II*, the self is a "zero point" (*Nullpunkt*), understood as a center of reference and orientation from which distances, times, etc., radiate outwards; and (6) in *Cartesian Meditations*, the transcendental ego is the source of time consciousness and is characterized as "*a connectedness that makes the unity of one consciousness.*"[46]

Husserl's difficulties in accounting for the transcendental ego parallel the corresponding difficulties associated with Kant's unity of apperception and Hegel's absolute Ego. With respect to the former, Husserl's phenomenology replaces the Kantian things-in-themselves with objects of conscious intention and the transcendental aesthetic (i.e., space, time, and causation) and analytic (i.e., categories of understanding) with the structures of consciousness. But in both cases, if one starts with an epistemological premise, in the case of Kant, that all knowledge originates in the empirical world, and, in the case of Husserl, that all knowledge is of phenomena as given to consciousness, and if one excludes any recognition of intuitive knowledge of self as substance, notwithstanding that such knowledge is given to the understanding or consciousness (as the case may be), then one is left with a conception of self that is a mere formal unity. And such a formal unity, whether of apperception or consciousness, is circular in precisely the way identified by the German Idealists because, in each case it requires for its self-understanding the existence of objects which are dependent upon it in the first place. And just as is the case with German Idealism, in the absence of recognition of self as substance, Husserl cannot escape the rudderless, incoherence of absolute Consciousness and a world that reduces to absolute Consciousness constituting itself as such. It is not difficult to see, therefore, how Husserl has left himself open to Heidegger's immanent critique.

Perhaps Husserl's greatest accomplishment is his placement of man in the world of his cognition so that it is no longer acceptable to treat epistemology as though it is a mere servant of scientific inquiry. In working out the implications of this simple idea, Husserl tells us that cognition is a unified activity that must be understood from the standpoint of consciousness as well as its objects, that instead of bringing *a priori* categories of empirical understanding to sensible objectivities, man brings an entire *a priori* conscious structure to the cognition of the objects of consciousness, which includes a multitude of regions and modes of taking what is presented to consciousness, and that, in so doing, man rises above other sentient creatures as what we have come to call the "agent of the truth" of the world. Having said all of this, it is difficult to depart from the study of Husserl's work without a sense that it never sufficiently liberates itself from Brentano's science of psychology and that, as a result, Husserl's epistemology is less about the world than it is about the mind of man in a way that leaves reality virtually unexamined. Although it is certainly unfair to both Brentano and Husserl to treat them as mere precursors to the sublime work of Heidegger, where the subject matter is, as it is in these pages, largely driven by ontology, doing so is a necessity.

---

46. Ibid., 168–174.

9

Being and Intelligibility

DASEIN[1]

Heidegger's philosophy is heavily dependent upon his own voluminous glossary of terms that are etymologically well-crafted but which render his exposition to be less accessible than may be desired, especially to we Anglophones. In recognition of the burden Heidegger imposes upon us in asking that we acquire a new philosophical lexicon to access his work, Heidegger offers as one of his foundational themes that post-Socratic western philosophy has neglected the fundamental question of Being and has, as a result, become so substantively and definitionally rigidified that it is impossible to offer a concrete exposition of Being without employing new terms which are not imbued with the mistaken nuances that attend modern philosophy. The most obvious example of Heidegger's definitional revolution is "*Dasein*," which is the term that is most central to his philosophy and which represents the human being's peculiar mode of Being and which literally translates from German to "Being-there" or "Being-open."

At the highest level, insofar as Heidegger's philosophy is relevant to the philosophical investigations in these pages, it may be regarded as a life-long "interrogation of Being" (to employ Heidegger's own description) by asking, over the course of several major works, three questions.[2] The first is the one already alluded to, namely, "What is the meaning of Being?" which Heidegger asks in *Being and Time*. The second question is, "Why are there beings at all instead of nothing?" which Heidegger asks in his *Introduc-*

---

1. In addition to my own study of the major works cited in this section, I have consulted certain secondary sources the authors of which, as noted authorities on Heidegger, have far greater access to the vast body of Heidegger's scholarship (some of which is not translated into English) and doubtlessly a broader and more insightful understanding of Heidegger's meaning. These sources include: Mulhall, *Routledge Philosophy Guidebook*; Sheehan, "Dasein"; and Wheeler, "Martin Heidegger."

2. There is at least one other question that would naturally be explored in a complete collection of Heidegger's work that, due to the scope of our inquiry and the interests of not enlarging an already long summary, we will not address in this book. That question is, "How does Being occur essentially?," which Heidegger addresses in *Contributions to Philosophy*, a work that although written in 1936–37, was not translated and published in English until after Heidegger's death but which has been recognized as among his more important works.

tion to Metaphysics. The final question is, "What is the ground (*grund*) of Being?" which is the subject of Heidegger's *The Principle of Reason*.

In recognition of the length of the ensuing review of Heidegger's rich and important investigations, it will be helpful to provide at the outset some detail of our plan. In this and the following two sections, after providing a brief background, we will undertake a more or less sequential analysis of Heidegger's response to the three questions posed above. However, as we will see from our review, notwithstanding the profundity of Heidegger's ontology, there remains in his work and that of his predecessor phenomenalists a gaping hole as regards the fundamental questions of ethics. Although some phenomenalists would argue otherwise, there is nothing compelling in the philosophy of Brentano, Husserl, and Heidegger itself that provides any ethical guidance other than a relativism that is left undiscussed except to the extent one might endeavor to extract it from Heidegger's call to revert to historical *Dasein*. Nevertheless, there are two distinct (although not mutually exclusive) possibilities for an objective ethics that emerge from a view of humanity that is compatible with the phenomenological perspective. One such ethical system is presented in the *Credo* of Jeff Bergner in his *Against Modern Humanism*, which takes the human Being as the open dative of self- and world-disclosure and explores how such a being, who is free to pursue his possibilities for Being *only within the boundaries of his historical, cultural, and personal history and talents, on the one hand, and the world into which he is thrown, on the other,* ought to comport himself or herself in life. Bergner's philosophy, which will be discussed in the fourth section of this chapter, is a highly moral (and admirable) one, which is based neither upon reason as such nor upon obedience to God. The other such ethical system is the one that, beginning with section five of this chapter, will be offered in the remaining pages of this book as part of the metaphysical system that we will complete using Heidegger's phenomenology as a springboard. Although, as a practical matter, our ethics is substantially compatible with Bergner's *Credo*, the philosophy presented here is based upon a fundamental recharacterization of *Dasein* as the being who is, in essence, *Being-towards-God*, and it is upon that understanding that our ethics will be based.

Heidegger's early, pre–*Being and Time* years were spent under the close tutelage of Husserl who, as we have seen, was deeply affected by his own study under Brentano. As a result, all three were profoundly and explicitly influenced by Aristotle. One of Brentano's earliest writings was *On the Several Senses of Being in Aristotle*, and the concept of intentionality, upon which his descriptive psychology is founded, harkens back directly to Aristotle. Similarly so with respect to Husserl's phenomenology, which is also fundamentally an exploration of the concept of intentionality, albeit one which expands its scope from the psychology of mental activity to the science of consciousness and employs additional methods of investigation which Husserl invents. Heidegger read and was greatly influenced by Brentano's work on Aristotle's theory of being and, as Husserl's protégé, Heidegger began his career as a phenomenologist. Although Heidegger shared with Brentano and Husserl the goal of a presuppositionless philosophy, Heidegger harbored, from his earliest years, a fundamental disagreement concerning their claims to success on this score. At the root of Heidegger's criticism is that the foundational concept of presentation or giveness, as the case may be, is itself a theoretical construct, the preconditions of which neither thinker has adequately explored. As a result, Heidegger rejects (to Husserl's great disappointment) phenomenology as a philosophy and, instead, adopts it as a mere method of investigation, and asserts, quite rightly, that the point of origin of philosophical investigation must be the question of the meaning of Being.

Heidegger's critique of phenomenology did not diminish his regard for Aristotle and it would not be an over-simplification to characterize Heidegger's own study of Being as phenomenological in method but neo-Aristotelian in substance. To address the deficiencies of Brentano and Husserl, Heidegger reverts to Aristotle, not for his concept of intentionality which inspired Brentano and Husserl, but for Aristotle's theories of knowledge and the teleology of Being. Heidegger interprets Aristotle's theory of knowledge as positing that every *meaningful* appearance of beings in their multiplicity of modes of Being involves an event in which a human being "takes a being as" something. Heidegger accepts Aristotle's description structurally but asserts that "taking as" is not grounded in multiple modes of presence, but in a temporal unity of intelligibility which Heidegger characterizes as "Being-in-the-World."[3] And this temporal unity grounds *Dasein's* teleology as well insofar as *Dasein* is always in the mode of projecting forward into its potentiality-for-Being. These matters will be explained in detail in the remainder of this section.

At the end of the first part of the previous chapter, we refrained from endeavoring to list all of the Husserlian concepts that would be adopted or expounded upon by Heidegger because they are simply too numerous and, indeed, some current scholars disagree with the mainstream view that Heidegger's ontological philosophy is a rejection of Husserl's phenomenology and instead prefer to characterize Heidegger as advancing the development of Husserl's work. There are many interesting arguments in favor of and against this point of view. Whether this view is correct, as a preliminary matter it will be helpful to note a few points of contrast between the two philosophers. One such difference is that, unlike Husserl whose philosophical investigations are for the most part epistemological and classificatory (in the sense of Kant with whom Husserl acknowledges the fundamental compatibility of his philosophy), Heidegger proposes what he calls a fundamental ontology, which attempts to describe Being in a concrete manner. The second major difference is that Husserl's subject matter is consciousness and its objects, whereas Heidegger's subject matter is *Dasein* and Being generally. A third difference is that, as just noted, Husserl's formal structure of the human side of cognition is built upon intentionality, whereas Heidegger's formal structure of *Dasein* is temporality, which although structurally quite similar to Husserl's conception of temporality, Heidegger asserts *constitutes Dasein's essential concern for its own Being.*

With this background, we turn to Heidegger's first great work, which is *Being and Time*, the avowed goal of which is the presentation of a concrete science of Being. Notwithstanding the fact that Heidegger abandoned the full work (the outline of the abandoned portion of the book was not excised from the introduction to the book) prior to

---

3. The term "world," which is not generally capitalized in the translations of Heidegger's work or in the related secondary literature, is used by Heidegger to connote the matrix of intelligibility that, as will be explained, is structured by human beings from the things found within the world as ordinarily understood. See 231–233. Hence, I have decided to do the unthinkable and capitalize the term "World" when using it in the Heideggerian sense.

its completion, *Being and Time* has greatly influenced the course of twentieth century philosophy, especially in continental Europe. The work surprises from the very first line, which quotes Plato's *Sophist* and which is translated by Heidegger as follows:

> For manifestly you have long been aware of what you mean when you use the expression "being." We, however, who used to think we understood it, have now become perplexed.

In doing so, Heidegger immediately directs us to the question of the necessity, structure, and priority of the question of Being, with the obvious implication that it remained unanswered in the thousands of years that transpired since it was raised by Plato and, indeed, Heidegger tells us that not only is that the case, but, far worse, we no longer even bother to concern ourselves with it. Heidegger assesses the sanctioning of the neglect of the question in the modern era by dogma that, because Being is the most universal concept, it is empty and impervious to definition and, further, that this circumstance is untroublesome because, to the extent that Being is susceptible of being understood, it is accessible to everyone in their ordinary thinking and language.

Heidegger tells us that although Being is the most universal and that its understanding is therefore included in everything, Being is neither a class nor a genus and was therefore understood by Aristotle as the "transcendental universal constituting a unity of analogy" (which is a view with which we are in agreement) and by Hegel as the "indeterminate immediate." But Heidegger draws a very different conclusion from the special ontological status of Being than does the modern mainstream. Heidegger tells us that, instead of concluding that Being is not a matter of philosophical concern, the only conclusion to be drawn from the supreme universality and indefinability of Being is that *Being is itself not an entity* and Heidegger insists that we must ask *what Being means notwithstanding that it is undefinable*. Heidegger buttresses his position in opposition to the modern mainstream by arguing that the fact that we continually, in our everyday discourse, employ the undefinable term, should only serve to highlight the importance of its investigation.

Heidegger tells us that, as a threshold matter, the question must be appropriately formulated and that the starting point in doing so is the observation that all questioning is a seeking of something that is guided beforehand by what is sought. Heidegger adds to that observation the deceptively simple one, which will run throughout his entire philosophy, that all interrogation of Being is itself conducted by a being and concludes that we must therefore identify the way in which we, as the being conducting the inquiry, understand Being in advance of asking the question of its meaning. Heidegger tells us that Being is *that which determines entities as such*:

> Everything we talk about, everything we have in view, everything towards which we comport ourselves in any way, is Being; what we are is Being, and so is how we are. Being lies in the fact that something is, and in its Being as it is; in [r]eality; in presence-at-hand (i.e., being as it naturally occurs outside of the context of having any meaning for *Dasein*); in subsistence; in validity; in *Dasein*; in the "there is."[4] (Parenthetical added.)

---

4. Heidegger, *Being and Time*, H6–7. All page references are to the later German editions as indicated in this work.

It should be pointed out immediately, because it runs to the heart of our differences with Heidegger, that one may agree with his characterization of Being as the determining characteristic of beings without acquiescing in the idea that Being is therefore excluded from being an entity itself. Because the elucidation of this point requires that the analysis conducted in the first three sections of this chapter be completed first, it will not be further mentioned until the latter parts of this chapter.

Returning to Heidegger's own analysis that Being is in *Dasein* gives us *ourselves* as a viable (indeed, according to Heidegger, the only viable) point of access to the meaning of Being:

> Looking at something, understanding and conceiving it, choosing, access to it—all these ways of behaving are constitutive of our inquiry and therefore are modes of Being for those particular entities which we, the inquirers, are ourselves. Thus to work out the question of Being adequately, we must make an entity—the inquirer—transparent in his own Being. The very asking of this question is an entity's mode of Being; and as such it gets its essential character from what is inquired about—namely, Being.[5]

Anticipating the complaint that his approach is circular, Heidegger tells us it is not the case because we can determine the nature of entities in their individual Being without having explicit any concept of Being and, therefore, there is no logical circularity in interrogating beings as to their Being. I understand this to mean (validly so) that, because we have an idea, however unphilosophical it may be, of how to employ the concept of Being in our ordinary usage, we can identify what we mean when we say something "is" by asking of that thing what makes it something that *is*. Heidegger tells us that, instead of being circular, the relationship between the inquiry, as a mode of Being (of *Dasein*), and that which is being interrogated is a "relatedness back and forth," and, as a result, *Dasein* is shown to be *the being that inquires into its own Being*.

Heidegger next introduces another foundational concept that adds detail to his theme that the philosophy that followed Aristotle, especially from Descartes onward, which treats itself as though it were an empirical science, is based upon the mistaken objectification of reality inherent in scientific investigations, which can only occur because science leaves unaddressed the ontologically most originary question of Being, which must precede all scientific investigations. Heidegger explains that defining the subject matter of a field of inquiry (such as empirical science) entails, as a threshold matter, interpretation of the subjects with respect to their basic state of Being and observes that the question of Being permeates *every* region of investigation and is the most fundamental one:

> The question of Being aims therefore at ascertaining the *a priori* conditions not only for the possibility of the sciences which examine entities as entities of such and such a type, and, in so doing, already operate with an understanding of Being, but also for the possibility of those ontologies themselves which are prior to the ontical sciences and which provide their foundations. *Basically, all ontology, no matter how rich and firmly compacted a system of categories it has at its disposal, remains blind and perverted from its ownmost aim, if it has not first*

---

5. Ibid., H7.

> *adequately clarified the meaning of Being, and conceived this clarification as its fundamental task.*[6]

This is a point that is not too far removed from Kant's criticism of the mainstream empirical conception of truth as conformity of reason to its object on the grounds that for such a definition to be meaningful reason must first have grasp of its objects.

Having established the ontological importance of the question of Being, Heidegger turns to the question of its ontical (i.e., empirical) importance and concludes that its priority extends there as well. Heidegger tells us that *Dasein* is ontically distinguished by the fact that, in its very Being, *Being is an issue for it* and that, inasmuch as Being is an issue for *Dasein*, it is a constitutive state of *Dasein's* Being and, therefore, *Dasein* must be said to have a relationship *towards its* Being, which is itself one of Being. In other words, for Heidegger, *Dasein's* explicit understanding of its Being is an ontic characteristic which, unlike many other such characteristics, renders the issue of its Being ontologically important for *Dasein*.

Heidegger next introduces another foundational concept, which he will describe in detail phenomenologically, namely, that *Dasein* always understands itself *in terms of its existence and the possibilities presented to it thereby*. As a result, *Dasein's* pre-ontological understanding of its Being extends to "something like" a world and to the Being of each being that is presented to *Dasein* in the world. These characteristics render *Dasein* as both the ontologically and ontically prior entity with the import being that fundamental ontology can only be had in the *existential analytic of Dasein*:

> *Dasein* accordingly takes priority over all other entities in several ways. The first priority is an ontical one: *Dasein* is an entity whose Being has the determinate character of existence. The second priority is an ontological one: *Dasein* is in itself "ontological," because existence is thus determinative for it. But with equal primordiality *Dasein* also possesses—as constitutive for its understanding of existence—an understanding of the Being of all entities of a character other than its own. *Dasein* has therefore a third priority as providing the ontico-ontological condition for the possibility of any ontologies. Thus *Dasein* has turned out to be, more than any other entity, the one which must be interrogated ontologically.[7]

It would not be an over-generalization to describe the remainder of *Being and Time* as the working out of what Heidegger has already described as the close connection between the Being of *Dasein* and Being (in general); indeed, as we will see, for Heidegger, although the existence of mind-independent reality is undeniable, the question of Being is one that has no meaning in the absence of *Dasein*.

With this, Heidegger has successfully validated (if not achieved the justification of the necessity of) the investigation of the Being of *Dasein* as the way to understand Being. But Heidegger is immediately confronted with a philosophical difficulty, which is that the ontico-ontological priority of *Dasein* means that although *Dasein* is ontically closest to itself, the ontological priority of *Dasein*, which is based upon its manner of Being, means that manner of Being is concealed *from itself from within itself*. In other words,

6. Ibid., H11.
7. Ibid., H13.

although *Dasein* can capably recognize as an ontical matter that it is concerned with its own Being, the ontology of *Dasein's* manner of Being, which includes self-concern and self-investigation, is not a matter that is subject to empirical observation and it therefore remains hidden within *Dasein*. Therefore, access to the Being of *Dasein* depends upon identifying a method of analysis which enables *Dasein* to *show itself from within itself* and that, in turn, requires examination of *Dasein* in its *everydayness* (i.e., the way in which *Dasein* comports itself in and to the world in its everyday life). From such an examination, which is to be conducted phenomenologically, Heidegger hopes to identify the formal structures of the Being of *Dasein* that are characteristic of it. Heidegger recognizes, however, such structures can provide only a provisional understanding of the Being of *Dasein*; they do not provide the meaning of *Dasein*, which must be elicited from them by a higher level of analysis of them. And even then we will not have completed our inquiry because a third level of investigation will be required by reinterpreting the provisional understanding of *Dasein* in the context of its meaning so elicited. In other words, we will begin with an assessment of how man comports himself generally in the world, which will yield a structural understanding of man, which can finally be examined to determine what the essential elements (i.e., those elements that make man *Dasein*) of that structure are.

We just noted Heidegger's observation that *Dasein* always understands itself in terms of its existence and the possibilities presented to it thereby. By possibilities, Heidegger does not mean the discrete contingencies of everyday life but rather *possible ways of Being towards which Dasein may press forward*. Because of the forward-looking nature of *Dasein's* self-understanding, it should not surprise us that our provisional understanding of *Dasein's* existential structures will yield that temporality is critical to the Being of *Dasein*. So, to complete the analysis of the meaning of the Being of *Dasein*, it will be necessary first to justify the priority of *Dasein's* temporal character and then to reinterpret the structures of *Dasein* provisionally identified in the context of their temporality.

It is interesting to note that, unlike Aristotle's (and Kant's and Husserl's) categorical investigation and Hegel's triadic method of logical investigation, Heidegger's interpretation of the question of Being represents a process of interpretation and reinterpretation until one has arrived at the most fundamental level of understanding. Neither should it surprise us that Heidegger's understanding of temporality, although phenomenological in nature and similar to Husserl's, is uniquely his own and differs importantly from his mentor's in that Heidegger emphasizes the future as the mode of temporality in which *Dasein* discloses its primordial concern for its Being which Heidegger calls "care"[8] and which represents a radically new phenomenological interpretation of *Dasein*. In other words, unlike for Kant and Husserl, where temporality is a phenomenon that is associated with reason, for Heidegger, temporality is *Dasein's* essential mode of Being.

---

8. It should be acknowledged that the use of the word "care" instead of the more syntactically comfortable word "concern" is deliberate. Both words are terms of art for Heidegger. "Care" is the term that comprises *Dasein's* ontological structure and is used for that purpose in the sense that *Dasein*, as the being for whom its Being is an issue, cares about (i.e., attaches fundamental importance to) itself. "Concern," on the other hand, is used in the sense of matters with which *Dasein* may from time to time be concerned (i.e., paying attention), usually in its everyday activities and comportments.

We turn next to a summary, albeit a lengthy one, of what Heidegger calls appropriately the "existential analytic" (of *Dasein*). This is Heidegger's first level of analysis of the Being of *Dasein*. As the being for whom its own Being is an issue, *Dasein* may be understood to be concerned about its existence existentially. So, although Heidegger's terminology is a bit strange to the uninitiated, it makes sense that Heidegger would assert, on a phenomenological basis, that *Dasein's* basic engagement with the entities of the empirical world is as "equipment," that is, as entities that are more or less relevant to the satisfaction of *Dasein's* existential concerns. And, again, strange as it may appear at first blush, Heidegger's conception is compatible with the common sense notion that from the standpoint of evolutionary success, *Dasein* (in similar fashion to all other sentient organisms) should encounter the empirical world through a lens that highlights what is most relevant to it its survival as a species. In any case, Heidegger tells us that our most primordial encounter with such entities is in manipulating them for the sake of our own purposes and, as a result, calls such entities, when encountered in this way, "ready-to-hand." Entities that are not *ready-to-hand*, that is to say, not experienced as being meaningful to such concerns, are called by Heidegger "present-at-hand" and are sometimes referred to as "Things." *Present-at-hand* entities may broadly be understood as the objective, mind-independent entities understood in the standard empirical manner. Readiness-to-hand and presence-at-hand constitute the two categories of encounter with the world and, as a result, comprise the entirety of the world except for *Dasein*, which, as the being who brings the two categories to its cognition, is *in* neither category (but, to be clear, *Dasein* is in the world). It is important to note that, depending upon the context in which it is encountered by *Dasein*, an entity may be both ready-to-hand and present-at-hand and we see immediately the profundity of the importance of *Dasein's* attitude in the manner in which it experiences reality. Consider, as an example, one used by Heidegger, namely, *Dasein's* encounter with a hammer. Our experience with a hammer may be had scientifically or, perhaps more precisely, theoretically (as an engineer might do), in which case, it occurs in the traditional subject-object structure as being present-at-hand and is a mere Thing to be studied. But our experience with a hammer may also be had in the course of fulfilling a task that is existentially meaningful to us (such as roofing a house), in which case it is the act of hammering that overwhelms the distinction between the hammering subject and the hammer with which the subject fastens a nail and, indeed, the experience takes on the character of a structurally unified, absorbed engagement that is not subject-object in nature. When *Dasein* is in a scientific or theoretical mode, it assumes the perspective of an independent investigator, which is a particular mode of its Being, and its task is to categorize, explain, and predict the behavior of present-at-hand entities. When *Dasein* is fully engaged in a world of ready-at-hand entities (we will hereinafter refer to the world considered equipmentally, as the "World"), its experience is quite different and it is on this difference that Heidegger wishes to focus.

For Heidegger, the World is a "totality of involvements" or a "network of intelligibility" comprising equipmental relationships that is experienced by *Dasein* according to its projects and concerns. When *Dasein* uses a hammer in the fulfillment of a task, the hammer loses its character as a World-independent entity (i.e., a present-at-hand object) and instead is understood relationally as part of such a totality (similarly to Hegel's notion that each entity in the universe can only be understood in relation to each other such entity) and, indeed, Heidegger tells us that there really is no such thing as "an equipment."⁹ The relation of *Dasein* (i.e., its *involvements*) as the being who determines its projects and concerns varies according to each aspect of an experience and includes the following relationships or engagements: *with-which; in-which; in-order-to; towards-this;* and, most important of all, *for-the-sake-of-which*. Michael Wheeler offers examples of his involvements in writing an article on Heidegger as follows:

> Thus I am currently working with a computer (a *with-which*), in the practical context of my office (an *in-which*), in order to write this encyclopedia entry (an *in-order-to*), which is aimed towards presenting an introduction to Heidegger's philosophy (a *towards-this*) for the sake of my academic work, that is, for the sake of my being an academic (a *for-the-sake-of-which*).[10]

The last type of involvement, for-the-sake-of-which, is the most important one because it is asserted by Heidegger to lay at the end of all of the totalities of *Dasein's* involvements and it provides the analytical connection between the idea that *Dasein* is constantly choosing between the Being that will characterize its self-understanding and the not-Being that it rejects and, therefore, determines the way in which *Dasein's* World is intelligible to it.

Having so depicted the World, the next and most obvious question is whether and how *Dasein* may be characterized as existing *in* it. Here, Heidegger's analysis follows neatly from his categorial understanding of entities. If *Dasein* is the origin of its unique, equipmental understanding and is engaged with its World as the entity that experiences the World in unity with it, *Dasein* cannot, in its usual, non-scientific mode of Being, be said to be *contained in* the World in the Cartesian sense of space and time. Instead, another mode of description is required to convey that *Dasein* is *in relation to* a World that reflects its projects and concerns and with which it is "familiar" pre-ontologically and with which, in its actual existence, it dwells as an entity that is unified with it. Heidegger describes this relation as "Being-in-the-World."

Heidegger continues to elucidate his concept of what he calls the "worldhood" of the World by contrasting it with Cartesianism. As is to be expected, Heidegger's critique is cast in terms of his own brand of phenomenology. It will be recalled that early on in this book we presented Descartes as unjustifiably bisecting the psychosomatic unity of the human being into soul and body, and in the preceding chapter we presented Husserl's separate criticism of Descartes that, in attempting to doubt everything, Descartes neglected to doubt his own methodology. We now add to these Heidegger's criticism of Descartes that the Cartesian view is fundamentally scientific in nature and as such represents a theoretical view of the world that is at odds with the philosophically more important equipmental World of *Dasein's* rational experience. Heidegger characterizes Descartes as presenting the world, including *Dasein*, as a collection of present-at-hand entities and ascribing *Dasein's* spatial relation with the world as being contained in the Cartesian, extension-based space that came to represent the empirical mainstream view. In contrast, we have the view of Heidegger already presented, namely, that *Dasein* is, at

---

9. Heidegger, *Being and Time*, H97.
10. See, Wheeler, "Martin Heidegger," §2.2.3.

the most fundamental epistemological level, in unified relation to its objects as Being-in-the-World. For Heidegger, *Dasein dwells* in relation to the World in a spatial manner, but that spatiality is not at all Cartesian, which cannot possibly apply to *Dasein* because it is not a present-at-hand Thing. To the contrary, Heidegger asserts that equipmental space is *functional space defined by Dasein-centered totalities of involvements.*

In the course of Heidegger's criticism of Descartes, Heidegger provides a profoundly important elucidation, which is that in *Dasein's* experience of reality, which is Being-in-the-World, it is in relation to entities *qua* equipment and that to achieve the theoretical Cartesian understanding of reality it is necessary to prescind from the World its *Dasein*-given meaning. In other words, epistemologically the raw material of reality is not laying there, present-at-hand, for constitution by *Dasein* as meaning-imbued and ready-to-hand—instead, the World and its equipment is present to *Dasein* as such *ab initio* and the Cartesian, present-at-hand world of Things is a theoretical reduction in which *Dasein* is contained in the world as the subject of the cognition of the objects (Things) with which it co-exists. In still other words, the Cartesian world of Things presupposes the ready-at-hand World and not the other way around.

After completing his sojourn with Descartes, Heidegger returns to his existential analytic of *Dasein*, this time addressing himself to the question of what he calls the "who" of *Dasein*. Here the analysis is subtle and a bit obscure and it goes in a surprising direction. Heidegger starts with the observation that in every case, *Dasein* is an entity that is "I myself" but he cautions us that this is merely an ontologically constitutive state of Being. Ontically, we distinguish ourselves from all other entities by referring to our own "I" as a present-at-hand subject. Again, we are cautioned not to be misled—additional questioning must be undertaken to determine whether the "I" as so understood "does proper justice to the stock of phenomena belonging to everyday *Dasein*" and we must be careful to avoid the obvious temptation to take the giveness of the "I" as requiring a phenomenological investigation that disregards everything else that is given to the "I" including the world and other "I's." Indeed, such an approach is contrary to the one that is appropriate because it disregards the fundamental unity of *Dasein's* experience (i.e., its Being-in-the-World). Recognizing this state of affairs demonstrates that the giveness of the "I" is merely a non-committal formal indicator which, upon phenomenological analysis, may indicate something that is, in some particular mode of Being, the opposite of the ordinary understanding, which is to say that in some contexts, such as when the "I" loses (in a manner which will be explained shortly) itself, the persistent "I-hood" of experience may manifest itself in a "not-I." And in fact, this turns out to be precisely the case most of the time.

To get at the proper interpretation of "I-hood" we must begin with Being-in-the-World. It follows from *Dasein's* essential Being-in-the-World and from the fact that much of the equipment found there is for the sake of other beings who share similar concerns and are in other important respects (to be identified) similarly situated (such beings are called by Heidegger, the "Others" or the "they"), that the World discloses another mode of *Dasein's* being as "Being-with." Heidegger tells us:

> By "Others" we do not mean everyone else but me—those over against whom the "I" stands out. They are rather those from whom, for the most part, one does not

> distinguish oneself—those among whom one is too.... By reason of this with-like Being-in-the-[W]orld, the [W]orld is always the one that I share with Others.[11]

Being-with Others is different from Being-with equipment or Things because, unlike equipment and Things, Others, who like the "I," relate to the World through its equipment, are not "in" the world as ready-to-hand or present-at-hand but are also *in relation to* the World. As a result, *Dasein* cannot relate to Others in a concerned mode of Being as it does to the equipment in its World. Heidegger refers to the special Being-with Others and the special interrelations with Others as "*Dasein*-with" and "solicitude" (*fürsorge*), which apparently is only a rough translation of the German and which seems to mean concern for the welfare of others. To arrive at an understanding of the "who" of *Dasein*, it is therefore necessary to conduct a phenomenological examination of the *Dasein*-with in its everydayness to determine what its existential structures are. And in these special relationships, Others are freed from the environmental world by *Dasein* and it becomes evident that *Dasein*-with, as a way of Being, is *essentially for-the-sake-of Others*. The for-the-sake-of-ness of *Dasein*-with manifests itself in selflessness (e.g., charity) and in conformity (i.e., doing what one does) and discloses an ontologically important structure of *Dasein*, namely, that in most circumstances, as Heidegger foreshadowed, the "I-hood" of *Dasein* manifests itself as a "not-I." In a very important passage, Heidegger asserts this and asks the next obvious question:

> One's own *Dasein*, like the *Dasein*-with of Others, is encountered proximally and for the most part in terms of the with-[W]orld with which we are environmentally concerned. When *Dasein* is absorbed in the [W]orld of its concern—that is at the same time in its Being-with Others—it is not itself. *Who* is it then who has taken over Being as everyday Being-with-one-another?[12]

The answer to Heidegger's rhetorical question is interesting and foundational. *Dasein*, in its Being-with Others (*Dasein*-with), comports itself in certain ways which disclose certain of its and the they's existential characteristics, namely, distantiality (awareness of the way one differs from Others), averageness (conformity to social norms), levelling down (noiseless suppression of the exceptional), publicness (that which comprises distantiality, averageness, and levelling down), the disburdening of one's Being (the ceding personal responsibility by appropriating the judgments of the they), and accommodation (the disburdening of *Dasein* in its everydayness by the they). Because *Dasein*, by appropriating the they in its everydayness, acts existentially and is essentially the "they-Self," it is distinguished from the authentic self, which is the self that, as we shall see, takes hold of, as owner, its *Dasein*.

Up to this point Heidegger's elucidation of *Dasein* as Being-in-the-World has focused on *the World* in relation to which *Dasein* dwells, which is to say he has provided an ontological depiction of the World and the modes of Being that characterize *Dasein* in its relationship to the World. But that still leaves the question of what it means for *Dasein* to be *in relation to* the World and it is to this question that Heidegger next turns

---

11. Heidegger, *Being and Time*, H118.
12. Ibid., H125.

his attention, with the bold promise that analysis of the "Being-in" aspect of the Being of *Dasein*, will "pave the way to grasping the primordial Being of *Dasein* itself. . . ."[13]

Heidegger begins by reminding us (once again) that "Being-in" is an essential kind of Being of *Dasein* and that in conducting our investigation we must take care not to break-up the "Being" and the "in." Heidegger elucidates:

> The entity which is essentially constituted by Being-in-the-[W]orld is itself in every case its "there." According to the familiar signification of the word, the "there" points to a "here" and a "yonder." The "here" of an "I-here" is always understood in relation to a "yonder" ready-to-hand, in the sense of a Being towards this "yonder"—a Being which is de-severent, directional, and concernful. *Dasein's* existential spatiality, which thus determines its "location," is itself grounded in Being-in-the-[W]orld. The "yonder" belongs definitely to something encountered within-the-[W]orld. "Here" and "yonder" are possible only in a "there"—that is to say, only if there is an entity which has made a disclosure of spatiality as the Being of the "there." This entity carries in its ownmost Being the character of not being closed off. In the expression "there" we have in view of this essential disclosedness. By reason of this disclosedness, this entity (*Dasein*), together with the Being-there of the [W]orld, is "there" for itself.[14]

In this passage, it is interesting to note the significance of Heidegger's break from Cartesian spatiality. Heidegger has made clear that to "Be-in" is to "Be-there" at the point where the World is disclosed to *Dasein* as such and that these are essential elements of *Dasein* insofar as *Dasein* is at the epicenter of its own phenomenal experience in which it opens up the World *in its relation to* the World.

Heidegger's exposition of Being-in (the Being of the "there") proceeds in two parts. The first is the exposition of Being-in in terms of the existential constitution of the "there," which will be in terms of "understanding" and "state-of-mind," and the second is in terms of the everyday Being of the "there" which is the "falling" of *Dasein* (as the they-Self). As will be explained, state-of-mind and understanding are characterized equiprimordially by "discourse," which Heidegger defines as *the articulation of intelligibility*. As he frequently does, Heidegger reminds us that the exposition is existential in nature and therefore is not a description of something present-at-hand but of ways for *Dasein* to be in its everydayness.

For Heidegger, the ontological state-of-mind connotes what we ontically understand as our mood or manner of attunement, but unlike the standard psychological depiction, these states-of-mind are not internally generated responses to mind-independent reality but rather manifestations of "how one is" in its "thereness," by which I understand Heidegger to mean that they are ways of Being *in relation to* the World and, as such, are an inseparable part of it. And, indeed, Heidegger tells us that *Dasein is* the "there" of its state-of-mind.

Heidegger characterizes the facticity of our moods as the "that-it-is" and our "thrownness," which is an important Heideggerism that describes the *manner* in which *Dasein* is there in its Being-in-the-World. In this regard, it is important to remember

---

13. Ibid., H131.
14. Ibid., H132.

that the World, itself, is *Dasein's* relation to all that which is ready-to-hand. If I am depressed, the World opens up to me in darkness and gloominess and I am attuned to the burdensomeness of Being-in-the-World and, if I am elated, then I turn away from these things to Being-in a very different World. Importantly, it is in our thrownness that we find ourselves in relation to the World, as Heidegger says "not in the sense of coming across itself by perceiving itself, but in the sense of finding itself in the mood that it has."[15]

In addition to disclosing *Dasein's* thrownness, *Dasein's* state of mind has two other phenomenologically important aspects. The first is that it discloses *Dasein* to itself as Being-in-the-World as a whole, which enables *Dasein* to direct itself towards something. The second is that insofar as *Dasein's* state of mind determines the way in which the World is disclosed *Dasein's* state of mind is itself part of Being-in-the-World. Heidegger expounds:

> Letting something be encountered . . . has the character of becoming affected in some way; we can see this more precisely from the standpoint of state-of-mind. But to be affected by the unserviceable, resistant, or threatening character of that which is ready-to-hand, becomes ontologically possible only in so far as Being-in as such has been determined existentially beforehand in such a manner that what it encounters within-the-world can "matter" to it in this way. The fact that this sort of thing can "matter" to it is grounded in one's state-of-mind; and as a state of mind it has already disclosed the world—as something by which it can be threatened, for instance. Only something which is in the state-of-mind of fearing (or fearlessness) can discover that what is environmentally ready-to-hand is threatening. *Dasein's* openness to the world is constituted existentially by the attunement of a state-of-mind.[16]

Heidegger tells us that state-of-mind is one of the existential structures in which the Being of the "there" maintains itself and that equiprimordial with it in constituting the Being of the "there" is "understanding." Heidegger notes that a state-of-mind always has its understanding and *vice versa*. For Heidegger, understanding "is the existential Being of *Dasein's* own potentiality-for-Being [and] it is so in such a way that this Being discloses in itself what its Being is capable of."[17] To explain the structure of *understanding as always pressing forward into possibilities*, Heidegger adopts as his own term of art "projection" and tells us that the understanding *projects Dasein's* Being upon its "for-the-sake-of-which" and that *Dasein* is *thrown* into the kind of Being which he calls *projecting*, which occurs not as comporting towards a plan but as Being the totality of its possibilities and as always understanding itself as such. Heidegger says:

> Only because the Being of the "there" receives its [c]onstitution through understanding and through the character of understanding as projection, only *because it is what it becomes (or alternatively, does not become), can it say to itself "Become what you are" and say this with understanding.*[18] (Emphasis added.)

15. Ibid., H135.
16. Ibid., H137.
17. Ibid., H144.
18. Ibid., H145.

It is essential to understanding Heidegger's philosophy to recognize that he has just told us that *Being is becoming*. It is this notion, which Heidegger formally describes as *Dasein* understanding itself in terms of the totality of its potentiality-for-Being and continually pressing forward into those possibilities which matter to it, that will ultimately ground his assertion that *Dasein* is to be fundamentally interpreted in terms of temporality and that the vulgar notions of time are derivative from it. But we are not quite ready for that yet. Having completed his exposition of the existential constitution of the "there" with the discussion of states-of-mind and understanding, Heidegger turns to the completion of his final preparatory task, namely, the description of the everyday Being of the "there" and the falling of *Dasein*. Heidegger characterizes this dimension of Being as "fallenness," which is not intended to be pejorative (as in a fall from grace) but instead to connote that *Dasein*, in its circumspection and absorption with its World, is lost in the publicness of the they and has therefore fallen from itself as an *authentic* potentiality-for-Being into *inauthentic* Being-with-one-another, which is characterized by what Heidegger calls idle talk, curiosity, and ambiguity.

Thus far, *Dasein's* ontological structure, which is holistically conceived, may be defined (as Heidegger explicitly does) in its average everydayness as "Being-in-the-[W]orld which is falling and disclosed, thrown and projecting, and for which its ownmost potentiality-for-Being is an issue, both in its Being alongside the "[W]orld" and in its Being-with Others."[19] But this does not go far enough to explain *Dasein* and with it the meaning of Being. What is missing from this definition is *its own ontological foundation*. Heidegger tells us that "[t]he Being of *Dasein*, upon which the structural whole as such is ontologically supported, becomes accessible to us when we look all the way through this whole to a single primordially unitary phenomenon which is already in this whole in such a way that it provides the ontological foundation for each structural item in its structural possibility."[20] In other words, the provisional understanding of *Dasein* in its everydayness that has been achieved must itself be questioned regarding its ontology to see whether there is a more fundamental phenomenon that characterizes each of the elements in the provisional definition. This is the second level of interpretation.

As we have just seen, *Dasein* knows itself through state-of-mind and understanding. Success in identifying the foundational ontological phenomenon underlying the formal structure of *Dasein* in its average everydayness will depend upon whether there is a state-of-mind in which *Dasein's* ownmost understanding of itself will be disclosed to itself. Not surprisingly, Heidegger is able to identify such a state-of-mind and the phenomenon it discloses. The former is what Heidegger calls "anxiety" and the latter is what he calls "care."

The first question, then, is what is so special about anxiety that it brings *Dasein* before itself in its own Being and discloses what sort of entity *Dasein* is? It turns out that it is anxiety that motivates *Dasein* to flee from its authentic Being and to turn towards Being-with Others and Being-alongside the World in its inauthentic mode of Being. Anxiety is not the same as fear but it is what makes fear possible. Fear is always about something in the World that is threatening. Anxiety is not about any entity at all but

19. Ibid., H181.
20. Ibid.

instead about the indefinite—about Being-in-the-World as such, and not in the face of anything within-the-World. It is in the state-of-mind that is anxiety, therefore, that the World is disclosed to *Dasein* as World. Anxiety, therefore, removes the possibility of *Dasein* understanding itself inauthentically in terms of the World into which it falls and discloses to *Dasein* its authentic potentiality-for-Being-in-the-World. Heidegger tells us:

> Anxiety throws *Dasein* back upon that which it is anxious about—its authentic potentiality-for-Being-in-the-[W]orld. Anxiety individualizes *Dasein* for its ownmost Being-in-the-[W]orld, which as something that understands, projects itself essentially upon possibilities. Therefore, with that which it is anxious about, anxiety discloses *Dasein* as Being-possible, and indeed as the only kind of thing which it can be of its own accord as something individualized in individualization.[21]

In projecting itself upon its possibilities for Being, *Dasein* is revealed as being both *free* and *ahead of itself in its Being*.[22] With this, we arrive at the final formal characterization from which, as we will soon see, we can interpret *Dasein* in terms of temporality, namely, as "ahead-of-itself-Being-already-in-(the-[W]orld) as Being-alongside (entities encountered within-the-[W]orld)."[23]

For Heidegger, entities *are*, albeit in a special way to be discussed, independent of *Dasein*, but Being *is* only in the understanding of *Dasein* (and any other Being to whom *something like an understanding of Being* belongs). As noted, in Heidegger's understanding, Being is not itself an entity but something that is characteristic of entities (as we shall also see, as their *ground*). Accordingly, a question arises as to the relationship between the Being of *Dasein* and the manner in which other entities may be said *to be*. The fact that *Dasein* is for the most part falling into the they-Self means that it is in the world in a mode of Being in which it takes the world as present-at-hand. As a result, *Dasein* tends to interpret Being as meaning "Being in general" and it thus acquires a meaning that is equivalent to "Reality" (understood as a world of Things and sometimes referred to as "the Real"). So one way that entities (other than *Dasein*) may be said to be is in the world as "Things." However, such an interpretation is particular only to one of the two primary modes of *Dasein*, and is therefore both one-sided and limited and makes clear the necessity that, to understand Being, one must understand the connection between Being and Reality in all of the fullness of Being (i.e., including, in any event, *Dasein*'s authentic mode).

Reality is commonly understood as the "external world" which is consistent with *Dasein*'s fallen interpretation of it. As a result of this interpretation, the question arises as to whether the Real can be understood to exist independently of consciousness. In modern philosophy, the question is routinely asked without any understanding of the extent to which the Being of entities whose very existence is being put into question has been clarified. Heidegger tells us that "[t]he question of whether there is a world at all and whether its Being can be proved, makes no sense if it is raised by *Dasein* as Being-in-the-World" (i.e., as Being *in relation to* the World) and then asks rhetorically "who else would raise

---

21. Ibid., H187–88.
22. It is important to note that freedom is part of the Being of *Dasein*.
23. Heidegger, *Being and Time*, H192.

it?"[24] In other words, because *Dasein* is the site at which the world is disclosed along with the Being of *Dasein*, the very posing of the question answers it affirmatively.

Heidegger refers us to Kant to frame the discussion. In Kant's "Refutation of Idealism," Kant calls the failure of philosophy to have proven the existence of mind-independent reality the "scandal of philosophy." Kant's proof of empirical reality is based upon the empirical character of the very consciousness which asks it: "The mere consciousness of my own *Dasein*—a consciousness which, however, is empirical in character—proves the *Dasein* of objects in the space outside of me."[25] Kant's argument proceeds on the basis of our experience of time. In Heideggerian terms, Kant treats each human consciousness as present-at-hand together with the multiplicity of the representations that are internally given to it in a process that is understood as *change*. For there to be a determinate temporal character there must be permanence against which change can be recognized as such, either within or outside of consciousness. But, if consciousness itself exists temporally (i.e., in time) as present-at-hand and experiences the changes within itself (i.e., the multiplicity of representations), the permanence against which its being in time must be external to it. What is externally permanent is the condition which makes it possible for the changes "in me" to be present-at-hand. Heidegger characterizes Kant as having proven that entities which are changing and entities which are permanent are present-at-hand together. But, as we have just seen, this is a one-sided proof that presupposes that consciousness is exclusively inauthentic (i.e., present-at-hand). Heidegger says, "But the Being-present-at-hand of the physical and the psychical is completely different ontically and ontologically from the phenomenon of Being-in-the-World."[26]

According to Heidegger, the scandal of philosophy is not that the proof of external reality has yet to be given, *but that any such proof is expected and attempted over and over again.* Such expectations arise because of the mistaken conceptual separation of Being and the world of beings, which arises because of the failure to recognize that *Dasein's* Being is Being-in-the-World. On this false premise, the object becomes to prove the existence of a world independently of *Dasein* and outside of it. And, as we have just noted, the illusion upon which the false premise is based arises because *Dasein* buries itself in the world in its inauthentic they-Self.

The subject matter of the scandal philosophy is the "pure presence-at-hand" of Things. But Reality, as understood by *Dasein*, is the totality of its engagements as readiness-to-hand, present-at-hand, or Others. All modes of Being of entities within-the-world are founded ontologically upon the worldhood of the World, and accordingly, the phenomenon of Being-in-the-World. Reality, therefore, refers always back to care as the way of Being in which *Dasein* is in-the-World. Even so, Heidegger tells us that "the fact that Reality is ontologically grounded in the Being of *Dasein*, does not signify that only when *Dasein* exists and as long as *Dasein* exists, can the Real be as that which

---

24. Ibid., H202.
25. Ibid., H203, quoting Kant, *Pure Reason*, B275.
26. Ibid., H204.

in itself is."²⁷ In one of the most interesting and important passages of *Being and Time*, Heidegger explains:

> Of course only as long as *Dasein* is (that is, only as long as an understanding of Being is ontically possible), "is there" Being. When *Dasein* does not exist, "independence" "is" not either, nor "is" the "in-itself." In such a case this sort of thing can be neither understood or not understood. In such a case even entities within-the-word can neither be discovered nor lie hidden. *In such a case* it cannot be said that entities are, nor can it be said that they are not. But *now*, as long as there is an understanding of Being and therefore of presence-at-hand, it can indeed be said that *in this case* entities will still continue to be.²⁸

So the question and its answer are intelligible only because it is being asked by *Dasein* in the context of *Dasein*'s understanding of its own and the Being of Things. If *Dasein* no longer is, then what remains becomes *unintelligible but not nothing*. It must be mentioned in passing here, for later elucidation, that this is another point with which we are in profound disagreement with Heidegger; indeed, it is the position of the philosophy expounded in these pages that Being and intelligibility are the same and that the logical structure of the world empowers its persistence even in the absence of all of the sentient beings of the world.

With this (and a brief discussion of truth which will be postponed until the summary of *Introduction to Metaphysics*), Heidegger's preparation for the exposition of *Dasein* as temporality is complete. As we turn to the question of temporality, it will be helpful to remind ourselves that the reason for Heidegger's relentless interrogation of *Dasein* is to arrive at an answer to the question of the meaning of Being in general, which Heidegger hopes to obtain by first identifying *Dasein*'s essential Being. Heidegger appropriately tells us that in order to arrive at *Dasein*'s essence, we must reach a primordial interpretation of the Being of *Dasein*, which means that our interpretation must extend to the *whole* of *Dasein*. In arriving at care as the most primordial interpretation of *Dasein* the formal structure has been provided but the existential analysis of care remains phenomenologically incomplete in two respects. First, because the characterization says nothing about *Dasein*'s beginning or end, it does not address the finite nature of *Dasein*. Second, until now, the existential analysis of *Dasein* has not covered its *authentic* Being. So, in order to arrive at an answer to the question of the meaning of Being in general, it will be necessary to provide an existential interpretation of care as a formal characteristic of *Dasein* in its finiteness and in its authentic mode of Being.

Heidegger begins to address these questions by recognizing a difficulty which risks rendering his whole project unfeasible. What is required is an interpretation of *Dasein* in its totality, that is, its Being-a-whole. However, if, under the aegis of care, *Dasein* is always ahead-of-itself, the question arises as to how to understand the end of all of *Dasein*'s possible relations which must occur in a death that *Dasein* itself can never experience (i.e., we cannot experience the no-longer-Being that attends death because only Beings can experience the World). In other words, if we cannot experience death ontically, then

---

27. Ibid., H212.
28. Ibid.

it appears that we cannot determine its character ontologically in its Being-a-whole. Heidegger's solution to this problem is not to amend the concept of care but instead to assert that although the totality of authentic *Dasein*, that is, its Being-a-whole, can never include its own death, it does include, as an outer boundary, *the possibility of its own death*.

It is therefore important to interpret the possibility of death (not death itself) in terms of care. With respect to projection, because care includes Being-ahead-of-itself in its possibilities, care must always include Being-towards-the-end (i.e., death), which as we have just noted is always one of such possibilities. Heidegger calls Being-towards-Death (as a possibility) "anticipation." With respect to thrownness, Being-towards-the-end is a possibility into which *Dasein* has been thrown and which is revealed to *Dasein* as *anxiety*. In the inauthentic mode of Being that characterizes fallenness, Being-towards-the-end is disclosed in its everydayness, in which death is acknowledged by the they but in depersonalized and ambiguous terms, which convert anxiety into a mere fear which the they insists must be faced with a stiff upper lip, so that in its everydayness Being-towards-Death is a "constant fleeing in the face of death." Each individual *Dasein's* death, more than any other possibility, uniquely belongs to it insofar as it is specific to it and it is the moment when it ceases to be in relation to all of the other entities in the World. In light of the foregoing, Heidegger expresses the full ontological conception of death as "*Dasein's ownmost* possibility—non-relational, certain and as such indefinite, not to be outstripped . . . [and] in the Being of this entity towards its end."[29] Heidegger characterizes Being-towards-Death in terms of anticipation as "anticipation reveals to *Dasein* its lostness in the they-Self, and brings it face-to-face with the possibility of being itself, primarily unsupported by concernful solicitude, but of being itself, rather in an impassioned freedom towards death—a freedom which has been released from the [i]llusions of the 'they', and which is factical, certain of itself, and anxious."[30]

So far, so good, but there is still a piece missing from the puzzle. If death is *Dasein's* ownmost possibility, it must have an authentic dimension, even if *Dasein* is able to flee from it. However, if Being-towards-Death is grounded in care and care is characterized by the three dimensions of projection, thrownness, and fallenness, and if fallenness is inauthentic, the question is whether and how Heidegger can account for Being-towards-Death in terms of care. If Heidegger cannot do so, then care is not the primordial structure of *Dasein* that accounts for the *whole* Being of *Dasein*. So it would seem that Heidegger must either abandon care or provide, in addition to the other dimensions of care, a fourth dimension that will, in lieu of fallenness, operate as an *authentic mode* of care.

In a methodologically consistent manner, Heidegger defines the task as identifying an authentic potentiality-for-Being that will be disclosed (Heidegger says "attested") as an ontical possibility by *Dasein* itself. Because *Dasein* is, in normal circumstances, lost in the they of everydayness, its possibilities-for-Being are *inauthentic*, unless and until something allows it to find its authentic possibilities. What is needed is an ontical potentiality-for-Being-its-Self (authentically) and Heidegger claims that such is provided by what we commonly understand as the "voice of conscience." Heidegger is quick to point out that the sort of conscience to which he is referring is neither a materially

29. Ibid., H258–59.
30. Ibid., H266.

reducible nor a theological phenomenon, but rather something in the Being of *Dasein* that discloses to inauthentic *Dasein* its potentiality-for-Being-its-Self (authentically). And as a basic state of *Dasein*, it is constituted by state-of-mind, understanding, falling, and "discourse" (by virtue of which we hear it).

For Heidegger, conscience is a "call," which is a type of discourse that can be heard above the inauthentic idle talk and other noise of the they which bombards *Dasein* in its everydayness. *Dasein* is the subject of the call (discourse) of conscience. The call reaches the they-Self of concernful Being-with-Others and calls *Dasein* to its ownmost (authentic) self. Significantly, in keeping with Heidegger's assertion that the call to conscience is not a call to morality, Heidegger tells us that the call is contentless:

> But how are we to determine what is said in the talk that belongs to this kind of discourse? *What* does the conscience call to him to whom it appeals? Taken strictly, nothing. The call asserts nothing, gives no information about world-events, has nothing to tell. Least of all does it try to set going a "soliloquy" in the Self to which it has appealed. "Nothing" gets called to this Self, but it has been summoned to itself—that is to its ownmost potentiality-for-Being. The tendency of the call is not as to put up for "trial" the Self to which the appeal is made; but it calls *Dasein* forth (and "forward") into its ownmost possibilities, as a summons to its ownmost *potentiality-for-*Being-its-Self.[31]

If *Dasein* is the subject of the call, then who is the caller? Heidegger tells us that conscience is the call of care, with the caller being *Dasein* itself, which in its thrownness is anxious about its potentiality-for-Being. So it is *Dasein*, in its inauthentic everydayness which summons itself to its ownmost (authentic) potentiality-for-Being. Heidegger tells us that the call of care does not speak to us in terms of an ideal or universal potentiality-for-Being, but rather in terms of an individualized one that belongs to the *Dasein* being called, that the nature of the call is, ontically, a declaration of "Guilty!"[32] or "not-Guilty!," and that *Dasein*'s concept of guilt can only originate from the interpretation of its own Being. He goes on to formalize existentially guilt as "Being-the-basis for a Being which has been defined by a 'not'"—that is to say, as "*Being-the-basis of a nullity.*" Although Heidegger's prose on this subject is particularly obscure, I am understanding this in the overall context of his presentation to mean that the call of conscience is a call from inauthentic *Dasein* to authentic *Dasein* to *take responsibility* for those potential ways of Being which *Dasein* does not actualize in the continuous course of choosing a way of Being at each moment of its Being-in-the-World. This makes especial sense in a phenomenological context where "not-Being" constitutes absence, which is a way of Being and not the negation of existence. So, although *Dasein* is proximally and for the most part Being-inauthentic, because *Dasein* is care it is always subject to the call of conscience, which means that it must be responsible for its way-of-Being and its ways-of-not-Being, both of which are determined from the manifold potential ways of Being that are available to it at each moment. We can summarize the foregoing as meaning that the call of con-

---

31. Ibid., H273.

32. From the context (in which Heidegger expressly disavows a normative connotation), I am understanding the translation of the German *schuldig* to "guilty" to be intended to connote "to be wanting" or "falling short."

science, which is an ontical occurrence, attests to *Dasein* that it always has an authentic, ownmost potentiality-for-Being, which is in *Dasein* itself. Conscience attests by calling *Dasein* to Being-guilty (i.e., to take responsibility for its potentiality-for-Being). Hearing the call (which Heidegger calls wanting to have a conscience) allows one's ownmost Self to take action in itself of its own accord in its Being-guilty and represents, phenomenally, authentic potentiality-for-Being.

According to Heidegger, hearing the call is a way in which *Dasein* discloses itself to itself. As is to be expected, this disclosedness is constituted by discourse and state-of-mind. The state of mind is anxiety about the uncanniness of Being-towards-the-end, so wanting to have a conscience entails a readiness for anxiety. Because the discourse of the call is contentless and one-sided, *Dasein* listens to it but does not respond. This mode of discourse is therefore called "reticence." The distinctive and authentic disclosedness attested to by conscience, which Heidegger calls "resoluteness," is thus reticent self-projection upon one's ownmost Being-guilty, in which one is ready for anxiety. Heidegger tells us:

> Resoluteness, as *authentic Being-one's-Self*, does not detach *Dasein* from its [W]orld, nor does it isolate it so that it becomes a free-floating "I." And how should it, when resoluteness as authentic disclosedness, is authentically nothing else than *Being-in-the-[W]orld*? Resoluteness brings the Self right into its current concernful Being-alongside what is ready-to-hand, and pushes it into solicitous Being with Others.[33]

In other words, resoluteness does not entail *Dasein*'s drawing itself into itself in order to treat the World as present-at-hand, but instead calls *Dasein* to reinterpret the World in accordance with its authentic potentiality-for-Being.

A final point to be emphasized before completing the preparation for the interpretation *Dasein*'s authentic potentiality-for-Being-a-whole, and temporality as the ontological meaning of care, is the relationship between resoluteness and irresoluteness. In this context, it is helpful to remember that the issue of conscience as a call of care arises because it is an ontical occurrence which "attests" to an authentic potentiality-for-Being which required the addition of *discourse* to the three dimensions of care (thrownness, projection, and fallenness) that comprise inauthenticity. If, in hearing the call of conscience, *Dasein* is delivered to its ownmost, authentic way-of-Being, pronounced "Guilty!" (i.e., responsible for its own life choices), and freed from the "they," then any decision by *Dasein* to return to an inauthentic mode of Being must also be freely and responsibly made. And inasmuch as *Dasein* is subject to the call of conscience while in such a mode, then it is never fully free from the prospect of being called back to authenticity, anxiety, and Being-towards-the-end. *Dasein* always has the potentiality-for-Being authentic and inauthentic and the responsibility for each such possibility.

With *anticipation* (i.e., Being-towards-Death) and *resoluteness* (i.e., authentic potentiality-for-Being as exhibited ontically and understood existentially), Heidegger has identified two of the three pieces necessary to complete the existential exposition of the potentiality-for-Being-a-whole required for validation of the ontological adequacy of

---

33. Heidegger, *Being and Time*, H298.

understanding *Dasein* as care. What remains is to connect them so that the ontical phenomenon of resoluteness attests not just to authentic potentiality-for-Being in general but to potentiality-for-Being-towards-Death specifically, which is always, as Heidegger puts it, the uttermost possibility which lies ahead of every factical potentiality-for-Being of *Dasein*. And Heidegger claims that *resoluteness* in its very meaning accomplishes just that.

Heidegger is finally prepared to unveil the meaning of the Being of care, which, he told us in the introduction, would be in terms of temporality. Heidegger's exposition will focus on the concept of Self, which is so central to the philosophy presented in these pages. Interestingly, Heidegger presents a metaphysically new characterization of Self—one which subsists, but is neither substance nor mind nor mere unity of experience:

> Ontologically, *Dasein* is in principle different from everything that is present-at-hand or Real. Its "subsistence" is not based on the substantiality of a substance but on the "*Self-subsistence*" of the existing Self, whose Being has been conceived as care. The phenomenon of the Self—a phenomenon which is included in care—needs to be defined existentially in a way which is primordial and authentic, in contrast to our preparatory exhibition of the inauthentic they-Self. Along with this, we must establish what possible ontological questions are to be directed towards the "Self," if indeed it is neither substance nor subject.[34]

Heidegger promises that this method will clarify the phenomenon of care so that it may be interrogated as to its ontological meaning and, in arriving at that, "temporality will have been laid bare," and tells us that in temporality we get a "conception of the entire phenomenal content of *Dasein's* basic existential constitution in the ultimate foundations of its own ontological intelligibility" and further that "[t]emporality gets experienced in a phenomenally primordial way in *Dasein's* authentic Being-a-whole, in the phenomenon of anticipatory resoluteness."[35]

To recapitulate, we have before us *Dasein* as having been characterized ontologically as care, which as a unified structure comprises thrownness (Being-already-in-a-World), fallenness (Being-alongside), and projection (Being-ahead-of-itself). Care, however, does not give us the whole of *Dasein* nor its authentic potentiality-for-Being; instead it gives us the condition for the possibility of the ontic existence of the potentiality-for-Being-a-whole. The question is how can *Dasein* exist as a unified Being whose essence is care? Not surprisingly, answering this question requires reversion to the only *Dasein* that each of us knows essentially in our existence, namely, the "I" or the "Self" that is each *Dasein*. And, also not surprisingly, for exposition of the Self, Heidegger begins with a discussion of Kant's transcendental Ego.

Heidegger's position on Kant is that Kant is correct in rejecting the ontical theses that the soul is substance but Kant fails to achieve an appropriate ontological interpretation of Selfhood. The gist of Heidegger's criticism is that Kant's "I think" is, as the form of representation of empirical objects, itself treated as "the constant Being-present-at-hand of the 'I' along with its representations" without giving any consideration to the "I think something" and its ontological presupposition of the World. If one takes the

---

34. Ibid., H303.
35. Ibid., H303–4.

World into account correctly, it will be seen as co-determining the state of Being of the "I" and, therefore, must be considered ontologically in that relationship. Although Kant avoids severing the "I think" from the "something" that it thinks, in Kant's philosophy *the objects of thought remain indefinite as to their Being* and so, therefore, must the "I think." For Heidegger, the "I (think something)" is always Being-in-the-World, which provides the clarity necessary for its further interrogation. But even this is not sufficient because *Dasein* interprets itself differently depending upon its manner of Being. In its everydayness, *Dasein* treats the "I" inauthentically as the "they-Self," which, although self-same, is self-forgetful, simple, and empty.[36] Even though one "is that with which one concerns oneself" it does not mean that, philosophically speaking, we need to lose ourselves, so we need to keep in mind that the "I" that is ontologically important for elucidation of the meaning of Being is the *authentic* one, the one for which Being is an issue and which is itself *care* (which expresses itself in both the inauthentic and authentic modes). Heidegger summarizes the implications as follows:

> If the ontological constitution of the Self is not to be traced back either to an "I"-substance [Descartes] or to a "subject" [Kant], but if on the contrary, the everyday fugitive way in which we keep on saying "I" must be understood in terms of our *authentic* potentiality for Being, then the proposition that the Self is the basis of care and constantly present-at-hand, is one that still does not follow. Selfhood is to be discerned existentially only in one's authentic potentiality-for-Being-one's-Self—that is to say, in the authenticity of *Dasein's* Being as *care*.[37]

Accordingly, it is *authentic* care that constitutes the Self and it is anticipatory resoluteness that illuminates the Self-constancy that characterizes authentic Being-in-the-World. In other words, when we speak of Self, we are speaking of a constant *authentic* Self and not the entirety of *Dasein*, which, insofar as it is constituted by care, includes the absence of Self which characterizes irresolute fallenness of the they-Self. Heidegger says:

> *Care does not need to be founded in a Self. But existentiality, as constitutive for care, provides the ontological constitution of Dasein's Self-constancy, to which there belongs, in accordance with the full structural content of care, its Being-fallen factically into non-Self-constancy. When fully conceived, the care-structure includes the phenomenon of Selfhood. This phenomenon is clarified by [i]nterpreting the meaning of care; and it is as care that Dasein's totality of Being has been defined.*[38]

Heidegger's motivation in identifying Selfhood with *authentic* care (as opposed to the whole of the care structure which includes the inauthentic they-Self) is twofold: first, to highlight *existential Dasein* as Being-in-the-World in a way that is self-subsistent and not present-at-hand, and second, to make manifest the authentic Self that provides the constancy necessary to articulate *Dasein* as a unified, potentiality-for-Being-a-whole.

Having accomplished that, Heidegger is now finally in a position to provide the promised reinterpretation of the Self in terms of temporality. Near the beginning of *Being and Time*, Heidegger tells us that when he says that "*Dasein* is in such a way as

36. Ibid., H321–22.
37. Ibid., H322.
38. Ibid., H323.

to be something which understands something like Being," he means that "whenever *Dasein* tacitly understands and interprets something like Being, it does so with time as its standpoint" and that, accordingly, "[t]ime must be brought to light—and genuinely conceived—as the *horizon* of all understanding of Being and every way of interpreting it"[39] (emphasis added). It should be obvious that Heidegger does not intend to show that *Dasein* interprets itself in its Being as existing in what we have previously referred to as "transcendent" time (i.e., the objective time of worldly processes and events) because that would mean that *Dasein* is essentially *Being-in-time* and, as such, merely present-at-hand. Instead, since Heidegger has defined *Dasein* as care, his objective will be to explain how care is essentially temporal. As we shall see, there is a clear relationship between Heidegger's phenomenological depiction of time and that of Husserl, and it will be helpful in understanding Heidegger's conception to bear in mind that, whereas Husserl's characterization of time-consciousness is oriented toward cognition and therefore centered around the present, Heidegger's conception will be determined by his ontological understanding of Dasein as teleologically concerned with its ownmost potentiality-for-Being and therefore centered around the future. In a similar vein, we will also see that Heidegger will supplant Husserl's notion that consciousness of immanent time is the presupposition of all cognition with the more radical idea that transcendent time is an *abstraction from the temporality of Dasein*, the latter of which is therefore primordial temporality.

We begin by reminding ourselves of the structure of *Dasein's* Being as consisting of existence, facticity, and falling, which in turn yields that *Dasein* means "ahead-of-itself-Being-already-in-(the-World) as Being-alongside (entities encountered within-the-World)." It is not at all hard to see how each of the elements of this characterization contains a temporal component and it is upon this observation that Heidegger rests his assertion that the "primordial unity of the structure of care lies in temporality."[40] "Being-ahead-of-itself" (i.e., projection or pressing ahead into one's possibilities) is futuristic in the sense of being forward-looking, "Being-already-in-the-World" (i.e., thrownness) is "having been" and backwards-looking, and "Being-alongside" the objects of one's concern connotes the present. What Heidegger seeks to extract from the language of temporality is a horizon in which the forwardness of "Being-ahead" and the "having been-ness" of "Being-already-in-the-World" provide the conditions for the possibility of *Dasein's* essential character of having its potentiality-for-Being be an issue for it. So Heidegger tells us that Self-projection upon the "for-the-sake-of-oneself" is grounded in the future and therefore the future is the primary meaning of existentiality; *Dasein's* Being is *based upon* thrownness and always *exists* has "having been" and never as an entity "with a bit of it past already" (in the sense of present-at-hand entities that no longer exist); and that the "making present" of "Being-alongside" is included in both projection and fallenness which constitute the "there" of *Dasein*. Thus, for so long as an individual *Dasein* exists, it exists as always having been and always caring about its potentiality.

39. Ibid., H17.
40. Ibid., H327.

Heidegger asserts:

> The future, the character of having been, and the [p]resent, show the phenomenal characteristics of the "towards-oneself," the "back-to," and the "letting-oneself-be-encountered-by." The phenomena of the "towards ... ," the "to ... ," and the "alongside ... ," make temporality manifest as the ἐκστατικόν (*ecstases*) pure and simple. *Temporality is the primordial "out-side-of-itself" in and for itself.*[41]

Heidegger calls the "towards ... ," the "to ... ," and the "alongside ... " of temporality "ecstases" because they disclose the unity of *Dasein* to itself by comprising its constitutive elements so that they stand out as its (phenomenological) moments. Heidegger tells us that temporality does not arise as a cumulative sequence of *ecstases* but that temporality temporalizes itself in their equiprimordiality. Heidegger explains this in a sentence that is difficult but important to grasp: "Primordial and authentic temporality temporalizes itself in terms of the authentic future and in such a way that in having been futurally, it first all awakens the [p]resent."[42]

It is helpful in understanding Heidegger's characterization of temporality to note that the common understanding of our sequential passage through space and time is at odds with its phenomenal presentation in which each of us is always *here and now* and that from the perspective of here and now we are each *always and everywhere* a "having-been," a "being," and a "possibility-of-being," with the implication that we cannot go back to the past or forward into the future as they are commonly understood because they never really exist as such, and are, instead, conditions of the possibility of our Being (here and now). The three elements of *Dasein's* temporal structure are (phenomenological) moments of an indivisible unity but have the described temporal character as providing *horizons for the intelligibility of the process* of Being or, as Heidegger earlier expressed it, becoming what one is. Ontologically, *Dasein* does not have a past, a present, and a future—it has only its care, which is thrown projection plus fallenness/discourse. It is only in ontic existence that the common notions of time, which are fully derivative of *Dasein's* temporality, come into view as *Dasein's* past, present, and future.

Perhaps an example will help. Among my potentialities-for-Being is Being-a-philosopher. As I press forward into the possibility (*projection*), I read, study, think, and write about philosophical issues, all for-the-sake of Being-a-philosopher. In so doing, I am alongside the World of books, desks, computers, etc. (*fallenness*), which I can manipulate toward that end. The existing philosophical literature, the World in which it arose, my education in schools already in Being when I began to project upon the potentiality-for-Being-a-philosopher, and the intellectual capabilities that I inherited, are the foundation (*thrownness*) which ground that potentiality and from which I may project myself onto it. Significantly, nowhere in the foregoing description of my Being-towards-philosophy is there reference to a date, time, timespan, or *state of being* that lies in the future, is in the present, or occurred in the past, and, ontologically speaking, the description is complete even though it makes no reference to the ordinary time that we understand as a succession of "nows."

41. Ibid., H328–329.
42. Ibid., H329.

In common parlance, *Dasein* is a unity that is always in the figurative motion of becoming itself and never in that stasis of having achieved its potentiality for Being. *Dasein* is the totality of its potential and it is not an actuality that is anything other than its potentiality. Understood in this way, *Dasein* is essentially a process of pressing forward into its own possibilities (projection) which cannot be realized because they are always merely potentialities. Moreover, *Dasein* is not a free-floating Being that presses forward from nothingness but instead does so from the context of its world-historical circumstances, its cultural circumstances, its own history, and its own aptitudes (which collectively constitute thrownness) which are also in constant flux. *Dasein* presses forward into what matters to it by engaging with the entities in its World as they are disclosed to it (concerned fallenness). At each step in the process *Dasein* may "use up" its possible ways of Being by choosing one way of Being and eschewing the others but all that accomplishes is to alter *Dasein*'s thrownness and present *Dasein* with a new understanding of itself as constituted by a new set of potential-ways-of-Being. It should be noted, however, that even this last characterization seems to be overly imbued with the vulgar understanding of temporality and that instead of speaking in terms of a temporally sequential consumption of possible ways of Being it would be better to speak in terms of *Dasein*'s disclosing itself to itself in its pressing forward into, and its repetitive reinterpretation of, its potentiality-for-Being.

It should also be noted that *Dasein*'s understanding of itself temporally differs according to whether it is an authentic or inauthentic mode of Being. Authentically, the anticipatory process of *Dasein*'s pressing forward is described by Heidegger as coming towards one's ownmost self by coming back to one's ownmost self, by which I understand him to mean that one's potentiality-for-Being is always understood from the standpoint of one's authentic thrownness and that pressing forward is not a temporal going ahead and leaving behind but instead a continuous reinterpretation of one's care. The way in which authentic *Dasein* understands itself as temporally Being-in-the-World is called a "moment of vision" and the process of authentic temporalizing is called "repetition." The repetitive temporalizing constitutes *Dasein* as a historical Being and is called "historicizing." When *Dasein* is in an inauthentic mode, as the they-Self, it presses forward toward its possibilities from a having-forgotten (its authentic self) and toward a future in which it awaits its authentic possibilities (i.e., its authentic self).

With this understanding, we are now in a position to inquire of Heidegger as to the derivative connection between his conception of the temporality of care and its relation to ordinary time. For Heidegger, there are two philosophically important senses in which time is commonly understood. The first is what Heidegger calls World time and the second is what Heidegger calls ordinary time. World time is time that is characterized in accordance with the meaning that *Dasein* brings to the World. It is significant, datable, spanned, public, sequential, or successive and it is part of the structure in which we understand the ready-to-hand World. Ordinary time is the Newtonian "container" which holds extended objects (i.e., the present-at-hand). So, ontologically speaking, we have a hierarchy in which *Dasein*, for whom its Being is an issue, is always thrown into a World (of equipment) in which it projects itself upon its *potentiality-for-Being*. This World is understood in an "equipmental" World-time, which is embedded in originary time as one of its *ecstases* and "flattened-out" into a "before" and an "after" which opens up the present of our engagements as we project ourselves onto our potentiality-for-Being, and ordinary time is merely an objectified, abstracted structure from which *Dasein's* care has been prescinded leaving only the span of World time within it.

In the interest of clarification, it will be helpful to briefly revert to our earlier summary of Heidegger's position on the existence of mind-independent Reality in the context of our discussion of temporality. As noted, Heidegger does not doubt that there is a real world that is independent of *Dasein* but, because Heidegger's understanding of Being and temporality are unabashedly transcendental, the world of time and space and the intelligibility of the Being of beings requires *Dasein*; in other words, it is *Dasein* that brings temporality into the world of Reality; however, the latter may be said to be constituted in *Dasein's* absence.

At the end of Part I of *Being and Time*, after reminding us that philosophy is "universal phenomenological ontology, [which] takes its departure from the hermeneutic of *Dasein*, which as an analytic of existence, has made fast the guiding-line for all philosophical inquiry at the point where it *arises* and to which it *returns*,"[43] Heidegger provides the following assessment of what has been accomplished in Part I and what remains to be accomplished in Part II:

> Something like "Being" has been disclosed in the understanding-of-Being which belongs to existent *Dasein* as a way in which it understands. Being has been disclosed in a preliminary way, though non-conceptually; and this makes it possible for *Dasein* as existent Being-in-the-[W]orld to comport itself *towards entities*— towards those which it encounters within-the-[W]orld as well as towards itself as existent. *How is this disclosive understanding of Being at all possible for Dasein?* Can this question be answered by going back to the *primordial constitution-of-Being* of that *Dasein* by which Being is understood? The existential-ontological constitution of *Dasein's* totality is grounded in temporality. Hence the ecstatical projection of Being must be made possible by some primordial way in which ecstatical temporality temporalizes. How is this mode of the temporalizing of temporality to be [i]nterpreted? Is there a way which leads from primordial *time* to the meaning of *Being*? Does time itself manifest itself as the horizon of *Being*?[44]

As it turns out, Heidegger is about to take a radically different approach to answering the questions he raises at the end of *Being and Time*—one that is not a repudiation of his exposition of *Dasein* but which nevertheless requires him to leave his great interrogation of *Dasein* behind, only half completed.

THE BEING OF BEINGS

Had Heidegger completed his *phenomenological* analysis of the Being of beings it is not difficult to see where he would likely have come out. *Dasein* has revealed itself from within itself as the being for whom its own Being is an issue, the being whose Being is Being-there, the being whose Being is openness to the World, the Being whose essential

43. Ibid., H436.
44. Ibid., H437.

Being is Being-with, the being whose Being consists of the totality of its possibilities and who is always choosing among ways to be and not be. Since *Dasein's* Being is co-determined with the world as a unified whole, the Being of non-*Dasein* beings would be expected to be ontologically that which is disclosed to *Dasein* as presenting itself from within itself to *Dasein*. And, as we will now see, that is where Heidegger comes out notwithstanding his employment of a vastly different methodology.

But why did Heidegger feel the need to dramatically change his manner of investigation? Apparently, as Heidegger was working out the implications of *Dasein's* temporality, the importance of the historical aspects of thrownness became increasingly apparent to him to the point where Heidegger concluded that understanding Being from any starting point within modern philosophy (including phenomenology) is impossible because the mistaken modern concept of Being as a Thing reaches back all the way to the inception of metaphysics with Plato and Aristotle. If the current objective of philosophy is, as it should be, to *reset* ontology in a way that will enable historical *Dasein* (i.e., man's historical Being) to project itself forward on a sound footing, the task is not so much a phenomenological one as it is a historical one, and the appropriate methodology must be the hermeneutic analysis of ancient Greek philosophy. Moreover, with regard to the last point, in Heidegger's view, although the seed of the annihilation of ontology may have been sewn by Plato, the degeneration got going in earnest with the *translation of ancient Greek philosophy to Latin* by virtue of which the original understanding of the meaning of Being developed by the pre-Socrates was utterly perverted. Heidegger's methodology and starting point, then, will be the hermeneutic investigation of the pre-Socratic philosophers, with a special emphasis on the etymological usage by the pre-Socratics of the Being-related language.

For the purposes of our further investigations, we will focus on two of Heidegger's works. The first is the lecture series that is embodied in *Introduction to Metaphysics*. The second, *The Principle of Reason*, is a shorter work which embodies a subsequent lecture series. After completion of our analysis of these two works, we will finally be in a position to use Heidegger's work as a springboard to discovery of our own, quite different, interpretation of the meaning of Being.

Introduction to Metaphysics proceeds in discrete sections the enumeration of which will assist in organizing our presentation: (1) the most originary question is identified, provisionally, which, as it turns out, is the *Why* question; (2) the *Why* question then gives way to the more originary question: How does it stand with Being?; (3) the meaning of Being, as understood by the pre-Socratics is identified as *phusis*, which means "emerging abiding sway," by grammatical and etymological analysis of pre-Socratic philosophy; (4) the ontology of *phusis* is provisionally worked out in terms of its priority and its presencing to *Dasein*; (5) the four manners in which Being, as a concept, is commonly considered restricted (i.e., fenced in) by the scope of other related concepts (Being versus becoming, Being versus seeming, Being as thinking, and Being versus the "Ought") is shown to be philosophically unfounded and such concepts are shown to be incorporated in and subsumed by Being; and (6) Being is shown to be the *ousia* (substance) of beings. All of the foregoing is presented under the thematic umbrella of identifying and correcting the mistaken path of modern philosophy that began with the seeming innocuousness of Plato's theory of Ideas and culminated in the incoherence of Hegel's Absolute.

With respect to the *Why* question, Heidegger tells us that it is broadest in scope and limited only by Nothing, deepest in that it seeks the ground of everything, and most originary in that it is implicit in all other questions (including its being presupposed by science). Heidegger then lays out the theme of his turn towards etymological hermeneutics by placing philosophy in historical context and asserting its importance as it unfolds historically. Specifically, Heidegger argues that although modern philosophy began to veer off course with Plato's theory of Ideas, its fate was not sealed until classic philosophy was translated from Greek to Latin. Here, Heidegger introduces *phusis* as the fundamental Greek word for beings as such and tells us that *phusis* was translated to *natura* (i.e., nature) in Latin, which means, instead, birth. In pre-Socratic philosophy *phusis*, as the emerging abiding sway, was understood as *the fixed continuity of that which arises from the concealed*. In Heidegger's historical view, the translation of *phusis* to *natura* underpins the movement from ancient ontology to the modern philosophy of science. Heidegger tells us:

> *Phusis* as emergence can be experienced everywhere: for example, in celestial processes (the rising of the sun), in the surging of the sea, in the growth of plants, in the coming forth of animals and human beings from the womb. But *phusis*, the emerging sway, is not synonymous with these processes, which we still today count as part of "nature." This emerging and standing-out-in-itself-from-itself may not be taken as just one process among others that we observe in beings. *Phusis* is being itself, by virtue of which beings first become and remain observable.[45]

In highlighting what Heidegger regards as the fundamental error of modern philosophy, Heidegger emphasizes the difference between studying beings as such and the question of Being. Heidegger proposes to investigate not what is characteristic of beings but what is characteristic of Being.

Heidegger proposes to unfold the *Why* question by means of the question of Nothing. Heidegger at first acknowledges that the phrase "instead of Nothing" contained in the *Why* question appears superfluous. Heidegger tells us that at first blush the *Why* question would appear to be identical with the question of "why are there beings at all?," which, so formulated, clearly and unequivocally seeks the ground of Being, and that, not only is the reference to Nothing apparently superfluous but *that the idea of Nothing is logically contradictory and incoherent.* Nothing, after all, is *no thing*. But that is precisely the point that Heidegger wants to have understood. For Heidegger, modern philosophy is the home of logic and reason and not the home of Being and speaking of Nothing in philosophical terms is therefore an affront to modern philosophy and suborns nihilism. However, there is a hidden presupposition in this position and its rejection is the ground upon which Heidegger's entire thesis will stand; namely, that logic has priority over all that there is, including Being. Heidegger readily agrees that talking about Nothing is unscientific, but his fundamental point is that because logic is dependent upon Being,

---

45. Heidegger, *Introduction to Metaphysics*, 11. Page references are to the 1953 edition of *Einführung in die Metaphysik* published by Max Niemeyr Verlag (Tübingen).

and not the other way around; logic can never be the tribunal in which Being is to be judged. Heidegger concludes that science is derivative of philosophy and, transgressing the border into mysticism, that philosophy, properly understood, stands in a "higher domain and rank of spiritual *Dasein*" where it keeps company only with poetry which is constituted (when good) by an essential superiority of spirit.[46]

Heidegger next turns to the *Why* question itself. On its face, the question interrogates beings by asking what makes a being a Being instead of a non-Being. But in so doing, it is really asking an even more fundamental question, namely, the ground for the fact that beings *are*. And that is a question not about beings but about the being of beings, which we have been calling *Being* all along. So the question that has been identified as most originary is seen to presuppose an even deeper question, which Heidegger formulates as: How does it stand with Being? And this is precisely the question that modern philosophy has forgotten all about.

After a lengthy discussion of the historical disintegration of philosophy, culture, and spirit that coincides with the philosophical and linguistic misunderstanding that ensued as a result, Heidegger turns to a grammatical and etymological exposition that focuses on the understanding of Being in terms of the pre-Socratic Greek language, which may be summarized as follows. The grammar of the ancient Greeks developed under the influence of their conception of Being. In the infinitive form (to be) the definite meanings of Being are blurred so that it is no longer clear what it means for something to be. The substantive (Being) fixes and objectifies the blurring so that it becomes a name for something indefinite. The word *Being* is a leveling off, to the point of emptiness and evanescence, of three root meanings, namely *es*, *bhū*, and *wes*. *Es* is the oldest, from the Sanskrit, and means life, living, that from which out of itself and in itself stands and goes and reposes. *Bhū*, which is Indo-Germanic, belongs to the Greek *phuo* and means to emerge, hold sway, to come to a stand from out of itself and to remain standing. In its original meaning it connoted coming to presence and appearing and coming into the light, illuminating, and shining forth. *Wes* is also Germanic and appears in the inflection of the German word *sein* and means to dwell, to abide, to sojourn. From the three stems we derive three originary meanings: living, emerging, abiding. These three meanings have died out in the abstract indefiniteness of the word "to be."

Accordingly, it serves to ask: Does the emptiness and indefiniteness of the word "being" mandate that our inquiry be abandoned? Must we turn, as modern philosophy has done, to a scientific investigation of beings as such as the horizon at which our knowledge is delimited? Heidegger's answers to these questions are of course in the negative for it cannot escape our notice that in our everyday experience we are surrounded by all sorts of entities and know that they are beings and exist. Says Heidegger:

> We understand the word "Being," and hence all its inflections, even though it looks as if this understanding were indefinite. We say of what we thus understand, of whatever *opens itself up* to us somehow in understanding, that it has meaning. Being, insofar as it is understood at all, has a meaning. To experience and conceive

---

46. Ibid., 29.

of Being as what is most worthy of questioning, to inquire especially about Being, then means nothing other than asking about the meaning of Being.[47]

And, indeed, Heidegger's argument proceeds that we, as *Dasein*, have an understanding of Being as implicit in our very constitution of care, for how else can we be the being for whom its own Being is an issue? And this understanding of the Being of *Dasein* must therefore be of the highest rank. For Heidegger (as well as transcendent realism), this is a fact that modern philosophy cannot (even though it attempts to) ignore.

Heidegger's analysis next takes a completely different turn. This time he seeks to understand Being in terms of four specific limitations that have been placed upon it over the history of philosophical inquiry. These are Being and becoming, Being and seeming, Being and thinking, and Being and the Ought, and they are presented in the order in which they have appeared in the history of philosophy. Heidegger's intention is to show that, contrary to common understanding, Being is not restricted by these related concepts and that, instead, Being, as the originary concept and ground of all beings, encompasses and subsumes them.

With respect to *Being* in contradistinction to *becoming*, as might be expected, Heidegger refers us to Parmenides and Heraclitus, two of his heroes. The modern understanding of distinction between Being as having completed the process of becoming is a perversion of the originary meaning of Being and reflects, says Heidegger, a completely artificial opposition of the two pre-Socratics that has been mistakenly adopted by modern philosophy. Instead, asserts Heidegger, Being is the emerging sway and as such represents perdurance in the face of change. In other words, the *Being* of a thing is its *becoming* what it is.

With respect to *Being* in contradistinction to *seeming*, Heidegger tells us that the modern understanding that Being represents the actual and that seeming represents illusion is also incorrect. Upon etymological analysis, seeming is shown to have three modes of meaning: manifestation or self-showing; luster and glow; and semblance or appearance; with the first such modes being primary and comprehending the other two, secondary meanings. As was the case with the first-discussed restriction of Being, the second restriction is seen to be illusory because Being, as the emerging sway, is in itself the seeming or appearing of that which presents itself. And here Heidegger makes the important connection between Being and truth:

> The emerging sway is an appearing. As such, it makes manifest. This already implies that Being, appearing, is a letting-step-forth from concealment. Insofar as Being as such *is*, it places itself into and stands in *unconcealment, aletheia*. . . . [T]he Greek essence of truth is possible only together with the Greek essence of Being as *phusis*. On the grounds of the unique essential connection between *phusis* and *alethiea*, the Greeks could say: beings as beings are true. The true as such is in being. This says that what shows itself in its sway stands in the unconcealed. The unconcealed as such comes to a stand in showing itself. Truth, as un-concealment, is not an addendum to Being.
>
> *Truth belongs to the essence of Being*. . . .[48]

---

47. Ibid., 63–64.
48. Ibid., 77–78.

With respect to *Being* in contradistinction to *thinking*, we come to the heart of Heidegger's misgivings with modern philosophy and, accordingly, a somewhat deeper analysis is required. Heidegger begins by observing that the opposition between Being and thinking is different from the three others because thinking is not merely put forth in contrast to Being as a faculty by which Being is purported to be understood, but thinking is put over and above Being. As noted earlier, by "thinking," Heidegger means the free re-presenting by *Dasein* to itself of that which appears in order to analyze by means of identifying applicable universals. And thinking occurs under formal rules of thought which we have understood since Aristotle as logic. Logic is the science of *logos*, which is understood here as meaning *assertion*. But, Heidegger tells us that it is by no means clear that thinking is the application of logic and his task is, therefore, to show how its misconstrual as such arose. Heidegger tells us that it began with the introduction by Plato of his theory of Ideas and the development by the Platonic-Aristotelian schools of the rules of logic. Originally, *phusis* and *logos* were closely connected. *Logos* did not mean thinking, understanding, and reason. *Logos* originally meant gathering or bringing together in a process of comparing and contrasting. To make the point, Heidegger reverts yet again to Heraclitus, analyzing two fragments as follows:

> What is said of *logos* here corresponds exactly to the authentic meaning of the word "gathering." But just as this word denotes both 1) to gather and 2) gatheredness, *logos* here means the gathering gatheredness, that which originally gathers. *Logos* does not mean sense or word or doctrine and certainly not the sense of a doctrine but instead the originally gathering gatheredness that constantly holds sway in itself.[49]

Heidegger concludes that "*Logos* is constant gathering, the gatheredness of beings that stands in itself, that is, Being."[50]

Having conjoined *phusis* and *logos* in their original usage, it is now incumbent upon Heidegger to show how they became separated in subsequent philosophy and how logic rose to a position of supremacy over Being. Not surprisingly, Heidegger attributes the inception of the disjunction to a misinterpretation of a famous statement by Parmenides that "thinking and Being are the same." The misinterpretation turns on the meaning of "*noein*" which, according to Heidegger, etymologically means *apprehending* (not thinking) with the consequence that Parmenides is misunderstood to mean that "to be is to think or reason." Instead, Parmenides's meaning is "belonging-together reciprocally are apprehending and Being"—in other words, that Being consists in the apprehension of what is present to it and that apprehension is nothing less than the *coming into Being of man*. As it progressed, the disjunction coalesced around a change in the interpretation of another closely related word, that is, "*eidos*," which means *idea*. Originally, *eidos* stood for that which is apprehended. The *eidos* of something originally meant what is seen in it as it appears, the *look* of something, that "within which and as which the thing comes-to-presence. . . . " Considered in this way, the idea of something has two aspects. The first is that it represents the appearance of that which appears and the second is that it

---

49. Ibid., 98.
50. Ibid., 100.

represents the *what* of a being. Plato's theory of Ideas, in which the appearance of a thing was reduced to an imperfect copy of the Idea of the thing, formalized the diremption. Heidegger summarizes these circumstances as follows:

> However, as soon as the essence of Being comes to consist in whatness (idea), then whatness, as *the* Being of beings, is also what is most in being about beings. On the one hand, whatness is now what *really is, ontōs on*. Being as idea is now promoted to the status of what really is, and beings themselves, which previously held sway, sink to the level of what Plato calls *mē on*—that which really should not be and really *is* not either—because beings always deform the idea, the pure look by actualizing it, insofar as they incorporate it into matter. On the other hand, the *idea* becomes the *paradeigma*, the model. At the same time, the idea necessarily becomes the ideal. What is produced by imitation really "is" not, but only participates in Being, *methexis* (participation). The *chōrismos* (separation) has been ripped open, the cleft between the idea as what really is, the prototype and archetype, and what really is not, the imitation and likeness.[51]

Heidegger goes on to explain that the reinterpretation of *phusis* as idea is accompanied by a corresponding change in the interpretation of *logos*. In the inception, *logos* is the occurrence of unconcealment. But because the gathering that characterizes *logos* is expressed in language (discourse) its nature changes from speaking about beings (as such) to speaking about ideas and gets reinterpreted as assertion. The truth of disclosure is supplanted by the truth of correctness and truth itself becomes a mere property of *logos*. As a result, *logos,* instead of being the gathering gatheredness of that which appears, becomes a proposition to be tested against beings and Being. Being becomes Being-in-a-state, which can be tested against the *logos*, ontology becomes the theory of categories, and *logos* becomes the categorial determination of Being. *Ousia* becomes substance. And with the ascent of the Idea and its categories, all that remained for Western philosophy was to work out the implications. The reinterpretation of Being as thinking requires reinterpretation of becoming, which becomes mere *motion*, and seeming, which becomes *illusion*. And the reinterpretation of Being as Idea gives rise to the Idea of all Ideas, the Idea of the Good. The separation between the Idea of the Good and all the lesser Ideas culminates in rationality's highest achievement, the grounding of morality in Kant's categorical imperative.

To summarize Heidegger's analysis, in the entire history of philosophy, only the pre-Socratics were on the right track to understanding Being. The degeneration of ontology began with Plato's interpretation of Being, which had been understood by the pre-Socratics as *phusis*, as *eidos*. The etymological meanings of the critical Greek terms, especially *logos* and *ousia*, were irretrievably lost when Western scholarship became Latin scholarship. The truth of disclosure became the truth of propositions. Being as Idea culminated in Hegel's Absolute idea and in Kant's moral philosophy.

Heidegger is determined to restore ontology to its pre-Socratic footing so that Western culture can start anew on a sound philosophical basis. Such a beginning must recognize that Being is unrestricted, Being is becoming, Being is appearance, and Being

---

51. Ibid., 140–41.

is prior to and encompasses thinking and, to the extent it might be fairly said to exist, the Ought. Heidegger concludes that Being is the ground of all there is.

THE GROUND OF BEING

In *Being and Time* and *Introduction to Metaphysics*, Heidegger has asked and answered two of the three questions that we will cover in these pages. *Dasein*, as the temporal being for whom his own Being is an issue and as the site at which the world opens up in its disclosure and apprehension, is itself the *meaning* of Being. Surely, without *Dasein*, beings other than *Dasein* would continue to be, but they would no longer be apprehended in the manner that they are by *Dasein*. Temporality, including originary time, World time, and ordinary time, would not exist as such. Beings could not be said to be *in time*. Neither could beings be said to have any meaning, because beings receive their meaning from *Dasein*. Beings would merely be present-at-hand. But *Dasein* is in the World and beings are disclosed to *Dasein* as *phusis* and they are so apprehended. Being is the ground of all beings.

Still, there remain some obvious questions. If Being is the ground of all beings, what is the ground of Being? If Being is not an entity, can it be said to have a ground? How can something exist that is not a being? Or is the question of the existence of Being a tautology?

In *The Principle of Reason*, Heidegger addresses these questions through the vehicle of Leibniz's law: *Nihil est sine ratione* (Nothing is without reason). Heidegger, acting quite naturally, reverses the double negatives and shows that the principle states that everything has a reason. But Heidegger explains that Leibniz deliberately formulated the principle in the double negative so that it does not appear as an assessment that invites testing by, for example, scientific method and which can never be proven. By formulating Leibniz's law in the double negative, Leibniz is free to argue that it is a rule of thought that is "directly illuminating," (i.e., that is known by direct intuition).

Heidegger tells us that the principle of reason is no ordinary rule of thought (if there can be such a thing). His explanation is as follows. The other such rules, all of which have been previously examined in these pages, apply as they should, to logical thinking. A thing is identical with itself. A thing cannot be and not be. If a thing is equal to another and that other thing is equal to a third thing, then the first thing is equal to the third. But the principle of reason says that everything has a reason and, as so understood, seems to apply to all of the other rules of thought and, importantly, in the word "reason," which it contains it speaks also to itself. *The principle of reason is, therefore, the principle of all principles.*

But, Heidegger tells us, even this status is insufficient to comprehend the importance of Leibniz's law. Not only does the scope of the principle of reason make it unique but so also does the way it operates within the act of thinking. The principle of reason is a *modus vivendi* lying at the foundation of our pre-ontological cognitive acts. We are by nature cognitive agents and, as such, we always seek proximate and sometimes the most remote causes of things. We ask "why" over and over again until we are at the edge of the abyss (*abgrund*) of reason. So even if we never heard of the principle of reason we would still operate existentially under its enduring spell.

Heidegger next identifies an important difficulty with this characterization of the principle of reason. We said a moment ago that the principle of reason speaks to itself. But that seems to create a circularity that cannot be abided. Two possibilities therefore emerge. One such possibility is that the principle of reason is not within its own jurisdiction and, therefore, the principle of reason does not require that there be a reason to support it. But this involves a contradiction. The other such possibility is that the principle of reason requires that it have a reason itself and that any such reason also have a reason, and so on, so that the principle of reason is, by its own operation, incoherent. So, like the first possibility, the second possibility seems to be unacceptable on its face. If the principle of reason does not have a reason, then the principle of reason is false. Heidegger's way out of the conundrum is dubious at best. He asks whether, in applying the principle of non-contradiction to the principle of reason, we act mindlessly. He notes that the principle of non-contradiction is a keystone of scientific reasoning to be sure, but, tells us that, ever since Hegel's *Science of Logic*, philosophy must acknowledge the possibility that the fact that something contradicts itself does not mean that it is not real. So where does this leave us with respect to the principle of principles? Heidegger provides an answer that we will soon call into question: "The [p]rinciple of [p]rinciples without reason—for us this is inconceivable. But what is inconceivable is by no means unthinkable, given that thinking does not exhaust itself in conceiving."[52] What is implicit in Heidegger's attempted escape is what was explicit in *Introduction to Metaphysics*; namely, that Being is to be privileged over logic. However, in yielding to this disappointing conclusion, Heidegger fails to consider a third possibility, which is the one that we will adopt and which is that the principle of reason, as the principle of all principles, speaks to itself necessarily and without circularity and in so doing *is its own ground*.

Heidegger is nevertheless prepared to press onward with his exposition of the principle of reason, this time by appeal to the following etymology. As the principle of principles, the principle of reason requires that everything about which it speaks must have a reason, whether or not it speaks to itself. We accept the principle of reason because we regard it as axiomatic, but in saying something is a principle or an axiom we are almost always too glib and must take care to be clear about our meaning. The Latin word for principle is "*principium*." "*Principium*" means that which contains the *ratio* of something else. A principle is an *axiom* to the Greeks. In Greek, "*axiom*" means that which I find worthy and "worthy" means to bring something to shine forth in that countenance in which it finds its repose, and to preserve it therein. The principle of principles is the "*principium-id quod primum*," which means that "which has been grasped, captured, and thus contains what is first, and in this manner is that which stands first in rank." In German, these all connote "Grund-Satz," which although directly translatable to the Greek as "*hypothese*" (hypothesis) was used by Plato to mean "that which already lies at the basis of something else and which always already has come to light through this other, even if we people do not immediately or always expressly notice it." We begin now

---

52. Heidegger, *Principle of Reason*, 18.

to see where Heidegger is heading, that is, on the path that leads to *phusis* and to *logos* and to Being itself and to the identification of Being with intelligibility.

Heidegger returns to Leibniz. Leibniz calls the principle of reason a *principium grande*, a mighty principle. He says that *Nihil est sine ratione seu nullus effectus sine causa* (nothing is without reason, or no effect is without a cause), thereby rendering the principle of reason equivalent to causality. But he also says "there are two supreme [p]rinciples for all proofs, the [p]rinciple—it goes without saying—of contradiction and the [p]rinciple *reddendae rationis*" which says that "for every truth [true proposition] the reason can be rendered." Thus, the *principium rationis* is the *principium reddendae rationis*. It runs to the heart of cognition: In Latin cognition is *representatio*. Heidegger tells us:

> What is encountered is presented to a cognizing I, presented back to and over against it, made present. According to the *principium reddendae rationis*, cognition must render to cognition the reason for what is encountered—and that means give it back (*reddere*) to cognition—if it is to be discerning cognition. . . . Therefore, for Leibniz the [p]rinciple of [r]eason is the fundamental principle of rendering reasons.[53]

So, the principle of reason is not only the first rule of thought and the *modus vivendi* of *Dasein*, but it is also the fundamental principle of cognition itself, and what is *mighty* about the principle is that it pervades, guides, and supports all cognition that expresses itself in sentences or propositions.

The interpretation of the principle of reason as a principle of cognition raises a profoundly important question the elucidation of which will motivate Heidegger throughout the remainder of *The Principle of Reason*. This question may be stated thusly: as a principle of cognition is the principle of reason restricted only to that which is discernible or does it mean that nothing can be said to be if it cannot be cognized? Heidegger makes unmistakably clear how the *principium reddendae* rationis identifies Being with intelligibility:

> Cognition is a kind of representational thinking. In this presentation something we encounter comes to stand, to a standstill. What is encountered and brought to a standstill in representational thinking is the object. For Leibniz and all modern thinking, the manner in which beings "are" is based in the objectness of objects. For representational thinking, the representedness of objects belongs to the objectness of objects.
>
> But then again the *principium rationis* as the *principium reddendae rationis* says that this representational thinking and what it represents, that is, the object in its obstancy, must be a founded one. The obstancy of the object amounts to the manner in which the object as such stands, which means, is. So the strict formulation of the *principium rationis* as the *principium reddendae rationis* is not a restriction of the principle of reason; rather, the *principium reddendae rationis* is valid for everything that is an object, which means here everything that "is." Accordingly, the strict formulation of the *principium rationis* as the *principium reddendae rationis* contains a very specific and decisive explanation of what the unrestricted [p]rinciple of [r]eason says: nothing is without reason. This now says: something "is," which means, can be identified as being a being, only if it is stated in a sentence that satisfies the fundamental [p]rinciple of [r]eason as

53. Ibid., 22.

the fundamental principle of founding. What is mighty about the [p]rinciple of [r]eason displays its power in that the *principum reddendae rationis*—to all appearances only a [p]rinciple of cognition—also counts, *precisely in being the fundamental principle of cognition, as the [p]rinciple for everything there is.*[54] (Emphasis added.)

But, Heidegger tells us, even this does not exhaust the might of the mighty principle. The *principium reddendae rationis* means that reasons are not indeterminately and indifferently present but instead that beings may be said to exist only insofar as they appear to reason as a *founded* cognition:

> Only what presents itself to our cognition, only what we en-counter such that it is posed and posited in its reasons, counts as something with secure standing, that means, as an object. Only what stands in this manner is something of which we can, with certainty, say "it is."[55]

At this point, Heidegger has delivered all that he considers important in Leibniz's development of the principle of principles, which can be summarized as Leibniz's recognition that the principle of reason is no mere rule of thought but instead is the mighty principle of the cognition of all that may be said to be, and Heidegger is now ready to part company with Leibniz over its implications, which for Leibniz include proof of the existence of God. Heidegger explains that the principle of reason is a normative principle in the Leibnizian system because it is related to everything there is and that it applies to all *Natura* including all being, nature, and history. Leibniz tells us that "[t]here is a reason in Nature why something exists rather than nothing." Leibniz also tells us that "[t]his reason (in the "Nature" of things according to which they have the inclination to exist rather than not to exist) must be in some sort of real being, or in its cause," and, finally, "(that being in which necessarily exists as the highest reason) is usually named with one word: GOD." Leibniz calls God the "*ultimo ratio Rerum*" (the "highest existing reason of all things"). So we see that Leibniz's characterization of the mighty principle extends it to all that there is and can be thought or said to be, including God, as the First Cause. However, Heidegger accepts the modern mainstream criticism of the First Cause on the basis that it is circular insofar as the principle purports to prove the existence of the same God upon whose existence the principle itself depends:

> Taken to its extreme, [the First Cause argument] means that God exists only insofar as the principle of reason holds. One immediately asks in turn: to what extent does the principle of reason hold? If the principle of reason is the mighty [p]rinciple, then its bepowering is a sort of effecting. In fact ... Leibniz speaks of an efficacy, an *efficere* that accrues to the supreme principles. However, (according to the principle of reason) all effecting requires a cause. But the first cause is God. So the [p]rinciple of [r]eason holds only insofar as God exists. But God exists only insofar as the [p]rinciple of [r]eason holds. Such thinking moves in a circle.[56]

---

54. Ibid., 23.
55. Ibid., 27.
56. Ibid., 28.

Heidegger cautions, however, that we should not conclude that Leibniz "acquiesced" in the circularity or that the circularity fully eviscerates the mighty principle. And with this Heidegger makes a subtle distinction that will unfold as his fundamental theme throughout the remainder of his lecture series, namely, the distinction between reason and Being as the subject of the principle of reason:

> What still remains [valid in Leibniz's thinking] is the insight into that upon which everything depends: the [p]rinciple of [r]eason is the [p]rinciple that pervasively bepowers everything insofar as reason, according to the strict formulations of the fundamental principle, insists that each thing that is, is (exists) as a consequence of . . . , which is to say, by virtue of the express, complete fulfillment of the demand of reason. . . .
> The *principium reddendae rationis* requires that all cognition of objects be a self-grounding cognition and, along with this, that the object itself always be a founded—which means, securely established-object.[57]

So how does reason "securely establish" an object? The answer is in the completion of the object's conditions of its own possibility. Heidegger explains:

> Reason, which insists on its being rendered, at the same time requires that it, as a reason, be sufficient, which means, completely satisfactory. For what? In order to securely establish an object (*Gegenstand*) in its stance (*Stand*). In the background of the definition of sufficing, of sufficiency (of *suffectio*), there is the guiding idea of Leibnizian thinking—the idea of *perfectio*, that is, of the completeness (*Vollständigkeit*) of the determinations for the standing (*Stehen*) of an object (*Gegenstand*). Only in the completeness of the conditions for its possibility, only in the completeness of its reasons is the status (*Ständigkeit*) of an object through and through securely established, perfect. . . . [T]he title of the [p]rinciple of [r]eason reads, when thought strictly and completely: *principium reddendae rationis sufficientis*, the fundamental principle of rendering sufficient reasons.[58]

Heidegger continues his interpretation more deeply by restating the mighty principle as "Nothing is without a why" in order to employ as a vehicle a wonderful verse from the poetry of Angelus Silesius:

> The rose is without why: it blooms because it blooms,
> It pays no attention to itself, asks not whether it is seen.[59]

Heidegger points out that in the poem the rose is without a "why" (a seeking of its ground) but yet has a "because" (ground) and it exists, unlike *Dasein*, without any concern for its own being. So the mighty principle holds in the case of the rose *qua* object (of our cognition) but not for the rose in its rose-being (in its own right). And this brings us to a new understanding of the mighty principle, in which lies Heidegger's most fundamental of all assertions: the mighty principle tells us that reason demands that reasons be rendered in all cognition of objects, but it tells us nothing about reason itself. In Heidegger's hands, the principle of reason states nothing directly about the

---

57. Ibid.
58. Ibid., 33.
59. Ibid., 35.

essence of reason and it tells us nothing about from whence the mighty principle makes its demands. For Heidegger, the principle of reason is a principle of Being and it reads in a completely different intonation: "*Nihil est sine ratione*"—every being (as a being) has a reason.[60] So we see that the mighty principle, by way of the example of the rose, shows us that grounds (*grund*) can stand in manifold relationships to us as the cognizing creature. Compare animals and inanimate objects. According to Leibniz (as we saw in chapter 2, "The Death and Resurrection of Metaphysics"), every being is a living being and as such is a representation-striving being. But it is only *Dasein* who can bring before itself grounds of things *qua* grounds. Like the rose, other living things are grounded in their existence but do not live according to reasons. They have a because but not a why. Reason grounds our cognition of objects in Being but it is not, as such, in the Being of such objects.

Heidegger elucidates as follows. The question arises as to whether reasons are always associated with objects, either as "why's" or "because's," or whether they can become dissociated from objects and still be reasons. The question calls upon the principle of reason for some particulars about the essence of reason itself. We see *in the second intonation* that the subject is "every being" and the predicate is "has a reason." It is definitely a statement about Being. The principle of reason represents reason in an essential way, certainly, but it speaks to beings not reason as such. This representation of reason allows it sufficient scope to serve as the guiding principle in the derivation and founding of propositions. The principle of reason itself is under this intonation underivable and therefore the sort of thing that limits thinking. But if we listen to the principle of reason we will hear what it says "to Being belongs something like a ground." Heidegger rephrases the idea simply: "Being : Ground, the same."

Heidegger comes now to the fundament of the analysis embodied in the three volumes under consideration in these pages. The principle of reason, "Nothing is without reason" and "every Being is with reason" contain "is" as their copulas. But Being implies the "is" and renders it redundant. Therefore, the principle of reason means that Being and reason belong together. Heidegger tells us:

> Being and ground/reason belong together. Ground/reason receives its essence from its belonging together with [B]eing *qua* [B]eing. Put in the reverse, [B]eing reigns *qua* [B]eing from out of the essence of ground/reason. Ground/reason and [B]eing ("are") the same—not equivalent—which already conveys the difference between the names "[B]eing" and "ground/reason." Being "is" in essence: ground/reason. Therefore [B]eing can never first have a ground/reason which would supposedly ground it. Accordingly, ground/reason is missing from [B}eing. Ground/reason remains at a remove from [B]eing. Being "is" the abyss in the sense of such a remaining-apart of reason from [B]eing. To the extent that [B]eing as such grounds, it remains groundless. "Being" does not fall within the orbit of the [p]rinciple of [r]eason, rather only beings do.[61]

For Heidegger Being : Ground, the same, but Being itself is ungrounded.

---

60. Ibid., 39–40.
61. Ibid., 51.

BERGNER'S CREDO

To my knowledge, Heidegger never offered what we would normally regard as a traditional ethics but instead challenges us to return to the openness of Being so that human history can play itself out on a philosophically sound basis. Certainly, Heidegger decries the contemporary epoch which he asserts begins with Plato's objectification of reality as Idea and ends with Nietzsche's nihilism and results in the utter oblivion of Being. As a result, Heidegger is sometimes said to be a cultural relativist. But I think this misses Heidegger's point altogether. Heidegger is anything but a subjectivist and he certainly regards the historical-cultural epochs in Western history from Plato onwards to be predicated upon a profoundly flawed understanding of the essence of humanity. Doubtless, there is a theme in Heidegger's thinking that naturally flows from his idea that reality is *aletheia* that truth is not an absolute entity that is frozen throughout the ages, but that nowise implies that the *mode du jour* is what it *ought* to be, and Heidegger's main emphasis is that precisely opposite the case has prevailed for more than two and a half millennia.

The case that an understanding of the Being of man as *Dasein* does not rule out objective justice is well made by Bergner in *Against Modern Humanism*. Although Bergner is not an avowed phenomenologist or phenomenological ontologist, his philosophy is explicitly compatible with Heidegger's core understanding of the human being as the agent of unconcealment. Bergner traces the history of the West from a different perspective than does Heidegger but reaches a similar conclusion, namely, that modern humanism is ungrounded. Nevertheless, Bergner's thesis is uniquely his own and quite startling. Bergner treats in sequence ancient Judaism, ancient Greece, medieval Christianity, modern philosophy through German idealism, and, finally, modern material reductionism, and identifies the core understandings of each epoch and shows how each relates to the others. For the ancient Jews, the understanding of the human being was membership in the tribe, but insofar as it is based upon faith in Yahweh and not reason its doctrines are not philosophically founded. For the ancient Greeks, the human being is understood primarily as soul (*psuche*) and the theme as developed through Aristotle is striving toward living a completely human life. The most jarring event in Western history was the birth of Jesus, whose teaching propelled the West into Christianity. During the Christian epoch, the human being came to be understood as a psychosomatic unity possessed of the freedom to turn toward or away from God, which represents a melding of the Greek notion of man as body and soul with the Hebrew emphasis on the centrality of religion in human life. As we have seen, modern idealism began with Descartes's division of the human being into body and mind and ended with Hegel's Absolute Ego. And here comes what is perhaps Bergner's most interesting observation: although contemporary mainstream materialism rebukes idealism in general and especially German idealism, it surreptitiously retains the notion of the Ego as the center of its moral philosophy, even though on its own reductionist principles this position is utterly indefensible.

Bergner's other innovation is with respect to the question of how human beings conceived as revealers of Being ought to live. Bergner begins with the observation that human philosophical understanding is achieved by individual effort and requires pushing forward "beyond every limited view, toward the fullness of what is human" without any guarantee of success:

> What does such a life look like? What is a life which expresses beyond all essentialist views of human beings as tribal members, as souls, as embodied wills, or as minds? What is a life which is open to the fullness of human being, but which understands that such openness is not infinite and complete, but is always somehow rooted in the finitude of a persisting self-awareness? How shall we come truly to know ourselves?[62]

In "Credo," the final chapter of *Against Modern Humanism*, Bergner addresses four areas of human Being, namely, the relationship of man to Nature, to other human beings, to the gods, and in internal life. Inasmuch as Bergner's work is an exposition of the case against humanism, much of his presentation is by way of contrast with other main lines of philosophy, which we will summarize in passing. But what is most interesting to us in our own search for the meaning of Being is not only what Bergner has to say positively about how we ought to live but also the way in which Bergner derives his ethics from his Heideggerian-compatible view of man as the agent of disclosure of the world.

We begin with man's relationship to Nature. Bergner's argument is as follows: As revealers of Being, it is one of our fundamental characteristics to regard Nature with wonderment. We share with Nature our Being and we human beings and Nature reciprocally bring to each other the elements of our unique relationship. Nature is in a certain sense an "idea" of our own making but only to the extent that it is by virtue of human cognition that the world of external things comes out of its concealed potentiality to actuality. Nature can be known only through human classifications and therefore the emergence of Nature into the light of human understanding is dependent upon human understanding. But none of this implies that the human Ego creates, determines, or owns in any way Nature. Neither is the world arbitrary. Nature is given (*es gibt*) to human beings in its relationship of shared Being with us. Accordingly, to be fully human is to recognize our co-determinacy with Nature, to recognize our shared Being with Nature, to regard nature with wonder and gratitude, and to be attentive and open to Nature as it continues to reveal itself and us out of itself and ourselves.

Bergner drives home the point against modern humanism as follows:

> To look upon the world and all within it, including our own [B]eing, as "given" is bound to invoke a certain wonder or surprise. It may, depending on the temperament of the observer, also generate responses from pious gratitude to Schopenhauerian disgust—but wonder is the underlying and more or less inevitable response of anyone who has ever contemplated all that is given to him. This sense of wonder is far from the sense of creative mastery of the contemporary ego. It is far from the idea that the external world is merely given its qualities on loan by the freely creative ego. It is far from the idea that the external world is merely "standing reserve" waiting to be shaped and utilized by the creative ego. It is far from being a "mere pensioner" on human ego.[63]

---

62. Bergner, *Against Modern Humanism*, 238.
63. Ibid., 238–39.

With respect to our relationship to other human beings, Bergner's starting point is the importance of the social context we inherit in our Being in the world. We cooperate with, struggle with, exchange language and meaning with, and build social and political institutions with other human beings. We seek to understand how things are with each other and through our institutions we seek an understanding of what justice is. Bergner takes on directly Hume's naturalist fallacy (i.e., that "ought" cannot be derived from "is") by identifying many ways in which the notion of "ought" is imbedded in our cognition, our language, and our everyday expectations of one another. In this regard, Bergner offers the example of a table. When we characterize a table we communicate that the relevant entity has certain characteristics that it *ought* to have in order to truly constitute a table. Bergner proposes that it is most appropriate to root the idea of justice in a proper description of a human being because, in so doing, we avoid the obstacles that mainstream philosophy puts in the path of the determination of justice. We thereby avoid the naturalist fallacy, altruistic ethics, or the need to conjure up a world of moral sentiments that, somehow, exists in an obligatory way alongside fact-based science. In order to do that, we first need to understand the difference between "facts" and "values" and how they appear in cognition. Bergner tells us that the notion of contemporary egoism that Ego creates science and scientific things in order to serve its intentions is completely erroneous:

> For surely in the world of day-to-day activity—from a mother and a child to the struggles of people to find justice in a political order—the reality is everywhere exactly the opposite. What one calls something, how one conceives of it and describes it, is everywhere and always pointing toward how one should orient oneself toward it (that is, its meaning). How one thinks of the nature or origin of anything always points in the first instance to some conclusion about it—that is, what is its importance, its significance, its meaning.[64]

Bergner offers two emotionally charged examples of what he asserts is the character of human beings to learn from one another and to contend with one another in the search to understand the objects, institutions, and practices appropriate to justice. Bergner's purpose is not to take sides on the issues he presents but rather to show that the political contentiousness is attributable to a disagreement as to how to understand and characterize issues. The first example offered by Bergner is the issue of abortion. Bergner argues that the agreement with respect to the fact that abortion entails termination of a fetus is trivial and that the real controversy surrounds whether abortion constitutes the exercise of a right to choose or the murder of a human being—in other words, the question at issue is how to describe what an abortion *is*. The second example offered by Bergner is that of terrorism. Bergner frames the question as being whether terrorism is the taking of innocent lives for political purposes or the taking of guilty lives in furtherance of some moral end. Bergner's point is that these debates do not arise from disagreement as to "moral sentiments," but instead arise from the meanings imbedded in how we describe events. Underlying Bergner's analysis is the notion that human beings bring meaning to that which is presented to them as a unified cognitive act and

64. Ibid., 246.

do not, as the contemporary mainstream would assert, attribute meaning to objective entities and events on a basis that is secondary to cognition. What is to be said about the meaning that human beings contribute to cognition? Meaning is neither dispassionate nor merely instrumental to our ends but is rooted in our efforts to orient ourselves to the world, and justice is, concomitantly, the outcome of our efforts to understand how we ought to comport ourselves in the fullness of our humanity in the social and political context of our personal circumstances. But justice acquires an objective content in that understanding and requires us to accept ourselves "as members of our social context and not as a potentiality-bearing ego." Bergner tells us that society is not an arbitrary limitation upon our Being nor a hindrance to realizing our humanity but an important part of what it means to be human. Bergner admonishes:

> If you are a father, act like a father. If you are a husband, act like a husband. If you are a citizen of America, act like one. These are not roles—they are each a genuine portion of your human [B]eing. These features of your [B]eing are not to be cast off at will. Act according to the manifold fullness of the human [B]eing which you are. Do not do so because there is a reward which will maximize your potential to be or to do something else. What after all would be the point of being able to be something else?[65]

Living according to a principle of realizing the fullness of our humanity has at least three other implications. One is that one ought to live a full life, not one that is governed by obsession with one or two aspects (such as our work) of the manifold of our human experience. The second implication is that just as it is the case with respect to our relationship to Nature that Nature does not determine our conduct, neither should our social context preclude us from exercising our own free judgment where we determine justice requires. The final implication is that it is unlikely that we will ever identify a perfect justice that will inform each and every aspect of our lives and should therefore measure our lives in their entirety against the dictates of justice.

With respect to the gods, Bergner's fundamental notion is that "we should seek from the standpoint that there may be a god or gods and a fully human life requires us to seek to know their [B]eing and their will."[66] Although Bergner's religious thinking extends all the way to openness regarding the possibility that superior or supreme beings who are generally beyond our reach may appear or communicate in some form at their discretion, Bergner's openness to the possible existence of God (or gods) is subject to several major qualifications that, broadly speaking, are injunctions against dogmatism. Bergner's argument is that it is philosophically unacceptable to rationalize our own personal or social desires through the medium of religion, or to anthropomorphize the gods, either explicitly or through conception of God having characteristics that are analogous to human willing and human capacity for action, or to speculate concerning the existence of an afterlife the existence of which nowise follows from the existence of God. As to the last, Bergner argues instead that openness and fullness of Being require focus upon life in this world.

---

65. Ibid., 250.
66. Ibid., 253.

With respect to interior life, Bergner starts from the standpoint that we are all that we are in the broadest sense, including our body, time and place, social relations, and the ways that forces outside of us act upon us. It follows that any attempt to find ourselves by looking "inside" for a pure and essential ego disregards our fundamental Being. And, indeed, openness (i.e., being open to that which presents itself) requires that we allow others to act upon us. Bergner contrasts his view of the nature of the human being with the pure Ego of modern humanism by noting that the latter "is a mythological private 'place' which cannot be acted upon, which cannot be shaken, and which is pure freedom itself" and "if the pure freedom of ego were shaped by what is outside, it would no longer be free."[67]

It follows that our uniqueness derives from our world—not from the separateness of our ego but from our relationships with entities and others and with the gods. Bergner observes that we recognize our uniqueness and persistence in the finitude of our relationships and that in such recognition we are able to recognize the uniqueness of others and thereby transcend ourselves. Thinking is how we transcend our limits, space and time, our relationships and circumstances. Ironically, thinking is our most selfish activity yet it is the means by which we transcend our selfishness. We can transcend our situation by seeing it as our situation. We live a gift not a self-creation.

THE MEANING OF BEING

It is a simple task to find reasons to laud the work of Brentano, Husserl, Heidegger, and Bergner. Indeed, with respect to the work of Heidegger, which will receive most of our attention from here on out, a case can be made that it ranks with Plato, Leibniz, and Kant as the deepest and most profound in all of philosophy, although in my opinion, Plato remains, after more than 2,500 years, without equal. In evaluating Heidegger, especially as he is generally received among contemporary philosophers, it seems almost obligatory to mention that his work carries the regrettable baggage of his political affiliation with the National Socialist movement in World War II–era Germany and his questionable professional distancing from his mentor, Husserl, who was born Jewish and upon whose shoulders Heidegger's work undeniably stands. Notwithstanding that Hitler and his followers bear most of the responsibility for the mind-boggling carnage that occurred during that epoch, it is to be hoped that Heidegger's work will receive broader and fairer consideration on its own merits with the passage of time. Those who allow their personal views about Heidegger to preclude thoughtful consideration of his work only deny themselves the important philosophical experience of his phenomenological ontology.

Having acknowledged the rank of this phenomenological line of philosophy, it must also be stated that the work of Brentano, Husserl, and Heidegger is deeply flawed in ways that will illuminate the path to be followed in our own pursuit of the meaning of Being. Brentano presents a clear and well-thought-out structure of the psychology of thought, which is quite different from the mainstream idea that meaningful mental activity is reducible to logic and logically deduced reality and, in that structure, Brentano has planted the seeds of the phenomenological philosophy that was to follow closely

---

67. Ibid., 260–61.

upon its heels; nevertheless, in Brentano's adoption of Aristotle's intentionality and his focus on its objects, Brentano presents a one-sided psychology that is far too narrow to achieve philosophical greatness in its own right. Husserl was quick to address this shortcoming in Brentano's work. Husserl's accomplishments include not only the broadening of the domain of his science of consciousness to include that phenomenon together with its objects, but also the development in full of forceful phenomenological methods and articulating the important task of providing a presuppositionless philosophy. However, Husserl's shortcomings are precisely those which are identified by Heidegger in his immanent critique, namely, Husserl's adoption of transcendental subjectivism and his unrecognized presupposition of Being in his critique of consciousness.

Heidegger's greatest accomplishments include: his identification of the meaning of Being as the most originary question and, as such, the one that is implicit in all other questions and assertions; his opening up of the question by means of the interrogation of *Dasein* by phenomenological means; his etymological analysis of the pre-Socratics; and his hermeneutic analysis of Leibniz's principle of reason through which he recasts what was originally intended to be a logical principal into a principle of Being *qua* ground. The interrogation of *Dasein* yields the being who is concerned with its own Being, the being who discloses itself and the World to itself from within itself, the *there* of Being-at-the-point of the opening up of the world, the being who is the totality of its possibilities, the being who is always ahead-of-itself in its care, and the being that temporalizes itself in its self-understanding. One need not embrace this characterization of the human being in its entirety to appreciate that it is a breathtaking portrayal and one that represents a much needed broadening out of Kant's observation that man brings to cognition certain *a priori* concepts that govern his cognition of reality. As we have seen, Heidegger, motivated by his ever-growing concern for the development of historical *Dasein* and his profound discomfort with the linguistically ambiguous terminology bequeathed to philosophy by modern philosophy, abandoned the phenomenological methodology of *Being and Time* for the historical etymological hermeneutics of his subsequent work. The change in methodology does not, however, appear to have impacted Heidegger's results—the result of his analysis of Being in general and of the ground of Being, which is that Being is *phusis*, the emerging abiding sway, and that Being grounds all beings but is itself ungrounded, follows consistently from his phenomenological exposition of *Dasein*.

But Heidegger goes awry in several outcome-determinative respects. Taking Heidegger's errors in chronological order, the first occurs in *Being and Time* where he dismisses the substance of factical morality in his ontological analysis of the phenomenology of *Dasein* with the result that his notion of conscience is functional (as the alarm which awakens *Dasein* from fallenness) but contentless (in its silence). Heidegger's second mistake is seen most clearly in *Introduction to Metaphysics*, where he explicitly treats the possible solutions to the question of the relative priority of Being and logic as though they are binary instead of tertiary (i.e., logic is secondary to Being, Being is secondary to logic, and Being and logic are, to employ Heidegger's terminology, equiprimordial). As a result of this error, Heidegger fails to see that Being and logic must be treated as the unified, ontologically primordial phenomenon, in which Being is understood as the emerging-abiding sway that discloses itself from within itself *in a fundamentally and essentially logical* way. The third major error that Heidegger makes is his misattribution of the reason for scientific philosophy gaining priority over ontology of Being to the ascendance to supremacy of *logos* over *phusis*, which he asserts was rigidified with the advent of Christianity at which time *logos* was translated into Latin as meaning "word" instead of "gathering gatheredness." Although this mistake does not undercut the validity or value of Heidegger's etymological hermeneutic of the pre-Socratics, it causes Heidegger to misdirect his attack against logic and to misplace the historical tipping point, which we have argued from the outset occurs with the Cartesian decapitation of the soul from the body. The final error that Heidegger makes is a consequence of the second one, namely, the failure to recognize that the principle of reason has three (not two) intonations, with the last such intonation, <u>Nihil</u> est <u>sine</u> <u>ratione</u>, being read to mean that *Nothingness* is *irrational*, from which we must conclude that Being is necessary and therefore its own ground.

Bergner's *Against Modern Humanism* is a scathing and penetrating indictment of German idealism and the secular materialism that surreptitiously adopts the Egoism of the former and Bergner's *Credo* provides a celebratory ethics that is an objective antidote to relativism. As such, Bergner's *Credo* represents a welcome and deeply thought out filling-in of the gaping ethical hole in the philosophy of Heidegger and his phenomenological predecessors. Heidegger's notion of Being-towards-its-ownmost-potentiality and Bergner's notion that a human being *ought* to live a fully human life seem to draw heavily on Aristotle's teleology, which asserts the natural movement of beings (in their becoming) towards their *telos* or completeness (perfection). If one begins with the premise, as Bergner does, that it is dogmatic to assert that God exists, then it is impossible to find fault with the substance of his *Credo*, all of which follows from his ontological characterization of human beings as revealers of Being, and I would even go so far as to assert that Bergner comes as close to overcoming Hume's naturalist fallacy as is philosophically possible on a non-theological basis. Indeed, if we all heeded Bergner's *Credo*, the world would doubtless be much more human and humane and a morally better place. Certainly, just as stones must be stones and dogs must be dogs, humans must be human beings, and, if part of being human is acting according to a moral principle, then we ought to do that, even if the principle itself is grounded in our own humanity. So, in that sense we can say with confidence along with Bergner that one ought to live openly and with gratitude, that one ought to take Nature and others into account and welcome interaction with them, and that one ought to live fully in the world in which one finds himself thrown. But if one rejects the premise that the existence of God is not demonstrable, then, without rejecting the substance of Bergner's *Credo* (except insofar as it is predicated on his own, uniquely open agnosticism), we can go much further in our characterization of Being and the Being-towards of the human Being—all the way to *Being-towards-God*.

With that, we have finally arrived at the point where, from these words onward, we can focus on providing the philosophical basis for the existence of God, the manner in which he can only be understood within the human capacity to understand, and the moral implications of his existence and our understanding of it. Heidegger tells us that questioning is a process in which the questioner has at the outset some idea about what he seeks. We have just articulated whither we are heading. In the remainder of this chapter, our vehicle will be a critical examination of Heidegger's great work as summarized in the previous pages. We have already identified our main points of difference. After correcting for Heidegger's errors, we will recharacterize *Dasein* (which is a nomenclature we will shortly abandon to avoid any confusion between the *Dasein* of Heidegger and our own view of the human being) as the being who is fundamentally moral in nature and who is guided in his moral journey through his possibilities for Being by a Supreme Principle of Being and Intelligibility that is fundamentally and definitionally good.

We will consider our criticisms of Heidegger not in the chronological order in which they are presented above, but in the order that is most suited to a cohesive exposition. The question of the relative priority of Being and logic is the most important question of all and the ontological subordination of logic along with the Cartesian error of dividing man into body and soul represent the two most disastrous errors of modern philosophy. The first demotion of logic occurred with Kant in his privileging of the categories of empirical understanding over the logic that he deemed to be abstracted from it. In the instant case, by placing Being over and above logic, Heidegger makes substantially the same error as Kant and, in Heidegger's resulting acceptance of Nothing as a delimiter of Being, Heidegger pays a comparably heavy price. Heidegger's motivation, which is to purge historical *Dasein* of the scientific metaphysics that led to modern nihilism, is noble enough. However, the problem with modern metaphysics is not that it holds logic, which we have asserted is embedded in the ontology of all objects, in too high esteem, but rather the problem that Heidegger identifies at the outset of his philosophy, namely, that scientific philosophy, in its exclusive focus on *beings*, presupposes an understanding of *Being* that it does not have the tools to investigate and therefore never offers.

This brings us to a point that was mentioned in chapter 1, "Introduction," that requires addressing prior to continuing with our critique of Heidegger's ontology. It was there asserted that the traditional scientific approach to metaphysics, with its emphasis on beings and its presupposition of their Being, remains a valid methodology as long as one understands what is presupposed by that approach. In our initial cut at metaphysics we asserted that in order for there to be objective knowledge there must exist a self-conscious thinker, objective rules of thought, and an orderly world comprising only objects that are, or inherit from, logical objects. Heidegger might fairly object that this approach presupposes the Being of the objects we reduced by thought experiment to logical objects and the world in which all such objects and we as their thinker exist. From the strict standpoint of Heidegger's ontology, although we are certain that the present-at-hand world exists independently of the mind of man, it must forever remain unintelligible to us. But under our initial approach, there is nothing to preclude us from acknowledging all of our presuppositions and accepting, provisionally, that the empirical and theoretical are as they are commonly understood to be and again, provisionally, to bring them before our reason to see how they are constituted. And the result of that examination, which must still be regarded as provisional, is that logical objects are the originary beings of all cognition. The fact that the analysis presupposes Being does not render it invalid; instead, it merely requires additional examination of our presuppositions to see whether they are necessary or may be eliminated or whether they are inconsistent with our provisional conclusions. In other words, that we assess logical objects to equate with the very Being we are presupposing does not, without more, negate the notion that the human being, is fundamentally a revealer of Being and that cognition is part of a unified act involving a cognizing "I" and an object of cognition.

The examination commences by seeking, as does Heidegger, an understanding of Being through the interrogation of *Dasein* and proceeds with the subsequent elucidation of the Being of beings. For present purposes, we can adopt all of Heidegger's relevant interpretation in *Being and Time* and in *Introduction to Metaphysics* (other than the privileging of Being over logic) all the way to the characterization of Being as *phusis*, which is the emerging abiding sway, which is identity through change. We ask: How do we experience and understand *phusis*? And also: Is there a more primordial way of understanding the essence of the emerging abiding sway? The answer to the first question is that the emerging abiding sway is everywhere and always experienced as the manifestation of *the unity among manifolds,* which is temporalized in the case of ready-to-hand and present-at-hand objects and which is experienced all at once in the case of theoretical objects. To answer the second question, we must see whether we can identify a further ontological reduction of the unity among manifolds. Indeed we can: to be intelligible, the emergence of the emerging abiding sway cannot be haphazard, but instead occurs in an orderly fashion and, as a result, *the unity of* phusis *is always and everywhere reducible to the unity of logical objects.* Our provisional understanding remains intact after this second cut of analysis—it seems correct that we cannot understand unity among manifolds, identity through change, or the emerging abiding sway, except through the ontology of logical objects.

We have one more step to complete before we can conclude that the phenomenological understanding of *phusis* implies its logicality, which is to turn our inquiry back to the interrogation of *Dasein* itself to see whether the elements of its ontology (as given by Heidegger) may themselves be understood in terms of the logical unity among manifolds. At the various levels of his interpretation, Heidegger characterizes *Dasein* as temporality, care, and Being-in-the-World, as the totality of its potential-for-Being, and as various versions of what Bergner appropriately calls the revealer of Being. It will be remembered that the temporality of *Dasein* arises as a result of its having the character of "ahead-of-itself-Being-already-in-(the-World) as Being-alongside (entities encountered within-the-World)," which we have already characterized in turn as a *unity that is always in the figurative motion of becoming itself* and never in the stasis of having achieved its potentiality for Being. At root, temporality is, therefore, a manifestation of orderable unity among manifolds, is undeniably logical in its structure, and underlies the intelligibility of *Dasein*. Considered as care, *Dasein* is thrown projection plus fallenness/anxiety. Again, *Dasein* is understood as an orderable unity of relation among the individual elements of care (i.e., thrownness, projection, and fallenness or anxiety). As the totality of its potential-for-Being, *Dasein* is yet again an orderable unity among manifolds. The unity is the individual *Dasein* considered as a totality and the manifold is the individual *Dasein*'s potentiality which is orderable in many different ways including the ways in which at each moment *Dasein*'s potentiality depends upon its thrownness which in turn depends in part upon the decisions that *Dasein* has already made with respect to its potentiality-for-Being. In other words, *Dasein*'s potentiality-for-Being is anything but random, its order relates to its thrownness, and its thrownness is temporally ordered. Heidegger tells us that *Dasein*'s character as Being-in-the-World depends upon *Dasein*'s having an understanding of "something like Being" and "something like a World," but, yet again, we can go deeper ontologically. All that *Dasein* must bring to rational experience in order to understand something like Being and something like the world of its re-presentation is *an intuition of orderable unity among manifolds*. With such an understanding, both Being and World may readily be assembled by *Dasein* in its intuitional interpretation of that which is presented to it. We have already seen that Being as *phusis* is orderable unity among manifolds, and World, as the totality of *Dasein*'s engagements, is the (temporally) orderable unity among the manifold of such engagements.

We conclude that cognition, whether scientifically or phenomenologically understood, whether of objects considered as mind-independent or as re-presented to a cognizing "I," occurs with respect to objects which are or which inherit from logical objects and are in that sense and to that extent fundamentally logical. Cognition is not illusory or random. Cognition is structured in a sequential, countable, and magnitudinal way. And, indeed, Leibniz's mighty principle—the *principium reddendae rationis* which is the principle of cognition accepted by Heidegger and which says that *cognition must render to cognition the reason for what is encountered*—tells us precisely that. Cognition can only occur if it is logical and logicality cannot ensue except under the ontology of logical objects. Logic is the logic of logical objects, not something independent of them, and the Being of all such objects is their intelligibility. *Logic is the articulation of Being.*

Characterizing Being (or anything else for that matter) as being pre-logical is, accordingly, incoherent and renders ontology mere gibberish. If it were otherwise, the question would immediately arise how it is possible that *Dasein* can utilize a pre-logical sense of Being to experience (constitute) itself or the entities that disclose themselves to it as an entity that is a logical unity among manifolds. In other words, if *Dasein* has pre-knowledge access to an unformed and ambiguous sense of Being from which it may so constitute itself and the other entities in the world, then there is no other explanation for the ontical structure of such entities other than that it must correspond to that sense of Being in all important respects of their presencing, including, most importantly, the logical structure of objects of thought and the spatio-temporal characteristics of extended objects. Such an unformed and ambiguous sense of Being would remain irretrievably mired in its own unintelligibility. We must ask: How is it possible to assemble logic from objects whose cognition is given solely through the intuition of the pre-logical? The answer is that it is not.

Another way of making the same point against Heidegger in his own terms is that if logic is not fundamental to Being, reason under the principle of principles must be treated as part of the peculiar ontology of *Dasein* and not part of an orderly Reality. In other words, if logic is not codeterminate with and of Being, then it must be something that *Dasein* itself brings with it in its Being in relation to the World. In such event, the ontical fact of reason would have profound ontological importance for *Dasein*, which would have to be understood as the being whose mode of Being includes the logical interpretation of a disorderly world. But what would ground such interpretation? The temporality that temporalizes experience is subject to a prior logical structure (thrownness as past, projection as future, and Being-alongside as present) that it does not create. And so must be Reality, else, not only would Silesius's rose be without a why but it would also be without a because and no human reason would be able to make sense of it. It is indeed odd that Heidegger, who made so much of the identity of Being and ground and of Being and intelligibility, could find it possible to place one above the other.

At this point it is worth reverting briefly to our earlier, traditional analysis of the logical structure of space and time to consider whether it withstands our new understanding of Being as it relates to the question of the reality of the world independent of the human mind. Two questions must be asked. How does our position on the logical structure of objects relate to the question of the existence of reality independently of the human mind? Does the existence of a mind-independent reality, the logic of which is not sourced in the human intellect, negate the notion of the human being as the revealer of being? The answer to the first question is precisely the same as earlier given. Man does not create reality, but rather interprets reality and his ability to interpret it objectively depends upon the mind-independent existence of objects which inherit from logical objects—in other words, reality must be ordered logically independently of any human overlay upon it. The answer to the second question is, decidedly not. Logical order is the only constraint which necessarily must be placed upon mind-independent reality. The manner in which that order is interpreted by the human being in the process of cognition is *decidedly human*. The human being may bring either or both of temporality and spatiality to the cognition of objects because both are logically structured. Naïve realism is not necessarily implied by the logical structure of reality and indeed, for reasons earlier expounded upon, it is probably not the better view. And, *Dasein*, as the being concerned with its own Being and with Being in general is *the only entity that can attribute Being as such to reality. Dasein* remains the revealer of Being, even in a logically structured world.

We have observed on more than one occasion that Heidegger's position on this issue is another manifestation of the sort of error committed by Kant in limiting logic to the transcendental and prioritizing the categories of understanding over it. The difficulty of so doing remains the same in each case. Objective knowledge cannot be subjectively sourced. To the contrary, as we have seen, objective knowledge depends upon mind-independent, self-justifying *a priori* rules of thought, an empirical reality that is orderly in a manner that may be understood under the aegis of general logic, and consciousness of self as a persistent, rational entity. To be sure, *Dasein* plays an important role in that trilogy but its role does not place it above the orderly universe in which it dwells in its *Being-in-the-World*. *Dasein* cannot impose the conditions of objective knowledge upon a chaotic world in which it also exists; chaos cannot produce order from chaos. *Dasein* can only reveal the world in its objectivity. In this regard, it is particularly telling that Heidegger characterizes Being as ground. But we must immediately ask: as ground of what? The answer startles: Because ground is always *the ground of something* it cannot be thought to occur in the absence of the predication that it grounds. Being is not ground but *grounded predication*. And, as we know from Leibniz, imbedded in the very notion of grounded predication is what we call reason or logic. If Being were ungrounded, then all that it grounds would also be ungrounded; the very notion calls to mind the ancient conception of the world as sitting on the back of an elephant which stands on the back of a turtle. Even worse, if Being were ungrounded, then it would be unintelligible and therefore unthinkable.

This brings us nicely to perhaps the most important consequence of Heidegger's mistaken privileging of Being over logic. Heidegger correctly recognizes that the principle of reason in its first intonation is the first and highest principle of thought and that in its second intonation it is not merely a principle of reason but also one of Being. *Nihil est sine ratione* (the first intonation) means that there is a sufficient reason for everything. *Nihil est sine ratione* (the second intonation) means that every being has a ground which is Being itself. But Heidegger, in his zeal to make the case against scientific metaphysics, is blind to the obvious connection between the two intonations, which gives rise to a third and ontologically highest intonation. *Nihil est sine ratione* means that *Nothing(ness) is irrational* (and incoherent) and that, therefore, Being is necessary and, therefore, Being is *its own ground*. Indeed, conversely paralleling Heidegger's grammatical strictness in his assertion that, to avoid the redundancy of the copula when Being is the subject of a sentence, it is necessary that it merely be directly related to its predicate (where he pronounces "Being and ground: the same"), we should avoid connecting Nothingness with something via the copula and state "Nothing(ness): irrational," or to emphasize the third intonation, "*Nihil: sine ratione.*"

It will be recalled that Heidegger takes great care to avoid the apparent circularity of attempting to prove the existence of God as the uncaused cause through employment of the principle of reason, which Heidegger asserts along with the modern mainstream depends upon the existence of God in the first place, and that his solution is not to discard the principle but rather to restrict its applicability to beings and not to reason itself. Although Heidegger's avoidance of this difficulty does not preclude him from advancing wonderfully far in the remainder of his investigations, it does prevent him from reaching the end that is implicit in his starting point. Heidegger's conclusion is that Being and ground are the same but that Being itself is the ungrounded (*abgrund* or abyss). This conclusion follows from his restriction of the principle of reason and his placement of Being above logic. But observe what happens when one corrects for the latter error. If, as we have seen, Nothingness becomes irrational, then Being becomes (if you will) *necessary*. And, as the ontologically most originary concept, it cannot be grounded by anything else but it also cannot, due to its necessity, be itself ungrounded. *Instead, Being must be its own ground*. So when we say "Being and ground: the same," we mean it literally and fully. Being, as grounded predication, is both subject and predicate. It is the ground that grounds itself, the ground of grounds.

This idea strikes us as odd at first blush because, considered in this way, Being is, of course, unlike any ordinary being, but it shows itself as quite familiar upon only a little examination. The idea is nowise circular. We have seen that all beings in their grounded predication inherit the logicality of logical objects. Being, as the grounded predication of beings, is that which renders beings intelligible. Being is that which empowers the mighty principle and makes possible the rendering to reason of reasons. Being is intelligibility itself. And, as such, Being must render itself as intelligible—nothing else can do that. *Being is therefore the intelligibility of all that is intelligible, including intelligibility itself.* Being is intelligibility turned upon itself. It is the light that illuminates all that may be illuminated and seen, including the illuminating light itself. Being is the *ultimo ratio Rerum,* the Supreme Principle of Being and Intelligibility and also itself. Its familiarity can be seen simply by considering the following: we not only think logically about the world but we also think about logic itself and when we do so we turn our reason upon itself. And it is here that we reach what is truly called *direct intuition.* Direct intuition is reason's self-justification. Reason rests comfortably with itself because there is no other place for reason to go. Reason does not rest at axioms or principles. The logicality of Being is known by the direct perception of the irreducible; Being, intelligibility, and logical predication are what the mind sees when it thinks, which is to say *when it represents the irreducible to itself and looks to see what is there.* Our familiarity with Being as its own ground can also be seen in the ancient self-identification of God to Moses: "I AM THAT I AM," which is thought to have been written in the book of Exodus sometime during the sixth and fifth centuries BC about an event that is thought to have transpired nearly one thousand years earlier, which it is interesting to note is also approximately one thousand years before Thales, the first of the known pre-Socratics.

We can and must go further than merely equating Being and intelligibility. In idle conversation (and idle philosophy) we far too often jumble together words that in themselves have meaning but when placed together are contradictory and incoherent. This happens, as we have just seen, when we speak of Nothingness, which is inconceivable and unthinkable and yet appears to be meaningful only because we are very familiar with the absence of individual entities. This also happens when we attribute to God powers that are beyond our ability to conceive, which is indeed tempting for trivially obvious reasons. But what powers could we think that we are speaking of when we say that they are unintelligible or beyond conception? *For similar reasons, we must be clear that intelligibility is not a limit but that which encompasses all that there can be said to be.* To say that there can be something else is to muddle together the concept of Being with something other than Being, which is, of course, a self-contradiction.

We can now move on to consideration of Heidegger's first-described error, which is his failure to give proper ontological weight to substantive factual morality. We must first consider with some specificity which of the ontological characteristics of *Dasein* we are prepared to accept. As we did in the discussion of unity among manifold, we can survey *Dasein* from the top down, starting with temporality. In that regard, Heidegger's work can fairly be viewed as a neo-Kantian working out of time as an *a priori* condition of the possibility of empirical experience. We have previously agreed with Kant that time is not an empirical, mind-independent entity but rather a reflection of the way in which the human being organizes what it presented in sensory experience. Heidegger's reduction of ordinary time to a series of temporally structured occurrences in which *Dasein* presses forward into and repetitively reinterprets its potentialities in its Being-towards-Death has the advantages of internalizing the empirical sensation of ordinary time in a manner that is logical and fully consistent with our own notion of intelligibility. However, it is ontologically dependent upon the structure of care from which it is deduced. That structure includes thrownness, projection, and fallenness or anxiety. To be sure, these elements of *Dasein*'s ways-of-Being are for the most part unique to the human being and seem to be important in a categorial way. With respect to thrownness, it is beyond dispute that how we comport ourselves in the world is fundamentally, but not exclusively, dependent upon our historical, cultural, and social circumstances. With respect to projection and fallenness, it is also safe to say that when we are absorbed in the world (Being-alongside and Being-with) we are largely if not completely free from the anxiety that accompanies our awareness of our finitude and when we are so aware we are unable to stay consciously in the moment and always seem to be oriented to the future. Whether the significance of projection also accompanies fallenness seems less than clear. With respect to anxiety, there can be no doubt that the human being seems uniquely ill-at-ease in the world, even to the extent of devising many strategies and preoccupying itself with many diversions for the purpose of quelling its characteristic *angst*. Whether Heidegger is correct in attributing anxiety to *Dasein*'s Being-towards-Death or his concern for his own Being-moral we will discuss in a moment. But first we can summarize thusly: Heidegger's characterization of *Dasein* as the being for whom its own Being is an issue is a wonderful and almost unfathomably pithy reduction of the essential human Being.

It is striking that Heidegger, who is so astute at identifying that which is factical in *Dasein* and which has existential importance, completely misses the mark on the fact of morality. This is the case all the more so because Kant, in making the fact of morality the centerpiece of his moral philosophy, puts all subsequent ethical philosophers in the posture of having to address it. Nevertheless, the closest that Heidegger comes to acknowledging the fundamental importance of moral behavior is in his exposition of conscience, which, supporting as it does his foundational concept of anticipatory resoluteness, cannot accommodate such an important mistake without undercutting his entire philosophy. In *Being and Time*, Heidegger gives morality only cursory mention (treating common morality as presumptively representing error) and instead asserts that the importance of conscience lies in that fact that it calls *Dasein* from inauthentic fleeing of Being to authentic care for its ownmost finitude in Being-towards-Death. But Heidegger's concept of conscience is utterly an empty one which disregards the substantive facticity of morality, and the factical nature of moral behavior means that *Dasein*'s care does not blindly project in Being-towards-the-end but, in selecting among its potentiality-for-Being, that *it acts under a moral principle* (which it often disregards) the urgency of which is imbedded in the finitude of *Dasein* and which *gives Dasein an ontologically moral character*.

From a phenomenological perspective, we are fully justified in accepting the facticity of *Dasein*'s morality (as what Heidegger would call an *existentiell*), but we need to connect it on an existential basis with *Dasein*'s fundamental concern for its own Being. In other words, we need to show that there is a basis in the Being of *Dasein* for morality. Morality, as experienced by *Dasein*, consists of two elements. The first is an understanding of good and bad, right and wrong. The second is an understanding that the idea of goodness is obligatory for *Dasein*. In order to have an understanding of good (and its absence, not-good), *Dasein* must have an understanding, not just of Being (as Heidegger asserts) but of perfection, (i.e., *perfect Being*). It should go without saying that such an understanding cannot come from *Dasein*'s factical existence. Instead, it can only come from *Dasein*'s pre-ontological understanding of beings as logical objects and *the logical necessity of Being*. And *Dasein*'s understanding of the obligatory nature of morality, (i.e., what Heidegger refers to as the "Ought"), derives also from the logical necessity of Being, in particular from the fact that Being is its own ground. Although these two ideas will be worked out in detail in the following chapters we can observe here that we have already identified the source of the moral obligation under which *Dasein* operates, namely, the Supreme Principle of Being and Intelligibility.

Moral facticity requires recharacterization of Heidegger's concept of conscience to accord more closely with the common understanding and his concept of anticipatory resoluteness as an authentic potentiality-for-Being-*moral* in *Dasein's* Being-towards-Death. Heidegger's understanding of the movement of *Dasein* calls upon Aristotle for its inspiration. Aristotle understood perfection as the possession by a thing of its *telos*. For Aristotle, an entity is perfect only when it achieves the Being of what it is to be in its own essence, that is, its ownmost Being. For Aristotle, all real entities participate in their *telos* and continually strive, without success, towards its possession. In Heidegger's philosophy, *Dasein*, as the being for whom its own Being is an issue, is always striving not for possession of an essential *telos* as such but for its ownmost potentiality for Being, which it alone is free (within the context of its own thrownness) to determine. Seen in this way, Heidegger's *Dasein* is another example of modern egoism. Bergner seeks, quite effectively, to reign *Dasein*, the revealer of being, back into moral objectivity, which, by adopting an implicitly Aristotelian view of Being, Bergner successfully accomplishes to the extent that it can be done without taking a view on the existence of God as the source of morality. For Bergner, because man's essence is openness and wonderment, he should strive always to its possession and should comport himself in the world accordingly.

Bergner's innovation may guide us further. Under our recharacterization of *Dasein*, authentic, ownmost potentiality for Being requires action in accordance with a moral principle whose source is external to him. Unlike all other beings, man, for whom Being is an issue, is not limited merely to possession of a *telos* that is limited and measured by his capabilities. Man, unlike all other Beings, knows of perfection and therefore can and does *consciously* strive for a *telos* which he can never possess. It is true that most men are anxious about their death when confronted with it but I do not believe this to be the source of anxiety that is ontologically significant, and I would note that of the too many *natural* deaths I have personally witnessed *not a single one* was faced by the dying with fear—indeed it seems that what is feared most often is not death in and of itself but *untimely* death. Man is the only being who understands his own imperfection and who also knows that in his finitude he can never achieve perfection. We have accepted broadly the character of self as described generally by Heidegger in *Being and Time* as *Dasein* insofar as is meant that man is the being who is peculiarly concerned about his Being and who, at each moment, acts under a compulsion to lead his life in a manner in which he must choose between the being he will be from among all the other possibilities that exist and to which he is open. But man cannot and does not choose among his potential ways-of-Being without regard for the Ought because he cannot ignore it even if he tries. In Being-towards-the-end, man is not mere Being-towards-Death but instead he is Being-towards-perfection, which is to say, that he is Being-towards-God and his anxiety is attributable to the impossibility of his ever achieving success. Man may orient himself toward God but he can never achieve perfect godliness. And the call of conscience is exactly as it is commonly understood, which is a call to an authentic way of Being-towards-God.

Interpreting *Dasein* as Being-towards-God may require an additional and important amendment to Heidegger's characterization. It will be recalled that, for Heidegger, *Dasein* is neither Cartesian "I"-substance nor Kantian "subject," but is instead potentiality-for-Being-one's-Self (as care). This means that *Dasein* is always and everywhere in relation to an empirical World as the point at which the World opens up. *Dasein's* World as defined by Heidegger is limited to the ready-to-hand, the present-at-hand, Others, and *Dasein's* own care. But when one considers the World to which *Dasein* is in relation to include transcendent reality, including, especially, God, it is no longer clear that *Dasein's* Being is coterminous with its own, self-interpreted physicality. This has two implications. The first is that *Dasein* may indeed be the soul that we have argued from the outset is disclosed to itself from within itself as a persistent, morally obligated and substantive entity. The second is that if *Dasein's* ownmost potentiality-for-Being includes relation with God, *Dasein's* care may include on a teleological basis the self-overcoming of its ownmost temporality.

Of the issues we have identified with the work of Heidegger, there remains to be addressed only Heidegger's historical misplacement of the irretrievability of the obliteration of Being at the hands of those who translated the Gospel according to St. John the Evangelist into Latin. As we have thematically emphasized, Being and logic go hand in hand and, therefore, although the ontology of Being must embrace logic and its relations, a scientific-based metaphysics is subject to too many inherent difficulties, which we have already elucidated, for it to supersede ontology. However, although it cannot be denied that the term "*logos*," from which the English word "logic" was translated into the term "word," Heidegger's argument that the definitive historical development in this regard was the advent of Christianity and the identification in the Gospel of St. John the Evangelist of Jesus as being the *Logos*, that is, the Word, is uncharacteristically superficial and demonstrably incorrect.

Heidegger bases his argument for the completion of the ascendance to primacy of logic over Being on the idea that insofar as Jesus is the Word, Jesus is the mediator between God and man who conveys the commandments of God (the Father) to humanity. The case in rebuttal begins with the gospel itself:

> In the beginning was the Word, and the Word was with God, and the Word was God. The same was in the beginning with God. All things were made by him; and without him was not any thing made that was made. In him was life; and the life was the light of men. And the light shineth in darkness; and the darkness comprehended it not.[68]

It is especially striking that in this very passage, where Jesus is identified as the Word, the full depiction of Jesus has nothing to do with commandments but instead emphasizes Being and disclosure and it does so to a large degree in terms that are precisely those upon which Heidegger's etymological exposition relies! It is of course true that Jesus is characterized as the Word. But it is also true in the same passage that he is

---

68. John 1:1–5 (NAB).

characterized as God, the maker of all things, and the light of men. Elsewhere in the same gospel as well as in the synoptic gospels, Jesus self-characterizes as the Good Shepherd, the Beginning and the End, the Alpha and the Omega, the Truth, the Life, and the Way (to God, the Father). These characterizations are not in any way superseded by Jesus's characterization as the Word, but are rather embellishments on its meaning. Ironically, they too reflect virtually all of the ways in which Heidegger characterizes *phusis* (emerging sway) or its synonyms including *phainesthai* (lighting-up, self-showing, appearing), *logos* (gathering gatheredness and circle[69]), and *aletheia* (truth). Jesus is the appearance of God as a man and is explicitly characterized as light and truth and, as the Good Shepherd, what else is he other than the One *who gathers his flock* (not randomly, but according to a principle of those who listen to the truth (i.e., hear his voice). Moreover, even at the end of the Scholastic period (let alone at the advent of Christ), that the *Word* is clearly understood in a special way that belies Heidegger's position is evidenced by the hermeneutics of St. Thomas Aquinas: (1) the Word cannot be a human or angelic word because it precedes humans and angels and because it was not made since all things were made by it, and so Jesus can only be the Word of God; (2) the Word differs from human words because it is expressive of all that is in God and not of imperfect human understandings; (3) the term Word is chosen to convey the idea of Jesus as having come *to manifest* the Father; (4) the term Word is chosen over the term notion (*ratio*) to reflect that although the Son exists in the Father he has the operative world-creative power; (5) the prefatory phrase "in the beginning (*arche*, which means principle, beginning, and origin, among other things)" conveys that Jesus is the *principium* (principle), in the sense in which life is said to be "in" God and, as a principle, is honored as determining all and, by reference to other passages in the Old and New Testaments, the Word connotes Wisdom and Truth; and (6) that the Son is said to be "in" the Father because he has the same essence (consubstantiality) as Father.[70]

It would seem, then, that the characterization of Jesus as the Word is intended to connote that he, along with God the Father, *is the Supreme Principle of Being and Intelligibility* who, together (as One) are the source of all meaning that human beings bring with them to the world and without whom all meaning would be closed off from us. Consider, in this regard, what Heidegger has to say about the special meaning-giving meaning of the word Being:

> Suppose that there were no indeterminate meaning of Being, and that we did not understand what this meaning signifies. Then what? Would there just be one noun and one verb less in our language? No. *Then there would be no language at all.* Beings as such would no longer open themselves up in words at all; they could no longer be addressed and discussed. For saying beings as such involves understanding beings as beings—that is, their Being-in advance. Presuming that we did not understand Being at all, presuming that the word "Being" did not even have that evanescent meaning, then there would not be any single word at all. We ourselves could never be those who say. We would never be able to be

---

69. Heidegger himself makes especial note of Fragment 10e of Heraclitus in which it is written: "Gathered in itself, the same is the beginning and the end in the circumference of the circle."

70. See, Aquinas, *Commentary on the Gospel of St. John*, Part I, Chapter 1.

those who we are. For to be human means to be a sayer. Human beings are yes- and no-sayers only because they are, in the ground of their essence, sayers, the sayers. That is their distinction and also their predicament. It distinguishes them from stone, plant, and animal, but also from the gods. Even if we had a thousand eyes and a thousand ears, a thousand hands and many other senses and organs, if our essence did not stand within the power of language, then all beings would remain closed off to us—the beings that we ourselves are, no less than the beings that we are not.[71]

If this book were a work of apologetics, we would, of course, make much, much more of St. Thomas's hermeneutics of the Gospel of St. John the Evangelist. However, to be clear, the point of the foregoing biblical hermeneutics is *not* apologetics but rather to show that the translation of "*Logos*" to "Word" does not pave the way for a scientific metaphysics that excludes ontology and instead, taken in full context, shows that Christianity has always considered the Son and the Father as representing the same, perfect, and ontologically supreme Being and not mere logic. In fairness, it should be mentioned that during the Scholastic period, which immediately preceded the advent of modern philosophy, theology became unabashedly Aristotelian and, indeed, this was the era of the formulization of the various Aristotelian logical arguments for the existence of God. However, two additional points preclude attributing the ascendance of scientific metaphysics to the Latin scholarship of the church during this (or any other) period. The first is that the early and medieval church first resisted philosophy and then embraced it only in the context of *faith seeking understanding* and not *vice versa*. The second is that *the church also resisted science* and, as we have repeatedly asserted, modern philosophy is fairly understood in the context of an unabated, centuries-long rebellion against the church. Accordingly, we continue to maintain that the usurpation by modern science of philosophical territory over which it can never have authority begins with Descartes.

There is one final point to be made in connection with Heidegger's misplacement of the rigidification of scientific philosophy at the advent of Christianity which has been saved for last because it has much broader implications. In the preceding pages, we have discussed various views of the nature of man, including the reductionist views of scientific philosophy, Descartes's dualism, Leibniz's monads, and the Ancient Greek conception of man as soul. In considering and rejecting each of these, we have adopted yet another conception, which is the psychosomatic unity bequeathed to us by Christianity. Although Heidegger does not adopt this or any of the other views in his characterization of *Dasein*, there is an undeniable compatibility between *Dasein* and the view of man as a psychosomatic unity. The compatibility exists on two grounds. The first and most obvious one is in Heidegger's emphasis of the unity among manifolds (*phusis*) that characterizes Being. The second is a bit more subtle and it arises out of *Dasein's* Being-in-the-World. In its Being-in and its Being-with, *Dasein* is, along with Others, disclosed to itself from within itself as part of the (physical) World. But *Dasein*, as Being-there, is more than a mere physicality (which would render it present-at-hand)—it is the unified point of relationship with the World at which the world, including its own being as *self-interpreted physicality*, is opened up to it. Seen in this light, the distinction between

---

71. Heidegger, *Introduction to Metaphysics*, 62–63.

Dasein and the view of man as a psychosomatic unity, if there is one, pales. The points to be made as a result are twofold. First, since the view of man as a psychosomatic unity is compatible with *Dasein*, it is difficult to maintain that scientific philosophy was predestined by the advent of Christianity and, instead, that misfortune should, as we have been asserting all along, be laid at the feet of Descartes. Second, we may accept *Dasein*, recharacterized as the revealer of Being who is Being-towards-God, without abandoning our view of man as a psychosomatic unity.

So, where do we stand in our conception of the Being of the human being? We do not need to accept phenomenology as a philosophy or phenomenological ontology as the correct interpretation of human rational experience to recognize the important contributions of Brentano, Husserl, and Heidegger, and of Bergner's ethical interpretation of the last. Aided by their work, we see more clearly that natural science is nowise philosophy, that man is both a philosophical and a moral being, and that man brings with him in the act of cognition a pre-ontological understanding of something like Being and something like a world, but that he does so under the rubric of a prior understanding of the necessary logicality of things (i.e., logical objects). With our understanding of the formal meaning of Being as self-grounding intelligibility, a great lamplight has been lit to show the path we must follow to understand the meaning of Being in its other, normative sense. As we have seen, if Being formally is intelligibility, then Nothing (not-Being) is incoherent and therefore impossible and the grounds of Being must be self-contained. This is the foundation upon which understanding of the Supreme Principle of Being and Intelligibility as transcendently real must be predicated. And, as we will begin to see immediately, understanding that principle does not come without its own, formidable demands and the moral freedom to perform them.

10

Duty and Desire

MORALITY AND AGAPE

There is no other area of metaphysics that demonstrates the futility of material reductionism with more clarity than the question of the existence and nature of moral obligation. The dilemma that reductionists face on this issue, which is one of their own making, is how to reconcile their own intuition of morality, which may be presumed generally to be held in common with the rest of us, with a human experience that they steadfastly insist is materially reducible, for there is nothing in the empirical world other than man's own moral sensibility which contains even a whiff of what is commonly understood as moral obligation.

This can be seen to be true as a matter of fact and is necessarily true as a matter of reason. As Thomas Hobbes so famously states, in the state of nature "the life of man, [is] solitary, poor, nasty, brutish, and short." Because the empirical world is one of material scarcity in which all life is in constant competition for survival, it is difficult to understand how morality might in any way arise or be useful, other than as a self-justifying requirement that is external to the empirical world. Indeed, in an environment that is as competitive as our earthly one, theoretical reason would seem to dictate that self-interested pursuit of survival and not altruistic behavior should prevail and, as a matter of fact, such seems to be generally true throughout the animal kingdom. Even in the case of highly rational social animals such as human beings, who are capable of appreciating the benefits of joining forces against a hostile environment (and each other), the best that can be rationally hoped for seems to be action in accordance with a set of sociopolitical rules of convenience, not necessary, universal, and objective principles of morality that often bind an individual to act against his own selfish interest or desire. The social contract is, after all, just that—an agreement among members of society to comport themselves in a certain way, which reduces to consensual rules of action and omission, the violation of which is remedied sociopolitically, and not one of moral obligation.

Moreover, even in a benign world, the absence of material underpinnings for moral obligation would obtain. This is because of the theoretical impossibility of *naturally* deriving any moral obligation, which is commonly known as the "is-ought problem" or the "naturalist fallacy," and is described most famously by David Hume in the following passage from *A Treatise of Human Nature*:

> In every system of morality, which I have hitherto met with, I have always remarked, that the author proceeds for some time in the ordinary ways of reasoning, and establishes the being of a God, or makes observations concerning human affairs; when all of a sudden I am surprised to find, that instead of the usual copulations of propositions, is, and is not, I meet with no proposition that is not connected with an ought, or an ought not. This change is imperceptible; but is however, of the last consequence. For as this ought, or ought not, expresses some new relation or affirmation, 'tis necessary that it should be observed and explained; and at the same time that a reason should be given; for what seems altogether inconceivable, how this new relation can be a deduction from others, which are entirely different from it. But as authors do not commonly use this precaution, I shall presume to recommend it to the readers; and am persuaded, that this small attention would subvert all the vulgar systems of morality, and let us see, that the distinction of vice and virtue is not founded merely on the relations of objects, nor is perceived by reason.[1]

Given nature's impetus toward selfish disregard of the interests of others, material reductionists are faced with only two choices in considering the problem of ethics, namely, eschewing moral obligation altogether or attempting to conjure it up out of the nature of man himself, who, it must be remembered, is considered by these philosophers to be materially reducible and, therefore, the difficulty of pursuing this latter course is compounded by the need to identify the source of morality not in the brute matter of the human organism but in organic being comprising it. Because, as has been said, the denial of moral obligation is considered by most credible philosophers to be unpalatable, the question immediately arises as to what possible strategies empiricists might employ in explaining (and justifying) an organic, human-based morality. One such possibility is that morality itself is the subjective creation of man, which is to say that moral obligation arises either because human beings desire that it should exist or because it is a human characteristic to hold each other accountable for considering the interests of all human beings when determining how to act. The other possibility is that moral obligation arises out of the theoretical reason to which man's empirical intellect somehow has access.

It takes only a little analysis to see that subjective moral theories contain the naturalistic fallacy. However deeply held the desire of man for the safety, regularity, and predictability that a moral society offers may be, these needs cannot support the existence of moral obligation because they are merely facts of human experience which are analytically no different than any other common human needs, such as food, shelter, or procreation. Similarly, the fact that most mentally healthy human beings are empathetic by nature is a fact that may explain altruism, but it cannot explain the common sense of moral obligation, again because the source of intention of the empathy is a *subjective desire* to act out of concern for the object of such intention and, indeed, a lack of

---

1. Hume, *Treatise of Human Nature*, 302. It should be noted that, in the final sentence of this paragraph, Hume is also asserting that morality is not known to man by direct intuition, which is a position that will be contested throughout this chapter. We have already seen that Bergner contests the natural fallacy. See 264.

empathy may logically subject one to characterization as pathological, but, without an independent source of moral obligation, that does not support a charge of immorality. Finally, all subjective approaches contain a fundamental flaw, namely, that any moral obligation that purports to arise by individual or group fiat can be disposed of by the same whim that created it and therefore any purported subjective moral obligation is illusory.

As it happens, ethical arguments that are based on theoretical reason are available to rationalists and empiricists alike, but their specifics depends upon whether one considers reason itself to arise ontologically out of direct intuition, as is the case with the rationalists, or by inference from empirical experience, as is the case with the empiricists. Whatever the metaphysical bent of their proponents may be, all of these arguments fail because it is not possible compellingly to connect rationally determined action with an *obligation* to act rationally. In other words, although theoretical-reason-based arguments may be able to identify rational conduct, they must also show that all such rationally identified action is both *per se good* and *obligatory* in order to offer a satisfactory ethics, neither of which can be demonstrated. These are particularly acute difficulties because the facts that in a state of nature theoretical reason dictates self-interested behavior and that there are many theoretical-reason-based ethical systems which yield diverse results, some of which disregard individual rights altogether, make clear that something is missing when one looks to reason alone for morality. Moreover, when theoretical-reason-based arguments are advanced by empiricists, they are attended by the additional challenges of first justifying the existence of an empirically based rationality and then justifying its applicability to moral concerns prior to advancing any ethics that might be predicated upon it.

So here is the dilemma awaiting empiricism at the terminus of its moral argument: if one accepts that all knowledge originates in the senses, then there is no valid basis for asserting that moral obligation exists. If one wishes to adhere to empiricism, one must accept the conclusion that man is either fully determined by mechanistic forces of nature or completely free to do as he pleases (which, ironically, as we will see in the discussion of free will in the next chapter, is not freedom at all) without any moral obligation.

It follows that if one accepts the existence of moral obligation one must also accept that its grounds are both external to the morally conscious beings obligated under it and outside of sensible reality. We have already made the case for a similar metaphysical structure in the context of objective human theoretical knowledge so that knowledge of objective moral good might arise on similar grounds should come as no surprise. However, as has just been pointed out in debunking theoretical reason as a possible ground of morality, there is nothing about theoretical reason, even as it is presented under transcendent realism as existing as part of the broader *Logos,* which suggests any obligatory element and we should therefore suspect that mere objective knowledge of good is insufficient to support any obligation to act in accordance with it. Indeed, for objective moral goodness to be obligatory it must be more than an *idea* of goodness—it must be *intentional* goodness. Therefore, if necessary and universal moral obligation exists, there is only one possible explanation for it, namely, that it arises as a result of, and is therefore dependent upon, direct perception of a universally constituent *Agape* and such a will must be regarded under any conception, literal or metaphorical, as being definitionally divine in nature. Accordingly, our conception of the *Logos* must be expanded to include divine *Agape* and our conception of the universe will necessarily take on a distinctly moral character.

THE FACT OF MORALITY

Man feels himself intuitively to be subject to moral obligation, that is, to act under an obligation that is independent of, and superior to, his subjective desires for a purpose understood by him to be good. When man acts in accordance with his moral obligation he typically feels justified and, when he does not, he typically experiences a sense of guilt. In any event, moral obligation is widely felt to exist regardless of how individual men may view the desirability of compliance with it or the specifics of its dictates in a given set of circumstances.

A distinction should be made between discharge of an objective moral obligation and altruistic behavior in which man makes a subjective decision to act for the sake of good based upon his relative valuation of the gratification such an act will bring. In the latter case, such acts occur even when there is no moral obligation to undertake them. Because such a decision, however culturally praiseworthy it may be, is not morally *obligated* it neither entails moral freedom[2] nor satisfies any moral obligation. Altruistically motivated people may be worthy of admiration because their desires naturally correspond to, or even exceed the dictates of, moral obligation, but sight must not be lost of the fact that they act rightly without any conflicting subjective desire to the contrary that is of greater or equal magnitude. To be clear, the conduct of a saint that exceeds the demands of morality because of the profundity of his or her love of God is altruistic and is not the sort of behavior that is of interest to us in this chapter.

A distinction should also be made based upon the motivation of the subject who complies with a moral obligation. Truly ethical behavior requires both good conduct and good motive. A person who makes a subjective decision to honor an obligation does not act morally. Take for example, a person who decides to tell the truth, not because it is the right thing to do but because doing so will advance his own selfish interests. In such a case, expedience happens to fall on the side of truth and although the conduct is right, the motive is hardly praiseworthy, which is another way of saying that the person is acting in the absence of a good will. It follows that the critical question for the purposes of determining whether the behavior fulfills moral obligation is whether the actor would have satisfied the moral obligation irrespective of any subjective desire to do so.

Moral obligation has been both historically and cross-culturally prevalent. In western culture, the Ten Commandments are a paradigmatic and compelling example.

---

2. We are here making a distinction between freedom, considered as the ability to choose subjectively among morally neutral alternatives, and moral freedom, considered as the freedom to take action based upon objective moral principles. Determinists would argue that neither freedom exists. Phenomenologists would argue that both such freedoms exist phenomenologically and are indistinguishable. In these pages, we are concerned only with the second sort of freedom and, although, it would seem that the phenomenologists have the better of the argument with the determinists with respect to freedom generally we hold that the two sorts of freedoms are significantly different and we will, for the sake of argument, contrast moral freedom with determinism.

Although instances of moral conduct occur around us all the time, the source of moral obligation has been hotly disputed because it is ineluctably related to the larger question of whether God exists. As a result, whether the phenomenon is real or merely a psychological or sociological phenomenon is a question that has appropriately received much attention over the entire course of the history of philosophy. By its very nature, the stakes attending its answer are high.

As noted, that human beings often act with what they regard to be moral motives is what Kant called "the fact of morality," and that fact, together with the fact that moral obligation is an object of *apparent* internal intuition (that is to say that most people believe that they intuitively know that they have an obligation to act morally), must be the starting point for any meaningful discussion of the basis of ethics. It is sometimes argued by those who do not recognize moral obligation or who consider it to be subjective, that the fact that commonly accepted notions of moral behavior have varied across cultures and historically within cultures demonstrates that moral obligation is not objective or universal or accessible by internal intuition. This argument merits careful consideration, which will be provided shortly; however, for the moment, it need only be pointed out that in all these circumstances there is present *some* notion of moral obligation, which even in the presence of relatively abhorrent dictates can easily be shown to include a common core of morally obligated conduct, and, therefore, the fact of morality remains. That philosophical significance should be attached to such differences does not follow necessarily from the fact that they may exist, because, for example, they may only show moral evolution over the course of history or that although conduct must definitionally be in service of a necessary and universal understanding of moral obligation, the specifics of morally obligated conduct may very well depend upon contingent historical and cultural circumstances and capabilities.

THE POSSIBILITY OF OBJECTIVE PRACTICAL REASON

In chapter 4, "The Possibility of Objective Knowledge," we considered a fundamental question posed by Thomas Nagel, namely: How is it possible that radically contingent creatures such as human beings have access to universally valid methods of objective thought? In that chapter, reason was divided along customary lines into two types, namely, theoretical reason and practical reason. Of course, such a division is for heuristic purposes and there is only one and the same reason which is accessible to man. In that discussion, we posited three preconditions of objective thought, namely: (1) mind-independent, self-justifying *a priori* rules of thought; (2) an empirical reality that is orderly in a manner that may be understood under the auspices of general logic; and (3) consciousness of self as a persistent, rational entity. Under this understanding, for there to be objective theoretical knowledge all thought and all objects of thought must be governed by metaphysically existing, self-justifying logical rules the direct intuition of which is the defining characteristic of objectively rational entities. In other words, there must be a mind-independent rational structure to things, which we have been referring to here as the *Logos*. Also in that chapter, we asserted objective, internal intuition of the transcendent objects of soul (and, by implication, of *Agape*) and provided its grounds on the basis of direct perception, analytical intuition, and the empirical fact of morality. Our task here is to investigate *Agape* specifically as the source of moral obligation and to see whether the results of that investigation mandate the expansion of the preconditions of objective thought in order to accommodate practical reason as well.

Practical reason is the faculty by which a rational being determines how it *ought* to behave. Unlike theoretical reason, practical reason is concerned with the determination and instantiation of objects for *moral* ends. Although theoretical reason is employed in connection with practical reason, and practical reason may therefore be said to be dependent upon theoretical reason, practical reason is concerned not merely with the apprehension and comprehension of objects but also with *their being brought into existence through the exercise of the will of the knowing subject in accordance with a moral principle*. Theoretical reason is therefore, as its name implies, merely theoretical, whereas practical reason is by its nature *willful* insofar as practical reason requires that its objects be realized in fact and must therefore always include a deliberate action or omission to act. It should be mentioned here in passing, to be explored in detail in the sequel chapter, that in order for an entity to act morally it must enjoy the freedom to do so (as opposed to being the agent of action that is merely an event in a mechanistically determined sequence that results in a particular object presumed (incorrectly, on this state of affairs) to be morally required) and also that, since at least Hume, the existence of freedom has been one of the central matters of philosophical debate. For present purposes, it will be assumed that moral freedom exists and attention will be focused on the question that is relevant to the preconditions of objective human moral experience, namely, the nature of practical reason, and the question of whether moral freedom exists will be left to the sequel chapter. This approach is warranted because, as will be seen in the subsequent discussion on moral freedom, the existence of moral obligation gives rise to the freedom to fulfill it, and not the other way around, as is sometimes held. In other words, we consider moral freedom not as a precondition to objective moral behavior but rather the consequence of moral consciousness. Also before moving on, it is worthwhile to observe that the direct intuition of human freedom supports the fact of morality and poses yet another dilemma for the reductionists, namely, to deny freedom's existence altogether or to explain freedom in amoral terms.

Given that practical reason is dependent upon theoretical reason as a means to moral ends, it follows that the preconditions of theoretical reason are also preconditions of practical reason. But the impossibility of deriving moral obligation from empirical facts or theoretical reason alone tells us that although such preconditions are necessary for practical reason they cannot be sufficient for it. What must be sought, then, are one or more additional preconditions of objective moral knowledge. The starting point in identifying the additional preconditions of practical reason is consideration of what it means to say that a rational being *ought* to behave in a certain way or, in other words, what it means to have a moral obligation to do something. A moral obligation is a special type of duty. Duties arise in various ways, including as a matter of law, contract, social custom, religion, and morality. Legal duties are obligations imposed under rules the compliance with which may be enforced by a governmental authority. In the case of criminal laws, criminal penalties may be imposed upon criminal perpetrators, including the taking of property, the deprivation of liberty through incarceration, and, in some cases, corporal or capital punishment. Civil duties arise under rules governing the conduct of private citizens toward one another, including the law of contract and the law of torts, and are also enforced by governmental authorities. Social obligations are rules of conduct that arise by custom or other social arrangement and the violation of which is not generally a matter of governmental interest. In cultures where freedom of worship obtains, religious duties arise as a matter of faith freely chosen and the enforcement of which is left to the discretion of religious authorities or, it is often presumed, God. Each of these systems constitutes a code of conduct that is enforced by the will of a sanctioning authority, whether it is a government, society, religious body, or God; in other words, the duties expressed in each system arise by the *will* of the sanctioning authority itself or the constituents from whom its authority arises. Without such will, duty would be mere idea and could not be said in any meaningful way to constitute obligation.

For the past two millennia in the Western World, the Judeo-Christian ethical system has informed commonly accepted moral norms and, therefore, is worthy of consideration on a philosophical basis without any inference as to its religious truth. At the core of this system lie the Ten Commandments and the Golden Rule. The first four of the Ten Commandments express the duty of man to God and the last six express the duty of man to other men. The Golden Rule, famously articulated by Jesus but first appearing in the book of Leviticus of the Old Testament, which was written approximately 1300 BC, requires love of God, other human beings, and self. Of particular interest, the Golden Rule mandates treatment of other beings as *ends-in-themselves* and is predicated upon the notion that all human beings are equally beloved by God. Significantly, this same rationale informs the Declaration of Independence, the second paragraph of which begins with the words: "We hold these truths to be self-evident, that all men are *created equal, that they are endowed by their Creator* with certain unalienable Rights, that among these are Life, Liberty, and the pursuit of Happiness" (Emphasis added.)

Structurally, moral obligation may be analyzed in similar fashion to any other duty. In addition to the required conduct itself, moral obligation must include the following principals: (1) an object on whose account the obligation arises or other objective source of such obligation; (2) an obligor who is obligated by that object or source to act morally; and (3) the beneficiary of the moral obligation. Under the Golden Rule, God is the account object who, under clause (1), requires action in accordance with his divine will, each human being is an obligor under clause (2), and God and each human being is a beneficiary under clause (3), with the duty being to instantiate divinely moral objects by action toward God, fellow man, and self with *agape*, that is, unqualified good will. By way of contrasting example and as will be discussed at length shortly, under Kant's ethical system, human rationality is the source of obligation required under clause (1) and the duty is to act in a manner that may be universalized as a moral law. In any event, it is clear that the obligor cannot also be the source of its own obligation as it is asserted to be under relativistic systems, because, in that case, there would be only mere, subjective desire.

There is nothing about human beings, including that they are both theoretically and practically rational, that confers the status of moral beneficiary upon them without validation by an account entity or other source of moral obligation. It is no coincidence that the foundational principle underlying the Founding Fathers's assertion of independence from the royal tyranny of British colonial rule in the Declaration of Independence is that the ground of individual human rights is equal endowment by the Creator. At best, without some such validation, human beings are merely rational creatures possessed of subjective moral consciousness and it is in the nature of subjectivism that each human being, acting freely under its own moral compass, may disregard any notion that other human beings are independently worthy of moral status. Subjectivism may be superficially self-justifying, but without reference to any objective idea of *good-in-itself*, it cannot require that one rational being accord another treatment as an *end-in-itself*; to the contrary, in a world of survival of the fittest, mere theoretical reason may dictate otherwise and, even if it does not do so, it may yield ethics that are not at all considerate of individual rights. Although human *moral* rationality provides grounds for treatment of others as *ends-in-themselves*, the rationale does not lie in the nature of man as such but rather in the nature of a will that is *good-in-itself*; as will be shown, the special moral status of human beings arises because *good-in-itself* (considered as the account object) points to morally knowledgeable beings both as its objects and, as will be developed shortly, the means of its own instantiation.

For something to be morally good, it must be *good-in-itself*, without reference to anything else. If good were good by reference to something else, then that something else would be ontologically and morally antecedent to what is good in the first instance and so on. There would be no resting point. So, just as is the case with theoretical reason, practical reason must be self-justifying, it must stop at that which is *good-in-itself* and, as is the case with the rules of theoretical reason, *good-in-itself* must be accessible as such to direct intuition. In this context, to say that *good-in-itself* must be self-justifying is another way of saying that when practical reason rests upon *good-in-itself* as its object, it knows it to be good without anything more than practical reason and the theoretical reason which serves it.

Any theoretical concept of goodness that does not include within it the requirement that it be given effect is empty and can be shown to be so. No mere thing, no matter how useful in many circumstances it may be, can be shown to be good (by reference to our direct intuition of it) in all circumstances. Providing food, shelter, water, and/or love to those in need of it may often be morally required. Yet, although they are all useful in many contexts, they are not good in and of themselves. They can be misused in destructive and immoral ways. Food may be the object of gluttony, shelter may be given to murderous fugitives, water may be the cause of drowning, and love may be obsessive or unwanted. This is the reason that Kant so famously states: "Nothing can possibly be conceived in the world, or even out of it, which can be called good, without qualification, except a good will."[3] Only the will to do good, which operates in obedience to the requirement of *good-in-itself* that it be brought into effect, is present in all circumstances in which moral behavior occurs. Mere theoretical goodness, if it existed independently of a self-included requirement that it be effectuated, at most would yield knowledge of what object is desirable in the circumstances. It would illuminate that which is good for goodness' sake, but that would still leave a gap between knowing that something is desirable and being obligated to make it happen, not unlike the gap between knowing something

3. Kant, *Groundwork*, 10.

is rational and being required to act rationally. Clearly, those who see the goodness of providing food and shelter to the needy yet fail to recognize any personal obligation to do so commit the moral *error* of disconnecting the object, which is to comfort those in need, from any personal obligation to provide such comfort.

Practical reason is concerned not only with understanding or identifying that which is *good-in-itself* as a mere idea but also with understanding the nature and extent of any related empirical obligation to act or omit from acting in accordance with that idea. But from whence does that obligation arise? Moral obligation cannot arise on the part of the knowing party (as obligor) because what is considered to be an obligation would be a mere desire which could be avoided at the whim of the purported obligor. The obligation cannot be in the nature of a rule because the understanding that it must be followed could not be contained within the rule itself but instead would require independent authority. In order for *good-in-itself* to include within itself the necessity of its own instantiation it must require that those who know it act upon it. Unlike theoretical reason, which is theoretically compelling (i.e., a thinker is not rationally free to deny logic), for *good-in-itself* to be morally compelling it must itself be in the nature of will, which means that it must be self-instantiating, *Agape* and its beneficiaries must be objects of *Agape*. In other words, there can be no moral obligation without there being an ontologically supreme will that at once defines what is good and, by its own will, requires it to be done. We have seen that the human being is a revealer of Being. We now see that the human being is something more: the human being is a revealer of *Agape*. *One cannot know what is good without also knowing that one is obligated by the very nature of the concept itself (as account object) to bring it into being.* Morally conscious entities, as revealers of *Agape*, are therefore morally obligated entities who, in harmonizing their will with *Agape*, instantiate it (to the extent of their ability) and, in doing so, act morally.

Although practical reason requires theoretical reason for its implementation, *Agape* is not dependent upon it for the determination of its objects. The preconditions of objective practical reason are twofold: there must be a source of moral obligation and an entity that can know and discharge it in the empirical world. The former is *Agape*, which is part of the *Logos* and the latter is an autonomous soul, which by its nature must be morally conscious (from which consciousness its freedom will arise). The preconditions of practical knowledge, then, include all of the preconditions of theoretical knowledge and, additionally, that the moral subject have access to *Agape*, including apprehension of the intentionality of *Agape* (which will be left for later discussion) and that the moral subject is *Agape*'s object. We can identify the preconditions of all objective human understanding, both theoretical and practical, as follows: (1) mind-independent, self-justifying *a priori* rules of thought; (2) an empirical reality that is orderly in a manner that may be understood under the auspices of general logic; (3) consciousness of self as a persistent, rational, and morally-obligated entity (i.e., as *soul*); and (4) mind-independent, self-justifying divine *Agape*.

In asserting the dependence of morality on divine *Agape* on a take-it-or-leave-it-basis, we have thrown down the gauntlet to the material reductionists and other empiricists. It should not surprise us that whether there is anything that is *good-in-itself* is a matter of intense (and emotional) philosophical debate and that in the current state of secularist and relativist bias that characterizes reductionist philosophy the view that there is no such thing is clearly the majority view. Accordingly, since Kant, the contemporary mainstream has gone to extraordinarily painful lengths to avoid the necessary relation between morality and God and its status as such mandates consideration, however wrongheaded it may be.

The preconditions of human understanding of objective moral obligation provide a useful source of identifying the questions by which conflicting ethical systems may be judged, including: (1) By what standard do such systems assert that right conduct is to be determined? (2) Under such systems, what sort of entities may be subject to moral obligation? (3) What degree of consciousness is required under such systems for moral obligation? and (4) What degree of freedom is required under such systems for moral obligation? It will streamline our discussion if we give these questions names so, henceforth, they will be referred to as the "Moral Standard Problem," the "Entity Problem," the "Consciousness Problem," and the "Free Will Problem," respectively.

The answer provided by transcendent realism to the Moral Standard Problem has been posited as having *Agape* as its referent. Because moral obligation is a question of practical reason, which under transcendent realism in turn requires access to the *Logos*, the answers to the Entity Problem and the Consciousness Problem are intertwined here. Access to the *Logos*, to the full extent available to human beings, requires that human beings must be *thinking selves* and that for consciousness to occur the self of conscious thought must be a persistent entity that is distinguishable from the thoughts it may have. It is possible, although by no means certain, that other sentient earthly beings (cats, dogs, elephants, and porpoises are obvious candidates) meet the criteria of thinking selves. Certainly, these and other highly intelligent animals display a high capacity to receive via their special sensory mechanisms and process enormous amounts of empirical data. They often display in their play and social behavior what appears to be the type of objective thought that we would associate in ourselves with consciousness. Clearly, such animals operate under a capacity of *present awareness*. But we need take care not to read more into their behavior than necessary to explain it and, to my knowledge, although there are instances in which animal behavior may appear to be altruistic, there is no compelling evidence that any of it is engaged in with concern for their own Being or any concept of future or any moral motives. Accordingly, there is no reason to believe that any such animals have access to practical reason and it is indeed possible that attributing even *thinking-self* status to such animals is merely fanciful anthropomorphism. Nevertheless, as a theoretical matter, we can reasonably distinguish between thinking selves who also have direct intuition of *Agape* and those who do not by referring to the former as *souls* and the latter as *selves*.

The answer provided by transcendent realism to the Free Will Problem, the exposition of which has been left to the sequel chapter, is that in order for moral obligation to exist, not only must the subject of moral obligation be free to discharge such obligation without regard for any subjective desire to the contrary that the obligor might have but that his moral consciousness will provide him with that freedom. The apparent simplicity, straightforwardness, and indisputability of this assertion belie the complexity that inheres in the Free Will Problem. Reductionists, whose views are governed by the laws of physics (whether they are regarded as causal or probabilistic), find it impossible to account for true freedom and therefore postulate illusory substitutes as being sufficient support for the ethical claims that they nevertheless are unwilling to relinquish. At the other extreme, most laymen simply assume that they are free to do as they please in all things, including, for example, to choose what dessert they would like to eat, but careful consideration yields that the apparent freedom to choose among subjective desires such as between having a chocolate or vanilla ice cream cone may be chimerical because any selection may be (or, for philosophical purposes, may be presumed to be) fully materially reducible and, therefore, fully determined. The conclusion that will be reached in the sequel chapter is that moral freedom exists in the ability to choose to refrain altogether from accommodating subjective desire and instead to follow an independent objective moral *requirement*. The main distinction that must be made and understood for purposes of, and which will be assumed in, the discussion in this chapter is that objectivity alone is insufficient for freedom because the decision to act objectively will always be a permissibly subjective one unless the objective alternative includes within itself, as its own end, an *obligation*. That is to say, for moral obligation to exist there must be an authoritative moral law that is independent of the obligor. Although objective knowledge is a necessary condition of the existence of moral obligation it is not a sufficient one because, by itself, it is devoid of obligation. As a result, mere objectivity supports altruism but not morality. It follows that the moral freedom to refrain altogether from accommodating subjective desire and instead to follow an objective moral requirement can be had only by morally conscious beings (i.e., souls). So a refinement to the Entity Problem is warranted to include the element of moral freedom, with the distinction between theoretically conscious and morally conscious entities now being between *thinking selves* and *autonomous* souls, respectively.

SUBJECTIVE REDUCTIONISM

Few philosophers, classic, middle ages, or modern, have been willing to deny the existence in man of real moral obligation. It is probably safe to say that this is due in whole or in part to the force with which man *intuitively feels* morally obliged, the distasteful consequences of the denial of moral obligation which are generally recognized regardless of philosophical attitude, and the empirically incontestable fact that people are expected to and frequently act as though they are under an obligation to be moral. The fact of apparent direct intuition of moral obligation places the burden of the argument on any philosophy that suggests that either there is no such moral obligation or that it arises out of natural causes (i.e., is materially reducible) and apparent direct intuition of moral obligation is illusory. This is by no means a small point. A material reductionist who asserts that there is no such thing as moral obligation because any such purported obligation cannot be reduced to material terms must then explain in material terms the phenomenon of illusory moral obligation. Alternatively, a material reductionist who desires to argue that moral obligation exists as a materially reducible phenomenon must explain precisely how that is the case and, in doing so, must satisfactorily address in material reductionist terms the Moral Standard Problem, the Entity Problem, the Consciousness Problem, and the Free Will Problem.

One modern philosopher of great significance who is willing to deny the existence in man of real moral obligation is Hume. Hume holds that moral distinctions are not derived from reason but from moral sentiments, such as feelings of approval and disapproval. For Hume there are first order passions which may be considered by reason but only at the instance of a second order passion to do so. Hume directly challenges reason-based ethics by asserting that reason alone cannot be a motive to the will, but rather is always the "slave of the passions." Nagel, arguing for a reason-based ethics, suggests that no matter how many orders of desire are involved in a considered action, an agent can always analyze them from both a personal and impersonal standpoint and further that, when objective reason is introduced into consideration, because human action is no longer based upon pure passion human actors may be held accountable for actions based upon an assessment of conformity to reason. There are many problems with Nagel's analysis (which will be considered in greater detail in discussing objective empirical ethics below). Here it will suffice to point out that (1) the decision whether to act in accordance with theoretical reason and not subjective desire is itself a subjective decision which may be valued and reached relative to other subjective desires, (2) introducing objective analysis as a possibility is one thing but introducing it as a moral imperative is quite another and requires justification itself, and (3) even if one can be held to conduct based solely on its rationality (legal systems do this all the time by imposing a reasonable person standard of conduct) the underlying premise of ethics based upon such an idea, namely, that theoretically rational conduct equates to moral conduct, cannot be justified by reference to theoretical reason alone. In other words, the assertion that one is morally required to act in accordance with theoretical reason is a matter not of theoretical reason but of *practical reason*. Reason will not allow us to rest upon theoretical reason in answering moral questions; in other words, we do not have direct intuition of any *obligation* to act rationally. This is precisely the point that Hume is making and Nagel has not succeeding in discrediting it.

Hume's offering is of a classic, agent-relative ethics, which ultimately reduces to absolute ethical skepticism. Hume's argument is based upon individual psychology. Hume argues that, because only moral *sentiments* exist, there can be no basis for valid moral criticism of any individual human action. The ethical principle implicit in Hume and other subjectivist philosophies is that each individual should act in accordance with his own individual maxims, which is the same as saying that there is no moral obligation at all for an individual cannot be *required* to act as he wishes. The statement that there is no moral obligation is, of course, an ethical statement in itself but, because it does not entail a denial of objective theoretical reason, it is not self-contradictory and must be taken seriously.

There are other subjectivist positions that are agent-neutral and which do not deny the existence of moral obligation. These philosophies typically approach ethics from a sociological standpoint. In essence, agent-neutral subjectivist arguments state that morality is simply a fact of human nature that is socially determined. These philosophies generally do not intend to understate the importance of moral conduct but they require that it must be considered equally along with other features of human social behavior.

The agent-neutral nature of these philosophies notwithstanding, their ethics is relativistic across culture and across history; under them, the individual, by his own human nature, is morally subject only to the requirements of the society of which he is a member. Sophisticated arguments have been advanced in support of development of the agent-neutral subjectivist ethics, including, most recently, evolutionary game theory, which purports to show how natural selection might lead to ethical norms in social animals.

Both agent-relative and agent-neutral subjectivist positions draw weak consolation from the fact that moral reason (as commonly understood) sometimes seems to yield contradictory results historically and cross-culturally. The fact of such contradictions is undeniable and cannot be glossed over. However, these sorts of contradictions are not disproof of objective moral obligation; rather, they merely show that man's understanding (or misunderstanding) of moral obligation may be subject to contingencies of culture and history or that man's determination to discharge his moral obligation may be flawed to the point of deliberate denial or mischaracterization of it. Such moral discrepancies doubtlessly reflect the strength of man's materially reducible characteristics, such as man's social and herd instincts, which are often contrary to moral behavior and which therefore may be said to illustrate both the extent of the moral challenge facing empirical beings and their freedom to act or not act morally. That societies have engaged in systematic atrocities does not show that its members are free of moral obligation but only that other, baser human instincts may for periods of time prevail over it, and that when such instincts are embraced at a societal level the magnitude of the illusion of their moral acceptability and the associated depravity correspondingly increase. Such moral discrepancies may simply mean that societal contradictions need to be considered as ethical mistakes of a sociological nature and support a conclusion that man is both free to act immorally and also to rationalize, individually or collectively, immoral conduct. Obvious examples include genocide, cannibalism, and slavery. Clearly, such conduct is morally wrong and requires understanding, but, although it demonstrates great human weakness, it is not proof that there is no such thing as objective moral obligation. The particular immorality of such conduct is especially apparent to those of us who are fortunate to live in societies that are not physically or economically dependent upon their being embraced for survival. Philosophers must take great care not to infer more than is warranted from the occurrence of such phenomena.

The subjectivist positions as a whole are fraught with too many difficulties to withstand scrutiny. For one thing, as has already been noted, subjective obligation is illusory because anything that is subjective may be overridden by other subjective considerations. This is not just a theoretical matter. In the current moral climate, the subjectivist argument, however unsound it may be, has indeed yielded abject hedonism and the glorification of licentiousness, and some would argue has oriented modern western culture away from the pursuit of moral advancement to pandering to the lowest common denominator; indeed, history may yet record such subjectivism as a major cause of the downfall of modern society should it occur. Another issue for subjectivist ethical systems is that, whether acknowledged or not, they entail a rejection of moral freedom because all action that is subjectively taken reduces to action taken in furtherance of subjectively determined desires even where the end is objectively rational. Although skeptical subjectivists may be willing to give up freedom along with objective morality, they may only do so on the grounds of radical skepticism, which has been discredited in earlier chapters, and must explain the phenomenon of how human beings come to have an intuition of freedom that they regard as illusory. In spite and because of these insurmountable difficulties, the agent-neutral subjectivists desperately seek to explain moral accountability on something less than freedom as it is commonly understood. These subjective theories are generally part of a material reductionism, are built on the same defective foundation, and are advanced on an analytic basis, without addressing some or all of the Entity Problem, the Consciousness Problem, or the Free Will Problem, which they simply treat as if they do not exist. As a result, they cannot contain a justified ethics.

Subjectivism confuses laws (i.e., subjective rules of socially required behavior, whether rational or not) with moral obligation, which must be self-justifying and absolutely obligatory. Sociological or psychological explanations of why man has come to establish rules are not explanations of why man feels himself to be morally obliged to conduct himself in certain ways, including, sometimes, to obey those rules even where the risk of being held to account is nil or to defy those very rules for a moral purpose (e.g., civil disobedience for human rights) where it is likely that he will be held to account for such defiance. That mankind has historically demonstrated a desire for the rule of law (whether the lawmaking is reposed in a democratically elected parliament or a dictator) and that such laws often require conduct in common with moral obligation are beyond dispute. However, the explanation of the origin and authority of societal laws may very well be largely or wholly sociological and, therefore, have little or nothing to do with morality.

The subjectivists have painted themselves into a corner. They seek to deny objective and universal moral obligation and so they must explain why it is an illusion. In order to do that, they must (1) explain in subjective terms the intuition of moral obligation, and (2) either show that such obligation is compelling notwithstanding its subjective origins or accept the fact that it does not exist. The subjectivists fail on both counts. Sociological or psychological explanations are mere speculation, generally fly in the face of Darwinian evolution, and always reduce to moral skepticism. Although it is not self-contradictory to hold that there is no such thing as moral obligation that position cannot be maintained without access to objective reason, which cannot be explained in materialist terms (or any subjective terms because that would be a contradiction in terms), and therefore is only available to non-reductionist philosophies. The best that the subjectivists can do is to say that real moral obligation cannot be explained materially, which is, of course, true. But to assert that because it cannot be explained materially it does not exist is mere dogma, which is both inconsistent with, and largely unexplanatory of, human experience. In the end, this too must be defended by reference to an objective reason the access to which they are denied by the terms of their own philosophy.

SECULAR DEONTOLOGICAL ETHICS

Secular deontological systems are rule-based approaches that typically start with the empirical fact of a core of common moral judgments and seek to show how such judgments may be comprehended under one or more rational laws. It is important to understand what is meant by reason in the context of objective secular deontology. Because these philosophies must operate without any ontological reference (i.e., no direct intuition of mind-independent moral law), their project is to apply theoretical reason in the context of human action to make moral claims. In other words, the objective is to show that *practical* reason is a special category of theoretical reason and that moral conduct consists of the application of theoretical reason to the contingent circumstances of everyday life.

That theoretical reason can yield self-evident truths within its own domain is undeniable not only because theoretical reason is self-evidently true but also because to deny it would be a claim of theoretical reason. However, to show that theoretical reason is also able to yield self-evident moral truths, one has to assert that rationality equates to morality. The assertion that moral action is rational action is itself a *moral* claim which is clearly not self-evident in the way that *modus ponens* or the rest of theoretical reason is. If it is not self-evident, or cannot be seen to be so after having been broken down into elements each of which is self-evident, then the statement cannot be analytic *a priori* and, therefore, its grounds must be identified on a synthetic *a priori* basis. This is why the secular deontological project must be to survey empirically man's moral actions and to see whether and how they might be justified rationally. Kant, whose categorical imperative represents the paradigmatic secular deontological ethical rule, expressly embraces this approach.

The fundamental problem with these approaches is that even where they yield a result that is consistent with our common understanding of morality they can never bridge the gap between reason and obligation. So, for instance, they may be able to argue that suicide is irrational but they cannot justify the conclusion that therefore suicide is immoral. This problem manifests itself in several ways. First, the project of developing synthetic *a priori* ethics is a circular one. Empirically moral conduct cannot be identified unless you know what is being sought after in the first place. Take, for example, truth-telling. We might agree that there is a moral obligation to tell the truth. But how do we know that? We cannot resort to theoretical reason as the source of the obligation without first assuming that rationality equates to morality. But that is precisely what the secular deontologists are seeking to prove when they undertake to identify moral conduct to determine its nature. Even if the plan is to identify conduct that is presumed to be of a moral character, the circularity problem is not solved, because the rationale of the presumption must first be explained without reference to any *a priori* notion.

Second, a closely related issue arises when one considers the origin of moral conduct from a secular deontological perspective. If the secular deontological project is to avoid superfluity, it must identify a rational principle which explains moral judgments that is generally not knowingly applied in the actual making of such judgments. In other words, the premise of secular deontological ethics is that human beings engage in moral conduct, such as truth telling, without knowing why they are morally obliged to do so. Such a state of affairs would require that morally conscious beings have direct intuition of particular moral laws (such as the requirement to tell the truth), even though they do not have direct intuition of a unifying *a priori* principle that comprises each one. This seems highly unlikely, if not altogether impossible, and, in any case, requires a direct intuition that is denied by secular deontologists.

Third, because theoretical reason does not contain within itself its own end, it is not equivalent to practical reason. Theoretical reason cannot identify a moral end but only identify how to achieve it once it is independently identified and, unfortunately, reason can also identify how to achieve ends which are immoral. Theoretical reason serves both the passions and the will, not just a morally good will. If theoretical reason were an end in itself, the presence of immoral conduct (which is deemed to be irrational) would demonstrate free will and not the moral neutrality of theoretical reason. However, because theoretical reason is not an *end-in-itself*, the presence of immoral behavior demonstrates the instability of the secular deontological claim; it cannot be *rational* to observe a reason-based code of conduct if others will not do the same. Instead of asking what a rational person should do in a given set of circumstances, secular deontological systems should ask what a rational person should do in a given set of circumstances recognizing that many will not act in a manner that is consistent with theoretical reason. Oddly, this problem may be characterized as the pursuit of a universal rational rule where one of the operating assumptions must be that reason will not necessarily be observed by all of the participants. The result is that reason might very well dictate a different outcome where it was given that all persons would follow it than it would where it was known that only some persons would follow it. The secular deontological rule that one should treat others as he wishes to be treated has no rational answer to the rejoinder: "Why should I do that when most people will not treat me the same way?"

Finally, it should be observed that, in the absence of an acknowledged non-theoretical understanding of what is good, theoretical reason can justify many dramatically different systems, for example, utilitarianism (maximize the aggregate happiness of society at the expense of the individual), individual natural rights (respect rights of individuals even if the cost to society yields a net loss of total happiness), and totalitarianism (the ends justify the means and/or the strong should rule the weak). Strictly speaking, under common parlance, these outcome-based systems are usually not considered to be deontological; however, the point remains that theoretical reason is wholly unable to fulfill the task of explaining morality without pointing to a transcendent source.

KANT AND NAGEL

The difficulties attending secular deontological ethical approaches are fully manifest in Kant's moral system, which is, not surprisingly, the most formidable and meticulously formulated example of them. Kant starts with the fact that man possesses what he regards as moral knowledge. We *know*, for example, that it is immoral to lie, to steal, to commit adultery, and to kill other human beings. The question is: How can it be shown that we are prohibited by moral law from such conduct? Because, in Kant's view, moral laws (like all laws) are by their very nature both universal and necessary, moral knowledge must be *a priori*. However, because, for Kant, all knowledge originates in the senses, we cannot have direct intuition of our moral obligations. According to Kant, moral knowledge, therefore, must be *synthetic*; that is, we come to understand our moral obligation by making moral judgments through the exercise of our will in response to the contingencies of the empirical world. Kant's goal is, therefore, to identify the principles according to which our reason operates when it directs to the will to act morally. In other words, Kant is attempting to identify the *a priori* knowledge underlying moral judgments.

To demonstrate that morality (and moral philosophy) is not empirical in character, Kant argues that morality must be founded upon reason:

> Everyone must admit that if a law is to have, i.e., to be the basis of an obligation, it must carry with it absolute necessity; that, for example, the precept, "Thou shalt not lie," is not valid for men alone, as if other rational beings had no need to observe it; and so with all the other moral laws properly so called; that, therefore, the basis of obligation must not be sought in the nature of man, or in the circumstances in the world in which he is placed, but *a priori* simply in the conception of pure reason.[4]

Kant proclaims his objective to be the identification of the supreme principle of morality. Although the answer to the question of how one ought to act in a given set of circumstances can only be had by the employment of reason, it is readily apparent that the rational process in reaching moral judgments is of a completely different nature than the rational process involved in cognition. It is therefore important for Kant to delineate between reason, insofar as it performs its cognitive function, and reason, insofar as it considers moral choice, even though both are aspects of one and the same rational faculty. In its cognitive function, reason is concerned with *understanding* the objects presented to it by the senses. In its moral function, reason is concerned with *producing* its objects in accordance with its ideas to the extent of its physical capability to do so. The latter faculty is a function of the will, through which man is able to implement moral choices; in other words, it is through will that morally conscious beings accomplish moral ends. It follows that moral knowledge is not a process of cognition of that which is theoretically good, but rather a process of determining what a rational being ought to endeavor to bring about, which is to say, how a rational being should exercise its will.

It will be recalled that for Kant's statement to avoid tautology he must provide content to the concept of good will and show how it is good in itself. It has already been seen that for Kant the transcendental Ideal (i.e., God, as the *Ens Perfectissimum*) is definitionally *good-in-itself*, but, as will be discussed shortly, because for Kant belief in God can only be founded on moral knowledge and not the other way around, equating moral obligation with the will of God can only be a matter of faith and not knowledge. Therefore, for Kant, moral claims can only avoid dogma if they are not based upon recourse to supersensible reality and are fully understandable in rational terms. In short, Kant's goal is to show that moral obligation is the requirement of objective reason and that moral conduct is rational conduct.

According to Kant, reason dictates that man must act at all times for the sake of duty and not for his own desire and that a will to act for the sake of duty is therefore a good will. For Kant, duty requires action out of reverence for moral law and, as noted, for a moral law to be such, it must be necessary and universal, which means that it must be comprehensible as a matter of *a priori* reason. Kant concludes that, to avoid subjective desire and ensure that duty is the object, reason dictates that one ought to act "only on

---

4. Ibid., 5.

that maxim whereby thou canst at the same time will that it should become a universal law."[5] Kant's point is that if one cannot logically universalize his conduct (in all of its circumstances), then it cannot be moral. Kant offers the prohibition against lying as an example of how the categorical imperative operates in practice. Consider an individual who determines to lie because it is expedient to do so; because the success of his lie depends upon the assumption that people are obligated to tell the truth, it is impossible to universalize the maxim that it is permissible to lie for the sake of expedience. In other words, the maxim that one may lie where it is expedient is logically unstable. Kant offers other examples, including prohibitions against suicide and disregarding needs of the poor, which need not be analyzed here. Nevertheless, to be clear, Kant's categorical imperative is a rule by which prospective conduct (or personal maxims of action) can be evaluated but it does not, in and of itself, provide specific rules of conduct.

Kant's formulation certainly satisfies the criterion of universality, but something more is required to connect Kant's formulation with the necessity that it be obeyed; that is to say, the universalization of conduct supplies the level of generality required for a law but it does not, by itself, supply the requisite element of obligation. Recognizing this, Kant expressly asks the question of whether it is *necessary* that rational beings act in accordance with the law as stated. Kant contends that, if it should be so, he will have succeeded in identifying the combination of universality and necessity for his moral law to be *a priori* and, therefore, determinable by reference to reason alone. It should be remembered that Kant's Copernican revolution is in response to Hume, who held that reason cannot be the ground of morality and instead merely serves the passions. Kant has reached a critical juncture; if Kant can show that a reason-based moral principle contains within itself the necessity that it be obeyed, he will have responded with overwhelming force to Hume's moral skepticism. Kant reminds us that will is a faculty of *a priori* reason that is exercised for an *end*. It follows that if reason contains within itself its own end, then the ground of the necessity of the moral law will also lie within it. And Kant asserts that this is precisely the case. According to Kant, morality requires that human beings and all other rational creatures must act only where their conduct may be universalized *because it is rational to do so* and their *will*, which determines its own ends and is itself a faculty of reason, *ought* to have rational conduct as its end. Moreover, Kant asserts that, because reason contains within itself its own end, all rational creatures, by virtue of their rationality, must be treated as *ends-in-themselves*:

> If then there is a supreme practical principle or, in respect of the human will, a categorical imperative, it must be one which, being drawn from the conception of that which is necessarily an end for everyone because it is an end in itself, constitutes an objective principle of will, and can therefore serve as a universal practical law. The foundation of this principle is: rational nature exists as an end in itself. Man necessarily conceives his own existence as being so; so far then this is a subjective principle of human actions. But every other rational being regards its existence similarly, just on the same rational principal that holds for me: so that it is at the same time an objective principle, from which as a supreme practical law all laws of the will must be capable of being deduced. Accordingly, the practical imperative

---

5. Ibid., 28.

will be as follows: So act as to treat humanity, whether in thine own person or in that of any other, in every case as an end withal, never as means only.[6]

To complete his moral philosophy, Kant has one more problem to address. It is readily apparent that moral action can only occur if man is free to fully disregard his deterministic desires and to act solely out of reverence for the moral law. Stated more formally, for Kant, moral freedom is a necessary precondition of moral action. But since the sensible world yields only deterministic action, for Kant freedom can only be a transcendental Idea that belongs in supersensible reality and, as such, can never be proved. As a result, for Kant to remain true to his premise that the categories of understanding can never be applied beyond the sensible world, he must stop short of declaring that man is morally obligated and content himself with the conclusion that what man regards as moral knowledge is, at best, only possibly the case.

Although Kant has, by his own terms, exhausted the limits of knowledge, because morality requires the assumption of a supersensible freedom, Kant wishes to show that the assumption is reasonably made. To do that, Kant is effectively compelled to cross the border into a *noumenal* reality in which he is generally uncomfortable. The first, and most obvious question that Kant must address, arises as a direct result of the position in which Kant's epistemology places him, namely, how to reconcile the assumption of freedom with human nature about which only empirical knowledge may be had. Because Kant's empirical epistemology precludes him from being able to prove the very freedom that his rationalist ethics requires, he may not avoid making an assumption about the existence of freedom as a *noumenal* idea. Because Kant has identified by reference to *a priori* reason alone the categorical moral law, even if he were temperamentally capable of abandoning his moral claims because they depend upon supersensible freedom, he may not permissibly do so. This means that even though freedom can only exist as a *noumenal* phenomenon, it differs from other possible *noumenal* phenomena, such as a logical first cause, because unlike the latter, freedom must be assumed to support the moral law that pure reason alone states must exist. In other words, we do not know whether the empirical world, which we know exists, requires a first cause, but we do know that moral obligation, which we also know exists, requires moral freedom. Kant therefore has only one way to go. Kant must conceptually bifurcate man into a material being, who can be *known* to be fully determined, and a *noumenal* being (i.e., a soul) who must (and can only) be *assumed* to exist in order to support the moral freedom that is the supreme principle of morality. Predictably, the assumption of a soul forces Kant even farther into supersensible reality. Because *noumenal* entities exist outside of space-time, the immortality of man's soul must also be presumed. Finally, by a complicated line of reasoning that will not be discussed in further detail here, in order to reconcile the disconnect between virtue and happiness which exists in the material world, Kant postulates God, as the cause of Nature, which does not include God, in which human will is fully in harmony with morality and moral beings therefore attain perfect happiness that corresponds to their virtue.

---

6. Ibid., 33.

Not surprisingly, Kant's sojourn into the supersensible subjected him to harsh criticism from the modern empiricists and, sadly, may be responsible for the merits of his remarkable deontological ethics to be under appraised. Nevertheless, it cannot be denied that the many difficulties which generally attend secular deontological ethical systems already described above apply specifically to Kant's deontological ethics. For one thing, although Kant wishes to begin with duty he cannot define it without reference to an external standard, which he infers from empirical moral judgments that are made without knowledge of that standard. Although Kant's practical methodology parallels his epistemological methodology, the process is fundamentally different because it is one thing to make epistemological inferences from an objective empirical reality that is independent of the rational being to whom such reality is presented and quite another to attempt to infer the rational principle behind judgments that are made without reference to it and yet which must depend upon it in the first place. The analysis is not the same as attempting to elicit principles of cognition from a reality that is presented to the senses because, in the case of moral conduct, the conduct that is the subject of analysis is said to originate within the same rationality that is considering it. If humans knowingly judge their action in accordance with the categorical imperative, then its discovery and presentation by Kant is superfluous; if not, then how is it that they know how they should act?

Another problem arises because the universality of the categorical imperative as formulated fails to take into account the persistence of immorality in the everyday human behavior from which it is synthetically derived. Why should one act only on that maxim whereby he can at the same time will that it become a universal law, when he knows with certainty that others will not do the same? That would be irrational, not rational. People sometimes tell the truth and sometimes lie. Kant's proof of the logical instability of expedient lying may or may not be theoretically sound but it is not practically sound where it can be said with certainty that universal truthfulness will never come into being. Therefore, if Kant wishes to found his ethics on the synthetic fact of morality, he must also take into account the inevitable and persistent *fact of immorality* in human conduct. And the presupposition of that task is that one already knows how to distinguish between moral and immoral acts.

Yet another problem arises because acting without regard to one's own interest is not a duty unless the object of the action is an *end-in-itself*. Kant is correct that theoretical reason supplies its own *grounds* but incorrect that in doing so it makes itself its own end. Theoretical reason cannot be its own end because, although it is self-justifying, theoretical reason is not self-instantiating, it does not intend itself as its own end (or any other end for that matter), and is not in the nature of will. *Modus ponens* and the rest of the *Logos* that are available to theoretical reason supply the rules of thought, but they are wholly indifferent as to whether they are used for any particular end. *Agape*, as it is available to practical reason, is anything but indifferent as to its ends; indeed, it morally obligates all entities that have access to it to instantiate it in their conduct. Therefore, theoretical reason is *logically* necessary but not *practically* necessary and it can only show the way to rational conduct, not *oblige* such conduct.

Moreover, even if Kant were correct that reason is its own end, it does not follow that rational beings should be treated as *ends-in-themselves*. That thought may not exist without a thinker is consistent with human experience, but clearly all rational beings, even of a given species, are not equal in thought and there is no rationale for treating them equally *that is solely based upon theoretical reason.* The diremption between the necessity of reason and the moral status of beings with access to it is most tellingly demonstrated by the fact that when Kant asserts that each rational entity is by virtue of its rationality an *end-in-itself*, he not only offers argument for the necessity of the categorical imperative, *but he unwittingly substantively changes it!* This is a mortal blow because if the explanation of the necessity of the rule effects a substantive change in the rule itself, then it is clear that the rule did *not* contain its own necessity within itself. Specifics are warranted. Kant's categorical imperative is that one ought to act "only on that maxim whereby thou canst at the same time will that it should become a universal law." However, true this may be, by itself it allows for widely diverse ethical systems, including utilitarian systems, natural rights systems, and other systems that are designed to favor certain classes of rational beings where there is a rational basis for discrimination. But when one introduces the notion that each rational being is an end-it-itself, then only natural rights systems are justified.

In *The Last Word,* Nagel attempts to show how an objectivist secular deontological system might be based upon theoretical reason *alone*, thereby avoiding the ontological assumptions required to be made in Kant's system. In doing so, Nagel asserts entitlement to take for granted that there is no external moral reference underpinning ethical choice. Nagel's conclusion is that reason requires (1) that any ethical system be universal (Nagel calls this generality), which is to say that the reasons for action must apply to all rational beings in the same circumstances; and (2) choosing between agent-relative and agent-neutral reasons, with the latter being the better choice. The first claim reflects the universal nature of reason itself, so, as a requirement of a secular deontological ethics, it can hardly be controversial. The second claim reflects Nagel's observation that man's reason enables him to recognize that he is one individual among many similar persons and to view himself both from a first-personal perspective and also from the objective impersonal perspectives from which he is regarded by others. From this peculiar ability, Nagel argues that man can effectively generalize the value that he attributes to himself to others and therefore conclude that he should treat others as he would like to be treated.

Although Nagel's project is far more limited than Kant's, in these two points it is very similar. However, to complete his offering, Nagel must also address the question of free will. In this, Nagel has two advantages over Kant. The first is that Nagel is staunchly anti-reductionist and therefore not bound by any deterministic impulse. The second is that Nagel is not subject to the same constraints as Kant of having set forth a comprehensive epistemology with respect to which his discussion of freedom must be harmonized.

Nagel launches his attack against determinism on two fronts. With respect to theoretical reason, Nagel argues that determinism, which if true must apply to thought as well as to more clearly physical phenomena, is an assault on reason itself, which, because like all such assaults it can be conducted only by recourse to reason, is unstable:

> Suppose you became convinced that *all* your choices, decisions, and conclusions were determined by rationally arbitrary features of your psychological makeup or by external manipulation, and then tried to ask yourself what, in the light

of this information you should do or believe. There would really be no way to answer the question, because the arbitrary causal control of which you had become convinced would apply to whatever you said or decided. You could not simultaneously believe this about yourself and try to make a free, rational choice. Not only that, but if the very belief in the causal system of control was itself a product of what you thought to be reasoning, then it too would lose its status as a believe freely arrived at, and your attitude toward it would have to change. (Though even that is a rational argument, whose conclusion you are no longer in a position to draw!)[7]

Nagel's second ground is based upon the existence of objective reason. He starts by noting that the general deterministic skepticism with respect to all conduct hereinabove discussed may be raised about practical reason alone. In this respect, the argument would be that determinism renders practical reason altogether illusory. Nagel's rebuttal is that even if one believed that what appear to be moral judgments are in fact due to arbitrarily determined factors, it is always possible for one to step back and, taking such factors into account, ask how one *ought* to act. In response to the argument that any such assessment is itself the result of mechanistic forces, Nagel asserts that the fact that our practice is to engage persistently in moral judgment manifests our best judgment that we are in fact free to act. Nagel states: "Freedom requires holding oneself in one's hands and choosing a direction in thought or action for the highly contingent and particular individual that one is, from a point of view outside oneself, that one can nevertheless reach from oneself."[8]

Even Nagel's more limited project cannot withstand analysis. For one thing, Nagel's starting point that there is no external moral reference for ethical conduct is an unsupported hypothesis even upon Nagel's own understanding. It will be recalled from the discussion in chapter 4, "The Possibility of Objective Knowledge," that Nagel considers the explanation for human access to universally valid methods of objective to be undiscoverable, so all he has to work with in this regard is the mere fact of objective reason. If the source of objective reason remains out of reach, then on what basis is it permissible to assert that apparent direct intuition of moral obligation is illusory? Second, Nagel's arguments that all humans are morally equal by virtue of their mere humanity and that theoretical reason attaches sufficiently high value to life to arrive at what we regard as moral obligation are utterly unconvincing. Nagel is certainly correct that each person is justified in presuming that others attach similar value to themselves, but that observation says nothing about whether one ought to recognize that value. Mere theoretical reason can never tell us how highly any life should be valued, or even whether the same value should be attached to the unborn, the aged, and the mentally ill. That this is so has become increasingly and tragically clear in the era of modern humanism which is predicated upon a denial of external moral obligation.

We have in Kant a system and in Nagel an outline for a system which are largely compatible. Both require generality of rules and respect for individual rights. However, neither Kant nor Nagel succeeds in justifying his claims of the sufficiency of theoretical

---

7. Nagel, *Last Word*, 115.
8. Ibid., 118.

reason as warrant for practical reason, the necessity that the offered general rules be followed, or even that each individual ought to be treated as an *end-in-itself*.

That theoretical reason cannot yield absolute truths in the domain of practical human action suggests either that there are no such absolute truths—this is the subjectivist position that has been earlier discredited—or that ethics cannot be had by mere application of theoretical reason. But it does not mean that Kant and Nagel are wrong in identifying universality, necessity, and treatment of individuals as *ends-in-themselves*. To the contrary, I believe they are correct. But that raises immediately the question of how they can be so if their arguments are flawed. My answer is simple and I believe the only one, namely, that they, along with the rest of us, have an internal intuition of *Agape* which informs their conclusions to the contrary, whether they are willing to recognize it or not.

INTERNAL INTUITION OF AGAPE

Early on in this chapter, it was asserted that if moral obligation exists, then morally conscious beings must have, by virtue of their reason, direct knowledge of the existence and content of *Agape*. *Agape* was described as being self-justifying and self-instantiating *good-in-itself* without discussion of what its content might be. A distinction was made between the mere idea of goodness and *Agape*. Conceptual goodness is merely an object of theoretical reason and, as such, does not include itself as an *end*. *Agape* is self-justifying in a manner that is analogous to theoretical reason. We know by direct and analytical intuition that theoretical reason gives its own grounds and, accordingly, reason may comfortably rest when it reaches a theoretically satisfactory explanation of the questions that it might consider. For *Agape* to be the source of moral obligation it must, in a similar way, offer an answer to the question of how a morally conscious being ought to act in a given set of circumstances in a manner which can be seen by practical reason to be good, thereby affording practical reason a comfortable resting point. But *Agape* is something uniquely more than the theoretical insofar as *Agape* is also self-instantiating. In addition to being understood by internal intuition as self-justifying, *Agape* is understood as that object of reason which, because it determines itself as its own end, is an end in itself. *Agape* therefore morally *obligates* practical reason to determine that its end be to instantiate *Agape* and, when practical reason so determines, moral action is the result.

In justifying the claim that self-instantiating *Agape* is the directly intuited source of moral obligation, sufficient content must be provided to the concept of *Agape* so that it may be instantiated in the empirical contingencies of everyday life and then it must be shown that moral obligation, as so understood, is available to reason without reference to the empirical contingencies to which it might be applied or without deduction from theoretical reason. In other words, what we are looking for is a moral law that is not only universal, necessary, and self-justifying, but also that is self-instantiating and known generally to human beings. I believe that there is such a law and that it is known to virtually all as the essential element in Judeo-Christian morality alluded to earlier in this chapter, namely, that one must act in all matters to the best of his or her ability with equal consideration given to the interests of oneself and all other affected morally conscious entities (this law will henceforth be referred to as the "Moral Law"). Until now, we have refrained to the extent possible from explicitly identifying *Agape* with God, considering the former only as the ontologically supreme principal of morality. However, it is important to note that, if one substitutes God for *Agape* or identifies God as its source, the Moral Law can be seen to be a formal restatement of the commandments identified by Jesus as the most important of all:

> One of the scribes who had listened to them debating appreciated that Jesus had given a good answer and put a further question to him, "Which is the first of all the commandments?" Jesus replied, "This is the first: Listen, Israel, the Lord our God is the one, only Lord, and you must love the Lord your God with all your heart, with all your soul, with all your mind and with all your strength. The second is this: You must love your neighbour as yourself. There is no commandment greater than these."[9]

The rule that one must act in all matters with equal consideration given to the interests of oneself and all other affected morally conscious entities is both universal, insofar as it applies to all conduct, and necessary, insofar as it binds all morally rational creatures. It is self-justifying, which is to say that we intuitively know that it is good without reference to any other source, and self-instantiating, because the object of *Agape*, which is *good-in-itself* and described in the rule, is realized in each instance in which the moral law is obeyed out of reverence for it. In other words, by willing in conformity with *Agape*, a morally conscious being instantiates it. Significantly, unlike Kant's categorical imperative, the rule articulated here contains within itself its own object and its own necessity.

It might be objected that, if the Moral Law were directly intuited, disgraceful phenomena such as slavery, genocide, and cannibalism could never occur or prevail for any length of time. That such phenomena may merely reflect man's shortcomings or societal denial of moral obligation, and not the nonexistence of the Moral Law, has already been explained. But I also believe that these phenomena more often than not are accompanied by a delusionary rationalization that the subjects of such abomination are less than human than their oppressors and therefore not entitled to the natural rights accorded to morally conscious beings under the Moral Law.

Having posited a universal, necessary, self-justifying, and self-instantiating moral law, the question that must finally be addressed is whether that law is known by internal intuition. This question may be answered in three ways, namely, by process of elimination of all other means of knowledge, by direct appeal to the epistemological process by which moral knowledge is obtained, and by appeal to human moral experience. Each of these means will now be employed.

The process of eliminating all types of philosophical approaches to the question of moral obligation other than internal intuition has been undertaken and completed in this chapter (subject to the justification of freedom as being dependent upon *Agape* to be provided in the sequel chapter). Radical moral skepticism, typified by Hume, has been discounted as being inconsistent with the fact of morality and generally being subject to the dispositive criticisms of radical skepticism generally. Materialist reductionist philosophies have also been disposed of as being incapable of providing satisfactory answers to the

---

9. Mark 12:28–31 (NAB).

Moral Standard Problem and the Consciousness Problem and, as we will see in the sequel chapter, to the other presuppositions of morality (i.e., the Free Will Problem and the Entity Problem). Subjective deontological philosophies have been shown to reduce to moral skepticism, which was rejected in the discussion of Hume. Objective, secular deontological philosophies have been shown to be unable to connect rational conduct with moral conduct. That leaves internal intuition as the only possible explanation of moral obligation.

That moral obligation must logically be known only by internal intuition is also demonstrable. Because practical reason is employed in answer to the question of how one ought to act in the empirical world, the moral philosopher is immediately presented with a bit of a conundrum. If moral experience is not to be found in the empirical world independently of the conduct of morally conscious beings, then the question arises as to how to connect *a priori* practical reason with empirical conduct. Kant's resolution to the problem is to examine moral knowledge with the goal of identifying the *a priori* elements in moral judgments and, in so doing, Kant hopes to identify the fundamental rational principles according to which human beings make moral judgments. For Kant, moral knowledge is therefore synthetic *a priori*. The problem with Kant's approach is that he treats each instance of moral conduct as if it is an empirical event and not the instantiation of a universal and necessary object of reason. But as we have seen this is a circular process because human beings are assumed to be ignorant of the categorical imperative when they engage in the moral conduct from which the categorical imperative is derived. To avoid the circularity implicit in seeking moral obligation on a synthetic basis, for a secular deontological approach to have any hope of success it would have to seek the common thread in moral judgments on an analytical basis. In analytical statements, such as "all bachelors are unmarried," the predicate of the sentence is contained in the concept of the subject. Because moral judgments entail the application of an *a priori* law to a contingent judgment, such as "I am required by the Moral Law to tell the truth in court," moral judgments may not be understood analytically. Instead, it can be seen that the Moral Law must be internally intuited and moral conduct must be a matter of applying the internally intuited moral law to empirical conduct. In the case of the Moral Law, reason stops at *Agape* and rests comfortably there. That is not to say that the Moral Law cannot be examined by reason; to the contrary, it must withstand the tests of universality, necessity, self-justification and self-instantiation, and in so doing its access to reason by direct intuition becomes apparent.

The final argument for internal intuition of moral obligation is internal intuition itself. The argument that direct perception is the final resting place for practical reason must also apply to direct perception; in other words, we can only know that we have direct perception by direct perception. To be clear, the arguments that have just been advanced in favor of the direct intuition of moral obligation based upon process of elimination and epistemology presume direct intuition. For example, it is argued that we know that *modus ponens* is true simply because its truth requires no explanation and we cannot even conceive of what sort of explanation might be available if we believed that we required one. But the conclusion that we know of the truth of *modus ponens* because we analytically intuit it depends upon our ability to experience its truth analytically, without reference to anything that is not directly or analytically intuited. Therefore, to complete the justification of direct perception of moral obligation we must offer an explanation of the experience as such.

I would like to start out on this topic by stating that my internal intuition of moral obligation includes, as it would seem it should, direct perception of not just the Moral Law but also its precondition, namely an autonomous soul. In the discussion had hitherto, I have gone to some lengths explaining my own direct perception of self as a morally conscious being. To avoid too much redundancy, I will only repeat here that my sense of self is as a persistent *noumenal* being who does not change with the passage of time or along with his own biology. I also have a direct perception of my own free will. That is to say, that in considering how I ought to act in a given set of circumstances, I not only assume my freedom but I know that it is real. My belief in my own freedom is based upon my direct perception of my own motives. When I act morally, not only do I know whether my action was out of reverence for the Moral Law or out of expedience, but I also understand the judgment that I make in undertaking such action to be qualitatively different than the judgment that I make when I choose between strawberry and chocolate ice cream. When I determine whether or not to act morally, I am judging between willing a morally required end or my own subjective end. When I choose the flavor of my desert, my judgment is how best to satisfy my own desire. This is not merely theoretical. There are, frankly, times when I act out of moral motive against a much greater subjective desire and in spite of a wish that no moral obligation existed; in other words, in such a case, I know that I have acted freely because in honoring a moral obligation any supporting subjective satisfaction is known to me to be of less personal value than the subjective satisfaction that would have attended serving my own subjective end. Any doubt that this is possible, may be eliminated by considering the ultimate sacrifice of a soldier for his country. It may not be seriously contended that the subjective satisfaction of doing so (which can only be felt prospectively) would outweigh the satisfaction of survival. The only possible argument is that the soldier would rather stand, fight, and die than turn and run, but in that case, the fact that the subjective satisfaction that would normally attend survival has been diminished or eliminated by the moral obligation is proof of the independence of the moral obligation that diminished or eliminated it.

Finally, I would like to describe my own experience of knowledge of the Moral Law itself. Certainly, that experience includes the totality of my consideration of it, including the presentation included in these passages. But my experience is fundamentally not as a mere being, or a mere thinking being, but as a fully autonomous, *morally conscious* being. The content of that experience is the same as the Moral Law, namely, that in all things I act subject to an obligation to treat all other morally conscious beings as ends, not means. The nature of that obligation is such that I feel myself to be the object of *Agape*, which means that I am both an end and the means by which *Agape* instantiates its ends. I can express this more directly in two ways. The first is that I cannot imagine myself as free from moral obligation; in other words I cannot think moral obligation away without changing my own intuition of the soul that I am. The second is even more direct, namely, that I cannot imagine, as a general maxim of my own behavior, treating other beings as means to my own personal satisfaction. If I try to imagine either, my own humanity utterly disappears and what is left behind is an unrecognizably grotesque character whom I would shudder to think of meeting.

I would like to close this chapter by referring once again to the Golden Rule of the book of Leviticus and two greatest commandments as given to us by Jesus in the Gospel of Mark (and also the Gospel of Matthew). My objective in doing so is not to make a religious point but rather a philosophical one. To the religious Jewish, the book of Leviticus, and to religious Christians, the book of Leviticus and Jesus's word, are the revealed word of God and, as such, are pure truth and to be taken on faith. On this, I concur. But the philosophical point is this: if the Bible did not reflect our own internal intuition, it would have been received differently than it has been and would have almost certainly faded away long ago. So it should be expected and not surprising that in identifying the Moral Law as reflecting the obligation to instantiate *Agape* that we arrive at a religiously familiar place. Some moral skeptics might argue to a different conclusion, namely, that the conformity of the Moral Law presented here to biblical teaching merely shows that the Moral Law has no greater significance than anything else that is learned at mother's knee. But that objection is completely unsound. It requires us to ask: where did mother, grandmother, and great grandmother learn it and how and why did human beings arrive at a conception of morality that is so patently at odds with their naturally short, nasty, and brutish lives?

11

Moral Freedom

THE DEPENDENCE OF FREEDOM ON AGAPE

Not only is it impossible for material reductionists to overcome the hurdle of identifying an empirical basis for moral obligation, but even if they could meet that challenge, they would face another similarly impassable obstacle, namely, that of justifying in material terms the freedom necessary for man to discharge that obligation. At the root of the materialist difficulties lies the impossibility of reconciling the natural sequence of materially determined (whether causally or probabilistically) events, which they assert describe all reality, with any notion that human beings are *morally* accountable for their actions. The classic and uncharacteristically laughably simplistic attempted empirical resolution to the difficulty is offered by Hobbes, who asserts that freedom exists where an agent finds "no stop in doing what he has the will, desire, or inclination to do."[1] But this line, including all of the refinements to it that continue to this day to be enthusiastically proposed by materialists, represents a transparent attempt to define the problem away by supplanting the concept of freedom with a concept of moral accountability that is completely independent of freedom; it merely asserts that one is responsible for one's actions unless they are compelled by external forces or engaged in under certain (but not all) circumstances in which one's mental capacity is compromised. But what Hobbes offers is a definition of *license*, not freedom.

The rationalists have done little better. Plato, Descartes, and Leibnitz are all mind-body dualists and accordingly cannot effectively connect the willing soul with the actions of a material body. Spinoza, a monist who equates reality with an all-encompassing God, is forced to reduce man to a mere mode of existence.

Not surprisingly, Kant stands in a class of his own on the question of free will because, although he is squarely an empiricist in epistemology, he is willing to speculate on free will as an unknowable Idea. As has already been explained in much detail, Kant identifies free will as the supreme principle of morality but, because Kant's empirical epistemology binds him to determinism and will not allow him to locate freedom in the material world, he must relegate freedom to a special type of *noumenal* phenomenon

---

1. Hobbes, *Leviathan*, 108.

which, unlike the *things-in-themselves*, must and can only be *presumed* to be real. Although Kant's moral philosophy is unsuccessful, there is genius in his formulation insofar as it detaches freedom from *mere* objective reason and associates freedom with moral obligation itself.[2] However, because Kant faithfully follows his unduly limited empirical epistemology to its conclusion, he gets the connection between freedom and moral obligation backward. Instead of moral obligation requiring freedom as its supreme principle or presupposition as Kant holds, *it is man's cognition of the Moral Law that provides him with the freedom to discharge it.* Indeed, it is moral consciousness that liberates man from the chains of subjective desire, including the needs for acceptance and approval that, as Hume noted, often attend otherwise apparently moral behavior, and it is moral consciousness that separates man from animal.

Although the phenomenologists are neither mainstream nor reductionists, given our regard for their methodology and Husserl's express characterization of phenomenology as transcendental idealism, we should make mention here that phenomenology requires approaching freedom from a completely different perspective than the philosophies just mentioned. Under phenomenology, freedom is simply given to consciousness, in the case of Husserl, and fundamental to *Dasein's* way of Being, in the case of Heidegger. With respect to the latter: How could *Dasein* be the temporalizing being for whom his own Being is an issue unless he were at liberty to be such? Indeed, it is doubtful that Heidegger would even recognize freedom as a meaningful concept for, under his ontology, the notion of determinism, which relies on material reductionism, must be understood to result from the obvious mistake of taking *Dasein* as a present-at-hand object.

Before moving on to a rebuttal of determinism on traditional grounds, a final point in critique of the phenomenologist position is necessary. Our reinterpretation of *Dasein* in chapter 9, "Being and Intelligibility," as not merely Being-towards-the-end but as Being-towards-God, which is based upon the codetermination of Being and logic, requires assessment of the impact of moral obligation on *Dasein's* possible ways of Being. Under our analysis, *Dasein* is not at liberty "to become who it is" without regard for the Moral Law and, indeed, the Being of *Dasein* ontologically includes a *telos* that is Being-toward the perfection that it can never achieve. Under Heidegger's ontology, the only restraint on *Dasein* is its *thrownness*, but under our reinterpretation of *Dasein*, moral obligation, which is necessary, universal, and transcendent, operates as a *constraint that is independent of* thrownness. As a result, it is not correct to say, as a phenomenologist might, that *Dasein's* Being is circumstantial but unregulated; rather, under our reinterpretation, *Dasein* must be understood as the being who *discloses itself to itself as Being-moral* (with "moral" being used to signify being subject to moral obligation). Whereas Heidegger might say that Being-moral is a type of not-Being insofar as it represents a denial of the authentic Self in favor of a mistaken notion of a moral Self, under our reinterpretation, precisely the opposite is the case, namely, that authentic Being *is* moral Being.

At this point, we will leave the discourse on phenomenology behind, and focus on the question of free will versus determinism as that question is traditionally considered.

---

2. There is a subtlety here that must be understood. Although Kant's categorical imperative is justified wholly by appeal to objective reason, Kant insists that freedom, its presupposition, may not be proved solely by appeal to objective reason.

For purposes of this discussion, we will accept the materialist premise that if man is reducible, then he must be fully determined. Of course, on that premise, *modus tollens* tells us that if man is free, then he is not materially reducible.

Man's intuition of freedom is such that, except where urgent biological necessities are concerned, he generally considers it to be applicable to all of his actions whether or not they are attended by ethical considerations. But a little reflection shows that this is not necessarily the case. There is a distinction between will and free will, the latter of which is, as its name implies, merely one type of the former. Will is a faculty of reason by which a rational entity realizes (i.e., brings about), to the extent of its capacity to do so, its objects in accordance with its ideas. Will is the rational faculty by which a rational entity implements all of its ends, including its subjectively *chosen* objects and its objectively required moral objects. Will requires conscious decision-making and action in furtherance of the decision consciously made. Will is reason in action. By contrast, that form of *freedom* which is of interest to us in these pages, namely *moral freedom,* is not freedom to determine the manner in which an entity will satisfy his subjective desires; instead, moral freedom consists in *the ability to act independently of one's subjective desires*. For the remainder of the discussion in this chapter, consistent with our acceptance of the reductionist premise, we will treat moral freedom as though it is the only alternative to determined action (i.e., we will not allow for the possibility of non-moral freedom).

Reductionists might tell us that the *illusion* of freedom is a consequence of the fact that man's reason gives him access to the fact that there may be one or more alternatives to each and every course of action chosen by him. But the fact that he is aware of, and may carefully consider alternative courses of action, does not imply that the choice he makes is anything other than materially determined. On the other hand, where ethical considerations are applicable, man may feel himself morally bound to act in a certain way, but, ironically, this is precisely the case in which man's moral freedom is manifest. Man's moral freedom depends fully on the fact that he may elect to heed the call of obligation in spite of his subjective desires.

It is not an overstatement to assert that the close association of choice among subjective desires or maxims of behavior, which will hereinafter be referred to as "choice" or, correlatively, "choosing," "chosen," or "to choose," and moral freedom, fuels much bad philosophy on this question. Most people do not consciously distinguish between choice, which under the traditional mode of discourse seems and for purposes of the discussion here will be presumed to be fully materially governed, and moral freedom, which depends upon knowledge of the transcendent Moral Law. Under the circumstances of the secular blind spot characterizing current day mainstream philosophy, neither do most philosophers. The situation is exacerbated by the fact that much of the time people make subjective *choices* either to engage in conduct that has the same object as truly moral behavior without recognizing the importance of the role played by motive or to place subjective desires ahead of moral obligation as if one has the moral right to do so. But a moral end, if chosen as the object of a subjective desire for approval, as Hume suggests is often the case, does not arise from the exercise of freedom and a decision to ignore moral obligation represents moral freedom only if one defines free will to include the freedom to refuse to discharge a moral obligation in favor of a materially determined desire.

The situation is also muddied by the presence in man of objective reason, which enables him to take into account the circumstances of other people who might be affected by his actions. Indeed, as noted in the prequel chapter, thinkers as capable as Nagel have suggested that man's ability to take into account the interests of others implies the freedom (and obligation) to act on that knowledge. But this is clearly not the case. The ability to consider others merely supports subjective choice in their favor whenever it is made. Morally conscious entities can only escape their own subjectivity if they act in satisfaction of a self-independent *obligation* that is indifferent to that subjectivity. That is what the Moral Law is and that is where moral freedom arises. Accordingly, the definition of free will that is important to philosophers cannot be a morally neutral one.

The prevalent philosophical confusion regarding free will is underscored by the fact that the best starting point in its consideration is not among the great philosophers but instead with the economists. Economics is the social science that is concerned with the manner in which human beings allocate the scarce resources available to them for satisfaction of their desires. It is the social science most directly concerned with the nature and implications of human *choice*. The presuppositions of the ironically called *free* market economics are that man intuitively feels himself to be free in all of his actions and that, in acting in the world, man employs his reason to attain satisfaction of his subjective desires to the extent of his resources. As it turns out, that satisfaction of such desires entails *choice* (not freedom) is of little or no interest to economists (except to the extent they seek, as a very small number sometimes do, to inject ethics into the market place) because their first order concerns are the allocation of resources and pricing of goods and services and not the moral consequences of the foregoing. For the economist, a free market is one in which its actors are allowed to apply their resources to the satisfaction of their needs in any manner that they see fit. Nevertheless, that such markets require unencumbered choice as their precondition, not moral freedom, neither affects the validity of the economic analysis or the capacity of the economic methodology to illustrate the difference between choice and freedom. That most economists do not recognize it as a philosophical issue is apparent from the fact that, when economists introduce any notion of objective ethics into economic behavior, it takes the form of imposing external rules that diminish their philosophically incorrect notion of a free market.

Although man employs objective reason in both ordering and determining how to attain his ends, where such ends are subjective in nature, under mainstream philosophical concepts, it seems clear that they are materially determined, or, at the very least, that there is no compelling reason to assume otherwise. Consider, by way of example, a hunter with a need for both food and shelter, each of which is a basic biological necessity where the end is survival. Given a certain set of conditions, the hunter may determine that he must first obtain sustenance before he can construct shelter. He may further determine that if he hunts abundant and easily trapped rabbit rather than more savory but difficult larger game he will have sufficient time to construct basic tools and use them to build a shelter before it becomes too cold for his survival. Under such circumstances, the hunter may have an *ordinal* schedule of desires for satisfaction during daylight as follows: (1) big game for consumption, (2) rabbit for consumption, (3) shelter tonight, and (4) tools for construction of a house. The schedule tells us not the order in which the hunter will pursue his ends but rather the order in which he would pursue his ends if they were all independently achievable. But the hunter also has a *cardinal* schedule of desires, which reflects the quantity of the value that the hunter associates with each end. Economists often heuristically express such valuation in hypothetical units of satisfaction (not unlike monetary units) called "*utils*" and we will follow that course. The amount of *utils* assigned to each end will be highest with respect to the most desired item and decline in accordance with the *ordinal* ranking. So, for example, our hunter may assign big game a value of 100 *utils*, rabbit a value of 75 *utils*, shelter a value of 50 *utils*, and tools a value of 10 *utils*. It will be observed that there are limits to what the hunter may accomplish in a day with his labor and available natural resources. If the hunter were able by his labor to obtain precisely all of these items and he valued all of them more than resting, we would conclude that the subjective value (to the hunter) of his labor is precisely 235 *utils*. However, if we assume that the hunter is not so capable and can only achieve satisfaction of some of his desires and in certain combinations since, for example, he must first produce tools before he can construct shelter, the rational course of action for the hunter, will be to allocate his resources to the attainment of ends whose aggregate value is the highest number of *utils* that the hunter can obtain in a day. Although the hunter's greatest yearning is for big game, to which he assigns a value of 100 *utils*, assume that the hunter cannot attain it without foregoing tools, shelter, and rabbit, to which he assigns an aggregate value of 135 *utils*. In this case, the hunter will settle for rabbit instead of larger game in order to have the time to build tools for the construction of shelter and to construct the shelter as well. It can be seen that, although the logic employed by the hunter to order his needs and develop a plan for their attainment is undeniably objective in nature, the hunter's ends are subjective and flow from his nature as an organic entity trying to survive in a state of nature. It is noteworthy that the specific items or their order tell us nothing about the emotional needs of the hunter. Even a pathological person, with no appreciation of moral obligation, has a utility schedule by which he determines how to act.

Now suppose the hunter's religion includes an absolute *requirement* that he spend an hour in prayer to the goddess Artemis prior to commencing any hunt. If the moral requirement to pray is to have any meaning at all, the hunter's subjective schedule of desires is irrelevant to the question of whether he *ought* to pray prior to hunting. Indeed, the moral requirement of prayer is akin to any objective *factor* which, to the extent that it limits the hunter's ability to satisfy all of his ends by consuming the time that would otherwise be available for their satisfaction, is, except as described below, like any other factor that contributes to the scarcity of the environment to fulfill his needs. Therefore, prayer may not be included in his ordinal schedule of subjective desires and the amount of value, if any, the hunter assigns to prayer may not be included in his cardinal schedule of desires. For the hunter, praying to Artemis is simply something that the hunter ought to do as a condition to his commencing satisfaction of his needs regardless of his subjective desire to tend to his pressing needs. In effect, the obligation to pray for an hour merely diminishes the aggregate utility of subjective ends the hunter may accomplish. If the hunter believes that there is sufficient time to pray, hunt rabbit, build tools, and construct shelter, his rational course is to accomplish those ends in that order. But what happens if the hour consumed in prayer will preclude the hunter's constructing shelter?

In that event the hunter has two options. He can *choose* to forego prayer in favor of satisfying his material needs or he can *freely elect* to satisfy his moral obligation to pray and only afterward hunt rabbit, and as a result he will be forced to risk the perils of spending the night exposed to the elements. If the hunter *chooses* the first option, he does so based solely on subjective grounds; indeed, it may be said that the total utility to the hunter of hunting and building shelter exceeds the *utility* to him of prayer. In that case he has *chosen* to violate the moral law by subjectively valuing satisfaction of his moral obligation and then choosing satisfaction of other needs over it. If, on the other hand, the hunter elects to pray first, it will either be because the utility of prayer to him exceeds the utility of the shelter that he will forego for one night or *because he correctly recognizes that the moral requirement is of such a nature that it precludes any valuation at all*. The first case might apply where the hunter's superstitions create an anxiety that can only be ameliorated by prayer, in which case the hunter will have made a subjective *choice*; he can be said to value the gratification (i.e., the relief from anxiety) received from prayer more highly than the discomfort of foregoing shelter. If, however, the second case is applicable, then, in obeying the moral requirement, the hunter has acted *freely of his subjective desires* altogether and there is no valuation involved. In that case, it may very well be true that the hunter subjectively values shelter more than prayer but nevertheless elects the latter because he understands the nature of his moral obligation. In that case, the hunter can be seen not to *choose* prayer but to freely elect prayer as his end, and in doing so, his action can be seen to be genuinely moral and fully independent of materially causal factors.

This example illustrates the great and fascinating diremption between conduct that is and is not attended by moral obligation. Conduct that is not so attended (if there is any) may be engaged in with great license but because, upon mainstream analysis, the course *chosen* will be materially determined, it cannot be said to be free. Conduct that is morally required admits of no subjective alternative or valuation. It is profoundly important to note that, under any philosophy that holds morality to be subjective, morality and freedom may not coexist. If morality is subjective to the willing subject, he will merely place his purported moral need on his subjective utility schedule and act in accordance with that. In such a case, morality may be said to be determined and there will be no freedom. If morality is measured against a subjective societal rule, then again the willing subject can simply place the cost of non-compliance on his utility schedule (i.e., in the form of avoidance of socially meted punishment) and determine whether a particular course of action is more valuable than the risk of paying dues to society. In both these cases, there is no meaningful moral imperative.

Before proceeding further, it should be noted that the above example is attended by the complicating factor that it is likely that the hunter errs in believing that praying to Artemis is morally obligated. That raises the question of whether action can be said to be free when it is sincerely taken in spite of subjective action to the contrary. The difficulty is less acute than it might otherwise seem because, for action to be moral, it must be in accordance with the Moral Law, not some other mistaken ethical standard (which can only be thought to be given to reason deterministically) and, it therefore seems better as a philosophical matter to take the position that freedom cannot arise by mistake, however well-intended the mistaken action might be.

Although, as noted, Kant brilliantly connects freedom with moral obligation, Kant's determinist empiricism leads him to conclude that that freedom cannot be proven to exist but, instead, must only be presumed to exist as a precondition of the fact of morality. I disagree. The proof of man's freedom lies in the fact that man sometimes acts as morally required in spite of contrary subjective desires and sometimes *chooses* not to do so. To demonstrate the veracity that man sometimes acts without regard for his subjective desires all one needs to do is examine his own motives. If I act to achieve a morally obligated end, even though I would prefer to do otherwise, I have privileged and direct knowledge that my motivation is morally pure and without consideration of my subjective desire. Those who would deny freedom (usually with an atheistic agenda) might argue that I only *think* that I am acting to satisfy a moral obligation and that, if I could fully understand my own psychology, I would find that my motivation to act morally was the result of a subjective, subconscious desire. There are two responses to this objection. One is that it is one thing to say that I may not know myself sufficiently well to understand why I might *choose* chocolate over strawberry ice cream, but it is quite another to say that I do not understand myself sufficiently well to understand that I am mistaken in my belief that, when I act morally, I only think that I am overriding a subjective desire to the contrary. In the former case, I know that I am making a subjective *choice* and might fully explain my motivation by saying that I *chose* chocolate *because I felt like it*. Where I elect to act morally in spite of a contrary desire, I will assert that my conduct is objectively determined to satisfy a moral obligation, *even though I felt like doing something quite different*. It should be noted that the question of my motive is not the correctness of my moral judgment but only my determination to follow a course that I assess to be morally required and that determination is one which, as a morally conscious being, I am undeniably privileged to make. A second response is that certain moral conduct cannot possibly be reasonably understood to be in furtherance of subjective desire. It would be absurd to suggest, for example, that one might subjectively prefer to endure torture and death over committing apostasy, yet there have been (and regrettably continue to be) many instances of people who have done (and are doing) so. In such cases, the only reasonable characterization is that the person who refuses to disavow his religion (whatever it might be) endures such treatment because he believes it is morally impermissible to commit apostasy regardless of the pain and suffering he will be required to endure as a result.

Freedom can also be proven to exist as the result of direct intuition of real moral obligation. The proof of freedom proceeds along the following lines:

1. If moral obligation exists, then it must be either subjective or objective in nature.

2. If moral obligation is subjective in nature, it is indistinguishable from any other subjective desire and may be ordered by man on a scale that includes subjective desires that are inconsistent with it.

3. If moral obligation may be ordered by man on a scale that includes subjective desires that are inconsistent with it, then some subjective desires may at the whim

of man be placed above it on such a list. (This is because if moral obligation were *required* to be ranked first on any list of subjective desires moral obligation could not be said to be subjective).

4. If some subjective desires may be placed above moral obligation on a scale of subjective desires, then moral obligation can be disregarded in favor of such subjective desires.

5. If moral obligation can be disregarded in favor of a subjective desire, then it is not a moral obligation, which, by its very nature, mandates action in spite of subjective desires.

6. Therefore, if moral obligation exists, it must be objective in nature.

7. If moral obligation is *objective obligation* (i.e., self-instantiating *Agape*), then it must be obeyed regardless of any subjective consideration.

8. Man sometimes satisfies his objective moral obligation in spite of and sometimes acts in furtherance of a contradictory subjective desire, without making any effort to satisfy his objective moral obligation.

9. If man sometimes satisfies his moral obligation in spite of a contradictory subjective desire, he must have the freedom to determine to satisfy his moral obligation without regard for his mechanistically determined subjective values.

10. Therefore, freedom exists.

The preceding syllogism shows that direct intuition of objective moral obligation, the warrant for which was discussed in the prequel chapter, implies that morally conscious entities possess free will. The implication is that one may not assert that moral obligation is subjective or that man is free even though there is no such moral obligation.

If freedom were concerned with morally neutral choices, such as whether to go out for a run or stay home and read, the conflict between the human intuition of freedom and the physical law of causation might be one for psychologists, not philosophers. However, freedom is most acutely considered to be a precondition or, in the case of transcendent realism, a coincident condition to moral responsibility and, because of the theological and sociological importance of moral responsibility, freedom in the context of moral responsibility must be one of the primary areas of concern for philosophers.

FREEDOM AND ACCOUNTABILITY

When a man disregards a moral requirement we believe ourselves to be justified in holding him morally responsible for his action. For such a belief to be rational, it must be based upon the premise that man is free to act morally. If a man's action is fully determined it makes no sense to criticize it on objective moral grounds. That is not to say that the right of the individual or society to defend against, punish, or deter certain sorts of conduct is at all dependent upon freedom. It merely means that for conduct to be immoral, it must be chosen in spite of the freedom to act morally. Ironically, a society may retain under all *moral* circumstances the right to address conduct that is *undesirable*, whether or not it is freely engaged in, especially because deterrence may serve as a factor even in causally determined conduct.

The nature of moral accountability and its close relationship to legal accountability merit additional consideration. In this regard, an example involving murder, one of the more heinous crimes, will be illuminating. Consider a scenario in which a husband, finding his wife engaging in an act of infidelity, determines to murder his wife and her lover in revenge even though he knows he will be arrested and incarcerated for life. In such an event, it can be said that the husband values revenge more highly than liberty. Before discovering his wife's indiscretion, the husband had a utility schedule that included a host of items the procurement of which required that he be at liberty. After his discovery, the husband places his act of revenge, which comes at the cost of long-term imprisonment or worse, as punishment, ahead of attainment of all of those items. If the husband commits the double murder both illegal and immoral action are involved. If the elements of the crime of murder are present, the husband will be held by the legal system of his society to account for his crime. If the murdering husband has the capacity to appreciate the moral wrongness of his act of revenge, we will hold him not only legally, but also morally, responsible for his action. In other words, we will assert that in this example, no matter how much liberty he is willing to give up to achieve vengeance, *he has no moral right to act in accordance with his utility schedule.* But how can this be so? Unlike the items on the utility schedule which are subjectively determined by the husband, *the prohibition against murder is objective, necessary, and universal.* Stated simply, we hold that one *ought* not to murder another, no matter how strong his sense of aggrievement or his desire for revenge.

Note that, because the prohibition against murder is objective, there is nowhere that compliance with it can be placed on the utility schedule, which, in our example, includes only the subjective desires of the husband. He might list "murdering traitorous lovers" above all of the actions that require his remaining out of prison, or even be willing to lose his own life as punishment, but it matters not how he values the act of vengeance; he is morally prohibited from acting upon his desire for revenge no matter what. Note also that we consider someone to be culpable even if his action is in response to (presumed) psychologically determined forces. That he was raised in a violent home, that his mother was unfaithful to his father and that his father then abandoned him, and other similar factors may be taken into account as a legal matter in considering his punishment for the crime, but they do not relieve him of the moral responsibility for an act of murder. Why do we hold someone accountable regardless of the materially determined factors behind his conduct? The reason is because, as a *rational actor*, he knows that his conduct is *per se* wrong and that, as a result, no matter the circumstances of his background, we consider him to have the freedom to follow the objective rule of moral reason in spite of his own subjective utility schedule that places preeminent value upon revenge. That is to say, we regard objective moral reason as being absolutely compelling and, as a result, absent exonerating circumstances,[3] moral reason affords rational entities the freedom to act in accordance with it no matter what the material factors are.

---

3. Such circumstances include necessity, duress, automatism, self-defense, mistake, and lack of capacity.

THE FAILURE OF COMPATABILISM

So far, we have considered freedom without reference to the metaphysical requirements of beings that might possess it, which we referred to in the prequel chapter as the Entity Problem. Instead, we have focused upon the distinction between subjective needs and objective moral requirements as they relate to all human action. We have noted that free will is the faculty of reason by which a rational entity may elect a morally correct course of action notwithstanding his materially determined desires. But it can be readily seen that a complete understanding of freedom requires analysis of the core definitional concepts of the Entity Problem in addition to the Free Will Problem and Moral Standard Problem. It cannot be gainsaid that any discussion of the problem of free will can only occur within the context of objective reason, including an understanding of what is morally right, which, under transcendent realism, means as part and parcel of the *Logos*. Because transcendent realism views man as a psychosomatic unity comprising body and soul, transcendent philosophy contains elements of monistic idealism and as a result offers a solution to the problem of free will that does not suffer from the infirmities of dualism or materialism. The answer provided by transcendent realism is that for an entity to be morally responsible, it must be a free, self-conscious, rational being (with a persistent self), with knowledge of its existence as an object of *Agape*. Under transcendent realism, moral reason *qua* reason is part of the *Logos* and, as such, is transcendent; although moral reason is applicable to empirical action, moral reason is not materially sourced but is a by-product of access to *Agape*, and moral freedom is nowhere found in the material world, except when it is brought to it by a rational being with direct access to the *Logos*.

Perhaps no topic other than the Free Will Problem so clearly demonstrates the bankruptcy both generally of analytical approaches to philosophical problems that do not start with a clearly articulated epistemology and in particular of compatibilist materialist reductionism. This is because, in either case, instead of addressing each of the several problems identified above as the essential components of the Free Will Problem, the treatment given by these philosophies is to eliminate some or all of them from consideration either expressly or by pretending they do not exist. Sometimes, the unstated underlying assumptions of compatibilists, such as that rational agency must be understood wholly in organic terms, may be divined. Oftentimes, such assumptions remain obscure. Although the Free Will Problem cannot be fully addressed without an understanding of moral justice (i.e., the Moral Standard Problem), most of the modern discussion assumes a common sense of moral justice and deliberately avoids exploration of how we come to have it or whether it is itself compatible with materialism, inappropriately relegating those questions to the study of ethics.

Because few modern philosophers are willing to follow a materialist reductionist premise to morally empty philosophies such as hedonism or nihilism or to acknowledge that the solution to the Free Will Problem might be outside their philosophical school and therefore call their entire project into question, the focus of modern philosophy has been almost exclusively on the question of whether determinism can be shown to be compatible with free will. One would have hoped that the obvious fruitlessness of this line of inquiry would have precluded its pursuit; however, because materialist reductionists cannot deny the intuition of freedom and sentimentally must accept some concept of moral obligation they seem to have no choice but to proceed in this fashion. In any event, following along with the argument, at least in broad chunks, will show both the unacceptability of the analytical approach to the question and the vacuity of the compatibilist arguments.

The course that modern compatabilism has chosen is one that is more commonly a part of politics than philosophy. Most people, informed by the ordinary meaning of words, would agree that moral accountability presupposes free will which is characteristic of mankind. More specifically, most people would agree that for a person to have been free to take a particular course of action, *he must have been able to take an alternative course of action*. For the layman, this goes without saying, because freedom of action is precisely how he experiences the world. In those rare cases where action is coerced (e.g., at the barrel of a gun) otherwise objectionable action is almost always excused. However, the compatibilists avoid taking on directly the question of how a fully determined entity could ever be said to choose freely from among two alternatives and attempt to redefine the question in a manner that is more manageable. The compatibilists propose to define "free will" as *the unique ability of persons to exercise control over their conduct in the fullest manner necessary for moral responsibility*. That this formulation is question-begging is totally ignored. Instead, the compatibilists hope to show a set of conditions upon which a being whose actions are considered to be mechanistically determined may be appropriately held accountable for them nevertheless. Rather than attempting the impossible task of explaining the human experience of freedom in material terms, the compatibilist project is to explain moral responsibility without any presupposition of freedom.

Compatibilists have advanced many creative propositions in their favor, including classic compatabilism, the argument against alternative possibilities, morally reactive attitudes, and new dispositionalism. Under classic compatabilism, which is the offering of both Hobbes and Hume, one is morally responsible for his actions if he does what he desires in the absence of coercion or external impediments. Under this view a person is not the ultimate source but the mediator in a long chain of causation. For the classic compatibilist, moral culpability merely requires congruity of desire and action. True freedom, as has been postulated in these pages, is irrelevant. Under the argument against alternative possibilities, which is offered by Harry Frankfurt, the fact that a person could not have done otherwise, does not mean that he did not freely choose to do as he did. An example in support of this thesis, is where Jones freely shoots Smith (believing that he had the freedom to do so) even though Black would have coerced him to shoot Smith had Jones not chosen to do so. There are at least two problems with Frankfurt's example. One is that it rarely applies to ordinary experience. The other is that Jones's decision to shoot Smith was freely taken regardless of whether he would have been coerced to do so had he decided otherwise. If one generalizes Frankfurt's example to ordinary human action, it may be restated that human action is always undertaken under an illusion of freedom and that such an illusion is sufficient for purposes of ethical responsibility. But if freedom is in fact known to be illusory, what is the basis for holding someone responsible for their actions? One possible answer is the intention of the person who engages in prohibited conduct, which is the answer proposed by P. F. Strawson. Under the morally reactive attitudes model offered by Strawson, responsibility depends not on freedom but upon whether *ill will* is present. The obvious problem with this (and Frankfurt's) formulation is that the ill will upon which moral responsibility is purported to be justified must itself be determined by materially reducible forces. To respond to this question, Strawson abandons philosophy altogether and resorts to sociology and psychology. Strawson argues that moral sociology is an inherent fact of human life and therefore cannot be changed by recourse to abstract philosophical concerns. Strawson also argues that we are psychologically incapable of abandoning moral responsibility so these arguments are a fool's errand. These arguments leave Strawson's position discreditable on the same grounds as the subjective argument for moral obligation provided in the prequel chapter.

New dispositionalism argues that sufficient freedom for moral accountability is present even though an action is the determined result of a given set of circumstances or laws because, under a different set of circumstances or laws, an action might have been different. Perhaps this is a way of saying that I am hard-wired to act immorally under certain conditions and not others and the fact that I act immorally under circumstances over which I have no control does not relieve me of responsibility. But this removes freedom from the equation altogether and places us at the mercy of circumstances beyond our control. Under some conditions, most people would commit immoral acts of some consequence. If the fact that one does and the other does not is completely dependent upon the luck of the draw, why would we hold one accountable and another not? If the answer is that under the circumstances in question, most people would not be disposed to commit the immoral act, then what is being offered is a subjective, sociological, and comparative explanation of culpability that has nothing to do with freedom or morality.

All of these compatibilist arguments, and other similar arguments, either disregard freedom altogether or seek to label as free something that appears to involve freedom at one level but that is fully determined at a higher level. In doing so, the compatibilists are substituting an argument that they must lose, namely, that determinism and freedom are compatible for an argument that requires resort to metaphysical considerations that they fail to address, namely, that determinism is incompatible with moral responsibility. A glaring example is the absence of any discussion of the Entity Problem. It would seem that under determinism a mere self-conscious organism would fit the bill. But materialist reductionism cannot explain self-consciousness and will not acknowledge that a mere material organism is ontologically different from dead matter. Instead, such an organism is characterized as an "agent" and regarded as merely a phase in a causal sequence. But that raises a question which reductionists cannot well answer: On what basis do you hold an ever-changing organism morally responsible for an act or omission that occurred at a prior time, perhaps when not a single atom present in the responsible party is the same as the atoms of the perpetrator? Another example is the absence of discussion of the Moral Standard Problem. In this regard, the compatibilists seem to assume without discussion that commonly held notions of morality are subjective but are nevertheless sufficient for analysis of moral responsibility. But, as noted, subjective standards neither support freedom nor moral responsibility. These deficiencies illustrate that analytical philosophy, which seeks to treat fundamental philosophical problems in isolation from one another and is here represented by compatabilism, is a flawed approach.

12

The Supreme Principle of Being and Intelligibility

THE NATURE OF THE SUBSISTENT WORLD

So far, we have posited that objective knowledge requires an orderly universe and rationally conscious entities with direct intuition of the structure and rules of thought. We have also posited moral obligation and the freedom to disregard subjective considerations in order to satisfy it, both of which depend upon morally conscious entities possessing direct intuition of *Agape*. In our journey to this point, we have rejected an ontologically closed empirical world as being insufficiently robust to explain its own intelligibility or to justify the common human experience of moral obligation. Although we have drawn much from Kant's epistemology, we have also rejected his transcendental "empiricism" as being circular in its presuppositions and mistaken in its conclusion that knowledge ends at the boundaries of the sensible world. Similarly, our examination of the three questions asked by Heidegger led us to the co-determination of Being and logic, the Supreme Principle of Being and Intelligibility, and the reinterpretation of *Dasein* as Being-towards-God. The *Logos*, as we have postulated it, comprising as it does the structure and rules of thought, the conditions of the intelligibility of objects of thought and of the senses, and the basis for moral obligation, contains within itself the necessity of its own existence independently of the souls who have direct intuition of it. The *Logos* is, as a result, neither empirical nor merely transcendental, but *transcendent*.

Some precision is required about what we mean when we say that the *Logos* is *transcendent*. In doing so, we are asserting that the *Logos* is necessary, universal, self-justifying, and self-instantiating and, therefore, that it has an enduring subsistence that is completely independent of the existence of any or all empirical beings. To make the point most forcefully, the complete disappearance of the empirical world and its inhabitants would not affect the subsistence of the *Logos*. If all non-divine, rationally conscious entities were to disappear, the *Logos* would subsist and, if other such entities were to reemerge, the *Logos* would be there, waiting to inform their Being.

The distinction between transcendent realism and Kant's transcendental idealism is far greater than the asserted scope of applicability of reason; indeed, the distinction is about the scope of valid human experience. Transcendental idealism is exclusively concerned with the applicability of pure reason to empirical experience, which it asserts is the only experience as to which empirical beings can attain knowledge. As a result of that assertion, Kant not only accepts, but also goes to great lengths to attempt demonstration of, the unknowability of the traditional objects of metaphysics, including, most importantly, the self as a real subsistent entity, which he does in spite of postulating the self (in the form of the unity of apperception) as the supreme principle of all synthetic (i.e., empirical) knowledge. In contrast, transcendent realism starts with direct intuition of self as a real, substantive entity and shows that the other objects traditionally considered to be the subject of metaphysics can be known epistemologically by the same direct intuition. The approach of transcendent realism is not new; to the contrary, it is common to many rationalist philosophies and dates back at least to Plato.

The grounds for the independent reality of the *Logos* are several. First, for an object to be intelligible, it must be orderly; otherwise, the apprehending subject would be imposing its own order on chaos (or, as some philosophers have it, nothingness) and therefore creating its own reality. Second, for the apprehending entity to make sense of an object, it must have intuition of an objective rationality that corresponds to the order of the object and which can inform that which is presented to the senses. If such rationality were subjective, then the apprehending subject would again be creating its own reality. Third, for objective knowledge to occur there must be a real and persistent, knowing self. Such a self is necessary to abstract such knowledge from empirical experience and to understand the Being of beings, including itself. Skepticism about the self is incoherent because it is the skepticism of a self and must be justified upon an objective reason to which it must deny itself access. Any attempt to conjure up from empirical reality a merely "formal" self cannot achieve such permanence, is circular in its dependence upon knowledge of the empirical reality of which it purports to be the presupposition, and compels a solipsistic conclusion. And the supplanting of individual persons with a single, absolute, and universal consciousness is unstable solipsism writ large and impossible to reconcile with the experience of the individuals whom it denies.

The question naturally arises as to how we should understand a world that is not given to the senses or whether it is even coherent to speak of transcendence as comprising a world. A good place to start in answering these questions is the simple observation that the empirical world, which is upon the common understanding conceptually separate from the transcendent world, is understood within the framework of space and time. Although, as has been considered at length, some empiricists take the view that space and time are real in the sense that they exist as an integral part of empirical reality independently of the experience of any sentient observer, we have expressed disagreement with that proposition and, following Kant, have argued in favor of the view that space and time are the forms of empirical cognition that human beings bring to the raw data presented to the senses. With that understanding, the empirical world is seen to be a world of material objects and relationships among such objects that are organized and understood by human reason in space and time. It is commonly stated that transcendent entities, if they exist, are by definition outside of space and time, which is sometimes glibly referred to as existing "nowhere and nowhen." Cute as this phraseology may be, it is utterly incomprehensible and, to the extent that meaning may be attributed to it, suggests that there is a physical universe and a transcendent universe that is somehow *located* apart from it. Such a conception flows from the mainstream empirical view of space and time as being part of empirical reality but that conception adds unnecessary complexity and, not surprisingly, by filling up an infinite universal topography, it presents a virtual blockade against anything that might be said to subsist non-empirically. However, if one adopts the view that space and time are merely the forms of cognition, it is readily apparent that to say that there is a transcendent reality simply means that *there is a reality to which the cognitive framework of space and time does not apply*. Rather than locating transcendent reality nowhere and nowhen, it is much clearer to say that terms which entail reference to spatial or temporal attributes are utterly inapposite to the consideration of transcendent reality and that transcendent reality is a non-empirical world of Being, not becoming, at least not in the temporal sense. Transcendent reality can only be understood within the terms that it provides itself, namely, the soul, general logic, freedom, the Supreme Principle of Being and Intelligibility, and *Agape* and not in terms of extension. Transcendent reality must therefore be ontologically over and above but not physically immanent in empirical reality.

It is not uncommon among empiricists to conclude from the foregoing that transcendent reality is therefore unthinkable, but nothing could be further from the truth. It has already been shown that the *Logos*, and not the empirical world, is the presupposition of knowledge, and that the structure and rules of theoretical reason are neither spatial nor temporal. To the contrary, they only appear (to some) to become so when they are brought by human reason to empirical experience in the process of cognition of its objects and relations. If one takes as axiomatic that all knowledge comes from the senses, then it follows that all knowable reality must be sensible and that reality may be defined in such a way that it requires extension. On the empirical premise, that is fair and reasonable. However, the empirical definition of reality may not be offered in proof of the empirical postulate upon which it depends. Axioms should be self-evident and expressly distinguished from hypotheses or postulates, which may be used as starting points for exploration of their own or their opposite's explanatory power. On this understanding the premise that all knowledge comes from the senses is not an axiom and, as a hypothesis, its lack of explanatory power is striking.

There is another phenomenon that occurs frequently in the materialist mitherings which, considered in the best light, spring from a mistake of reason, and which often take the form of *ad hominem* assault. I refer here to the willful refusal on the part of some materialists to distinguish between acknowledged fantasy and legitimate supersensible experience. Any reasonable person would admit that there is a genuine philosophical difference between the premise that the soul is substance and a story about unicorns, yet it is not uncommon for materialist philosophers to characterize their philosophical opposition as fairy tale believers or worse. Considered by itself, this phenomenon would be best treated with intellectual indifference and taken as a sign of the vacuity of the materialist position but I raise it as an issue because it lays bare an important intellectual strand in the history of philosophy. It is indisputable that the human impulse to seek the unconditioned often led primitive societies to conjure up supernatural explanations for phenomena whose causes could not be seen nor understood by the science of the time, which, in the light of subsequent science, came to be seen as naïve or even childish. However, it is a horrendous error to conclude from the historical success of science in paring back the unknown that there is no supersensible reality. It is no surprise that because pure science, the integrity of which should be beyond question, is a natural antidote for superstition, it may be seized upon as an ally for materialist philosophers, who, as a matter of tactics, would happily resort to lumping together fictional creatures and the human soul. But such an alliance should be embraced with caution, because science, considered within the limitations of its own field of inquiry, rather than supporting the empiricist position, demonstrates most strikingly the inability, already chronicled in these pages, of empiricism to explain most of human experience and natural history. In this regard, I would like to suggest that the Big Bang theory, which is widely accepted by current science as the explanation of the beginning of the material universe and which postulates a singularity of all matter and energy *prior to the commencement of space-time*, is not so much a scientific theory as it is a metaphysical one.

The argument about the thinkability of transcendent reality is also sometimes included in the discourse on the philosophy of language. Human experience includes and is generally limited to sense perception of empirical existing objects and consciousness of objects of thought, including such objects. Empirical objects are considered to be real, in the sense of existence separate and apart from the apprehending subject. Whatever the school of thought, it is undeniable that the names of empirical objects are most often taught by the technique of pointing and speaking their names. In contrast, objects of direct intuition are internally experienced apart from empirical reality and, because they are not extended, may not be pointed to. Materialists, who deny the existence (or subsistence) of anything that is not materially reducible have no choice but to contend (and no hesitation in doing so) that names of directly intuited objects, such as "soul," are meaningless because they have no empirical reference and are therefore incapable of being substantively communicated. But that is simply not the case. If we have common direct intuitions and objective rules of thought, then the mind may be directed to the objects of metaphysics (as long as they are not incoherent such as the idea of nothingness) and they may be clearly understood as such. Those of us who directly intuit our souls as substance have no doubt that they understand each other perfectly well when that is the topic of conversation.

Consider in this regard the irony of Wittgenstein's misconstruction of the self as a limiting condition to experience rather than as the direct perception of the essence of the living subject. In order to attempt to refute the self as substance, Wittgenstein must first point us to it in a way that can be understood. There is no doubt that he succeeds in that and, indeed, we understand what Wittgenstein means when he refers us to the self. We also understand what Wittgenstein means when he says something is a limiting condition. But we must reject Wittgenstein's challenge to the self as a limiting condition precisely because his argument is incoherent. I cannot assert that I do not exist. There cannot be a limiting condition to *my* experience that does not include *me*. It is not possible to assert in the third person that one's conception of self is illusory without assuming that it is not illusory in the first instance. Wittgenstein could avoid the instability of his argument by asserting that reality is a single, unified consciousness (as does Hegel), but that position is easily seen to be false based upon our own individual intuition of individual ego and the fact that there is a meaningful word "self" in our lexicon. In any event, the point here is not to rehash the arguments concerning the ontological importance of direct perception of the self but rather to show that not only do we have such direct perception but that we are capable of communicating intelligibly to one another about it even though it is not an extended object.

UNITY AND PREEMINENCE

To a large degree, metaphysics may be described as the pursuit by reason of the unconditioned explanation of human experience of reality, including the question of whether such a pursuit is even possible. Material reductionism operates in a causally closed empirical world and therefore can only offer the alternatives that the world is an infinite contingency or that it admits of and requires no explanation at all. Both have been advanced with ferocious zeal because their failure renders the theism their proponents so greatly dread a viable, if not the only reasonable, alternative, but neither such empirical characterization is even remotely satisfactory and together they seem more evidentiary of the prevailing secular agenda than they are persuasive. The discourse with respect to the viability of comprehending the empirical world as an infinite contingency is important, long, and nuanced, so it will be separately considered below in connection with the discussion of the ontological proofs of the existence of God. For the time being, it will be sufficient to anticipate that discussion by asserting that if an empirical infinite contingency were possible, it would have to be necessary in its totality (meaning that although each contingent event is explained by a causally prior contingent event, the entire infinite sequence must necessarily exist and could not have not existed) and, being necessary, contain within itself the explanation of its necessity in a way that satisfies reason, which it cannot do. Here is what Leibniz has to say on this issue in advancing his argument in favor of the mighty principle:

> But there must also be a sufficient reason for contingent truths or truths of fact, that is to say, for the sequence or connexion of the things which are dispersed throughout the universe of created beings, in which the analyzing into particular reasons might go on into endless detail, because of the immense variety of things in nature and the infinite division of bodies. There is an infinity of present and past forms and motions which go to make up the efficient cause of my present writing; and there is an infinity of minute tendencies and dispositions of my soul, which go to make its final cause.
>
> . . . And as all this detail again involves other prior or more detailed contingent things, each of which still needs a similar analysis to yield its reason, we are no further forward: *and the sufficient or final reason must be outside of the sequence or series of particular contingent things, however infinite this series may be.*[1] (Section numbers omitted.)

---

1. Leibniz, *Monadology*, §§36–37, 237–38.

In considering the shortcomings of the empiricist view, it is desirable to turn yet again to Kant because his transcendental philosophy represents a strict form of empiricism which at least attempts to address those shortcomings, unlike the modern material reductionism, which, for the most part, defends them by dogmatic assertion, if it acknowledges them at all. Kant recognizes that the pursuit of the unconditioned is natural to reason and serves important intellectual and practical purposes and, indeed, Kant's critical philosophy may be regarded as the attempt to delineate the epistemological boundary at which that pursuit leads from knowledge to dogma. Kant denies that there can be *knowledge* of the unconditioned principle of reality but asserts, instead, that because the existence of moral obligation requires the presumption of freedom and because freedom can only exist if there is a subsistent reality, moral obligation offers a justification for *belief* in subsistent reality, in the first instance, and, ultimately, in the *Ens Perfectissimum*. The transcendent philosophy presented in these pages asserts that Kant's constraint of epistemology to the sensible world is unsupportable on its own premises, that there is direct intuition of the unconditioned in human experience of objective theoretical reason and moral obligation, and that *Agape*, upon which the latter experience depends, must be understood as not merely self-instantiating but as *the Supreme Principle of human experience of all reality, transcendent and empirical*. By "Supreme Principle" of *all* reality, I mean that entity which explains Being as such, becoming, reason, and moral obligation. The assertions that human beings have direct intuition of the mind-independent, objective rules of thought and that moral obligation must be grounded upon a directly intuited, subsistent, and self-instantiating *Agape* have been explained and justified. It therefore remains to address the last such assertion, namely, that the *Agape* of direct intuition is ontologically supreme.

The claim that *Agape* is the Supreme Principle of reality contains two components. The first is that *Agape* is an ontologically unified and supreme entity. The second is that, as such, it is the ground of all Being and intelligibility. As was noted in chapter 10, "Duty and Desire," I have resisted to the extent possible without diminishment of the exposition of transcendent realism the obvious and inevitable identification of *Agape* as that of God as he is commonly understood in the Western world. My reason for doing so was to keep the focus of the presentation on metaphysics as opposed to religion but, if metaphysics leads ineluctably to the necessity of an ontologically supreme being, continuing to avoid reference to God must ultimately outlive that purpose and can only result in needless confusion and stilted syntax. In previous pages, I have made much about the impossibility of thought existing without its thinker and as a general matter the same must be true about will, which has been described in a previous chapter as reason or thought in action. Whether *Agape* appertains to a *supreme Being* considered as an entity or is pure, supreme *Agape* without any of the internal relations that could be understood as constituting such an entity is not knowable by man; nevertheless, given the identity between Being and intelligibility, *Agape* can only be thought to exist as a unity among a manifold and, therefore as the self-willing ground of all grounds.

It may be observed that any ontology that concludes in a place where reason may rest comfortably must end with the Supreme Being. The denial of the possibility of metaphysics, or the conclusion that the world simply is what it is, or the conclusion that there are a multiplicity of gods, all leave reason with the unanswered question: *Why?* That question can only be answered with finality by positing a rationally self-justifying and self-instantiating being. Reason, as Kant says, seeks the unconditioned, and, in doing so, it also seeks the self-justifying and the self-instantiating, and these cannot be found except in the Supreme Being. That is not to say that because we can ask the question of what the sufficient reason for all things (including itself) might be we must be able to answer it beyond asserting that reason demands that it be so, but it is to say that reason demands at least that much. This point is profoundly important. In asserting that reason does not require a First Cause, modern philosophy treats logic as a set of rules as opposed to the structure of Being. When one understands that Being is essentially grounded logical predication and, therefore, that Being and intelligibility are identical, the necessity of a Supreme Being and the necessity of its selfsame Supreme Principle becomes manifest.

There are many reasons to conclude that there can be one and only one Supreme Being. The first, and most compelling, is the nature of the Supreme Being and the logical road that is traveled to reach him. The Supreme Being is the *logically necessary* being of which there cannot be more than one. If one starts with the empirical world of caused entities, reason seeks a single uncaused entity. It does not seek multiple uncaused entities because more than one such entity is not *logically necessary* and, indeed, reason tells us that in either case a multiplicity of necessary beings is self-contradictory.

A second reason lies in the heart of moral obligation. It will be recalled that for moral obligation to exist, it must arise as the result of an object that is its own end, which means that there must be a self-instantiating *Agape* of which morally conscious beings have knowledge. If the only self-instantiating being behaved in what we understand (in our current circumstances) to be evil ways, we would not recognize them as such but would instead consider them to be good because we would have no other referent by virtue of which we could recognize them to be evil. The notion of *Agape* derives from the fact that the Supreme Being wills itself as its own object and in doing so obligates all beings who are conscious of it to will its objects as well. Therefore, the declarations that "the essence of the Supreme Being is existence," "the Supreme Being is *good-in-itself*," and that "the Supreme Being contains all perfections" are equivalent and *goodness equates all three to self-instantiation and self-justification*. In other words, under all conceivable circumstances we would recognize the self-instantiating and self-justifying will of the Supreme Being as *Agape* and therefore obligating our own wills. It is worth noting here, for development in the sequel chapter on *Agape*, that one enormously important consequence that follows from this point is that, if the Supreme Principle of all Being and intelligibility is *Agape*, then the universe cannot be morally neutral.

It follows from the concept that the Supreme Being is by nature *Agape* that there cannot be more than one source of our direct intuition of *Agape*. That is to say that neither reason nor our experience can include a multiplicity of morally good absolutes. Any conception of such a multiplicity is unstable because each being would be *good-in-itself* and therefore all such beings would intend (and instantiate) the same object and be one and the same God. If such sources were in conflict, then only one could be recognized as being good and the others would be evil by reference to it. This point may be understood as the application of Leibniz's doctrine of the identity of indiscernibles to the concept of *Agape* and it must be remembered that although that doctrine bears Leibniz's name it does not belong to him but is instead an expression of the very *Logos* under consideration. We can and do distinguish between good and evil, but not a multiplicity of goods.

It is important to note that (as will be explained in the sequel chapter on *Agape*) the fact that there may be more than one morally correct option in a given set of circumstances does not suggest or support the existence of a multiplicity of Moral Laws. The existence of diverse courses of conduct that might be considered to be good merely corresponds to the variety of outcomes that inhere in a diversely contingent world and the variety of morally obligated beings, each with its own capabilities and shortcomings, whose conduct is in question. There is and can only be a single Moral Law, namely, to act with *agape*. Such action may sometimes be affected in more than one way or require different conduct from persons who are differently situated.

It is also worth noting that the Scholastic arguments for the existence of God lead to a Supreme Being who is asserted to be unitary and absolute even though the deifying characteristics contained in such proofs differ. For example, the proofs of St. Thomas Aquinas yield that God is the Prime Mover, the Efficient Cause, the Necessary Being, the Most Perfect Being, and the Intelligent Designer. It is a common criticism of atheists that, even if these proofs were true, there is no reason to conflate them to a single Supreme Being. It is tempting to respond that such critics should at least abandon their atheism in favor of polytheism but the real point is that such critics mistake the multiplicity of arguments with a multiplicity of the objects of the arguments. The better response, therefore, is that the conception of God as *Agape*, to which reason leads as it seeks the unconditioned, self-instantiating, self-justifying, Supreme Principle of Being and Intelligibility, uniquely comprises all of these characteristics by its own definition. The self-instantiating nature of the Supreme Being means that it is the First Cause and the Sufficient Reason. Insofar as the Supreme Being is the Supreme Principle of Being and Intelligibility it must be the Most Perfect Being and the Intelligent Designer (for there can be no other). Finally, the Supreme Being's essence as pure will requires that it be the Prime Mover.

It follows from God's necessity and unity that he is the ontologically highest being. Given the necessary nature of God, because no other being can be necessary no other being can be ontologically higher. Theoretical reason seeks a single, highest principle of existence, the explanation of which would allow reason to cease its search for the answers to metaphysical questions. If there appeared to be more than one such pure being, reason would seek a higher principle that explained such multiplicity. *Reason, therefore, expects a unified pure being whose essence is Being and who is therefore the supreme principle of all other beings.* Multiple pure beings are not possible. If there were two beings whose essence was their existence then they could only be conceived of as being one and the same entity. This is Leibniz's principle of the identity of indiscernibles as it applies to the understanding of God as pure Being (and, again, merely expresses the fundamental logical nature of Being).

THE GROUND OF BEING AND INTELLIGIBILITY

To complete the ontological picture, the second step is to show why God must be regarded as the Supreme Principle of Being and Intelligibility. To a large degree, this has already been accomplished, at least implicitly, in the preceding chapters, based upon the grounds for the possibility of universal and objective knowledge and human moral experience. Moral obligation requires the existence of self-justifying, self-instantiating *good-in-itself*, to whom we have first referred as *Agape* and subsequently also as "God." Intelligibility requires not the moral but the theoretical elements of the *Logos*, both on the part of the knowing subject and the object that is to be known. Together, reason comprises both a theoretical faculty and a moral one and, with these faculties, access is given to God as the self-willing ground of all that there is and can be and of *the rationality by which* Agape *intends itself as its own end*. It is accurate, therefore, to say that God has manifested himself to human beings as the Supreme Principle of Being and Intelligibility by granting to human reason access to the *Logos*.

I believe that there is an ontological argument that fully supports the preceding analysis, which as far as I am aware has not previously been advanced. Because ontological proofs hold the prospect of a theistic conclusion that is not dependent upon notoriously unreliable sensible experience, such proofs are tantalizingly attractive to rationalist philosophers and correspondingly odious to materialist reductionists. For theists, the importance of an ontological approach to the problem of the existence of God is heightened by the fact that, as Kant pointed out and as will be explained below, other well-known arguments for the existence of God, including those commonly known (thanks to Kant) as the cosmological arguments and the teleological arguments, which depend for their conclusion upon human experience of empirical reality, seem to come to a point where they must *assume*, as an ontological matter, that the God whose proof is asserted exists.

The first ontological argument for the existence of God was offered by St. Anselm in the eleventh century and was immediately met with significant criticism. Although the debate over St. Anselm's and other formulations of the ontological argument has continued to the present day, it seems fair to say that so far the theists have failed to meet their burden of proof. This is because as a general matter the ontological proofs attempt to prove the necessity of God by including within the concept of his essence the very existence they seek to prove. In contrast, the key features of the argument that I will propose shortly are that reason alone can show that the world is necessary and that because the world is necessary it must contain at least one necessary object that by its nature must be a pure will that meets the common understanding of God. However, because certain of the premises and conclusions of the argument to be presented in these pages specifically address important aspects of the historical critique of traditionally formulated ontological proofs, either by adoption or refutation, the explication of the argument will be substantially aided by its being placed in historical context.

St. Anselm offers two historically important ontological proofs, both of which are relevant to the current discussion. His first proof depends upon the characterization of existence as a perfection that must be included in any conception of God as the *Ens Perfectissimum* and may be crudely paraphrased as follows:

1. I can conceive (as an idea) of a being who is the greatest possible being.
2. A being possessing the perfections of the greatest possible being and which also exists is greater than one that is merely an idea.
3. Therefore, the greatest possible being must exist.

St. Anselm's second proof depends not upon mere existence but rather upon *necessary existence* and may be again crudely paraphrased as follows:

1. I can conceive (as an idea) of a being who is the greatest possible being.
2. A being that necessarily exists is greater than a being that does not necessarily exist.
3. Therefore, the greatest possible being must necessarily exist.

A moment's analysis shows that, in the first proof, St. Anselm is arguing that the most perfect possible being must exist because existence is a perfection that the most perfect being must, by definition, have. In the second argument, St. Anselm has substituted necessary existence for existence, arguing that necessity, as opposed to mere possibility, is a perfection that must attend the concept of the most perfect being. The merit of these and other similar arguments has been debated since the moment they were first proposed, but it was Kant, seven centuries after St. Anselm, who appears to have dealt the telling blow to this type of formulation of ontological argument. With respect to the first proof, Kant disputes the claim that existence is a perfection, contending wholly in accordance with his categories of understanding that, instead, existence is a modality of an object under which the relationship of the object to the understanding is known from alternatives that include possibility, actuality, and necessity. This criticism is often summarized under the idea that *existence is not a predicate*, meaning that unlike other predicates (such as "redness" or "goodness") attributing existence to a subject adds nothing to its content. With respect to the second proof, Kant argues that the switch from existence to necessity renders the first premise meaningless as stated because it contains *sub silentio* the concept of a possible necessary being, which results from the merger of the subjects of the two premises, and is therefore totally meaningless, and that, as a result, the second proof reduces itself to the notion that the conceivability of a necessary being implies its real existence, which is a mere tautology.

In making these points, the particular form of ontological argument that Kant discusses is as follows:

1. I can conceive of an absolutely necessary (as opposed to merely possible) being.
2. The idea of a merely possible (and not actually existing) necessary being is a contradiction in terms.
3. Because the idea of an absolutely necessary being is possible, it must exist.

Kant argues that the intermediate premise is not correct because, for a necessary being to be merely possible, it must also be possible that it not exist and if one thinks of it as not existing one is not left with an idea of something that is not a reality but no idea at all. In other words, Kant's point is that a merely possible necessary being is not a self-contradictory concept, but rather a meaningless concept, which has been created by inserting one *modality*, namely, necessity, into the definition and then testing it against a *contradictory modality*, namely, possibility. To the counterargument that the concept of necessary being is unique insofar as its essence is its existence (and therefore its existence is a wholly analytic proposition), Kant replies that the counterargument entails a tautology because it inserts existence into a concept and then concludes that the thing must exist, which reduces to the assertion that an existing object exists.

Kant's presentation on this point includes one of his most famous passages:

> Being is evidently not a real predicate, that is, a concept of something that can be added to the concept of a thing. It is merely the positing of a thing, and of certain determinations in themselves. Logically, it is merely the copula of a judgment. The proposition, "God is omnipotent," contains two concepts, each having its object, namely, God and omnipotence. The small word is not an additional predicate, but only serves to posit the predicate in relation to the subject. If, then, I take the subject (God) with all its predicates (including that of omnipotence), and say, "God is," or "There is a God," I do not add a new predicate to the concept of God, but I only posit the subject in itself with all its predicates, and indeed posit the object in relation to my concept. Both must contain exactly the same, and nothing can be added to the concept, which expresses only possibility, by my thinking this object (through its expression, "It is") as absolutely given. And thus the actual does not contain more than the merely possible. A hundred actual *Talers* do not contain the slightest bit more than a hundred possible *Talers*, for as the latter signify the concept, the former the object and the positing of it in itself, it is clear that, if the former contained more than the latter, my concept would not express the whole object, and would not therefore be its adequate concept.[2]

Although there remain those who wish to argue that necessary existence is a predicate only when it refers to the *Ens Realissimum*, I think that, with some qualification, Kant is correct in this important point and will rely upon Kant's perspective in favor of a different theistic argument in the ontological proof that follows shortly. It should be pointed out, however, that Kant's assertion is much more clearly true in the context of his epistemological framework where logic is merely an abstraction from the categories of understanding. An argument might be made that existence is not a predicate with respect to an empirical subject, but where the subject is supersensible the case is less clear. For Kant, this is not a problem because he denies that knowledge of supersensible objects is possible. However, where, as is the case with transcendent realism, the epistemology included in a philosophical system does not so constrain logic, the consequences of attaching existence to a supersensible subject require additional analysis. In the case of ontological objects, at issue is not whether such an object is instantiated in sensible reality but whether an ontological being has *objective ontological reference*, by which is meant that a concept refers to an *instantiated* ontological entity. In such a case, it might be asked whether anything is added to the *idea* of an omniscient entity

---

2. Kant, *Critique of Pure Reason*, 627.

by saying that it has objective ontological reference and it seems that there is. The idea of an empirical object that is not self-contradictory may always possibly be instantiated in the empirical world. However, the modality of ontological objects is not the same as the modality of empirical objects. The categories of ontological objects include abstract ideas (such as those of logic, mathematics, and geometry) which do not and cannot have objective ontological reference, contingent ideas, such as the human soul, which can but do not necessarily have objective ontological reference, and God, who, if he is conceivable at all, must necessarily subsist as a *transcendently real object*. In such a case, necessary existence, being essential to the God-concept, cannot be removed from the God-concept to create an abstract idea of God without destroying the concept. In this respect, God is ontologically unique. So although necessary existence adds nothing to the God-concept, it is not because necessary-existence is a modality but because the modality of the God-concept includes necessary existence. The implication is as unique as the God-concept itself, namely, that although proponents of the ontological argument are correct that if God is conceivable he must exist, such proponents may not assert as an unjustified premise that they can conceive of God (considered as a necessary being) and must instead prove such conceivability.

Before moving on, I would like to make a thematic point which runs throughout these pages and is, I believe, telling against the prevalent analytical approach to philosophy. Kant's criticism of ontological arguments presumes Kant's epistemology, and appropriately so. To understand Kant's critique of ontological arguments, one must first understand the category of modality, to understand modality one must first understand the categories of understanding and the concept of judgments, and to understand these concepts one must understand how Kant views the relationship of logic to reason. The sophistry of analytic philosophy is that the epistemological presuppositions of analytical arguments are often unstated and/or inconsistently relied upon. I raise this point here because, although I am proposing to provide an ontological argument, it very much relies generally upon the *Logos* as being the objective and universal source of reason, which I hope to have justified well by now, and, as will be explained, the scope of reason as it is accessible to man.

Also, propaedeutic to the presentation of the ontological argument, it is necessary to return briefly to the discussion of the principle of sufficient reason, which was discussed at length in our consideration of Heidegger's analysis of Leibniz's work. That the principle of sufficient reason is correct by direct intuition can hardly be disputed, but it is disputed hotly nevertheless, particularly by secularist philosophers. In my opinion, the reason is more agenda- than reason-driven. The implications of the principle of sufficient reason, which include the existence of a necessary, self-instantiated Being (Heidegger notwithstanding), are simply too oriented toward theism to be accepted by modern mainstream philosophy. The challenges to the principle of sufficient reason come in the familiar way, either by denying the existence of universally objective reason itself or by asserting that any attempt to apply the principle of sufficient reason to the empirical world as a totality is a dogmatic overreach. In a curious philosophical move, rather than to reach an ontological conclusion, material reductionists are wont simply to assert (i.e., believe) that there are certain "brute" facts as to which no explanation can be expected or given. But the response to that assertion is simply to ask the question why it should be so and, metaphysically speaking, given the identity of Being and intelligibility, it cannot be the case. The materialist justifications have their roots in Kant's argument that the reach of reason is limited to cognition of empirical experience and, because we have no experience of the universe as a totality or anything outside of it, the principle of sufficient reason must cease applicability at the boundaries of the empirical world. Ironically enough, not only does Kant not deny the principle of sufficient reason but instead he elevates it to the status of an ordering principle of spatio-temporal cognition, but, although he does so, he is clear that its application is limited to empirical experience and therefore tells us nothing about the reason the world exists. Nevertheless, as has been discussed with some repetition in these pages, Kant's restriction of reason to empirical experience is a major philosophical error. When reason is liberated from that constraint, it is free to search until it rests comfortably in direct intuition. Those who hope to challenge the principle of sufficient reason on the basis that it too must have an explanation are therefore hopelessly lost.

The ontological argument for the existence of God that I wish to propose is as follows:

1. For something to be possible, it must be conceivable.
2. For something to be conceivable the rules of its conception (i.e., theoretical reason) must exist and apply to it.
3. Therefore, for something to be possible it must be conceivable in accordance with the rules of conception of objects of thought (i.e., logically possible).
4. The concept of "absolute nothingness" ("Absolute Nothingness") is unintelligible because it entails the absence of all that may possibly be, including the rules of its own conception.
5. Therefore, Absolute Nothingness is logically impossible.
6. Therefore, the rules of conception of objects must exist and the world must contain at least one conceivable object.
7. Under the rules of conception of objects, conceivable objects must either be necessary or contingent.
8. A contingent object, a limited set of contingent objects, and an infinite set of contingent objects all might not exist.
9. Therefore, for the world to exist necessarily, it must contain at least one object that is not contingent.
10. Therefore, for the world to exist necessarily, there must exist at least one object that is necessary.
11. A necessary object is one that does not depend for its existence upon the existence of any other object.
12. Under the rules of conception of objects, conceivable objects must have an intelligible reason for their necessary or possible existence.

13. Because existence is not a predicate, the fact of the existence of something cannot be an intelligible reason for its existence.
14. Therefore, a necessary object must contain within itself the explanation of its own existence other than the fact of its existence.
15. Therefore, for the world to necessarily exist there must be a necessary object that contains within itself the explanation of its existence (other than the fact that it exists) and the rules of its own intelligibility.
16. Such an object must intend itself as its own end in accordance with its own rules of conception.
17. Such an object must be understood to exist as the Supreme Principle of Being and Intelligibility.
18. We call the Supreme Principle of Being and Intelligibility "God."

Comment on point 1: For something to be possible, it must be conceivable. This premise is both a statement about the modality of objects and about the scope of reason. Because of the identity of Being and intelligibility, all Beings are by definition intelligible, which means that only that which is intelligible can conceivably *be* and, conversely, that which is inconceivable cannot *possibly be*. Statements to the effect that, as a general matter, human rationality may not be exhaustive of all that there is, seem to make sense but are in fact incoherent; to hold otherwise is to deny the identity of Being and intelligibility. Indeed, it is not even possible to meaningfully make statements about the limits of the reach of reason unless, by limitation, it is understood that reason reaches the full domain of all that may possibly be. All of this follows directly from our assertion that Being and intelligibility: the same. And it follows, of course, that modality and the other categories of understanding, and the logic that underpins them, may not be thought to apply to that which is not conceivable.

Comment on point 2: For something to be conceivable the rules of its conception (i.e., theoretical reason) must exist and apply to it. This premise is simply a statement about the structure of reason and its relationship to cognition. An object, whatever its modality, can only be conceived of, and understood in accordance with, the rules of thought which are constituent of the Being of the object as a logical object or an object that is a descendant of a logical object.

Comment on point 3: Therefore, for something to be possible it must be conceivable in accordance with the rules of conception of objects of thought (i.e., logically possible). This conclusion follows directly from points 1 and 2.

Comment on point 4: Absolute Nothingness is inconceivable because it entails the absence of all that may possibly be, including the rules of its own conception. This premise/conclusion follows from the preceding points because it shows that Absolute Nothingness entails its own unthinkability. It is also impossible to conceive of the absence of all that might possibly be (Absolute Nothingness) because the conception of Absolute Nothingness can only occur in accordance with the rules of thought which would not exist if nothing existed. Those who argue that they can think everything away are manifestly incorrect. I believe that their misconception arises as a fallacy of the composition of the fact that it is possible to think away any existing object. It will be remembered that this is the point that Heidegger tells us is true unless one privileges, as he does, Being above logic but, as we have shown, because of the identity of Being and intelligibility Heidegger is in grave error in doing so.

Comment on point 5: Therefore, Absolute Nothingness is logically impossible. It follows from points 3 and 4 that because Absolute Nothingness is inconceivable, it cannot be logically possible. Nothingness cannot exist because it would be something. Neither can Nothingness be said to not exist because that statement bespeaks of Nothingness again as though it were a nonexisting *something*. Nothingness is therefore illogical and incoherent. This is the meaning of the third intonation of the mighty principle.

Comment on point 6: Therefore, the rules of conception of objects must exist and the world must contain at least one conceivable object. Here, the world is set up in opposition to Absolute Nothingness and therefore as the container of at least one object (i.e., supersensible or sensible). The necessity of the world follows directly from the inconceivability of Absolute Nothingness. At first blush, it might seem that the inconceivability of Absolute Nothingness implies only that the rules of its conception need exist but that cannot be the case unless such rules are conceived, as Plato did, to have objective content. Under transcendent realism, the rules of the conception of objects constitute only the form of cognition of objects, therefore, although they may be spoken of as an abstract object, they do not have the objective content to stand alone in opposition to Absolute Nothingness. By this understanding, as the presupposition to intelligibility, the rules of conception cannot be abolished by anything that is conceivable but their logical existence is insufficient to objectify the world except as constitutive of Being. The rules of conception of objects are codetermining of and with Being and such rules cannot exist in the absence of all that is conceivable. I cannot think away all possible objects of thought and still retain the rules of their conception. Having said that, because the remainder of this proof leads to the necessity of pure will, which wills itself in accordance with its own rules of conception (which are given to theoretical reason), whether the Supreme Principle of Being and Intelligibility is objectified reason (akin to the Platonic Idea of the Good, which Plato understood to be pure Reality) or pure will, as I assert here, seems for the purposes of this proof to be a distinction without a difference insofar as they both represent the unconditioned explanation for the conceivable. In this proof, I opt for pure will over the Idea of the Good because, definitionally, will is reason's intention of an end and, therefore, by pure will, I mean a rational entity that has the power to intend itself as its own end, which, in accordance with reason, is the only conceivable explanation for the existence of a necessary object.

Comment on point 7: Under the rules of conception of objects, conceivable objects must either be necessary or contingent. This is a statement of the logical modality of objects of thought.

Comment on point 8: A contingent object, a limited set of contingent objects, and an infinite set of contingent objects all might not exist. The first two assertions follow from the definition of contingency. The last follows inductively from the fact that the addition of a contingent object to a limited set of contingent objects does not make the set any less contingent.

Comment on point 9: Therefore, for the world to exist necessarily, it must contain at least one object that is not contingent. If the world consisted of a set, infinite or otherwise, of infinite contingencies, then its existence would be happenstance.

Comment on point 10: Therefore for the world to exist necessarily, there must exist at least one object that is necessary. This follows from points 7 and 9. *Nota Bene*: It is sometimes argued that disjunctive contingencies (i.e., either A or B, where A and B are the only two possible contingencies) might satisfy a requirement that something must necessarily exist while avoiding the requirement of a necessary object but this is not correct because necessity is implied in the disjunction (i.e., "either A or B" means that "it is necessary that either A or B be true"). Consider the example of a coin toss, where, although the outcome of heads or tails is contingent, the coin must necessarily exist as a precondition and explanation of the disjunctive contingency of the outcome. Moreover, the explanation for the existence of a particular contingency cannot be the nonexistence of a correlated disjunctive contingency because such an explanation is circular (i.e., the nonexistence of the correlated disjunctive contingency would be explained by the existence of the correlated contingency) and because existence/nonexistence are not explanatory predicates.

Comment on point 11: A necessary object is one that does not depend for its existence upon the existence of any other object. This is true definitionally and logically.

Comment on point 12: Under the rules of conception of objects, conceivable objects must have an intelligible reason for their necessary or possible existence. This is a statement of the principle of sufficient reason.

Comment on point 13: Because existence is not a predicate, the fact of the existence of something cannot be an intelligible reason for its existence. As noted in the text preceding this discussion, I accept Kant's characterization of existence as a mere modality that describes the relationship of an object to reason. Therefore, to say something exists because it exists is a tautology. Even under Russell's characterization of existence as a quantity, to say there is one and only one because there is only one is also a tautology. Therefore, mere existence is not an explanation of existence.

Comment on point 14: Therefore, a necessary object must contain within itself the explanation of its own existence other than the fact of its existence. This follows from points 12 and 13.

Comment on point 15: Therefore, for the world to necessarily exist there must be a necessary object that contains within itself the explanation of its existence (other than the fact that it exists) and the rules of its own intelligibility. The explanation required by point 14 must be intelligible and also an explanation of intelligibility.

Comment on point 16: Such an object must intend itself as its own end in accordance with its own rules of conception. See the comment on point 6.

Comment on point 17: Such an object is the Supreme Principle of Being and Intelligibility. This follows from point 15, whether one accepts point 16 or not.

Comment on point 18: We call the Supreme Principle of Being and Intelligibility "God." This point follows from the preceding, whether one considers the Supreme Principle of Being and Intelligibility to be pure will or pure reality. Plato would call this the Idea of the Good. In Judeo-Christian text, Yahweh is "I AM WHO I AM" (Exod 3:14).

PLATO AND THE IDEA OF THE GOOD

In the comment on point 6, I minimized the distinction between Plato's Idea of the Good and transcendent realism's self-instantiating and self-justifying *Agape*, in each case as the Supreme Principle of Being and Intelligibility. That is possible only because the two concepts achieve the same ontological end, namely, to explain the full reach of reason, the existence of the world, the possibility of objective and universal knowledge, and moral experience. The two concepts, therefore, are more or less interchangeable for purposes of the ontological proof presented in these pages. But construing the Idea of the Good and pure *Agape* as fully the same would be putting a grotesque gloss on them. Platonic Idealism, including the Idea of the Good, which stands at its pinnacle, and transcendent realism, as an unabashedly theistic philosophy, representing as they do two rationalist philosophies are in certain respects compatible. Nevertheless, their differences are far greater in number than their similarities. Particularly relevant to the current discussion is the fact that Plato does not expressly identify the Idea of the Good with God (and, instead, at times, speaks of the Demiurge as the god-architect of the world) and does not connect the sublimity of the Idea of the Good with will in explaining how the world comes to be. On the other hand, the two philosophies are sufficiently broad in scope to contemplate the reality of the sensible world and a fully real transcendent world and, given their compatibility on the question of the Supreme Principle of Being and Intelligibility, it serves to explore Plato's philosophy in somewhat greater detail.

Plato, permissibly for his time, takes for granted that there is universal and objective knowledge. The purpose of his epistemology is therefore not to explain how that might be so but instead to identify with clarity what knowledge is. For Plato, such knowledge must be permanent and abiding, and it therefore cannot be found through sensation of ever-changing (i.e., becoming), particular sensible objects. Such a process can only yield unreliable opinion about the nature of an empirical world that is in a constant state of flux. For true knowledge, one must consider and comprehend the universal and unchanging, which Plato finds in what he calls Ideas or Forms and what the modern philosophical world refers to as universals. For Plato, the objects of the real world participate in the Ideas that characterize them and because such Ideas are permanent and universal and determine such objects, the Ideas are ontologically superior. For Plato, there is an Idea for every predicate of a subject and that Idea exists, with objective ontological reference, in a transcendent world that is ontologically separate from the sensible world. Plato generally does not distinguish hierarchically among the various Ideas with the exception of three normative ones, namely, Justice, Beauty, and Goodness. These Ideas are sometimes spoken of separately and sometimes as though they are the same Idea by Plato; however, his special reverence for the Idea of the Good is always manifest when reference is made to it. For Plato, the Idea of the Good stands in relationship to the other Ideas as such Ideas stand in relationship to the sensible world. That the Idea of the Good is the Supreme Principle of Being and Intelligibility follows from the participation of such other Ideas in the Idea of the Good and from the epistemological process in which the soul of the philosopher achieves the sublime, mystical vision of the Idea of the Good. Epistemologically, the philosopher proceeds first by contemplating sensible objects and then by achieving an understanding of the science of their apparent relationship, which leads to the universal Ideas, and finally, by seeking the ground for all such knowledge, the philosopher reaches the Idea of the Good and, in doing so, achieves, to the extent humanly possible, the understanding of reality and the intelligibility of reality. Only then can the soul of the philosopher joyfully cease its search for the unconditioned. For Plato, the Idea of the Good is indeed the cause and the explanation of reality and its intelligibility. Here follows one of the most celebrated passages in all of the history of philosophy in which Plato, speaking as Socrates to Glaucon in *The Republic*, makes the point:

> You will not misapprehend me if you interpret the journey upwards to be the ascent of the soul into the intellectual world according to my poor belief, which, at your desire, I have expressed—whether rightly or wrongly God knows. But, whether true or false, my opinion is that in the world of knowledge the idea of good appears last of all, and is seen only with an effort; and, when seen, is also inferred to be the universal author of all things beautiful and right, parent of light and of the lord of light in this visible world, and the immediate source of reason and truth in the intellectual; and that this is the power upon which he who would act rationally either in public or private life must have his eye fixed.[3]

The many difficulties surrounding Plato's philosophy have been analyzed and chronicled, starting with that great philosopher himself, and will not be further discussed in these pages. Nevertheless, Plato's rationalism has informed the other great rationalist systems of the history of philosophy, including most notably those of Descartes, Spinoza, and Leibniz, and because of the scope of its identification and treatment of epistemological and metaphysical issues, Plato's rationalism remains very much a viable, if not the most preferable, starting point for students of philosophy. Plato's theory of Ideas is still very much alive in the modern discourse on universals and numbers and the possibility of their objective existence.

Transcendent realism takes its approach to epistemology structurally from Kant, not Plato, and it adopts conceptually categories of understanding that are similar to Kant's. Transcendent realism has, therefore, no need for subsisting universal Ideas. These are supplanted by the ontologically prior logic of objects and their relations which underpins the categories and by the vagaries of the nature of sense perception itself. But in asserting the applicability logic beyond the sensible world, transcendent realism walks arm in arm with Platonic idealism, and arrives together with that philosophy at a Supreme Principle of Being and Intelligibility. Plato, as he has come down to us through the ages, merely describes the Idea of the Good in a mystical way that Plato himself characterizes as such. He does not fully justify the Idea of the Good by rational argument. Neither does Plato tell us whether it is in the nature of the explanation of the world, its direct cause, or pure will, and it must be remembered that elsewhere in his dialogues, Plato speaks of the Demiurge as the god who fashions reality from a seemingly preexisting neutral matter (interestingly, because such matter does not participate in the Ideas prior to the action of the Demiurge it is sometimes regarded by Plato as nothingness) by causing it to participate in the Ideas.

---

3. Plato, *Republic*, Book VII, 217.

For purposes of the ontological proof offered here, it can be seen that the Idea of the Good, as the Supreme Principle of Being and Intelligibility, seems to fill the bill of explanatory power required by the principle of sufficient reason, as well as providing the ground for the existence of the world. But it carries with it too much baggage, including the lack of a clear connection between it and its own instantiation. For my part, I can only understand the Idea of the Good as pure self-instantiating will, and I can only connect it with my own internal experience of moral obligation and external experience of the empirical world, if I characterize it as being in the nature of a Will that intends itself as its own end. The reasons for this perspective should be readily understandable from the contents of chapter 10, "Duty and Desire." The Platonic Idea of the Good, as I understand it, operating as it does by participation, seems entirely too passive to explain the *Logos* and all that actually exists. On another reading it may be that Plato, when he refers to the Idea of the Good as the universal author of all things beautiful and right, is expressing not just the *form* of that which is good but also identifying the entity in which *form and will are united* as the universal creative force, in which case I would withdraw the point (although I am uncertain as to what should be made of the Demiurge on such a reading). Of profound importance to transcendent realism as a comprehensive philosophy, it is only God, considered as pure *Agape* and not a passive Being, that solves, rationally and without resort to mysticism, the ontological puzzle. God is intelligible to us in precisely the way he has disclosed himself to us: as the Supreme Principle of Being and Intelligibility and as *Agape*.

OTHER ARGUMENTS FOR THE EXISTENCE OF GOD

The selective favor that Kant finds with modern material reductionists is due in significant part to his restriction of reason to empirical cognition generally and to his criticism of the Scholastic arguments for the existence of God. As has been mentioned, before adding his own moral argument, Kant grouped the traditional arguments into three categories, *viz.*, the ontological argument, the cosmological argument, and the teleological argument. In his critique, Kant selects as his starting point the disproof of the ontological argument because, as he correctly points out, the cosmological and the teleological arguments depend upon there being an uncaused being whose necessary existence cannot be shown solely by reference to the empirical world and therefore the cosmological and teleological arguments implicitly depend upon the ontological argument. Kant's strategy is effective, of course, only to the extent that his argument is that it is impossible to prove as an ontological matter that God exists. On the other hand, if one can show on an ontological basis that there is a self-instantiating being, then the cosmological and teleological arguments are sound. The ontological argument offered in these pages fits that bill. However, it should be noted that, unlike other such arguments, the one offered here begins with the necessity of the world without distinguishing between empirical and supersensible reality, and therefore can only be used in support of arguments that assume the contingency of the empirical world because it also shows that the material world is contingent.

THE SOUL

No concept is more central to transcendent realism than the soul, for it is the soul that is the essential precondition to moral self-consciousness and, as such, both the window to, and proof of, direct intuition of supersensible reality. The soul is directly perceived and the means by which all other direct intuition occurs. The soul is the persistent unity of the experience of an organic life that is in constant flux. The soul is the subject and object of its own self-consciousness. It is the subject of its own self-consciousness insofar as it is the being who thinks its thoughts. It is the object of its self-consciousness insofar as it is conscious of itself not merely as a thinker, but as a morally conscious being. The soul is the means by which man, as a psychosomatic unity, has access to objective, universal, and necessary truths of the *Logos* and to *Agape*. The soul is not just a mind, but it possesses a mind of a very special sort, one that not only has the faculty to consciously apprehend the sensible and the supersensible but also to determine its own ends in accordance with, or contrary to, the Moral Law.

As a philosophical concept, the soul has a history as long as literature itself. In the Homeric era, the soul was conceived of that which enlivens animate creatures and was thought to descend upon death to Hades where it would continue to exist as a shadow of its possessor. In the *Phaedo*, Socrates speculates on the immortality of the soul, which he identifies with the cognitive and intellectual features as well as the source of life, contrasting it with the perishable material world. In the *Republic*, the concept of the soul is refined to contain reason, appetite, and spirit. For Aristotle, the soul is a type of natural occurrence that defines the relationship between the form of a living being, considered as an organic mechanism with characteristic faculties, including in the case of man, mind, and the matter comprising it, and the soul is not capable of existing apart from the organism that it in-forms. By the time of Descartes, the soul had become identical with mind and by the time of Hume it was doubted to exist at all. Leibniz argues against materialism on the grounds that it cannot explain the existence of real beings and self-consciousness, both of which are characterized by a unity that cannot be achieved by the aggregation of its parts, and concludes that the world consists of soul-like substances, which are unified and unextended and which are endowed with the properties of the objects of which they are the foundation, including, in the case of sentient beings, consciousness. Kant, as has been noted, argued from a unity of apperception that is the mere form of representation of objects and not the representation of itself as an object that subsists (although he posits the existence of the soul as such as a matter of faith).

In these pages, I do not intend to speculate on the nature of the soul beyond that which can be known of it by direct perception and inference from other known facts of human experience. If one prescinds from human experience all that is explained or may conceivably, with scientific progress, be explained by empirical experience, one is left with the supersensible, including the *Logos*, and what comes from human access to it, namely, consciousness of self as a morally responsible being. The self of self-consciousness is directly perceived to be a persistent, unchanging, unified, morally responsible entity that knows itself as a thinking ontological object with faculties of cognition and will. The particular entity of which each person is self-conscious is, because of its moral character, what is referred to in transcendent realism as the soul. In our reinterpretation of Heidegger's *Dasein*, the soul is the being which we become when we become who we are.

The soul, so conceived and perceived, is decidedly *noumenal* in nature. Insofar as the soul may not be understood as a material phenomenon, it must be *noumenal* in the positive sense and understood as subsisting outside of the framework of space and time. But the association of each soul with a particular empirical being cannot be disregarded, so to the extent of that association, the soul must be understood as *noumenal* in the negative sense as well. Mind-body dualism has no basis and, as has been noted from the earliest of these pages, has led to the collapse of metaphysics as a meaningful discipline. To the extent that the soul is *noumenal* in the positive sense, it subsists and is not cognizable in a spatiotemporal way; whether lack of temporality implies eternality is a question that may not be answered in this life. Indeed, it seems that there are several possibilities, including that the soul is extinguished with the body upon death, that the soul persists as a completed Being, or that the soul progresses sequentially outside of space and time. As to the last possibility, in Heideggerian terms, it may be that upon death, although *Dasein's* potentiality for Being-in-the-World has come to an end, its mode of sequential progression continues in a different horizon. This possibility arises as the result of our recharacterization of *Dasein* as Being-towards-God and also not just Being-in-the-World but also Being in relation to transcendent reality and may imply that *Dasein's* ownmost potentiality for Being includes overcoming its own temporality.

With that, we have said all we can say about the metaphysics of the persistence of the soul. Nevertheless, we will indulge ourselves as did Kant with a bit of speculation that transgresses the boundary between philosophy and faith by making two points that seem to connect with our metaphysics but cannot be said to be anything other than speculation. The first is that it would seem odd if man's essential moral responsibility simply arose and departed with his corporeal existence because that would require asserting obligation without meaningful consequence. This is thematically consistent with Kant. The second is a related point, which follows from the connection of moral obligation with *Agape*. God, as he is known to reason, is *Agape*. Man, considered as a soul, is a morally conscious being possessed of freedom of will. In this way, man is similar to God with the important distinction that, unlike God, man can choose among ends but not create or define them. For man, virtue consists in reconciling his will with *Agape*. A perfect soul would intend in all things the identical ends as does God and, in doing so, would achieve unity of will with that of the divine. Ordinary men, being imperfect, are certainly at the time of death far separated in their Being from the divine, although, to the extent of the virtue they achieve in life, may be said to participate in divinity. Reconciliation between God and man would seem to require, then, either of two things. One is the opportunity to unify man's will with that of God in an afterlife. The other is to achieve consubstantiality in this life through the intermediation of a man whose will is perfect. Indeed, if such a man were to exist he could only be understood to be, in his essential Being, a God-man.

13

Agape (Αγάπη)

AGAPE, LOVE, AND UNQUALIFIED GOOD WILL

For the reasons that have been emphasized from the outset of this book, there is no topic which shines a light on the vacuous nature of empiricist philosophy more brightly than ethics. In the sensible world there is only causality or, if one prefers to deny it, probability, and as a result there can be no responsibility. If man has no freedom and no soul, what differentiates him from any animal and why should he behave differently? The thing that causes empiricists to squirm is that most are, empirically, just like the rest of us when it comes to conduct. They feel obliged to act justly and most often do and sometimes do not. They feel justified in holding others accountable for their actions. But they cannot validate their sense of obligation except upon the psychological grounds of having learned right from wrong at mother's knee.

Under transcendent realism, the core ethical principle is that all morally rational agents are required to act at all times with *agape*. The rationale is that, in so doing, such agents instantiate *Agape* whose will is done through them in the empirical world. Since *Agape* is self-instantiating and self-justifying *good-in-itself*, action in accordance with *Agape* is action in accordance with divine will and is morally required.

It is one of the unfortunate quirks of the English language that *"agape"* is most often translated into the word "love," because that term is one of the more amorphous ones and can have radically different meanings and connotations. The Merriam-Webster dictionary defines "love" as follows:

1. a (1) : strong affection for another arising out of kinship or personal ties—maternal love for a child (2) : attraction based on sexual desire : affection and tenderness felt by lovers—"After all these years, they are still very much in love." (3) : affection based on admiration, benevolence, or common interests—"love for his old schoolmates"
   b: an assurance of affection—"give her my love"

2. warm attachment, enthusiasm, or devotion—"love of the sea"

3. a: the object of attachment, devotion, or admiration—"baseball was his first love"

b (1) : a beloved person : darling—often used as a term of endearment (2) British—used as an informal term of address

4. a: unselfish, loyal, and benevolent (see benevolent 1a) concern for the good of another: such as (1) : the fatherly concern of God for humankind (2) : brotherly concern for others
b: a person's adoration of God

5. a god (such as Cupid or Eros) or personification of love

6. an amorous episode : love affair

7. the sexual embrace : copulation

8. a score of zero (as in tennis)

9. capitalized, Christian Science : God[1]

It can be seen that the definition of love has a wide variety of different meanings with a correspondingly wide range of moral implications. With respect to the definition of "*agape*," the dictionary points the reader to 4a of the definition of "love" provided above, which perhaps taken together with 4b, 5, and 9, approximates the use employed in these pages. However, a simpler definition will best align these dictionary definitions with the philosophy of transcendent realism and set a standard by which ethical conduct can be measured, so as used herein (and described in chapter 1, "Introduction") the term "*agape*" means *unqualified good will*. This definition encapsulates the full metaphysics of our understanding of *Agape* as self-instantiating, self-justifying, *good-in-itself* (will) as well as the practical standard of morally required behavior for the instantiation of *Agape* in empirical reality. More specifically, for purposes of articulating ethical conduct and attitude, in addition to free will (*agape*) and divine will (*Agape*), the term "*agape*" will be used in this chapter (a) in the case of God for man, to refer to God's unqualified good will for humanity, (b) in the case of man for God, to refer to sublime adoration by man for God as pure, creative *good-in-itself*, and (c) in the case of man for fellow man, to refer to unqualified brotherly good will, *without any requirement of personal affection.*

That man is an object of *Agape* means that man matters to God and, correlatively, that how man acts matters to God. It has just been argued in these pages (especially in chapter 10, "Duty and Desire") that it is morally required of human will that it endeavor to instantiate the divine will. The question that now needs to be answered is: How ought man to do that?

AGAPE AND ETHICAL BEHAVIOR

The following relevant observations may be made from the prior elucidation of transcendent reality: (1) man is a morally self-determining soul; (2) the sole principle of morality is to act in good will at all times; and (3) each soul is an object of the divine will (i.e., loved by God). From these three principles, a complete ethical system that is based on divine will, as the unconditioned principle of all reality, can be deduced and enumerated.

1. Merriam-Webster Online, s.v. "love." Accessed March 27, 2017. http://www.merriam-webster.com/dictionary/love. (Minor changes were made to punctuation.)

AGAPE (Ἀγάπη)

1. *The fundamental ethical principle is to act in good will at all times.* The divine will is a fact of man's experience, not a set of rules of behavior. Because the divine will is not a law, those who seek to find in it a specific code of conduct are doomed to disappointment. To say that a specific set of immutable laws cannot be derived from knowledge of the divine will is not to say that its principles are unclear, however. The fundamental core tenets are, not surprisingly, as set forth in the Bible, including both the New Testament (to love God and your fellow man) and the Ten Commandments.[2]

2. *Acting with* agape *is a call to reciprocate* Agape. If man understands that God's good will for him is absolute, unconditional, and, by definition, *good-in-itself*, then, logically, he must emotionally and morally embrace it. That is not to say that man is not free to reject God, which, to the contrary, is a freedom necessarily implied by moral obligation, but rather that, because the divine will is *good-in-itself*, rejecting God's love must be *evil*, which can never be justified. In a harsh and brutal world of scarcity, living by the light of God's divine will is often difficult and often requires behavior that is inconsistent with individual physical needs or human passions. That means that, although man may not always like the moral call to unify his will with the divine will, he *ought* always to endeavor to do it.

By adopting the divine as his own, man approaches union with God morally, that is, he chooses to instantiate *Agape* in the empirical world. Nontheists and other critics of the Judeo-Christian view of God often argue that no self-respecting God would demand that man love him and no perfect Being would be in need of anything, least of all man's *agape*. But this misses the nature of God's good will for man and may very well be attributable to the earlier described insufficiencies of the term "love" in this context. God does not "love" man in a needy, human way. *Agape* is in the nature of good will, that is, concern for, man as a moral agent and a means for the instantiation of *Agape* in the empirical world. God does not demand that man *love* him or need to be loved by man; this is implicit in the concept of free will. If God were not prepared to accept man's decision whether to conduct himself in a morally good way, God would not have given man free will, which is to say God would not have given to man moral consciousness. If God required that man utilize his freedom in a particular way, then man could not be said to be free. The divine will is simply a fact of the world as is man's freedom to disregard it. The good man will always have *agape* for God simply because the good man is precisely that. And that means that the good man's will is to the limited extent humanly possible always that the divine will, not his, be done.

3. *Because each soul is an object of* Agape, *each soul must be treated with* agape. If the divine will extends to every man, then each man must extend his own good will to each other man, whether he likes him or not. This is the reason that each person is an *end-in-itself* and not, as Kant has it, because each person is rational and therefore rationally capable of acting in accordance with the categorical imperative. If God's will is without qualification or condition, then so must be the good will of each man to each other. Man does not have to like his fellow man, but he does have to wish the best for him, and he does have to act accordingly. This is what it means to *love* your neighbor. It is helpful to consider the divine will in the context of the earlier analogy to parental love for children.

2. Mark 12:28–34 (NAB); Exod 20:1–17 (NAB).

Does not every parent feel every insult and injury suffered by their child and wish that they might suffer it instead? Does not every parent feel that what is done to their child is done also to them? So, if a man lies to, cheats, curses, does physical harm to, seeks revenge against, or wishes that ill should befall another man, is this not in direct contradiction to, and a refusal to instantiate in the empirical world, *Agape*? This is the underlying principle of all moral rules governing the relationship among men. It is not from empathy that man should consider his relationship with other men but from his personal relationship with and to God. Is it a sin therefore to tell a lie? If it is done with indifference or malice it must surely be so. But in answer to a commonly asked question, it cannot be a sin to deceive a murderer about the location of his intended victim because such deception would be an act of good will, in fact, for both the victim and the would-be murderer.

4. *Human existence is essentially moral existence.* Because man brings morality into the sensible world by acting freely pursuant to his direct intuition of *Agape*, if man were absent from the world, the world would in fact be precisely as it is understood to be from a materialist perspective. It would be a world where everything is governed by physical laws and determined by an endless chain of causes and effects (or probable outcomes). There would be no "ought" in the world and no reason to think that anything should be or occur differently from the way it is or is occurring. The harsh and brutal realities of competition for the world's scarce resources would still be harsh and brutal, but they would be so without moral implication. Without man, the world and life in it would be utterly meaningless, not because humanity is meaningful in itself, but because humanity is connected to *Agape*.

Man is, at least for a time, in the world, and he brings his ethos with him. Life is not meaningless. For man, every decision has a moral component. Whether he should eat, work, or sleep, whether he should hoard or share, whether he should take charge or defer to another, whether he should suffer violence or defend against it, are all, in a very real sense, moral decisions. Whatever man does, there is always an alternative that he could be doing, including refraining from doing anything.

5. *Man is a moral process.* Man must make each of these decisions, not in accordance with a set of hard and fast rules, but rather in accordance with the dictates of a personal good will that mirrors, to the best of his ability, the good will of God. If man does not do so, he does wrong. Man defines himself, in the deepest and most real terms, by what he wills to do and what he wills to be done. To ask what sort of person a man is morally is to ask what sort of person he is. To ask the question any other way is to ask what sort of animal he is. Aristotle holds that a man becomes virtuous by doing virtuous things. Although his meaning may have been a practical one (i.e., that doing good is habit forming), the truth of this position goes beyond behavior all the way to man's soul. If it is correct to infer man's eternal soul from his knowledge of the divine will, the conclusion is inescapable that the nature of a man's soul can only be understood in this world by the nature of his will, which, of course, determines his actions. Those actions must have defining consequences for his soul because disregard for the divine call must have consequences; otherwise, the divine call would be an empty whisper and man's free will would be meaningless. The failure to act morally cannot harm man *qua* animal; it can only degrade his soul. This is understood by man by direct perception and analytical intuition and is part of the *Logos*, notwithstanding its moral character.

AGAPE (Αγάπη)

Man is therefore in his essence a moral process and he must be seen and respected as such by his fellow man. The world is not simply a test of character, but an ongoing, interactive arena in which man defines his own soul. The challenges of the empirical world are presented to man one after another in space and time, and his responses to those challenges are not abstract but instead influence and alter the progression of events and circumstances, not just for him, but for those around him. Love for fellow man means that each man has a vested interest in the success of his fellow man in passing that test. By acting with *agape* for his fellow man, a man lightens the weight of reality as it bears down upon his fellow man, in effect, reducing his moral challenge and making it more achievable. By acting maliciously, a man has the opposite effect. If a man shares with a starving man, the starving man has less incentive to steal. If a man steals from another, he motivates his victim to respond in kind or with violence.

6. *Protecting the freedom of all souls to develop morally is paramount.* The two preconditions of morality are being the object of *Agape* and the *freedom* to act in accordance with the divine will. If man is a moral process, initiated and guided by God, then each man is fundamentally of equal dignity and value, and *it must be the gravest immorality to interrupt or interfere in that process*. That the moral requirement of non-mortal decisions is to act in good will has already been discussed. But there are two categories of action that are *intended to terminate the moral process altogether* and, as a result, require special consideration.

The first is to deprive man of his freedom to act morally. Any attempt to legislate or enforce the morality of others that extends beyond order and security is a deprivation of such freedom and interference in the relationship between God and man. Any attempt by one man to force another man be moral is a logical absurdity. Depriving a person of his free will by dictating moral principles to him either removes the moral character of his action altogether or places a heavy burden on its free exercise. This, of course, must be contrary to the divine will because the intent is to thwart it not, as is often asserted, to enforce it. If there were categories of offense attached to sinfulness, depriving a man of his moral freedom would be among, if not in fact the most, heinous. No religious interpretation that validates imposition of its values upon men by force can be valid. Religious fascism in all of its forms is an oxymoron.

Deprivation of freedom to be moral is not limited to compelling men to bow down to a god at the point of a gun. Societies that prohibit free worship, or inhibit or discourage private charity, including those which compel their citizens to be dependent upon government and not the assistance of fellow citizens freely offered, are fundamentally immoral. Government charity is not charity but a taking from one citizen and a giving to another (usually with an agenda that is utterly unrelated to good will) and as such it is a deprivation of the freedom of the citizen whose property is taken to act in accordance with the divine will. It is no coincidence that socialist and communist doctrine is almost always antagonistic to religion.

The second and most direct category of interference with man, considered as a moral process, is deprivation of life. It is easy to see that killing is wrong in all its manifestations, except, perhaps, in self-defense. The most direct category of life-taking is, of course, murder and the rationale for its characterization as depravity is obvious. If every man is a moral process who is valued by God, then terminating that process by depriving a man of his life is the most direct and severe affront to God, for it deprives God of the complete self-determination of the soul of an object of his unqualified good will.

The same must hold true for capital punishment. Society has, of course, a right to protect itself from violent criminals and it should do so. But such protection does not extend to capital punishment, which is no less the termination of a moral process the result of which might very well include repentance in the fullness of time, than is murder. Lifetime incarceration may be necessary for deterrence and protection of society, but extermination can never be.

Then there is the problem of abortion. Abortion is by definition the premature termination of a *thing*, but the thing in the case of human abortion is a *living moral process*. There can be no denying that at conception, a fetus has everything it needs to develop into a child of divine good will other than time and the nurturing environment of its mother's womb. It makes no difference whether a fetus is viable or not, because, at conception, the human organism is animate and the essential process of its biological and moral life is underway. *The moral process is a transcendent unity.* There is no "stage" in the moral process that is irrelevant or more or less important than another. There is no stage in which man becomes man; he is a unique moral process from the moment of conception. Viewed in this light, it is clear that abortion is the single greatest problem facing mankind at the start of the twenty-first century. The number of abortions in the United States alone exceeds one million annually. It is nothing less than a holocaust.

Finally, there is suicide and assisted suicide. That the termination of a human being as a moral process occurs at his own hands or at his request is irrelevant and, if anything, represents an act of rejection of divine good will. In the case of elderly or terminal human beings, the only moral answer is palliative care. Assisting in suicide is murder.

A question arises as to the characterization of those many men who assert that they hear no call to morality. Such men have in common a misunderstanding of the perfection of Being; they think that they can be complete, which is to say who they are as a human being, in and of themselves. Nothing could be further from the truth. Human beings are and must be toward-God, which is where perfection stands. Such misunderstandings may be simple failures of reason or psychologically sourced or combinations of both, but, in any event, they are failures and, at that, of a kind that is uniquely human. Even so, no matter how freely or frequently such men act immorally, until their last breath, they must still be regarded as having the capacity to reform their will in favor of *Agape*. As rational human beings, such men may come to see the error of their thinking. And, even if they do not have the intellectual capacity to do so, it is far beyond the wisdom of those of us who do to treat them differently from any other men, especially because we must presume that all men, not just the more intelligent or apparently more moral men, are the object of divine *Agape* and are therefore ends-in-themselves.

Of course, these are just of few of the larger moral issues confronting man in empirical reality. The practical, everyday issues are too numerous and circumstantial for analysis and, as a general matter do not admit of universal analysis under any other guideline than to act, in all things, with *agape*, which is precisely the point being made here.

Bibliography

Aquinas, St. Thomas. *Commentary on the Gospel of St. John*, translated by Fabian Larcher and James Weisheipl. Washington, DC: Catholic University of America Press, 2010.
Aristotle. *The Metaphysics*. Vol. 3 of *The Works of Aristotle,* translated by W. D. Ross. Oxford: Clarendon, 1928.
Ayer, Alfred J. *Language, Truth and Logic*. New York: Dover, 1952.
Bergner, Jeff. *Against Modern Humanism*. Norfolk, VA: Rambling Ridge, 2013.
Berkeley, George. *A Treatise Concerning the Principles of Human Knowledge*. Vol. 1 of *The Works of George Berkeley, D.D., Bishop of Cloyne*, edited by George Sampson. London: George Bell and Sons, 1897.
Blattner, William. "Temporality." In *A Companion to Heidegger*, edited by Hubert L. Dreyfus and Mark A. Wrathall, 311–24. Malden, MA: Blackwell, 2005.
Brentano, Franz Clemens. *Psychology from an Empirical Standpoint*, translated by Antos Rancurello, D. B. Terell, and Linda McAllister. New York: Routledge, 1995.
Castelvecchi, Davide. "What Do You Mean, the Universe Is Flat? (Part I)," Degrees of Freedom (blog), *Scientific American*, July 25, 2011. https://blogs.scientificamerican.com/degrees-of-freedom/httpb logsscientificamericancomdegrees-of-freedom20110725what-do-you-mean-the-universe-is-flat-part-i/.
Chesterton, G. K. *Othodoxy*. Sioux Falls, SD: NuVision, 2007.
Chorost, Michael. "Where Thomas Nagel Went Wrong." *The Chronicle of Higher Education*, May 2013. http://www.chronicle.com/article/Where-Thomas-Nagel-Went-Wrong/139129.
Copleston, Frederick. *Greece and Rome: From the Pre-Socratics to Plotinus*. Vol. 1 of *A History of Philosophy*. New York: Doubleday, 1994.
———. *From the French Enlightenment to Kant*. Vol. 6 of *A History of Philosophy*. New York: Doubleday, 1993.
———. *From the Post-Kantian Idealists to Marx, Kierkegaard, and Nietzsche*. Vol. 7 of *A History of Modern Philosophy*. New York: Doubleday, 1994.
Copleston, Frederick, and Bertrand Russell. "A Debate on the Existence of God." Debate on Third Program of the British Broadcasting Corp., 1948. http://www.biblicalcatholic.com/apologetics/p20.htm.
Descartes, René. *Meditations on First Philosophy*. Translated by Donald Cress. 3rd ed. Indianapolis: Hackett, 1993.
Dutton, Blake. "Benedict De Spinoza." *Internet Encyclopedia of Philosophy*. http://www.iep.utm.edu/spinoza/.
Editors of the Encyclopædia Britannica. "Causation." *Encyclopædia Britannica*, February 9, 2009. https://www.britannica.com/topic/causation.
———. "Conservation of Mass." *Encyclopædia Britannica*, July 19, 2011. https://www.britannica.com/science/conservation-of-mass.
Eshleman, Andrew. "Moral Responsibility." *The Stanford Encyclopedia of Philosophy*, edited by Edward Zalta. Winter 2016 ed. https://plato.stanford.edu/archives/win2016/entries/moral-responsibility/.
Flew, Antony. "Theology and Falsification," In *Reason and Responsibility: Readings in Some Basic Problems of Philosophy*, edited by Joel Feinberg, 48–49. Belmont, CA: Dickenson, 1968.

Bibliography

Guyer, Paul, and Rolf-Peter Horstmann. "Idealism." *The Stanford Encyclopedia of Philosophy*, edited by Edward Zalta. Fall 2015 ed. https://plato.stanford.edu/archives/fall2015/entries/idealism/.

Hanna, Robert. "Kant's Theory of Judgment." *The Stanford Encyclopedia of Philosophy*, edited by Edward Zalta. Winter 2016 ed. https://plato.stanford.edu/archives/win2016/entries/kant-judgment/.

Harris, William. "Heraclitus: The Complete Fragments." Middlebury College. http://community.middlebury.edu/~harris/Philosophy/heraclitus.pdf.

Hawking, Stephen, and Leonard Mlodinow. *The Grand Design*. New York: Bantam, 2010.

Hegel, Georg Wilhelm Friedrich. *The Phenomenology of Mind*. Translated by J. B. Baillie. 2nd rev. ed. Mineola, NY: Dover, 2003.

———. *The Phenomenology of Spirit*. Translated by A. V. Miller. Oxford: Oxford University Press, 1977.

Heidegger, Martin. *Being and Time*. Translated by John Macquarrie and Edward Robinson. Reprint ed. New York: Harper Perennial, 2008.

———. *Introduction to Metaphysics*. Translated by Gregory Fried and Richard Polt. 2nd ed. New Haven: Yale University Press, 2014.

———. *The Principle of Reason*. Translated by Reginald Lilly. Bloomington: Indiana University Press, 1996.

Heinzmann, Gerhard, and David Stump. "Henri Poincaré." In *Stanford Encyclopedia of Philosophy*, edited by Edward Zalta. Spring 2017 ed. https://plato.stanford.edu/entries/poincare/.

Hempel, Carl. "On the Nature of Mathematical Proof." In *The Philosophy of Carl G. Hempel*, edited by James H. Fetzer, 3–17. Oxford: Oxford University Press, 2001.

Hobbes, Thomas. *Leviathan*. Adelaide: The University of Adelaide, 2016. E-book.

Hoffman, Piotr. "Dasein and 'Its' Time." In *A Companion to Heidegger*, edited by Hubert L. Dreyfus and Mark A. Wrathall, 325–34. Malden, MA: Blackwell, 2005.

Hofstadter, Douglas R. *Gödel, Escher, and Bach: An Eternal Golden Braid*. New York: Basic Books, 1979.

Husserl, Edmund. *The Crisis of European Sciences and Transcendental Phenomenology: An Introduction to Phenomenological Philosophy*. Translated by David Carr. Evanston: Northwestern University Press, 1970.

———. *Ideas for a Pure Phenomenology and Phenomenological Philosophy, First Book: General Introduction to Pure Phenomenology*. Translated by Daniel O. Dahlstrom. Indianapolis: Hackett, 2014.

———. *Logical Investigations*. 2 vols. Translated by J. N. Finlay. New York: Routledge, 2001.

Hume, David. *An Enquiry Concerning Human Understanding*. 2nd ed. Oxford: Oxford University Press, 2002.

———. *A Treatise of Human Nature*. Vol. 1. Edited by David Fate Norton and Mary J. Norton. London: Oxford University Press, 2007.

Joad, C. E. M. *Guide to Philosophy*. New York: Dover, 1957.

Kant, Immanuel. *Critique of Pure Reason*. Translated and edited by Marcus Weigelt. New York: Penguin Classics, 2007.

———. *Groundwork for the Metaphysics of Morals*. N.p.: Digireads, 2005.

Kelly, Michael R. "Phenomenology and Time-Consciousness." *Internet Encyclopedia of Philosophy*. http://www.iep.utm.edu/phe-time/#1-11.

Kennefick, Daniel. "Testing Relativity from the 1919 Eclipse—A Question of Bias." *Physics Today*, March 2009, 37–42.

Korab-Karpowicz, W. J. "Martin Heidegger." *Internet Encyclopedia of Philosophy*. http://www.iep.utm.edu/heidegge/.

Leibniz, Gottfried Wilhelm. *The Monadology and Other Philosophical Writings*. Translated by Robert Latta. London: Clarendon, 1898.

Locke, John. *An Essay Concerning Human Understanding*. Oxford: Oxford University Press, 1975.

McKenna, Michael, and D. Justin Coates. "Compatibilism." *The Stanford Encyclopedia of Philosophy*, edited by Edward Zalta. Winter 2016 ed. https://plato.stanford.edu/archives/win2016/entries/compatibilism/.

McQuillan, Colin. "German Idealism." *Internet Encyclopedia of Philosophy*. http://www.iep.utm.edu/germidea/.

Moran, Dermot. *Introduction to Phenomenology*. London: Routledge, 2000.

Moore, A. W. *The Infinite*. 2nd ed. New York: Routledge, 2001.

Mulhall, Stephen. *Routledge Philosophy Guidebook to Heidegger and Being and Time*. 2nd ed. London: Routledge, 2005.
Nagel, Ernest, and James Newman. *Gödel's Proof*. New York: New York University Press, 2001.
Nagel, Thomas. *The Last Word*. New York: Oxford University Press, 2012.
———. *Mind and Cosmos*. New York: Oxford University Press, 2012.
———. "What Is It Like to Be a Bat?" *The Philosophical Review* 83 (October 1974) 435–50.
Plato, *The Republic*. Vol. 3 of *The Dialogues of Plato*. Translated by B. Jowett. London: Clarendon Press, 1892.
Popkin, Richard, ed. *The Columbia History of Western Philosophy*. New York: Columbia University Press, 1999.
Raatikainen, Panu. "Gödel's Incompleteness Theorems." In *The Stanford Encyclopedia of Philosophy*, edited by Edward Zalta. Spring 2015 ed. https://plato.stanford.edu/entries/goedel-incompleteness/#Mat.
Russell, Bertrand. *A History of Western Philosophy*. New York: Simon & Schuster, 1945.
———. *Introduction to Mathematical Philosophy*. London: George Allen & Unwin, 1929.
———. *The Principles of Mathematics*. 2nd ed. New York: Norton, 1937.
———. *The Problems of Philosophy*. Mineola, NY: Dover, 1999.
———. *Why I Am Not a Christian*. New York: Simon & Schuster, 1957.
Sheehan, Thomas. "Dasein." In *A Companion to Heidegger*, edited by Hubert L. Dreyfus and Mark A. Wrathall, 193–213. Malden, MA: Blackwell, 2005.
Searle, John R. *Mind: A Brief Introduction*. New York: Oxford University Press, 2004.
Smith, David. "Phenomenology." In *Stanford Encyclopedia of Philosophy*, edited by Edward Zalta. Winter 2016 ed. https://plato.stanford.edu/archives/win2016/entries/phenomenology/.
Smith, Joel. "Phenomenology." In *Internet Encyclopedia of Philosophy*. http://www.iep.utm.edu/phenom/#H8.
Sokolowski, Robert. *Introduction to Phenomenology*. New York: Cambridge University Press, 2000.
Spinoza, Bernard. "Ethics." In Vol. 1 of *The Collected Works of Bernard Spinoza*, edited and translated by Edwin Curley, 408–617. Princeton: Princeton University Press, 1985.
Wheeler, M. "Martin Heidegger." In *The Stanford Encyclopedia of Philosophy*, edited by Edward Zalta. Fall 2015 ed. http://plato.stanford.edu/archives/fall2015/entries/heidegger/.
Wittgenstein, Ludwig. *Tractatus Logico-Philosophicus*. London: Kegan Paul, Trench, Trubner & Co., 1922.

Name Index
(Includes Adjectival References)

Abraham, 11
Anaximander, 174
Anselm of Canterbury, 10, 16, 328–29
Aquinas, Thomas, 16, 175–76, 278, 327
Aristotle, 8, 16, 63n11, 71n23, 80, 121, 153, 166–67, 175, 187, 199, 201, 215, 225–27, 228, 230, 250, 254, 262, 267, 268, 276, 339, 344
Ayer, Alfred J., 18, 40, 113

Bergner, Jeff, 23, 105, 225, 262–66, 268, 270, 276, 280, 282n1
Berkeley, George, 12, 18, 29, 30–32, 34, 35, 45, 97–98, 204
Bolzano, Bernard, 177
Brentano, Franz Clemens, 4, 197–209, 210, 212, 213, 221, 222, 223, 225–26, 266–67, 280
Brouwer, L. E. J., 184, 187, 188–89
Brown, Thomas, 204
Burlati-Forti, Cesare, 182–83

Cantor, Georg, 83n36, 133, 134n4, 137, 138, 148n16, 175, 176, 177–88, 189, 191n20, 194
Castelvecchi, Davide, 93n51
Chesterton, G. K., 20
Copernicus, Nicolaus, 34, 99, 106, 154, 298
Copleston, Frederick, 14, 62, 66–67, 99

Darwin, Charles, 44, 294
Dedekind, Richard, 138, 177, 179
Descartes, René, 6, 11, 12, 22–30, 32, 35, 36, 38, 41, 45–46, 47–50, 52, 54, 56, 60, 67, 69n20, 94, 96, 97, 108, 176, 199, 204, 209, 214, 228, 232–33, 235, 245, 262, 268, 269, 277, 279–80, 308, 337, 339

Eddington, Arthur, 91n47
Einstein, Albert, 57n3, 91n47, 153–54, 158, 160, 161, 163
Elijah, 11
Euclid of Alexandria, 83, 93, 120, 152–53, 158, 159–62, 166, 169

Fraenkel, Abraham, 183
Fermat, Pierre de, 114
Fichte, Johann, 101–2, 105
Flew, Anthony, 17, 18, 40
Frankfurt, Harry, 318–19
Frege, Gottlob, 40, 133–34, 140, 176, 177, 202, 209

Gaon, Saadya, 80
Galilei, Galileo, 154, 178–79, 193–94
Gassendi, Pierre, 26–28, 30, 34–35, 38, 40, 50, 52, 105
Gödel, Kurt Friedrich, 143, 183, 184, 189, 190–92

Hartley, David, 204
Hawking, Stephen, 41, 45, 57n1
Hegel, Georg Wilhelm Friedrich, 13, 23, 26, 34, 38–39, 40, 48, 97, 101–5, 106, 123, 176, 209–10, 223, 227, 230, 231, 251, 255, 257, 262, 324
Heidegger, Martin, 2, 3, 4–5, 6. 7, 34, 50, 53, 131–32, 186, 197–200, 203, 204, 206, 208, 210, 215n23, 221, 223, 224–80, 309, 320, 331, 334, 340
Hempel, Carl, 134n4, 137–39, 146
Heraclitus, 6, 54, 153, 253, 254, 278n69
Hilbert, David, 184, 187, 192–94
Hitler, Adolf, 39, 48, 266

351

Name Index

Hobbes, Thomas, 281, 308, 318
Hofstadter, Douglas R., 192
Husserl, Edmund, 4, 186, 197–200, 202–3, 204, 208–23, 225–26, 230, 232, 246, 266, 267, 280, 309
Hume, David, 9, 11–12, 18, 23, 26–28, 30, 34–35, 37, 38, 39, 40, 42–43, 46, 47, 48, 49, 50, 51, 52, 53, 56–57, 59–60, 80, 87–88, 89, 105, 164, 165, 222, 264, 268, 282, 286, 292, 298, 304–5, 309, 310, 318, 339

Jesus, 11, 20, 25, 262, 277–78, 287, 304, 307
Joad, C. E. M., 21
John the Evangelist, 277–79

Kant, Immanuel, 2, 3, 7–16, 17, 19, 20, 23, 26, 29, 35–39, 40, 43, 45, 46, 47, 48, 49, 50, 52, 56–108, 109–10, 111–13, 116–17, 123, 124–25, 133–34, 139, 143, 146, 149, 150–73, 184–85, 187, 197, 199, 200, 201, 202, 204, 208, 209–10, 223, 226, 229, 230, 239, 244–45, 255, 266, 267, 269, 272, 274, 275, 277, 285, 287, 288, 290, 295, 296–305, 308–9, 314, 320–21, 325, 326, 328–35, 337, 338, 339, 340, 343
Kennefick, Daniel, 91n47
Kroenecker, Leopold, 183, 184

Lange, Friedrich Albert, 208
Leibniz, Gottfried Wilhelm, 6, 12, 29, 32–34, 35, 45, 50, 55, 56, 103, 130–31, 134, 163, 176, 256–61, 266, 267, 271, 272, 279, 324, 326–27, 331, 337, 339
Linnaeus, Carl, 121
Locke, John, 12, 18, 23, 26, 29–30, 34, 35, 41, 43, 45, 47, 54, 57, 89, 113, 201

Mark the Evangelist, 304n9, 307, 343n2
Marx, Karl, 17, 197
Maxwell, James, 158
Mill, James, 204
Mill, John Stuart, 17, 204
Moran, Dermot, 210, 212n17, 219, 221n43, 222
Moore, A. W., 175, 176n4, 181–82, 184n13, 189n19
Moore, G. E., 40
Moses, 11, 274

Nagel, Thomas, 17, 45n28, 110–11, 115, 121, 122, 222, 285, 292, 301–3, 311
Newton, Isaac, 44, 83, 91–92, 134, 157–58, 176, 248
Nietzsche, Friedrich, 17, 39, 48, 197, 262

Parmenides, 6, 10, 153, 175, 253, 254
Peano, Giuseppe, 133, 134–42, 144, 146
Peirce, C. S., 184
Plainer, A., 204
Plato, 4, 6, 35, 80, 127, 129, 133, 153, 167, 202, 209, 215, 216, 227, 250–51, 254, 255, 257, 262, 266, 308, 321, 334, 335, 336–38
Poincarè, Henri, 183, 184
Pythagoras, 133, 174

Russell, Bertrand, 13, 14, 17–18, 40, 82–93, 103–4, 130n2, 132–35, 138–44, 146, 148–49, 150, 152–53, 158–62, 176, 177–78, 182, 183, 185–86, 189–91, 193, 335

Schelling, Friedrich, 101–2, 105
Searle, John R., 23, 41–43, 48n29, 53, 56n1, 67, 123
Silesius, Angelus (aka Johann Angelus Silesius), 260, 272
Sokolowski, Robert, 214, 215, 216n28 and n30, 217n24, 218, 220n40, 221n43
Spencer, Herbert, 204
Spinoza, Baruch (aka Bernard and Benedict de), 12, 23, 26, 28–29, 34, 35, 45, 50, 56, 58, 101, 176, 204, 308, 337
Strawson, P. F., 318–19

Thales, 274
Theseus, 54

Wheeler, Michael, 232
Wiles, Andrew, 114
Wittgenstein, Ludwig, 23, 26, 40, 50, 51, 68, 97, 123, 185, 187, 188, 323–24

Zeno of Elea, 175, 176,
Zermelo, Ernst, 133, 141, 143, 183

www.ingramcontent.com/pod-product-compliance
Lightning Source LLC
Chambersburg PA
CBHW060506300426
44112CB00017B/2569